SAP H
Time Manag
Technical Reference and Learning Guide

MW00851381

SECOND EDITION

P. K. AGRAWAL

Formerly Program Manager
Tata Technologies Limited
Pune

PHI Learning Private Limited

Delhi-110092

2013

Rs. 550.00

SAP HR Time Management: Technical Reference and Learning Guide, Second Edition
P.K. Agrawal

© 2010 by PHI Learning Private Limited, Delhi. All rights reserved. No part of this book may be reproduced in any form, by mimeograph or any other means, without permission in writing from the publisher.

Warning and Disclaimer
While every precaution has been taken in the preparation of this book, the author and the publisher do not guarantee the accuracy, adequacy, or completeness of any information contained in this book. Neither is any liability assumed by the author and the publisher for any damages or loss to your data or your equipment resulting directly or indirectly from the use of the information or instructions contained herein.

Trademark Acknowledgements
SAP, SAPconnect, SAPNet, SAPoffice, SAPscript, ABAP, Basis, ECC are registered or unregistered trademark of SAP AG.

All product and service names mentioned in this book are registered or unregistered trademarks or service marks of their respective companies. Use of any product or service name in this book should not be regarded as affecting the validity of any trademark or service mark.

ISBN-978-81-203-4065-7

The export rights of this book are vested solely with the publisher.

Fourth Printing (Second Edition)   ...   ...   **August, 2013**

Published by Asoke K. Ghosh, PHI Learning Private Limited, Rimjhim House, 111, Patparganj Industrial Estate, Delhi-110092 and Printed by Rajkamal Electric Press, Plot No. 2, Phase IV, HSIDC, Kundli-131028, Sonepat, Haryana.

This book is dedicated to
SAP consultants and users
who deserve to understand SAP much better

Table of Contents

Each chapter is rated for its importance and relevance for functional consultants (FC), users (US), business process owners (PO) and senior managers (SM). In MR you can keep your own rating and in UL, your understanding level.

SAP Menu

Sequence number	SAP Menu (ECC 6.0)	Where covered	Why not covered
	▽ 🗁 SAP menu		
1	▷ 🗀 Office		Not TM
2	▷ 🗀 Cross-Application Components		Not TM
3	▷ 🗀 Collaboration Projects		Not TM
4	▷ 🗀 Logistics		Not TM
5	▷ 🗀 Accounting		Not TM
6	▽ 🗁 Human Resources		
6.1	⬡ PPMDT - Manager's Desktop		Not TM
6.2	▷ 🗀 Personnel Management		Not TM
6.3	▽ 🗁 Time Management		
6.3.1	▽ 🗁 Shift Planning		
6.3.1.1	▽ 🗁 Shift plan		
6.3.1.1.1	⬡ PP61 - Change shift plan	38.1.1	
6.3.1.1.2	⬡ PP60 - Display shift plan	38.1.1	
6.3.1.1.3	⬡ PP6C - Undo completed target pla⌐	38.1.10	
6.3.1.2	▽ 🗁 Requirements		
6.3.1.2.1	⬡ PP67 - Create	38.2.1	
6.3.1.2.2	⬡ PP63 - Change	38.2.1	
6.3.1.2.3	⬡ PP62 - Display	38.2.1	
6.3.1.3	▽ 🗁 Information system		
6.3.1.3.1	⬡ PP6A - Display personal shift plan	38.1.17	
6.3.1.3.2	⬡ PP6B - Display attendance list	38.1.17	
6.3.1.3.3	⬡ PP6C - Undo completed target pla⌐	38.1.10	
6.3.1.3.4	⬡ PP6I - Display temporary assignm⌐	38.1.17	
6.3.1.4	▽ 🗁 Settings		
6.3.1.4.1	⬡ PP64 - Choose plan version	38.1.16	
6.3.1.4.2	⬡ PP66 - Choose profile	38.1.1	
6.3.1.4.3	▽ 🗁 Entry objects		
6.3.1.4.3.1	⬡ PP65 - Simple maintenance	38.1.16	
6.3.1.4.3.2	⬡ PP01 - Detail maintenance	38.1.16	
6.3.1.4.4	▽ 🗁 Current settings		
6.3.1.4.4.1	⬡ S_AHR_61004989 - Specify sh⌐	38.5	
6.3.1.4.4.2	⬡ S_AHR_61004980 - Maintain s⌐	38.11	
6.3.1.4.4.3	⬡ S_AHR_61005002 - Define tim⌐	38.24	
6.3.1.5	▽ 🗁 Environment		
6.3.1.5.1	⬡ PPOME - Change organization and⌐	38.1.16	
6.3.1.5.2	⬡ PPPD - Display profile	38.1.16	
6.3.1.5.3	⬡ PPPM - Change profile	38.1.16	
6.3.1.5.4	⬡ PEPM - Profile matchup	38.1.16	

Sequence number	SAP Menu (ECC 6.0)	Where covered	Why not covered
5.3.2.7	▽ 🗀 Settings		
5.3.2.7.1	◇ S_AHR_61009123 - Create Evaluation Period		Payroll
5.3.2.7.2	◇ S_AHR_61008856 - Earliest Recalculation for	28.3	
5.3.2.7.3	◇ S_AHR_61010745 - Earliest Recalculation for	28.3	
5.3.2.8	▽ 🗀 Environment		
5.3.2.8.1	◇ PT80 - Subsystem Connection	25.3	
5.3.2.8.2	◇ PT68 - Activity Allocation	21.6	
5.3.2.8.3	◇ PU12 - Third-Party Payroll		OoS
5.3.3	▽ 🗀 Incentive Wages		
5.3.3.1	▽ 🗀 Time tickets		
5.3.3.1.1	◇ PW03 - Record	37.2	
5.3.3.1.2	◇ PW01 - Maintain	37.2	
5.3.3.1.3	◇ PW02 - Display	37.2	
5.3.3.2	▽ 🗀 Information system		
5.3.3.2.1	▽ 🗀 Working Time		
5.3.3.2.1.1	◇ PW61 - Time Leveling	37.26	
5.3.3.2.1.2	◇ PW62 - Working Times of Time- and Incen	37.26	
5.3.3.2.1.3	◇ PW63 - Reassignment Proposals for Wag	37.26	
5.3.3.2.2	▽ 🗀 Remuneration Statements		
5.3.3.2.2.1	◇ PW_CEDTX0_BEFORE - Before Gross Pa	37.26	
5.3.3.2.2.2	◇ PW_CEDTX0_AFTER - After Gross Pay	37.26	
5.3.3.3	▽ 🗀 Tools		
5.3.3.3.1	▽ 🗀 Tools selection		
5.3.3.3.1.1	▽ 🗀 Cluster		
5.3.3.3.1.1.1	◇ PT_CLSTB1 - Display Temporary Time	29	
5.3.3.3.1.1.2	◇ PT_CLSTB2 - Display Time Evaluation	30	
5.3.3.3.1.1.3	◇ PT_CLSTL1 - Display Individual Incen	37.2.14	
5.3.3.3.1.1.4	◇ PT_CLSTG1 - Display Group Incentive	37.2.14	
5.3.3.3.1.2	▽ 🗀 Recalculation		
5.3.3.3.1.2.1	◇ PW70 - Individual Incentive Wages	37.14	
5.3.3.3.1.2.2	◇ PW71 - Group Incentive Wages	37.14	
5.3.3.3.1.2.3	◇ PW72 - Withdrawal from Group	37.14	
5.3.3.3.2	◇ PU03 - Change payroll status	1.13.1	
5.3.3.4	▽ 🗀 Settings		
5.3.3.4.1	◇ S_AHR_61010096 - Earliest recalculation for	37.13	
5.3.3.5	▽ 🗀 Environment		
5.3.3.5.1	◇ PT80 - Subsystem connection	25.3	

Sequence number	SAP Menu (ECC 6.0)	Where covered	Why not covered
5.3.4	▽ 🗁 Time Sheet		
5.3.4.1	▽ 🗁 CATS Classic		
5.3.4.1.1	🞉 CAT3 - Display Working Times	36.1	
5.3.4.1.2	🞉 CAT2 - Record Working Times	36.1	
5.3.4.2	▽ 🗁 CATS for Service Providers		
5.3.4.2.1	🞉 CATSXT - Record Own Working Times	36.1.13	
5.3.4.2.2	🞉 CATSXT_ADMIN - Record Working Times	36.1.13	
5.3.4.3	▽ 🗁 Approval		
5.3.4.3.1	🞉 CATS_APPR_LITE - Approve Working Times	36.1.9	
5.3.4.3.2	🞉 ACTEXP_APPR_LITE - Approve Working Time	36.1.9	
5.3.4.4	▽ 🗁 Information System		
5.3.4.4.1	🞉 CATS_DA - Display Working Times	36.1.14	
5.3.4.4.2	🞉 CATSXT_DA - Display Working Times and Ta:	36.1.14	
5.3.4.4.3	🞉 CATSXT_DTL - Working Times and Tasks: Di	36.1.14	
5.3.4.4.4	🞉 CATC - Time Leveling	36.1.11	
5.3.4.4.5	🞉 CAT8 - Display Single Documents	36.1.14	
5.3.4.5	▽ 🗁 Transfer		
5.3.4.5.1	🞉 CATA - All Components		OoS
5.3.4.5.2	🞉 CAT7 - Accounting		OoS
5.3.4.5.3	🞉 CAT6 - Human Resources	36.1.10	
5.3.4.5.4	🞉 CATM - External Services		OoS
5.3.4.5.5	▽ 🗁 Plant Maintenance/Customer Service		
5.3.4.5.5.1	🞉 CAT9 - Transfer		OoS
5.3.4.5.5.2	🞉 IW46 - Postprocessing Confirmations		OoS
5.3.4.5.5.3	🞉 COFC - Postprocessing Actual Costs		OoS
5.3.4.5.5.4	🞉 COGI - Postprocessing Goods Movement:		OoS
5.3.4.5.6	▽ 🗁 Project System		
5.3.4.5.6.1	🞉 CAT5 - Transfer		OoS
5.3.4.5.6.2	🞉 CN30 - Postprocessing Confirmations		OoS
5.3.4.5.6.3	🞉 COFC - Postprocessing Actual Costs		OoS
5.3.4.5.6.4	🞉 COGI - Postprocessing Goods Movement:		OoS
5.3.4.6	▽ 🗁 Tools		
5.3.4.6.1	🞉 CATR - Reorganize Interface Tables	36.1.10	
5.3.4.6.2	🞉 CATSARCH - Archiving		OoS

SAP Customizing Implementation Guide

Sequence number	SAP Customizing Implementation Guide (ECC 6.0)	Where covered	Why not covered
4.9	▷ Financial Conditions		Not TM
4.10	▷ 📑 General Application Functions		Not TM
4.11	▷ 📑 Bank Directory		Not TM
4.12	▷ Payment Cards		Not TM
4.13	▷ SAP Business Partner		Not TM
4.14	▷ SAP Product		Not TM
4.15	▷ Master Data Synchronization		Not TM
4.16	▷ Predefined ALE Business Processes		Not TM
4.17	▷ 📑 Initial Data Transfer		Not TM
4.18	▷ 📑 Open Information Warehouse (OIW)		Not TM
4.19	▷ 📑 Internet/Intranet Services		Not TM
4.20	▷ Homepage Framework		Not TM
4.21	▷ Self-Services		Not TM
4.22	▷ Express Planning		Not TM
4.23	▷ 📑 Audit Management		Not TM
5	▷ Auto-ID Infrastructure		Not TM
6	▷ SAP xApp Resource and Portfolio Management (		Not TM
7	▷ 📑 Financial Accounting		Not TM
8	▷ Financial Accounting (New)		Not TM
9	▷ Financial Supply Chain Management		Not TM
10	▷ Strategic Enterprise Management/Business Ana		Not TM
11	▷ 📑 Controlling		Not TM
12	▷ 📑 Investment Management		Not TM
13	▷ 📑 Enterprise Controlling		Not TM
14	▷ 📑 Real Estate		Not TM
15	▷ Flexible Real Estate Management (RE-FX)		Not TM
16	▷ 📑 Logistics - General		Not TM
17	▷ 📑 Environment, Health and Safety		Not TM
18	▷ 📑 Sales and Distribution		Not TM
19	▷ 📑 Materials Management		Not TM
20	▷ 📑 Logistics Execution		Not TM
21	▷ 📑 Quality Management		Not TM
22	▷ 📑 Plant Maintenance and Customer Service		Not TM
23	▷ 📑 Customer Service		Not TM
24	▷ 📑 Production		Not TM
25	▷ 📑 Production Planning for Process Industries		Not TM
26	▷ 📑 Project System		Not TM
27	▷ Collaboration Projects		Not TM
28	▷ Collaboration Folders		Not TM
29	▷ 📑 Personnel Management		Not TM
30	▷ SAP E-Recruiting		Not TM

Sequence number	SAP Customizing Implementation Guide (ECC 6.0)	Where covered	Why not covered
31.3	Personnel Time Events		
31.3.1	General Settings		
31.3.1.1	Specify Communication Parameters	14.3	
31.3.1.2	Create Number Range for Time Events a	14.2	
31.3.1.3	Group Personnel Time Event Types	13.2, 13.3	
31.3.1.4	Set Groupings for Connections to the Su	13.6	
31.3.1.5	Enhancement for Link to Time Recording	25.1	
31.3.2	Personnel Time Events		
31.3.2.1	Set Up Attendance/Absences Groupings	13.4	
31.3.2.2	Maintain Attendance/Absence Reasons	13.5	
31.3.2.3	Determine Data to be Displayed at the Te	13.8, 28.6	
31.3.2.4	Set Groupings for Access Control	13.7	
31.3.2.5	Set Up Background Jobs		
31.3.2.5.1	Upload		SM36
31.3.2.5.2	Processing		SM36
31.3.2.5.3	Download		SM36
31.3.3	Employee Expenditures: External, Cafeteria,		
31.3.3.1	Determine Grouping for Employee Exper	26.3	
31.3.3.2	Maintain Wage Types	26.4	
31.3.3.3	Set Up Background Jobs		
31.3.3.3.1	Upload		SM36
31.3.3.3.2	Processing		SM36
31.3.3.3.3	Download		SM36
31.4	Plant Data Collection		
31.4.1	General Settings		
31.4.1.1	Create Number Range for Time Events a	14.2	
31.4.1.2	Group Work Time Event Types	13.2, 13.3	
31.4.1.3	Set Groupings for Subsystem Connectio	13.6	
31.4.1.4	Settings for the Logistics System		
31.4.1.4.1	Activate HR Integration		
31.4.1.4.2	Maintain Standard Value Keys (PP)		
31.4.2	Work Time Events from Logistics		
31.4.2.1	Schedule Background Jobs		
31.4.2.1.1	Process Work Time Events		SM36
31.4.2.2	Data Transfer to Incentive Wages		
31.4.2.2.1	Settings for Pair Formation	28.2	
31.4.3	Working Time Durations from Logistics		
31.4.3.1	Schedule Background Jobs		
31.4.3.1.1	Transfer Confirmations to Attendance		SM36
31.4.3.1.2	Transfer of Confirmations to Incentive		SM36

Sequence number	SAP Customizing Implementation Guide (ECC 6.0)	Where covered	Why not covered
31.5	▽ 🗎 Time Evaluation		
31.5.1	▽ 🗎 General Settings		
31.5.1.1	🗎 🕔 Define Settings for Pair Formation	28.2	
31.5.1.2	🗎 🕔 Schedule Time Evaluation		SM36
31.5.1.3	🗎 🕔 Set Modifier for Earliest Recalculation Da	28.4	
31.5.1.4	🗎 🕔 Set Earliest Recalculation Date for Pair F	28.3	
31.5.1.5	🗎 🕔 Determine Time Evaluation Period		
31.5.2	▽ 🗎 Time Evaluation Settings		Payroll
31.5.2.1	🗎 🕔 Set Personnel Subarea Groupings for Tir	2.4	
31.5.2.2	🗎 🕔 Group Employee Subgroups for the Pers	2.8	
31.5.2.3	🗎 🕔 Set Employee Groupings for the Time Ev	13.9	
31.5.2.4	🗎 🕔 Define Time Types	28.6	
31.5.3	▽ 🗎 Time Evaluation With Clock Times		
31.5.3.1	▽ 🗎 Initial Steps		
31.5.3.1.1	🗎 🕔 Set Controls	3.3	
31.5.3.1.2	🗎 🕔 Define Groupings	32.3.2	
31.5.3.2	▽ 🗎 Providing Time Data		
31.5.3.2.1	▽ 🗎 Work Schedule and Time Events		
31.5.3.2.1.1	🗎 🕔 Determine Breaks for Import		PCR
31.5.3.2.1.2	🗎 🕔 Import Work Schedule and Time E	32.4.9	
31.5.3.2.1.3	🗎 🕔 Import Work Schedule	32.4.23	
31.5.3.2.1.4	▽ 🗎 Dynamic Assignment Based on C		
31.5.3.2.1.4.1	🗎 🕔 Assign Daily Work Schedule C	3.19, 32.4.19	
31.5.3.2.1.4.2	🗎 🕔 Dynamic Assignment Based c	3.20, 32.4.20	
31.5.3.2.1.5	🗎 🕔 Process Time Events with Attenda	32.4.15	
31.5.3.2.2	▽ 🗎 Absences		
31.5.3.2.2.1	🗎 🕔 Provide Absence Data	32.4.13	
31.5.3.2.2.2	🗎 🕔 Provide Full-Day Absences Recor	32.4.16	
31.5.3.2.2.3	🗎 🕔 Adjust Absence Data	32.4.31	
31.5.3.2.3	▽ 🗎 Attendances		
31.5.3.2.3.1	🗎 🕔 Provide Attendance Data	32.4.14	
31.5.3.2.3.2	🗎 🕔 Provide Full-Day Attendances Rec	32.4.16	
31.5.3.2.3.3	🗎 🕔 Import Manually Recorded Overtin	32.4.17	
31.5.3.2.3.4	🗎 🕔 Process Work Center Substitution	32.4.11	
31.5.3.2.4	▽ 🗎 Reduced Working Hours		
31.5.3.2.4.1	🗎 🕔 Import Reduced Hours Data	32.4.4, 4.2	
31.5.3.2.4.2	🗎 🕔 Process Overlapping Leave/Redu	32.4.12	
31.5.3.2.5	▽ 🗎 Checking Time Data		
31.5.3.2.5.1	🗎 🕔 Use Test Procedures Infotype in T		PCR

Sequence number	SAP Customizing Implementation Guide (ECC 6.0)	Where covered	Why not covered
31.10	Management of Roles and Authorizations		
31.10.1	Time Management Authorizations		
31.10.2	Time Management Roles		
31.10.3	Maintain Roles		OoS
31.11	Information System		
31.11.1	Settings for Reporting		
31.11.1.1	Quota Statuses		
31.11.1.1.1	Define Reporting Quota Types	34.10.5, 34.9.6	
31.11.1.2	Employee Time and Labor Data		
31.11.1.2.1	Define Reporting Time Types	34.10.8, 34.10.9	
31.11.2	Set Value Limits for Cumulated Evaluatio	35.16, 35.17, 35.18	
31.12	Web Applications (ITS Version)		
31.12.1	Internet Work Schedule		ESS
31.12.2	Internet Time Accounts		ESS
31.12.3	Internet Time Statement		ESS
31.12.4	Leave Request (New)		
31.12.4.1	Link Absence Types and Workflow Te		ESS
31.12.4.2	Rule Groups for Absence Types and \		ESS
31.12.4.3	BAdI: Link Absence Types and Workfl		ESS
31.12.5	Leave Request (Old)		ESS
32	Payroll		Not TM
33	Training and Event Management		Not TM
34	SAP Global Trade Services		Not TM
35	Management of Internal Controls		Not TM
36	Incentive and Commission Management		Not TM
37	Discrete Industries		Not TM
38	Public Sector Management		Not TM
39	Integration with Other mySAP.com Components		Not TM
40	SAP Banking		Not TM

Reasons for 'why not covered'

Code	Reason
ABAP	The work done by ABAP consultants is out of scope of this book.
CS	Country specific functionalities are not covered.
ESS	You may consult a book on Employee Self Service.
MSS	You may consult a book on Manager Self Service.
Not TM	These nodes are not for Time Management
Obsolete	These functionalities of Time management are obsolete. They are replaced by other functionalities.
OoS	These are out of scope of this book.
PA	You may consult a book on Personnel Administration.
Payroll	You may consult a book on Payroll.
PCR	Time management consultants are expected to have competence to write PCRs.
SA38	Time management consultants are expected to know how to create variants of programs.
Schema	Time management consultants are expected to know how to copy and modify schemas.
SM36	Time management consultants are expected to know how to schedule programs in background.

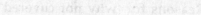

Preface

If you are a consultant or user of SAP HR Time Management, and at some point you did not know what the values in a particular field meant, or what would be the impact of selecting a particular value, this book is for you. If you did not know whether a certain functionality was supported by SAP, this book is for you. This book is also for you, if you did not know why your system was behaving in a certain way.

This book has evolved from the difficulty that each one of us experiences in 'Managing SAP'. As I constantly struggled, trying to understand the concepts of SAP and explore their linkages with other concepts, I found memory to be a major handicap. So I started taking notes. Before long, I could not find what I had written. Then I started reorganizing my notes. And finally I started feeling more comfortable. I knew where to write when I learnt something new, and I could find things I was looking for.

The notes improved continuously, and then came the desire to share them with others. Hence this book. While writing this book, I have tried to be as clear, crisp and comprehensive as possible.

This book is also meant for users of SAP, business process owners and senior managers of companies, who have implemented, or are in the process of implementation, or are planning to implement, or are evaluating SAP HR Time Management. Their need to understand the subject is not as comprehensive as that of functional consultants. How all these category of readers should use this book is described below.

How to use this book

There are two ways in which you can use this book. You can use it as a learning guide, and you can use it as a technical reference. When you use this book as a learning guide, you have to cover it in several iterations. Each iteration is designed to enhance your knowledge and prepare you for the next iteration.

In terms of job roles one can classify the readers as senior managers, business process owners, users, and functional consultants. Senior managers need to know only the important concepts, and what SAP can do for them. BPOs need to know more of SAP concepts and have a good idea of how to perform different tasks in SAP. Users need to have a thorough understanding of different tasks they have to perform in SAP and concepts underlying them. Functional consultants need to know everything, or at least everything important.

In the table of contents, each topic is classified in terms of relevance and importance for each category of user. Each topic is given A, B, C, or X rating for each category of user.

During each iteration, you can decide the role and importance level you intend to cover. You can select the role you are going to refer to in an iteration, based on your job role, but that is not essential. For example, if you are going to be a user of SAP, but do not know anything about SAP, you may select senior manager role in your first iteration. Having learnt important concepts, you may select BPO role in the next iteration. Finally you may select user role. Also, once you become a proficient user, you may go through the book from the perspective of a functional consultant.

In the table of contents, I have left two blank columns. Although I have given an importance rating to each topic, you can decide the importance based on your requirements. For example, if you are not implementing shift planning, or overtime, or availability, you may mark them as not relevant for you. Similarly, you can decide the importance rating. There is nothing sacrosanct about the rating given by me. You may note this rating in the blank column 'MR', meaning my rating. As you read a topic, you achieve a level of understanding. You can record it in the column 'UL', meaning understanding level. You may use A/B/C/X, or any other rating scale. After you complete an iteration, these columns will help you decide, which topics to revisit.

When you are reading this book, you need to work on the system. When you are reading only the important concepts as senior manager, it may be possible to read the book without hands-on experience. However, as you go deeper and deeper, working on the system becomes more and more necessary.

If you are using this book as a technical reference, apart from the table of contents and index, you can also locate the relevant material by using 'SAP Menu', and 'SAP Customizing Implementation Guide (IMG)'. Expanded tree of both the SAP menu and 'SAP Customizing Implementation Guide is given after the table of contents. Once you find the node in these structures, you are guided to the relevant chapter. If that node is not covered in the book, that is also mentioned along with the reason for not covering it. In such cases you have to look for information elsewhere; this book will not help you.

You can also use the structure of this book to keep your discoveries in an organized way. You can maintain a Word or Excel document where you record your discoveries either against page numbers or chapter numbers. You can also share your discoveries with me (agrawal.prem@gmail.com) and help make this book even more useful in future editions.

You can also use the structure of this book for guiding your discussion with the users and recording their input. That document will finally become the configuration-cum-user manual.

Acknowledgements

I am deeply indebted to my employer, my colleagues (particularly Sreedhar Raju, Milind Deval, Lopa Ganguly and Anand Dhodapkar), and my family, who contributed in different ways to make this book possible. I express my sincere gratitude to my publisher, PHI Learning Private Limited, for putting their trust in me and for improving the presentation of this book.

Individual social responsibility

There is no doubt that we must excel in our chosen profession. But our responsibility does not end there. Indeed, we have a greater responsibility of making the world a better place to live in—to address the challenges the world faces, to analyze, to find solutions, to share, to network, and to make a difference. You may have wondered about the diagram on the cover page; it is a plan for a city without traffic lights. There are four articles at the end of this book. You will perhaps find them interesting to read. In particular, think about Samay Daan. You are welcome to get in touch with me (agrawal.prem@gmail.com). Let us make a difference together. It is our Individual Social Responsibility.

P.K. AGRAWAL

Infotypes

1.1 INFOTYPE CONCEPTS

Functional Consultant	User	Business Process Owner	Senior Management	My Rating	Understanding Level
A	A	A	A		

SAP lets you keep a large amount of information about your employees. This is organized in logically related sets called *infotypes*.

The screenshot on the next page shows the organizational assignment (infotype 0001) of one employee. Apart from the time infotypes, which you would create, you would usually view the following infotypes.

0000	Actions
0001	Organizational Assignment
0002	Personal Data
0003	Payroll Status
0006	Addresses

In this chapter the above infotypes and the time management infotypes are explained to you, and some concepts which are common to all infotypes are also covered.

Personnel number

In SAP, an employee is uniquely identified by his eight-digit personnel number. Thus, even if two employees have identical names, you would be able to distinguish them from their personnel numbers. This number can be system generated or externally assigned.

1

Change Organizational Assignment

| | | | Org Structure | |

Pers.No.	121715		Name	Agrawal Prem
Pers.area	PNCV Pune CVBU			
EE subgrp	E4 DM		WS rule	WSRPG G SHIFT
Start	01.01.2005 to	31.12.9999	Chng 07.07.2006	QHRPKA000137

Enterprise structure

CoCode	0100	Tata Motors Limited			
Pers.area	PNCV	Pune CVBU	Subarea	CV9Z	TTL
Cost Ctr			Bus. Area		

Personnel structure

EE group	1	Permanent	Payr.area	P1	Pune CVBU MR
EE subgroup	E4	DM	Contract		

Organizational plan

Percentage	100.00	
Position	99999999	Integration: default po...
Job key	00000000	
Org. Unit	00000000	

Administrator

Group	PNCV
PersAdmin	
Time	
PayrAdmin	

SAP does not support alphanumeric employee identification. It is also possible to generate personnel numbers in different ranges for different units of an organization.

Validity period

Let us consider infotype 0001, which contains the employee's organizational assignment. What happens if a person is transferred? You can update this information in the system. However, what if you wanted to know where was he prior to this or in which grade an employee was during a particular period in the past? SAP recognizes that employee information may change over a period, and that you may want to know what it was in the past. Therefore, it lets you assign a validity period to each infotype record. You can even create infotype records for future. Thus, if you decide that an employee is going to be promoted, and that the promotion will be effective next month, you can enter this information in the system. It does not interfere with the current information or current processes. This is a very powerful feature of SAP.

Subtype

Some infotypes may have subtypes. For example, your company may have different types of leaves. All these are stored as subtypes of infotype 2001.

Time constraint

Since SAP lets you create data with validity period, sometimes you may have data conflicts. For example, can you be present and absent at the same time? To control such inconsistencies in data, SAP has a concept of time constraint.

For most infotypes, the validity period is in days and consistency is checked with other records of the same infotype.

However, for some time management infotypes, the record is for a time period (which may be part of a day) and its consistency is checked not only with other records of that infotype, but also with records of other infotypes.

For each infotype, time constraint is predefined by SAP. Functional consultants may change it if required. If a user ever finds inconsistent data, he can take it up with his consultant. It is the consultant's job to set the system such that data consistency is ensured.

Two-step data entry process: Maker checker concept

SAP permits a two-step data entry process in which one person enters the data, and another approves it. Technically, the first person creates a locked record, which the second person unlocks, with or without modification. The locked record is not used for any purpose and remains dormant waiting to be unlocked. When you create a new record, it could be delimiting the previous record. In case you create a locked record, this does not happen, but when you unlock the record, the same action takes place.

There are two ways of creating a locked record. The system can be so configured that when a user creates a record, it is always created locked. Alternatively, the user can create a record and lock it before saving.

Reason for change

When creating or changing an infotype, one can specify the reasons for change. During customizing, reasons for change for each infotype are created as per your needs.

Date of last change

This field is system-maintained, and is useful when one has to investigate suspect data changes.

User who changed object

This field is also system-maintained, and is useful when one has to investigate suspect data changes.

Historical record flag

If you mark a record 'historical', it is permanently stored in the database and is available for reporting. However, it cannot be changed.

Storing additional information with an infotype

For many infotypes SAP allows entry of free text associated with a record (Edit ➤ Maintain Text). This text is stored elsewhere and not in the infotype.

Infotype header

In any infotype screen, you see a header, which contains information that does not necessarily come from that infotype. For example, in most infotypes, the header would contain employee name, which comes from infotype 0002. Also, when you are viewing employee data for a past period, should the header information be for that period, or should it be for the current period? SAP lets you decide what information is to be shown in the header, and whether it should be for the current period or for the period of the infotype.

A user only needs to ensure that the data being displayed meets his requirement. If not, he should speak to his consultant. Also, note that the header information can vary from infotype to infotype.

Infotype screen

SAP usually has a large number of fields in each infotype. You may not need all of them. Therefore, during configuration, your consultant would decide what fields should be shown on the screen, whether they are mandatory, optional, and so on.

A user needs to ensure that the fields not needed by him are not shown on the screen, and that the field properties are right. If he doesn't like what he sees, he should talk to his consultant. Note that SAP provides the flexibility of having multiple screens for the same infotype. However, whether this feature is used or not depends on how critical is the need and the management policy.

1.2 INFOTYPE PROCESSES

Functional Consultant	User	Business Process Owner	Senior Management	My Rating	Understanding Level
A	A	A	A		

When you use transaction PA61 and enter personnel number, infotype, and subtype if applicable, you can create a new infotype record, or modify or delete an existing one. These are briefly described as follows.

Create

Normally when an infotype record is created, the start date is known but the end date is not known. This is to be represented by putting end date as 31/12/9999, which is the default date. When the infotype data changes, a new record is created where the changed information is specified with the date from which it is valid. Thus, there will be two records which will be valid on the start date of the second record. If this infotype has time constraint 1, SAP recognizes that the first record is no longer valid from the start date of the second record. Therefore, it automatically updates the end date of the first record to one day before the start date of the second record. In this way, SAP maintains time constraint 1 with minimal user effort. Also, if a record is created and its validity clashes with more than one existing record, the first existing record is delimited and the subsequent records are deleted. The system gives a warning in such cases.

Change

If you change data in an infotype (other than the data in primary key which cannot be changed) and save it, the old data is overwritten. It is not possible to know what the information was before the change was made.

Display

Using this method, an infotype record can be displayed for viewing.

Copy

If one wishes to enter data afresh, one creates a record, but if the data change is not much, it saves effort to copy and modify. Normally, create gives a blank screen, but in some cases, create also works as copy, e.g. for personal data infotype.

Delimit

Normally, creating a new record delimits the previous record. However, if a record is to be delimited without creating another, then this method can be used. Needless to say, it cannot be used for infotypes having time constraint 1.

Delete

An employee's infotype record can be deleted. The system behaviour depends on time constraint. If the time constraint is 1 and there is only one record, it cannot be deleted. If there are multiple records and the first record is deleted, the period of the second record is extended to cover the period of the first record as well. If any other record is deleted, the previous record's to-date is extended to cover the period of the deleted record as well. For infotypes having time constraint 2 or 3, a record can be deleted without causing any side effect.

Overview

Overview shows all records of an infotype. One can specify date range for which one wishes to see the records. It is also possible to select the record from the overview mode and go into maintain/display mode.

Exploring SAP

Using SAP effectively requires exploring. There are so many screens and so many fields and icons on each screen that no one can hope to explain everything to you. On top of that, your screen may change, or you may get a new window, depending on the data you enter, or the icon you press. Your best guide is your experience, a spirit of exploration, on-line help, and this book. However, the basic infotype processes, which appear as icons on the screen when you execute transaction PA30/PA61, have been explained as they cover important concepts related to infotypes.

1.3 ACTIONS (INFOTYPE 0000)

Functional Consultant	User	Business Process Owner	Senior Management	My Rating	Understanding Level
A	A	A	A		

1.3.1 Screen

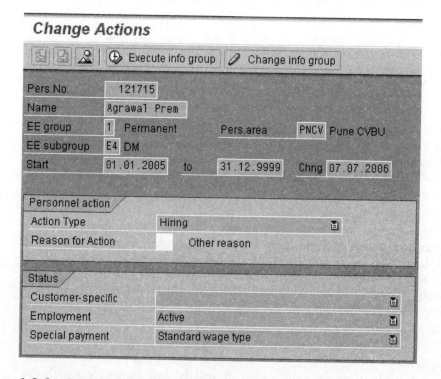

Change Actions

1.3.2 Purpose and Overview

Infotype 0000 shows you the important events during the employment of an employee, e.g. hiring, promotion, salary change and disciplinary action. It also shows you the employment status of an employee on a given day, which is very important information in terms of relationship between the employee and the company, and determines whether the employee's payroll is run or not.

Status	Description	Explanation
0	Withdrawn	These employees have left the company for good and no relationship with the company exists. Payroll is not run for withdrawn employees.
1	Inactive	These employees are not working for the company currently, but they are employed with the company, e.g. employees on study leave.
2	Retiree	These employees have left the company, but their relationship with the company continues in some form, e.g. for payment of pension.
3	Active	These employees are currently working for the company.

1.4 ORGANIZATIONAL ASSIGNMENT (INFOTYPE 0001)

Functional Consultant	User	Business Process Owner	Senior Management	My Rating	Understanding Level
A	A	A	A		

1.4.1 Screen

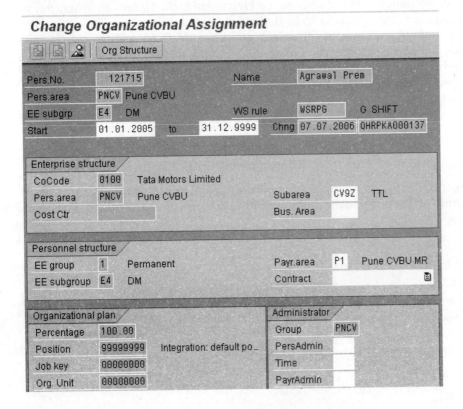

1.4.2 Purpose and Overview

Infotype 0001 is a crucial infotype in SAP-HR. It stores the employee's relationship with the organization. This relationship is in terms of his place in the organization (position), his physical location (enterprise structure), and the groups of employees (personnel structure) to which he belongs.

SAP realizes that the rules in an organization may not be uniform for all its employees. It caters to this requirement by giving you flexibility in two ways. Your rules may differ based on an employee's physical location. They may also differ based on the category (groups) of employees.

Based on physical location, the employees are divided in personnel areas and personnel subareas. Many rules, particularly rules in time management area, can depend on the PA and PSA, and thereby can be different for different employees.

Rules may also be different, for example, for executives and for workmen. SAP provides two attributes, employee group and employee subgroup, which can be assigned to employees, and based on which different rules can be applied to different employees. Unlike PA and PSA, which is a two-level hierarchy of locations, employee group and employee subgroup are independent attributes of an employee.

In an organization, both the number of PSAs as well as the number of EG + ESG combinations can be very large. When the rules depend on them, the rules have to be defined for each combination. This can become a Herculean task. Moreover, whenever a PSA, EG or ESG is added, the rules have to be defined for each combination. This difficulty is overcome by defining groupings of PSAs and groupings of EG + ESG combinations. For each purpose, say appraisal, you can create PS grouping and ES grouping. PSAs are grouped in PS grouping for appraisal, and EG + ESG combinations are grouped in ES grouping for appraisal. In this way, the flexibility is also retained and configuration of rules is also manageable.

This infotype also contains the employee's company code, business area and cost center, which are needed when you post employee-related costs in FI/CO module of SAP.

Payroll area forms groups of employees whose payroll is run together.

The time administrator is the employee's administrator for time recording. It can be used for assigning administrative tasks and authorization checks.

1.5 PERSONAL DATA (INFOTYPE 0002)

Functional Consultant	User	Business Process Owner	Senior Management	My Rating	Understanding Level
A	A	A	A		

1.5.1 Screen

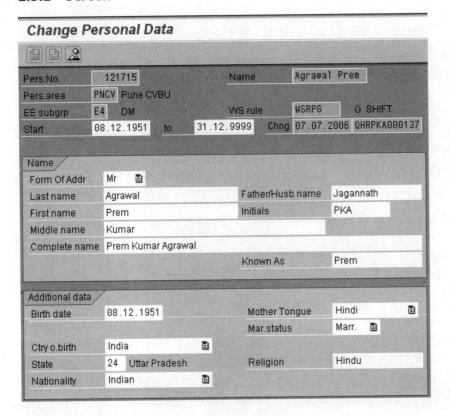

Change Personal Data

Pers.No.	121715	Name	Agrawal Prem
Pers.area	PNCV Pune CVBU		
EE subgrp	E4 DM	WS rule	WSRPG G SHIFT
Start	08.12.1951 to 31.12.9999	Chng	07.07.2006 QHRPKA000137

Name

Form Of Addr	Mr		
Last name	Agrawal	Father/Husb name	Jagannath
First name	Prem	Initials	PKA
Middle name	Kumar		
Complete name	Prem Kumar Agrawal		
		Known As	Prem

Additional data

Birth date	08.12.1951	Mother Tongue	Hindi
		Mar.status	Marr.
Ctry o.birth	India		
State	24 Uttar Pradesh	Religion	Hindu
Nationality	Indian		

1.5.2 Purpose and Overview

The personal data Infotype stores personal information of an employee. This infotype has time constraint 1, which means that an infotype data record must exist in the system at all times from the date the employee is hired. The validity start for the first record of the infotype 0002 is determined from the employee's date of birth, and not from the date of his joining the organization, as is the case for most other infotypes.

1.6 PAYROLL STATUS (INFOTYPE 0003)

Functional Consultant	User	Business Process Owner	Senior Management	My Rating	Understanding Level
A	A	A	A		

1.6.1 Screen

Change Payroll Status

| | | | Payroll correction | | | |

Pers.No.   121715   Name   Agrawal Prem

Pers.area   PNCV Pune CVBU

EE subgrp   E4   DM   WS rule   WSRPG

Chng 07.07.2006 QHRPKA000137

Payroll/retroactive accounting

Earl.pers. RA date   Accounted to

Run payroll up to   Earliest MD change   01.01.2005

Do not account after   Mast.data chng.bonus 01.01.2005   →

☐ Pers.no.locked   ☐ Payroll correction

Time evaluation

Earl.pers.rec.date   Pers.calendar from

PDC recalculation   01.01.2005

☐ PDC error indicator

Other data

Initial input   07.07.2006   13:56:40

1.6.2 Purpose and Overview

Infotype 0003 contains control data for an employee's payroll and time accounting. The system automatically creates this infotype when an employee is hired. Whenever an infotype is updated, which requires that the employee's payroll or time evaluation is to be run for a past period, the system automatically updates this infotype. The infotypes which result in retro accounting of payroll and time management are defined in table T582A.

You can control retro accounting at employee level for payroll and time management. You can temporarily stop the payroll of an employee by updating lock indicator. It controls whether an employee's payroll runs or not.

The earliest personal retroactive accounting date for time management enables you to restrict the earliest retroactive accounting period for time evaluation (including pair formation) for individual employees.

'Personal calendar from' specifies the date as of which the employee's personal calendar must be generated.

'PDC Recalculation' specifies the date on which the next time evaluation run should start. When time evaluation is complete, the date is set to the first day for which the report has not yet been run. This field is used for the retroactive accounting recognition in PDC Time Management.

PDC Error Indicator: The system automatically activates this indicator, if a personnel number is rejected in time evaluation.

There is no history maintained for this infotype. There is only one record which has the current status. Infotype 0003 can also be maintained using transaction PU03.

1.7 ADDRESSES (INFOTYPE 0006)

Functional Consultant	User	Business Process Owner	Senior Management	My Rating	Understanding Level
A	A	A	A		

1.7.1 Screen

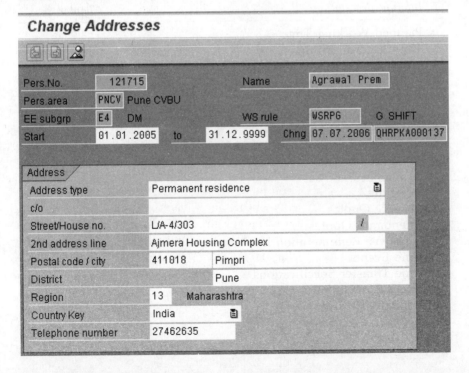

1.7.2 Purpose and Overview

The addresses infotype is used to store address information. All regular employees must have a permanent address, which is stored in subtype 1. This is mandatory for running payroll. In infotype 0006, you can maintain different types of addresses of an employee, e.g. permanent address, present address and emergency address. Different types of addresses are maintained as subtypes of infotype 0006 and identified by the address type field.

Time constraints of infotype 0006 are at subtype level. Thus, you may permit multiple emergency addresses, but allow only one permanent address.

1.8 TIME MANAGEMENT INFOTYPES

Functional Consultant	User	Business Process Owner	Senior Management	My Rating	Understanding Level
A	A	A	A		

Of the many infotypes you have in SAP, some may be called time management infotypes. As a time management user you are going to maintain them day in and day out. It is, therefore, very important that you understand them thoroughly; what information they contain, how to use them, and what is their impact. Each infotype is described in this book in considerable detail. The following table tells you which chapter to refer to, so that you understand the contents of each infotype clearly.

Infotype	Infotype description	Chapter
0007	Planned Working Time	3.2
0050	Time Recording Info	13.1
0080	Maternity Protection/Parental Leave	17.1
0081	Military Service	18.1
0082	Additional Absence Data	19.1
0416	Time Quota Compensation	10.1
2001	Absences	5.1
2002	Attendances	6.1
2003	Substitutions	4.1
2004	Availability	12.1
2005	Overtime	11.3
2006	Absence Quotas	7.1
2007	Attendance Quotas	9.1
2010	Employee Remuneration Info	16.1
2011	Time Events	14.1
2012	Time Transfer Specifications	15.1
2013	Quota Corrections	8.1
2050	Annual Calendar	5.16

(Contd.)

Infotype	Infotype description	Chapter
2051	Monthly Calendar	5.17
2052	Weekly Entry w/Activity Allocation	5.18
2500	Personal Work Schedule Times	1.10
2501	Employee Time and Labor Data	1.11
2502	Quota Statuses	1.12

1.9 SIMULATED INFOTYPES

Functional Consultant	User	Business Process Owner	Senior Management	My Rating	Understanding Level
A	A	B	C		

Usually data of an infotype is stored in a database table and can be read in ad hoc query. Some data is also stored in clusters, and cannot be queried using ad hoc query. This causes inconvenience as data from infotypes and clusters cannot be viewed together. SAP solves this problem by providing simulated infotypes. In time management, infotypes 2500, 2501 and 2502 are simulated infotypes. SAP does not store data in database tables for these infotypes, but they can be queried in ad hoc query and ABAP programs like any other infotype. However, you cannot see these infotypes using transactions PA20, PA30, PA51 and PA61.

1.10 PERSONAL WORK SCHEDULE TIMES (INFOTYPE 2500)

Functional Consultant	User	Business Process Owner	Senior Management	My Rating	Understanding Level
A	A	B	C		

The personal work schedule simulated infotype provides information from the personal work schedule. Personal work schedule is derived from the work schedule rule specified for an employee in infotype 0007. Substitutions from infotype 2003 are superimposed on it. No configuration is required for this infotype.

1.11   EMPLOYEE TIME AND LABOR DATA (INFOTYPE 2501)

Functional Consultant	User	Business Process Owner	Senior Management	My Rating	Understanding Level
A	A	B	C		

In this infotype, you can see data based on reporting time types. Reporting time types combine data from attendances and absences, time types, and wage types. Configuration in chapter 34.9.8 is done to map different reporting time types to their constituents.

1.12   QUOTA STATUSES (INFOTYPE 2502)

Functional Consultant	User	Business Process Owner	Senior Management	My Rating	Understanding Level
A	A	B	C		

You can use this infotype to see a comprehensive view of the absence and attendance quotas. Apart from data from infotypes 2006 and 2007, it can also take into account cluster data from table SALDO, which contains time balances. Since time balances can be used for taking time off, etc. by combining this data with infotype data, one gets a comprehensive picture. In order to use this infotype, configuration described in chapter 34.9.5 is necessary.

1.13   INFOTYPE MAINTENANCE

Functional Consultant	User	Business Process Owner	Senior Management	My Rating	Understanding Level
A	A	A	B		

1.13.1   Maintain Time Data

When you enter transaction PA61, you get the following screen, which is used to enter all infotypes for an employee.

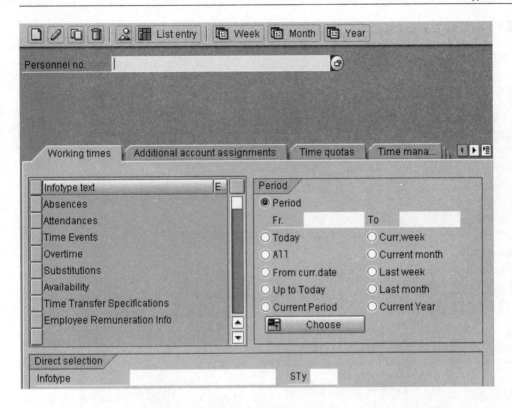

The 🔲 icon next to the 'Personnel number' field indicates that you can see the list of personnel numbers in the system. When you click on this icon, the system shows you a sub-screen, which can help you find an individual based on his name, etc.

Here you see some tabs, and in each tab, there are some infotypes. The tabs and infotypes in each tab are defined by your consultant. Wherever data in an infotype exists for an employee, it is displayed by a green check mark. You can select an infotype from a tab page, and perform activities, e.g. create, change, copy and delete; or you can enter infotype and subtype directly on the screen.

Now look at the box labeled 'Period'. SAP recognizes that employee information may change over a period of time. Therefore, you can have multiple records of an infotype for a personnel number. When you specify the period in this box, you will see only those records, which are valid during that period. Also, if you are creating a record, this period will be proposed as the validity period of the new record, which you can change if you like.

If you do not fill the period field, SAP uses a default value. This default is set by your consultant, and can be different for different infotypes.

Transaction PA51 is a display version of transaction PA61. Transactions PA30, PA20 and PU03 are similar to PA61 and PA51. Only these transactions don't have the calendar icons.

1.13.2 Fast Entry

When you enter transaction PA71, you get the following screen.

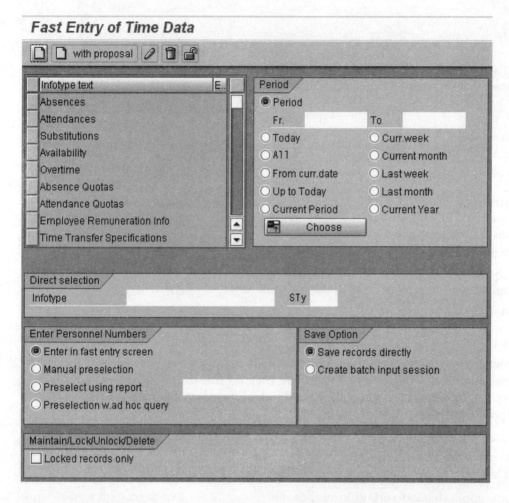

Fast Entry of Time Data

When you have to enter the data in bulk, entering it through normal SAP screens can be time consuming. SAP offers you alternative methods of data entry. Fast entry is a very good alternative. You can either select the infotype from the displayed list, or you may enter it directly. However, note that this method is available for limited infotypes only. Therefore, for some infotypes, you may get an error message.

The concept of period here is the same as that in transaction PA61. If no value is entered, a default value is picked up. You don't have to enter each and every personnel number manually. You can select the population using ad hoc query. You can also select the population using a report, where you can also use the organization structure to select the population.

Usually, you save the records directly, but if your list is too big, you can create a batch input session. If you select the check box, 'Locked records only', only locked records are selected, unlocked records are not selected. If you don't tick this checkbox, all records are selected.

Let us look at the simplest option; create records with personnel number entry in fast screen:

Personnel number	Type	Start	End	From	To	L	C
				02.03.2006	02.03.2006		I
				02.03.2006	02.03.2006		I
				02.03.2006	02.03.2006		I
				02.03.2006	02.03.2006		I

When you click on the 'Create' icon, fast entry data screen is displayed. You may take special note of 'lock indicator', which determines whether records will be locked or unlocked. Also take note of 'Operation indicator', which indicates whether the record will be inserted, changed or deleted. Here, it is being inserted.

In the above screen, you got from-date and to-date by default. You can get more fields by default, if you 'Create with proposal'.

Through Fast entry, not only can you create new records, but also change, delete, lock or unlock them. Suppose you want to change data of 10 employees for a certain period. Enter the period, enter the employees using manual preselection, and click on 'Change'. The system fetches and shows you the data, which you may change and save. In the same way, you can also delete, lock or unlock infotype records.

1.13.3 Maintaining Additional Data

SAP supports various features, e.g. activity allocation (chapter 21), cost assignment (chapter 22), external services (chapter 23), and different payments (chapter 24). If these are used in your organization, you may see relevant chapters to understand them.

These are applicable for certain infotypes. For example, you may create an attendance record with activity allocation. This data can be entered in infotype 2002 itself by clicking on the activity allocation icon. However, if there is more data, you may find that method time-consuming. You can use transaction PA62 to enter such data in an easy manner.

Employee Groupings

2.1 OVERVIEW

Functional Consultant	User	Business Process Owner	Senior Management	My Rating	Understanding Level
A	A	A	A		

SAP understands that your policies may not be the same for all employees. For example, the holidays may differ from area to area, taking into account local needs and statutory regulations. Similarly, attendance recording requirements for workmen may be different from those for executives. SAP lets you define different rules for different employees. It does so primarily on the basis of geographic locations (PA + PSA) and category of the employee (EG + ESG).

Since combinations of PA + PSA, as well as EG + ESG can be very large, it can become a nightmare to define the rules in the system. SAP, therefore, lets you create Personnel Subarea groupings (PS grouping) as well as Employee Subgroup groupings (ES grouping). Also, it lets you do so for each purpose. For example, you may have different policies for time recording, but uniform policy for work schedule. SAP lets you define it that way and use it appropriately.

PS groupings are defined in view V_001P_ALL, and ES groupings are defined in V_503_ALL. Other tables in this section are prerequisite for these two views. Both these sets of groupings are widely used in time management configuration.

All the needs of employee grouping are not met by these two views. You will encounter more groupings in this book. For example, some of the employee groupings are defined by a PCR called by function MOD. These groupings are used in time evaluation.

SAP also provides a feature, LLREP, which you can use to run different variants of reports, e.g. time statement, for different employees.

2.2 PERSONNEL AREA

Functional Consultant	User	Business Process Owner	Senior Management	My Rating	Understanding Level
A	A	A	A		

2.2.1 Purpose and Overview

View T500P contains the master list of personnel areas. SAP can be configured to apply different logic to different employees based on the personnel area to which they belong, particularly in the area of time management.

In SAP HR, you can use 'Features' to build customer specific logic to categorize employees and use different logic or default values for them. Personnel area is one of the important employee characteristics, which is often used to meet your requirements. For example, the personnel area is used to generate default values for an employee's payroll area.

Usually both PA and PSA are available for decision making in features, but feature NUMKR is an exception. You may have multiple personnel number ranges, and the range from which an employee gets his personnel number can depend on his personnel area, but not on his personnel subarea.

In SAP payroll and time management, there are Personnel Calculation Rules (PCRs), in which you can query employee characteristics and perform different operations, based on the result. PA is used in them.

Personnel area is an important manpower reporting parameter, although it is debatable whether it should be so. Ideally, manpower reporting should happen based on the organization structure. If you don't take this decision in the beginning itself, the manpower reporting will evolve around personnel area and personnel subarea. Once that happens, PA and PSA will start getting defined based on manpower reporting need. Then they will become more volatile. If you stick to the basic purpose of PA and PSA, which is to allow flexibility in defining company rules based on employee location, you will have much more stable PA–PSA regime.

Personnel area determines an employee's company code.

The authorization of users can be limited to specified personnel area. Note that PSA cannot be used for authorization check. If you have many personnel areas, it is useful to have a good naming convention. This can serve to group the personnel areas, either in ranges or using wild card characters. One of the places you can use these groupings in is authorization.

2.2.2 IMG Node

SM30 ➤ T500P

2.2.3 Screen

Personnel area	AR01	Oficina central Argentina

Personnel Areas

House No. and Street	San Martin 575
PO Box	
Postal Code	
City	Capital Federal
Country Key	AR
Region	00
County code	
City code	

2.2.4 Primary Key

Personnel Area

2.2.5 Important Fields

All fields are self-explanatory. You also need to maintain the address of the PA through the icon ▣.

2.3 ASSIGNMENT OF PERSONNEL AREA TO COMPANY CODE

Functional Consultant	User	Business Process Owner	Senior Management	My Rating	Understanding Level
A	A	A	A		

2.3.1 Purpose

This view of personnel area table T500P stores the linkage between personnel area and company code.

2.3.2 IMG Node

SM30 ≻ V_T500P

2.3.3 Screen

Change View "Assignment of Personnel Area to Company Code":

Pers.area	Personnel Area Text	Company Code	Company Name	Ctry grpg
1000	Hamburg	1000	IDES AG	01
1100	Berlin	1000	IDES AG	01
1200	Dresden	1000	IDES AG	01
1300	Frankfurt	1000	IDES AG	01
1400	Stuttgart	1000	IDES AG	01
1900	ALE Lissabon	2000	IDES UK	19
1901	ALE Porto	2100	IDES Portugal	19

2.3.4 Primary Key

Personnel Area

2.3.5 Important Fields

Company code

In SAP, company code is determined from personnel area. Company code is an important employee attribute, which determines from which company code the employee gets paid.

Country grouping

PA also determines the country grouping to which an employee belongs. A PA cannot span across multiple country groupings.

2.3.6 Caution

If you decide to split your company code and assign some personnel areas to a new company code or merge company codes, and therefore need to do the same or transfer a PA from one company code to another company code, you have a problem. If you were to change PA to company code relationship, and payroll for an employee ran with retro effect, the system would pay in the new company code and recover from old company code, because there is no date validity for personnel area table. Similarly, if a personnel area is no longer in use, it cannot be delimited or deleted. You have to depend on either user discipline, or write a user exit to prevent its use.

2.4 PERSONNEL SUBAREA

Functional Consultant	*User*	*Business Process Owner*	*Senior Management*	*My Rating*	*Understanding Level*
A	A	A	A		

2.4.1 Purpose and Overview

On the basis of physical location, a company code is divided into personnel areas, which are further divided into personnel subareas. On any given day, an employee belongs to one of the personnel subareas. View V_001P_ALL contains the list of PSAs.

SAP provides the flexibility to build different rules for employees in different locations, based on PSAs. Since PSAs could be many, they are grouped into PSA groupings for defining rules. However, the rules belong to different areas. For example, you want to group PSAs for appraisal. You also want to group PSAs for time recording. The way you want to group PSAs for appraisal may be different from the way you want to group PSAs for time recording. SAP lets you create separate groupings, one for each purpose. This view contains all the groupings for the PSAs.

Some countries also have country specific PS groupings, e.g. those in table T7IN0P for India. If the payroll does not run, giving error 'no currency in T001P', entry in table T500C is missing.

2.4.2 IMG Node

SM30 ➤ V_001P_ALL

2.4.3 Screen

PA	PA text	PSu...	PS text	Pr...	P..	A...	L...	T...	W...	H...	A...	TR...	A...	S...	PS ...	P...	L..	S..
IN01	IN Model ...	0001	Admin	1	40	40	40	40	IN	40	01	40		01	01		
IN01	IN Model ...	0002	Produ...	1	40	40	40	40	IN	40	01	40		03	01		
IN02	IN Model ...	0001	Admin	1	40	40	40	40	IN	40	01	40		01	01		
IN03	IN Model ...	0001	Admin	1	40	40	40	40	IN	40	01	40		01	01		

2.4.4 Primary Key

Personnel Area + Personnel Subarea

2.4.5 Important Fields

Personnel area, personnel subarea

A company code is divided into personnel areas, which are further subdivided into personnel subareas. An employee belongs to one of these personnel subareas. This view contains the properties of personnel subareas.

PS grouping for leave types

This field is obsolete.

Pay scale area

This is used to default pay scale area in infotype 0008. However, feature TARIF takes precedence over it.

Pay scale type

This is used to default pay scale type in infotype 0008. However, feature TARIF takes precedence over it.

PS grouping for absence and attendance types

The types of leave a company has are defined as absence types. Similarly, attendance types include training, business tour, etc. The properties of absence and attendance types are defined in table T554S. For example, you could specify that minimum duration of privilege leave is 3 days. SAP lets you configure different properties for different PSAs. For example, in one state the minimum duration may be 3 days, but in another state it may be 4 days. You could create 2 groups of PSAs, one for state 1 and another for state 2, and configure these rules in SAP.

PS grouping for substitution/availability types

The properties of substitution types (T556) and availability types (T557) can be different based on this grouping.

PS grouping for attendance and absence counting

Rules for Attendance/Absence Counting and Leave Deduction (T554X) depend on this grouping. This is an obsolete grouping. It was used when leave entitlement was kept in infotype 0005. Table T554X is also obsolete now.

Legal person

Your payroll consultant decides if this is needed. This defaults in infotype 0001.

PS grouping for time recording

This grouping is a key field in most tables related to time types, important among them being T555A Time Types, T555E Time Evaluation Messages, T555J Transfer to Time Types, T555K Transfer to Time Wage Types, and T555L Transfer to Absence Quotas.

PS grouping for time quota types

This grouping is a key field in most tables related to time quotas, important among them being T556A Absence Quota Types, T555L Transfer to Absence Quotas, T556C Counting Rule for Attendances and Absences, T556P Attendance Quotas, T556R Rules for Deduction Sequence for Absence Quotas, T556U Attendance/Absence Quota Compensation Types, T556W Wage Type Assignment for Att./Absence Quota Compensations.

PS grouping for premiums

This grouping is used in configuring different premiums in table T510P.

PS grouping for primary wage type and wage maintenance

This grouping is used to allow/restrict a wage type to certain PSAs. The values must be from 0 to 9. It is used in view V_511_B Define Wage Type Permissibility for each PS and ESG.

Statistics modifier

This field is required for reporting ASM and BIGA statistics in Switzerland.

PS grouping for appraisals

This grouping is a key field in tables related to appraisals: T513G Appraisal Groups, T513H Appraisal Criteria, T510B Appraisal Constants and T513PAPD PA-PD: Assign Appraisal Models to EE (sub)area/(sub)group.

Public holiday calendar

Public holiday calendar is defined at the PSA level.

PS grouping for work schedules

This grouping is a key field in T508A Work Schedule Rules, T508Z Assignment of PS Grouping for Work Schedules to Daily WS. Through the later table, it is key for T550A Daily Work Schedule, T550P Break Schedules, T551A Period Work Schedules, T551C Period Work Schedule Valuation, T552V Dynamic Daily Work Schedule Assignment, and T552W Dynamic Daily WS Assignment: Planned/Actual Overlap.

2.4.6 Caution

Lack of validity period in this table also causes problems. Suppose you have one holiday calendar for all PSAs, and you are in production environment for several years. Then you decide that some of your PSAs need to have a different holiday calendar. If you change PSA to holiday calendar assignment, you have a problem with retro. You have to create the holiday calendar from the day you went live, generate work schedules, make all the adjustments you did in those work schedules (e.g. change in off days). Alternatively, you create a new PSA, assign the new holiday calendar, and shift all employees of the old PSA to the new PSA. Also, you have to ensure that the old PSA is no longer used. There is no way of doing this in standard SAP. You have to enforce this discipline manually, or write a user exit so that the old PSA is not used from the date it is made invalid.

2.4.7 PS Grouping for Daily Work Schedules

You can club multiple PS grouping for work schedules into a single PS grouping for daily work schedules. PS grouping for daily work schedules is part of the primary key for the following tables:

T550A	Daily Work Schedules (DWS)
T550P	Break Schedules
T551A	Period Work Schedules (PWS)
T551C	Period Work Schedule Valuation
T552V	Dynamic Daily Work Schedule Assignment
T552W	Dynamic Daily WS Assignment: Planned/Actual Overlap

You may first determine PS grouping for daily work schedules required by you, based on DWS, PWS, break schedules, etc. Normally, the same can be used as PS grouping for work schedules (one-to-one correspondence). However, if you find that at work schedule rule level you need more flexibility, e.g. different start day for period work schedule, you may define more PS grouping for work schedules in view T508Z and link them to PS grouping for daily work schedules.

PS grouping	DWS grouping
01	01
02	02
03	03
04	04

2.5 EMPLOYEE GROUP

Functional Consultant	User	Business Process Owner	Senior Management	My Rating	Understanding Level
A	A	A	A		

2.5.1 Purpose

Employee groups let you categorize your employees for identification and reporting. Employee groups can be used in features and PCRs. You can use them to generate data entry default values; e.g. for payroll area. User authorization can be restricted based on employee groups. ES groupings are defined at employee group, employee subgroup level.

2.5.2 IMG Node

SM30 ➤ T501

2.5.3 Screen

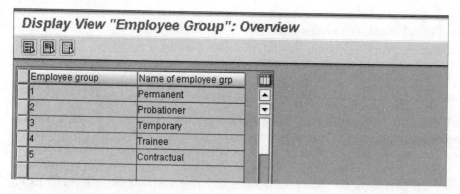

2.5.4 Primary Key

Employee Group

2.5.5 Important Fields

Employee group

You may use employee group to capture an important characteristic of employee, e.g. permanent, temporary and trainee. Since rules can be based on employee group, the employee attribute it represents should be chosen very carefully.

It is often useful to opt for a good naming convention. For example, if you have several type of trainees, each represented by an employee group, you may use the same first character, say T, for all of them. While defining authorizations you may specify T*, rather than list all types of trainees.

2.6 EMPLOYEE SUBGROUP

Functional Consultant	User	Business Process Owner	Senior Management	My Rating	Understanding Level
A	A	A	A		

2.6.1 Purpose and Overview

Employee subgroups let you categorize your employees for identification and reporting. They can be used in features and PCRs. You can use them to generate data entry default values; e.g. for payroll area. User authorization can be restricted based on employee subgroups. Employee subgroup is an independent categorization of employees and is not a further classification under employee group. ES groupings are defined at employee group, employee subgroup level.

2.6.2 IMG Node

SM30 ➤ T503K

2.6.3 Screen

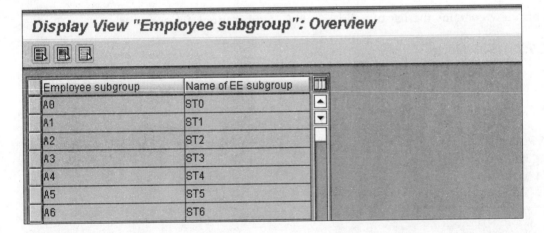

2.6.4 Primary Key

Employee Subgroup

2.6.5 Important Fields

Employee subgroup

You may use employee subgroup to capture an important characteristic of employee, e.g. grade. Since rules can be based on employee subgroup, the employee attribute it represents should be chosen very carefully.

It is often useful to use a good naming convention. For example, your employee grades may be classified as Executive, Officer, Supervisors and Operatives. If you followed a naming convention, which helps you identify the group of grades from the first character, it could help you while defining authorizations by specifying, for example, E* rather than listing each individual grade in that category.

2.7 COUNTRY ASSIGNMENT FOR EMPLOYEE GROUP/SUBGROUP

Functional Consultant	User	Business Process Owner	Senior Management	My Rating	Understanding Level
A	A	A	A		

2.7.1 Purpose

This view contains the list of valid EG, ESG combinations for a country.

2.7.2 IMG Node

SM30 ➢ V_T503Z

2.7.3 Screen

2.7.4 Primary Key

EG + ESG + Country Grouping

2.8 EMPLOYEE GROUP/SUBGROUP

Functional Consultant	User	Business Process Owner	Senior Management	My Rating	Understanding Level
A	A	A	A		

2.8.1 Purpose

Various SAP functionalities can be configured to work differently for different categories of employees. The employees can be categorized based on EG–ESG combination. There is a category (grouping) for each purpose. This view defines the linkage between EG–ESG combination and these groupings. The ES groupings need to be defined carefully and the linkage built.

2.8.2 IMG Node

SM30 ➤ V_503_ALL

2.8.3 Screen

E.	EE Gp Na...	ESgrp	EE ...	A...	E...	Tr...	E...	C...	E...	Pr...	A...	T...	WS...	Parti...
1	Permanent	1A	1A	1	2	2		3	A	1	1	1	2	☐
1	Permanent	1B	1B	1	2	2		3	3	1	1	1	2	☐
1	Permanent	2A	2A	1	2	2		3	3	1	1	1	2	☐
1	Permanent	2B	2B	1	2	2		3	3	1	1	1	2	☐

2.8.4 Primary Key

EG + ESG

2.8.5 Important Fields

ES grouping for personnel calculation rule

Personnel Calculation Rules (PCR) are used in payroll and time management. These rules can apply different logic to different employees based on ES grouping for PCR. In this field you assign the ES grouping for PCR to each combination of EG and ESG. Master list of ES grouping for PCR is predefined by SAP. The meanings of these groupings are fixed and must not be changed. Use value 3 for salaried employees.

ES grouping for primary wage types

This grouping is used to allow/restrict a wage type to certain employee group–employee subgroup combinations. The values must be from 0 to 9. It is used in view V_511_B Define Wage Type Permissibility for each PS and ESG.

Employee category

The data element is no longer used. It is now possible to define country-dependent work contracts in table T542A.

ES grouping for collective agreement provision

In SAP, you define different components of an employee's salary under different wage types. Since some payments can be based on employee attributes, e.g. his grade, SAP allows a wage type to be indirectly valuated based on five employee characteristics. ES grouping for CAP is one of them; others are pay scale type, pay scale area, pay scale group and pay scale level, which are defined in infotype 0008 at employee level.

ES grouping for work schedules

You determine which work schedules are permissible for which employee group–employee subgroup combinations using the ES grouping for the work schedule. This grouping is a key field in table T508A, Work Schedule Rules.

Activity status

This field is for Belgium.

Employment status

This field is also for Belgium.

Training status

This field is for Germany/USA.

ES grouping for time quota types

This grouping is a key field in most tables related to time quotas, important among them being T556A Absence Quota Types, T555L Transfer to Absence Quotas, T556C Counting Rule for Attendances and Absences, T556P Attendance Quotas, T556R Rules for Deduction Sequence for Absence Quotas, T556U Attendance/Absence Quota Compensation Types, T556W Wage Type Assignment for Att./Absence Quota Compensations.

ES grouping for appraisal

You can set up appraisal criteria dependent on ES grouping. This grouping is a key field in tables related to appraisals: T513G Appraisal Groups, T513H Appraisal Criteria and T513PAPD PA-PD: Assign Appraisal Models to EE (sub)area/(sub)group.

Participation in incentive wages

This field can take only 2 values: Participates/Doesnot participate in incentive wages. This indicator can be queried in payroll by the operation OUTWP with the feature INWID. In this way, you can check rule XW3 in payroll whether an employee participates in incentive wages. Incentive wage averages formed with function AVERA are only available for employee subgroups that participate in incentive wages.

Single-character flag

2.9 ES GROUPING FOR WORK SCHEDULES

Functional Consultant	User	Business Process Owner	Senior Management	My Rating	Understanding Level
A	A	A	A		

2.9.1 Purpose

This view contains master list of ES grouping for work schedules. It is assigned to an EG–ESG combination in table T503. Although this table is not a check table for table T503, do not use any value in table T503, unless it is specified in this table. Permissible work schedule rules are defined at PSAGWS + ESGGWS + Holiday calendar ID level. Work schedules are also generated at this level.

2.9.2 IMG Node

SM30 ➤ V_T508T

2.9.3 Screen

ES grpg	ES grouping for WS
0	Applicants
1	Hourly wage earners
2	Salaried employees
3	Executive
4	Executive - PH

2.9.4 Primary Key

Language Key + ES Grouping for Work Schedules

Work Schedule

3.1 OVERVIEW OF WORK SCHEDULE

Functional Consultant	User	Business Process Owner	Senior Management	My Rating	Understanding Level
A	A	A	A		

Time management compares the plan (when is the employee expected to work) with actual (when did the employee work, when was he absent and why) and draws various conclusions. This chapter deals with the various concepts in SAP, which helps you define when the employee is expected to work.

All employees of a company may not have the same working time. Some may work day shift, whereas some may work night shift. Some employees may even have flexi time. These different working patterns, including tolerance for late coming and early going, are defined as daily work schedule. You also define daily work schedules for off days.

Even if an employee has the same working time every day, he has weekly off. Therefore, you need to define the pattern in which the daily work schedules occur during a week. This is defined in the period work schedule. A period work schedule may define a weekly pattern, or it may define a 2-week or a 3-week pattern. These are useful when an employee works in different shifts in different weeks according to a pattern.

If there are employees who work the same pattern of shifts, but when one group of employees are working shift A, the other group is working shift B, you can use the same period work schedule, but have a different starting day. This is specified in the work schedule rule. The work schedule rule is assigned to an employee in infotype 0007. Thus, for each employee, for each day you can determine, from what time to what time is he expected to work.

During a day's work, an employee is permitted to take breaks. These breaks may be fixed, variable, dynamic or overtime. Breaks can be paid, unpaid or partly paid. These are defined in break schedule. Break schedules are assigned to daily work schedules.

Companies also have holidays. These are defined in holiday calendar. When the work schedule rule is defined, apart from the ES grouping and PS grouping for work schedule, it also depends on the holiday calendar. The holiday calendar consists of public holidays. The holidays may occur on the same date every year, or the date may differ from year to year.

It is common business practice to have half day holidays, which precede a full day holiday, or a weekly off day. You cannot define these in period work schedule because holidays are unpredictable. Even in the case of half day working before an off day, the half day working is expected to shift in case the off day is shifted. SAP solves this problem by defining a daily work schedule variant, and a rule to decide when this variant is applicable. Thus, even for half day working, the daily work schedule remains the same, but the rule selects a variant, which has its own definition of working time.

When you define holidays in holiday calendar, you assign them a holiday class. Usual values of holiday class are full day holiday and half day holiday. The value of holiday class for a normal working day is blank.

You can use holiday class to determine a daily work schedule variant. You can select a daily work schedule variant purely on the basis of the holiday class for the day. Thus, if you have a half day holiday, this information in conjunction with the daily work schedule gives you a variant, that determines the working time, which is for half day working. However, SAP lets you decide the daily work schedule variant in a more flexible way. You can select a daily work schedule variant based on three conditions:

➢ Holiday class for the day
➢ Holiday class next day
➢ Weekday

When all the three conditions are met, the specified variant is selected. If the condition is not met, the next line of the rule is examined. You can use this flexibility to say that a working day before a holiday has half day working, whereas a half day holiday, before a full day holiday, becomes a full day holiday.

As you can see, there can be multiple variants of a daily work schedule. You can have a 4-hour work schedule for half day holidays, while employees may work a 6-hour work schedule on Saturdays. The sequence in which you write the rule is also important, because as soon as the first match is found, the variant is selected.

SAP assigns a day type to each day of the employee. The day type provides the flexibility to deduct an absence from different quota, valuate an absence differently, pay different wage types, and implement your logic in time evaluation. For more details, see the overview of day type in view V_T553T. Apart from day type, period work schedule and daily work schedule can also affect quota deduction and time wage type generation.

Based on all the logic in the configuration, you generate a monthly work schedule, which is stored in table T552A. It is applicable to a group of employees, and contains daily work schedule, daily work schedule variant, public holiday class, day type and religious denomination key for each day. This table can be changed after generation to give effect to changes in work schedule made by your management, which cannot be incorporated in configuration.

Note that these manual changes would be lost if you regenerate the monthly work schedule for any reason. You must keep a record of such changes, so that they can be done again after work schedule is regenerated. Monthly work schedule is the basis of personal work schedule which also takes into account the employee's attendances, absences and substitutions.

3.2 PLANNED WORKING TIME (INFOTYPE 0007)

Functional Consultant	User	Business Process Owner	Senior Management	My Rating	Understanding Level
A	A	A	A		

3.2.1 Screen

Work schedule rule	
Work schedule rule	WSRPG
Time Mgmt status	9 9 - Time evaluation of planned times
☐ Part-time employee	

Working time			
Employment percent	100.00	☐ Dyn. daily work schedule	
Daily working hours		Min.	Max.
Weekly working hours	0.00	Min.	Max.
Monthly working hrs	0.00	Min.	Max.
Annual working hours	0.00	Min.	Max.
Weekly workdays			

3.2.2 Purpose and Overview

Infotype 0007 stores information relating to an employee's planned working time and time management status. The employee is assigned to a work schedule rule, which is a condensed specification of planned working time. The relationship between a work schedule rule and the planned working time is configured in time management.

Time management status determines whether an employee is expected to record attendance, or whether he's assumed to be working as per his work schedule, and is expected to merely record his absences, or whether he is not evaluated for time management at all.

Before the time evaluation program can be run for a particular employee, you must specify the time management status in infotype 0007. Otherwise the system cannot account the employee's time data with the time evaluation program.

3.2.3 Subtypes

This infotype has no subtypes.

3.2.4 Time Constraint

1 (Record must have no gaps, no overlappings)

3.2.5 Important Fields

Work schedule rule

Work schedule rule and related configuration determines when the employee is supposed to work. This includes shift timings, break timings, grace periods, weekly offs, holidays, etc. The default value of this field is determined by feature SCHKZ.

Time management status

Time management status determines whether your employee's time data is evaluated by time evaluation or not. Its default value is determined by feature TMSTA. You may see the list of values for time management status and their meanings in table T555U.

Part-time employee

You select this option if you want to reduce the planned working time of an existing full time work schedule rule to the percentage specified in the employment percent field. You also select this option if you have created a special work schedule rule for part-time employees. You can then use the part-time status of these employees as a criterion in statistical queries.

Employment percent

If you select part-time employee, enter employment percentage here. This is used to determine working hours per day, week, month and year. You may need to adjust the capacity utilization level in infotype 0008.

If you enter employment percentage, without ticking part-time employee, system automatically ticks it, opens all relevant fields, and ticks dynamic daily work schedule by default.

Daily/weekly/monthly/annual working hours

Out of these four fields, only one is open for entry, others are automatically calculated. Employment percent is also automatically calculated. Which field is open for input is decided by the feature WRKHR.

Weekly workdays

These are calculated automatically based on the work schedule rule. Changing this does not change weekly/monthly/annual working hours. When you create an infotype 0007 record, the default value of weekly workdays field comes from work schedule rule (table T508A). However, when you copy or change an infotype 0007 record, you have a choice of either retaining the value from infotype 0007 or getting it afresh from work schedule rule. This is determined by the feature WRKHR.

Dynamic daily work schedule (for part time workers)

This option is available when you select the part-time employee option and press 'Enter'. If you choose this option, the system reduces the planned working time determined by the work schedule rule to the percentage you enter in the employment percent field. When calculating an employee's new working time, the system uses the specifications from the daily work schedule for the work schedule rule. The system takes the start of work time from the daily work schedule as its starting point and taking into account the break schedule, adds the new number of planned hours. The end of work time from the daily work schedule is then brought forward in accordance with the percentage you specify.

Minimum and maximum fields (for part time workers)

These are specified at day, week, month and year levels for part-time workers. These fields are optional. They can be queried in time evaluation but have no influence on an employee's daily work schedule. To enter values in these fields, you must select the dynamic daily work schedule option.

3.2.6 Reports and Other Features

Daily work schedule (PT_DSH20)

If you want to see the details of a daily work schedule, you can see it by running transaction PT_DSH20. The user sees all the details of a daily work schedule, which has been configured by the consultant (see chapter 3.6).

Work schedule

When you click on [⊞ Work schedule] in any infotype, SAP shows you the work schedule for a month. For each day, it shows the daily work schedule, the daily work schedule variant, and the day type. It also shows the holiday class if it is not blank.

Personal work schedule (PT63)

Personal work schedule shows the daily work schedule, daily work schedule variant, day type, holiday class, period work schedule, holiday calendar and number of time infotypes.

Revaluate daily work schedules (PT_UTPR00)

Daily work schedule has an embedded break schedule. Paid breaks in the break schedule are included in planned working hours. If you change a break schedule such that hours of paid breaks are changed, then you need to update this field appropriately. This is done by executing transaction PT_UTPR00.

Revaluate planned working time (PT_UWSH00)

Infotype 0007 contains information about daily/weekly/monthly/annual working hours of an employee. These are based on his work schedule rule. If the definition of work schedule rule changes, infotype 0007 should be appropriately updated. Transaction PT_UWSH00, Revaluate Planned Working Time, is used to do that. In the rare event of this happening, your consultant will ask you to run this transaction.

Generate personal calendar (PT_BPC00)

You can use this transaction to generate personal calendar. However, it is better to set 'Admissibility indicator PC' field in table T582Z to 1. In that case the personal calendar is automatically maintained and there is no need to use this transaction.

Display personal calendar (PT_CLSTPC)

You can see one year calendar at a glance showing absences, holidays, etc. from cluster PC.

Personal calendar reorganization (PT_REOPC)

You can use this report to correct inconsistencies in personal calendar, if any, from cluster PC.

3.3 EMPLOYEE TIME MANAGEMENT STATUS

Functional Consultant	User	Business Process Owner	Senior Management	My Rating	Understanding Level
A	A	A	A		

3.3.1 Purpose

This view contains master list of time management status, which are assigned to employees in infotype 0007. Time management status determines how the employee's time data comes in the system.

3.3.2 IMG Node

SM30 ➤ T555U

3.3.3 Screen

TM status	Text
0	0 - No time evaluation
1	1 - Time evaluation of actual times
2	2 - PDC time evaluation
7	7 - Time evaluation without payroll integration
8	8 - External services
9	9 - Time evaluation of planned times

3.3.4 Primary Key

Employee Time Management Status

3.3.5 Important Fields

Employee time management status

Time Mgt status	Text	Meaning
0	No time evaluation	Time evaluation is not done for these employees.
1	Time evaluation of actual times	Employee considered present only if his attendance is recorded. Time evaluation is done for these employees for quota generation, overtime, formation of time types and time wage types, etc.
2	PDC time evaluation	For employees whose time evaluation is based on plant data collection.
7	Time evaluation without payroll integration	For absence quota generation using schema TQTA, when time evaluation is not implemented.
8	External services	You can use this status if you want to pay on the basis of work done by the employees of external service provider. These employees must be assigned personnel numbers in SAP.
9	Time evaluation of planned times	Employee is considered present unless his attendance/absence is recorded. Time evaluation is done for these employees also.

3.4 DEFAULT TIME MANAGEMENT STATUS

Functional Consultant	User	Business Process Owner	Senior Management	My Rating	Understanding Level
A	C	C	X		

3.4.1 Purpose

This feature determines default value of time management status in infotype 0007.

3.4.2 IMG Node

PE03 ➤ TMSTA

3.4.3 Screen

```
TMSTA DEFAULT VALUE FOR TIME MANAGEMENT STATUS
   |
   |____9
```

3.4.4 Fields for Decision Making

Company Code
Personnel Area
Personnel Subarea
Employee Group
Employee Subgroup
Country Grouping

3.4.5 Return Value

Default value of time management status

3.5 WORKING HOUR FIELDS CONTROL

Functional Consultant	User	Business Process Owner	Senior Management	My Rating	Understanding Level
A	C	C	X		

3.5.1 Purpose

In infotype 0007, there are four fields: Daily/Weekly/Monthly/Annual working hours. Out of these four fields, only one is open for entry, others are automatically calculated. The first part returned by this feature decides which of these fields is open for input.

When you create an infotype 0007 record, the default value of weekly workdays field comes from the work schedule rule (table T508A). However, when you copy or change an infotype 0007 record, you have a choice of either retaining the value from infotype 0007, or getting it afresh from the work schedule rule by specifying 'X' in the second part returned by this feature.

3.5.2 IMG Node

PE03 ➤ WRKHR

3.5.3 Screen

```
WRKHR Input control for working hour fields/weekly workdays
  |
  |——D/X
```

3.5.4 Fields for Decision Making

Company Code
Personnel Area
Personnel Subarea
Employee Group
Employee Subgroup
Country Grouping

3.5.5 Return Value

See Purpose.

3.6 DAILY WORK SCHEDULE

Functional Consultant	User	Business Process Owner	Senior Management	My Rating	Understanding Level
A	C	C	X		

3.6.1 Purpose

Daily work schedule

Daily work schedule defines how an employee works during a day; what are the timings, how much late coming or early going is tolerated, when does he have break, etc. In the case of flextime, you can specify planned, normal and core times.

Daily work schedule variant

It is common business practice to have half day holidays; the day before a holiday being half day; or a specific day, e.g. Saturday, being a half day. You cannot define these in period work schedule because holidays are unpredictable. SAP solves this problem by defining the following:

> Holiday class: For each holiday, you have a holiday class, whether it is a full day or a half day holiday. The value of holiday class for normal working day is blank.
> Daily work schedule variant: Your normal work timings are defined in the daily work schedule. In the variant you specify the work timings, which are to be used on special occasions. It is not necessary that they must be half day, they can be anything.
> Rules to determine variant: You have a need to use daily work schedule variant. You have defined the variant. How do you know on which day the variant should be used, instead of regular daily work schedule? These rules are defined in V_T550X and attached to a daily work schedule in V_T550A.
> In V_T550X, you define three conditions:
>   ‣ Holiday class for the day
>   ‣ Holiday class next day
>   ‣ Weekday
> When all the three conditions are met, the specified variant is selected. If any of the conditions is not met, the next line of the rule is examined.
> As you can see, there can be multiple variants of a daily work schedule. You can have a 4-hour work schedule for half day holidays, while employees may work a 6-hour work schedule on Saturdays. The sequence in which you write the rule is also important, because as soon as the first match is found, the variant is selected.

Daily work schedule variant selection is useful when variant selection is based on holiday class of the day or holiday class of the next day. If variant selection depends only on the weekday, you can define it as a different daily work schedule in the period work schedule. However, if you dynamically determine an employee's daily work schedule based on his clock-in time (T552V), this approach does not work. If there is a full day shift on week days and a half day variant on Saturday, the variant approach works; but different daily work schedule approach does not, as the clock-in time is the same.

3.6.2 IMG Node

SM30 ➤ V_T550A

3.6.3 Screen

The screen of daily work schedule is on the next page.

3.6.4 Primary Key

PS Grouping for Daily Work Schedules + Daily Work Schedule + Daily Work Schedule Variant + Sequential Number of Daily Work Schedule (Field not in use. Value always 01) + End Date

3.6.5 Important Fields

DWS grouping

DWS grouping for which you are defining the daily work schedule. Daily work schedule can differ based on DWS grouping.

Daily work schedule and variant

You can define either the basic daily work schedule or a daily work schedule variant.

Start and end date

The daily work schedule definition can vary over a period of time. Here you specify the validity period.

Planned working hours

Normally you do not fill this field. It gets determined by the system. In the case of fixed working hours, it equals planned working time + paid breaks. For flextime, it is normal working time + paid breaks.

Daily work schedule has an embedded break schedule. Paid breaks in the break schedule are included in planned working hours. If you change a break schedule such that hours of paid breaks are changed, then you need to update this field appropriately. This is done by executing transaction PT_UTPR00.

DWS grouping   01

Daily work schedule   AFTN   Afternoon Shift

Start Time	Exit
> 01.01.1990	31.12.9999

Planned working hours

Planned working hours   7.00   DWS selection rule   01

☐ No planned working hrs.

Working times

Fixed working hours

Planned working time   16:00 - 24:00

Flextime

Planned working time   [ ] - [ ]

Normal working time   [ ] - [ ]

Core time 1   [ ] - [ ]

Core time 2   [ ] - [ ]

Breaks

Work break schedule   AFTN

Tolerance time

Begin tolerance   [ ] - [ ]

End tolerance   [ ] - [ ]

Valuation

Min. working time   [ ]   Daily WS class   2

Max. working time   [ ]   ☐ Automatic overtime

Compensation time   [ ]

Additional hours   [ ]   Ind. for arbitrary use

Overtime infotype (2005)

Reaction to overtime   Reaction to OT in core time

No planned working hours

You create a daily work schedule even for off day and tick this field.

DWS selection rule

This rule would determine which work schedule variant is applicable. For more details, see chapter 3.8.

Planned working time (from and to) of fixed working hours

If you want your employees to follow fixed working hours, you specify the start and end time here. In the case of night shift, the To-time may be smaller than the From-time. The system interprets it correctly.

Planned working time (from and to) of flextime

In the case of flextime, the planned working time defines the limit of normal work. Working hours, which are recorded during this interval, are credited to a flextime account, while those outside are treated as overtime.

Normal working time

In the case of flextime, if clock-in/clock-out entries are missing because the employee has been absent, the system uses the normal working time to calculate the absence hours. It also computes planned working hours as the normal working time plus the paid breaks.

Core times 1 and 2

If employees work flextime, the core time defines the period during which they must be at work each day. You can define two core times. They should not overlap with breaks.

Work break schedule

A work break schedule stipulates when employees can take breaks, and how long the breaks may last. For more details, see 3.7.

Begin tolerance

If the employee comes during this period, the system assumes that he came at the planned time. The tolerance after shift start time allows an employee to come late, without being considered late. The tolerance before shift start time is needed to prevent the system from considering this period as overtime. Tolerances are processed in the schema by function DPTOL.

End tolerance

If the employee leaves during this period, the system assumes that he left at planned time. The tolerance before shift end time allows an employee to go early. The tolerance after shift end time is needed to prevent the system from considering this period as overtime. Tolerances are processed in the schema by function DPTOL.

Minimum working time

This field can be queried in a PCR to check whether the employee has put in the specified minimum amount of work for a day. It is read by operation HRS. In PCR TR40, this time is compared with time type 0003. If the employee has not worked the required minimum number of hours, a note is issued. You can write your own logic based on this field.

Maximum working time

This field can be queried in a PCR to check whether the employee has worked more than the specified maximum amount of work for a day. It is read by operation HRS. You can write your own logic based on this field. Balances are calculated in time evaluation only up to the maximum daily planned working time. Any attendances outside of this are not included in the calculation.

Compensation time

If your daily work schedule requires your employees to work more than what they are supposed to work as per agreement, you can assign this excess to compensation time. During time evaluation, the compensation time can be accumulated in a quota, which the employees can use in various ways provided by you.

This field can be queried in a PCR. It is read by operation HRS. You can see how to use it in PCR TR15.

Additional hours

This is a customer-specific field which can be used to calculate time balances in time evaluation. If you want to use the field, you have to write your own PCR and use operation HRS=SADD to specify how the values should be processed in time evaluation.

Daily work schedule class

When you define a daily work schedule, you can assign it a daily work schedule class (0 to 9). It can be used in the following ways:

➤ You can use it as a condition while defining rules for generating time wage types (T510S). In this way, you can generate different wage types depending on different daily work schedules.
➤ You can also use it as a condition while defining rules for quota deduction (T556C). In this way, you can apply different logic for quota deduction depending on different daily work schedules.
➤ When function P2001 imports the absences for the day being evaluated into table TIP, you specify whether that should happen only for workdays, or for all days. A workday is one where daily work schedule class is other than 0 and day type is 0 or 1. Thus, daily work schedule class 0 is not a workday.
➤ You can write your own PCRs, where you can use operation VARST (DPRCL) to query the daily work schedule class, and write logic based on it.

Automatic overtime

If this field is activated, employees doing this DWS do not need approval for doing overtime. However, to achieve this, you must have a PCR, e.g. TO15, which queries this field using operation VARST (OVPOS) and does the needful.

Indicator for arbitrary use

You can use this indicator to query customer-specific enhancements in time evaluation operations.

Reaction to overtime

In the case of flextime, working hours within planned working time are flextime, while those outside are overtime. If someone is entering overtime in infotype 2005 you may want to give an error message or warning, in case he enters time which is within planned working time, and hence does not qualify to be overtime. This indicator is only effective when recording overtime in infotype 2005. It does not affect processing of overtime records in time evaluation.

Reaction to overtime in core time

If someone tries to enter overtime in infotype 2005, which clashes with core time of his daily work schedule, you may want to give an error message or warning. This indicator is only effective when recording overtime in infotype 2005. It does not affect processing of overtime records in time evaluation.

Availability

In this field, in view V_550A_B, you can define whether this daily work schedule can be used in availability infotype 2004. For more details, see infotype 2004.

3.7 WORK BREAK SCHEDULE

Functional Consultant	User	Business Process Owner	Senior Management	My Rating	Understanding Level
A	C	C	X		

3.7.1 Purpose and Overview

This view contains break schedules which are included in daily work schedules. There are four types of breaks:

➢ Fixed Break—difference between Start and End matches sum of Paid and Unpaid.
➢ Variable Break—e.g. 15 minutes unpaid between 9:30 and 10:00.
➢ Dynamic Break—e.g. 15 minutes unpaid after 4 hours of work.
➢ Overtime Break—taken during overtime work (type 1 = O).

Breaks can be paid, unpaid or partly paid. Dynamic breaks are processed in the schema by function DYNBR TF10. Variable breaks are processed in the schema by function PBRKS. If you change a break schedule after it has been assigned to daily work schedules, you must revaluate daily work schedules using transaction PT_UTPR00.

3.7.2 IMG Node

SM30 ➤ V_T550P

3.7.3 Screen

	Grpg	Break	N.	Start	End	P	Unpaid	Paid	After	RefTim	Type 1	Type 2
	01	ERLY	03	12:30	12:45	☐		0.25				
	01	EXEC	01	12:00	12:30	☐	0.50					
	01	GLZ	01	09:30	10:00	☐	0.25					
	01	GLZ	02	11:30	13:30	☐	0.75					
	01	GLZ	03	22:00	22:10	☐	0.17				0	
	01	LATE	01	23:45	24:00	☐		0.25				
	01	LATE	02	02:00	02:30	☐		0.50				
	01	LATE	03	04:30	04:45	☐		0.25				
	01	M3	01			☐	0.25		4.00			

3.7.4 Primary Key

DWS Grouping + Breaks + Sequence Number

3.7.5 Important Fields

DWS grouping

The break definition can vary depending on DWS grouping.

Break

Name of break.

Sequence number

A DWS can have multiple breaks. Hence, a break schedule can have multiple parts, each identified by a sequence number.

Fixed break

E.g. from 12:30 to 13:00.

Start and end of break

Here you specify the actual break timings.

Previous day

You tick this indicator where the daily work schedule is for the previous day and the breaks are in the next calendar day.

Unpaid break

If the employee is not paid for the break period, you enter the break time here.

Paid break

If the employee is paid for the break period, you enter the break time here. It is also possible to enter part of the time in unpaid break and the rest in paid break.

Variable break

E.g. 15 minutes unpaid between 9:30 and 10:00.

You use the same fields as in fixed break. Only the duration of break is longer than the sum of paid and unpaid breaks.

Dynamic break

E.g. 15 minutes unpaid after 4 hours of work.

After

Number of hours the employee should work before taking a break from start of planned working time as stipulated in the daily work schedule. In time evaluation this is used by function DYNBR.

Reference time

In the case of dynamic break, whether the break starts after the planned working time or the normal working time.

Overtime break

This break is taken during overtime work (type 1 = O).

Break type 1

Here you can specify whether a break is normal break or overtime break.

Break type 2

This is a free field where you can specify a 1-character break type and use in PCR.

3.8 DAILY WORK SCHEDULE SELECTION RULE

Functional Consultant	User	Business Process Owner	Senior Management	My Rating	Understanding Level
B	X	X	X		

3.8.1 Purpose and Overview

It is common business practice to have half day holidays; the day before a holiday being half day; or a specific day, e.g. Saturday, being a half day. You cannot define these in period work schedule because holidays are unpredictable. SAP solves this problem by defining the following:

➤ Holiday class: For each holiday, you have a holiday class, whether it is a full day or a half day holiday. The value of holiday class for normal working day is blank.

➤ Daily work schedule variant: Your normal work timings are defined in the daily work schedule. In the variant you specify the work timings, which are to be used on special occasions. It is not necessary that they must be half day, they can be anything.

➤ Rules to determine variant: You have a need to use daily work schedule variant. You have defined the variant. How do you know on which day the variant should be used instead of regular daily work schedule? These rules are defined in V_T550X and attached to a daily work schedule in V_T550A.

➤ In V_T550X, you define three conditions:

▸ Holiday class for the day
▸ Holiday class next day
▸ Weekday

➤ When all the three conditions are met, the specified variant is selected. If any of the conditions is not met, the next line of the rule is examined.

➤ As you can see, there can be multiple variants of a daily work schedule. You can have a 4-hour work schedule for half day holidays, while employees may work a 6-hour work schedule on Saturdays. The sequence in which you write the rule is also important, because as soon as the first match is found, the variant is selected.

➤ One can understand that an employee's work schedule depends on holiday class for the day, holiday class next day and weekday. But would you expect it to change if the employee is absent? Although rare, but some companies want it and SAP provides for it.

➤ If an employee is absent for full day, for how many hours is he absent? SAP uses planned working hours of the daily work schedule to answer that question. Sometimes you do not want that to happen (see the document of the configuration node for view V_550X_B).

➤ On such occasions, SAP lets you change the daily work schedule variant. Since you may not want the same rule to apply for all absence types, the selection can depend on 'Absence type grouping to determine daily WS variants' which is an attribute of Absence type. The rule is defined in V_550X_B.

3.8.2 IMG Node

SM30 ➤ V_T550X (Record type 01), V_550X_B (Record type 02)

3.8.3 Screen V_T550X

Rule	No	Holiday class b123456789	Hol.cl.next day b123456789	Weekday 1234567	Variant
☐ 01	01	. . X	XXXXXXXXXX	XXXXXX	B
☐ 01	02	XX . XXXXXXX	XXXXXXXXXX	. . . . X . .	B
☐ 98	01	XXXXXXXXXX	XXXXXXXXXX	. . . . X . .	A
☐ 99	01	XXXXXXXXXX	XXXXXXXXXX	. . . . X . .	F

3.8.4 Screen V_550X_B

Rule	No	Holiday class b123456789	Hol.cl.next day b123456789	Abs./att. grpg 123456789	Weekday 1234567	Variant
☐ 01	01	XXXXXXXXXX	XXXXXXXXXX	. X	XXXXXX	A
☐ GB	01	XXXXXXXXXX	XXXXXXXXXX	. X	XXXXXX	I
☐ NL	01	XXXXXXXXXX	. XXXXXXXXX	XXXXXXXXX	XXXXXX	A
☐ PT	01	XXXXXXXXXX	XXXXXXXXXX	X	XXXXXX	V

3.8.5 Primary Key

Record Type + DWS Selection Rule + Sequence Number

3.8.6 Important Fields

Record type

This table is used for two purposes identified by Record type. Record type 01 is used for determining the variant when work schedule is generated (V_T550X). Record type 02 is used for determining the variant if it depends on attendance/absence types (V_550X_B).

DWS selection rule

The DWS selection rule is defined here and assigned to a daily work schedule in table T550A.

Sequence number

A rule consists of multiple lines. Each line has a condition part and a result part. The rule is scanned in the order of sequence number. If all components of condition are satisfied, the result is returned. Otherwise, the next line is examined.

Condition Part

In this part you define what conditions must be satisfied, for the variant to be selected. All conditions must be satisfied.

Holiday class

Here you enter the holiday class of the day. You can use this field to select a variant for half day holidays by entering holiday class 2 in this field. If other fields are fully filled, for a day that has holiday class 2, the condition is satisfied, and variant is selected.

Holiday class next day

The holiday class you enter here is checked against the holiday class of the next day. You can use this field to select a variant if you work less, or more, hours before a holiday. If you enter holiday class 1 in this field and other fields are fully filled then the variant is selected on the eve of a holiday.

Absence/attendance grouping

If you want the daily work schedule variant to be selected depending on attendance/absence type, then you create groups of attendances/absences. In T554S, you specify it for attendance/absence types in the field 'Attendance/Absence type grouping to determine daily WS variants', and define the rule in V_550X_B. This field is not applicable in V_T550X.

Weekday

The day of the week for which the rule line applies. 1 corresponds to Monday, and 7 to Sunday.

Result Part

In this part you define the DWS variant to be selected if the conditions are satisfied.

DWS variant

You specify the daily work schedule variant here, which is selected if the condition part is satisfied.

3.9 PERIOD WORK SCHEDULE

Functional Consultant	User	Business Process Owner	Senior Management	My Rating	Understanding Level
A	C	C	X		

3.9.1 Purpose

It It is common business practice that employees follow a regular working pattern. Some employees follow the same time every day. Others may come in morning shift for one week, evening shift next week, and the night shift the week after that. The pattern may repeat after three weeks.

SAP lets you create a period work schedule. The period work schedule can be of any length—one week, two weeks, three weeks, or even arbitrary number of days. For each day of the period (01 is Monday), you can specify the daily work schedule. If the number of days in a period is not divisible by seven, indicate the end of the period by entering a *. Note that even an off day is specified as a daily work schedule with zero planned hours.

3.9.2 IMG Node

SM30 ≻ V_T551A

3.9.3 Screen

Grpg	PWS	Period WS text	W...	01	02	03	04	05	06	07
01	3-WK	3week Rotating Shift	001	DAY	DAY	DAY	DAY	DAY	FREI	FREI
01	3-WK	3week Rotating Shift	002	AFTN	AFTN	AFTN	AFTN	AFTN	FREI	FREI
01	3-WK	3week Rotating Shift	003	NGHT	NGHT	NGHT	NGHT	NGHT	FREI	FREI
01	EXEC		001	EXEC	EXEC	EXEC	EXEC	EXEC	FREI	FREI

3.9.4 Primary Key

PS Grouping for Daily Work Schedules + Period Work Schedule + Week Number

3.9.5 Important Fields

PS grouping for daily work schedules

PS grouping for daily work schedules is determined from PS grouping for work schedules (T508Z), which is determined from PA + PSA combination (V_001P_ALL). PA + PSA of an employee are determined from infotype 0001.

Period work schedule

Period work schedule, which is being defined.

Week number

A period work schedule can be for one or more weeks. Here you specify the week number.

Daily work schedule

Here you specify the daily work schedule for each day of each week. Day 01 is Monday.

3.10 PERIOD WORK SCHEDULE VALUATION

Functional Consultant	User	Business Process Owner	Senior Management	My Rating	Understanding Level
A	X	X	X		

3.10.1 Purpose

A period work schedule has a counting class and a valuation class. Since table T551A, which contains period work schedule definition, has week level records, counting classes and valuation classes are assigned to period work schedules in these view.

3.10.2 IMG Node

SM30 ➤ V_T551C
SM30 ➤ V_551C_B

3.10.3 Screen V_T551C

	Grpg	Period WS	Description	Start Date	End Date	Cntg class
	01	$XQP		01.01.1990	31.12.9999	1
	01	3-WK	3week Rotating Shift	01.01.1990	31.12.9999	1
	01	GLZ	Flextime	01.01.1990	31.12.9999	5
	01	J001	6 TO 14:30	01.01.2001	31.12.9999	1

3.10.4   Screen V_551C_B

	Grpg	Period WS	Description	Start Date	End Date	Val.class for PWS
	01	$XQP		01.01.1990	⊡.12.9999	
	01	3-WK	3week Rotating Shift	01.01.1990	31.12.9999	
	01	GLZ	Flextime	01.01.1990	31.12.9999	5
	01	J001	6 TO 14:30	01.01.2001	31.12.9999	

3.10.5   Primary Key

PS Grouping for Daily Work Schedules + Period Work Schedule + End Date

3.10.6   Important Fields

PS grouping for daily work schedules

Counting class and valuation class assignment can be different for different PS grouping for daily work schedule.

Period work schedule

Period work schedule is the one to which counting class and valuation class are being assigned.

Start and end date

Over a period of time, counting class and valuation class for a period work schedule can change.

Valuation class for period work schedule

During time evaluation, you can generate time wage types, which get paid in payroll. When you define rules for generating wage types in view V_T510S, you can specify a number of conditions, which must be satisfied for generating these wage types. One of them is valuation class for period work schedule.

If, for example, you want to pay different rates to night shift workers, as compared to day shift workers, you can generate different wage types depending on period work schedule, which can result in different amounts being paid in payroll. Note that daily work schedule class can also be used for this purpose. Hence, you must decide which is the most appropriate method for meeting your objective.

Apart from its use in view V_T510S, you can also read this field in a PCR using operation VARST (TIMCL) and write your own logic. Valuation class can have a value from 1 to 9 and blank.

Counting class for period work schedule

In table T556C you define the rules for deducting quota for attendances and absences. If you want these rules to depend on period work schedule, you can define different counting classes and assign them to period work schedules. The rules for deducting quota can then depend on the period work schedule of the employee. For example, if you want to deduct 1 day, if an employee misses a day in fixed shift pattern, but 0.5 day if he misses a day in flex shift pattern, you can do so using this counting class. Note that here also you have an option of using daily work schedule class, and must decide which option is more suitable.

Counting class can have a value from 1 to 9 and blank.

Note that there are other counting classes also, e.g. Counting Classes for Absence Valuation, T554E.

3.11 WORK SCHEDULE RULE

Functional Consultant	User	Business Process Owner	Senior Management	My Rating	Understanding Level
A	C	C	X		

3.11.1 Purpose

The work schedule rule defines which period work schedule to use, and from which date does the cycling of the period work schedule start. It also specifies which rule to use to determine day types. Work schedule rule is assigned to an employee in infotype 0007.

3.11.2 IMG Node

SM30 ➤ V_T508A, V_508A_B

3.11.3 Screen V_T508A

ES grouping	1	Hourly wage earners	
Holiday calendar ID	01	Germany (Schleswig-Ho...	
PS grouping	26		
Work schedule rule	TH5D		

Start Time   Exit
> 01.01.1990 ⊕ .12.9999

Working time

Daily working hours	8.00		Monthly working hrs	173.00
Weekly working hours	40.00		Annual working hours	2080.00
Weekly workdays	5.00		Addnl monthly hours	

Work schedule generation

Period work schedule	TH5D	TH: 5Day
Ref. date for PWS	01.01.1990	
Start point in PWS	001	
Rule for day types	01	
Automatic generation		

Grouping for daily work schedule

DWS grouping   26

Reduced working hours

☐ WS rule for RWH

Alternative WS rule

Shift premium _____   Sickness indicator ▪

3.11.4 Screen V_508A_B

E...	ES grpg for WS	Hol.cal.ID	Text	PSG	WS rule	Start Date	End Date	Availability
1	Hourly wage earn...	01	German..	26	TH5D	01.01.1990	⊕.12.9999	☐
1	Hourly wage earn...	01	German..	26	TH6D	01.01.1990	31.12.9999	☐

3.11.5 Primary Key

ES Grouping for Work Schedules + Public Holiday Calendar + PS Grouping for Work Schedules + Work Schedule Rule + End Date

PSA affects the work schedule rule both through PS grouping as well as holiday calendar.

3.11.6 Important Fields

ES grouping for work schedules

For an employee, EG and ESG comes from infotype 0001. For this combination of EG and ESG, ES grouping for work schedules is specified in V_503_ALL, which is matched with this field.

Holiday calendar ID

For an employee, PA and PSA comes from infotype 0001. For this combination of PA and PSA, holiday calendar is specified in V_001P_ALL, which is matched with this field.

PS grouping for work schedules

For an employee, PA and PSA comes from infotype 0001. For this combination of PA and PSA, PS grouping for work schedules is specified in V_001P_ALL, which is matched with this field.

Work schedule rule

For an employee, the work schedule rule is specified in infotype 0007.

Start and end date

The period for which this definition is valid.

Daily working hours

The value you specify here is used as default value of daily working hours in infotype 0007.

Weekly working hours

The value you specify here is used as default value of weekly working hours in infotype 0007.

Monthly working hours

The value you specify here is used as default value of monthly working hours in infotype 0007.

Annual working hours

The value you specify here is used as default value of annual working hours in infotype 0007.

Weekly workdays

The value you specify here is used as default value of weekly workdays in infotype 0007.

Additional monthly hours

This field has country-specific uses.

Period work schedule

The period work schedule or shift pattern which is used by this work schedule rule.

Reference date and starting point for period work schedule

Specifying a period work schedule is not enough. You need to specify when it starts. These two fields determine that. The reference date determines the date the system uses as the reference point for generating the period work schedule. The starting point determines the day number in period work schedule which corresponds to reference date.

Rule for day types

The day type rule is attached to work schedule rule and determines day type for each day. For more details, see chapter 3.14 (T553A).

Automatic generation

In this field, you can determine how the system should react if the monthly work schedule has not yet been generated when the personal work schedule is set up.

Blank	The monthly work schedule is automatically generated by the system. The work schedule is, however, not saved in the database. The system outputs a message.
A	The monthly work schedule is automatically generated by the system. The work schedule is not saved in the database, however. The system does not output a message.
M	The monthly work schedule is not automatically generated. An error message appears.

DWS grouping

Work schedule rule is defined for a PS grouping for work schedules and the period work schedule is defined for a PS grouping for daily work schedule. Therefore, before you can access valid period work schedules, you need to determine PS grouping for daily work schedule. This relationship is defined in table T508Z. In the table, you can club multiple PS grouping for work schedules into a single PS grouping for daily work schedules. Therefore, for the PS grouping for work schedules, the value of PS grouping for daily work schedules, is determined and displayed here.

Work schedule rule for RWH

If your company uses infotype 0049 (Reduced working hours), you need to specify the work schedule rule here. Only those work schedule rules, where this indicator is ticked, are valid in infotype 0049.

Alternative work schedule rule

When you have reduced working hours condition, what work schedule rule (which is for RWH) should be applicable in place of this work schedule rule.

Shift premium

If you want to pay an additional percentage to those employees who follow this work schedule rule, you specify that here. This is automatically applicable when the employee is assigned this work schedule rule, and you do not have to go on changing his salary details every time he is assigned this work schedule rule.

Sickness indicator

This field is for Austria only.

Indicator showing if work schedule rule is allowed for availability

Only work schedule rules with this indicator can be entered in 'Availability based on a work schedule rule' in infotype 2004.

3.12 DEFAULT WORK SCHEDULE RULE

Functional Consultant	User	Business Process Owner	Senior Management	My Rating	Understanding Level
A	C	C	X		

3.12.1 Purpose

This feature returns the default work schedule rule in infotype 0007.

3.12.2 IMG Node

PE03 ➤ SCHKZ

3.12.3 Screen

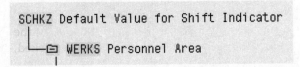

3.12.4 Fields for Decision Making

Company Code
Personnel Area
Personnel Subarea
Employee Group
Employee Subgroup
Country Grouping

3.12.5 Return Value

Work schedule rule

3.13 DAY TYPE

Functional Consultant	User	Business Process Owner	Senior Management	My Rating	Understanding Level
A	C	X	X		

3.13.1 Purpose

Day type

Day type is an important concept in SAP's work schedule. Each day of an employee's work schedule is assigned a day type. All days with a day type other than 0 or Blank are non-working days. Thus, day type is used primarily to classify non-working days.

Day type determination

An employee is assigned a work schedule rule in infotype 0007. A work schedule rule is assigned a rule for day types. A rule for day types determines day type depending on the day of the week and holiday class for the day.

Day types so determined are stored in table T552A, Monthly Work Schedule. Day types can also be directly specified for specific days in T553S. These are also taken into account. You can also directly change day type in table T552A. However, note that these direct changes get lost if the schedule is regenerated.

When you define substitution in infotype 2003, you can also specify day type.

In exceptional cases, you overwrite day type in time evaluation using operation DAYPG.

Day type use

Day type can influence the following:

➢ Quota deduction
➢ Payment/deduction for absence
➢ Time wage type selection
➢ Processing during time evaluation

Day type is used in the condition part of table T556C. In this way you can deduct for an absence from one or the other quota depending on day type.

When rules for absence valuation are defined in table T554C, you can define a day rule. The day rule can depend on the day type of current day and day type of the next day, and determine that the absence valuation line does not apply. In this way, you can assign an absence to different counting classes depending on day type, which may result in different payments.

In table T510S, you define how the time wage types are determined. This can be influenced by day type. Thus, you can pay under one wage type on national holidays, and under another wage type on local holidays. Using this flexibility, you can also pay at different rates.

In time evaluation, you can query day type using operation VARSTDAYTY. You can therefore write your logic based on day type. In schema TM00, standard PCRs TD90, TE20, TF10 use day type to determine what should happen. Function P2001 also uses the day type.

3.13.2 IMG Node

SM30 ➤ V_T553T

3.13.3 Screen

Day type	ShortTxt	Day type text
		Work/paid
0	WP	Work/paid
1	O/pd	Off/paid
2	O/upd	Off/unpaid
3	O/sp	Off/special day

3.13.4 Primary Key

Language Key + Day Type

3.14 DAY TYPE RULE

Functional Consultant	User	Business Process Owner	Senior Management	My Rating	Understanding Level
A	C	X	X		

3.14.1 Purpose

The day type rule is attached to a work schedule rule. It determines day type for each day. The day type is determined based on the holiday class of the day and the day of the week. There are predefined holiday classes, which are assigned to holidays. The holiday classes are:

Blank	Working day
1	Full day holiday
2	Half day holiday
3–9	User defined

For a day, you can determine holiday class. You also know whether it is Saturday/Sunday/other week day. Based on this combination, day type is determined.

3.14.2 IMG Node

SM30 ➤ T553A

3.14.3 Screen

	with holiday class	Weekday b123456789	Sat. b123456789	Sun. b123456789
Rule				
☐ 01	Gives day type	111	111	111
☐ 02	Gives day type	222	222	222
☐ 03	Gives day type	333	333	333
☐ 10	Gives day type	1111111	1111111	1111111

3.14.4 Primary Key

Day Type Rule

3.14.5 Important Fields

Weekday, Saturday, Sunday

On a weekday, if holiday class is blank, the day type you want is entered as the first character of the field. Next nine characters are for holiday classes 1 to 9. Similar is the case for Saturday and Sunday.

3.15 DAY TYPES FOR SPECIAL DAYS

Functional Consultant	User	Business Process Owner	Senior Management	My Rating	Understanding Level
A	C	X	X		

3.15.1 Purpose

Table T553A determines day type based on a rule. View T553S contains exceptions to that rule. It is used to define day type for some special days. It contains day type for specific dates. These must be defined for every day type rule.

While generating monthly work schedule, day type rule is determined from work schedule rule. Then the day type rule is applied to the characteristics of each day to determine its day type. However, if there is an entry in this view, the day type is taken from here. If the day type of a day is specified here, even if the monthly schedule is regenerated, the day type would be correct.

If you changed the day type in the monthly schedule directly, it gets overwritten if the monthly schedule is regenerated. Day type should be directly changed in monthly schedule only if you want to change day type only for some groups of employees.

3.15.2 IMG Node

SM30 ➤ T553S

3.15.3 Screen

Rule	Date	Day type	Day type text
11	16.02.2003	3	Off/special day
11	16.03.2003	3	Off/special day
11	31.08.2003	0	Work/paid

3.15.4 Primary Key

Rule for Day Types + Date for Special Day

3.16 PUBLIC HOLIDAY

Functional Consultant	User	Business Process Owner	Senior Management	My Rating	Understanding Level
A	B	B	C		

3.16.1 Purpose and Overview

Here you define public holidays. There are five types of public holidays:

➢ With fixed date
➢ With a fixed day from date
➢ Distance to Easter
➢ Is Easter Sunday
➢ Is a movable holiday

Apart from determining which day is a public holiday, it also determines what is the holiday class of the holiday, and whether it is applicable to people belonging to a specific religion only. Note that public holidays are client independent.

3.16.2 IMG Node

Transaction OY05   Factory calendar
Transaction SCAL   Factory Calendar with GUI

3.16.3 Primary Key

Public Holiday Key

3.16.4 Important Fields

Public holiday key

This is a system generated three-character key to uniquely identify each holiday.

Holiday rule

Which type of holiday it is:

(a) With fixed date (F)
(b) With a fixed day from date (W)
(c) Distance to Easter (V)
(d) Is Easter Sunday (V)
(e) Is a movable holiday (U)

3.16.5 Holidays: Fixed Dates

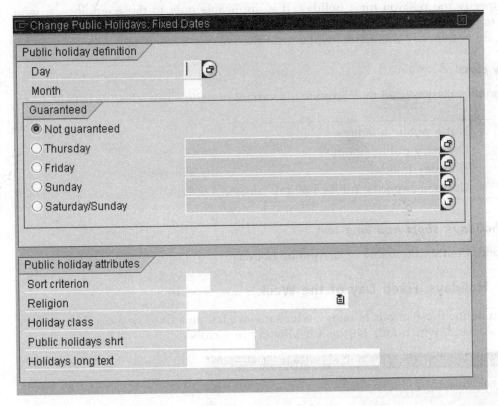

A holiday, which comes on a fixed month and date every year, e.g. new year.

Month and day

Here you specify the month and date on which the holiday is observed every year.

Public holiday guaranteed flag

In this field you specify what should happen if a public holiday falls on an off day. If the holiday is 'Not guaranteed', then it is not shifted. In case it falls on Thursday, Friday or Sunday, you could specify that it should be shifted to the previous day, or next day. If you chose Saturday/Sunday radio button, there is an additional choice where you can move Saturday to previous day and Sunday to next day.

Sort criterion

In this field, you can enter a three-character holiday sort key. The holidays can be sorted in alphabetical order with this key. If several holidays have the same sort criterion, they are also sorted by the text. You can use the sort criterion to display logically related holidays in a block, e.g. all holidays for a country.

Religion

If you specify the religion for a holiday, it is applicable only to those employees, who belong to that religion, as maintained in infotype 0002. Unless you intend to use this feature, do not specify this field, just because the holiday belongs to a religion.

Holiday class

Public holiday class is used to determine if a variant of daily work schedule is to be used.

Blank	Not a public holiday
1	Ordinary public holiday
2	Half-day holiday
3–9	Customer-specific public holiday classes

Public holidays: short and long text

These fields contain the name of the public holiday.

3.16.6 Holidays: Fixed Day of the Week

Here you define those public holidays, which always fall on a fixed day, e.g. Labour Day of New Zealand, which falls on the 4th Monday in October.

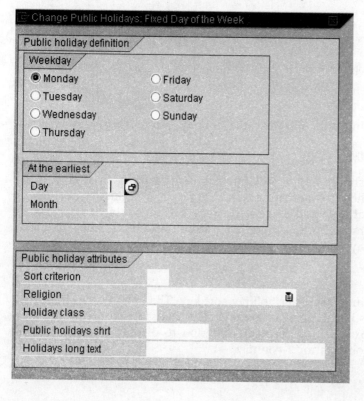

Weekday

Here you specify the day on which the holiday falls.

Earliest day and month

Here you specify the month in which the holiday falls and the earliest date.

3.16.7 Holidays: Distance from Easter, is Easter Sunday

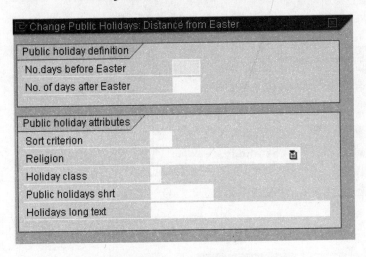

Number of days before or after Easter

Here you specify whether the holiday falls before or after Easter, and by how many days. If you define a holiday as 'is Easter Sunday', number of days before or after Easter fields are hidden.

3.16.8 Holidays: Movable Public Holidays

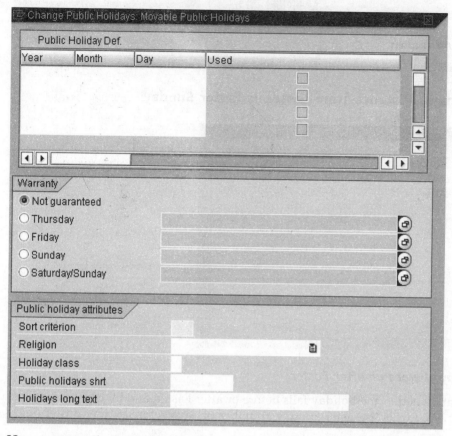

Here you specify those holidays, for which there is no fixed logic of occurrence. Here you can specify the date, month and year when they are observed.

3.17 PUBLIC HOLIDAY CALENDAR

Functional Consultant	User	Business Process Owner	Senior Management	My Rating	Understanding Level
A	B	B	C		

3.17.1 Purpose

Here you define holiday calendars, which are assigned to PSAs in table T001P. This holiday calendar is applicable to all employees in that PSA. It contains applicable holidays in a calendar. When Monthly Work Schedule (T552A) is generated, the holidays are picked up from this calendar. Note that the public holiday calendar does not contain weekly offs, which are there in factory calendar.

3.17.2 IMG Node

Transaction   OY05   Factory calendar
Transaction   SCAL   Factory Calendar with GUI

3.17.3 Screen

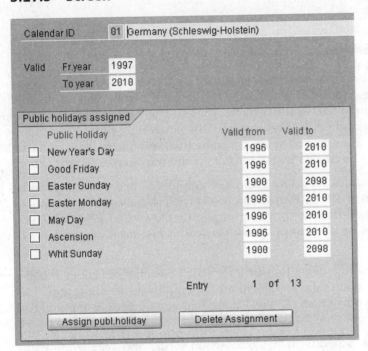

| Calendar ID | 01 | Germany (Schleswig-Holstein) |

Valid   Fr.year   1997
         To year   2010

Public holidays assigned

Public Holiday	Valid from	Valid to
New Year's Day	1996	2010
Good Friday	1996	2010
Easter Sunday	1900	2098
Easter Monday	1996	2010
May Day	1996	2010
Ascension	1996	2010
Whit Sunday	1900	2098

Entry   1   of   13

| Assign publ.holiday | Delete Assignment |

3.17.4 Primary Key

Public Holiday Calendar

3.17.5 Important Fields

Public holiday calendar

Public holiday calendar is assigned to PA + PSA in T001P, and thus becomes applicable to an employee based on his PA + PSA in infotype 0001.

Calendar validity: from year and to year

From which year to which year is the calendar valid.

Public holiday: valid from and valid to

Here you specify the list of public holidays in the calendar and their validity period. In a year, if the calendar is valid but the holiday is not, the calendar does not contain that holiday.

3.18 MONTHLY WORK SCHEDULE

Functional Consultant	User	Business Process Owner	Senior Management	My Rating	Understanding Level
A	C	C	X		

3.18.1 Purpose and Overview

Converting a work schedule rule into the characteristic of each day is a complex process as you will see from the description that follows. Hence SAP allows you to do this translation beforehand and store the result in table T552A. This is done by executing transaction PT01—Create work schedule. Transaction PT01 is wrongly put in SAP menu which is for users. If a user tries to run it on a productive system, he gets an error message. Work schedules must be created by the consultant and transported to production.

If you are creating work schedules for many groups of employees or for many periods, you may like to use transaction PT_SHF00, Create Period Work Schedule. Whereas in PT01, you can create work schedule only for one group of employees, in PT_SHF00, you can do it for multiple groups or all groups. Also, you can schedule it as a batch job, instead of executing online.

You can display this work schedule using transaction PT03. You can also change it using transaction PT02. The change you make applies to all the employees in the group. This is needed, for example, when you shift an off day. Changes in work schedule of individual employees are done through infotype 2003, Substitution.

You can also delete the work schedule using transaction PT02, and regenerate using PT01. Note that the changes you might have made in the work schedule are lost. Therefore, before you delete a work schedule, you may identify the changes you had made, and note them down. Unfortunately, there is no easy way of identifying these changes; you have to study the pattern. After you have recreated the work schedule, you need to determine whether those changes need to be made again.

You are normally not required to delete and recreate work schedule, except in the following circumstances: If holiday calendar is changed, period work schedule is changed, rule to determine daily work schedule variant is changed, day type selection rule is changed. All these changes are configuration changes done by your consultant. If he has changed any of these, he will also recreate work schedule and transport to production. The generated work schedule is stored in table T552A. This table applies work schedule rule to a period, and determines the following characteristics of each day.

➤ Daily work schedule
➤ Day type
➤ Public holiday class
➤ Daily work schedule variant
➤ Religious denomination key

From Work Schedule Rule (T508A), the PWS is determined. Using PWS (T551A) and DWS variant selection rule (T550X), the DWS and DWS variant are determined. Using holiday calendar (THOCI), and assignment of holidays to holiday calendar (THOC), holidays are determined. Using public holidays table (THOL) the holiday class and religion is determined.

From Work Schedule Rule (T508A), Day Type Selection Rule (T553A) is picked up. For the day, holiday class is also determined (see above paragraph). From both these, the day type is determined. Day types for special days (T553S) are also taken into account.

For an employee, all key data fields of this table can be determined and the characteristics of each day can be found. Thus, each record in this table gives the characteristics of each day of the month for a set of employees.

The monthly work schedule does not normally show the holiday class. But for a holiday, e.g. 1st May, it shows. In the case of a holiday, the DWS as well as the day type have to be changed.

3.18.2 IMG Node

Personnel Time Management ➤ Work Schedules ➤ Work Schedule Rules and Work Schedules ➤ Generate Work Schedules in Batch

Transaction   PT01   Create Work Schedule

3.18.3 Screen

ES grouping	2	DWS grouping	20	Monthly hours	150.00
Holiday calendar ID	M1	Period work schedule	M001		
PS grouping	20	Work schedule rule	M001		

Valid   February   2005   Chngd 14.01.2005   QHRLGA0011…

Work Schedule

Wk	D	MO	HC	D	TU	HC	D	WE	HC	D	TH	HC	D	FR	HC	D	SA	HC	D	SU	HC
05		01			02			03			04			05			06				
		M001			M001			M001			M001			M001			MOFF			MOFF	
06	07	08			09			10			11			12			13				
		M001			M001			M001			M001			M001			MOFF			MOFF	
07	14	15			16			17			18			19			20				
		M001			M001			M001			M001			M001			MOFF			MOFF	
08	21	22			23			24			25			26			27				
		M001			M001			M001			M001			M001			MOFF			MOFF	
09	28																				
		M001																			

3.18.4 Primary Key

ES Grouping for Work Schedules + Public Holiday Calendar + PS Grouping for Work Schedules + Work Schedule Rule + Calendar Year for Monthly Work Schedule Generation + Fiscal Period

3.19 DYNAMIC SHIFT CHANGE BASED ON CLOCK-IN TIME

Functional Consultant	User	Business Process Owner	Senior Management	My Rating	Understanding Level
A	C	C	X		

3.19.1 Purpose and Overview

What happens if an employee comes in a shift which is different from his schedule? You could take a strict view and mark him absent, or require the employee to apply for a change in his shift, and create a substitution. Some companies take a lenient view, and let the employee come in a different shift. They also want the system to allow it, without burdening the administrator with the task of creating substitutions.

You may configure SAP to dynamically change the DWS. There are two methods of doing it: (a) based on clock-in time and (b) based on overlap of planned and actual time. This view allows dynamic assignment of daily work schedule based on the clock-in times of an employee. Intervals are defined in this view which determine the DWS. If this method is to be used, function ACTIO TD30 should be active in the schema TM00. The entries should include the original DWS as well, in addition to alternate DWS.

If dynamic assignment of the daily work schedule is only to be carried out for specific employees, you may read the documentation on personnel calculation rule TD30. Note that this method cannot be used for determining daily work schedule, or its variant, if the clock-in time remains same. If an employee works full day on weekdays, and half day on Saturday, you cannot use this method, in case his clock-in time remains the same. You must use DWS variant to meet this requirement.

3.19.2 IMG Node

SM30 ➤ V_T552V

3.19.3 Screen

G..	PWS	D...	Start Date	End Date	Start	End Time	DWS	Variant	Var. ctrl	OrigD...
01	J001	01	01.01.1991	31.12.9999	04:00:00	12:00:00	J001		✔	☐
01	J001	01	01.01.1991	31.12.9999	12:01:00	20:00:00	J002		✔	☐
01	J001	01	01.01.1991	31.12.9999	20:01:00	23:59:00	J003		✔	☐

3.19.4 Primary Key

PS Grouping for Daily Work Schedules + Period Work Schedule + Type for Daily Work Schedule Assignment + End Date + Start Time

3.19.5 Important Fields

PS grouping for daily work schedules

Rules for dynamic assignment of DWS need not be same for the whole company. They can differ based on the employee's PS grouping for daily work schedules.

Period work schedule

Period Work Schedule to which it applies.

Type for daily work schedule assignment

Even within a PS grouping for daily work schedules, you can apply different rules to different employees based on this field. In time evaluation, this field is set by function MOD, PCR MODT, operation MODIF to value S.

Dynamic assignment of DWS is done through operation DYNDP, which is called in PCR TD30. Operation DYNDP is called with a parameter. Only if the parameter of the operation matches with the parameter of the employee (set by Operation MODIF), dynamic assignment of DWS takes place.

Start and end date

Specification of dynamic work schedule assignment can change with time.

Start and end time

If the clock time is within this interval, the daily work schedule and variant are selected.

Daily work schedule

The daily work schedule which will be assigned. You must include the normal DWS (one which the employee gets from the PWS before the dynamic assignment takes place).

Daily work schedule variant

If you want a fixed variant, you specify here.

Indicator: control of DWS variant from T550X

If you want the variant to be determined using table T550X, you tick this. Note that if you made a change in monthly work schedule, it would get overwritten by dynamic daily work schedule assignment.

Indicator: transfer of original DWS variant

If you do not want your original DWS variant to be overwritten, tick this field.

3.20 DYNAMIC SHIFT CHANGE BASED ON PLANNED/ACTUAL OVERLAP

Functional Consultant	User	Business Process Owner	Senior Management	My Rating	Understanding Level
A	C	C	X		

3.20.1 Purpose

This view allows a second method of dynamic assignment of daily work schedule, which is based on the overlap between planned and actual work time of the employee. If this method is to be used, function DYNWS should be activated in the schema TM00.

3.20.2 IMG Node

SM30 ➤ V_T552W

3.20.3 Screen

	G.	PWS	DW...	No.	Start Date	End Date	Daily WS	Variant	Var. ctrl
	01	M3		001	01.01.1996	31.12.9999	F-11		☐
	01	M3		002	01.01.1996	31.12.9999	S-11		☐
	01	M3		003	01.01.1996	31.12.9999	N-11		☐
	01	M3	01	001	01.01.1996	31.12.9999	F-11		☐

3.20.4 Primary Key

PS Grouping for Daily Work Schedules + Period Work Schedule + Type for Daily Work Schedule Assignment + Sequential Number + End Date.

3.20.5 Important Fields

PS grouping for daily work schedules

Rules for dynamic assignment of DWS need not be same for the whole company. They can differ based on the employee's PS grouping for daily work schedules.

Period work schedule

Period work schedule to which it applies.

Type for daily work schedule assignment

Even within a PS grouping for daily work schedules, you can apply different rules to different employees based on this field. In time evaluation, this field is set by function MOD, PCR MODT, operation MODIF to value S.

Dynamic assignment of DWS is done through function DYNWS. In the second parameter, you can specify the type. Only if the parameter of the function matches with the parameter of the employee set by Operation MODIF, dynamic assignment of DWS takes place.

Sequential number

This is purely a sequence number, through which you allow multiple daily work schedules, from which the most appropriate one is selected based on the overlap of planned and actual time.

Start and end date

Specification of dynamic work schedule assignment can change with time.

Daily work schedule

Here you specify the work schedules which are to be compared with actual times to determine the best fit.

Daily work schedule variant

If the daily work schedule is to be taken with a fixed variant, you specify that here.

Indicator: Control of DWS variant from T550X

If the daily work schedule is to be taken with a variant determined through table T550X, you tick this check box.

3.21 WORKING WEEK

Functional Consultant	User	Business Process Owner	Senior Management	My Rating	Understanding Level
C	X	X	X		

3.21.1 Purpose

You can define a working week which is different from a calendar week. You assign a working week to an employee in infotype 0007. In order to do that, you have to activate working week entry field in view T588M. The working week of an employee and its details can be queried in a PCR using operations OUTWP and VARST, and logic can be written based on it. You can set default value of working week of an employee using feature WWEEK.

3.21.2 IMG Node

SM30 ➤ T559A

3.21.3 Screen

Working week	Name of working week	Lngth	Start date	Start time
01	Working week Monday	07	01.01.1990	
02	Working week Friday 12 noon	07	05.01.1990	12:00:00
03	Working week Monday 12 midnght	07	01.01.1990	00:00:00

3.21.4 Primary Key

Working week

3.21.5 Important Fields

Working week, name

Working week id and its name.

Length of working week

The length of the working week need not be 7 days.

Start date of working week

This determines the day on which the working week starts.

Start time of working week

The working week can start from a particular time of the day.

3.22 DEFAULT WORKING WEEK

Functional Consultant	User	Business Process Owner	Senior Management	My Rating	Understanding Level
C	X	X	X		

3.22.1 Purpose

This feature returns the default working week in infotype 0007.

3.22.2 IMG Node

PE03 ➤ WWEEK

3.22.3 Screen

```
WWEEK Default value for working week

    └─▭ PERSK Employee Subgroup
    |
```

3.22.4 Fields for Decision Making

Company Code
Personnel Area
Personnel Subarea
Employee Group
Employee Subgroup
Country Grouping

3.22.5 Return Value

Working week

Substitution

4.1 SUBSTITUTIONS (INFOTYPE 2003)

Functional Consultant	User	Business Process Owner	Senior Management	My Rating	Understanding Level
A	A	A	A		

4.1.1 Screen

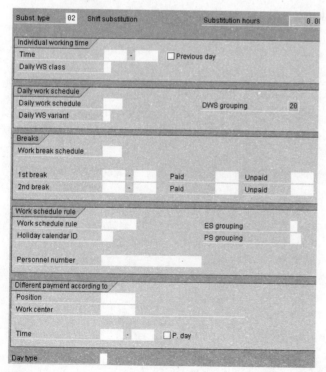

4.1.2 Purpose and Overview

Normally, an employee is expected to come to work as per his work schedule, which is determined from the work schedule rule assigned to him in infotype 0007. When time evaluation takes place, this plan is compared with the actual time he came to work, and various conclusions drawn. In case there is a temporary change in a person's work schedule, one would have to change his infotype 0007, which would get cluttered up. Moreover, it would provide only limited flexibility. SAP lets you change an employee's work schedule through infotype 2003 (substitutions), where it provides you much more flexibility.

➤ You can directly specify the working time of the employee.
➤ You can specify the daily work schedule.
➤ In both the above cases, you can specify the break timings.
➤ You can specify a work schedule rule, selecting from all the locations, and employee groups, and not merely from employee's own.
➤ You can specify a personnel number, whose work schedule this employee would follow.
➤ You can specify the basis for making different payments to the employee.
➤ You can directly specify the day type.

While doing substitution, collision with other infotypes is checked. It makes no sense, for example, if you say that an employee is going to be absent in infotype 2001, and that he is going to come in night shift in infotype 2003.

➤ Except for position substitutions, all types of substitution constitute a change to the employee's personal work schedule, as the system overwrites the original work schedule when you enter a substitution. Therefore, on any one day, the system can take only one substitution into account that changes the employee's planned working time.
➤ By combining a position substitution with other substitution types, you can change both the employee's planned working time and payment details.

Your substitutions can protect an employee's salary, if the indicator for shift change compensation in table T556 is ticked for the substitution type.

Your substitutions may not take into account reduced working hours, while counting absence. For more details, refer to Chapter 4.2.

Payment Data: There are three ways of making a different payment resulting from a substitution in the system:

➤ Position
➤ Different payment
➤ Substitution type. Substitution type can be queried in payroll schema XT00. Only reduced hours substitutions are queried and valuated in time evaluation.

4.1.3 Subtypes

Substitution type

4.1.4 Time Constraint

Z (Time constraint for time management infotypes -> T554Y)

4.1.5 Important Fields

Substitution type

This specifies the type of substitution you are doing. Substitution types are subtypes of infotype 2003. This value can be defaulted from feature VTART.

Substitution hours

This field is automatically computed by the system based on your input.

Individual Working Time

This is the most flexible method of substitution. Here you can directly specify the working time of the employee. You can also specify breaks along with individual working time.

Time (from and to)

Here you specify the time an employee is expected to work.

Previous day

If an employee is working night shift, his out swipe for 10th takes place on 11th. In such a case, you tick the previous day indicator.

Daily work schedule class

Even though SAP lets you specify the time, instead of a daily work schedule, it still needs to know the daily WS class, which you need to specify.

Daily work schedule

This is the most common method of substitution. If an employee is going to come in a different shift, you specify the shift, i.e. daily work schedule and its variant. You can also specify break schedule with it if you do not want the default break schedule to be used. You can also specify day type.

Daily work schedule and variant

Daily work schedule defines a day's work pattern, including start and end time, break timings, late coming and early going tolerances, etc. These are configured by your time management consultant. You assign that here. Only those daily work schedule and variant, which are applicable to the employee as per his DWS grouping, are shown in the list of daily work schedule.

DWS grouping

PS grouping for daily work schedule (DWS grouping) is determined by the system based on the employee's PA and PSA.

Breaks

Work break schedule

If you enter a break schedule here, this substitutes the break schedule assigned to the daily work schedule. You also need to specify the break schedule if you are specifying individual working time.

Break timings

If you want to give break to the employee, which do not follow any standard pattern, instead of specifying the break schedule, you can specify the actual timings. You can also specify whether they are paid, unpaid, or partly paid. If you specify a break schedule, or actual break hours, these take precedence over the break schedule defined in the daily work schedule.

Work schedule rule

You can specify a work schedule rule, selecting from all the locations and employee groups, and not merely from employee's own. Alternatively, you can specify a personnel number, whose work schedule this employee would follow.

Work schedule rule, holiday calendar ID, ES grouping, PS grouping

The definition of a work schedule rule can differ depending on ES grouping for work schedules, PS grouping for work schedules and holiday calendar. This section gives you the flexibility of assigning a work schedule rule to an employee, not only from his area, but also from other areas. When you select an item from the list of values, all the four fields get populated.

Personnel number

Very often, you are doing a substitution, because some other employee is absent or needs assistance. This person should follow the same work schedule as the person he is substituting. SAP lets you specify the personnel number of a person, whose work schedule is followed by the person for whom you are creating this substitution record. Note that the substitute employee only gets the work schedule of the employee he is substituting and not his authorizations.

Different payment according to

Here you can specify if this person is to receive payment as per a position, or a work center and for what time. If you only enter the position, the planned working time does not change. You can combine the substitution based on a position with all other types of substitution, enabling you to take advantage of other variations of the substitution.

Day type

Here you can explicitly specify the day type. This supersedes the day type determined in his personal work schedule.

4.2   SUBSTITUTION TYPE

Functional Consultant	User	Business Process Owner	Senior Management	My Rating	Understanding Level
A	C	C	X		

4.2.1   Purpose

This view defines various types of Substitutions.

4.2.2   IMG Node

SM30 ➤ V_T556

4.2.3   Screen

	PSG	Sub...	Substitution type text	Time cstr. class	Chg.comp.	RWH subs.
	01	01	Foreman substitution	01	☐	☐
	01	02	Shift substitution	02	☐	☐
	01	03	RWH substitution	01	☐	☑
	01	04	Workers comp.substitution	01	☐	☐

4.2.4   Primary Key

PS Grouping for Substitution/Availability Types + Substitution Type

4.2.5   Important Fields

PS grouping for substitution/availability types

Based on their PA and PSA, employees are grouped in different PS groupings for substitution/availability types. For the same substitution type, the properties can differ based on this grouping.

Substitution type

You can create various substitution types, which help you understand the kind of substitution or reason for substitution. The details of substitution are specified in infotype 2003.

Time constraint class

While doing substitution, collision with other infotypes are checked. It makes no sense, for example, if you say that an employee is going to be absent in infotype 2001, and that he is going to come in night shift in infotype 2003. The collision checks are based on time constraint class. For more details see chapter 5.3 (V_554Y_B).

Indicator for shift change compensation

Shift change compensation ensures that an employee does not lose out financially by working a substitution. If the shift change compensation field is active, the difference between two levels of remuneration for a substitution can be adjusted automatically in payroll.

Reduced hours substitution indicator

Your company might declare that due to bad weather, employees need to work only 4 hours on a particular day, instead of normal 8 hours. This would be done through substitution. However, if an employee is absent, would you like to count his absence as 4 hours, or 8 hours? If your company wants to count it as 4 hours, you do not tick this. If you want to count it as 8 hours, you tick this.

4.3 DEFAULT SUBSTITUTION TYPE

Functional Consultant	User	Business Process Owner	Senior Management	My Rating	Understanding Level
A	C	C	X		

4.3.1 Purpose

You can use this feature to assign default value for substitution type, when you create an infotype 2003 record.

4.3.2 IMG Node

PE03 ➤ VTART

4.3.3 Screen

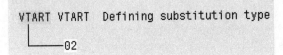

```
VTART VTART  Defining substitution type
  └──────02
```

4.3.4   Fields for Decision Making

Company Code
Personnel Area
Personnel Subarea
Employee Group
Employee Subgroup
Period Work Schedule
Work Schedule Rule
Country Grouping

4.3.5   Return Value

Substitution type

5

Absence

5.1 ABSENCES (INFOTYPE 2001)

Functional Consultant	User	Business Process Owner	Senior Management	My Rating	Understanding Level
A	A	A	A		

5.1.1 Screen Number 2001 Quota Deduction

Entry screen 2001 is used for absence types which require quota deduction. When you enter an absence type with quota deduction, the system checks the existing quotas. The absence record can only be stored if sufficient quota is available. If sufficient quota is available, the system updates the quotas automatically. In customizing you determine which absence types you want to be deducted from which absence quota types.

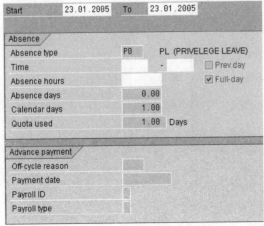

85

5.1.2   Screen Number 2000 Absences (General)

Entry screen 2000 is used for all absences that do not require any special processing. The system displays payroll hours and days on this screen.

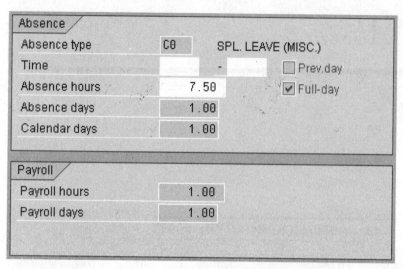

5.1.3   Screen Number 2008 Work Incapacity (General)

This Screen 2008 is used for all absence types that are related to automatic continued pay. The screen includes special fields and additional subscreens to store and check data for continued pay and sick pay supplements. The system also displays payroll hours and days here.

Additional Information		
Relationships	/	
Days credited		
End of continued pay		
End of sick pay		
Notific. to employer		00:00
Confirmation		00:00
Start doctor's cert.		
Superior		
Reference number		
Abs. due to accident		
Work capacity pct.		

5.1.4 Purpose and Overview

If you have information that an employee is not going to work as scheduled, you would keep that information in infotype 2001. For some absence types, e.g. maternity and military service, there are special infotypes. Their special functionality is designed only for certain countries. There are some fields in infotype 2001, which store country-specific features for recording incapacity to work for Germany, France, the Netherlands, Austria, and Great Britain/Ireland. There are several screens of infotype 2001 of which the following are very important.

> ➢ General absences (screen 2000)
> ➢ Absences with quota deduction (screen 2001)
> ➢ Absences relating to an incapacity to work (screen 2008)

You can enter full day absences, or part day absences. Full day absences can be for one or more days. In the case of part day absences, start and end date must be the same. If you enter absence hours, start time and end time are determined (depending on the settings made in feature HRSIF). Similarly, you can enter start time and end time, in which case absence hours are determined. Break timings are taken into account during such determination. Start time and end time are always within scheduled working hours. If the actual start time and end time are not within scheduled working hours, you may have to do a substitution (infotype 2003) first.

Absences with quota deduction are absences that are deducted from an employee's absence entitlement. You can only record these absences for employees who have sufficient absence quota in the absence quotas infotype (2006). Absences relating to incapacity to work result in computation of continued pay, sick pay, etc. These features are country-specific.

You can click on the icon 🎦 Personal work schedule to see the work schedule of the employee for a period. This schedule takes into account any substitution you may have made.

You can do activity allocation, cost assignment, external services and different payment for infotype 2001. See chapters 21, 22, 23 and 24 on these topics for more details. You can use the absences infotype (2001) to transfer costs and work performed data to the Accounting and Logistics components.

5.1.5 Quota Deduction for Absences

The linkage for absence quota deduction is as follows: Absence (PA2001) ➢ Absence type (V_554S_Q) ➢ Counting Rule (T556C) ➢ Deduction Rule (V_556R_B) ➢ Quota type (T556A).

Quota deduction takes place when absence entries are made in infotype 2001. This entry contains absence type, whose properties are defined in table T554S. One of the attributes of absence type is counting rule which takes us to table T556C. In a counting rule, you define deduction rule, which takes us to V_556R_B. If you are not using a deduction rule, you can directly specify quota type. In the deduction rule, you define quota type from which absence is to be deducted.

Finally, when quota deduction takes place, the details are stored in table PTQUODED, Deduction of Time Quotas. It is necessary to know which absence was deducted from which quota record because if the absence record is deleted, the quota deduction has to be reversed.

5.1.6 Attendance/Absence Days and Hours, Payroll Days and Hours

You come across these terms in this infotype, as well as in many other places. You need to know how they are calculated. Holiday in the table below means day type is not equal to 0. No other logic is used. Off day in the table below means planned hours is 0.

Planned working hours

Holiday	Off day	Normal day	Full/ Partial	Condition	Planned working hours
Y	Y		N.A.		0
		Y	N.A.		Planned working hours

Absence hours

Holiday	Off day	Normal day	Full/ Partial	Condition	Absence hours
Y			*		0
	Y	Y	Full		Planned working hours
	Y		Partial		Record cannot be created
		Y	Partial		From the screen

Attendance hours

Holiday	Off day	Normal day	Full/ Partial	Condition	Attendance hours
Y	Y	Y	Full		Planned working hours
Y	Y	Y	Partial		From the screen

Calendar days

Holiday	Off day	Normal day	Full/ Partial	Condition	Calendar days
Y	Y	Y	Full		1
Y	Y	Y	Partial		0

Attendance/Absence days

Holiday	Off day	Normal day	Full/ Partial	Condition	Attendance/Absence days
Y	Y	Y	*	PWH=0	0
Y	Y	Y	*	AAH>=PWH	1
Y	Y	Y	*	Otherwise	AAH/PWH

Payroll hours

Holiday	Off day	Normal day	Full/ Partial	Condition	Payroll hours
Y	Y	Y	*		AAH multiplied and rounded as per the counting rule

Payroll days

Holiday	Off day	Normal day	Full/ Partial	Condition	Payroll days
Y	Y	Y	*	AAH>=PWH	1 multiplied and rounded as per the counting rule
Y	Y	Y	*	Otherwise	AAH/PWH multiplied and rounded as per the counting rule

If you want to multiply payroll hours and days by a factor, you can implement BAdI TIM00ATTABSCOUNTING (Multiply Payroll Hours and Payroll Days). If you want to generate new values for payroll hours and days, but using a factor is not sufficient for your requirements, you can use BAdI PT_ABS_ATT_COUNTRY (Free Determination of Payroll Hours and Payroll Days).

5.1.7 Subtypes

Absence type

5.1.8 Time Constraint

Z (Time constraint for time management infotypes -> T554Y)

5.1.9 Important Fields

Start and end date

Here you specify the period of absence. Depending on the settings made in table T554S, the system issues either a warning or error message if the 'from date' or 'to date' of the record falls on an employee's day off.

Absence type

All absences are created against predefined absence types. Absence types are subtypes of infotype 2001 and are configured in table T554S.

Start and end time

For absences, which last less than one day, you can give start and end time. Start and end time, previous day indicator, and absence hours fields are enterable only if end date is same as start date.

Start and end time must be within scheduled working time. If you enter a start time, which is before the start time of the employee's daily work schedule, the system changes it to the start time of the daily work schedule. Similarly, you cannot enter the end time after the end time of the employee's daily work schedule. If the times you enter cover the full day, the time fields are blanked out, and full day indicator is ticked. If the actual start time and end time are not within scheduled working hours, you may have to do a substitution (infotype 2003) first.

Previous day indicator

If you have a night shift, e.g. from 22:00 hours till 06:00 hours on the next day, all times till 06:00 hours must be assigned to the previous day. This indicator is automatically determined by the system.

Absence hours

If start and end time are blank and you enter absence hours, the system assumes the start time as start of shift, and computes end time, based on absence hours (provided configuration in feature HRSIF requires it to do so). If there are breaks during that period, the end time is appropriately delayed.

Between start time, end time and absence hours, you can enter any two fields; the third is calculated by the system.

Full day

The absence times are relevant only if the absence is not a full day absence. In most cases, where the absence is a full day absence, this indicator is ticked. Where the absence record is for multiple days, this indicator is automatically ticked.

Absence days

Absence days are determined by the system by taking into account the holidays and weekly offs.

Calendar days

The calendar days are the number of days between the start and end dates of a record. They are displayed by the system.

Quota used

Quota used is determined by the system as per the logic in overview of 'Quota deduction for Absences'. If there is no quota deduction, this field is not shown.

Advance payment

If you pay for absences, e.g. payment for annual leave, and wish to pay in advance, you need to have necessary time management configuration in place. In that case you populate off-cycle reason, payment date, payroll id, payroll type and run off-cycle payroll.

Payroll hours

Depending on your configuration, payroll hours can be different from absence hours.

Payroll days

Depending on your configuration, the system may determine the payroll days to be different from absence days. This is usually done when the number of working hours is not same on all days.

Additional information

Absences relating to incapacity to work result in computation of continued pay, sick pay, etc. These features are country-specific.

5.1.10   Reports

Attendance/absence data: Overview (PT64)

This report shows PA/PSA wise attendance/absence data summary. It can be expanded to show employee level details, and further expanded to show absence types. However, this report does not show the absence dates. It calls program RPTABS20.

Attendance/absence data: Calendar view (PT90, PT90_ATT)

Calendar view is very similar to annual calendar. Additional facilities include statistics, legend, seeing only selected attendances and absences if you so desire and highlighting of holidays. However, you cannot create attendances/absences directly from here, which is possible in annual calendar. It calls program RPTABS50.

Attendances/absences: Multiple employee view (PT91, PT91_ATT)

This report is also like calendar view, but instead of showing data of one person for multiple dates, it shows data of multiple persons for a single date. It calls program RPTABS60.

Overview graphic of attendances/absences (PT65)

This report shows a graphic view of Attendances/Absences. If you click on an attendance/absence, it opens the corresponding record. It calls program RPTLEA40.

Recalculate attendance/absence records (PT_UPD00)

The program creates a batch input session for revaluating absence and attendance records. A revaluation can be necessary if work schedule data on which the valuation is based changes after the absence or attendance is entered. It calls program RPTUPD00.

5.2 ATTENDANCE AND ABSENCE TYPES

Functional Consultant	User	Business Process Owner	Senior Management	My Rating	Understanding Level
A	B	B	C		

5.2.1 Purpose and Overview

When you have information about an employee's absence, you enter it in infotype 2001. One of the most important information about an absence is absence type. You would like to know if the employee is absent because he is on privilege leave or casual leave, or is he absent because of injury on work. This view maintains the characteristics of absence types (as well as attendance types which are covered later). These characteristics can change with time. They may also be different for different PS grouping for absence and attendance types.

An absence type is assigned a time constraint class which ensures that data across infotypes is not contradictory. For example, you cannot have both attendance and absence record for the same day. For more details, see chapter 5.3 (V_554Y_B).

SAP has provided different screens for different purposes. For example, the screen for absences, which leads to quota deduction, is different from the screen for absences, which does not lead to quota deduction. You can select a suitable screen for an absence type.

In many companies, employees are entitled to a specified amount of leave. For such absences, you can link absences to quota deduction. You can directly specify the quota type from which the absence can be deducted. You can also build a more complex rule for quota deduction, through counting rule (T556C), which you can assign to an absence/attendance type.

SAP lets you view the personal calendar of an employee showing a crisp view of the full month. There, instead of showing attendance/absence types, you see absence/attendance category, which is only one character. You can also create an attendance/absence from the calendar view. If you have many attendance/absence types linked to the same absence/attendance category, you have to choose while creating the attendance/absence.

You can group absence types in different time evaluation classes, which you can query in time evaluation and process differently, according to the rules you write.

If you record absence and attendance of your employees in infotypes 2001 and 2002, and your employees do not record time at attendance recording terminals, you use a different method of time evaluation. In this, the processing type and time type is determined by function TYPES using table T555Y, based on processing type/time type classes of the attendance/absence type. This processing type/time type class for an attendance/absence type is defined here.

Absences have an impact on payroll. You may want to deduct an employee's salary if he is absent. Or, you may want to pay him a vacation allowance if he is on vacation. The complete link from absence type to payroll result has been explained in this chapter where the field absence valuation rule is discussed.

While generating quota, you can specify if quota should be reduced in the case of absences. You can also specify if absences below a threshold level should not lead to quota reduction. You can also specify that while generating quota, absences above a given number should not lead to quota reduction.

5.2.2 IMG Node

SM30 ➤ T554S

5.2.3 Primary Key

PS Grouping for Absence and Attendance Types + Attendance or Absence Type + End Date

5.2.4 Important Fields

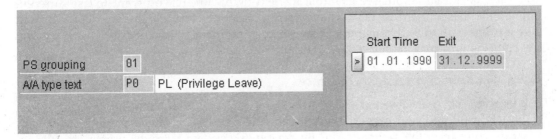

PS Grouping for absence and attendance types

PS grouping for which properties of absence type are being defined.

Attendance or absence type

Attendance or absence type, whose properties are being defined.

Start and end date

Period for which properties of attendance or absence type are being defined.

Attendance or absence indicator

This view contains both attendance types (P) and absence types (A).

Availability for an attendance/absence

If a person has an absence record, then normally he is not available. If he has an attendance record, which shows he is occupied, then again he is not available for other activities. However, if there is an attendance record, which shows that he is present but not occupied, he can be used. It is therefore necessary to know for which attendance/absence types the person is available, and for which he is not. This is specified here. The system permits you to indicate availability even for absence types, although these are less common. This information can be used in the integration of time management with the training and event management, shift planning, and logistics capacity planning, etc. If a person is not available, you cannot plan work for him in logistics.

Absence type grouping to determine daily work schedule variants

An employee is expected to work as per his daily work schedule. If he is absent for full day, the system uses the same timings to determine the number of absence hours. However, you may have a situation (see example in field help), where you want to use different timings for these absences. If you have such a situation, to each absence type, you can give a number (1 to 9) in this field. You can then define a rule in V_550X_B, where you can use this grouping to select DWS variant.

Check end date of attendance/absence

Suppose you have an absence record from 1st January 2005 to 10th January 2005 of an absence type PL, and your properties for this absence type have changed on 5th January 2005. What do you expect the system to do? By default, the system takes the properties valid on the start date of the absence record. However, if this is not acceptable to you, you check this field. The system gives an error. Then you split the absence record from 1st to 4th and 5th to 10th, so that the properties of absence type can be applied without any conflict.

Screen for recording absences or attendances

Here you specify the screen you want when entering absences in infotype 2001. The most likely values are: 2001 Quota deduction, 2000 Absences (general) and 2008 Work incapacity (general).

There are other screens that are suitable for specific countries. You should spend some time to determine which screens are best for you.

Time constraint class

The time constraint class is used to check for collisions between Time Management infotypes (2001 to 2013). It allows you to specify different regulations for checking for collisions between individual subtypes. How to design time constraint classes and how to specify the rules to ensure that you do not have conflicting data, e.g. an employee is both present and absent at the same time, is discussed in chapter 5.3 (V_554Y_B).

Attendance/absence class

This field is of no general use.

Input checks		
First day is day off	W	Minimum duration
Last day is day off	W	Maximum duration 999
Non-working period		Unit R Payroll days
☑ Second date required		

Reaction indicator when first day is a day off

Normally, you would enter absence only when the employee is working. If you entered an absence such that the first day of the absence period is an off day, what would you like the system to do? You can choose to give an error, a warning, information, or quietly accept the entry.

Reaction indicator when last day is a day off

If you entered an absence such that the last day of the absence period is an off day, what would you like the system to do? You can choose to give an error, a warning, information, or quietly accept the entry.

Reaction indicator for non-working period

Normally, you would enter absence only when the employee is working. If you entered an absence such that the entire period is non-working, what would you like the system to do? You can choose to give an error, a warning, information or quietly accept the entry.

Second date required

When you create an absence record in infotype 2001, start and end date could be defaulted based on settings in V_T582A. If you think that this default could be dangerous for some absence types, you tick this field. If the field is activated, the system does not use default values from V_T582A.

Minimum duration in days

You can use this field to enforce a company policy, e.g. privilege leave must be minimum 3 days.

Maximum duration in days

You can use this field to enforce a company policy on maximum duration of an absence. However, one can enter multiple records to bypass this check.

Unit for minimum/maximum number of days

The minimum and maximum duration can be specified in calendar days, attendance/absence days, or payroll days.

Counting and quota deduction			
Quota type		Counting rule	040
Grpg att./abs. for counting		☑ Quota deduction	
Manual leave deduction		☐ Deduction over interval end	

The fields on the left hand side of this picture is for infotype 0005, which is obsolete. The field 'Quota deduction over interval end' does not appear in view V_554S_A, which is for attendances.

Attendance or absence quota type

If an absence type results in quota deduction, here you can directly specify the quota type from which the deduction should take place. Quota type 99 is deducted from infotype 0005. Quota types 01–98 for absences are deducted from infotype 2006.

Grouping of attendance and absence types for counting

Earlier SAP used to keep leave entitlements in infotype 0005. That is obsolete now, and you have absence quota (infotype 2006) instead. This grouping is required for leave deduction from infotype 0005. Deduction rule is specified in T554X.

Indicator for manual leave deduction

In this field, you determine whether absence quota type 99 (leave) can be reduced manually from infotype 2001.

Blank	Changes cannot be made manually
1	Only number fields can be overwritten
2	All fields can be changed

Counting rule

SAP offers a very powerful mechanism to decide how an absence should be counted for quota deduction. The linkage for absence quota deduction is as follows: Absence (PA2001) ➢ Absence type (V_554S_Q) ➢ Counting Rule (T556C) ➢ Deduction Rule (V_556R_B) ➢ Quota type (T556A). The Counting rule specified here is the link between V_554S_Q and T556C.

Quota deduction

If this checkbox is ticked, only then quota deduction takes place.

Deduction over end of deduction interval

In absence quotas you can define deduction interval. You can deduct from these quotas only if the absence period lies within the quota deduction interval. Some companies allow deduction as long as the start date lies within the quota deduction interval, even if some part of the absence is outside it. In such cases, you tick this field. This field is only for absence types.

Absence/attendance category

SAP lets you view the personal calendar of an employee showing a crisp view of the full month. There, instead of showing attendance/absence types, you see absence/attendance category, which is only one character. You can also create an attendance/absence from the calendar view. If you have many attendance/absence types linked to the same absence/ attendance category, you have to choose while creating the attendance/absence. The master list of absence/attendance category is defined in T554P and assigned here.

Attendance/absence type

This field is used in payrolls of Great Britain, Finland, France and Austria. It has a master table V_T5A4Q. This table is not covered in this book.

Indicator: Store attendance/absence in personal calendar

If you activate this field, the assigned absence category can be displayed in the personal calendar. You can also create an absence record from calendar.

Class for time evaluation

If you want to process different absence types differently in time evaluation, you can classify them into different classes here. This field is not used in any configuration. However, it can be read through operation VARABCAT and used in PCR for different purposes. SAP provides PCR TP10, where this field is used. You may examine that PCR to determine whether you need that PCR, with or without modification. If yes, you decide the appropriate value for this field.

Processing type/time type class

If you record absence and attendance of your employees in infotypes 2001 and 2002, and your employees do not record time at attendance recording terminals, you use a different method of time evaluation. In this, the processing type and time type is determined by function TYPES using table T555Y, based on processing type/time type classes of the attendance/absence type. This processing type/time type class for an attendance/absence type is defined here.

```
Payment data
Absence valuation rule              02
Abs./att.cat.for payroll
```

Absence valuation rule

Absences have an impact on payroll. You may want to deduct an employee's salary if he is unauthorized absent, but may want to pay if he is on approved leave. In payroll, this is called factoring. It is done in the following way:

- For an absence type, you define absence valuation rule (this field of table T554S).
- For an absence valuation rule, you define counting class in table T554C.
- All absences, which have the same counting class are accumulated in function PARTT in payroll.
- These are accessed through variables e.g. TKAU01. T indicates partial period, K is calendar days; AU is absences and 01 is counting class. TKAU** indicates absences belonging to all counting classes.
- You use these variables to compute partial period factors in PCR INP1 (or equivalent for your country).
- You assign partial period factors to wage type in processing class 10 (view V_512W_D).

The absence valuation rule can also be read through operation VARABVCL in PCRs, where you can write your own logic.

Absence/attendance category for payroll

This field is for Austria and Germany only.

```
Supplementary absence data
☐ Supplementary abs. data
Sickness tracking subtype
Accident data subtype
```

The fields in this view are only for absences, and not for attendances. For certain absences, the data stored in infotype 2001 is not enough. You need more data. This is kept in infotype 0082. You would wish to coordinate the entries of infotype 0082 and infotype 2001. Moreover, you would like to do the entries together. SAP lets you do that. You can create infotype 2001 entries from infotype 0082 themselves. SAP identifies these correlated entries through object type field. It also lets you change infotype 2001 entry in infotype 0082.

However, you do not want one to enter absence types which are not appropriate for a subtype of infotype 0082. To control this, SAP lets you define two subtypes of infotype 0082 for each absence type in table T554S. When you create an infotype 0082 record with a certain subtype, you can enter only those absence types, for which you have allowed this subtype in table T554S.

Supplementary absence data

If you activate this field, you can enter the data for infotype 2001 from the screen of infotype 0082.

Sickness tracking subtype and accident data subtype

In these two fields you can keep subtypes of infotype 0082. When you create an infotype 0082 record, and enter an absence type there, the system checks whether that subtype of infotype 0082 is present in any of these fields. If it is not found in either of these fields, you cannot create the absence record.

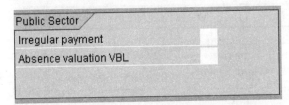

The fields in the above block are only for absences, and not for attendances. Also, they are only for Germany.

Indicator for irregular payment

This field is for Germany only.

Absence valuation VBL

This field is no longer used in table T554S. Use the V_5D0A_E view instead.

When you are generating absence quota, you do it for the period the employee has worked. Further, you may want his entitlement to be reduced to the extent he was absent during this period. Some companies would tolerate small absences and not reduce the quota an employee is entitled to. Also, in the case of long absences, some companies take a lenient view and reduce quota entitlement only partially. The fields in the above block provide this functionality. These fields are only for absences, and not for attendances.

Minimum number of calendar days for reduction for quota generation

Number of calendar days for each accrual period up to which an absence is not to cause the generated quota entitlement to be reduced. Only the absence days above this value contribute to the reduction.

Maximum number of calendar days for reduction for quota generation

Here you can put a ceiling on the number of days, which leads to a reduction in quota entitlement. In case the absence is above this figure, reduction in quota entitlement considers the figure specified here, instead of the actual figure.

Reduction indicator for quota generation

Days on which an employee is not active may make it necessary to reduce his quota accrual. Inactive days are usually a result of employees joining or leaving the company. However, you may also like to consider certain absence types as inactive. These are specified by ticking this field. Only absences lasting one or more days can be treated as inactive.

5.3   TIME CONSTRAINT REACTION FOR TIME MANAGEMENT INFOTYPES

Functional Consultant	User	Business Process Owner	Senior Management	My Rating	Understanding Level
A	B	B	C		

5.3.1   Purpose and Overview

For personnel administration infotypes you define time constraints which determine whether you can have multiple records of the infotype on the same day. Time constraints prevent data in an infotype, which does not make sense. They ensure data consistency within an infotype.

However, time management is different in two ways. First, in PA, whether multiple records can or cannot coexist is checked at day level; whereas in time management, it is checked at time level. Second in PA, there is no data consistency required across infotypes as each infotype is independent, whereas in time management, the data must make sense across infotypes.

It makes no sense, for example, if you say that an employee is absent in infotype 2001, and that he is present in infotype 2002. This data consistency check is performed across the following infotypes of time management: 2001, 2002, 2003, 2004, 2005, 2006, 2007, 2011, 2012 and 2013. When you enter a record in a time management infotype for a time, for which a record already exists, it is called collision, and the system has to decide whether

> ➤ the old records can coexist with the new record (N), or
> ➤ the old records can coexist with the new record but a warning is given (W), or
> ➤ the old records cannot coexist with the new record (E), or
> ➤ the old record is delimited (A).

The data consistency check needs to be performed at subtype level. It is possible that you may allow an employee to be on privilege leave (a subtype of infotype 2001), and attend training (a subtype of infotype 2002) at the same time, but may not allow privilege leave with attending to a customer.

This means that you have to make a matrix, which contains all time management infotypes + subtypes as its rows as well as its columns. Then for each cell you define whether the two records can coexist (N), can coexist with warning (W), cannot coexist (E), or the old record is delimited (A).

This definition also needs to be put in SAP. SAP reduces this configuration by a concept called time constraint class. If there are subtypes of an infotype, which have identical behaviour as far as collisions are concerned, you can group them together in a time constraint class. Then, you create a similar matrix, but the rows and columns are not infotype + subtype; instead this time the rows and columns are infotype + time constraint class. This is what you enter in view V_554Y_B.

5.3.2 IMG Node

SM30 ➢ V_554Y_B

5.3.3 Screen

| Infotype | 2001 |
| Time con. class | 01 |

Reaction when there is an overlap with existing infotype records

Infotype	Infotype text	Time cstr. class	Reaction indicator
2001	Absences	01	E
2001	Absences	02	A
2001	Absences	03	E
2001	Absences	04	E
2001	Absences	05	E

5.3.4 Primary Key

Infotype + Time Constraint Class

5.3.5 Important Fields

Infotype and time constraint class (header on the screen)

Infotype and time constraint class for which the collision reaction is being defined.

Infotype and time constraint class (columns on the screen)

Infotype and time constraint class with which the collision reaction is being defined.

Reaction indicator

When a record of an infotype + subtype (and therefore time constraint class) already exists, and for the same time another record of an infotype + subtype (and therefore time constraint class) is entered, should the system allow it or not. You enter here what the system should do, by choosing from one of the following:

A	The old record is delimited, all collisions are displayed. The part of the old record that overlaps with the new record is deleted.
E	The new record cannot be created. The system displays an error message.
W	The new record can be created without the old record being changed. The system displays a warning.
N	The new record can be created without the old record being changed. The system does not display a warning.

5.4 COUNTING RULE FOR ATTENDANCES AND ABSENCES (FOR QUOTA DEDUCTION)

Functional Consultant	User	Business Process Owner	Senior Management	My Rating	Understanding Level
A	C	X	X		

5.4.1 Purpose

In this view you define how the quota deduction should take place for those attendances and absences, where it is relevant. The counting rule is assigned to an absence/attendance type. Thus, when an absence record is entered in infotype 2001 or an attendance record in infotype 2002, the system knows which counting rule to call for quota deduction. The counting rule consists of three parts: applicability, counting and deduction rule.

In counting, you can define a quota multiplier. It is not necessary, that for an absence of 1 day, the quota should get deducted by 1 day only. You can deduct the quota by 1 day or 0.5 day or 2 days by specifying different values of quota multiplier. Also, you can do rounding of the days to be deducted from the quota.

In deduction rule, you assign a rule, which specifies, in T556R, the quota from which deduction will take place.

You can specify different counting logic and deduction rule for different conditions. These are specified in applicability. For example, you can specify that on weekdays, 1 day absence is counted as 1 day, but on Saturdays and Sundays, it is counted as half days. SAP offers a variety of attributes, which can be used in building conditions. You have to ensure that rules are defined for every possible condition.

5.4.2 IMG Node

SM30 ➤ T556C

5.4.3 Screen

ESG Time quota types	1
PS grpg tm quota typ	01
Counting rule	001 Paid work
Sequential no.	001

Applicability of rule

Conditions for current day

Weekday

☑ Monday	☑ Wednesday	☑ Friday	☑ Sunday
☑ Tuesday	☑ Thursday	☑ Saturday	

Holiday class

- ☑ Not a public holiday
- ☑ Holiday class 1 - public hol.
- ☑ Holiday class 2 - public hol.
- ☑ Holiday class 3 - public hol.
- ☑ Holiday class 4 - public hol.
- ☑ Holiday class 5 - public hol.
- ☑ Holiday class 6 - public hol.
- ☑ Holiday class 7 - public hol.
- ☑ Holiday class 8 - public hol.
- ☑ Holiday class 9 - public hol.

Day type

- ☑ Work acc. to work schedule
- ☐ Day type 1: Day off
- ☐ Day type 2: Day off
- ☐ Day type 3: Day off
- ☐ Day type 4: Day off
- ☐ Day type 5: Day off
- ☐ Day type 6: Day off
- ☐ Day type 7: Day off
- ☐ Day type 8: Day off
- ☐ Day type 9: Day off

Conditions for work schedule

Counting class for period work schedule

- ☑ Counting class 0
- ☑ Counting class 1
- ☑ Counting class 2
- ☑ Counting class 3
- ☑ Counting class 4
- ☑ Counting class 5
- ☑ Counting class 6
- ☑ Counting class 7
- ☑ Counting class 8
- ☑ Counting class 9

Daily work schedule class

- ☑ Daily work schedule class 0
- ☑ Daily work schedule class 1
- ☑ Daily work schedule class 2
- ☑ Daily work schedule class 3
- ☑ Daily work schedule class 4
- ☑ Daily work schedule class 5
- ☑ Daily work schedule class 6
- ☑ Daily work schedule class 7
- ☑ Daily work schedule class 8
- ☑ Daily work schedule class 9

Condition for planned hours

- ☐ Planned hours = 0
- ☑ Planned hours > 0

Condition for absence/attendance

- ☑ < 1 day
- ☑ Full-day

Counting

Hours

Quota multiplier	100.00 %
Rounding rule	
◉ Multiply first	
○ Round first	

Days

Quota multiplier	100.00 %
Rounding rule	
◉ Multiply first	
○ Round first	

Deduction rule

Absence quotas

Within entitlement	002
Over entitlement	

Attendance quotas

Within entitlement	001	Approved ov..
Over entitlement		

5.4.4 Primary Key

ES Grouping for Time Quota Types + PS Grouping for Time Quota Types + Rule for Attendance and Absence Counting + Counting Type + Sequential Number.

Apparently, counting type is an obsolete field. It has two possible values, A and Q. The table contains only value Q in this field. Both views of this table do not show this field.

5.4.5 Important Fields

ES grouping for time quota types

For the same absence type (and therefore counting rule), the counting rule definition can differ based on ES grouping for time quota types.

PS grouping for time quota types

For the same absence type (and therefore counting rule), the counting rule definition can differ based on PS grouping for time quota types.

Rule for attendance and absence counting

The rule for attendance and absence counting, which is being defined is assigned to an absence/attendance type in Table T554S.

Sequential number

The counting rule consists of multiple parts. It is scanned in the order of sequential number. When the condition is satisfied, the counting logic and deduction rule are picked up.

Applicability of rule

You can specify different counting logic and deduction rules for different conditions. These are specified in applicability. For example, you can specify that on weekdays, 1 day absence is counted as 1 day, but on Saturdays and Sundays, it is counted as half day. SAP offers the following attributes, which can be used in building conditions.

Weekday

For which days it is applicable.

Holiday class

For which public holiday class it is applicable (determined via T552A).

Day type

For which day type it is applicable (determined via T552A).

Counting class for period work schedule

For which counting class it is applicable. These counting classes are groupings of period work schedule, and assigned to them in T551C. Thus, for different period work schedules, you can have different counting rules based on counting class for period work schedule.

Daily work schedule class

For which daily work schedule class it is applicable (determined via T552A ➤ T550A).

Condition for planned hours

Is it applicable for planned Hours 0, or > 0, or both (determined via T552A ➤ T550A).

Condition for full day, part day

Applicable for full day absence records, partial day absence records, or both.

Counting

Counting can take place in hours or days. You specify the following:

Quota multiplier

Here you can define a quota multiplier. It is not necessary that for an absence of 1 day, the quota gets deducted by 1 day only. You can deduct the quota by 1 day or 0.5 day or 2 days by specifying different percentage in quota multiplier.

Rounding rule

Before you deduct the absence from quota, you may want to round it. In that case, you specify the rounding rule here, which you define in table T559R.

Multiplication/rounding sequence

Here you can define whether you want to do rounding first and then multiplication, or vice versa.

Deduction Rule for Absence Quotas

Deduction rules determine how attendances and absences are deducted from quotas. An employee can have balances in multiple quota types. In the deduction rule, you can specify which absence type deducts from which quota type, and in case there is no balance in that quota type, from which other quota type it deducts.

You can define two rules; one for within entitlement, and the other for over entitlement. Both these must have the same time unit. The absences are deducted from quotas using the within entitlement deduction rule. However, if all quotas are exhausted and absence is still not fully covered, then it uses the over entitlement deduction rule, and deduct from quota types which permit the quota to go negative.

Deduction Rule for Attendance Quotas

There are no separate counting rules for attendance quotas and absence quotas. Once the condition is satisfied, it works for both attendances and absences. This section is same as above. The above section applies for absences, this for attendances. The rule for deduction within entitlement and over entitlement must have the same time unit, but deduction rules for absence quotas and deduction rules for attendance quotas can deduct in different time units.

5.5 DEDUCTION RULES FOR ABSENCE QUOTAS

Functional Consultant	User	Business Process Owner	Senior Management	My Rating	Understanding Level
A	C	X	X		

5.5.1 Purpose

Deduction rules are used for two purposes:

➢ Deduction of attendances and absences from quotas. For this purpose, the deduction rules are assigned to counting rules in table T556C.
➢ Deduction from quotas in the case of quota compensation. For this purpose, the deduction rules are assigned to quota compensation type in table T556U.

You may use the same rules for both purposes, or you may have different rules. While designing the rules, you should try to meet the requirement with minimum number of rules possible.

Deduction rules determine how attendances and absences or quota compensation are deducted from quotas. In SAP, an employee can have quotas of multiple quota types. Also, for each quota type, there can be multiple records. When quota deduction has to take place, you have to specify from which quota type the deduction should take place, and if there are multiple records of that quota type, in what order they should be selected for deduction. You have to also specify what should happen if there is no balance and whether deduction should take place from other quota types.

5.5.2 IMG Node

SM30 ➢ V_556R_B, V_T556R (Deduction Rules for attendance quotas)

5.5.3 Screen

				Start Time	Exit
ESG Time quota types	1				
PS grpg tm quota typ	01			> 01.01.1990	31.12.9999
Deduction rule	040	Privilege Leave			

Unit of relevant absence quota types

○ Hours   ◉ Days

Absence quota types

Absence quota type	Quota text	Unit
39	Lapsable PL Extension	Days
40	Privilege Leave	Days

Quota type sequence for further deduction

◉ No further deduction
○ Sort all other quota types in ascending order
○ Sort all other quota types in descending order

Deduction priority

Quota types	3 Priority 3			
Valid from date	Not Relevant		◉ Ascending	○ Descending
Valid to date	2 Priority 2		◉ Ascending	○ Descending
Deduction from	Not Relevant		◉ Ascending	○ Descending
Deduction to	1 Priority 1		◉ Ascending	○ Descending

5.5.4 Primary Key

ES Grouping + PS Grouping + Quota Type + Deduction Rule + End Date

5.5.5 Important Fields

ES grouping for time quota types

The properties of a deduction rule can be different for different ES grouping for time quota types.

PS grouping for time quota types

The properties of a deduction rule can be different for different PS grouping for time quota types.

Quota type

This field is not seen on the screen. The table contains deduction rules for both absence and attendance types in the same table. This field determines whether the deduction rule is for absence (A), or it is for attendance (P). Deduction rules for absence types are accessed through view V_556R_B. Deduction rules for attendance types are accessed through view V_T556R. The screen of V_T556R is same as that of V_556R_B, except that in the last block, the last two fields, deduction from and deduction to are not on the screen. Note that the deduction rules for absences and attendances are mutually exclusive.

Deduction rule

The deduction rule being defined. It is assigned to a counting rule in table T556C. For quota compensation, it is assigned to quota compensation type in table T556U.

Start and end date

This signifies the period for which this definition is valid. The properties of the deduction rule can change with time.

Time unit

Is the deduction in hours or days?

Deduction sequence for attendance/absence quota types

Here you can specify up to 100 quota types. The deduction takes place in the sequence in which you have specified quota types.

Quota type sequence for further deduction

During quota deduction, if it is found that the need for deduction is not fulfilled even after considering all quota types specified above, the system needs to know what it should do. If you specify 'No further deduction', you get an error message for the absence/attendance/quota compensation record, which required quota deduction.

If however, you want deduction to take place from other quota types, you specify whether these other quota types should be selected in ascending or descending order. The system goes in that order until the need for deduction is fulfilled.

Deduction priority

In SAP, an employee can have quotas of multiple quota types. Also, for each quota type, there can be multiple records. In the above steps, the system would have determined the quota types from which the deduction would take place. It now needs to determine from which records the deduction should take place. The fields listed in this section are attributes of absence quota record. Here you specify in what priority the fields are to be taken first and whether they should be sorted in ascending or descending order.

5.6 ROUNDING RULE

Functional Consultant	User	Business Process Owner	Senior Management	My Rating	Understanding Level
A	C	C	X		

5.6.1 Purpose

In this view you define rounding rules. These are used for quota deduction (T556C) and quota generation (T559L). SAP provides a flexible method where you can define how rounding should take place. You can divide the total range, for example 0 to 1, to which rounding should apply into sub-ranges by defining lower and upper limit of each sub range. Then for each sub-range, you define target value. If your sub-ranges are regular, instead of defining multiple records, you can tick the field 'Roll interval'.

5.6.2 IMG Node

SM30 ➤ V_T559R

5.6.3 Screen

RoRul	Name	No.	Lower limit	Incl.	Upper limit	Incl.	Target value	Roll.
01	Round up or down...	001	0.50000	☑	1.50000	☐	1.00000	☑
02	Round percentag...	001		☐	0.25000	☐		☐
02	Round percentag...	002	0.25000	☑	0.75000	☐	0.50000	☐
02	Round percentag...	003	0.75000	☑	99,999.99999	☑	1.00000	☐

5.6.4 Primary Key

Rounding Rule + Sequential No.

5.6.5 Important Fields

Rounding rule

Rounding rule which is defined.

Sequential number

For the purpose of rounding, you divide the total range into sub-ranges. Each sub-range is created as a record, identified by sequential no.

Lower limit, upper limit and target value

When you are rounding a value, if the value falls between the lower and upper limit, it is rounded to the target value.

Inclusion of lower limit, inclusion of upper limit

Suppose you have a single interval 0 to 1, which you want to round to 0.5. If the value is exactly zero or exactly 1, do you want it to be rounded to 0.5? Perhaps not. In that case, you remove the tick of both inclusion of lower limit and inclusion of upper limit.

Roll interval

Rounding rule 01 in the screen shot above is a good example of how this field works. You want all fractions to be rounded to the nearest integer. You define that values between 0.5 and 1.5 should be rounded to 1. Then you tick roll interval. Now, if the value is between 1.5 and 2.5, it is rounded to 2, and so on.

Note that if you are rolling the interval, you cannot tick both 'Inclusion of lower limit' and 'Inclusion of upper limit'. This is because if a value is equal to the lower or upper limit, the system will find two target values. You will therefore get an error message. However, if you tick any of the two, the value will be rounded as specified. If you tick none, then values at boundary, in this case 0.5, 1.5, 2.5, etc. will not be rounded.

5.7 ABSENCE VALUATION

Functional Consultant	User	Business Process Owner	Senior Management	My Rating	Understanding Level
A	X	X	X		

5.7.1 Purpose

In this view you define how the absences affect payroll. Configuration nodes of this view are in payroll section of IMG. An absence type is assigned an absence valuation rule in table T554S. The rule is defined here. You can valuate an absence in various ways, depending on how you want to pay, or not pay, for it in the payroll. There are four ways, in which you can valuate an absence:

> ➢ Form counting classes
> ➢ Valuation using constants/averages
> ➢ Valuation using the 'as if' principle
> ➢ Special processing

If you form counting classes, SAP collects all absences in a counting class and populates variables AUnn or APnn (nn is the counting class, and U/P indicate whether it is unpaid or paid) in function PAB. These cumulations are further processed in function INP1 to compute /8 series wage types. /8 series wage types are used in PCR XVAL to factor the wage types.

Valuation using constants/averages creates the wage types to be paid in payroll.

The 'as if' principle of absence valuation means paying employees exactly as if they had worked.

In special processing, you can specify a PCR, which is used to valuate the absence.

Most of this configuration is in payroll section of IMG. Only V_554C_E is in time management.

5.7.2 IMG Node

SM30 ➢ V_T554C

5.7.3 Primary Key

Country Grouping + Employee Grouping for Absence Valuation + Absence Valuation Rule + Indicator for Absence Valuation in Offcycle Payroll + End Date

5.7.4 Important Fields

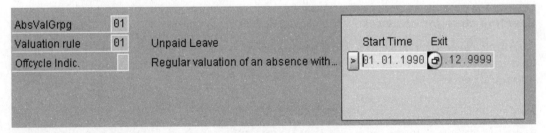

Employee grouping for absence valuation

This field is set in time evaluation by function MOD, PCR XMOD (MODIF A=) in schema XT00. Since the value of this field is set by a PCR, this table can be read only in time/payroll schema.

Absence valuation rule

Absence valuation rule which is being defined.

Indicator for absence valuation in offcycle payroll

Note the significance of this field. This is part of the primary key. It means that absence valuation can happen differently for regular and offcycle payroll. Possible values are:

Blank	Regular valuation of an absence without OC indicator
O	Valuation in offcycle payroll run
R	Valuation in the regular payroll run with OC indicator

Start and end date

Absence valuation rule can differ from period to period.

Form count.classes					
CC for absences	Cntg class text	Paid	Percentage	Day rule	Text for day ru
11	Unpaid absences	☐	100.00		

If you form counting classes, SAP collects all absences in a counting class and populates variables AUnn or APnn (nn is the counting class, and U/P indicate whether it is unpaid or paid) in function PAB. These cumulations are further processed in function INP1 to compute /8 series wage types. /8 series wage types are used in PCR XVAL to factor the wage types.

Counting-class for absences

Counting classes for absences are used to form 'buckets' to valuate paid and unpaid absences. They can be used for period factoring to determine a reduction in salary for unpaid absences.

Paid

Tick this checkbox if absences are to be paid. This determines whether the absence is cumulated under AUnn or APnn.

Percentage of absences

If counting classes are created, you can determine the percentage of the absence that is included in the respective counting class. The total of all percentages need not be 100%.

Day rule

Day rule serves as an on/off switch. If you want an absence type to go into different counting classes depending on the properties of the day, you can create different day rules. Then you create one record for each counting class here, and assign it the appropriate day rule. Depending on the properties of the day, one of the day rules is on, and the absence goes in that counting class. It must be ensured that on each day, exactly one rule is turned on. For more details, see V_T554R.

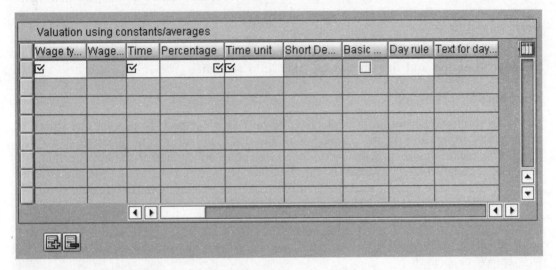

You can use this screen if you want to valuate absences using constants/averages. You can also maintain it through VV_T554C_D.

Wage type

Wage type is for valuating the absence. You can enter up to 15 wage types.

Time

This indicator specifies when the absence should be valuated. There are several methods of controlling the date on which the money is paid out.

B	Valuation in first payroll period	The entire absence should be valuated during the payroll period in which the absence starts.
I	Valuation in current payroll period	The absence should be valuated during the payroll period in which the absence actually occurred.
E	Valuation in last payroll period	The entire absence should be valuated during the payroll period in which the absence ends.
Z	Valuation per day	The absence should be valuated daily

Percentage

You use the absence percentage rate to determine what percentage of the absence time (in the specified time unit) should be valuated using a constant or average.

Time unit

The time unit specifies the unit of the number field of a wage type: calendar days/ absence days/absence hours/payroll days/payroll hours. For more details, see field help.

Basic pay split

Activate the basic pay split field if the employee's organizational unit has changed during the payroll period and this should be taken into account.

Day rule

Day rule serves as an on/off switch. If you want an absence type to generate different wage types depending on the properties of the day, you can create different day rules. Then, you create one record for each wage type here, and assign it the appropriate day rule. Depending on the properties of the day, one of the day rules is on, and the absence generates that wage type. It must be ensured that on each day, exactly one rule is turned on. For more details, see V_T554R.

```
Valuation using the 'as if' principle
  ☐ Time WType selection
```

The 'as if' principle of absence valuation means paying employees exactly as if they had worked. This includes bonuses that form part of the employee's planned working time. Overtime is not taken into account when absences are valuated using the 'as if' principle. You can also maintain it through VV_554C_E0.

Time wage type selection

Use this indicator to specify whether the absence should be paid exactly as if the employee had worked. If you activate the field, the employee is paid as normal for the absence. Bonuses for overtime, Sunday work, etc., which the employee may have received had he/she worked as normal, are not taken into account here unless you specify otherwise.

```
Special processing
  Personnel Calc.Rule  [      ]
  Time                 [  ]
  ☐ Operation ID
```

Here you can specify special processing for absence valuations. You do this using a personnel calculation rule that controls the special processing you require. You can also maintain it through VV_T554C_B.

Personnel calculation rule

The standard SAP system contains tables, personnel calculation schemas, and personnel calculation rules for absence valuation. If the options they provide are not sufficient for your purposes, you can specify special processing for absence valuation. To do this, you create a personnel calculation rule in which you define your own rules for absence valuation.

Time

This indicator specifies when the absence should be valuated. There are several methods of controlling the date on which the money is paid out.

B	Valuation in first payroll period
I	Valuation in current payroll period
E	Valuation in last payroll period
Z	Valuation per day

Operation ID

This field is applicable only for infotype 0005. For more details, see field help.

5.8 ABSENCE VALUATION RULES

Functional Consultant	User	Business Process Owner	Senior Management	My Rating	Understanding Level
A	X	X	X		

5.8.1 Purpose

This is just the master list of absence valuation rules. The rule is defined in T554C. This configuration is in payroll section of IMG.

5.8.2 IMG Node

SM30 ➤ V_T554L

5.8.3 Screen

Val.rule	Description
01	Unpaid Leave
02	Paid Leave
03	Unpaid Partial Absc.

5.8.4 Primary Key

Country Grouping + Absence Valuation Rule

5.9 COUNTING CLASSES FOR ABSENCE VALUATION

Functional Consultant	User	Business Process Owner	Senior Management	My Rating	Understanding Level
A	X	X	X		

5.9.1 Purpose

Counting classes are used in order to form 'buckets' to valuate paid and unpaid absences. Only the master list is defined here. For more details, see V_T554C. This configuration is in payroll section of IMG.

5.9.2 IMG Node

SM30 ≻ V_T554E

5.9.3 Screen

CountingCl	Cntg class
01	Paid Absences
11	Unpaid absences
12	Unpaid abs Partial

5.9.4 Primary Key

Country Grouping + Counting Class for Absences

5.10 DAY RULES FOR ABSENCE VALUATION

Functional Consultant	User	Business Process Owner	Senior Management	My Rating	Understanding Level
A	X	X	X		

5.10.1 Purpose and Overview

A day rule is a set of conditions. Each condition consists of the following sub-conditions:

➢ Holiday class of the current day and previous day
➢ Day type of the current day and previous day
➢ Planned hours are zero or not, for the current day and the previous day
➢ Day of the week

For any given day, you can determine whether a condition is satisfied or not. You do that for all the conditions in the day rule, and determine whether the day rule is satisfied or not. The day rule thus works as an on/off switch.

In table T554C, you specify the counting class in which an absence type goes. If you want an absence type to go into different counting classes, depending on the properties of the day, you can create different day rules, and assign them to respective counting classes. Depending on the properties of the day, one of the day rules is on, and the absence goes in that counting class. It must be ensured that on each day, exactly one rule is turned on. Day rule is also assigned to wage types in valuation using constants/averages in T554C and works in the same way. This configuration is in payroll section of IMG.

5.10.2 IMG Node

SM30 ➢ V_T554R

5.10.3   Screen

Day rule	01	On workdays
Sequential no.	00	

Conditions set for holiday class

	Prev. day	Curr. day
Holiday class BLANK - no public holiday	☑	☑
Holiday class 1 - public hol.	☑	☑
Holiday class 2 - public hol.	☑	☑
Holiday class 3 - public hol.	☑	☑
Holiday class 4 - public hol.	☑	☑
Holiday class 5 - public hol.	☑	☑
Holiday class 6 - public hol.	☑	☑
Holiday class 7 - public hol.	☑	☑
Holiday class 8 - public hol.	☑	☑
Holiday class 9 - public hol.	☑	☑

Conndition set for day type

	Previous day	Current day
Day type BLANK: Work according to personal work s...	☑	☑
Day type 1: Day off	☑	☐
Day type 2: Day off	☑	☐
Day type 3: Day off	☑	☐
Day type 4: Day off	☑	☐
Day type 5: Day off	☑	☐
Day type 6: Day off	☑	☐
Day type 7: Day off	☑	☐
Day type 8: Day off	☑	☐
Day type 9: Day off	☑	☐

Condition set for weekday

Monday	☑
Tuesday	☑
Wednesday	☑
Thursday	☑
Friday	☑
Saturday	☑
Sunday	☑

Conditions set for planned hours

	Prev. day	Curr. day
Plnd hrs > 0	☑	☑
Plnd hrs = 0	☑	☐

5.10.4 Primary Key

Day Rule + Sequential Number

5.11 BREAKDOWN OF ABSENCES AFTER QUOTA DEDUCTION

Functional Consultant	User	Business Process Owner	Senior Management	My Rating	Understanding Level
C	X	X	X		

5.11.1 Purpose

Normally absence valuation does not depend on the absence quota type from which the absence is deducted. However, if it does, here you can define a substitute absence valuation rule depending on the absence quota type, and its validity period, from which the absence is deducted.

5.11.2 IMG Node

SM30 ➢ V_T554A

5.11.3 Screen

	ValRl	Text	PSG	ESG	AQTyp	Quota text	No	Valid ...	End Date	Comp.	Diff.	Year	V...	Description
	01	Cu...	17	1	01	Normal le..	01	01.01...	31.12...	=		1996	02	Leave entit...
	01	Cu...	17	1	01	Normal le..	02	01.01...	31.12...	=		1997	03	Leave entit...
	01	Cu...	17	1	01	Normal le..	03	01.01...	31.12...	=		1998	04	Leave entit...
	01	Cu...	17	1	01	Normal le..	04	01.01...	31.12...	=		1999	02	Leave entit...
	01	Cu...	17	1	01	Normal le..	05	01.01...	31.12...	=		2000	03	Leave entit...
	01	Cu...	17	1	01	Normal le..	06	01.01...	31.12...	=		2001	04	Leave entit...
	01	Cu...	17	1	02	Non-paid ..	01	01.01...	31.12...				11	Collective ...

5.11.4 Primary Key

Country Grouping + Absence Valuation Rule + PS Grouping for Time Quota Types + ES Grouping for Time Quota Types + Absence Quota Type + Sequence Number + End Date

5.11.5 Important Fields

When an absence is to be valuated, the absence valuation rule is determined in table T554S. If you want to use a different rule depending on the absence quota type from which it is deducted, do the following:

Enter the original absence valuation rule in the first column; enter the absence quota type from which the absence is deducted in the appropriate column, and enter the substitute absence valuation rule in the last column. After you have filled the remaining columns, the system substitutes one absence valuation rule by another depending on the absence quota type from which the absence is deducted.

If you also want the substitution to depend on the validity period of the absence quota, you use the Comparison, Difference and Calendar year fields. The example in SAP helps explain how these fields are to be used.

Comp	Diff	Year	Meaning, such as
=	–	1998	Leave year 1998
=	0	–	Current leave year (start date of payroll period)
=	–1	–	Leave from previous year
<	0	–	Leave from prior years
–	–	–	Always

5.12 SYMBOL FOR ATTENDANCE AND ABSENCE

Functional Consultant	User	Business Process Owner	Senior Management	My Rating	Understanding Level
A	B	B	X		

5.12.1 Purpose

This view contains master list of one character attendance/absence category, which is assigned to an attendance/absence type (T554S) and displayed in personal calendar.

5.12.2 IMG Node

SM30 ➤ V_T554P

5.12.3 Screen

PSG	A/A cat.	Att./absence category text
01	A	Advance Leave
01	C	Unpaid leave
01	D	Blood Donation

5.12.4 Primary Key

Language Key + PS Grouping for Absence and Attendance Types + Absence/Attendance Category.

5.12.5 Important Fields

PS grouping for absence and attendance types

Absence/attendance categories can vary depending on the PS grouping for absence and attendance types.

Absence/attendance category and text

SAP lets you view the personal calendar of an employee showing a crisp view of the full month. There, instead of showing attendance/absence types, you see absence/attendance category which is only one character. You can also create an attendance/absence from the calendar view. If you have many attendance/absence types linked to the same absence/attendance category, you have to choose while creating the attendance/absence.

5.13 PROCESSING TYPE/TIME TYPE ACCORDING TO ATTENDANCE/ABSENCE CLASS

Functional Consultant	User	Business Process Owner	Senior Management	My Rating	Understanding Level
A	X	X	X		

5.13.1 Purpose and Overview

During time evaluation, each time pair in internal table TIP is assigned a time id, a processing type and a time type. The time id indicates the position of the time pair in relation to work schedule, e.g. core time, breaks, overtime, etc. The processing type is used for determining time wage type. The time type is used for storing time balances, which may be used for granting an absence quota to the employee, etc.

If your employees record clock times, all these functions are performed by function TIMTP. It first determines the time id. Then it uses table T555Z for determining the processing type and the time type of a time pair.

If your employees do not record clock times, all these functions are performed by function TYPES. It gets the Ptype/Ttype class of the attendance/absence type from table T554S and using it gets the processing type and the time type from table T555Y. These are updated in table TIP.

5.13.2 IMG Node

SM30 ➤ T555Y

5.13.3 Screen

PS grpg	Group	P/T	Start Date	End Date	PairType1		PairType2		PairType3	
☐ 01	01	00	01.01.1990	31.12.9999	P	1100	A	1200	P	1300
☐ 01	01	01	01.01.1990	31.12.9999	P	1101	A	1201	P	1301
☐ 01	01	02	01.01.1990	31.12.9999	P	1102	A	1202	P	1302
☐ 01	01	03	01.01.1990	31.12.9999	P	1103	A	1203	P	1303

5.13.4 Primary Key

PS Grouping for Time Recording + Time Type Determination Group + Processing Type/
Time Type Class + End Date

5.13.5 Important Fields

PS grouping for time recording

The processing type/time type determination depends on PS grouping for time recording,
which is determined from V_001P_ALL.

Time type determination group

In time evaluation, this field is set by function MOD, PCR MODT value T. Thus, this table
can be read only in a schema.

Processing type/time type class

This is determined for an attendance/absence type in T554S.

Start and end date

This is the validity period of the record.

Processing type and time type for pair type 1

Here you specify the processing type and time type for pair type 1 (when employee is at
work).

Processing type and time type for pair type 2

Here you specify the processing type and time type for pair type 2 (when employee is
absent).

Processing type and time type for pair type 3

Here you specify the processing type and time type for pair type 3 (when employee is working off-site).

5.14 CLOCK TIME GENERATION IN ATTENDANCE AND ABSENCE

Functional Consultant	User	Business Process Owner	Senior Management	My Rating	Understanding Level
A	X	X	X		

5.14.1 Purpose

When you record absences (infotype 2001) or attendances (infotype 2002) of less than one workday, you may specify hours. Here you can specify whether these should be converted in clock times using the daily work schedule, or not. If your employees record time at time recording systems, it is necessary to do this conversion. However, if they do not record time, you have an option. This affects the schema design.

5.14.2 IMG Node

PE03 ➤ HRSIF

5.14.3 Screen

```
HRSIF Recording atts./absences without clock times
  └──── 0
```

5.14.4 Fields for Decision Making

Personnel Area
Personnel Subarea
Employee Group
Employee Subgroup
Employee Time Management Status
Work Schedule Rule

5.14.5 Return Value

1   Hour can be recorded without clock times.
0   Clock times are generated.

5.15 ILLNESS TEXTS

Functional Consultant	User	Business Process Owner	Senior Management	My Rating	Understanding Level
C	X	X	X		

5.15.1 Purpose and Overview

In infotype 2001, there are two fields, illness code and illness description. If you enter illness code the illness description comes automatically. Otherwise, you can enter illness description yourself. The illness description, which automatically comes based on illness code, is maintained here.

5.15.2 IMG Node

SM30 ➤ T572B

5.15.3 Screen

Illness Texts		
Language	Illness	Description
EN	A41000	Influenza
EN	A41012	Intestinal flu
EN	B12001	Broken leg
EN	B12002	Broken arm
EN	C00012	Unknown

5.15.4 Primary Key

Illness Identifier

5.16 ANNUAL CALENDAR (INFOTYPE 2050)

Functional Consultant	User	Business Process Owner	Senior Management	My Rating	Understanding Level
A	A	A	B		

5.16.1 Screen

Annual calendar

Month	1	5	10	15	20	25	30
01 January	.	C	.	D C	. V	.	.
02 February	Z	.		.	.	.	▪▪▪
03 March		. K		. U	.	V . .	
04 April	.		.		.		▪
05 May	.		.	Z .		. C C C	
06 June		.		. K .		.	▪
07 July	.		.		.	K K .	
08 August	.	.		. .	Z .	H H H H H H H H H	
09 September	.			. .		.	.
10 October	.		. . .		Z K K H H H H	K	
11 November	. H H H H .		.	.		.	▪
12 December	.	. H H H H H H H H		.		.	

5.16.2 Purpose and Overview

> The infotypes, you have seen so far, store data. However, infotypes 2050, 2051, and 2052 are different. They show data from infotypes 2001 (Absences) and 2002 (Attendances) in a convenient calendar format. They also let you change data in these infotypes.
> You can get infotype 2050 screen from transaction PA61 or PA30. In PA61, you can also reach this by clicking on [📅 Year] icon. Here, you can view or change data.
> The dots in the calendar represent non working days.
> When you enter the appropriate code in the calendar, and save, corresponding absence/ attendance record is created.
> If one code corresponds to multiple absence types, or attendance types, you get a pop up window, where you select the absence type, or attendance type, which you want to create.
> If you enter same absence type, or attendance type, for several consecutive days, the system creates only one record with appropriate validity period.

5.17 MONTHLY CALENDAR (INFOTYPE 2051)

Functional Consultant	User	Business Process Owner	Senior Management	My Rating	Understanding Level
A	A	A	B		

5.17.1 Screen

Monthly calendar								
Wk FD LD	Monday	Tuesday	Wednes...	Thursday	Friday	Saturday	Sunday
53 01 - 02						OFF	JHF7
						A	AE
01 03 - 09	J007	J007	J007	J007	J007	JHF7	OFF
	AE	AE	C AE	AE	AE	AE	A
02 10 - 16	J007	J007	J007	J007	J007	JHF7	OFF
	AE	AE	D AE	C AE	AE	AE	A
03 17 - 23	J007	J007	J007	J007	J007	JHF7	OFF
	AE	V AE	AE	AE	AE	AE	A
04 24 - 30	J007	J007	J007	J007	J007	J007	JHF7
	AE	AE	A	AE	AE	AE	AE
05 31 - 31	J007						
	AE						

5.17.2 Purpose and Overview

➤ Infotype 2051 shows data from infotypes 2001 (Absences) and 2002 (Attendances) in a convenient monthly calendar format. It also let you change data in these infotypes.

➤ You can get infotype 2051 screen from transaction PA61 or PA30. In PA61, you can also reach this by clicking on 🔲 Month icon. Here, you can view or change data.

➤ Non-working days in the calendar are shown in red color.

➤ In the monthly calendar, you also see the employee's daily work schedule with variant. You can also see what other time infotypes exist for the day; A indicates Absence quota, E Time event. You can double click on these letters to see details.

➤ When you enter the appropriate code in the calendar, and save, corresponding absence/attendance record is created.

➤ If one code corresponds to multiple absence types or attendance types, you get a pop up window, where you select the absence type or attendance type, which you want to create.

➤ If you enter same absence type, or attendance type, for several consecutive days, the system creates only one record with appropriate validity period.

5.18   WEEKLY CALENDAR (INFOTYPE 2052)

Functional Consultant	User	Business Process Owner	Senior Management	My Rating	Understanding Level
A	A	A		B	

5.18.1   Screen

Week	6 Saturd...	7 Sunday	1 Monday	2 Tuesd...	3 Wedn...	4 Thurs...	5 Friday	
53 / 01	01.01.05	02.01.05	03.01.05	04.01.05	05.01.05	06.01.05	07.01.05	
	OFF	JHF7	J007	J007	J007	J007	J007	
Standard	0.00	0.00	0.00	0.00	0.00	0.00	0.00	0.00
Abs. hrs	0.00	0.00	0.00	0.00	8.00	0.00	0.00	8.00
Att. hrs	0.00	0.00	0.00	0.00	0.00	0.00	0.00	0.00
Rec.hours	0.00	0.00	0.00	0.00	8.00	0.00	0.00	8.00
Rest	0.00	0.00	0.00	0.00	0.00	0.00	0.00	0.00

D	Start Date	End Date	Hrs	From	To	P	Type	Att./absence type	C	E..	Cost Ctr	Order
3	05.01.2005	05.01.2005	8.00				X0	LWOP (AUTHORISED)				

5.18.2   Purpose and Overview

➤ Infotype 2052 shows data from infotypes 2001 (Absences) and 2002 (Attendances) in a convenient weekly calendar format. It also lets you change attendance data, but you cannot change absence data from here.

➤ You can get infotype 2052 screen from transaction PA61, either by entering infotype 2052, or by clicking on [📅 Week] icon. Here, you can view or change data.

➤ You can also get infotype 2052 screen from transaction PA30. The navigation is Goto ➤ List entry. You can also change data here.

➤ In the weekly calendar, you also see the employee's daily work schedule with variant, standard hours, absence hours, attendance hours, sum of absence and attendance hours, and remaining time (planned hours for which there is no absence or attendance).

➤ Standard hours can either come from planned time or from a time type. You can specify the logic of determining that in feature TIMTA.

➤ In the lower part, you have space to enter data. You can only enter attendances, not absences. If you specify day number, which is displayed in the line titled Week, the system generates start and end date.

➤ You can create default attendance/absence type using enhancement PTIM2005 and check completeness using enhancement PTIM2006.

➤ If your week does not start from Monday, you can set that in feature LDAYW.
➤ In this infotype, you directly enter the attendance type (not its corresponding code). When you save, appropriate attendance record is created.

5.19 DAILY STANDARD TIME DETERMINATION

Functional Consultant	User	Business Process Owner	Senior Management	My Rating	Understanding Level
B	X	X	X		

5.19.1 Purpose

This feature lets you determine daily standard time for your employees, which is used in infotype 2052. The standard time can be based either on time type or personal work schedule. You can also specify whether the absence times are taken into account or not while forming balances.

5.19.2 IMG Node

PE03 ➢ TIMTA

5.19.3 Screen

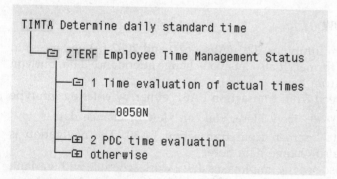

5.19.4 Fields for Decision Making

Personnel Area
Personnel Subarea
Employee Group
Employee Subgroup
Employee Time Management Status

5.19.5 Return Value

Daily standard time

5.20   LAST DAY OF A WEEK

Functional Consultant	User	Business Process Owner	Senior Management	My Rating	Understanding Level
B	X	X	X		

5.20.1   Purpose

This feature determines last day of a week. In this way you can specify when your week starts, which is used in infotype 2052.

5.20.2   IMG Node

PE03 ➤ LDAYW

5.20.3   Screen

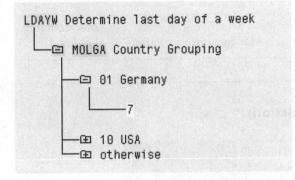

```
LDAYW Determine last day of a week

  └─⊟ MOLGA Country Grouping

       ├─⊟ 01 Germany

       │      └──7

       ├─⊞ 10 USA
       └─⊞ otherwise
```

5.20.4   Field for Decision Making

Country grouping

5.20.5   Return Value

Last day of a week

Attendance

6.1 ATTENDANCES (INFOTYPE 2002)

Functional Consultant	User	Business Process Owner	Senior Management	My Rating	Understanding Level
A	A	A	A		

6.1.1 Screen No 2050 (Quota Deduction)

Start	24.01.2005	To	24.01.2005

Attendance

Attendance type	10	CERTIFIED NO PUNCH
Time		☐ Prev. day
Attendance hours	7.50	☑ Full-day
Attendance days	1.00	
Calendar days	1.00	

Overtime comp. type	Depends on wage type	▤
Eval.type atts/abs		▤

6.1.2 Screen No 2051 (No Quota Deduction)

Start	23.01.2005	To	23.01.2005

Attendance

Attendance type	30	TRAINING
Time		-		☐ Previous day
Attendance hours	6.50	☑ Full-day
Attendance days	1.00	
Calendar days	1.00	

Payroll

Payroll hours	6.50	
Payroll days	1.00	
Overtime comp. type	Depends on wage type	📄
Eval.type atts/abs		📄

6.1.3 Purpose and Overview

In this infotype, you store information about an employee's presence, other than what comes from time recording terminals. The information in this infotype is not created on the basis of inference. If you want to assume that an employee is present, unless otherwise indicated, you should use time management status 9 in infotype 0007. You should not create records in infotype 2002. However, if you have data coming from employees, e.g. in CATS or from time administrators, who are creating records based on approved forms, e.g. for business travel or training or based on signed muster, you would keep the data here.

You can enter full day attendances or part day attendances. Full day attendances can be for one or more days. In the case of part day attendances, start and end date must be the same. If you enter attendance hours, start time and end time are determined (depending on the settings made in feature HRSIF). Similarly, you can enter start time and end time, in which case attendance hours are determined. Break timings are taken into account during such determination. Unlike absence times, attendance times can extend beyond an employee's daily planned working time.

You can use the attendance infotype 2002 to transfer costs and work performed data to the Accounting and Logistics components. You can click on the icon [ ] Personal work schedule to see the work schedule of the employee for a period. This schedule takes into account any substitution you may have made. You can do activity allocation, cost assignment, external services and different payment for infotype 2002. See chapters 21, 22, 23 and 24 on these topics for more details.

6.1.4 Quota Deduction for Attendances

The linkage for attendance quota deduction is as follows: Attendance (PA2002) ≻ Attendance type (V_554S_Q) ≻ Counting Rule (T556C) ≻ Deduction Rule (V_T556R) ≻ Quota type (T556A). Quota deduction takes place when attendance entries are made in infotype 2002. This entry contains attendance type, whose properties are defined in table T554S.

One of the attributes of attendance type is counting rule, which takes us to table T556C. In a counting rule, you define deduction rule, which takes us to V_T556R. If you are not using a deduction rule, you can directly define quota type. In the deduction rule, you define the quota type from which the attendance is deducted.

Finally, when quota deduction takes place, the details are stored in table PTQUODED Deduction of Time Quotas. It is necessary to know which attendance was deducted from which quota record because if the attendance record is deleted, the quota deduction has to be reversed.

6.1.5 Subtypes

Attendance type

6.1.6 Time Constraint

Z(Time constraint for time management infotypes -> T554Y)

6.1.7 Important Fields

Start and end date

Here you specify the period of attendance. Depending on the settings made in customizing, the system issues either a warning or error message if the 'from date' or 'to date' of the record falls on an employee's day off.

Attendance type

All attendances are created against predefined attendance types. Attendance types are subtypes of infotype 2002, and are configured in table T554S.

Start and end time

For attendances, which last less than one day, you can give start and end time. Start and end time, previous day indicator and attendance hours fields are enterable, only if end date is different from the start date.

Previous day indicator

If you have a night shift, e.g. from 22:00 hours till 06:00 hours on the next day, all times till 06:00 hours must be assigned to the previous day. This indicator is automatically determined by the system.

Attendance hours

If start and end time are blank, and you enter attendance hours, the system assumes the start time as start of shift, and computes end time, based on attendance hours (provided configuration in feature HRSIF requires it to do so). If there are breaks during that period, the end time is appropriately delayed.

Between start time, end time, and attendance hours, you can enter data in any two fields; the third is calculated by the system. Unlike absence times, attendance times can extend beyond an employee's daily planned working time.

Full day

The attendance times are relevant only if the absence is not a full day absence. In most cases, where the attendance is a full day attendance, this indicator is ticked. Where the attendance record is for multiple days, this indicator is automatically ticked.

Attendance days

Attendance days are determined by the system by taking into account the holidays and weekly offs.

Calendar days

The calendar days are the number of days between the start and end dates of a record. They are displayed by the system.

Quota used

Quota used is determined by the system as per the logic built into configuration of time management. If there is no quota deduction, this field is not shown.

Payroll hours

Depending on your configuration, payroll hours can be different from attendance hours.

Payroll days

Depending on your configuration, the system may determine the payroll days to be different from attendance days. This is usually done when the number of working hours is not same on all days.

Overtime compensation type

If the employees have a choice of deciding whether they want to receive payment, or time off, or a combination of the two, that choice is captured here. For more details, see chapter 11.4 (T555R).

Blank	Depends on wage type
1	Remuneration
2	Time off plus overtime rate
3	Compensation (time off)

Evaluation type for attendances/absences

This is a free indicator for attendances, which is specified in an infotype 2002 record. You can query it using operation VARPR in a personnel calculation rule, and write your own logic to handle the attendance record differently in time evaluation. It cannot be used for absences.

6.1.8 Reports

Attendance/absence data: Overview (PT64)

This report shows PA/PSA wise attendance/absence data summary. It can be expanded to show employee level details, and further expanded to show absence types. However, this report does not show the absence dates. It calls program RPTABS20.

Attendance/absence data: Calendar view (PT90, PT90_ATT)

Calendar view is very similar to annual calendar. Additional facilities include statistics, legend, seeing only selected attendances and absences if you so desire and highlighting of holidays. However, you cannot create attendances/absences directly from here, which is possible in annual calendar. It calls program RPTABS50.

Attendances/absences: Multiple employee view (PT91, PT91_ATT)

This report is also like calendar view, but instead of showing data of one person for multiple dates, it shows data of multiple persons for a single date. It calls program RPTABS60.

Overview graphic of attendances/absences (PT65)

This report shows a graphic view of attendances/absences. If you click on an attendance/absence, it opens the corresponding record. It calls program RPTLEA40.

Recalculate attendance/absence records (PT_UPD00)

The program creates a batch input session for revaluating absence and attendance records. A revaluation can be necessary if work schedule data on which the valuation is based changes after the absence or attendance is entered. It calls program RPTUPD00.

Attendance check (PT62)

When you run attendance check program using transaction PT62, you get a selection screen, which gives you more flexibility than when you run it from time management pool. Hence, this program is explained with respect to that transaction.

The purpose of this program is to show you the status of employees who are expected to be present at a given date and time. The expected presence takes into account the employee's daily work schedule, substitution and dynamic substitution.

Pers.No.	Employee/app.name	Stat.	Status text	TET	Meaning	TimeUnit	A/AType	Att./abs. type text	Time
110858	Sahasrabudhe Shashikant	1	At work	P10	Clock-in	08:26:00			
111048	Gracias Noel	7	Full-day At work				W0	CERTIFIED ATTD. (MISC.)	
111417	Kamat Shashikant	5	Full-day Absent				M0	SL (Sick Leave Certifd)	
111426	Sawant Shrikant	1	At work	P10	Clock-in	06:28:00			
111431	Sapre Satich	1	At work	P10	Clock-in	08:27:00			

This program is very useful for knowing which employees are present or absent at any given time. However, the following may dampen the enthusiasm somewhat:

➤ This program cannot be run unless time evaluation has been run. Therefore, if you are in a hurry to find out which people have or have not reported for the job at the start of the shift, you have to wait until the time evaluation is done first.
➤ You can't see the daily work schedule of the employees in this list.
➤ If you tick the checkbox 'Evaluate work schedule', the records selected change. It is not clear why that happens.
➤ Take care to select employment status 3 in the selection screen if you want the system to show only active employees.

6.2 EVALUATION TYPE FOR ATTENDANCES

Functional Consultant	User	Business Process Owner	Senior Management	My Rating	Understanding Level
C	X	X	X		

6.2.1 Purpose

This view contains the master list of evaluation type for attendances, which is specified in an infotype 2002 record. You can query it using operation VARPR in a personnel calculation rule, and write your own logic to handle the attendance record differently in time evaluation. It cannot be used for absences.

6.2.2 IMG Node

SM30 ➤ V_T554H

6.2.3 Screen

Evaluation Type for Attendances/Absences	
Eval.type	Name

6.2.4 Primary Key

Evaluation Type for Attendances/Absences

Absence Quota

7.1 ABSENCE QUOTAS (INFOTYPE 2006)

Functional Consultant	User	Business Process Owner	Senior Management	My Rating	Understanding Level
A	A	A	A		

7.1.1 Screen

From	01.01.2004	To	31.12.2004	Chg.	22.01.2005	PKAGRAWAL

Absence quota

Category	30	Casual Leave
Time		-
Quota number	8.00000	Days
Deduction	3.00000	⮞ Neg. deduction to 0.00000
Deduction from	01.01.2004	
Deduction to	31.12.2004	

7.1.2 Purpose and Overview

Infotype 2006 stores absence quota information for an employee. Note that an employee may have several records of each absence quota type. Absence quota may be created in the following ways:

- Manually in infotype 2006
- Automatically using program RPTQTA00
- By function QUOTA (Automatic quota generation, quota correction)
- By function P2013 (Quota correction for concurrent employment)
- By function P2012 (Time transfer)
- By operation UPDTQ

Quota records can be system generated, or manually created. System generated records cannot be edited. They may be corrected through infotype 2013, which may add to, subtract from, or replace the quota record of infotype 2006.

Quotas are deducted for absences (infotype 2001) and quota compensation (infotype 0416). For each Absence type you can specify whether quota deduction takes place. If yes, the quota type from which deduction takes place, and of the multiple records of quota types, what logic is followed to select the record? If the quota type is exhausted, it is also possible to deduct from alternate quota types.

Deduction of quota on account of absences can be restricted by using the deduction from and deduction to fields of absence types. However, for deduction of quota on account of quota compensation, there is no such feature. Therefore, as per your company policy, if a quota becomes unusable, it is best to create quota compensation without payment, thereby avoiding the risk of unintentional quota compensation.

You may permit negative balances for some quota types within specified limits. You can see all quotas for an employee in transaction PT50 (Quota Overview).

7.1.3 Subtypes

Absence quota type

7.1.4 Time Constraint

Z (Time constraint for time management infotypes -> T554Y)

7.1.5 Important Fields

Start and end date

This signifies the period for which the quota is given. There may be some type of quotas which are accrued. In these cases, this period is in the past. But there may be some quota types, where the quota is given in advance. In these cases, this is a future period.

Absence quota type (Category) and text

Each absence quota is for an absence quota type. Absence quota types are subtypes of infotype 2006.

From and to time

You can use this field to restrict quota deduction. Only absences during the specified time period can be deducted. These fields are not relevant where the quota is maintained in days.

Quota number and unit

This field contains the quota accrued/granted, along with the unit.

Deduction

Quota deduction, which has taken place so far, either because of absences, or because of quota compensation.

Deduction from and to

Through these fields you can restrict the period during which an employee can avail the quota through absences. If no entries are made in these fields, the validity period of the quota record determines the period in which the quota can be deducted. Quota compensation does not take these fields into account.

Negative deduction to

Depending on your configuration in T556A, some quota types may have negative balances. However, it cannot go below the figure in this field (zero or negative value).

7.1.6 Reports

Revaluate leave quota (PT_BPC10)

If counting rule for attendances and absences (for quota deduction) changes, and you have future dated attendance/absence records, you need to revaluate the quota deduction. You run this program RPTBPC10 to do that.

Create leave entitlement (PC00_M99_TLEA30)

You can use this report to create your employees' Leave Entitlement (infotype 0005) for a leave year. Note that infotype 0005 is now obsolete.

Leave accrual (PT_ILVA00)

You can use program RPILVA00 to generate employees' leave entitlement, based on the time data of the past calendar year.

Transfer remaining leave from infotype 0005 (PT_LEACONV)

This report enables you to transfer employees' remaining leave entitlements from infotype 0005 to absence quotas in infotype 2006.

Generate absence quotas (PT_QTA00)

This is the main program for generating absence quotas. You may see 'Absence Quota Generation' for more details.

7.1.7   Infotypes 0005 and 0083

The old leave functions for leave entitlements used infotypes Leave Entitlement (0005) and Leave Entitlement Compensation (0083). These have been replaced by infotypes 2006 and 0416 respectively.

7.2   NUMBER RANGE FOR ATTENDANCES, ABSENCES AND TIME QUOTAS

Functional Consultant	User	Business Process Owner	Senior Management	My Rating	Understanding Level
A	X	X	X		

7.2.1   Purpose

If you want to use attendance or absence quotas, you must create intervals for two number ranges. To deduct attendances and absences from the quotas, you must clearly identify attendance/absence records and attendance/absence quota records by assigning them a number.

7.2.2   IMG Node

Transaction PT10	Number Range Maintenance: PTM_DOCNR
Transaction PT11	Number Range Maintenance: PTM_QUONR

7.2.3   Screen

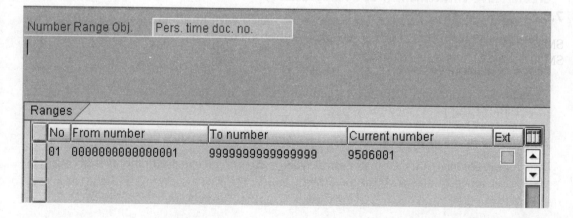

Number Range Obj.	Quota doc. no.

Ranges				
No	From number	To number	Current number	Ext
01	0000000000000001	9999999999999999	2079000	

7.3 ABSENCE QUOTA TYPE

Functional Consultant	User	Business Process Owner	Senior Management	My Rating	Understanding Level
A	C	C	X		

7.3.1 Purpose

An employee can have various types of absence quotas. Different types of absences, e.g. privilege leave, sick leave, etc. may be permitted only if the employees have respective quotas, and deductions would take place from them. Some of the important properties of the absence quotas are:

➤ Is the quota maintained in days or hours?
➤ Can the quota balance become negative? If yes, what is the limit?
➤ Can the quota be financially compensated?
➤ Is the quota automatically generated in time evaluation?

7.3.2 IMG Node

SM30 ➤ V_T556A
SM30 ➤ V_556A_B (see chapter 7.6)

7.3.3 Screen

ESG Time quota types	1			Start Time	Exit
PS grpg tm quota typ	01				
Absence quota type	40	Privilege Leave		> 01.01.1990	.12.9999

Absence Quota Type

Recording

Time/measurement unit	Days	Start time	
Time constraint class	02	End time	

Transfer rem. entitlement ☐

Deduction

Neg. ded. to	60.00000-	Rounding	4

Payroll-relevant data

No comp. ☐

E...	P...	A...	Quota text	Start Date	End Date	Unit	No ge...	Incre...	Repla...	NegDed	TCC
1	01	30	Casual leave	01.01.1990	31.12.9999	Hours	◉	○	○		01
1	01	35	Maternity Leave	01.01.1990	31.12.9999	Days	◉	○	○		04
1	01	39	Lapsable PL ...	01.01.1990	31.12.9999	Days	◉	○	○		04
1	01	40	Privilege Leave	01.01.1990	31.12.9999	Days	◉	○	○	60.00000-	02

7.3.4 Primary Key

ES Grouping for Time Quota Types + PS Grouping for Time Quota Types + Absence Quota Type + End Date

7.3.5 Important Fields

ES grouping for time quota types

Properties of absence quota type can depend on ES grouping for time quota types.

PS grouping for time quota types

Properties of absence quota type can depend on PS grouping for time quota types.

Absence quota type and text

Absence quota type being defined.

Start and end date

Period for which this record is valid.

Time unit

The quota can be maintained in hours/days.

Time constraint class

The time constraint class is used to check for collisions between time management infotypes (2001 to 2013). It allows you to specify different regulations for checking for collisions between individual subtypes. How to design time constraint classes and how to specify the rules to ensure that you do not have conflicting data, e.g. an employee is both present and absent at the same time, is discussed in chapter 5.3 (V_554Y_B).

Start time and end time

If you create an absence quota type with the hours time unit, you can specify default values for the start and end times. The system proposes the default values when you create absence quota in infotype 2006. In infotype 2006 these fields are used to restrict quota deduction.

Transfer remaining entitlement

You tick this field if you want to transfer leave from infotype 0005 to 2006. After you tick this field, you have to run the report RPTLEACONV for the actual transfer to take place.

Negative deduction

In this field you enter the limit of negative value for the quota type. The balance for the quota type cannot go below this.

Rounding

This field is now obsolete, as rounding now takes place through rounding rule defined in table T556C. This was used when leaves were stored in infotype 0005.

No compensation

If you tick this field, quota compensation is not allowed for this quota type.

No generation/increase/replace (view V_556A_B)

This field is available only in view V_556A_B and not in view V_T556A. It determines whether absence quota is generated automatically using function QUOTA in time evaluation, and if yes, whether it increases, or replaces, an earlier record with the same key. The radio buttons you select from are No generation, Increase, Replace. If you select No generation, you can either create the quota manually in infotype 2006, or create using the Generate Absence Quotas report (RPTQTA00).

7.4 ABSENCE QUOTA GENERATION

Functional Consultant	User	Business Process Owner	Senior Management	My Rating	Understanding Level
A	C	X	X		

7.4.1 Methods of Absence Quota Accrual

There are three methods of generating absence quotas.

Manual

You can directly create absence quota by making a manual entry in infotype 2006. The system can propose the validity period, deduction period, absence quota(s) and entitlements automatically. Manually created absence quotas can be changed in infotype 2006 directly.

Automatic using RPTQTA00

You can grant absence quota for an entire period in advance. Default values are proposed by the system when creating an infotype record. The quota is immediately available after accrual. There is no automatic recalculation. Quota is stored in infotype 2006 and can be corrected manually.

Automatic accrual in time evaluation using function QUOTA

This method is used primarily, when an employee earns the absence quota. In many companies, the employees earn their privilege leave on account of their attendance. These scenarios are suitable for quota accrual using function QUOTA. Function QUOTA can consider time types, which are summarized information about an employee's attendance, absence and work schedule, while granting quota. It can do proportionate calculation after a calculation period. Transfer of absence quota to infotype 2006 can be controlled. In the case of retro changes in time data, this function automatically recalculates the quota.

Quota correction

Automatically generated quotas cannot be corrected directly. It can only be corrected through infotype 2013 'Quota Correction'. The corrections are also transferred to infotype 2006, but the trail of external changes is maintained. This is done by function QUOTA in time evaluation. In the case of concurrent employment, it is done by function P2013.

Time transfer

Function P2012 processes infotype 2012 where you can transfer balances in time types, wage types and absence quotas from one to another. In some companies, the employees accumulate their overtime hours, from which they can take time off.

Operation UPDTQ

You can use operation UPDTQ to create absence quota. This operation can be used in function P2006, which processes table ABWKONTI, or other functions, e.g. P2007 or POVT.

7.4.2 IMG Node

SM34 ➤ VC_T559L

7.4.3 Screen

Dialog Structure
🗁 Selection rules
🗀 Quota types
🗀 Base entitlement
🗀 Validity/deduction interval
🗀 Validity period for default values
🗀 Reduction rules
🗀 Reduction indicators for absences
🗀 Rounding rules

7.4.4 Overview

Most rules pertaining to quota generation are defined in selection rules (T559L). Both function QUOTA in time evaluation and report RPTQTA00 use this table to generate quotas. The rules are categorized as: applicability, accrual period, base entitlement, accrual entitlement, transfer time and total entitlement. In this table, multiple selection rules can apply to an employee which lead to multiple absence types getting generated.

Applicability	This determines whether a selection rule is applicable to an employee or not. The applicability can depend on a date, e.g. probation completion date from infotype 0019, when the employee joined the company, and whether the employee is challenged.
Accrual period	When the quota is generated, it is generated for an accrual period. You specify the frequency of automatic quota accrual.
Base entitlement	Rule for base entitlement is defined in T559E and assigned to selection rule. Base entitlement can depend on age and seniority.
Accrual entitlement	Here you specify what should happen when accrual takes place. Should it be reduced for part time or inactive employees; should it be rounded, should it be limited to a specified maximum, etc.
Transfer time	If in view V_556A_B, you have specified that the quota is automatically generated, then you see this tab, where you specify when this quota is transferred to infotype 2006. You can also specify if the transfer should take place in packages of fixed days or hours.
Total entitlement	You can also specify rounding rule and maximum entitlement at total level.

Certain properties, e.g. whether quota generation takes place or not (and if it does, whether it increases or replaces an earlier quota record with the same key), the extent of negative deduction possible, and the time constraint class, are specified at quota type level (V_556A_B). These are used both by function QUOTA, as well as RPTQTA00.

Base entitlements define the basic entitlement of an employee and the period for which it is. Base entitlements can depend on seniority and age. The entitlement may be constant, or you may determine it in time evaluation. The rule is defined in table T559E, and assigned to a selection rule in T559L.

In SAP, absence quotas are not defined at quota type level. For the same quota type, there may be multiple records, e.g. one for each year. Since the quotas are generated automatically, the system must know what should be the 'From Date' and 'To Date', before creating an infotype record. This period is determined based on the settings in T559D. Also, an infotype 2006 record has a valid deduction period, during which quota can be deducted. These values in automatic quota generation are also determined based on settings in T559D. The validity period specified in this table is used only by function QUOTA. Absence quota generation report RPTQTA00 and online creation of infotype 2006 use the setting in table T559V. Table T559V provides the default start and end date when you create infotype 2006 record, either manually or through program RPTQTA00.

When absence quota accrual takes place, you may want to reduce the quota for employees who work only part time. You can define the rule to do that in table T559M. Also, you may not want to give full quota to an employee, who has either joined in between, or left in between. You may also not want to give full quota to employees, who are absent. These rules are also defined in table T559M. The rules for quota reduction due to absenteeism may be applicable only for certain absence types. This is specified in view V_554S_M.

Rounding rules for quota generation are defined in T559R.

7.5 SELECTION RULES

Functional Consultant	User	Business Process Owner	Senior Management	My Rating	Understanding Level
A	X	X	X		

7.5.1 Purpose

This view defines rules for automatic absence quota generation.

7.5.2 IMG Node

SM34 ≻ VC_T559L ≻ Selection rules (V_T559L)

7.5.3 Primary Key

ES Grouping for Time Quota Types + PS Grouping for Time Quota Types + PS Grouping for Time Recording + Quota Type Selection Rule Group + Selection Rule for Absence Quota Types + End Date.

7.5.4 Important Fields

			Start Time	Exit
ESG for time quotas	1			
PSG for time quotas	01		01.01.1990	31.12.9999
PSG for time rec.	01			
Quota type sel. grp	90			
Selection rule	040	Privilege Leave		
Absence quota type	40	Privilege Leave		

ES Grouping for time quota types

Absence quota generation rules can be different for different groups of employees.

PS grouping for time quota types

Absence quota generation rules can be different for different PS groupings for time quota types.

PS grouping for time recording

Absence quota generation rules can be different for different PS groupings for time recording.

Quota type selection rule groups

In time evaluation, this field is set by operation MODIF Q=XX. Alternatively, use the feature QUOMO to set the quota type selection rule group based on other organizational assignments.

Selection rule for absence quota types

Each selection rule is associated to one absence quota type. Since an employee may be entitled to multiple types of absence quotas, in this field he gets associated with multiple selection rules. Each of these match with one record in base entitlement.

Start and end date

Validity of the record.

Absence quota type

Absence quota type which is generated for the selection rule.

This tab determines whether a selection rule is applicable to an employee or not. The applicability can depend on a date, e.g. probation completion date from infotype 0019, when the employee joined the company, and whether the employee is challenged. If some employees are not going to satisfy the applicability criteria, you have to see whether they are not entitled to the absence type specified in the selection rule. If they are, additional rules must be written so that they can get the absence quota. Since one absence quota can be generated through multiple rules, one also has to ensure that an employee does not get the same absence quota through more than one rules.

Earliest accrual point

If your company has a policy that employees do not get absence quota when they are on training or on probation, you can implement those policies using this field. Here you specify the type of date before which the accrual should not take place, and specify the date for the employee in infotype 0019.

Entry date from and to

If you wish to apply more favorable rules for long-time employees than for new employees, you can specify a date range here. The rule applies only to those employees, who joined the company during that period.

Challenge group, degree of challenge from and to %

If you wish to apply this rule only to certain challenge groups, and to employees whose challenge % is within a range, you can specify that here. The challenge information about an employee is maintained in infotype 0004. If you wish to use this feature, you have to do configuration for infotype 0004, and maintain the employee data there.

Applicability	Accrual period	Base entitl.	Accrual entitl.	Total entitl.

○ Daily
○ Month
◉ Calendar year
○ Time evaluation period
○ Payroll period
○ Other period
○ Rel. to date type
　 Length

☐ Take Account of Change of Work Center/Basic Pay

When the quota is generated, it is generated for an accrual period. On this tab, you specify the frequency of automatic quota accrual.

Accrual point for leave entitlement

Quota accrual frequency can be daily/monthly/calendar year/time evaluation period/ payroll period/other period/rel. to date type.

Period parameter (for other period)

In the case of other period, you specify the frequency (period parameter) to be used.

Date type, relative position, time unit (for relative to date type)

Period is defined in relation to a date type from infotype 0041 and the number of days or months; for example, the date the employee joined the company, with a period of one month.

Take account of change of work center/basic pay

Suppose an employee leaves in the middle of the month, and your quota accrual is monthly, does he get quota for the days in the last month? If you tick this field, he gets pro rata quota.

Applicability	Accrual period	Base entitl.	Accrual entitl.	Total entitl.

Rule for base entitlement   001

Base Entitlement

Number	Day bal.	PeriodBalance	Unit	Base Period	FromS
30.00000			Days	Calendar year	

Calculation of Seniority

Calculation Process

Key Date for Determining Seniority	Key Date for Determining Age
● For Exact Day	● For Exact Day
○ Start ... ○ End of Accrual Period	○ Start ... ○ End of Accrual Period
○ Start ... ○ End of Base Period	○ Start ... ○ End of Base Period
○ Date Type	○ Date Type

Rule for base entitlement defined in T559E is assigned here, and the screen shows its details. Base entitlement can depend on age and seniority.

Rule for base entitlement

How much quota an employee is entitled to is defined in table T559E. That rule is assigned here. The details of the rule are displayed below the rule number.

Calculation process

SAP HR Benefits module lets you define a calculation process, which you can use for calculation of seniority. If you have complex rules to determine seniority, you can specify it in T525P and related tables, and specify here.

Key date for determining seniority

If your quota entitlement depends on seniority, you need to determine the seniority. Counting for seniority starts from the day the employee joins; but what is the end date? Is it the start of accrual period, or end of accrual period? You specify your choice here.

Date type

If you chose date type as the key date for determining seniority, you specify here the date type from infotype 0041 which is to be taken.

Key date for determining age

This field is similar to key date for determining seniority, and determines the end date for determining age.

Date type

If you chose date type as the key date for determining age, you specify here the date type from infotype 0041 which is to be taken.

Applicability	Accrual period	Base entitl.	Accrual entitl.	Transfer time

Calculated pro rata according to accrual period

- ⦿ Pro rata calculation
- ◯ No pro rata calculation

Multiplication with time balance

- ⦿ No multiplication
- ◯ Day balance
- ◯ Period balance

Reduction, rounding, max. entitlement

Reduction rule	05	Reduction acc. ...	Reduction quota	
Rounding rule				
Max.entitlement		Days	Maximum exceeded	

In accrual entitlement, you specify what should happen when accrual takes place. Should it be reduced for part time or inactive employees; should it be rounded or should it be limited to a specified maximum, etc.

Pro rata calculation of accrual entitlement

If the Accrual period is different from the base period, is the entitlement proportionately reduced? You should carefully decide whether your base period and accrual periods are going to be same or different. If they are different, this setting is important. Usually, you would use no pro rata option, when you choose replace option in V_556A_B.

Multiplication with time balance

You may want to take a person's working into account, for determining his absence quota. Do look at reduction rules (T559M), where you can reduce absence quota for days before joining and after leaving, and specified absences. Then look at base entitlement (V_T559E), where you can determine base entitlement itself based on time types. If you still want to multiply the quota accrual with a time type, you use the following fields.

No multiplication

If you don't want the accrual entitlement to be multiplied by a time balance, you choose this radio button.

Multiplication by day balance of time type

If you want the quota accrual to depend on the day balance of a time type, you choose this radio button and specify the time type here. In this way, you can control the absence quota type selection based on the actual working time performed. You can use either a pre-defined time type, or your own time type, which you have defined in T555A.

Multiplication by period balance of time type

If you want the quota accrual to depend on the period balance of a time type, you choose this radio button and specify the time type here. In this way you can give quota only for the days when the employee was present, and deny it for the days when he was absent.

Reduction rule for quota entitlements

When absence quota accrual takes place, you may want to reduce the quota for employees who work only part time. You can define the rule to do that in table T559M. Also, you may not want to give full quota to an employee, who has either joined in between, or left in between. You may also not want to give full quota to employees, who are absent. These rules are also defined in table T559M. The reduction rule which applies to the selection rule is specified here.

Rounding rule

Having determined how much quota has accrued to the employee, you may want to round it before crediting. You define the rounding rule in table T559R, and assign it to the selection rule here.

Maximum accrual entitlement

You can use this field to define an upper limit for the accrual entitlement. This is particularly useful if you determine quota entitlements based on hours worked.

Reduction quota

If a reduction takes place, the reduction can be put in the quota specified here. You can use it as per your company policy.

Absence quota if maximum entitlement is exceeded

If maximum permitted accrual entitlement is exceeded, and hence only the maximum entitlement is credited, the balance can be put in this quota. You can use it as per your company policy, e.g. monetary compensation.

Accrual period	Base entitl.	Accrual entitl.	Transfer time	Total entitl.

- ◉ Upon accrual
- ○ Per calendar year
- ○ Per time evaluation period
- ○ Per payroll period
- ○ Other period
- ○ Date type
- ○ Transfer rule

Transfer packages   Days

If in view V_556A_B, you have specified that the quota is automatically generated, then you see tab where you specify when this quota is transferred to infotype 2006. You can also specify if the transfer should take place in packages of fixed days or hours.

Time of transfer to leave entitlement

Here you specify when quota transfer should take place. This is done by selecting the appropriate radio button, e.g. upon accrual, per calendar year, etc. For some options, additional information is required.

Period parameter (for other period)

If you specify other period, you have to specify the frequency (period parameter).

Date type

If quota transfer should take place based on date type, you specify the date type.

Transfer rule

If you want to specify a more complex logic, you can define a transfer rule and assign it here. For that you have to configure tables T559G, T5QIA and T5QIT, which are for Australia.

Transfer packages

If you want to transfer a fixed size of quota only, you can specify a value here. Whenever quota crosses this number, this number is transferred. The balance is retained for further accumulation.

Applicability	Accrual period	Base entitl.	Accrual entitl.	Total entitl.

Rounding rule   80   Round up to nearest half

Max. entitl.   300.00000   Days

☐ Settlement of existing quota entitlements

This tab defines the limit on total entitlement.

Rounding rule

The rounding rule here is applied to total entitlement.

Maximum total entitlement

Here you specify the maximum total entitlement.

Settlement of existing quota entitlements

If an employee applies for leave in the next year for which the quota is still not generated, you can not enter his application in the system. SAP provides a solution for this. You create a manual absence quota and enter his application. When the quota is generated, only the incremental quota is generated, if this field is ticked.

7.6 QUOTA TYPES (AUTOMATIC GENERATION)

Functional Consultant	User	Business Process Owner	Senior Management	My Rating	Understanding Level
A	X	X	X		

7.6.1 Purpose

Quota types are defined in table T556A. While most properties of quota type are defined in view V_T556A, properties related to automatic generation can be defined only in view V_556A_B. These radio buttons determine whether absence quota are generated automatically using function QUOTA in time evaluation, and if yes, whether it increases, or replaces, an earlier record with the same key. The radio buttons you select from are No generation, Increase, Replace. If you select No generation, you can either create the quota manually in infotype 2006, or create using the Generate Absence Quotas report (RPTQTA00).

7.6.2 IMG Node

SM34 ≻ VC_T559L ≻ Quota types (V_556A_B)

7.6.3 Screen

E...	P...	A...	Quota text	Start Date	End Date	Unit	No ge...	Incre...	Repla...	NegDed	TCC
1	01	30	Casual leave	01.01.1990	31.12.9999	Hours	●	○	○		01
1	01	35	Maternity Leave	01.01.1990	31.12.9999	Days	●	○	○		04
1	01	39	Lapsable PL ...	01.01.1990	31.12.9999	Days	●	○	○		04
1	01	40	Privilege Leave	01.01.1990	31.12.9999	Days	●	○	○	60.00000-	02

7.7 BASE ENTITLEMENT

Functional Consultant	User	Business Process Owner	Senior Management	My Rating	Understanding Level
B	X	X	X		

7.7.1 Purpose

Base entitlements define the basic entitlement of an employee and the period for which it is. Base entitlements can depend on seniority and age. The entitlement may be constant, or you may determine it in time evaluation. The rule is defined in table T559E, and assigned to a selection rule in T559L.

7.7.2 IMG Node

SM34 ≻ VC_T559L ≻ Base entitlement (V_T559E)

7.7.3 Screen

ES grpg for time quotas	1
PS grpg for time quotas	06
PS grpg for time recording	01

	Start Time	Exit
>	01.01.1990	31.12.9999

Absence quota type	01	Leave Mon-Fri
Rule for base entitlement	001	
Sequential no.	001	

Base entitlement

Seniority	-	🗐
Age	-	🗐

Entitlement

Constant	2.08333	Days
Day balance		
Period balance		

related to period

- ◯ Calendar year
- ◯ Accrual period
- ◯ Time evaluation period
- ◯ Payroll period
- ◉ Other period — Every 4 weeks 🗐
- ◯ Rel. to date type — 🗐
  - Lngth — 🗐

7.7.4 Primary Key

ES Grouping for Time Quota Types + PS Grouping for Time Quota Types + PS Grouping for Time Recording + Absence Quota Type + Rule for Base Entitlement for Leave Accrual + Sequential number + End Date.

7.7.5 Important Fields

ES Grouping for time quota types

Base entitlement can be different for different groups of employees.

PS grouping for time quota types

Base entitlement can be different for different PS groupings for time quota types.

PS grouping for time recording

Base entitlement can be different for different PS groupings for time recording.

Absence quota type and rule for base entitlement

In Table T559L, absence quota type and rule for base entitlement are independent attributes of selection rule. It is possible that the same absence quota type has different rules for base entitlement and different employees get different quota.

Sequential number

You define multiple sub-rules because the rules can depend on seniority and age. The rule where the seniority and age conditions are met is picked up.

Start and end date

Validity period of the record.

Base Entitlement

Entitlement can depend on seniority and age.

Seniority from and to with time unit

By defining a seniority interval, you can specify special rules for determining an employee's base entitlement according to his or her seniority. The specified start of the interval is inclusive and the end is exclusive. How to compute seniority is specified in table T559L to which it is linked.

Age from and to with time unit

By specifying an age interval, you can define special rules based on an employee's age. The start of the interval is inclusive, the end exclusive. How to compute age is specified in table T559L to which it is linked.

Entitlement

Entitlement is generated during time evaluation or batch job.

Constant

You can specify the base entitlement as a constant in this field.

Day balance, period balance

In this view, you can specify base entitlement according to an employee's age or seniority. However, if that is not sufficient for your purposes and you want to use other criteria, SAP lets you do that. You can define a time type in which you compute the base entitlement and specify that time type here. Since a time type has a day balance, and a period balance, you can specify either day balance or period balance. The PCR should be inserted in the schema before function CUMBT and QUOTA.

Related to Period

Related to period (base period)

Here you specify the period for which the entitlement is. You do so by choosing from the listed options (radio buttons), e.g. calendar year, time evaluation period, payroll period, etc. By entering the base period, you specify the period for which the corresponding base entitlement is valid.

Period parameter (for other period)

In the case of other period, you specify the interval (period parameter) to be used.

Date type, relative position, time unit (for relative to date type)

Period is defined in relation to a date type from infotype 0041 and the number of days or months; for example, the date the employee joined the company with a period of one month.

7.8 VALIDITY/DEDUCTION INTERVAL

Functional Consultant	User	Business Process Owner	Senior Management	My Rating	Understanding Level
B	X	X	X		

7.8.1 Purpose

In SAP, absence quotas are not defined at quota type level. For the same quota type, there can be multiple records, e.g. one for each year. Since the quotas are generated automatically, the system must know what should be the 'From Date' and the 'To Date', before creating an infotype record. This period is determined based on the settings here. Also, an infotype 2006 record has a valid deduction period, during which quota can be deducted. These values in automatic quota generation are also determined based on settings here. The validity period specified in this view is used only by function QUOTA. Absence quota generation report RPTQTA00, and online creation of infotype 2006, use the setting in table T559V.

7.8.2 IMG Node

SM34 ➢ VC_T559L ➢ Validity/deduction interval (V_T559D)

7.8.3 Primary Key

ES Grouping for Time Quota Types + PS Grouping for Time Quota Types + Absence Quota Type

7.8.4 Important Fields

ESG Time quota types	1
PS grpg tm quota typ	06
Absence quota type	01 Leave Mon-Fri

ES grouping for time quota types

The definition of validity/deduction interval can depend on ES grouping for time quota types.

PS grouping for time quota types

The definition of validity/deduction interval can depend on PS grouping for time quota types.

Absence quota type

Absence quota type for which you are defining validity/deduction interval.

Validity interval

Valid from	Valid to
○ Calendar year	○ Calendar year
○ Time evaluation period	○ Time evaluation period
○ Payroll period	○ Payroll period
○ Accrual period	○ Accrual period
○ Base period	○ Base period
○ Transfer time	○ Transfer time
● Other period 37 Holiday year -	● Other period 37 Holiday year...
○ Date type	○ Date type
○ Start ● End	○ Start ● End
Relative position	Relative position 364 Days

Valid from

When you create infotype 2006 records, you have to specify their start and end date. When quotas are system generated, what these dates should be is determined by the validity interval settings you do here.

Here you only specify a validity period for absence quotas that are generated during time evaluation. Fields for entering the validity period are therefore only available for absence quotas for which you have selected replace or increase in the generating quotas allowed in time evaluation step.

Type of time interval and start or end of an interval

SAP gives you a wide choice which you can use to define how you want the valid from date to be determined. It can be start (or end) of the calendar year, payroll period or base period etc.

Period parameter (for other period)

In the case of other period, you specify the interval (period parameter) to be used.

Date type, relative position, time unit (for relative to date type)

Period is defined in relation to a date type from infotype 0041 and the number of days or months; for example, the date the employee joined the company with a period of one month.

Valid to

Valid to is defined in the same way as valid from.

Deduction interval		
Deduction from		**Deduction to**
● Start of validity interval		● Start of validity interval
○ End of validity interval		○ End of validity interval
Relative position	1 Days 📄	Relative position 12 Months 📄
No deduction before	📄	No deduction after 📄

When you create infotype 2006 records, you have to specify their deduction interval. When quotas are system generated, what these dates should be is determined by the deduction interval settings you do here.

Deduction from and relative position

You can set your deduction interval with respect to validity interval and offset it if you like. For example, your deduction interval may start three months after the validity interval starts or you may define your deduction interval to start nine months before the end of the validity interval.

No deduction before

Here you can specify, and thus further restrict, that no deduction should take place before a specified date. The date of specified type is picked up from infotype 0019.

Deduction to and relative position

You can set your deduction interval with respect to validity interval and offset it if you like. For example, your deduction interval may end three months after the validity interval ends or you may define your deduction interval to end 15 months after the start of validity interval.

No deduction after

Here you can specify, and thus further restrict, that no deduction should take place after a specified date. The date of specified type is picked up from infotype 0019.

7.9 VALIDITY PERIOD FOR DEFAULT VALUES

Functional Consultant	User	Business Process Owner	Senior Management	My Rating	Understanding Level
B	X	X	X		

7.9.1 Purpose and Overview

This view provides the default start and end date when you create infotype 2006 record, either manually, or through program RPTQTA00.

When you manually create a record, the validity from date and the validity to date specified in this view are proposed as default start date and end date. For this to happen, in table T582A, for infotype 2006, the fields create w/o start and create w/o end should be blank.

When you generate absence quotas using program RPTQTA00, you either specify both dates, one date, or no date. If you specify one date, the program takes the interval from this table, which contains that date. If you do not specify any date, the system takes the current date, and finds the interval from this table.

Note that in this table the validity period is not defined at absence quota type level, but at quota type selection rule group level (which is determined using feature QUOMO).

Since quota type is not a decision-making field in feature QUOMO, the default validity period cannot depend on quota type.

7.9.2 IMG Node

SM34 ≻ VC_T559L ≻ Validity period for default values (T559V)

7.9.3 Screen

ES grpg for time quotas	1
PS grpg for time quotas	01
Quota type sel. grp	01

Valid from date
- ● Calendar year
- ○ Time evaluation period
- ○ Payroll period
- ○ Other period
- ○ Date type
- ● Start ○ End
- Rel. position

Valid to date
- ● Calendar year
- ○ Time evaluation period
- ○ Payroll period
- ○ Other period
- ○ Date type
- ○ Start ● End
- Rel. position

7.9.4 Primary Key

ES Grouping + PS Grouping + Quota Group

7.9.5 Important Fields

Validity period defined here is similar to the validity period defined for automatic quota generation (V_T559D). Some of the choices, e.g. base period, are not applicable here. One major difference is that here the definition is for quota type selection rule group (which is determined using feature QUOMO), instead of quota type. Since quota type is not a decision-making field in feature QUOMO, the default validity period cannot depend on quota type.

7.10 REDUCTION RULES

Functional Consultant	User	Business Process Owner	Senior Management	My Rating	Understanding Level
C	X	X	X		

7.10.1 Purpose

When absence quota accrual takes place, you may want to reduce the quota for employees who work only part time. You can define the rule to do that here. Also, you may not want to give full quota to an employee, who has either joined in between, or left in between. You may also not want to give full quota to employees, who are absent (see V_554S_M). These rules are also defined here. The reduction rule, which is defined here, is assigned to selection rules in table T559L.

7.10.2 IMG Node

SM34 ≻ VC_T559L ≻ Reduction rules (T559M)

7.10.3 Screen

7.10.4 Primary Key

Reduction Rule

7.10.5 Important Fields

Reduction rule

Reduction rule being defined.

Reduction rule for part-time employees: basic data

If you have a part-time employee, his entitlement can be reduced based on:

➢ No reduction
➢ Based on employment percentage in infotype 0007.
➢ Based on capacity utilization percentage in infotype 0008.
➢ Weekly workdays in infotype 0007 divided by the number of days in view V_T510I.

Reduction rule for part time employees: key date

If the reduction has to take place, the date on which this quotient should be calculated, is specified here.

Reduction rule for inactive days

Days on which an employee is not active may also make it necessary to reduce the entitlement. Inactive days are usually as a result of employees joining or leaving the company. However, you may also like to consider certain absence types as inactive. These are specified by ticking 'Reduction indicator for quota generation' field in V_554S_M. In this case, the reduction quotient is determined by counting the number of payroll days in relation to the accrual period. You can specify a percentage of inactive days and specify different reduction rules if actual percentage is below or above this specified percentage.

Reference period

Do you want inactive days to be counted with respect to accrual period or base period?

Percentage of inactive calendar days, to percentage, from percentage

Inactive days can be due to an employee joining or leaving the company, or due to certain absences. You compute the percentage of the employee's inactive days within the accrual/base period. If that percentage is less than the specified percentage value, the reduction specified in 'To percentage' takes place. If that percentage is greater than or equal to the specified percentage value, the reduction specified in 'From percentage' takes place.

7.11 REDUCTION INDICATORS FOR ABSENCES

Functional Consultant	User	Business Process Owner	Senior Management	My Rating	Understanding Level
B	X	X	X		

7.11.1 Purpose and Overview

When you accrue absence quota, you may want to reduce it if the employee is absent. However, you may not want to do it for all absences, but only for specified absences. Here you can define the absences which are considered for quota reduction.

Even for these absences, you may not want to reduce quota if the absences are few. You can specify that limit. Further, if an employee is having too many problems, and has too many absences, you may not want to penalize him fully, but only to an extent. In that case, you can specify the maximum number of days, which is taken for quota reduction.

7.11.2 IMG Node

SM34 ➤ VC_T559L ➤ Reduction indicator for absences (V_554S_M)

7.11.3 Screen

PSG	A/AType	A/A type text	Valid From	End Date	Min. days	Max. days	Reduction
01	A0	IOW (INJURY ON ...	01.01.1900	31.12.9999			☐
01	ALWP	AUTH. LWOP FOR...	01.01.1990	31.12.9999			☑
01	B0	ROAD ACCIDENT	01.01.1900	31.12.9999			☐
01	C0	SPL. LEAVE (MIS...	01.01.1990	31.12.9999			☐

7.11.4 Important Fields

Minimum number of calendar days for reduction for quota generation

Number of calendar days for each accrual period up to which an absence is not to cause the generated quota entitlement to be reduced. Only the absence days above this value contribute to the reduction.

Maximum number of calendar days for reduction for quota generation

Here you can put a ceiling on the number of days, of quota reduction. In case the absence is above this figure, quota reduction considers the figure specified here, instead of the actual figure.

Reduction indicator for quota generation

Days on which an employee is not active may make it necessary to reduce his quota accrual. Inactive days are usually as a result of employees joining or leaving the company. However, you may also like to consider certain absence types as inactive. These are specified by ticking this field.

7.12 ROUNDING RULE

Functional Consultant	User	Business Process Owner	Senior Management	My Rating	Understanding Level
A	C	C	X		

You may see Rounding Rule (V_T559R) in chapter 5.6.

7.13 QUOTA TYPE SELECTION RULE GROUP DETERMINATION

Functional Consultant	User	Business Process Owner	Senior Management	My Rating	Understanding Level
B	X	X	X		

7.13.1 Purpose

This feature is used to determine Quota Type Selection Rule Group, which is used in table T559L (Automatic Absence Quota Generation) and table T559V (Validity Period: Absence Quotas for Default Values).

7.13.2 IMG Node

PE03 ≻ QUOMO

7.13.3 Screen

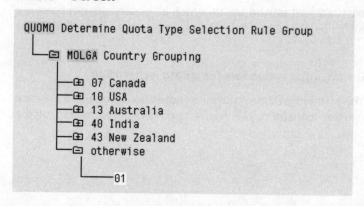

7.13.4 Fields for Decision Making

Company Code
Personnel Area
Personnel Subarea
Employee Group
Employee Subgroup
Country Grouping
PS Grouping for Leave Types
Pay Scale Type
Pay Scale Area
Pay Scale Group
Pay Scale Level
Work Schedule Rule
Personnel Number
Work Contract
Contract Type

7.13.5 Return Value

Quota Type Selection Rule Group

7.14 ENHANCEMENTS FOR QUOTA TYPE SELECTION

Functional Consultant	User	Business Process Owner	Senior Management	My Rating	Understanding Level
C	X	X	X		

7.14.1 Purpose

You can use the SAP enhancement HRPTIM03 for quota type selection to refine the criteria available for creating absence quotas in the following areas:

Exit	Area
EXIT_SAPLHRV_001	Applicability of the selection rule
EXIT_SAPLHRV_002	Defaults for processing accrual entitlements determined by time evaluation
EXIT_SAPLHRV_003	Rules for reducing quota entitlements
EXIT_SAPLHRV_004	Defaults for determining base entitlements
EXIT_SAPLHRV_005	Default for transfer: Change results of quota generation
EXIT_SAPLHRV_006	Processing individual regulations for determining the employee's entry and leaving dates

Quota Correction

8.1 QUOTA CORRECTIONS (INFOTYPE 2013)

Functional Consultant	User	Business Process Owner	Senior Management	My Rating	Understanding Level
A	A	B	C		

8.1.1 Screen

Start   30.01.2005

Absence quota type   30   Casual leave

Change accrual entitlement

Quota number   Days

◉ Increase generated entitlement
○ Reduce generated entitlement
○ Replace generated entitlement

Change transfer time

Transfer   Do not change transfer time

8.1.2 Purpose and Overview

If your absence quotas are system generated, you cannot change them in infotype 2006. This infotype lets you do manual adjustment to these quotas, if need be. This can be done only for those absence quota types, which are system generated, i.e. where Increase/ Replace radio button is selected in view V_556A_B.

You can increase, reduce or replace the quota by the value you specify. Quota correction is transferred to infotype 2006 only when the time evaluation is run. You can delay it further by specifying that it should be transferred only when the next entitlement is due.

Time evaluation carries out a recalculation starting on the day for which you have entered the quota correction. You can view the results of the quota correction in the quota overview (transaction PT50).

8.1.3 Subtypes

Absence quota type

8.1.4 Time Constraint

Z (Time constraint for time management infotypes -> T554Y)

8.1.5 Important Fields

Absence quota type

When you create infotype 2013 record, you specify the absence quota type as subtype on the initial screen. The list of value there shows only those absence quota types, which are relevant for the employee, by considering his ES grouping & PS grouping. Further, quota correction can be done only for those absence quota types, which are system generated, i.e. where Increase/Replace radio button is selected in view V_556A_B.

Quota number

Here you enter the number of days/ hours by which the quota is to be increased, reduced or replaced.

Increase/Reduce/Replace

Through these radio buttons, you decide whether the quota is to be increased, reduced or replaced.

Transfer accrued entitlement

Quota correction is not transferred to infotype 2006 unless the time evaluation is run. When the time evaluation is run, there is this quota correction waiting to be transferred, as well as there may be some entitlements generated till then. You can specify whether both should be transferred now, only correction should be transferred now, or even correction should be transferred only with the next scheduled transfer of entitlement. In the last case, the quota correction is not available in infotype 2006 for deduction until the next scheduled transfer.

Do not change transfer time	The quota correction is not processed until the time at which time evaluation normally transfers the calculated entitlement to the absence quotas infotype (2006). In this case, the quota correction does not appear immediately in infotype 2006, so you cannot deduct an absence or quota compensation from the value of the quota correction.
Transfer collected entitlement immediately	The quota correction is processed in the next time evaluation run. If you run time evaluation directly for the employee, the value of the quota correction and any entitlement already accrued by time evaluation are available for deduction in the absence quotas infotype (2006) directly afterwards.
Only transfer quota correction immediately	The quota correction is processed in the next time evaluation run. If you run time evaluation directly for the employee, the value of the quota correction is available for deduction in the absence quotas infotype (2006) directly afterwards.

Attendance Quota

9.1 ATTENDANCE QUOTAS (INFOTYPE 2007)

Functional Consultant	User	Business Process Owner	Senior Management	My Rating	Understanding Level
A	A	A	A		

9.1.1 Screen

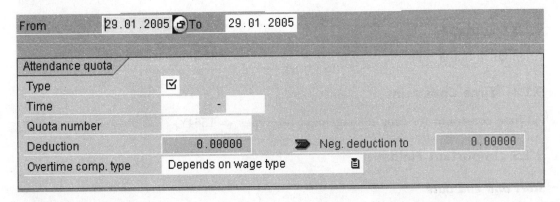

9.1.2 Purpose

Attendance quotas are used where you want to restrict entries in attendance infotype 2002. For example, you may use it to define how much training an employee is allowed. Attendance quotas are also used to approve overtime.

Attendance quota records are manually created. Note that an employee may have several records of each attendance quota type. You may permit negative balances for some quota types within specified limits. Attendance quota can be deducted in the following ways:

➢ Quotas are deducted for attendances (infotype 2002). For each attendance type you can specify whether quota deduction takes place. If yes, the quota type from which deduction takes place, and of the multiple records of that quota type, what logic is followed to select the record? If the quota type is exhausted, it is also possible to deduct from alternate quota types.

➢ In time evaluation, overtime can be deducted from infotype 2007 (operation GENOT is called in a PCR to do this). Thus, it can be used for overtime approval. Also, if you use time evaluation, you can use the overtime compensation type field to control whether overtime is to be remunerated or converted to time off.

➢ You can also use this infotype to create a general overtime approval for an employee. You do this by creating an attendance quota of zero hours. In this case, the attendance quota must be deducted automatically by time evaluation.

Deduction of quota on account of attendances can be restricted by using the deduction from and deduction to fields of attendance types. There are three ways of specifying the duration of the attendance quota:

➢ Detailed specification of the attendance quota (specify both interval and hours)
➢ Flexible attendance quota within a fixed time frame (specify only interval and not hours)
➢ Flexible attendance quota within a fixed period (specify neither interval nor hours)

You can see all quotas for an employee in transaction PT50 (Quota Overview). Attendance quotas cannot be generated automatically. Attendance quotas cannot be compensated financially.

9.1.3 Subtypes

Attendance quota type

9.1.4 Time Constraint

Z (Time constraint for time management infotypes -> T554Y)

9.1.5 Important Fields

Start and end date

This signifies the period for which the quota is given. There may be some type of quotas which are accrued. In those cases, this period is in the past. But there may be some quota types, where the quota is given in advance. In those cases, this is a future period.

Attendance quota type and text

Each attendance quota is for an attendance quota type. Attendance quota types are subtypes of infotype 2007.

From and to time, quota number and unit

When you create attendance quota for overtime, you can specify the time duration during which the employee is expected to work overtime. The system compares actual overtime done with that approved, and only the overlapping time period is recognized as overtime done and approved.

If you specify time interval which overlaps with schedule, the overlapping period is still considered overtime. This can be useful for flextime schedules.

If you specify time interval for attendance quota record, which is valid for more than one day, the approved period is valid for each day.

Instead of specifying time period, you can specify the number of hours approved. If you do so, overtime done is approved to the extent of hours entered here.

If you specify quota number for attendance quota record, which is valid for more than one day, you are specifying total number of hours, which can be used during the validity period. It is not interpreted as the number of hours each day.

Deduction

Quota deduction which has taken place so far because of attendances.

Negative deduction to

Depending on your configuration, some quota types may permit negative balances. However, it cannot go below the figure displayed in this field (zero or negative value).

Overtime compensation type

If the employees have a choice of deciding whether they want to receive payment, or time off, or a combination of the two, that choice is captured here. For more details, see chapter 11.4 (T555R).

Blank	Depends on wage type
1	Remuneration
2	Time off plus overtime rate
3	Compensation (time off)

9.2 ATTENDANCE QUOTA TYPE

Functional Consultant	User	Business Process Owner	Senior Management	My Rating	Understanding Level
A	C	C	X		

9.2.1 Purpose and Overview

This view contains the master list of attendance quota types.

9.2.2 IMG Node

SM30 ➢ V_T556P
SM30 ➢ V_556P_B

9.2.3 Screen V_T556P

```
ESG Time quota types          1
PS grpg tm quota typ         05                    Start Time    Exit
Att. quota type              10  Works council approval    > 01.01.1900  31.12.9999

Attendance Quota Type
Time/measurement unit    Hours          Time constraint class      01
 Times
  Start time        [    ]
  End time          [    ]

 Deduction
  ⦿ Deduction through time evaluation
  ○ Deduction through attendances

  Neg. ded. to       [        ]
```

9.2.4 Screen V_556P_B

E..	P...	QType	Quota text	Start Date	End Date	TmTy...	Alt.TT	Onl...
1	05	10	Works council approval	01.01.1900	🖉.12.9999			☐
1	07	01	Seminar/Course	01.01.1990	31.12.9999			☑
1	07	02	Business Trip	01.01.1990	31.12.9999			☑
1	07	03	Banked Overtime	01.01.1990	31.12.9999			☐

9.2.5 Primary Key

ES Grouping for Time Quota Types + PS Grouping for Time Quota Types + Attendance Quota Type + End Date

9.2.6 Important Fields

ES grouping for time quota types

Properties of attendance quota type can depend on ES grouping for time quota types.

PS grouping for time quota types

Properties of attendance quota type can depend on PS grouping for time quota types.

Attendance quota type and text

Attendance quota type being defined.

Start and end date

Period for which this record is valid.

Time/measurement unit

Here you specify whether the quota is maintained in hours or days.

Time constraint class

The time constraint class is used to check for collisions between time management infotypes (2001 to 2013). It allows you to specify different regulations for checking for collisions between individual subtypes. How to design time constraint classes and how to specify the rules to ensure that you do not have conflicting data, e.g. an employee is both present and absent at the same time, is discussed in chapter 5.3 (V_554Y_B).

Start time and end time

If you create an attendance quota type with the hours time unit, you can specify default values for the start and end times. The system proposes the default values when you create attendance quota in infotype 2007. In infotype 2007 these fields are used to restrict quota deduction.

Deduction through time evaluation or attendances

Here you specify whether deduction is going to happen through time evaluation, or whether attendances are deducted through online entry in infotype 2002.

Negative deduction to

In this field you enter the limit of negative value for the quota type. The balance for the quota type cannot go below this.

Time type, alternative time type

When overtime is worked, it is checked for approval specified in attendance quota in infotype 2007. Attendance quota specifies attendance quota type. If overtime is approved, it is accumulated in the time type specified in this field. If overtime is not approved, it is accumulated in the time type specified in the alternative time type field.

10 Quota Compensation

10.1 TIME QUOTA COMPENSATION (INFOTYPE 0416)

Functional Consultant	User	Business Process Owner	Senior Management	My Rating	Understanding Level
A	A	A	A		

10.1.1 Screen

When you create an infotype 0416 record, you specify a compensation method. That compensation method determines the manner of quota compensation, which are:

➤ Fixed time quota type, or compensation rule (screen 1)
➤ User specified time quota type, or compensation rule (screen 2)
➤ Free compensation (screen 3)

Compensation methods where time quota type, or compensation rule, is predefined

For these compensation methods the user has no flexibility. He just specifies the 'No. to compensate'. The system takes care of everything.

Compensation specifications		
Time quota type	40	Privilege Leave
Compensation rule	000	
No. to compensate		
☐ Do not account		

Compensation methods where time quota type, or compensation rule is not predefined

For these compensation methods the user can enter either time quota type or compensation rule.

Comp. method	1003 Personal Time Off payout

Compensation specifications	
Time quota type	
Compensation rule	
No. to compensate	
☐ Do not account	

▐▌ Compensation using default ✓
▐▌ Manual compensation

Free compensation

For this compensation method the user does not wish to use time quota type or compensation rule.

Comp. method	1003 Personal Time Off payout

Compensation specifications	
Time quota type	00
Compensation rule	000
No. to compensate	0.00000
☐ Do not account	

▐▌ Compensation using default
▐▌ Manual compensation ✓

Absence quotas

	ATy	Quota text	Entitl.	Unit	Comp.	Rem.	WT	Amount	Curr...	▨	Dedu
	30	Casual Leave	8.00000	Days		5.00000				☐	01.01.

10.1.2 Purpose and Overview

SAP lets you pay your employees in lieu of their leave entitlement. You would enter the number of days you want to pay for in infotype 0416, and specify the compensation method. Quota compensation can be done only for absence quotas and not for attendance quotas. Quota compensation usually results in

> ➤ quota deduction (rules defined in T556U), and
> ➤ payment (rules defined in T556W).

The quota deduction takes place immediately, but payment takes place when the payroll is run. Not all quota types can be compensated. For each quota type, you can define whether it can be compensated or not. There are three methods of quota compensation

> ➤ Based on time quota type
> ➤ Based on compensation rules
> ➤ Free compensation

If your deduction is based on time quota type, the deduction takes place directly from the time quota of that type. In case there are multiple records of time quota of that type, they are sorted by start date for deduction purpose.

Compensation rules offer more flexibility. You can specify more than one time quota type, from which deduction can take place. In case an employee has multiple quota types from which deduction is possible, you also specify how to decide priority.

If you specify neither time quota type, nor compensation rule, it is a method of free compensation. If you use this method, you can specify either time quota type, or compensation rule, when you create infotype 0416 record.

If you want still more flexibility, you can click on [Manual compensation] . This opens up all the fields in the lower part of the screen, where you can directly specify the wage type and amount, apart from other information. If there are multiple records for an absence quota type, you can also decide the record from which you want the deduction to take place.

If you want to permit free compensation, the permitted wage types must be allowed for infotype 0416 in table T512Z.

You can also compensate absence entitlements that have already expired or that are not yet available for deduction. The validity and deduction periods of absence quotas are not taken into account when entitlements are compensated. Note that you cannot prevent this from happening. If your company policy is not to compensate expired entitlements, you must create infotype 0416 records with 'Do not account' ticked on.

You can specify in customizing how you want each time quota compensation method to be remunerated. For example, you can specify that you want the compensation to be dependent on the validity period of the deducted quota. Thus, last year's quota can be compensated only at last year's rates, and not at current rates.

If you want to know which quota will be reduced by compensation, you may click on

[Compensate] icon or use menu path Edit ➤ Compensation ➤ Calculate. This will show the anticipated changes to the quota without saving the data record.

You can compensate all of an employee's quotas at the same time. This process is recommended if, for example, an employee leaves the company. You must be able to perform free compensation to be able to do this. The menu path is Edit ➤ Compensation ➤ Entire remainder.

10.1.3 Subtypes

Time quota compensation method (type)

10.1.4 Time Constraint

3 (Record may include gaps, can exist more than once)

10.1.5 Important Fields

Compensation method

The compensation method determines how the quota deduction takes place. Compensation methods are subtypes of infotype 0416.

Time quota type

If your deduction is based on time quota type, the deduction takes place directly from the time quota of the type indicated here. In case there are multiple records of time quota of that type, they are sorted by start date for deduction purpose.

Compensation rule

Compensation rules offer more flexibility. You can specify more than one time quota type, from which deduction can take place. In case an employee has multiple quota types from which deduction is possible, you also specify how to decide priority.

Number to compensate

Here you specify the number of days or hours for which the quota is to be compensated.

Do not account

If you tick this field, only quota deduction takes place, but no compensation is made. You can use this feature to lapse quota.

Wage type

In the case of free compensation, you can directly specify the wage type. The permitted wage types must be allowed for infotype 0416 in table T512Z.

Amount and currency

You can directly enter the amount to be compensated.

10.1.6 Default Values in Manual Compensation

In free compensation, you must specify the quota number to be compensated. If you do not specify the wage type and amount, they are determined by the system. If you specify both number and amount, wage type is determined by the system. You can also choose to specify all the three, viz. number, amount and wage type. More details are given as follows:

Number			The wage type is determined using customizing table T556W (Assign Wage Types to Quotas to be Compensated). The wage type is valuated by personnel calculation rule X015 in schema XT00 (where X = country indicator)
Number	Amount		The amount entered is the total amount for the compensation. It is transferred, without being multiplied by the number, to the wage type specified in the customizing table T556W (Assign Wage Types to Quotas to be Compensated)
Number	Amount	Wage type	The wage type is valuated, without being multiplied by the number, using the specified amount.

10.2   QUOTA COMPENSATION TYPES

Functional Consultant	User	Business Process Owner	Senior Management	My Rating	Understanding Level
A	B	C	X		

10.2.1   Purpose and Overview

There are three methods of quota compensation.

➤ To use compensation using deduction rules, enter the quota deduction rule in this view.
➤ Alternatively, you may use compensation of individual quotas, by entering the quota type directly. In case there are multiple records of time quota of that type, they are sorted by start date for deduction purpose.
➤ If you specify neither of the two here, the user has a choice of specifying either quota type, or compensation rule. He can also enter compensation manually.

Time quota compensation is entered in infotype 0416. Compensation methods defined here are subtypes of infotype 0416. When compensation is entered, you need to know which rule to use for quota deduction, and which wage type to compensate in (defined in T556W, key fields determined here).

10.2.2   IMG Node

SM30 ➤ V_T556U

10.2.3 Screen

	ESG	PSG	Comp.meth.	Description	Rule	Description	QTy.	Quota text
	1	01	1000	PL Encashment			40	Privilege Leave
	1	01	9999	Accrued PL encash ...	046	Accrued PL en...		
	1	01	CLL	CL Lapse			30	Casual leave

10.2.4 Primary Key

ES Grouping for Time Quota Types + PS Grouping for Time Quota Types + Quota Type (Attendance/Absence Quota) + Time Quota Compensation Method.

Quota type field is not in any view. SAP defaults it to A.

10.2.5 Important Fields

ES grouping

Quota compensation methods can differ depending on ES grouping for time quota types.

PS grouping

Quota compensation methods can differ depending on PS grouping for time quota types.

Compensation method

Time quota compensation method which is being defined.

Deduction rule, quota type

There are three methods of quota compensation.

➢ Based on time quota type
➢ Based on compensation rules
➢ Free compensation

If you assign a quota type here, quota deduction takes place from that quota type. The user has no choice when he is creating an infotype 0416 record.

If you assign a deduction rule (defined in T556R) here, quota deduction takes place as per that rule. The user has no choice when he is creating an infotype 0416 record.

If you enter none of these two, the user can choose either a quota type, or deduction rule, when he is creating an infotype 0416 record. He can also go for free compensation, where he can not only specify the absence types to be compensated, but the wage type and amount as well.

10.3   WAGE TYPE ASSIGNMENT TO QUOTA COMPENSATION METHOD

Functional Consultant	User	Business Process Owner	Senior Management	My Rating	Understanding Level
A	C	X	X		

10.3.1   Purpose

This view is used to assign wage types to quota compensation method. It permits different wage types to be associated to compensation for different years.

10.3.2   IMG Node

SM30 ➤ V_T556W

10.3.3   Screen

	E	P..	Co...	Description	Q..	Quota text	No.	C	Diff.	Year	% fa...	WT	Long text	Valid From	End Date
	1	01	1000	PL Encashme...	40	Privilege Leave	000	=			100.00	1405	PL Encash	01.01.2001	31.12.9999
	1	01	1010		50	Sick Leave	000	=			100.00	1415	SL Encash	01.01.2001	31.12.9999
	1	01	9999	Accrued PL en...	40	Privilege Leave	000	=			100.00	1405	PL Encash	01.01.2001	31.12.9999

10.3.4   Primary Key

Country Grouping + ES Grouping for Time Quota Types + PS Grouping for Time Quota Types + Quota type (Default Absence) + Time Quota Compensation Method + Attendance or Absence Quota Type + Number of Wage Type Rule if Key is Identical + End Date

10.3.5   Important Fields

ES grouping for time quota types

Wage types for a quota compensation method can depend on ES grouping for time quota types.

PS grouping for time quota types

Wage types for a quota compensation method can depend on PS grouping for time quota types.

Time quota compensation method

Time quota compensation method for which wage type is being defined.

Absence quota type

Wage types for a quota compensation method can depend on the absence quota type.

Number of wage type rule

Some companies may want to compensate current year's quota in a different way than last year's quota. If you have such a scenario, you can specify it in this view. This view offers you a method of creating different wage types for different year's quotas, the logic for which is specified in 'Comparison, Difference, Calendar year' fields. To enable this feature, you need multiple lines in this view. These lines are identified by this field, which is like serial number.

Start and end date

Period for which the record is valid.

Comparison, difference, calendar year

You can compensate quotas of different years at different rates by compensating them using different wage types. You can use these fields to build conditions which evaluate to 'true' or 'false'. When the condition will be 'true', the corresponding wage type will be selected. How to use these fields is explained through an example in SAP Help.

Comp	Diff	Year	Meaning, such as
=	–	1998	Leave year 1998
=	0	–	Current leave year (Start date of payroll period)
=	–1	–	Leave from previous year
<	0	–	Leave from prior years
–	–	–	Always

% factor

Percentage factor used to multiply the number field of the compensation. You can use this field if you want to deduct quota for 1 day, but compensate for 0.5 or 1.5 days.

Wage type

Wage type in which the quota is compensated.

Overtime

11.1 FUNCTIONALITY OVERVIEW

Functional Consultant	User	Business Process Owner	Senior Management	My Rating	Understanding Level
A	A	A	A		

In the case of overtime one is primarily interested in three things:

➢ Overtime done by an employee.
➢ Overtime approved by the management.
➢ Whether to remunerate overtime or compensate by attendance quota or both.

Overtime done by an employee is derived from his recorded time or attendance infotype 2002 by comparing it with his work schedule. The time outside the work schedule is overtime. If the work schedule is dynamically determined, the changed work schedule is considered. The overtime can also be recorded in infotype 2005. In this case there is no comparison done with work schedule.

Overtimes are not recognized unless management approves them. SAP provides various methods of overtime approval.

➢ Entries in infotype 2005 do not require any approval. It is presumed that overtime is approved before they are entered in infotype 2005.
➢ You can have automatic approval of overtime of all employees. This is done by PCR TO16.
➢ You can also have automatic approval of overtime of specific employees. This is done by PCR TO10. The employees are identified in infotype 0050.
➢ You can also have automatic approval of overtime for all employees working in a particular shift (daily work schedule). This is done by PCR TO15. The daily work schedules, for which overtime approval is automatic, are identified in table T550A.

➢ Other overtime approvals are entered in the system by creating an attendance quota in infotype 2007. The quota is deducted when overtime is approved in time evaluation in PCR TO20.

For those time pairs, which are recognized as approved overtime, function GWT creates time wage types and inserts them in table ZML. The rules for generating time wage types are defined in table T510S (Time Wage Type Selection Rule).

The wage types in table ZML may be paid, compensated by time off, or a combination of both. For some wage types, company rules may permit an employee to choose from these options. These specifications come from processing class 17 of wage type. If employee has an option, that information, overtime compensation type, comes from the infotypes. Function POVT processes table ZML and PCR TC40 creates appropriate time type balances in table TES. It also creates entries in table DZL where the employee needs to be paid.

If the company permits the employees to choose the method of compensation, this too is supported. For more details, see chapter 11.4 on Overtime Compensation Types.

Accumulated time balances can also be converted into wage types later, either by function LIMIT or by specific time transfer through infotype 2012.

11.2 TECHNICAL OVERVIEW

Functional Consultant	User	Business Process Owner	Senior Management	My Rating	Understanding Level
A	B	C	X		

Time evaluation with clock times	Overtime technical overview (Subset of schema TM00)
Provide time pairs and daily WS P2011	The employee's attendance is imported in table TIP from infotype 2011
Provide attendance data of the day P2002	The employee's attendance is imported in table TIP from infotype 2002
Provide overtime data of the day P2005	You can enter overtime data in infotype 2005, instead of 2002. In the daily work schedule table T550A, you define whether records in infotype 2005 can be created. If they are allowed, you can also restrict them from being created during core time.
	In time evaluation, overtime records from infotype 2005 are imported in table TIP by function P2005, which sets pair type '1', origin indicator 'O', overtime compensation type from the record and time id 01, 07 and 08 (overtime pair, unpaid overtime break, paid overtime break).

(Contd.)

Time evaluation with clock times	*Overtime technical overview (Subset of schema TM00)*
Set PTYPE/TTYPE for overtime PTIP TD40 GEN	These time pairs are further processed by PCR TD40, which sets the processing type of the overtime pairs imported from infotype 2005 to 'M' and adds hours in time type 0040.
Assign time type to time pair TIMTP	This function compares the work schedule TZP and actual time in TIP, and creates multiple records in TIP based on their overlap. The time outside the work schedule is overtime. If the work schedule is dynamically determined, the changed work schedule is considered. After this, these records are evaluated for time identifier and pair type. Based on these, processing type and time type is determined from T555Z. Depending on the source of attendance, absence information, the time type is usually 0310, 0320 or 0330.
Calculate overtime with quota 2007 01 GOT TO20 01	Function GOT with PCR TO20 compares the overtime done with attendance quota in infotype 2007. It also checks that the employee has completed his planned working hours. It also ensures that the employee's normal working hours + overtime does not exceed the maximum working hours for a day, which you specify in table T511K (TGMAX). If all the prerequisites are met, the overtime pair is assigned the processing type M and the corresponding time type for overtime. Attendance quota in infotype 2007 is appropriately reduced. It is necessary that the attendance quota type in table T556P is deductible through time evaluation. Since function GOT does not select time pairs with processing type M, the time pairs of infotype 2005 are not considered for the approval process set up by this function.
Evaluate overtime approval in I0050 PTIP TO10 GEN	If an employee has standard overtime approval in infotype 0050, this step converts an unapproved overtime pair into an approved one (processing type M). It also ensures that the employee has worked the planned hours before getting overtime, and that his total work including overtime do not exceed TGMAX value in table T511K.
Evaluate overtime approval in daily WS PTIP TO15 GEN	If an employee has a daily work schedule for which 'Automatic overtime' is allowed in the Daily Work Schedule (V_T550A), this step converts his unapproved overtime pair into an approved one (processing type M). It also ensures that the employee has worked the planned hours before getting overtime, and that his total work, including overtime, does not exceed TGMAX value in table T511K.

(Contd.)

Time evaluation with clock times	*Overtime technical overview (Subset of schema TM00)*
Determine overtime without approval PTIP TO16 GEN	This step converts an employee's unapproved overtime pair into an approved one (processing type M) unconditionally. It also ensures that the employee has worked the planned hours before getting overtime, and that his total work, including overtime, does not exceed TGMAX value in table T511K.
Wage type selection for overtime GWT M ZML	At this point, all overtime pairs are identified by processing type M. Function GWT generates time wage types from time pairs in table TIP, according to the rules in table T510S, Time Wage Type Selection Rule, and inserts them in table ZML.
Overtime compensation POVT TC40 GEN	The wage types in table ZML may be paid, compensated by time off, or a combination of both. For some wage types, company rules may permit an employee to choose from these options. These specifications come from processing class 17 of wage type. If employee has an option, that information, overtime compensation type, comes from the infotypes. Function POVT processes table ZML and PCR TC40 creates appropriate time type balances in table TES. It also creates entries in table DZL where the employee needs to be paid.
Form day balances RTIP TR10	This PCR adds day balances of time types 0310, 0320 and 0330 into 0301.
Flextime balance/overtime/ productive hrs ACTIO TR30	This PCR computes day balance in time type 0040 by adding time types 0041, 0042 and 0043.
Limits for time balances LIMIT	If you wish to limit the overtime time types at day level, you configure the same in table T559P, and function LIMIT applies it at day level.
Update balances, wage types CUMBT	Function CUMBT transfers the contents of table DZL to table ZL, which is read in payroll by function ZLIT.
Transfer excess flextime to overtime P2007 TS20 GEN	The PCR TS20 transfers the overtime balance in excess of GLMAX in table T511K to attendance quota. The quota is generated by operations UPDTQ and COLTQ.
Adjust flextime balance LIMIT	If you wish to limit the overtime time types at period level, you configure the same in table T559P, and function LIMIT applies it at period level in final processing.

Important fields of table TIP for processing overtime

Field	Values
Pair type	1, 3
Time id	01 (unapproved overtime), 07, 08, 09
Processing type	M (Overtime pair)
Time type	See list below
Overtime compensation type	
Origin indicator for time pairs	O (for infotype 2005)

Important operations in overtime

Operation	Description
ADDZL	Cumulate in time wage types table
OUTOT	Provide data on overtime wage types
GENOT	Generate time pairs for overtime
UPDTQ	Accrue absence quota
COLTQ	Increase amount of quota taken

Important time types in overtime

Time type	Description
0040	Overtime worked
0041	Overtime to compensate
0042	Overtime to remunerate
0043	Overtime basic/time off
0301	Overtime
0310	Overtime Attendance
0320	Overtime Absence
0330	Overtime Off-site
0407	Overtime offset
0410	Time off from overtime
0411	Overtime exceeding quota

11.3 OVERTIME (INFOTYPE 2005)

Functional Consultant	User	Business Process Owner	Senior Management	My Rating	Understanding Level
A	A	A	A		

11.3.1 Screen

```
Overtime
  Time                                      -              ☐ Prev.day
  Overtime hours
  Overtime comp. type      Depends on wage type          📋


Breaks
  Break 1          -            Unpaid              Paid
  Break 2          -            Unpaid              Paid
  Break 3          -            Unpaid              Paid
  Break 4          -            Unpaid              Paid
```

11.3.2 Purpose

You can use the overtime infotype (2005) to enter hours worked in addition to the employee's planned working time specified in the daily work schedule. The overtime infotype (2005) is normally used if time evaluation is not implemented. Time evaluation evaluates overtime automatically. You can use this infotype:

➤ If you record your employees' actual times in the attendances infotype (2002). This allows you to document overtime hours separately.
➤ To store special overtime data, that is, on overtime that is paid at a different rate than usual.

In the daily work schedule table T550A, you define whether records in infotype 2005 can be created. If they are allowed, you can also restrict them from being created during core time.

In time evaluation, these records are imported in table TIP by function P2005, which sets pair type '1', origin indicator 'O', overtime compensation type from the record and time id 01, 07 and 08 (overtime pair, unpaid overtime break, paid overtime break). These time pairs are further processed by PCR TD40, which sets the processing type of the overtime pairs imported from infotype 2005 to 'M'.

Since function GOT does not select time pairs with processing type M, these time pairs are not considered for the approval process set up by that function. For these time pairs, time wage types are generated by function GWT.

11.3.3 Subtypes

No subtypes

11.3.4 Time Constraint

Z (Time constraint for time management infotypes -> T554Y)

11.3.5 Important Fields

Start and end time

Here you specify the start and end time for overtime.

Previous day indicator

You tick this if the end time is on the next day.

Overtime hours

You can enter the hours directly without specifying the start and end time. If you enter start and end time, it is computed by the system. If you enter breaks, unpaid break times are subtracted from the overtime hours.

Overtime compensation type

If the employees have a choice of deciding whether they want to receive payment or time off or a combination of the two, that choice is captured here. For more details, see chapter 11.4 (T555R).

Blank	Depends on wage type
1	Remuneration
2	Time off plus overtime rate
3	Compensation (time off)

Breaks

You can specify up to 4 breaks, specifying the start time, end time, and whether the break is paid, unpaid or partially paid. Unpaid break times are subtracted from overtime hours.

11.4 OVERTIME COMPENSATION TYPES

Functional Consultant	User	Business Process Owner	Senior Management	My Rating	Understanding Level
A	C	C	X		

11.4.1 Purpose and Overview

When an employee does overtime, a company may want to

➢ Pay the employee.
➢ Give the employee time off.
➢ Use a combination of payment and time off.

In SAP, wage types for overtime are generated in table ZML.

A company may want to use different policies for different wage types. These are specified in processing class 17 of the wage type. You can use this flexibility to generate different wage types for officers and workers, and pay one category, and give time off to another.

Some companies want to give the choice to employees and let the employees choose the method of compensation. SAP supports this functionality. It lets the company specify the wage types for which the employees have a choice, and the wage types for which the employees have no choice. This is specified in processing class 17 of the wage type.

The employee choice comes as overtime compensation type in infotypes 2002, 2005, 2007 and 2010. It can also come from Cross-Application Time Sheet (CATS). You write a PCR (see TC40 for guideline) to process them appropriately. If the employee does not make any choice, the default behaviour is also defined in the processing class, and implemented through the same PCR.

11.4.2 IMG Node

SM30 ➢ T555R

11.4.3 Screen

O..	Text
	Depends on wage type
1	Remuneration
2	Time off plus overtime rate
3	Compensation (time off)

11.4.4 Primary Key

Overtime Compensation Type

12 *Availability*

12.1 AVAILABILITY (INFOTYPE 2004)

Functional Consultant	User	Business Process Owner	Senior Management	My Rating	Understanding Level
B	B	B	B		

12.1.1 Screen

Availability type ☑

Availability with fixed time

Time [   ] - [   ] ☐ Prev.day

Or according to daily work schedule

Daily work schedule [   ]
DWS grouping [20]
Daily WS variant [   ]

Or according to work schedule rule

ES grouping [   ]
Holiday calendar ID [   ]
PS grouping [   ]
Work schedule rule [   ]

12.1.2 Purpose and Overview

There are situations where you do not need a person to be physically present, but to be available in case a need arises. Availability is work performed outside of an employee's planned working time. When you create availability, the system does not overwrite the employee's work schedule.

You need to specify the timings for such availability. Infotype 2004 lets you do that. There are three methods of specifying availability.

➤ Availability with fixed time

- ‣ Use this availability variant if an employee has availability duty for a specific interval of time. This particular variant is intended primarily to record periods of availability that are outside the employee's planned working time specified in the daily work schedule.
- ‣ For flextime daily work schedules, the period of time should also be outside the normal working time. If availability periods overlap with times stipulated in the employee's daily work schedule, the system displays a warning, but still allows you to create the record.
- ‣ In on-call duty the times specified are not interpreted as an interval for on-call duty, but indicate the start and end times of a complete on-call record.

➤ Availability according to daily work schedule

- ‣ Use this availability type for planned working times or availability times stipulated in the daily work schedule. Unlike availability with fixed time, these times may overlap those specified in the employee's work schedule. In this way, you can enter an availability that is valid during an employee's normal working time.
- ‣ For this availability type, you can only use the daily work schedules that you have defined as permitted in V_550A_B.

➤ Availability according to work schedule rule

- ‣ You use this availability type if you want to take into account the work cycle specified in the period work schedule. The times of this availability type may also overlap the work schedule.
- ‣ For this availability type, you can only use the work schedule rules that you have defined as permitted in V_508A_B.

Availabilities can be paid for, either based on availability types or based on different payment. Availabilities are imported in the schema by function P2004. Note that this function is not there in schemas TM00–TM04. Hence, if you want to process availability, you have to include this function in the schema.

12.1.3 Subtypes

Availability type

12.1.4 Time Constraint

Z (Time constraint for time management infotypes -> T554Y)

12.1.5 Important Fields

Availability type

In this field, you enter the type of availability, selecting from the master list applicable to your company.

Availability type	☑

Availability with fixed time		
Time	–	☐ Prev.day

Start and end time

For on-call availability, the start time is for 'from date', and end time is for 'to date'. For other availabilities, the duty is from start time to end time each day.

Previous day indicator

This indicator is set if the end time is on the next calendar day.

Or according to daily work schedule	
Daily work schedule	
DWS grouping	20
Daily WS variant	

PS grouping for daily work schedules

For an employee, this is determined from his PA and PSA.

Daily work schedule and variant

There are some daily work schedules, which are permitted to be used for availability (see V_550A_B). You can assign one of those here.

Or according to work schedule rule	
ES grouping	
Holiday calendar ID	
PS grouping	
Work schedule rule	

View V_508A_B shows the work schedule rules, which are permitted to be used for availability. When you select one of them, all the four fields get populated.

12.2 AVAILABILITY TYPE

Functional Consultant	User	Business Process Owner	Senior Management	My Rating	Understanding Level
B	B	C	X		

12.2.1 Purpose

This view contains the master list of availability types.

12.2.2 IMG Node

SM30 ➤ V_T557

12.2.3 Screen

PSG	AvailType	Availability type text	Avail.ty...	TCC	Avail	Cal	Shift	Shift
01	01	On-call duty	R	01		◉	○	○
01	02	Availability <=10%	1	02		◉	○	○
01	03	Availability <=25%	2	02		◉	○	○
01	04	Availability <=40%	3	02		◉	○	○

12.2.4 Primary Key

PS Grouping for Substitution/Availability Types + Availability Type

12.2.5 Important Fields

PS grouping for substitution/availability types

The definition of availability type can change depending on the PS grouping for substitution/availability types.

Availability subtype and text

Master list of availability types which you use in infotype 2004.

Internal key for availability duty

This field is for use in German payroll only.

Time constraint class

You have to carefully choose the time constraint class, particularly where the absences can co-exist with availability and where they cannot.

Availability for on-call duty

You use availability to specify whether an employee is available for other work activities if he or she has been assigned this availability type. For example, if you assign an employee an availability that has been flagged as 'not available', the employee cannot work any more shifts during this availability.

0	Not Available
1	Available
3	Available On-call
9	Not Relevant

Availability type

This specifies whether the availability type refers to an on-call duty, an availability duty or an availability shift.

12.3 DAILY WORK SCHEDULES: PERMISSIBILITY FOR AVAILABILITY

Functional Consultant	User	Business Process Owner	Senior Management	My Rating	Understanding Level
B	C	X	X		

12.3.1 Purpose

This view defines which daily work schedules are permitted for availability.

12.3.2 IMG Node

SM30 ➢ V_550A_B

12.3.3 Screen

Grpg	Daily ...	Variant	Daily WS text	Start Date	End Date	Availability
01	EXEC		8-4:30	01.01.1990	31.12.9999	☐
01	F-11		Early shift	01.01.1990	31.12.9999	☐
01	FLEX		Flexible	01.01.1990	31.12.9999	☐
01	FREI		Off	01.01.1990	31.12.9999	☑

12.4 WORK SCHEDULE RULE: AVAILABILITY

Functional Consultant	User	Business Process Owner	Senior Management	My Rating	Understanding Level
B	X	X	X		

12.4.1 Purpose

This view defines which work schedule rules are permitted for availability.

12.4.2 IMG Node

SM30 ➤ V_508A_B

12.4.3 Screen

E...	ES grpg for WS	H...	Text	PSG	WS rule	Start Date	End Date	Availability
1	Hourly wage earn...	01	Germany (S...	26	TH5D	01.01.1990	31.12.9999	☐
1	Hourly wage earn...	01	Germany (S...	26	TH6D	01.01.1990	31.12.9999	☐
1	Hourly wage earn...	08	Germany (B...	01	GLZ	01.01.1990	31.12.9999	☑
1	Hourly wage earn...	08	Germany (B...	01	KUG	01.01.1990	31.12.9999	☐

Time Recording

13.1 TIME RECORDING (INFOTYPE 0050)

Functional Consultant	User	Business Process Owner	Senior Management	My Rating	Understanding Level
A	A	B	C		

13.1.1 Purpose and Overview

Infotype 0050 is the chief coordinator between SAP and time recording systems. Here you maintain information to control recording of attendance and other time events.

Infotype 0050 is used only if employee time data is accounted using the time evaluation program. Infotype 0050 must be created for each employee who will enter data at a time recording terminal.

The number on your id card does not have to be personnel number. It can be any other unique number, which can be linked to personnel number through the linkage stored here. Further, in the case of loss of an id card, you can issue a new one, and also ensure that the old one cannot be used for time recording any longer.

SAP, in conjunction with a suitable time recording system, supports a variety of functionalities; some of which are described here.

When employees clock-in or clock-out, the data they generate is called time events. SAP supports a variety of time events, e.g. start of break, end of break, etc., and not just clock-in and clock-out. Apart from time events, SAP can also capture work events.

SAP recognizes that all employees may not be permitted to use all time events, or work events. This is achieved in the following steps:

> Define time event groups in table T705F.
> Assign time event groups to an employee in infotype 0050.
> Download time event groups to employee linkage to time recording system using message type HRCC1DNPERSO (HR-PDC: Download HR Mini-Master).
> Define time events, which are a part of a time event group in table T705P, and download to the time recording system using message type HRCC1DNTEVGR (HR-PDC: Download time event type groups).
> The time recording system then uses this information to allow an employee to record only those types of time events, which he is permitted to record.

Employees can also specify attendance/absence reasons at the time recording system, which is collected and processed by SAP. In order to ensure that an employee uses only those attendance/absence reasons, which he is allowed to use, the following steps are required:

> Define grouping of attendance/absence reasons in table T705I.
> Assign grouping of attendance/absence reasons to an employee in infotype 0050.
> Download grouping of attendance/absence reasons to employee linkage to time recording system using message type HRCC1DNPERSO (HR-PDC: Download HR Mini-Master).
> Define attendance/absence reasons, which are part of a grouping of attendance/absence reasons in table T705A, and download to the time recording system using message type HRCC1DNATTAB (HR-PDC: Download permitted attendance/absence reasons).
> The time recording system then uses this information to allow an employee to record only those attendance/absence reasons, which he is permitted to record.

Employees can also record expenditures at the time recording system, which is collected and processed by SAP. In order to ensure that an employee uses only those expenditures, which he is allowed to, following steps are required:

> Define grouping for employee expenses in table T705J.
> Assign grouping for employee expenses to an employee in infotype 0050.
> Download grouping for employee expenses to employee linkage to time recording system using message type HRCC1DNPERSO (HR-PDC: Download HR Mini-Master).
> Define employee expenditure, which are a part of a grouping for employee expenses in table T705K, and download to the time recording system using message type HRCC1DNEXTWT (HR-PDC: Download permitted external wage types).
> The time recording system then uses this information to allow an employee to record only those expenditures, which he is permitted to record.
> Employee expenditures are uploaded from time recording systems using message type HRCC1UPEXTWT (HR-PDC: Upload external wage types). They are stored in table TEXLGA.
> The Run batch input sessions (RPIEWT04) report then creates data records for the infotypes 2010 or 0015.

SAP permits two type of access control—access control according to sites and access control according to time. The first is implemented as follows:

> Define groupings for connection to subsystem in table T705T.
> Assign groupings for connection to subsystem to an employee in infotype 0050.
> Download grouping for connection to subsystem to employee linkage to time recording system using message type HRCC1DNPERSO (HR-PDC: Download HR Mini-Master).
> Define the access control restrictions on the time recording system.
> The time recording system then uses this information to control access of an employee as per his authorization.
> Groupings for connection to subsystem are also used to restrict access to work centers. These are defined in tables T705R and CRHD.

SAP's access control according to time is implemented as follows:

> Define access control groups (time-restricted) in table T555O.
> Assign access control groups (time-restricted) to an employee in infotype 0050.
> Download access control groups (time-restricted) to employee linkage to time recording system using message type HRCC1DNPERSO (HR-PDC: Download HR Mini-Master).
> Define time profiles for each access control group on the time recording system.
> The time recording system then uses this information to control access of an employee as per his authorized time profile.

Employees can see their time balances on the time recording system. This is implemented as follows:

> Define the fields for which you want to show employee balances in table T555I.
> Download the time/quota/incentive wages balances for employees to time recording system using message type HRCC1DNBALAN (HR-PDC: Download employee balances).
> The time recording system then displays this information to the employees.

SAP lets you assign a personal code for a person in infotype 0050, which is downloaded to time recording system. This contains the employee's personal code which he must enter at the time recording terminal to be granted access.

SAP also lets you assign a mail indicator for a person in infotype 0050, which is downloaded to time recording system. When the employee records time, the mail indicator is interpreted by the time recording system, and a message is shown.

Usually, the rules to be applied during time evaluation depend on the employee's organizational assignment. However, if your requirements are not satisfied by that, SAP provides you more flexibility as under:

> Create employee grouping for the time evaluation rule in table T555N.
> Assign these groupings to an employee in infotype 0050.
> Write a PCR, where you query this grouping using operation OUTTI, parameter ABART. Depending on the value write your logic.
> Call the PCR in time evaluation schema.

HR mini-master record is downloaded regardless of the employee's status. Therefore, when an employee leaves the company, you must delimit infotype 0050, if you do not want left employees to interact with the system.

13.1.2 Screen

Time ID	
Time rec.ID no.	☑
ID version	

Interface data		Time variables	
Time event type grp	☑	Grpg for TE rule	
Subsystem grouping	☑	Flextime maximum	
Grpg. att./absence	☑	Flextime minimum	
EE expenses grpng	☑	Time bonus/deduction	
Access control group		Standard overtime	
Mail indicator		Additional indicator	
Personal code			

13.1.3 Subtypes

No subtypes

13.1.4 Time Constraint

2 (Record may include gaps, no overlappings)

13.1.5 Important Fields

Time ID	
Time rec.ID no.	☑
ID version	

Time recording ID number

This is the number on your id card. It cannot exist for any other personnel number. When recorded time data is loaded in SAP, the system uses this to determine the personnel number.

ID version

If your employee loses his id card, he should be given a new id card with the same time recording id number, but of next version. If the employee swipes his old id card, this information in infotype 0050 detects that and makes it an invalid swipe.

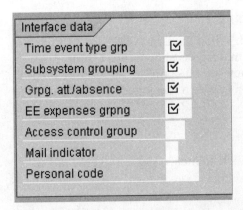

Interface data comprises information required by the time recording terminals.

Work time event type group

In SAP, when you record time, it is associated with a time event type, which describes what type of time event it is. You can group the event types, and assign it to an employee here, thus restricting him from recording event types, which he is not authorized to record.

Grouping for connection to subsystem

You must enter the subsystem grouping for employees who clock-in/out at a time recording terminal. This field specifies the time recording terminals to which an employee's mini-master records are downloaded.

Also, if you want to control access to your sites, you need to define your site access policies. You may not give same access to all the employees. Hence you need to divide your employees in groups. This grouping is used for that purpose. It is downloaded to the time recording systems and work centers. Based on the group to which an employee belongs, the time recording system/work center decides what access he is allowed.

Grouping of attendance/absence reasons

If your time recording terminal allows employee to enter attendance/absence reasons, you can create groups of attendance/absence reasons, and assign to an employee. In this way you prevent him from entering attendance/absence reasons, which he is not allowed to.

Grouping for employee expenses

This grouping allows the employee to enter only those types of employee expenses at time recording terminals, which he is allowed to.

Access control group

The time recording system can carry out time-restricted access control by referencing the access control groups.

Mail indicator

If you enter a mail indicator here, it is downloaded. When the employee records time, the mail indicator is interpreted by the system, and a message is shown. For example, if you want to communicate to some employees that they are to come in night shift on 10th February, you can do so. Alternatively, you could just give a message that the employees should contact their supervisor for shift change.

Personal code

This field contains the employee's personal code, which he must enter at the time recording terminal, to be granted access.

Time variables	
Grpg for TE rule	
Flextime maximum	
Flextime minimum	
Time bonus/deduction	
Standard overtime	
Additional indicator	

Here you can set special indicators that can be queried in time evaluation. These indicators are user-definable and can be queried and processed in user-specific personnel calculation rules.

Employee grouping for time evaluation rule

Usually, the rules to be applied during time evaluation depend on the employee's organizational assignment. However, if your requirements are not satisfied by that, you can create the groupings here, which you can query in time evaluation and write your logic in PCRs based on these. In these PCRs, you query this grouping using operation OUTTI, parameter ABART.

Flextime maximum and flextime minimum

In standard SAP, you maintain the minimum and maximum flextime which applies to all employees. If you want to control these at employee level, you can store them here. These are not processed by the standard system. You need to write the PCRs to use these.

Time bonus/deduction

Here, you can maintain a general time bonus or deduction for an employee. This is not processed by the standard system. You need to write the PCRs to use this.

Standard overtime

If a person works overtime, your company may have an approval process, without which the overtime is not recognized. Alternatively, you may not require an approval process. This can be set at global level. You can also specify at employee level that overtime does not require approval, by putting X in this field.

In time evaluation, PCR TO10, along with PCRs TO16 and TO11, ensure that you have worked the planned hours before getting overtime, and that your total work, including overtime, does not exceed TGMAX in table T511K.

Additional indicator

This is a free field for you to define and use.

13.2 WORK TIME EVENT TYPE GROUPS

Functional Consultant	User	Business Process Owner	Senior Management	My Rating	Understanding Level
A	C	X	X		

13.2.1 Purpose and Overview

SAP recognizes that all employees may not be permitted to use all time events, or work events. This is achieved in the following steps:

➢ Define time event groups in table T705F.
➢ Assign time event groups to an employee in infotype 0050.
➢ Download time event groups to employee linkage to time recording system using message type HRCC1DNPERSO (HR-PDC: Download HR Mini-Master).
➢ Define time events, which are part of a time event group in table T705P, and download to the time recording system via message type HRCC1DNTEVGR (HR-PDC: Download time event type groups).
➢ The time recording system then uses this information to allow an employee to record only those types of time events, which he is permitted to record.

13.2.2 IMG Node

SM30 ➢ T705F

13.2.3 Screen

T..	Text
1	All time events
2	Pers. time events w/off-site
3	Pers. time events w/o off-site

13.2.4 Primary Key

Work time event type group

13.3 TIME EVENT TYPES IN WORK TIME EVENT TYPE GROUPS

Functional Consultant	User	Business Process Owner	Senior Management	My Rating	Understanding Level
A	C	X	X		

13.3.1 Purpose and Overview

SAP recognizes that all employees may not be permitted to use all time events or work events. This is achieved in the following steps:

➢ Define time event groups in table T705F.
➢ Assign time event groups to an employee in infotype 0050.
➢ Download time event groups to employee linkage to time recording system using message type HRCC1DNPERSO (HR-PDC: Download HR Mini-Master).
➢ Define time events, which are a part of a time event group in table T705P, and download to the time recording system via message type HRCC1DNTEVGR (HR-PDC: Download time event type groups).
➢ The time recording system then uses this information to allow an employee to record only those types of time events, which he is permitted to record.

13.3.2 IMG Node

SM30 ➢ T705P

13.3.3 Screen

Ti...	Tim...	Tm.event type text
02	P10	Clock-in
02	P11	Change
02	P15	Start of break
02	P20	Clock-out

13.3.4 Primary Key

Work Time Event Type Group + Time Event Type

13.3.5 Important Fields

Work time event type group

Work time event type group to which the time event types are assigned.

Time event type

When you record time, it is associated with a time event type, which describes what type of time event it is, e.g. clock-in, clock-out. These are predefined by SAP and include both time events and work events.

13.4 GROUPING OF ATTENDANCE/ABSENCE REASONS

Functional Consultant	User	Business Process Owner	Senior Management	My Rating	Understanding Level
B	X	X	X		

13.4.1 Purpose and Overview

Employees can also specify attendance/absence reasons at the time recording system, which is collected and processed by SAP. In order to ensure that an employee uses only those attendance/absence reasons, which he is allowed to, the following steps are required:

➢ Define grouping of attendance/absence reasons in table T705I.
➢ Assign grouping of attendance/absence reasons to an employee in infotype 0050.
➢ Download grouping of attendance/absence reasons to employee linkage to time recording system using message type HRCC1DNPERSO (HR-PDC: Download HR Mini-Master).
➢ Define attendance/absence reasons, which are part of a grouping of attendance/ absence reasons in table T705A, and download to the time recording system via message type HRCC1DNATTAB (HR-PDC: Download permitted att./absence reasons).
➢ The time recording system then uses this information to allow an employee to record only those attendance/absence reasons, which he is permitted to record.

13.4.2 IMG Node

SM30 ➢ V_T705I

13.4.3   Screen

Grpg. att./absence	Text
001	SAP default 001
002	SAP default 002

13.4.4   Primary Key

Grouping of Attendance/Absence Reasons.

13.5   ATTENDANCE/ABSENCE REASONS FOR SUBSYSTEM

Functional Consultant	User	Business Process Owner	Senior Management	My Rating	Understanding Level
B	X	X	X		

13.5.1   Purpose and Overview

Employees can enter their absence and attendance reasons directly at the terminal if the configuration of your time recording system supports this function. The system uses this information to create a partial day absence record for the period the employee was absent. The absence type of the record depends on the absence reason. Thus, you may allow employees to go for doctor's appointment, but deduct salary if he has gone to bank.

Employee can also enter an absence reason to indicate that he will be absent on the subsequent day, or why was he absent on the previous day. An absence or attendance reason can be entered with both clock-in (P10) and clock-out (P20) time events.

SAP allows you to specify which employees are allowed to enter what set of attendance/ absence reasons. In order to ensure that an employee uses only those attendance/ absence reasons, which he is allowed to, the following steps are required:

➤ Define grouping of attendance/absence reasons in table T705I.
➤ Assign grouping of attendance/absence reasons to an employee in infotype 0050.
➤ Download grouping of attendance/absence reasons to employee linkage to time recording system using message type HRCC1DNPERSO (HR-PDC: Download HR Mini-Master).
➤ Define attendance/absence reasons, which are part of a grouping of attendance/absence reasons in table T705A, and download to the time recording system via message type HRCC1DNATTAB (HR-PDC: Download permitted att./absence reasons). This is done using program RPTCC103 (HR-PDC: Download attendance/absence reasons).
➤ The time recording system then uses this information to allow an employee to record only those attendance/absence reasons, which he is permitted to record.

In time management schema TM00, attendance/absence reasons are processed in the following steps:

> PTIP TD80 GEN: If the employee enters attendance/absence reason, this PCR generates a locked record of partial absence for current day or full day absence for subsequent or previous day, and puts it in TIP.

> ACTIO TD90: If the current day is a day off (daily work schedule class '0' or day type > '0'), the automatically generated record is extended by one day.

After the locked records are created by attendance/absence reason, they have to be unlocked and time evaluation has to be rerun.

13.5.2 IMG Node

SM30 ➤ V_T705A

13.5.3 Screen

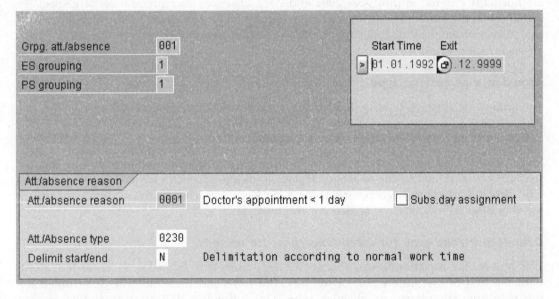

13.5.4 Primary Key

Grouping of Attendance/Absence Reasons + ES Grouping for Work Schedules + PS Grouping for Absence and Attendance Types + Attendance/Absence Reason + End Date.

13.5.5 Important Fields

Grouping of attendance/absence reasons

Attendance/absence type, which is determined from attendance/absence reason, can be different for different groupings of attendance/absence reasons. Grouping of attendance/absence reasons for an employee is specified in infotype 0050.

ES grouping for work schedules

Attendance/absence type, which is determined from attendance/absence reason, can be different for different ES groupings for work schedules.

PS grouping for absence and attendance types

Attendance/absence type, which is determined from attendance/absence reason, can be different for different PS groupings for absence and attendance types.

Start and end date

Validity period of the record.

Attendance/absence reason

If you work with time recording, employees can enter attendance and absence reasons when they clock-in or clock-out at the terminal. The attendance and absence types which are normally entered in infotypes 2001 and 2002, absences and attendances, are specially coded when the system is customized so that they can be processed by the terminals. You can correct or enter these codes manually in the time events infotype in the attendance/absence reasons field.

Attendance or absence type

Attendance or absence type is determined from attendance/absence reason.

Subsequent day assignment for attendance/absence reasons

You can set the subsequent day assignment indicator if you want an attendance or absence reason to be assigned to the subsequent day. If an attendance or absence reason flagged with this indicator has been recorded for a clock-in or clock-out, the system generates a full-day attendance/absence record for the next day.

Delimit start/end time for attendance/absence reasons

If a reason for an attendance/absence of less than one workday is recorded along with the first or last time event of the day, the start/end time must be determined for the resulting attendance or absence pair. The following delimitation indicators are used:

Blank	Delimitation is controlled in rule processing
C	Delimitation according to core work time
N	Delimitation according to normal work time
P	Delimitation according to planned working time

13.6 GROUPINGS FOR CONNECTION TO SUBSYSTEM

Functional Consultant	User	Business Process Owner	Senior Management	My Rating	Understanding Level
B	X	X	X		

13.6.1 Purpose

SAP permits two type of access control—access control according to sites and access control according to time. The first is implemented as follows:

➤ Define groupings for connection to subsystem in table T705T.
➤ Assign groupings for connection to subsystem to an employee in infotype 0050.
➤ Download grouping for connection to subsystem to employee linkage to time recording system using message type HRCC1DNPERSO (HR-PDC: Download HR Mini-Master).
➤ Define the access control restrictions on the time recording system.
➤ The time recording system then uses this information to control access of an employee as per his authorization.
➤ Groupings for connection to subsystem are also used to restrict access to work centers. These are defined in tables T705R and CRHD.

13.6.2 IMG Node

SM30 ➤ V_T705T

13.6.3 Screen

Subsystem grouping	Text
001	SAP default 001
002	SAP default 002

13.6.4 Primary Key

Grouping for connection to subsystem

13.7 TIME PROFILES

Functional Consultant	User	Business Process Owner	Senior Management	My Rating	Understanding Level
B	X	X	X		

13.7.1 Purpose and Overview

SAP's access control, according to time, is implemented as follows:

➤ Define access control groups (time-restricted) in table T555O, for each PS grouping for time recording.
➤ Assign access control groups (time-restricted) to an employee in infotype 0050.
➤ Download access control groups (time-restricted) to employee linkage to time recording system using message type HRCC1DNPERSO (HR-PDC: Download HR Mini-Master).
➤ Define time profiles for each access control group on the time recording system.
➤ The time recording system then uses this information to control access of an employee as per his authorized time profile.

13.7.2 IMG Node

SM30 ➤ V_T555O

13.7.3 Screen

PSG	Access control group	Text
01	00	ALL LOCATIONS
01	01	GENERAL OFFICE
01	02	SAP default

13.7.4 Primary Key

PS Grouping for Time Recording + Access Control Group

13.8 PDC MASTER RECORD INFORMATION

Functional Consultant	User	Business Process Owner	Senior Management	My Rating	Understanding Level
B	X	X	X		

13.8.1 Purpose and Overview

Employees can see their time balances on the time recording system. This is implemented as follows:

> Define the fields for which you want to show employee balances in table T555I.
> Download the time/quota/incentive wages balances for employees to time recording system using message type HRCC1DNBALAN (HR-PDC: Download employee balances). This is done using program RPTCC102 (HRPDC: Download employee time balances).
> The time recording system then displays this information to the employees.

The data you display to employees can depend on ES grouping and PS grouping. These are downloaded in HR mini-master.

13.8.2 IMG Node

SM30 ➤ V_T555I

13.8.3 Screen

ESG	PSG	Info field no.	Start Date	End Date	Info fld	Hrs-min
1	01	0	01.01.1901	31.12.9999	ARD	☐
1	01	1	01.01.1901	31.12.9999	DATE	☐
1	01	2	01.01.1901	31.12.9999	URLR	☐
1	01	3	01.01.1901	31.12.9999	URLB	☐

13.8.4 Primary Key

ES Grouping for Work Schedules + PS Grouping for Time Recording + Info Field Number + End Date

13.8.5 Important Fields

ES grouping for work schedules

Note that there is no ES grouping for time recording. That is why ES grouping for work schedules is used.

PS grouping for time recording

Information downloaded to employees can be different for different PS grouping for time recording.

Info field number

This determines the sequence in which the fields are shown.

Start and end date

Validity period.

Info field

Info field contents are predefined and include attendance/absence quotas and incentive data. For more details, see field help.

Hours–minutes format

Tick in this format for seeing data in hours—minutes format, instead of hours format (with fractional value in decimal).

13.9   EMPLOYEE GROUPING FOR THE TIME EVALUATION RULE

Functional Consultant	User	Business Process Owner	Senior Management	My Rating	Understanding Level
B	X	X	X		

13.9.1   Purpose and Overview

Usually, the rules to be applied during time evaluation depend on the employee's organizational assignment. However, if your requirements are not satisfied by that, SAP provides you more flexibility as under:

➤ Create employee grouping for the time evaluation rule in table T555N.
➤ Assign these groupings to an employee in infotype 0050.
➤ Write a PCR, where you query this grouping using operation OUTTI, parameter ABART. Depending on the value write your logic.
➤ Call the PCR in time evaluation schema.

13.9.2   IMG Node

SM30 ➤ T555N

13.9.3 Screen

	Grpg for TE rule	Text
	1	Full Day VDN 01
	2	Full Day VDN 02
	3	Full Day VDN 03

13.9.4 Primary Key

Employee Grouping for the Time Evaluation Rule

Time Events

14.1 TIME EVENTS (INFOTYPE 2011)

Functional Consultant	User	Business Process Owner	Senior Management	My Rating	Understanding Level
A	A	A	A		

14.1.1 Screen

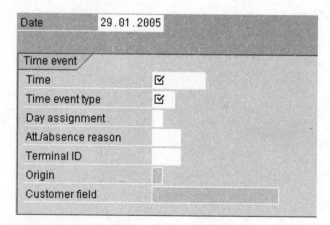

14.1.2 Purpose and Overview

Time data collection

Your employees may record the time when they come to work, or when they leave. They may also record when their lunch break starts and ends. In SAP parlance, these are called 'time events'. Your employees may also record work events, e.g. starting set-up of a machine, etc. This data needs to be transferred to SAP for further processing.

Time event data collection process may be manual, scheduled or automatic depending on the settings. Time data collection process ends with updation of TEVEN table with recorded times. There may also be reverse flow of data to time recording systems.

Time event data is collected from time recording systems. Time recording systems differ in their capability. Apart from recording the personnel number and time, when a person swipes, they may have the capability of recording the type of event, e.g. clock-in or clock-out, reason code and expenditure. The system may also be able to apply restrictions, e.g. valid personnel number and time restrictions. It may also have the capability of displaying balances for which it may download data from SAP. If the time event type is not recorded in the system, SAP may automatically determine it from the employee's attendance status at the time it is entered.

Time/work event data may also be collected from other modules of SAP and is called Plant Data Collection (PDC). It may be used for the calculation of incentive wages, etc.

Table TEVEN

Table TEVEN contains the data collected from the time recording terminals. The data can also be entered manually in infotype 2011. Time events can only be recorded for employees who take part in time recording. This must be specified in the planned working time infotype (0007). The employee must also be assigned an authorization for the required time event types in the time recording information infotype (0050).

The data contained in a record is for one time event. Each time event is given a sequential number which is used for referring to it in the entire system. Pairing of time events is done during time evaluation.

This is the only table that does not follow the table naming convention for infotypes; the table name is TEVEN, not PA2011. It also does not have the first two includes that all infotypes have.

Program SAPCDT45, HR PDC: Posting Personnel Time Events report reads the data from table CC1TEV and stores it as time events in infotype 2011 (table TEVEN).

14.1.3 Primary Key

Sequential Number for PDC Messages

14.1.4 Subtypes

No subtypes

14.1.5 Time Constraint

Z (Time constraint for time management infotypes -> T554Y)

14.1.6 Important Fields

Date and time

When an employee swipes his card, the date and time displayed on the time recording terminals are captured along with the employee id. These are stored in these fields.

Time event type

Time event types, e.g. clock-in, clock-out, start of break and end of break, are predefined by SAP. However, all time event types may not be applicable to the employee who is swiping. SAP determines the work time event type group of the employee from infotype 0050, and the event types permissible to that group from T705P. These are available here for selection.

Day assignment

The day assignment specifies whether a time event is assigned to the current day or to the previous day. If the indicator is blank when time evaluation is run, it is set automatically during pair formation and table TEVEN is updated:

=	The time event is assigned to the current day
<	The time event is assigned to the previous day

You can override this automatic assignment by making a manual entry:

+	The time event should be assigned to the current day
–	The time event should be assigned to the previous day

Attendance/absence reason

While recording time, employees can enter attendance and absence reasons when they clock-in or clock-out at the terminal. You can correct or enter these codes manually in this field.

Terminal ID

This information is useful for investigating complaints or errors in time recording.

Origin

This field is system-controlled and shows whether the time event was entered at subsystem, or it was entered or changed manually.

Customer field

This field is user-definable and can be filled in an enhancement.

14.2 NUMBER RANGE FOR TIME EVENTS AND ACCT ASSIGNMENT DATA

Functional Consultant	User	Business Process Owner	Senior Management	My Rating	Understanding Level
A	X	X	X		

14.2.1 Purpose

In SAP, all time events are given a sequential number. This node controls allotment of that number.

14.2.2 IMG Node

Transaction PA06   Number Range Maintenance: PD_SEQ_NR

14.2.3 Screen

14.3 COMMUNICATION PARAMETERS

Functional Consultant	User	Business Process Owner	Senior Management	My Rating	Understanding Level
A	X	X	X		

14.3.1 Purpose

At this node you specify the parameters that are used for communication between the SAP system and the time recording system. Here you determine whether you want to work with the Plant Data Collection: Employee Times and Expenditures Interface (HR-PDC), which is BAPI-based transfer, or with Communication Channel 1 (CC1), which is transceiver-based transfer. The settings are stored in table CC1PAR.

14.3.2 IMG Node

Transaction PT41   Customizing CC1 Communication Param.

14.3.3 Screen

HR-PDC/CC1 - active version

Upload parameters
Message receiver:

14.3.4 Primary Key

Communication Channel

14.3.5 Important Fields

HR-PDC/CC1-active version

This field determines whether an external time recording system is integrated with time management, via the HR-PDC interface or via CC1. They can also operate in parallel.

Message receiver

Administrator who should receive notification if an error occurs.

14.3.6 Remarks

You can also set up the connection from external time recording systems using sequential files. The sample Upload time events from sequential files (RPTEUP10) report is provided for this purpose. The sample Download mini-master record to sequential files (RPTEDO00) report provides the time recording system with HR mini-master records.

14.4 TIME EVENT TABLES

Functional Consultant	User	Business Process Owner	Senior Management	My Rating	Understanding Level
A	B	X	X		

14.4.1 Table CC1TEV, Temporary Buffer for Time Events from CC1

Table CC1TEV contains time events data, which is uploaded but not posted. On posting the data is put in TEVEN, and deleted from CC1TEV. It is a temporary buffer for time events coming from CC1.

All time postings recorded in the attendance recording system are read and uploaded to the SAP system using CC1 and stored in table CC1TEV. Program SAPCDT45 (HR PDC: Posting Personnel Time Events) reads the data from table CC1TEV and stores it as time events in infotype 2011 (table TEVEN). Successfully processed time events are deleted from table CC1TEV.

In case a personnel number is locked, the processing of the personnel time event is put on hold. The time event is not deleted from table CC1TEV and is available for the next posting. In case an error occurred when checking the time event, unprocessed time events are placed in time management pool.

14.4.2 Table CC1ERH, Incorrect Time Events from CC1, Header Information

When data loading goes in error, e.g. no authorization, a record is created in table CC1ERH.

14.4.3 Table CC1ERM, Incorrect Time Events from CC1, Error Messages

When data loading goes in error, e.g. no authorization, records of error messages are created in table CC1ERM.

14.4.4 Table CC1ERP, Incorrect Time Events from CC1, Postings

When data loading goes in error, e.g. no authorization, records of data are created in table CC1ERP. This table contains the records, which have gone in error. In addition to this table, header information goes in table CC1ERH, while messages go in table CC1ERM.

14.4.5 Table PDSNR, Sequential Number for PDC Messages

All PDC messages have a unique sequential number. This is stored in table PDSNR. This table contains only one record containing the last number.

Time Transfer

15.1 TIME TRANSFER SPECIFICATIONS (INFOTYPE 2012)

Functional Consultant	User	Business Process Owner	Senior Management	My Rating	Understanding Level
A	B	B	B		

15.1.1 Screen

Start	29.01.2005	To	29.01.2005

Time transfer specification		
Time transfer type	☑	Earned PL for Prev. Year
Number of hours		Hours

15.1.2 Purpose

Time transfer specifications allow you to change the time balances calculated for individual employees in time evaluation. Time transfer can transfer a time type, wage type or absence quota to another time type, wage type, or absence quota. In this infotype, you just specify the number of hours. This is read in time evaluation and the transfer specified for the time transfer type takes place.

Time transfer specifications are always made with reference to a specific validity date. If you specify a validity period, the system carries out a time transfer on each day of the period.

15.1.3 Subtypes

Employee time transfer type

15.1.4 Time Constraint

Z (Time constraint for time management infotypes -> T554Y)

15.1.5 Important Fields

Time transfer type

The time transfer type determines what kind of transfer takes place.

Number of hours

The number of hours determines the quantum of transfer.

15.2 EMPLOYEE TIME TRANSFER TYPE

Functional Consultant	User	Business Process Owner	Senior Management	My Rating	Understanding Level
A	B	C	C		

15.2.1 Purpose and Overview

SAP allows you a very simple, flexible, and powerful mechanism to transfer balances in time type, absence quota, and wage type, from one to another. For transfer of one hour under a time transfer type you specify how much it adds to, or subtracts from which time types, absence quotas, and wage types. All these are independently defined. Thus, you can

> Transfer from a time type to another time type(s), absence quota(s), wage type(s), or any combination of these.
> Similarly, you can transfer from absence quota or wage type to any time type(s), absence quota(s), wage type(s), or any combination of these.
> It is also not necessary that you must transfer. You could just credit time types, absence quotas or wage types.
> Similarly, you could just debit, without crediting anything.

Time transfers are defined as under:

> You specify the time transfer types in table T555P.
> You specify how the time transfer type affects time type balances in table T555J.
> You specify how the time transfer type affects wage types in table T555K.
> You specify how the time transfer type affects absence quota balances in table T555L.

You specify the time transfer for a time transfer type in infotype 2012. You run time evaluation to effect the transfers. If the function P2012 is called without parameter, it uses the specifications in T555J, T555K, T555L and T555P. Alternatively, a PCR (e.g. TR20) can be passed as the parameter, which specifies the processing logic.

All the transfers would take place together. If any one part cannot take place (e.g. if the quota becomes negative due to transfer, which is not permitted), other parts do not take place either.

Note that SAP provides you flexibility of changing daily and monthly balances of time types by using operations ADDDB and ADDMB. Similarly, you can update absence quotas through operation UPDTQ. Similarly there are operations FILLW, GENOW, GENTW and ADDZL, which can update wage types. These operations provide limitless opportunities to change time types, absence quotas and wage types in time evaluation. You may want to write your PCRs to meet your requirement. Some of standard SAP PCRs, like the examples below, also provide these functionality.

➤ There are PCRs, which effect time transfer. You may activate function P2007 TS20 GEN if the flextime balance should be transferred automatically at the end of the period to absence quota 02 (time off entitlement from BDE) if it exceeds the maximum permitted value, and the employee has sufficient attendance quota.

➤ You may also decide whether you want to delimit the flextime balance if it exceeds a certain value, or make a wage deduction if it falls short of a minimum value. If not, deactivate function ACTIO TS30.

Time balance transfers also take place in LIMIT function as per specifications in view V_T559P.

15.2.2   IMG Node

SM30 ➢ V_T555P

15.2.3   Screen

PSG	TrTy	Time transfer type text	Start Date	End Date	TmT...	Con
01	0005	Revision: Flex balance	01.01.1901	31.12.9999		
01	0098	Revision: Leave taken/yr	01.01.1901	31.12.9999		
01	0100	Flex to FV, remun. diff.	01.01.1901	31.12.9999	0005	>
01	0101	Flex to FV, off for diff.	01.01.1901	31.12.9999	0005	>

15.2.4   Primary Key

PS Grouping for Time Recording + Employee Time Transfer Type + End Date

15.2.5 Important Fields

PS grouping for time recording

Definition of employee time transfer type depends on PS grouping for time recording.

Employee time transfer type and text

These fields contain time transfer types and their description.

Start and end date

Validity period of the record.

Time type

This field can be used to provide a default value in the number field of infotype 2012. If you enter the time type in this field, the balance of the time type appears in infotype 2012 by default.

Condition for target time type

If you enter a condition in this field, the time type is only set to the value of the number field in the time transfer specifications infotype (2012) if the condition is fulfilled.

15.3 TIME TRANSFER TO TIME TYPES

Functional Consultant	User	Business Process Owner	Senior Management	My Rating	Understanding Level
A	C	X	X		

15.3.1 Purpose

This view specifies the time types which are credited or debited if a time transfer takes place. To understand time transfers, see purpose and overview of Chapter 15.2, employee time transfer type.

15.3.2 IMG Node

SM30 ➤ V_T555J

15.3.3 Screen

	PSG	TrTy	Time transfer type text	Tim...	Time type text	+/-	%	Min.	Max.
	01	0005	Revision: Flex balance	0005	Flextime balance	+	100.00	9999.99-	9999.99
	01	0005	Revision: Flex balance	0710	Repost flextime	+	100.00	9999.99-	9999.99
	01	0098	Revision: Leave taken...	0098	Annual leave taken	+	100.00	9999.99-	9999.99
	01	0100	Flex to FV, remun. diff.	0005	Flextime balance	+	100.00	9999.99-	9999.99

15.3.4 Primary Key

PS Grouping for Time Recording + Employee Time Transfer Type + Time Type

15.3.5 Important Fields

PS grouping for time recording

Definition of employee time transfer type depends on PS grouping for time recording.

Employee time transfer type

For each employee time transfer type you specify the time types which are credited and the time types which are debited.

Time type

For an employee time transfer type, you can add to, or subtract from, the balances of several time types.

Sign

Here you specify whether you want to add to or subtract from the balance of the time type.

Percentage transfer allocation

If you wish to transfer the balance from one time type to two time types, one receiving 60%, and the other 40%, you can use this field to specify that. It is also not necessary that these percentages add to 100. You can debit one time type by 100%, and credit another time type by 50%, if you so wish.

Minimum value for time type

If you want that the balance in a time type does not go below a lower limit on account of time transfer, you specify that value here.

Maximum value for time type

If you want that the balance in a time type does not cross an upper limit on account of time transfer, you specify that value here.

15.4   TIME TRANSFER TO WAGE TYPES

Functional Consultant	User	Business Process Owner	Senior Management	My Rating	Understanding Level
A	C	X	X		

15.4.1   Purpose

This view specifies the wage types which are credited or debited if a time transfer takes place. To understand time transfers, see Purpose and Overview of Chapter 15.2, Employee Time Transfer Type. Wage types are put in table DZL, from where they go into table ZL.

15.4.2   IMG Node

SM30 ➤ V_T555K

15.4.3   Screen

	PSG	TrTy	Time transfer type text	Wage t...	Wage Type Long Text	+/-	%	Info
	01	0100	Flex to FV, remun. diff.	MM10	Overtime 25%	-	100.00	M
	01	0740	OT remun. to OT time ...	MM10	Overtime 25%	-	100.00	M
	01	0741	OT time off to OT rem...	MM10	Overtime 25%	+	100.00	M
	02	OKCA	Pay on-call duty accou...	OKC0	On-call shift	+	100.00	S

15.4.4   Primary Key

PS Grouping for Time Recording + Employee Time Transfer Type + Country Grouping + Wage type

15.4.5   Important Fields

PS grouping for time recording

Definition of employee time transfer type depends on PS grouping for time recording.

Employee time transfer type

For each employee time transfer type you specify the wage types which are credited and the wage types which are debited.

Wage type

Wage type from which addition or subtraction takes place. Wage types are put in table DZL from where they go into table ZL.

Sign

Here you specify whether you want to add to or subtract from the wage type.

Percentage transfer allocation

If you wish to transfer the balance from one time type to two wage types, one receiving 60%, and the other 40%, you could use this field to specify that. It is also not necessary that these percentages add to 100. You may credit only one wage type by 50%, if you so wish.

Information type (S/M/A)

The wage types, which are created, go in internal table DZL. This table has a field, Information type (S/M/A). The value you enter here goes in that field, and can be used for subsequent processing. Possible values are: S (planned work), M (overtime), and A (absence).

15.5 TIME TRANSFER TO ABSENCE QUOTAS

Functional Consultant	User	Business Process Owner	Senior Management	My Rating	Understanding Level
A	C	X	X		

15.5.1 Purpose

This view specifies the absence quotas which are credited or debited if a time transfer takes place. To understand time transfers, see Purpose and Overview of Chapter 15.2, Employee Time Transfer Type.

15.5.2 IMG Node

SM30 ➤ V_T555L

15.5.3 Screen

PSG	TrTy	Time transfer type text	ES grpg	PSG	AQTyp	Quota text	+/-	%
01	0101	Flex to FV, off for diff.	1	01	02		-	100.00

15.5.4 Primary Key

PS Grouping for Time Recording + Employee Time Transfer Type + ES Grouping for Time Quota Types + PS Grouping for Time Quota Types + Absence Quota Type

15.5.5 Important Fields

PS grouping for time recording

Definition of employee time transfer type depends on PS grouping for time recording.

Employee time transfer type

For each employee time transfer type you specify the absence quotas which are credited and the absence quotas which are debited.

ES grouping for time quota types

Transfer of absence quota because of employees time transfer depends on ES grouping for time quota types.

PS grouping for time quota types

Transfer of absence quota because of employee time transfer depends on PS grouping for time quota types.

Absence quota type

Absence quota type which is credited or debited.

Sign

Here you specify whether you want to add to or subtract from the absence quota.

Percentage transfer allocation

If you wish to transfer the balance from one time type to two absence quotas, one receiving 60%, and the other 40%, you could use this field to specify that. It is also not necessary that these percentages add to 100. You may credit only one absence quota by 50%, if you so wish.

Employee Remuneration

16.1 EMPLOYEE REMUNERATION INFO (INFOTYPE 2010)

Functional Consultant	User	Business Process Owner	Senior Management	My Rating	Understanding Level
A	A	B	B		

16.1.1 Screen

Date　　　　29.01.2005

Remuneration info

Wage type	
Number of hours	
Number/unit	/
Amount	
Currency	INR
Extra pay/valuation	/
Pay scale group/level	/
Position/work center	
Overtime comp. type	Depends on wage type
Premium	
External document number	

16.1.2 Purpose

The purpose of infotype 2010 is to make payments related to time management. Normally time management related wage types are automatically generated. This infotype permits you to enter them directly. You can also use the concept of different payment.

16.1.3 Subtypes

Wage type

16.1.4 Time Constraint

T (Time constraint is based on subtype or subtype table)

16.1.5 Important Fields

Wage type

The wage type under which you want to make the payment.

Number of hours, number/unit, amount and currency

For a wage type, you can specify the number, rate or amount. Which of these can be entered depends on the wage type properties. Payroll works further on these, e.g. to convert number into amount.

Overtime compensation type

If the employees have a choice of deciding whether they want to receive payment or time off or a combination of the two, that choice is captured here. For more details, see chapter 11.4 (T555R).

Blank	Depends on wage type
1	Remuneration
2	Time off plus overtime rate
3	Compensation (time off)

External document number

Here you can keep a document Number.

Different payment

You may see chapter 24 on different payment for explanation of all other fields. In this infotype, these fields appear on the main screen instead of a separate window.

Maternity Leave

17.1 MATERNITY PROTECTION (INFOTYPE 0080)

Functional Consultant	User	Business Process Owner	Senior Management	My Rating	Understanding Level
A	B	C	C		

17.1.1 Screen

```
Maternity data
Pregnancy notification date    ☑          Sequence number  01
Expected date of delivery      ☑
Actual date of delivery
Date officially reported
Type of birth


Absences
Att./.. Att./abs. type text          Start        End
```

17.1.2 Purpose and Overview

The maternity protection infotype (0080) is an enhancement of the absences infotype (2001). It enables you to record all absences related to maternity protection and parental leave. You can decide whether you want to use this infotype only for female employees, only for male employees, or both. This is configured in feature MASEX.

Absences entered in maternity protection are also stored automatically in the absences infotype. The absences you enter in this infotype must be present in view V_T554V.

After you enter the expected date of delivery, the system can default the values based on the settings in table T554M. You can change these dates. Depending on the settings in T554M, you may get warning or error. If you change expected or actual date of delivery, you can recalculate the absence (Edit ➤ Recalculate absence).

When you save the record, the absence record is saved in infotype 2001. If the absence type requires quota deduction, it is done. If quota deduction fails, infotype 2001 is not saved, but infotype 0080 is already saved.

17.1.3 Subtypes

No subtypes

17.1.4 Time Constraint

3 (Record may include gaps, can exist more than once)

17.1.5 Important Fields

Pregnancy notification date

In this field, you specify the date on which the employer is informed of the pregnancy.

Expected date of delivery

In this field you can enter the date on which delivery is expected. The system uses this date to calculate the anticipated absence for the employee. If the actual date of delivery field contains an entry, calculations are based on that date instead.

Actual date of delivery

After you enter the actual date of delivery, you may 'Recalculate absences'. If you do that, the system automatically changes the entries in the absences infotype (2001) on the basis of the changed data.

Date officially reported

In this field, you specify the date on which the pregnancy was reported to a supervisory authority.

Type of birth

You may be given different periods of leave depending on the type of birth. For example, a normal birth may require shorter leave than a caesarean birth. The leave period you specify in view V_T554M can depend on the type of birth. In infotype 0080, you specify the type of birth, and the leave period is computed from this.

Absences

Absences shown/entered in this part of the screen are saved in infotype 2001. You can have more than one absence corresponding to an entry in infotype 0080.

17.2 PARENTAL LEAVE ELIGIBILITY

Functional Consultant	User	Business Process Owner	Senior Management	My Rating	Understanding Level
B	C	C	X		

17.2.1 Purpose

This feature, determines whether maternity protection/parental leave infotype 0080 can be created for females, males or both.

17.2.2 IMG Node

PE03 ➤ MASEX

17.2.3 Screen

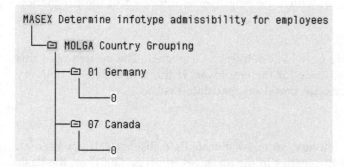

17.2.4 Fields for Decision Making

Company Code
Personnel Area
Personnel Subarea
Country Grouping

17.2.5 Return Value

0 Allowed for female and male employees
1 Allowed for female employees only
2 Allowed for male employees only

17.3 ABSENCE: INPUT CHECKS

Functional Consultant	User	Business Process Owner	Senior Management	My Rating	Understanding Level
B	X	X	X		

17.3.1 Purpose

This node (V_T554S) appears in configuration to remind you that you need to create the absence types you require for infotype 0080. You may create the absence type required, and set all its properties. For more details, see chapter 5.2 (T554S).

17.4 TYPES OF BIRTH

Functional Consultant	User	Business Process Owner	Senior Management	My Rating	Understanding Level
B	X	X	X		

17.4.1 Purpose

This view contains the master list of types of birth for each PS grouping for absence and attendance types. Maternity leave granted to an employee may depend on the type of birth.

17.4.2 IMG Node

SM30 ➤ V_T554G

17.4.3 Screen

PS grouping	Birth Type	Birth type text
01		Normal birth
01	01	Premature/multiple
03		Due dates
03	A	Termination of pregnancy
03	N	Normal birth

17.4.4 Primary Key

Language Key + PS Grouping for Absence and Attendance Types + Type of Birth

17.5 MATERNITY LEAVE RULES

Functional Consultant	User	Business Process Owner	Senior Management	My Rating	Understanding Level
B	C	X	X		

17.5.1 Purpose and Overview

In this view, you define periods for maternity protection and parental leave. The system uses these periods to calculate absences automatically. You can define different periods according to each PS grouping for attendance and absence types and birth types. You can define an allowance period for parental leave to reflect legal requirements or requirements stipulated by the collective agreement. You can also define the latest application date by which the employee must have put in a request for parental leave.

17.5.2 IMG Node

SM30 ➤ V_T554M

17.5.3 Screen

PS grouping	01
Att./abs. type	0500
Birth Type	Normal birth

Start Time   Exit
➤ 01.01.1990 ⌖ .12.9999

Rule Table: Absences for Maternity Protection

Calculation of dates
- ● Min.before   006 W   Weeks
- ○ Max.before   006
- ● Min.after   008 W
- ○ Max.after   008

Dates
- Min.duration
- Max.duration
- Allow. period
- Min.appl.period

Technical settings

Gender	2	Symbolic prog. name	
		Previous absence	
Indicator 1		Indicator 2	
Delivery date	Do not include day of birth in calculation of period	

17.5.4   Primary Key

PS Grouping for Absence and Attendance Types + Attendance or Absence Type + Type of Birth + End Date

17.5.5   Important Fields

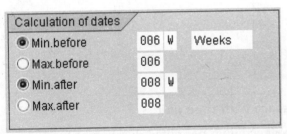

			Start Time	Exit
PS grouping	01		> 01.01.1990	.12.9999
Att./abs. type	0500			
Birth Type		Normal birth		

PS grouping for absence and attendance types

Leave entitlement may vary across locations within a company.

Attendance or absence type

You can have multiple absences for a birth type. All these are defaulted when you enter type of birth in infotype 0080, and 'Recalculate absence'.

Type of birth

Type of birth for which you are specifying default absences.

Start and end date

Validity period of the record.

Calculation of dates			
⦿ Min.before	006	W	Weeks
◯ Max.before	006		
⦿ Min.after	008	W	
◯ Max.after	008		

Minimum/maximum period before delivery

The minimum/maximum period before delivery specifies how long before the expected date of delivery the employee's maternity protection must start. If you make an entry in this field, it can be taken as the default value to calculate the employee's absence. You can change these dates in infotype 0080. Depending on the settings here, the system can give you error or warning.

Reaction indicator for protection period before delivery

You can use this indicator to determine how the system should react if the minimum or maximum protection period before delivery is not observed when absence data is recorded in infotype 0080, maternity protection. The possible system reactions are as follows:

Blank	No reaction.
E	Error message, the data record cannot be saved in this form.
W	Warning message, the data record can be saved.

Minimum/maximum period after delivery

The minimum/maximum period after delivery specifies how long after the expected date of delivery the employee's maternity/paternity leave should end. If you make an entry in this field, it can be taken as the default value to calculate the employee's absence. The system also uses the field for check purposes if an absence has been changed or a new one has been entered.

Reaction indicator for protection period after delivery

You can use this indicator to determine how the system should react if the minimum or maximum protection period after delivery is not observed when absence data is recorded in infotype 0080, maternity protection.

Time unit

This field specifies the unit of time for all fields in this block.

Dates		
Min.duration		
Max.duration		
Allow. period		
Min.appl.period		

Minimum/maximum duration of an absence with time unit

You can specify both the minimum and the maximum permitted duration of an absence for maternity protection or parental leave. This field cannot be referenced to generate default values.

Reaction indicator if absence duration is incorrect

You can use the reaction indicator to define how the system should react if the minimum or maximum duration is not observed when an absence is recorded in infotype 0080, maternity protection.

Allowance period with time unit

Here you can specify the time interval during which an employee is entitled to take parental leave, e.g. an employee is entitled to parental leave in the three years following the birth of his/her child.

Minimum application period with time unit

The minimum application period for parental leave specifies the date by which the employee must request leave.

Reaction indicator for allowance period and application period

You can use the reaction indicator to define what the system should do if the allowance period is not observed or if the minimum application period is not observed.

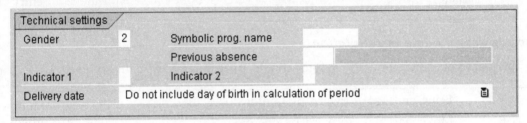

Gender key

Here you can define whether the rule is applicable to females, males or both.

Symbolic program name

The symbolic program name can be set by the individual customer.

Previous absence

If you enter a previous absence type in this field, you create a link between two absence types. You can thus define that the current absence may not begin before the previous one has ended.

Indicator if actual delivery date was after expected date

You can use this indicator to control the recalculation of absences if the actual delivery date was later than expected. The control options are as follows:

Blank	The absence should be extended. All validations are based on the actual delivery date.
1	The absence should be extended but may not exceed the maximum period following the expected delivery date. The validation for the maximum end date of the absence is based on the expected delivery date, the validation for the minimum end date on the actual delivery date.
2	The absence is not recalculated. The validation is based on the expected delivery date.

Indicator if actual delivery date is before expected date

You can use this indicator to control the recalculation of absences if the actual delivery date was earlier than expected.

Blank	The absence should be shortened. All validations are based on the actual delivery date.
1	The absence should remain as it is, based on the expected delivery date. The maximum period after delivery may not be exceeded. The validation of the maximum end date of the absence is based on the actual delivery date, the validation of the minimum end date on the expected date of delivery.
2	The absence is not recalculated. The validation is based on the expected date of delivery.

Include delivery date in calculation

In this field you define how the system should treat the date of delivery itself.

X	Bring end date forward by one day
B	Move start date forward by one day
Blank	Do not include day of birth in calculation of period

17.6 DEFAULTS FOR ABSENCE TYPES

Functional Consultant	User	Business Process Owner	Senior Management	My Rating	Understanding Level
B	X	X	X		

17.6.1 Purpose

This view can be used for infotypes 0080 and 0081. When you create an infotype 0080 record, you can enter an absence record on the same screen. However, all absence types may not be permitted for this purpose. Here you maintain those absence types, which can be entered there. You can indicate absences that the system should propose automatically by activating the default absence type field.

17.6.2 IMG Node

SM30 ➤ V_T554V

17.6.3 Screen

Infotype	PSG	Att./Absenc...	Att./abs. type text	Start Date	End Date	Defa...
0080	01	0500		01.01.1900	31.12.9999	☑
0080	01	0600		01.01.1990	31.12.9999	☐
0080	01	0605		01.01.1990	31.12.1991	☐
0080	03	0600	Maternity relief	01.01.1992	31.12.9999	☑
0080	03	0610	Grace leave	01.01.1992	31.12.9999	☑

17.6.4 Primary Key

Infotype + PS Grouping for Absence and Attendance Types + Attendance or Absence Type + End Date

17.6.5 Important Fields

Infotype

This view can be used for infotypes 0080 and 0081.

PS grouping for absence and attendance types

Different PS grouping for absence and attendance types may allow different attendance or absence types in infotypes 0080 and 0081.

Attendance or absence type

Attendance or absence types which are allowed in infotypes 0080 and 0081.

Start and end date

Validity period of the record.

Default

If you select this field, the absence type is automatically proposed. In infotype 0080, even the values are computed, but in infotype 0081 the values have to be entered manually.

Military Service

18.1 MILITARY SERVICE (INFOTYPE 0081)

Functional Consultant	User	Business Process Owner	Senior Management	My Rating	Understanding Level
A	B	C	C		

18.1.1 Screen

Military/non-military service

Service type

Military rank

Unit

Register date

Sequence number   01

☐ Military duty

Absences

Att./...	Att./abs. type text	Start Date	End Date	

18.1.2 Purpose and Overview

The military service infotype (0081) is an enhancement to the absences infotype (2001). You use this infotype for absences related to military and civil services. Absences entered in military service are automatically stored in the absences infotype. You can maintain the absences further in the absences infotype.

18.1.3 Subtypes

Service type

18.1.4 Time Constraint

3 (Record may include gaps and can exist more than once)

18.1.5 Important Fields

Service type

Here you enter the type of military/civil service which are defined in table T591A for infotype 0081.

Military rank

Here you enter the military rank which are defined in V_T554D.

Military duty

Mark this checkbox if the employee is obligated to serve in the military.

Unit

Here, you can either enter the unit, where the service is being performed, or you may just identify whether it is military service or community service.

Registration date

Date on which the employee registers for the service.

Absences

Absences are defaulted based on your configuration. You can change them. They are saved to infotype 2001.

18.2 MILITARY SERVICE ELIGIBILITY

Functional Consultant	User	Business Process Owner	Senior Management	My Rating	Understanding Level
B	C	C	X		

18.2.1 Purpose

This feature is used to determine eligibility of male and female employees for infotype 0081, military service.

18.2.2 IMG Node

PE03 ➢ DFSEX

18.2.3 Screen

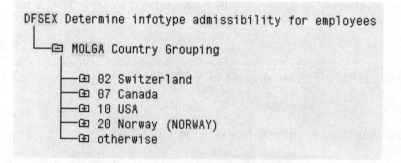

```
DFSEX Determine infotype admissibility for employees
  └──⊟ MOLGA Country Grouping
        ├──⊞ 02 Switzerland
        ├──⊞ 07 Canada
        ├──⊞ 10 USA
        ├──⊞ 20 Norway (NORWAY)
        └──⊞ otherwise
```

18.2.4 Fields for Decision Making

Company Code
Personnel Area
Personnel Subarea
Country Grouping

18.2.5 Return Value

0 Allowed for female and male employees
1 Allowed for female employees only
2 Allowed for male employees only

18.3 ABSENCE: INPUT CHECKS

Functional Consultant	User	Business Process Owner	Senior Management	My Rating	Understanding Level
B	X	X	X		

18.3.1 Purpose

This node (V_T554S) appears in configuration to remind you that you need to create the absence types you require for infotype 0081. You may create the absence type required and set all its properties. For more details, see chapter 5.2 (T554S).

18.4 DEFAULTS FOR ABSENCE TYPES

Functional Consultant	User	Business Process Owner	Senior Management	My Rating	Understanding Level
B	X	X	X		

18.4.1 Purpose

You may see chapter 17.6, as this view (V_T554V) is for both infotype 0080 and infotype 0081.

18.5 SERVICE TYPE

Functional Consultant	User	Business Process Owner	Senior Management	My Rating	Understanding Level
B	X	X	X		

18.5.1 Purpose

You can have various subtypes of infotype 0081, representing various types of military service. You create these subtypes in table T591A, view VV_T591A_0081___AL0.

18.6   PERIODS OF MILITARY SERVICE

Functional Consultant	User	Business Process Owner	Senior Management	My Rating	Understanding Level
B	X	X	X		

18.6.1   Purpose

In this view, you define the maximum duration of absences for each type of service. The system validates these periods when an absence is entered in infotype 0081. The periods you enter in this view are not binding and can be exceeded.

18.6.2   IMG Node

SM30 ➤ V_T554W

18.6.3   Screen

18.6.4   Primary Key

PS Grouping for Absence and Attendance Types + Attendance or Absence Type + Service Type + End Date

18.6.5   Important Fields

PS grouping for absence and attendance types

Periods of military service can be different for different locations.

Attendance or absence type

You may allow multiple absence types for military service. Depending on the absence type chosen in infotype 0081, the duration is picked up from this view.

Service type

Service duration can be different for different types of service.

Start and end date

Validity period of the record.

Military service duration and time unit

Here you define the maximum duration of absences for each type of service. The system validates these periods when an absence is entered in the military service infotype 0081. The periods you enter in this view are not binding and can be exceeded.

18.7 MILITARY SERVICE RANKS

Functional Consultant	User	Business Process Owner	Senior Management	My Rating	Understanding Level
B	X	X	X		

18.7.1 Purpose

This view contains the master list of military ranks. When you create an infotype 0081 record, you enter the military rank of the employee. It must be from the master list maintained here.

18.7.2 IMG Node

SM30 ➢ V_T554D

18.7.3 Screen

Military rank	Text
000	Gunner
001	Private
002	Private first class
003	Lieutenant

18.7.4 Primary Key

Language Key + Military Rank

Additional Absence Data

19.1 ADDITIONAL ABSENCE DATA (INFOTYPE 0082)

Functional Consultant	User	Business Process Owner	Senior Management	My Rating	Understanding Level
A	B	C	C		

19.1.1 Screen

Event		
Subtype	0001	Illness tracking
Case number		
Description		
Reported on		Time reported 00:00:00
Date of illness	☑	Illness time 00:00:00
Estimated costs		

Locational details of event	
Personnel area	
Personnel subarea	

☐ Claim for ind.accident

19.1.2 Purpose and Overview

There may be certain absences about which you need to know in more detail. For example, you may want to know more about illnesses and accidents.

What you want to know about illness would be different from what you want to know about accident. You do so by creating different subtypes of infotype 0082. You are free to define as many subtypes as you need in table T591A.

For each subtype, you define the information you want to keep. These are called events. Even though the name 'event' may not be very appropriate, it lets you keep different types of information. The events for a subtype are defined in table T572E. These events are shown when you click on 'Variable data' icon.

For each event, SAP provides you certain fields. However, all the fields may not be appropriate for an event. For example, event date is not appropriate for 'Treated by', but is appropriate for 'Treatment'. Hence, when you define properties of an event in table T572E, you decide the fields which are enabled for an event, and the fields which are disabled.

For each event, SAP lets you keep a comment. For some events, you may want to allow free text, whereas for some events, you might permit a selection only from a set of predefined comments. These are configured in table T572G.

Coordination of infotypes 0082 and 2001

Infotype 0082 contains additional data for absences. The data for absences is still kept in infotype 2001. You would wish to coordinate the entries of infotype 0082 and infotype 2001. Moreover, you would like to do the entries together.

SAP lets you do that. You can create infotype 2001 entries from infotype 0082 itself. SAP identifies these correlated entries through object type field. It also lets you change infotype 2001 entry in infotype 0082.

However, you do not want one to enter absence types which are not appropriate for a subtype of infotype 0082. To control this, SAP lets you define two subtypes of infotype 0082 for each absence type in table T554S. When you create an infotype 0082 record with a certain subtype, you can enter only those absence types, for which you have allowed this subtype in table T554S.

You can also maintain your own text containing details not captured in structured format.

19.1.3 Subtypes

Subtypes of additional absence data

19.1.4 Time Constraint

T (Time constraint is based on subtype or subtype table)

19.1.5 Important Fields

Subtype

You can keep various types of additional absence data. These are identified as subtypes of infotype 0082.

Case number

You may use this field to link this record with physical case papers.

Description

Here you keep a brief description of illness, accident, etc.

Reported on, time reported

The date and time on which the illness/accident is reported.

Date of illness, time of illness

The date and time on which the illness/accident occurred.

Estimated costs, currency

You can use these fields to keep an estimate of costs.

Personnel area and subarea

Here you keep details of where the event occurred.

Claim for industrial accident

Here you specify if this is an industrial accident.

Variable data

If you click on the variable data icon, you see the following screen. Here, you can enter additional absence data. The events on this screen will differ depending on the subtype, but for each event, the following fields are available. For an event, some of the fields are disabled in configuration table T572E.

Event data (Maximum of 25 entries)

Event Data

EI	Description	Yes	Event Date	Time	End Event	DI	Comments
01	Treatment	☐		00:00:00			
02	Treated by	☐		00:00:00			
03	Follow-up treatment	☐		00:00:00			
04	Certificate	☐		00:00:00			
05	Work restrictions	☐		00:00:00			

Event indicator

Events are information you want to keep in infotype 0082. For each subtype, there can be multiple events. Event indicator identifies the event. For each event, you define the properties in table T572E. These properties determine which of the event details can be entered, and which cannot.

Yes

This field indicates the validity of the given detail.

Event date and time

The date and time when the event began.

End of event

The date when the event ended.

Description indicator and comment

Here, you can keep details of the event. SAP lets you keep both codified description as well as free description. If you have defined a set of descriptions, from which one must be selected, you do so in DI field. If it is a free description, you enter it in comments field.

Absences

If you click on the absences icon, you get the following screen.

Event		
Event type	0001	Illness tracking
Case number		
Description		

Absence Data			
Type	Description	From	To

Infotype 0082 contains additional data for absences. The data for absences is still kept in infotype 2001. You would wish to coordinate the entries of infotype 0082 and infotype 2001. Moreover, you would like to do the entries together.

SAP lets you do that. You can create infotype 2001 entries from infotype 0082 itself. SAP identifies these correlated entries through object type field. It also lets you change infotype 2001 entry in infotype 0082.

However, you do not want one to enter absence types, which are not appropriate for a subtype of infotype 0082. To control this, SAP lets you define two subtypes of infotype 0082 for each absence type in table T554S. When you create an infotype 0082 record with a certain subtype, you can enter only those absence types, for which you have allowed this subtype in table T554S.

Maintain text

You can also maintain your own text containing details not captured in structured format by clicking on the 'Maintain text' icon.

19.2   SUBTYPES OF ADDITIONAL ABSENCE DATA

Functional Consultant	User	Business Process Owner	Senior Management	My Rating	Understanding Level
B	X	X	X		

19.2.1   Purpose

You can have various subtypes of infotype 0082, representing various types of additional absence data, e.g. illness tracking. Here you create these subtypes in table T591A, view VV_T591A_0082___AL0.

19.3   CONTROL TABLE FOR ADDITIONAL ABSENCE DATA

Functional Consultant	User	Business Process Owner	Senior Management	My Rating	Understanding Level
B	X	X	X		

19.3.1   Purpose

In this view, you define the events which can be stored on a subsequent screen of the additional absence data infotype (0082).

19.3.2   IMG Node

SM30 ➤ V_T572E

19.3.3 Screen

Infotype	0082	Additional Abs. Data
Subtype	0001	Illness tracking
Event ind.	05	Work restrictions

Organizaitonal possibilities for event fields

☐ Yes/No?   Text attributes   T 🔄

☑ Start date?   ☑ End date?
☐ Time indicator

Default values   1   ☑ Multiple

19.3.4 Primary Key

Infotype + Subtype + Event Indicator

19.3.5 Important Fields

Infotype

This view is used for infotypes 0076 and 0082.

Subtype

Subtype for which events are being defined.

Event indicator

Events are information you want to keep in infotype 0082. For each subtype, there can be multiple events. Event indicator identifies the event. For each event, you define the properties in table T572E. These properties determine which of the event details can be entered and which cannot be entered.

Yes/no field for internal medical service

This field determines whether yes/no field in infotype 0082 is enterable or disabled.

Text field attributes

SAP lets you enter event details in infotype 0082. For some events, you want to allow a selection only from predefined options. For some events, you would allow free entry. For some other events, only a numerical value would be appropriate. You can set these options here. In the case of predefined options, you also need to define these options in table T572G.

Start date allowed

If the event occurs on a date or over a period, you would enable this field so that start date can be entered in infotype 0082.

End date allowed

If the event occurs over a period, you would enable this field so that end date can be entered in infotype 0082.

Time indicator

If it were appropriate to record the time when the event took place or began, you would enable this field, so that start time can be entered in infotype 0082.

Control for default values

You store events data in infotype 0082. If you have not stored events data in an infotype 0082 record, and you click on variable data icon, the system shows you all the events for that subtype. You then store some events and save the record. When you go to that screen next time, it shows you the events for which you entered data. But for the remaining events, it shows you some but not others (of course you can create those events by explicitly entering them). This behaviour is controlled by this indicator. If you enter 1, the event is not shown after some events have been entered. This value is suitable for the events that are expected to be known from the beginning. If you enter value 2, the event is always shown.

Multiple entry of events

There are some events, which can occur multiple times, e.g. seeing a doctor. For such events, you tick this field.

19.4 PERMITTED VALUES FOR EVENTS

Functional Consultant	User	Business Process Owner	Senior Management	My Rating	Understanding Level
B	X	X	X		

19.4.1 Purpose

SAP lets you enter event details in infotype 0082. For some events, you want to allow a selection only from predefined options. These predefined options are configured here.

19.4.2 IMG Node

SM30 ➤ V_T572G

19.4.3 Screen

Permitted Values for Events						
Infotype	Subtype	Event ind.	De...	Description	STy.	Description
0082	0001	01	01	First aid	Additional Abs. Data	Treatment
0082	0001	01	02	Hospital	Additional Abs. Data	Treatment
0082	0001	01	03	At home	Additional Abs. Data	Treatment
0082	0001	02	01	Physician	Additional Abs. Data	Treated by

19.4.4 Primary Key

Infotype + Subtype + Event Indicator + Description Indicator

19.4.5 Important Fields

Infotype and text

Note that infotype text is in column titled STY.

Subtype

Subtype of infotype 0082.

Event indicator and description

Note that event text is in the last column 'Description'.

Description ID and description

Here you define the comments one can choose from for an event when one is entering data in infotype 0082.

19.5 SUPPLEMENTARY ABSENCE DATA

Functional Consultant	User	Business Process Owner	Senior Management	My Rating	Understanding Level
B	X	X	X		

19.5.1 Purpose and Overview

The fields in this view are only for absences and not for attendances. For certain absences, the data stored in infotype 2001 is not enough. You need more data. This is kept in infotype 0082.

You would wish to coordinate the entries of infotype 0082 and infotype 2001. Moreover, you would like to do the entries together. SAP lets you do that. You can create infotype 2001 entries from infotype 0082 itself. SAP identifies these correlated entries through object type field. It also lets you change infotype 2001 entry in infotype 0082.

However, you do not want one to enter absence types, which are not appropriate for a subtype of infotype 0082. To control this, SAP lets you define two subtypes of infotype 0082 for each absence type in table T554S. When you create an infotype 0082 record with a certain subtype, you can enter only those absence types, for which you have allowed this subtype in table T554S.

19.5.2   IMG Node

SM30 ➤ V_554S_P

19.5.3   Screen

	PSG	A/AType	A/A type text	Valid From	End Date	A	ST...	STy.
	05	0200	Sickness	01.01.1900	31.12.9999	✔	0001	0002
	05	0230	Doctor's/dentist's a	01.01.1900	31.12.9999	☐		
	05	0300	Special leave	01.01.1900	31.12.9999	☐		
	05	0500	Maternity leave	01.01.1900	31.12.9999	☐		
	05	0600	Parental leave	01.01.1900	31.12.9999	☐		

19.5.4   Primary Key

PS Grouping for Absence and Attendance Types + Attendance or Absence Type + End Date

19.5.5   Important Fields

Additional absence data

If you activate this field, you can enter the data for infotype 2001 from the screen of infotype 0082.

Sickness tracking subtype and accident data subtype

In these two fields you can keep subtypes of infotype 0082. When you enter an absence type while creating an infotype 0082 record the system checks whether that subtype of infotype 0082 is present in any of these fields. If it is not found in either of these fields, you cannot create the absence record.

Flextime

20.1 OVERVIEW

Functional Consultant	User	Business Process Owner	Senior Management	My Rating	Understanding Level
A	A	A	A		

In SAP, flextime is implemented primarily through time types. In definition of flex working hours, you define planned working time. The time worked by the employee during this time is accumulated as flex hours worked. Hours worked outside these hours are accumulated as overtime. Both these are accumulated in time types.

Unless there is approved absence, the employee is expected to be at work during core time. If he is not, this can be accumulated in time type, core time violation. If there were any rules pertaining to flextime, overtime or core time violation, they are implemented through PCRs.

At period end, you need to decide what to do with the flextime balance. Do you want to generate a wage type and take it to payroll? What to do if there is a deficit? What to do if there is excess? Do you want to convert into overtime or absence quota? Do you want it to lapse, if it is beyond certain limit? There are facilities to handle all these. Implementation is company specific.

20.2 DEFINITION OF FLEX WORKING HOURS

Functional Consultant	User	Business Process Owner	Senior Management	My Rating	Understanding Level
A	A	A	A		

When you define daily work schedule in table T550A, you define whether the employees are expected to work flextime or not. If yes, you define planned working time, normal working time and core times if any.

```
Flextime
Planned working time        [    ]  -  [    ]
Normal working time         [    ]  -  [    ]
Core time 1                 [    ]  -  [    ]
Core time 2                 [    ]  -  [    ]
```

Planned working time (from and to)

In the case of flextime, the planned working time defines the limit of normal work. Working hours, which are recorded during this interval, are credited to a flextime account, while those outside are treated as overtime.

Normal working time

In the case of flextime, if clock-in/clock-out entries are missing because the employee has been absent, the system uses the normal working time to calculate the absence hours. It also computes planned working hours as the normal working time plus the paid breaks.

Core times 1 and 2

If employees work flextime, the core time defines the period during which they must be at work each day. You can define two core times. They should not overlap with breaks.

Activity Allocation

21.1 ACTIVITY ALLOCATION

Functional Consultant	User	Business Process Owner	Senior Management	My Rating	Understanding Level
B	C	C	C		

21.1.1 Purpose and Overview

Many companies want to determine the cost of a particular project, or the profit made on a particular order. They keep account of expenses incurred on that particular project or order. Some of the work on these projects or orders is done by other parts of the company. While there is no external payment involved, the company wants to debit the project or order by the price of these activities, and credit the cost objects which performed these activities. This is the scenario supported by Activity Allocation.

You maintain the master list of activity types using transactions KL01 and KL02 in controlling or through view V_CSLA_CORE in SM30. You can do activity allocation in the following infotypes by clicking on Activity allocation :

> ➢ Absences (2001)
> ➢ Attendances (2002)
> ➢ Employee Remuneration Info (2010)

You can create default values for activity allocation using enhancement PTIM2001 and check activity allocation data using enhancement PTIM2004.

The two controlling objects involved in internal activity allocation are called the sender (of the service) and the receiver (of the service). Scheduled costs are calculated in controlling on the basis of activity types. In the normal course, the cost center which produces the activity is debited with the actual cost. When you do activity allocation, the producer cost center also becomes the sender cost center, and is credited by the value of the activity, while the receiver cost object is debited by the same amount.

If you find the activity allocation icon inactive in infotype 2001, 2002 or 2010, you can activate them in table T582Z. If it is active there, see view V_582A_C. The fields which are available for activity allocation can be configured in V_T588N. If you want the fields to be different for different groups of employees, you can create a feature and link it in table T588O. After the fields available for activity allocation are determined in V_T588N, the system selects the most appropriate screen from table TCOBL, which is maintained using transaction OXK1.

Activity allocation data is transferred to controlling by running the report RPTPDOC0. This report needs to be scheduled to run periodically. You also need to create two number ranges, which are used by posting documents created by this report. If activity allocation is already carried out in another component, then activity allocation does not occur in Time Management.

21.1.2 Screen

21.2 CONTROL TABLE FOR PA TIME MANAGEMENT

Functional Consultant	User	Business Process Owner	Senior Management	My Rating	Understanding Level
B	X	X	X		

21.2.1 Purpose

This view can be used to deactivate the following features for time infotypes

➢ Different payment
➢ Cost assignment
➢ Activity allocation
➢ External services

Some of the check boxes are grayed out, indicating that these features are not available for those infotypes. Where the check boxes are white, you have the option to enable or disable the feature. If you do not plan to use some feature, it is better to disable it to prevent unintended use.

21.2.2 IMG Node

SM30 ➤ T582Z

21.2.3 Screen

Infotype	Infotype text	Pers.cal.	Impor...	Impor...	S.no.	Rem...	Cost a...	Act. all...	Ext. s...
2001	Absences	1	01	01	4000	✔	✔	☐	☐
2002	Attendances	1	01	01	4050	✔	✔	✔	✔
2003	Substitutions		01	01	4100	✔	✔	☐	☐
2004	Availability		01	01	4150	✔	✔	☐	☐
2005	Overtime		01	01	4200	✔	✔	☐	☐

21.2.4 Primary Key

Infotype

21.2.5 Important Fields

Infotype

Infotype whose properties are being defined.

Personal calendar

The HR time management system maintains a personal calendar showing an employee's absences and, if required, attendances. This indicator enables you to determine which infotypes are taken into account when the personal calendar is maintained. Only infotypes 2001 and 2002 can be used. You can use report RPCLSTPC (transaction PT_CLSTPC) to display the personal calendar.

Blank	No update in personal calendar
1	Update in dialog (PAxx transactions)
2	Update via generation report RPTBPC00

It is recommended that you use value 1 here. In this option, the calendar is automatically maintained. In option 2, the user has to run the specified report periodically.

Import period

When you import time infotypes, it happens for current month. Here you can enter the number of months by which it should be brought back.

Import period

When you import time infotypes, it happens for current month. Here you can enter the number of months by which it should be taken forward.

Screen number

Here you specify the screen for list entry

Remuneration specification

If you disable this field, the different payment icon for the infotype is disabled.

Cost assignment

If you disable this field, the cost assignment icon for the infotype is disabled.

Activity allocation

If you disable this field, the activity allocation icon for the infotype is disabled.

External services

If you disable this field, the external services icon for the infotype is disabled.

21.3 ACCOUNT ASSIGNMENT SCREEN

Functional Consultant	User	Business Process Owner	Senior Management	My Rating	Understanding Level
C	X	X	X		

21.3.1 Purpose and Overview

When you use cost assignment, activity allocation, or external services, you get a screen as shown in chapters 21.1.2, 22.1.2 and 23.1.2. SAP allows you to customize this screen, so that the users see only those fields, which are implemented. Apart from simplifying the screen, this prevents entry of unwanted data. This is achieved in the following way.

In view T588O, you specify function modules for cost assignment (RP_TIME_COBL_002), activity allocation (RP_TIME_COBL_001) and external services (RP_TIME_003). For each of these, you decide whether the screen is same for all employees. If yes, leave the field 'Feature' blank. However, if you want different screens for different groups of employees, you enter the name of a feature in the field 'Feature'.

Function Module	Feature
RP_TIME_003	
RP_TIME_COBL_001	
RP_TIME_COBL_002	
RP_TRAVEL_COBL_1200	TRVCO
RP_TRAVEL_COBL_1700	TRVCO

In the feature specified in view T588O, you create groups of employees and return a variable key identifying each group. Then, in view V_T588N, you specify the properties of each field for a function module, variable key combination.

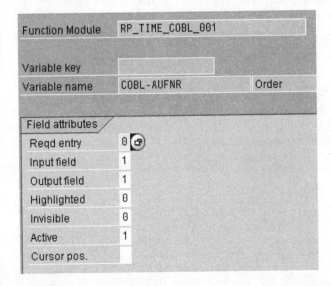

Function Module	RP_TIME_COBL_001	
Variable key		
Variable name	COBL-AUFNR	Order

Field attributes		
Reqd entry	0	
Input field	1	
Output field	1	
Highlighted	0	
Invisible	0	
Active	1	
Cursor pos.		

SAP provides a number of sub-screens, which you can see by running transaction OXK1. You can change their priority and 'Active' flag. You can also define your own screen. The fields decided by you are compared with the screens available in this transaction, and the most suitable screen is selected and shown. When multiple screens meet your requirement, the screen with highest priority is selected.

Subscreen	1001	BusArea/CCtr		
Priority	3	☑ Active		

Field Name	Position	With Text	
Accounting Indicator	0	☐	▲
Activity Type	5	☐	▼
Asset	0	☐	
Business Area	1	☐	
Business Process	0	☐	
CRP Calculation	0	☐	
Commitment item	0	☐	
Company Code	0	☐	
Controlling Area	0	☐	
Cost Center	3	☑	

21.4 NUMBER RANGE FOR ADDITIONAL TIME DATA

Functional Consultant	User	Business Process Owner	Senior Management	My Rating	Understanding Level
B	X	X	X		

21.4.1 Purpose

Additional time data for the controlling component is stored in the transfer table COIFT. The report RPTPDOC0 generates posting documents for activity allocation in controlling from the data in table COIFT. Each posting document is assigned a unique reference document number and is stored in tables HRAAHDR and HRAAITM. Sequence Number in table COIFT uses the number range from here.

21.4.2 IMG Node

Transaction PA05   Number Range Maintenance: RP_COIFT

21.4.3 Screen

Number Range Obj.	Table COIFT

Ranges

No	From number	To number	Current number	Ext
01	0000000001	9999999999	0	☐

21.5 NUMBER RANGE FOR POSTING DOCUMENTS (ACTIVITY ALLOCATION)

Functional Consultant	User	Business Process Owner	Senior Management	My Rating	Understanding Level
B	X	X	X		

21.5.1 Purpose and Overview

Additional time data for the controlling component is stored in the transfer table COIFT. The report RPTPDOC0 generates posting documents for activity allocation in controlling from the data in table COIFT. Each posting document is assigned a unique reference document number and is stored in tables HRAAHDR and HRAAITM. Reference document number in tables HRAAHDR and HRAAITM uses the number range from here.

21.5.2 IMG Node

Transaction PT12   Number Range Maintenance: HRAA_PDOC

21.5.3 Screen

Number Range Obj.	HR posting documents

Ranges

No	From number	To number	Current number	Ext

21.6 DATA TRANSFER TO ACTIVITY ALLOCATION

Functional Consultant	User	Business Process Owner	Senior Management	My Rating	Understanding Level
B	X	X	X		

21.6.1 Purpose

Data for the controlling component (additional time data) is stored in the transfer table COIFT. Transaction PT68, report RPTPDOC0, generates posting documents for activity allocation in controlling from the data in table COIFT. Each posting document is assigned a unique reference document number and is stored in tables HRAAHDR and HRAAITM. Report RPTPDOC0 needs to be run periodically, so that the posting documents are created. This may be done by scheduling a job, which will run report RPTPDOC0 at regular intervals.

21.6.2 IMG Node

Time management ➢ Integrating time management with other SAP applications ➢ Recording specifications for activity allocation ➢ Schedule data transfer to activity allocation.

21.6.3 SAP Menu

Transaction PT68   Activity Allocation

Cost Assignment

22.1 COST ASSIGNMENT

Functional Consultant	User	Business Process Owner	Senior Management	My Rating	Understanding Level
A	A	A	A		

22.1.1 Purpose and Overview

Personnel costs are most commonly charged to the employee's master cost center which is maintained in infotype 0001. When payroll is run, this cost center is transferred to table WPBP, from where it is picked up when accounting document is created.

However, if an employee is deployed to another cost center, you may like to charge his costs to the cost center where he is deployed. This can be done by changing the cost center in infotype 0001 itself. However, this may not be possible, if the employee's cost center is derived from the position to which he is assigned.

Either because you don't want to change the employee's master cost center as the deployment is a temporary one, or because you are not allowed to change the cost center as it is derived from the position, you may not change the cost center in infotype 0001.

In such cases, you may specify that the employee's cost be charged to another cost center in infotype 0027 (cost distribution). Infotype 0027 gives you a number of options:

➢ You can specify whether you want to charge wages/salaries or travel costs to the new cost center.
➢ You can specify that the cost be born between multiple cost centers in the proportions you define.
➢ You can specify other cost objects, e.g. purchase order, sales order and WBS element.

SAP provides you even more flexibility. You may want to charge a specific payment, e.g. bonus, or a specific time, e.g. training, to a different cost object. You can achieve that by doing cost assignment of a specific infotype record. You can do cost assignment in payroll infotypes 0014, 0015 and 0267. Similarly, you can specify cost assignments in time management infotypes 2001 (absences), 2002 (attendances), 2003 (substitutions), 2004 (availability), 2005 (overtime) and 2010 (employee remuneration info). You can create default values for cost assignments using enhancement PTIM2002.

When employees enter their time data at external time recording systems, they can also record information regarding cost assignment there at the same time. This data can be uploaded to the SAP system and stored in the time events infotype (2011).

You can control the infotypes where cost assignment can be done (tables T582A and T582Z), which fields are available and their properties (table T588N), and whether the fields and their properties can differ from employee to employee (table T588O). All these tables are discussed in chapter 21.

Personnel costs are determined in payroll (PY) and transferred to Controlling (CO). Controlling objects (such as cost centers) are debited with these primary costs in Controlling. Costs can be assigned to various controlling objects. In the case of cost assignment, the data is transferred from payroll to accounting through cluster table C1.

All these methods are for transfer of actual costs. SAP also lets you transfer cost on the basis of activity performed which is priced. For more details, see chapter 21, activity allocation.

If you click on   Cost assignment   in an infotype, you get the following screen where you can define whom to charge the costs.

22.1.2 Screen

External Services

23.1 EXTERNAL SERVICES

Functional Consultant	User	Business Process Owner	Senior Management	My Rating	Understanding Level
C	X	X	X		

23.1.1 Purpose and Overview

You can use this component if you want to pay on the basis of work done by the employees of external service provider. External employees must have their own personnel numbers in SAP HR. You must maintain infotypes 0000, 0001, 0003 and 0007. Other infotypes are optional. Since payroll is not calculated for external employees, you should either assign them a separate payroll area or include them in a payroll area for which you do not run payroll.

External employees must be assigned to the time management status 8 (external services) in the planned working time infotype (0007). To determine and account for overtime, night work, Sunday work, and so on, a work schedule rule must be assigned to the external employees in the planned working time infotype (0007).

You can record information about external employees only in infotype 2002 (see chapter 21.2, table T582Z). You can also record information about purchasing document, item number, service number and job. You can create default values for external services using enhancement PTIM2003.

Recorded time data is processed in time evaluation schema TM02. Standard time evaluation contains a specifically designed process for evaluating external services. Time evaluation identifies the times spent performing services that have a greater value (overtime, night work, Sunday work and so on). This information on services with a higher value can be compared with basic purchasing data so that the external services are posted with other service numbers there.

The compensation for the service depends on the qualifications of the employee, the type of activity, the time the activity is performed, and so on. It is specified in Materials Management—Purchasing. Times entered are processed in time evaluation. A resulting service number is derived from the wage types generated and the service number recorded. The resulting service number is decisive for the remuneration of the service.

The following configuration is done in time management. Many of these are covered in chapter 21.

➤ You permit external services for infotype 2002 in table T582Z.
➤ In table T588N you specify the fields available and their properties. If you do not want to use job key, it can be hidden. The function module is RP_TIME_003.
➤ If you want the fields to be different for different employees, you can specify a feature in table T588O.
➤ You maintain number ranges for table COIFT.
➤ You customize time evaluation schema TM02 as per your needs.
➤ You specify wage types permitted for transfer from time evaluation to MM-SRV module in view V_T510X.

For details of data flow, see SAP help (SAP Library ➤ Human resources ➤ Personnel time management ➤ Integrating time management with other components ➤ External services ➤ Data flow for integration of external services)

23.1.2 Screen

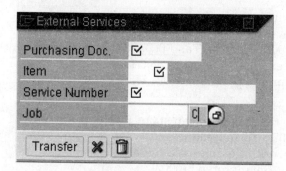

23.2 WAGE TYPES PERMITTED FOR TRANSFER TO MM-SRV

Functional Consultant	User	Business Process Owner	Senior Management	My Rating	Understanding Level
C	X	X	X		

23.2.1 Purpose

Here you maintain the wage types that are generated in time evaluation. These wage types are permitted for transfer to MM_SRV module.

23.2.2 IMG Node

SM30 ➢ V_T510X

23.2.3 Screen

Wage type	Wage Type Long Text

23.2.4 Primary Key

Country Grouping + Wage Type

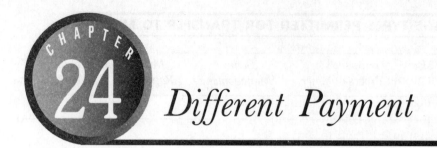

Different Payment

24.1 DIFFERENT PAYMENT

Functional Consultant	User	Business Process Owner	Senior Management	My Rating	Understanding Level
B	C	C	C		

24.1.1 Screen

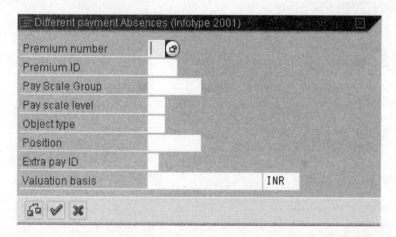

24.1.2 Purpose and Overview

You can store information on payment in time infotypes 2001, 2002, 2003, 2004, 2005, 2010 and 2011 in addition to just time data. In this way, employees can receive a special rate of remuneration for certain work activities. The specifications on a different payment are entered via an additional window in the infotype, which opens when you click on the icon ⊕ . However, in infotype 2010, employee remuneration information, these fields are directly on the screen. In the standard system, the data is passed on to the payroll to be queried and processed. The subtypes of certain time infotypes can also have an influence on payment (for example, the subtypes substitution type and availability type).

There are several methods of making 'Different Payment'. Note that you should only use one of the options for assigning a different rate of payment. An exception is the premium, which you can assign in addition to one of the other options.

➢ Assigning a premium
➢ Payment according to a different pay scale
➢ Payment according to the specifications for a different position
➢ Correcting payroll results

24.1.3 Assigning a Premium

You can assign an employee a premium for particular work activities or working conditions. The premium is selected according to a premium number and a premium indicator. You can either assign a premium on its own or together with other options.

24.1.4 Payment according to Pay Scale

You can use the pay scale group and pay scale level fields to enter data on payment for a particular work activity.

In infotype 0008, the employee is expected to receive payment under various wage types. Some of these wage types may be indirectly evaluated, using various employee attributes including his pay scale group and pay scale level.

If you specify pay scale group and pay scale level here, indirect valuation of wage type is done using the values specified here, rather than those specified in infotype 0008.

24.1.5 Payment according to a Position

You can use the fields—object type and position—to assign the payment for the work activity according to the specifications for a different position.

24.1.6 Correcting Payroll Results

The extra pay and valuation fields can be used to correct the results of payroll. Not every wage type is valuated using a fixed amount in payroll. The payroll program calculates a valuation basis during the payroll run which is used to valuate a wage type. The valuation basis is derived from the basic pay and the payments and deductions. You can change the valuation basis for the specified period in the valuation and extra pay fields. Enter an amount in the valuation field. The extra pay indicator determines how the new valuation basis is formed.

➤ If you enter + in the extra pay field, the amount in the valuation field is added to the valuation basis calculated in payroll.
➤ If you enter – in the extra pay field, the amount in the valuation field is deducted from the valuation basis calculated in payroll.
➤ If you do not make an entry in the extra pay field, the valuation basis calculated for the wage type in payroll is replaced by the specified amount.

Time Data Collection

25.1 SAP'S INTERFACE WITH TIME RECORDING SYSTEMS

Functional Consultant	User	Business Process Owner	Senior Management	My Rating	Understanding Level
A	A	B	B		

SAP needs to closely interact with time recording systems. The data collected by the time recording systems needs to be loaded in SAP. On the other hand, SAP data needs to be made available to time recording systems, so that they can provide rich functionality, and behave intelligently, rather than acting as dumb data collection terminals. SAP helps the time recording systems support the following functionalities:

➤ Recording time events (such as clock-in/clock-out entries, off-site work, breaks)
➤ Recording employee expenditures (such as company cafeteria data)
➤ Recording attendance/absence reasons
➤ Recording different payments
➤ Recording cost assignments
➤ Access control
➤ Displaying information for employees at recording terminals

While providing these functionalities, time recording systems ensure that only valid data is recorded, and access control is correctly granted. This is based on the employee data and other master data downloaded from SAP.

There are two methods of data transfer: transceiver-based transfer (old method) and BAPI-based transfer (new method). This book describes the latter. The data transfer takes place through ALE. SAP provides the time recording systems, both employee master data, as well as configuration data. The time recording systems provide SAP the attendance data and expenses incurred by employees.

Different types of data transfers are identified through message types. The message types pertaining to data transfer between SAP and time recording systems begin with HRCC1. You can see these message types by using transaction WE81. Transaction WE82 shows the link between message type and IDoc type. The data transferred by an IDoc type can be seen using transaction WE30. You select the segment, select segment attributes in 'Edit', and click on segment editor to see the data transferred. SAP downloads the following data to the time recording systems:

➢ HR-PDC: Download HR mini-master
➢ HR-PDC: Download employee balances
➢ HR-PDC: Download time event type groups
➢ HR-PDC: Download permitted attendance/absence reasons
➢ HR-PDC: Download permitted external wage types
➢ HR-PDC: Download objects (such as positions)
➢ HR-PDC: Download cost centers
➢ HR-PDC: Download internal orders
➢ HR-PDC: Download work breakdown structure element

SAP triggers the time recording systems to upload the following data and the time recording systems then upload it in SAP:

➢ HR-PDC: Upload request for time events (request is downloaded from SAP)
➢ HR-PDC: Upload time events
➢ HR-PDC: Upload request for external wage types (request is downloaded from SAP)
➢ HR-PDC: Upload external wage types

SAP provides user exits under enhancement HRPTIM05 (transaction SMOD) to further customize these download and upload processes.

25.2   TIME DATA RECORDING

Functional Consultant	User	Business Process Owner	Senior Management	My Rating	Understanding Level
A	A	B	B		

You must first determine what you want your employees to do at the time recording terminals. Accordingly, you configure your time recording system and SAP. You also communicate the same to the employees.

You may expect the employees to swipe their id cards to clock-in and clock-out. You may also want your employees to swipe at the start and end of breaks. These rules may be different for different groups of employees. You can also set up your system in such a way that an employee does not have to specify whether he is clocking in or clocking out. If his current status is absent he is assumed to be clocking in, otherwise clocking out.

In addition to this basic time recording, you may want an employee to provide the following additional information:

Cost center	If the employee is working for a cost center other than his own.
Internal order	If the employee is working for a specific order.
WBS element	If the employee is working for a project.
Position	If you want to pay the employee depending on the position for which he has worked. When clocking-in, the employee enters the position for which he will perform tasks in the following hours. After the upload, employee is assigned the pay scale of this alternative position and paid accordingly.
Attendance/absence reason	If the employee is expected to record the reasons for attendance/absence at time recording terminals.

The employees can also enter expenditures incurred by them. This data is passed to the payroll module, which deducts the amount from the employees' salary.

25.3 SCREEN

Functional Consultant	User	Business Process Owner	Senior Management	My Rating	Understanding Level
A	A	B	C		

If you run transaction PT80, the following screen appears.

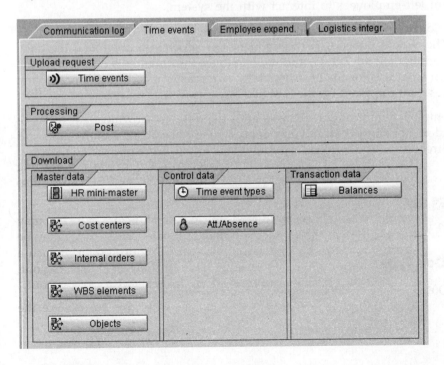

25.4 HR MINI-MASTER DOWNLOAD

Functional Consultant	User	Business Process Owner	Senior Management	My Rating	Understanding Level
A	A	B	C		

25.4.1 Purpose and Overview

HR Mini-Master is downloaded to the time recording systems using program RPTCC101 (HR-PDC: Download HR Mini-Master Record). The time recording systems use this data along with other master data to do the following:

➢ Determine the employee id from the card id. It also ensures that the employee is not using a card that has been replaced.
➢ Check the permissibility of the time event type entered by the employee.
➢ Check the permissibility of attendance/absence reasons entered by the employee.
➢ Check the permissibility of expenditures entered by the employee.
➢ Display employee name at the time recording terminal.
➢ Perform access control based on locations and/or time.
➢ Display employee balances.

Downloading an HR mini-master record is necessary for processing both time events and employee expenditures. HR mini-master record is downloaded regardless of the employee's status. Therefore, when an employee leaves the company, you must delimit infotype 0050 if you do not want left employees to interact with the system.

When you run the downloading program, you should specify a period for which the data is downloaded. This would depend on the frequency at which you download the data. If you are downloading data for 7 days, and the employee information is different on the first two days from what it is for the next five days; two master records are downloaded so that correct rules can be applied for the first two days, as well as for the next five days.

Note that if the employee information changes after the data are downloaded, the time recording system does not know of it, and may apply wrong rules. It is therefore important to determine the frequency of download carefully, and to perform special downloads if required.

25.4.2 Message Type

HRCC1DNPERSO

25.4.3 Basic IDoc Type

HRCC1DNPERSO01

25.4.4 Data Transferred

Position	Field name	Data element	Export length
1	SOURCE_SYS	LOGSYS	10
2	TIMEID_NO	DZAUSW	8
3	FROM_DATE	BEGDA	8
4	TO_DATE	ENDDA	8
5	TIMEID_VERSION	PT_ZAUVE	1
6	PERNO	PW_PERNR	8
7	EDIT_NAME	EMNAM	40
8	SORT_NAME	SMNAM	30
9	LANGU	SPRAS	1
10	LANGU_ISO	LAISO	2
11	PS_GRPG_ATT_ABS_TYPE	PT_MOABW	2
12	COUNTRY_GROUPING	MOLGA	2
13	SUBSYSTEM_GROUPING	BDEGR	3
14	ES_GRPG_WORK_SCHED	PT_ZEITY	1
15	ACCESS_CONTROL_GROUP	PT_ZANBE	2
16	PERSONAL_CODE	PT_ZPINC	4
17	MAIL_INDICATOR	PT_ZMAIL	1
18	ATT_ABS_REASON_GRPG	GRAWG	3
19	EXT_WAGETYPE_GRPG	GRELG	3
20	TIME_EVENT_TYPE_GROUP	PT_PMBDE	2
21	COMP_CODE	PW_BUKRS	4
22	COSTCENTER	KOSTL	10
23	CUSTOMER_FIELD_1	PDC_USRDN	20
24	CUSTOMER_FIELD_2	HR_USRFLD	40

25.5 COST CENTERS DOWNLOAD

Functional Consultant	User	Business Process Owner	Senior Management	My Rating	Understanding Level
A	A	B	C		

25.5.1 Purpose and Overview

You may want your employees to record the cost center for which they are working when they record their time. You would then want to ensure that the employees can only enter those cost centers which are permitted for this purpose. These may be a subset of all the cost centers you have.

To perform this validation, you download the permitted cost centers to the time recording systems using program: RPTCC107 (HR-PDC: Download Cost Centers). You download only permitted cost centers by creating cost center groups in controlling module and specifying cost center groups (in addition to the company code, plant and profit center), for which you want to download the cost centers when you run the download program.

The cost centers are downloaded with their validity period, so that the check is correctly performed.

25.5.2 Message Type

HRCC1DNCOSTC

25.5.3 Basic IDoc Type

HRCC1DNCOSTC01

25.5.4 Data Transferred

Position	Field name	Data element	Export length
1	SOURCE_SYS	LOGSYS	10
2	COMP_CODE	PW_BUKRS	4
3	COSTCENTER	KOSTL	10
4	COSTCENTER_GRP	PT_KSGRU	15
5	FROM_DATE	BEGDA	8
6	TO_DATE	ENDDA	8
7	COCNTR_TXT	COCNTR_TXT	20

25.6 INTERNAL ORDERS DOWNLOAD

Functional Consultant	User	Business Process Owner	Senior Management	My Rating	Understanding Level
B	C	X	X		

25.6.1 Purpose and Overview

You may want your employees to record the internal order for which they are working when they record their time. You would then want to ensure that the employees can only enter those internal orders which are permitted for this purpose. These may be a subset of all the internal orders you have.

To perform this validation, you download the permitted internal orders to the time recording systems using program: RPTCC111 (HR-PDC: Download Internal Orders). You download only permitted internal orders by creating internal order group in controlling module, and specifying internal order groups (in addition to the controlling area, company code and plant) for which you want to download the internal orders when you run the download program.

25.6.2 Message Type

HRCC1DNINORD

25.6.3 Basic IDoc Type

HRCC1DNINORD01

25.6.4 Data Transferred

Position	Field name	Data element	Export length
1	SOURCE_SYS	LOGSYS	10
2	COMP_CODE	PW_BUKRS	4
3	ORDER	AUFNR	12
4	ORDER_GRP	PT_AUFGR	15
5	ORDER_NAME	AUFTEXT	40

25.7 WORK BREAKDOWN STRUCTURE ELEMENT DOWNLOAD

Functional Consultant	User	Business Process Owner	Senior Management	My Rating	Understanding Level
B	C	X	X		

25.7.1 Purpose and Overview

You may want your employees to record the project for which they are working when they record their time. You would then want to ensure that the employees can only enter those projects which are permitted for this purpose. These may be a subset of all the projects you have.

To perform this validation, you download the permitted projects to the time recording systems using program: RPTCC108 (HR-PDC: Download Work Breakdown Schedule Elements). You download only permitted projects by specifying the controlling area, company code and plant, for which you want to download the projects when you run the download program.

25.7.2 Message Type

HRCC1DNWBSEL

25.7.3   Basic IDoc Type

HRCC1DNWBSEL01

25.7.4   Data Transferred

Position	Field name	Data element	Export length
1	SOURCE_SYS	LOGSYS	10
2	COMP_CODE	BUKRS	4
3	WBS_ELEMENT	PS_POSID	24
4	WBS_ELEMENT_GRP	PT_POSIDGR	15
5	WBS_SHORTTEXT	CHAR40	40

25.8   POSITIONS DOWNLOAD

Functional Consultant	User	Business Process Owner	Senior Management	My Rating	Understanding Level
B	C	X	X		

25.8.1   Purpose and Overview

If you have a policy of paying your employees differently when they work for a position other than their normal, you need that data for making payment. You may ask the employees to themselves record the position for which they are working when they record their time. Otherwise this task has to be performed by a supervisor. You would then want to ensure that the employees do not enter invalid positions.

To perform this validation, you download the permitted positions to the time recording systems using program: RPTCC110 (HR-PDC: Download Objects). You can download positions, jobs and work centers. The objects that you want to download are specified in the selection screen.

25.8.2   Message Type

HRCC1DNOBJID

25.8.3   Basic IDoc Type

HRCC1DNOBJID01

25.8.4 Data Transferred

Position	Field name	Data element	Export length
1	SOURCE_SYS	LOGSYS	10
2	OBJECT_TYPE	OTYPE	2
3	OBJ_ID	OBJEKTID	8
4	OBJ_ID_GRP	PT_OBJGR	15
5	FROM_DATE	BEGDA	8
6	TO_DATE	ENDDA	8
7	LANGU	SPRAS	1
8	LANGU_ISO	LAISO	2
9	OBJ_ID_TXT	STEXT	40

25.9   TIME EVENT TYPE GROUPS DOWNLOAD

Functional Consultant	User	Business Process Owner	Senior Management	My Rating	Understanding Level
B	C	X	X		

25.9.1 Purpose and Overview

When your employees record time, you would want to ensure that they only record them against the time event types, which they are allowed. All employees may not be allowed the same set of time event types. Therefore, you define the time event type groups in T705P and assign them to an employee in infotype 0050. When you download HR mini-master, the time event type group associated with an employee is also downloaded.

The time recording system now needs to know which time events are allowed for that time event type group. For this purpose, information in T705P also needs to be downloaded. Also, this data needs to be downloaded only when configuration in table T705 changes. The downloading is done by program: RPTCC105 (HR-PDC: Download Time Event Type Groupings).

25.9.2 Message Type

HRCC1DNTEVGR

25.9.3 Basic IDoc Type

HRCC1DNTEVGR01

25.9.4 Data Transferred

Position	Field name	Data element	Export length
1	SOURCE_SYS	LOGSYS	10
2	TIME_EVENT_TYPE_GROUP	PT_PMBDE	2
3	TEVENTTYPE	RETYP	3

25.10 PERMITTED ATTENDANCE/ABSENCE REASONS DOWNLOAD

Functional Consultant	User	Business Process Owner	Senior Management	My Rating	Understanding Level
B	C	X	X		

25.10.1 Purpose and Overview

Employees can enter their absence and attendance reasons directly at the terminal if your time recording system supports this function. The system uses this information to create a partial day absence record for the period the employee was absent. The absence type of the record depends on the absence reason. Thus, you may allow employees to go for doctor's appointment, but deduct salary if he has gone to bank.

Employee can also enter an absence reason to indicate that he will be absent on the subsequent day, or why was he absent on the previous day. An absence or attendance reason can be entered with both clock-in (P10) and clockout (P20) time events.

SAP allows you to specify, which employees are allowed to enter what set of attendance/absence reasons. In order to ensure that an employee uses only those attendance/absence reasons, which he is allowed to, the following steps are required:

➢ Define grouping of attendance/absence reasons in table T705I.
➢ Assign grouping of attendance/absence reasons to an employee in infotype 0050.
➢ Download grouping of attendance/absence reasons to employee linkage to time recording system using message type HRCC1DNPERSO (HR-PDC: Download HR Mini-Master).
➢ Define attendance/absence reasons, which are a part of a grouping of attendance/absence reasons in table T705A, and download to the time recording system via message type HRCC1DNATTAB (HR-PDC: Download permitted att./absence reasons). This is done using program RPTCC103 (HR-PDC: Download Attendance/ Absence Reasons).
➢ The time recording system then uses this information to allow an employee to record only those attendance/absence reasons, which he is permitted to record.

Based on the absence or attendance reason entered by the employee, the system generates a partial day absence or attendance record for the current day, or a full-day record for the previous or subsequent workday. Attendance/absence reasons are processed by PCRs TD80, TD81 and TD90.

25.10.2 Message Type

HRCC1DNATTAB

25.10.3 Basic IDoc Type

HRCC1DNATTAB01

25.10.4 Data Transferred

Position	Field name	Data element	Export length
1	SOURCE_SYS	LOGSYS	10
2	ATT_ABS_REASON_GRPG	GRAWG	3
3	PS_GRPG_ATT_ABS_TYPE	PT_MOABW	2
4	ES_GRPG_WORK_SCHED	PT_ZEITY	1
5	ATT_ABS_REASON	PT_ABWGR	4
6	FROM_DATE	BEGDA	8
7	TO_DATE	ENDDA	8
8	LANGU	SPRAS	1
9	LANGU_ISO	LAISO	2
10	ATT_ABS_REASON_TEXT	PT_ABANGRT	30

25.11 EMPLOYEE BALANCES DOWNLOAD

Functional Consultant	User	Business Process Owner	Senior Management	My Rating	Understanding Level
B	C	X	X		

25.11.1 Purpose and Overview

Employees can see their time balances on the time recording system. This is implemented as follows:

➤ Define the fields for which you want to show employee balances in table T555I.
➤ Download the time/quota/incentive wages balances for employees to time recording system using message type HRCC1DNBALAN (HR-PDC: Download employee balances). This is done using program RPTCC102 (HRPDC: Download Employee Time Balances).
➤ The time recording system then displays this information to the employees.

The data you display to employees can depend on ES grouping and PS grouping. These are downloaded in HR mini-master.

25.11.2 Message Type

HRCC1DNBALAN

25.11.3 Basic IDoc Type

HRCC1DNBALAN01

25.11.4 Data Transferred

Position	Field name	Data element	Export length
1	SOURCE_SYS	LOGSYS	10
2	TIMEID_NO	DZAUSW	8
3	PERNO	PW_PERNR	8
4	SUBSYSTEM_GROUPING	BDEGR	3
5	INFO_FIELD_1	PW_INFO	13
6	INFO_FIELD_2	PW_INFO	13
7	INFO_FIELD_3	PW_INFO	13
8	INFO_FIELD_4	PW_INFO	13
9	INFO_FIELD_5	PW_INFO	13
10	INFO_FIELD_6	PW_INFO	13
11	INFO_FIELD_7	PW_INFO	13
12	INFO_FIELD_8	PW_INFO	13
13	INFO_FIELD_9	PW_INFO	13
14	INFO_FIELD_10	PW_INFO	13
15	TIME_EVAL_MAIL_INDICATOR	MAILK	1
16	CUSTOMER_FIELD_1	PDC_USRDN	20
17	CUSTOMER_FIELD_2	HR_USRFLD	40

25.12 UPLOAD REQUEST FOR TIME EVENTS DOWNLOAD

Functional Consultant	User	Business Process Owner	Senior Management	My Rating	Understanding Level
A	B	C	X		

25.12.1 Purpose and Overview

Uploading the time events in SAP is triggered by SAP. You run program RPTCC106 (HRPDC: Download Upload Request for Time Events), which downloads to time recording system, an upload request for time events. This is done for a specific time recording system. On receiving the upload request, the time recording system uploads the time event data.

25.12.2 Message Type

HRCC1REQUPTEVEN

25.12.3   Basic IDoc Type

HRCC1REQUPTEVEN01

25.12.4   Data Transferred

Position	Field name	Data element	Export length
1	SOURCE_SYS	LOGSYS	10

25.13   TIME EVENTS UPLOAD

Functional Consultant	User	Business Process Owner	Senior Management	My Rating	Understanding Level
A	B	C	X		

25.13.1   Purpose and Overview

The time data recorded by the time recording system needs to be uploaded in SAP. This happens in two steps:

➢ SAP downloads a request to the time recording system to upload data.
➢ The time recording system uploads the data.

The personnel time events uploaded in SAP are stored in the table CC1TEV. These time events can be processed using the report SAPCDT45 (transaction PT45). The time events can then be displayed and changed manually in the time events infotype (2011).

25.13.2   Message Type

HRCC1UPTEVEN

25.13.3   Basic IDoc Type

HRCC1UPTEVEN01

25.13.4   Data Transferred

Position	Field name	Data element	Export length
1	SOURCE_SYS	LOGSYS	10
2	TEVENTTYPE	RETYP	3
3	TERMINALID	TERID	4
4	LOGDATE	LDATE	8
5	LOGTIME	LTIME	6

(Contd.)

Position	Field name	Data element	Export length
6	PHYSDATE	PHDAT	8
7	PHYSTIME	PHTIM	6
8	TIMEID_NO	DZAUSW	8
9	PERNO	PW_PERNR	8
10	ATT_ABS_REASON	PT_ABWGR	4
11	OBJECT_TYPE	OTYPE	2
12	OBJ_ID	OBJEKTID	8
13	COMP_CODE	BUKRS	4
14	COSTCENTER	KOSTL	10
15	ORDER	AUFNR	12
16	WBS_ELEMENT	PS_POSID	24
17	CUSTOMER_FIELD_1	PDC_USRUP	20
18	CUSTOMER_FIELD_2	HR_USRFLD	40

25.14   PERSONNEL TIME EVENTS POSTING

Functional Consultant	User	Business Process Owner	Senior Management	My Rating	Understanding Level
A	A	B	X		

25.14.1   Purpose and Overview

When the time events are loaded from time recording systems, they are loaded in CC1TEV table. This is done so that the data loading process does not have to deal with data validation. This is done using program SAPCDT45.

The time event data is then posted to TEVEN and NT1 tables. On successful posting, time events are deleted from table CC1TEV. If due to some problem, the same time events are loaded in CC1TEV again, the system will attempt to post them in table TEVEN again, where they already exist. SAP gives you the following choices which you can specify in V_T705B.

➢ Load the time event again in table TEVEN
➢ Ignore the time event
➢ Enter the time events in the error pool

Regardless of your choice, the time events are deleted from CC1TEV.

Sometimes events may be left in the interface table CC1TEV because the personnel number was locked. These time events are accessed again when the report is run the next time. If time events with errors cannot be posted to time management, you can run program RPAFRV00 to post process them.

Employee Expenditure Collection

26.1 SCREEN

Functional Consultant	User	Business Process Owner	Senior Management	My Rating	Understanding Level
B	C	X	X		

| Communication log | Time events | Employee expend. | Logistics integr. |

Upload request

>)) Expenditures

Processing

☐ Create session   🗔 Post   🗑 Reorganize

Download

Master data

▦ HR mini-master

▥ Expenditures

Control data

🕐 Time event types

26.2 OVERVIEW

Functional Consultant	User	Business Process Owner	Senior Management	My Rating	Understanding Level
B	C	X	X		

Employees can record expenditures at the time recording system which is collected and processed by SAP. In order to ensure that an employee uses only those expenditures, which he is allowed to, the following steps are required:

➤ Define grouping for employee expenses in table T705J.
➤ Assign grouping for employee expenses to an employee in infotype 0050.
➤ Download grouping for employee expenses to employee linkage to time recording system using message type HRCC1DNPERSO (HR-PDC: Download HR mini-master).
➤ Define employee expenditures, which are permitted for a grouping for employee expenses in table T705K. This table also contains the link between employee expenditures and internal wage types.
➤ Download employee expenditures, which are permitted for a grouping for employee expenses to the time recording system via message type HRCC1DNEXTWT (HR-PDC: Download permitted external wage types). This is done using program RPTCC104 (HR-PDC: Download employee expenditures).
➤ The time recording system then uses this information to allow an employee to record only those expenditures, which he is permitted to record.
➤ Uploading the employee expenditures in SAP is triggered by SAP when you run program RPTCC109 (HRPDC: Download upload request for employee expenditures).
➤ Employee expenditures are uploaded from time recording systems using message type HRCC1UPEXTWT (HR-PDC: Upload external wage types). They are stored in table TEXLGA.
➤ SAP provides user exits under enhancement HRPTIM05 (transaction SMOD) to further customize these download and upload processes.
➤ You run program RPIEWT00 (Batch input session for employee expenditures), to convert employee expenditures into internal wage types, create a batch to insert records in infotype 0015 or infotype 2010, and update the status in table TEXLGA to indicate that the expenditure is processed.
➤ You run program RPIEWT04 (Batch Input: Process sessions in batch) to create data records for the infotypes 2010 or 0015 by starting background processing for batch input sessions.
➤ Since the data in table TEXLGA is not deleted when you insert them in infotype 0015 or 2010, you periodically run program RPIEWT02 (Reorganize Table TEXLGA—Employee Expenditures), to delete records from table TEXLGA.

26.3   GROUPING FOR EMPLOYEE EXPENSES

Functional Consultant	User	Business Process Owner	Senior Management	My Rating	Understanding Level
C	X	X	X		

26.3.1   Purpose and Overview

This view contains the master list of grouping for employee expenses. SAP uses the following terms interchangeably: employee expense, employee expenditure, and external wage type. Grouping for employee expenses is assigned to an employee in infotype 0050. This assignment is downloaded to time recording systems in HR mini-master. The time recording systems also receive data on which employee expenditures are permitted for a grouping for employee expenses. When an employee enters expenditure, this data is used for validation.

26.3.2   IMG Node

SM30 ➤ V_T705J

26.3.3   Screen

Grouping for EE expe	Text
001	SAP default 001
002	SAP default 002

26.3.4   Primary Key

Grouping for Employee Expenses

26.4   EMPLOYEE EXPENDITURES FROM SUBSYSTEM

Functional Consultant	User	Business Process Owner	Senior Management	My Rating	Understanding Level
C	X	X	X		

26.4.1   Purpose and Overview

This view contains the employee expenditures that are permitted for a grouping for employee expenses. This data is downloaded to the time recording system. The time recording system also has the data on an employee's grouping for employee expenses, downloaded in HR mini-master. By linking these two, it knows the expenditures permitted for each employee, and is able to accept or reject an expenditure entered by an employee. This view also contains the linkage between employee expenditure and wage type, which is used to convert expenditure data in payroll deductions.

26.4.2 IMG Node

SM30 ➤ V_T705K

26.4.3 Screen

Ctry Grouping	01

Employee Expenditures from Subsystem

	Exp.	EE ...	End Date	Valid From	Wage...	Wage type	Wage Type Long Text	T...	Unit text
	001	EWT1	31.12.9999	01.01.1900	Lunch	M725	CompanyAnnivsry 25..		
	002	EWT1	31.12.9999	01.01.1900	Lunch	M725	CompanyAnnivsry 25/8		

26.4.4 Primary Key

Grouping for Employee Expenses + Country Grouping + Employee Expenditures + End Date

26.4.5 Important Fields

Country grouping

Wage types for employee expenditures can differ from country to country.

Grouping for employee expenses

An employee is assigned a grouping for employee expenses in infotype 0050. This allows him to enter a set of expenditures, which are defined in this view.

Employee expenditures

Here you define which employee expenditures are valid for each grouping. When an employee enters expenditure, his grouping is determined from infotype 0050. If the expenditure is found here, it is accepted, otherwise rejected.

Start and end date

Validity period of the record.

Wage type long text

This is the wage type the employee specifies.

Wage type and text

When an employee's expenditure is deducted, it is deducted using the wage type specified here.

Time/measurement unit and text

The unit used for wage type.

26.5 PERMITTED EXTERNAL WAGE TYPES DOWNLOAD

Functional Consultant	User	Business Process Owner	Senior Management	My Rating	Understanding Level
C	X	X	X		

26.5.1 Purpose and Overview

The time recording system has the data on an employee's grouping for employee expenses, downloaded in HR mini-master. It also needs the data on which employee expenditures are permitted for a grouping for employee expenses to validate employees' expenditure entries. In SAP this data is stored in table T705K. Here it is downloaded to time recording systems using program RPTCC104 (HR-PDC: Download employee expenditures). This data needs to be downloaded only when table T705K changes.

26.5.2 Message Type

HRCC1DNEXTWT

26.5.3 Basic IDoc Type

HRCC1DNEXTWT01

26.5.4   Data Transferred

Position	Field name	Data element	Export length
1	SOURCE_SYS	LOGSYS	10
2	EXT_WAGETYPE_GRPG	GRELG	3
3	COUNTRY_GROUPING	MOLGA	2
4	EXTERNAL_WAGETYPE	EXLGA	4
5	FROM_DATE	BEGDA	8
6	TO_DATE	ENDDA	8
7	WAGETYPE_UNIT	PT_ZEINH	3
8	WAGETYPE_UNIT_ISO	ISOCD_UNIT	3
9	LANGU	SPRAS	1
10	LANGU_ISO	LAISO	2
11	WAGELTEXT	LGTXT	25
12	UNIT_TEXT	TEXT20	20

26.6   UPLOAD REQUEST FOR EXTERNAL WAGE TYPES DOWNLOAD

Functional Consultant	User	Business Process Owner	Senior Management	My Rating	Understanding Level
B	B	X	X		

26.6.1   Purpose and Overview

Uploading the employee expenditures in SAP is triggered by SAP. You run program RPTCC109 (HRPDC: Download upload request for employee expenditures), which downloads to time recording system an upload request for employee expenditures. On receiving the upload request, the time recording system uploads the employee expenditure data.

26.6.2   Message Type

HRCC1REQUPEXTWT

26.6.3   Basic IDoc Type

HRCC1REQUPEXTWT01

26.6.4   Data Transferred

Position	Field name	Data element	Export length
1	SOURCE_SYS	LOGSYS	10

26.7 EXTERNAL WAGE TYPES UPLOAD

Functional Consultant	User	Business Process Owner	Senior Management	My Rating	Understanding Level
B	B	X	X		

26.7.1 Purpose and Overview

The employee expenditures recorded by the time recording system needs to be uploaded in SAP. This happens in two steps:

➢ SAP downloads a request to the time recording system to upload data.
➢ The time recording system uploads the data.

The employee expenditures uploaded in SAP are stored in the table TEXLGA. These employee expenditures can be processed using the report RPIEWT00 (Create Batch Input Session for Employee Expenditures). The report generates primary wage types from the employee expenditures that can be processed further in SAP Payroll. Data records are then created with these primary wage types in the employee remuneration info infotype (2010) or additional payments infotype (0015). The upload takes place separately for each time recording system.

26.7.2 Message Type

HRCC1UPEXTWT

26.7.3 Basic IDoc Type

HRCC1UPEXTWT01

26.7.4 Data Transferred

Position	Field name	Data element	Export length
1	SOURCE_SYS	LOGSYS	10
2	TEVENTTYPE	RETYP	3
3	TERMINALID	TERID	4
4	LOGDATE	LDATE	8
5	LOGTIME	LTIME	6
6	PHYSDATE	PHDAT	8
7	PHYSTIME	PHTIM	6
8	TIMEID_NO	DZAUSW	8
9	PERNO	PW_PERNR	8
10	EXTERNAL_WAGETYPE	EXLGA	4

(Contd.)

Position	Field name	Data element	Export length
11	NUMBER_EXT_WAGETYPE	HRAZL	9
12	WAGETYPE_UNIT	PT_ZEINH	3
13	WAGETYPE_UNIT_ISO	ISOCD_UNIT	3
14	AMOUNT_EXT_WAGETYPE	HRBET	11
15	CURRENCY	WAERS	5
16	CURRENCY_ISO	ISOCD	3
17	CUSTOMER_FIELD_1	PDC_USRUP	20
18	CUSTOMER_FIELD_2	HR_USRFLD	40

26.8 BATCH INPUT SESSION FOR EMPLOYEE EXPENDITURES

Functional Consultant	User	Business Process Owner	Senior Management	My Rating	Understanding Level
B	B	X	X		

26.8.1 Purpose and Overview

The program RPIEWT00 does the following:

➢ Read table TEXLGA.
➢ Convert employee expenditures, into internal wage types using table T705K.
➢ Create a batch input session, which inserts records in infotype 0015 or infotype 2010.
➢ You specify the infotype, in which the records should be inserted, on the selection screen.
➢ You also specify the validity date of the records inserted in the infotype.
➢ When processing is complete, the status is updated in table TEXLGA.

SAP also provides the flexibility of overwriting default currency, and additional authorization controls. For details, see program help.

26.9 PROCESSING OF SESSIONS IN BATCH

Functional Consultant	User	Business Process Owner	Senior Management	My Rating	Understanding Level
B	B	X	X		

26.9.1 Purpose and Overview

Program RPIEWT04, Batch Input: Process sessions in batch, is used to create data records for the infotypes 2010 or 0015. It automatically generates the session name, which depends on parameter EWT in your user profile.

26.10 REORGANIZATION OF TABLE TEXLGA (EMPLOYEE EXPENDITURES)

Functional Consultant	User	Business Process Owner	Senior Management	My Rating	Understanding Level
B	B	X	X		

26.10.1 Purpose and Overview

Since the data in table TEXLGA is not deleted when you insert them in infotype 0015 or 2010, you periodically run program RPIEWT02 (Reorganize Table TEXLGA—Employee Expenditures) to delete records from table TEXLGA.

26.11 INCORRECT BATCH INPUT SESSIONS PROCESSING

Functional Consultant	User	Business Process Owner	Senior Management	My Rating	Understanding Level
B	B	X	X		

26.11.1 Purpose and Overview

Report RPIEWT03 scans for incorrect sessions and starts batch input processing.

Logistics Integration

27.1 OVERVIEW OF PLANT DATA COLLECTION (PDC)

Functional Consultant	User	Business Process Owner	Senior Management	My Rating	Understanding Level
B	B	C	C		

In SAP logistics, employees record confirmations, which describe the progress of a job and are used for planning and controlling in logistics. They also document the performance of the employee who carried out the work. This data can affect an employee's remuneration. Logistics confirmations must be recorded with a personnel number or id number if they are to be transferred to time management. The confirmations can come from the following SAP application components:

➢ SAP Production Planning (PP) and Process Control (PP/PI)
➢ SAP Plant Maintenance and SAP Customer Service (PM/CS)
➢ SAP Project System (PS)

There are two types of confirmations: work time events and durations.

➢ Work time events: The confirmations recorded in Production Planning and Control (PP) are time event-related. The transferred data is stored in table EVHR in time management. The confirmations are then posted as work time events to the time events infotype (2011). Time tickets are generated from the work time events and can be transferred to incentive wages if required.

➢ Durations: Processing duration of production orders, maintenance orders, networks, and so on, is confirmed in logistics. In other words, the confirmation specifies the time worked as a number of hours. The transferred data is stored in table LSHR in time management. The data can either be posted to incentive wages as time tickets, or to the attendances infotype (2002) as attendances. You can only use this procedure if time management is integrated with all of the above logistics components.

They result in two types of outputs: time tickets or attendances.

> Confirmations from Plant Maintenance and Service Management (PM) and Project System (PS) are usually posted as attendances as they do not generally involve performance-based remuneration such as in piecework.
> Confirmations from Production Planning and Control are posted as time tickets if remuneration is performance-based (as in piecework wages).

In most cases, confirmations are recorded at front-end time recording systems for plant data collection and uploaded to the relevant logistics components in the SAP system. Certified interfaces provide the connection to the subsystem. However, data can also be recorded online in logistics.

Plant data collection transfers the relevant employee data from the above logistics application components to time management. This reduces the work involved in data entry. An additional advantage is that target values and specifications are also transferred from logistics along with the actual data. In this way, labor utilization rates can be determined when time tickets are created in incentive wages. The labor utilization rate affects the rate of remuneration, especially in piecework and premium wages. When the confirmations are transferred from logistics to time management, the data is written either to table EVHR or table LSHR. A plant data sequence number (PDSNR) is assigned to each entry in the tables.

Time wage types are formed during time evaluation in the time management component. They are referenced in the gross part of payroll. Time ticket data from incentive wages is also converted to the relevant wage types in the gross part of payroll. The data determined in the time management component can be accessed by the payroll component. The payroll data can be transferred to SAP controlling for cost accounting.

27.2 SCREEN

Functional Consultant	User	Business Process Owner	Senior Management	My Rating	Understanding Level
B	B	C	X		

27.3 WORK TIME EVENTS PROCESSING

Functional Consultant	User	Business Process Owner	Senior Management	My Rating	Understanding Level
B	B	C		X	

The confirmation data is transferred from production planning and control to time management and stored in table EVHR. The Post Work Time Events from CC2 (SAPCDT46) program does the processing:

➢ The work time events are read from table EVHR.

➢ The work time events open and close pairs. This information is updated in the pair table PT.

➢ Time tickets are also opened, updated and closed. Time tickets are saved to the time ticket table WST. The most important information in a time ticket is the time worked between two (or more) time events. The duration between two work time events is calculated from the employee's daily work schedule and breaks, and written to the last work time event. The time ticket also contains a reference back to the processed order in the form of the PDSNR number.

➢ The assignment of time tickets to pairs is specified in the link table AT.

The time pairs and time tickets are saved separately for each employee and period to tables PT (pair table), WST (time tickets), and AT (link table) in cluster B2, database PCL2.

The time events are saved in table TEVEN. For work time events, data is also saved in table TEVEN_MORE. The processed time events are deleted from table EVHR. If there is a time event that could not be processed as the personnel number was already locked by another transaction, it remains in table EVHR and is processed the next time. Work time events with errors are stored in a pool and deleted from table EVHR.

The incoming work time events from logistics contain an actual time that was determined by pair formation in logistics. Pair formation in time management also determines an actual time, which is generally more exact, since it is based on work schedules relating to persons. It therefore differs from the actual time from logistics. The differences resulting from comparing pair formation in both time management and logistics are transferred to logistics by program RPTIST00.

Generated time tickets are linked with work time events. They are linked with the time pair as well. The generated time tickets can be passed on to incentive wages. In this case, planning data is read from logistics and entered in the time ticket, enabling a performance-based valuation in payroll.

If the logistics confirmations contain information on the cost centers to be debited, this data is included in time evaluation and in incentive wages, and is also passed on to payroll.

27.4 DURATIONS PROCESSING

Functional Consultant	User	Business Process Owner	Senior Management	My Rating	Understanding Level
B	B	C	X		

The program RPWI1100 (Integration with Logistics: Read Interface File and Generate Session) creates a batch input session to retrieve confirmations using the interface table LSHR between the logistics and HR. It can also be run using transaction PW41. There is an older version of this program RPWI1000. If there are any batch input sessions with errors, they are processed using program RPWI3000.

Confirmations retrieved are stored either as time tickets or as attendances in one session. This is specified on the selection screen.

It is often necessary for confirmations from Plant Maintenance (PM) and Project System (PS) to be handled as attendances, because the labor utilization rate is not necessarily calculated there. Confirmations from Production Planning (PP) are posted as time tickets in incentive wages if a determination of the labor utilization rate is needed for the employee's compensation.

The program, RPWI2000 (Batch Input: Process sessions in batch), processes batch input sessions. You can select the sessions you want to be processed, including sessions with errors.

The program, RPWI4100 (Integration with Logistics: Reorganize Interface File), deletes the groups of confirmations from the interface table LSHR.

Time tickets are saved to cluster L1 for individual incentive wages and cluster G1 for group incentive wages. Attendances are updated in the attendances infotype (2002).

Time Evaluation Configuration

28.1 PAIR FORMATION: STATUS TABLE

Functional Consultant	User	Business Process Owner	Senior Management	My Rating	Understanding Level
A	B	C	C		

28.1.1 Purpose

This view determines how the time pairs are formed. When the pair formation is error free, when a new pair is started, when an existing pair is closed, etc. This view is maintained by SAP.

28.1.2 IMG Node

SM30 ➤ TPT_PAIRSTAT2

28.1.3 Screen

	From state	Ti...	U...	To state	Cont...	Clos...	Close	New	C...	E..	Pair form. status
	Start ...🗐	A10	A10	1 At work 🗐	☐	✔	☐	✔			2 No clock-in 🗐
	Start ...🗐	A20	A20	1 At work 🗐	☐	✔	☐	✔			2 No clock-in 🗐
	Start ...🗐	A30	A30	1 At work 🗐	☐	✔	☐	✔			2 No clock-in 🗐
	Start ...🗐	A40	A40	1 At work 🗐	☐	✔	☐	✔			2 No clock-in 🗐
	Start ...🗐	B10	B10	1 At work 🗐	☐	✔	☐	✔			2 No clock-in 🗐

28.1.4 Primary Key

Attendance or Absence Status in Pair Formation + Time Event Type

28.1.5 Important Fields

From state, time event type

At any point of time, an employee has a state. He may be at work or on break or absent, etc.

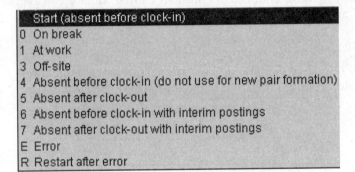

```
Start (absent before clock-in)
0  On break
1  At work
3  Off-site
4  Absent before clock-in (do not use for new pair formation)
5  Absent after clock-out
6  Absent before clock-in with interim postings
7  Absent after clock-out with interim postings
E  Error
R  Restart after error
```

This view explains what happens when an employee is in a particular state (from state), and a time event is recorded (time event type).

Unique time event type

In SAP, time event P01 is clock-in/clock-out. If the employee is at work, it means that he has clocked-out. If he is not at work, then it means that he has clocked-in. This interpretation is defined in the field. Where no interpretation is required, unique time event type is same as time event type.

To state

When an employee has a state, and a time event is recorded, the state of the employee would change. This is shown in this field.

Continue

This field is used only for interim postings. If between your clock-out and clock-in, there is an interim posting, you want two complete pairs, one from clock-out to interim posting, and another from interim posting to clock-in. The first two events form the first time pair. The third event, instead of starting a new time pair, ends the new time pair taking the ending event of previous time pair as the starting event of the new time pair.

Closed

When time events are converted in time pairs, normally the first event starts a time pair and the next event ends it. This process continues. However, if you have one missing time event, all subsequent pairs are wrongly formed. For example, if the entries are P15 (Start of break), P25 (End of break), and P20 (Clock-out), it is obvious that the employee forgot to clock-in. The first pair should have no starting time event, only ending time event P15. This is achieved through a tick in this field. It indicates that the time event should create new closed time pair.

Close

A tick in this field indicates that if there is an open time pair, it should be closed. For example, if an employee is at work, and time event P20 is recorded, then the pair should be closed. If there is no open pair, nothing is done. In contrast 'Closed' field creates an incomplete pair. Fields 'Closed' and 'Close' are mutually exclusive.

New

A tick in this field indicates that a new time pair should be started. Different combinations of 'Closed', 'Close' and 'New' fields result in different behaviour. These are summarized as follows:

Closed	Close	New	Open pair exists	Remarks
X	X			Closed-close combination not valid
X	Blank	X	Y	Close open pair, start new pair
X	Blank	X	N	Create an incomplete pair with ending time event, start new pair
X	Blank	Blank	Y	Close open pair
X	Blank	Blank	N	Create an incomplete pair with ending time event
Blank	X	X	Y	Close open pair, start new pair
Blank	X	X	N	Start new pair
Blank	X	Blank	Y	Close open pair
Blank	X	Blank	N	?
Blank	Blank	X	Y	Start new pair, do not close old.
Blank	Blank	X	N	Start new pair
Blank	Blank	Blank		Only for error and information entry.

Customer adjustment

Here you can specify a PDC processing status. It can be used for determining system reaction specified in view V_T705B.

Error

In the case of error, you may want to give an error message. In other cases, you may sometimes want to give an information message. In this field you define the number of message type.

Pair formation status

When a time event starts a new pair, or closes an existing pair, is the pair error free, or what the type of error is.

28.2 PDC PROCESSING STATUSES

Functional Consultant	User	Business Process Owner	Senior Management	My Rating	Understanding Level
A	X	X	X		

28.2.1 Purpose

When time events data comes, it must make sense. For example, a clock-in followed by another clock-in does not make sense.

You need to specify what to do in such situations. This is done in this view. You must be clear, and have user agreement on these settings, before you work on the time evaluation schema. If certain conditions are prevented through settings here, you need not deal with them in schema.

There is a reaction set for all processing statuses in the standard system. If you want to obtain information on the reaction of pair formation for specific statuses, you may use the F1 help documentation for the status field or the F4 help documentation for the reaction field.

28.2.2 IMG Node

SM30 ➤ V_T705B

28.2.3 Screen

P.	Status	Processing status text	Start Date	End Date	Reaction
01	A00	Repeated posting of time events	01.01.1900	31.12.9999	
01	A01	First record of day	01.01.1900	31.12.9999	
01	A02	Assigning a Record to a Day or a Subsequent Day	01.01.1900	31.12.9999	
01	A03	Employee has day off - start/end of day is estimated	01.01.1900	31.12.9999	

28.2.4 Primary Key

PS Grouping for Time Recording + PDC Processing Status + End Date

28.2.5 Important Fields

PS grouping for time recording

Time recording settings can be different for different locations.

Start and end date

These can be used if you want to change system behaviour from certain date.

PDC processing status and reaction

A00	Repeated posting of time events	If an employee swipes his card twice at the same time or if the data loading takes place twice, two time events are generated. You can decide whether to allow them, ignore them, or put them in error pool.
A01	First record of day	
A02	Assigning a record to a day or a subsequent day	Obsolete
A03	Employee has day off—start/end of day is estimated	
A04	Employee has day off—start/end of day is estimated	
A05	Time events which follow in quick succession	If an employee records two time events within a short period, the system can process both time events, or ignore the first. The span of time is defined in A06.
A06	Value limit for time events which follow in quick succession	See above.
A07	Assigning a time event to the current or previous day	If an employee is at work and swipes clock-out, the time event is assigned to previous day. Alternatively, if the swipe is within the previous day's work schedule, it is assigned to previous day. Here you can specify the time after the end of the previous day's work schedule, within which the time event is assigned to the previous day.
A10	Clock-in or clock-out	If your system does not differentiate between clock-in and clock-out, you enter '1' here. The system converts the entries in 'P01', and whether it is clock-in or clock-out depends on whether the employee is at work or not.
A11	Start or end of off-site work	Same as above for off-site work. The entries are converted in 'P03'.

(Contd.)

C01	Employee is absent and makes an 'end of off-site work' entry	If the employee is absent, i.e. not working off-site, and he records end of off-site work, the system may either give error, or allow it for further processing in time evaluation.
C02	Employee is absent and makes a 'clock-out' entry	If the employee is 'absent' and the record being processed is a clock-out, the system may either give error, or allow it for further processing in time evaluation.
C03	Employee is absent and makes a 'start of off-site work' entry	Similar to C02
C04	Employee is absent and makes a 'start/end of off-site work' entry	If the employee is absent, and the record being processed is for off-site work, the processing can be cancelled with error, or an 'open' pair without begin information can be generated.
C05	Employee is absent and makes a 'start of break' entry	If the employee is absent, he cannot be taking break. You may want to put it in error or handle it in time evaluation.
C11	Employee is at work and makes a 'clock-in' entry	If the employee is at work, he cannot be clocking in. You may want to put it in error or handle it in time evaluation.
C12	Employee is at work and makes an 'end of off-site work' entry	If the employee is at work, he cannot record 'end of off-site work'. You may want to put it in error or close the time pair.
C21	Employee is working off-site and makes a 'clock-in' entry	If the employee is working off-site and makes a 'clock-in' entry, you may want to put it in error or let the clock-in entry also end the off-site work.
C22	Employee is working off-site and makes a clock-out entry	If the employee is working off-site and makes a clock-out entry, you may want to put it in error, or close the time pair.
C31	Employee is on break and makes 'clock-in' entry	If the employee is on break and makes 'clock-in' entry, you may want to put it in error, or let the clock-in end the break.
F03	No account assignment	
F04	No account assignment: Depth of search	
F07	Time event finds time ticket already filled with data	

(Contd.)

F08	Determining productive set-up and machine time
G01	Posting time tickets
G02	Supplying actual times to logistics
L00	Repeated posting of work time events

28.3 EARLIEST RECALCULATION DATES FOR TIME MANAGEMENT

Functional Consultant	User	Business Process Owner	Senior Management	My Rating	Understanding Level
A	B	C	X		

28.3.1 Purpose

This view specifies the earliest recalculation date for four recalculation categories: pair formation, time evaluation, time statement and incentive wages. The system will not do retro accounting before the date specified here in each category.

28.3.2 IMG Node

SM30 ➤ V_T569R

28.3.3 Screen

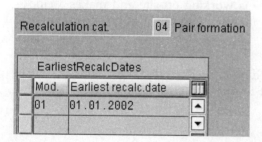

28.3.4 Primary Key

Modifier for Determining Earliest Recalculation Date + Recalculation Category

28.3.5 Important Fields

Recalculation category

Recalculation category	Text for recalculation category
1	Incentive wages
2	Time evaluation
3	Time statement
4	Pair formation

Modifier for determining earliest recalculation date

Table T569R contains earliest recalculation dates, which can vary for different employee groups. Hence, they are made dependent on modifier for determining earliest recalculation date. This modifier can be determined in feature TIMMO based on employee's organizational assignment.

Earliest recalculation date

Recalculation is not permitted before this date.

28.4 GROUPING FOR EARLIEST RECALCULATION DATE

Functional Consultant	User	Business Process Owner	Senior Management	My Rating	Understanding Level
A	X	X	X		

28.4.1 Purpose

Feature TIMMO determines the modifier for determining earliest recalculation date, which is used to access table T569R.

28.4.2 IMG Node

PE03 ➢ TIMMO

28.4.3 Screen

```
TIMMO Defining the modifier for table T569R

    └──── 01
```

28.4.4 Fields for Decision Making

Company Code
Personnel Area
Personnel Subarea
Employee Group
Employee Subgroup
Country Grouping

28.4.5 Return Value

Modifier for determining earliest recalculation date.

28.5 TIME TYPE DETERMINATION

Functional Consultant	User	Business Process Owner	Senior Management	My Rating	Understanding Level
A	B	B	C		

28.5.1 Purpose

During time evaluation, each time pair in internal table TIP is assigned a time id, a processing type and a time type. The time id indicates the position of the time pair in relation to work schedule, e.g. core time, break and overtime. The processing type is used for determining time wage type. The time type is used for storing time balances, which may be used for granting an absence quota to the employee, etc.

If your employees record clock times, all these functions are performed by function TIMTP. It first determines the time id. Then it uses this table T555Z for determining the processing type and the time type of a time pair. The processing type and the time type of a time pair depend primarily on the time id of the time pair and the pair type (not at work, at work, recorded absence, offsite work).

If your employees do not record clock times, all these functions are performed by function TYPES. It gets the 'Ptype/Ttype class' of the attendance/absence type from table T554S, and using it gets the processing type and the time type from table T555Y. These are updated in table TIP.

28.5.2 IMG Node

SM30 ➤ V_T555Z

28.5.3 Screen

PSG	Group	ID	Start Date	End Date	PairType0	PairType1	PairType2	PairType3
☐ 00	02	01	01.01.1900	31.12.9999				
☐ 00	02	02	01.01.1900	31.12.9999				
☐ 00	02	05	01.01.1900	31.12.9999				
☐ 01	01	01	01.01.1900	31.12.9999		0310	0320	0330
☐ 01	01	02	01.01.1900	31.12.9999	- 3020	P 0110	A 0120	P 0130

28.5.4 Primary Key

PS Grouping for Time Recording + Time Type Determination Group + Time Identifier for Daily Work Schedule + End Date

28.5.5 Important Fields

PS grouping for time recording

Usually processing type/time type determination does not depend on employee location. But SAP provides the flexibility in case you need it.

Time type determination group

In time evaluation, this field is set by function MOD, PCR MODT value T.

Time identifier for daily work schedule

Time identifier is the position of a time pair in relation to daily work schedule. Function TIMTP determines it by comparing plan time and actual time.

Time identifier	Description
01	Overtime (time outside of daily work schedule)
02	Fill time
03	Core time
04	Core time break
05	Fill time break
06	Paid break
07	Unpaid overtime break
08	Paid overtime break
09	Overtime break

Start and end date

Validity period.

Time types and processing types for pair types 0, 1, 2 and 3

Here you define the time types and processing types which should be assigned depending on pair type and time id. Time types and processing types can also vary based on PS grouping for time recording and time type determination group.

Pair type	Description
0	Non-recorded absence or employee is on break. The employee is not at work and it has not been recorded. If there are gaps in time pairs, function TIMTP creates the required pairs, and assigns them pair type 0.
1	Employee is at work. If the employee is recording time, there is appropriate time event, e.g. clock-in. If he is recording deviations from daily work schedule, this comes from planned time. It is imported to time evaluation using function P2011 or P2000.
2	Employee is absent with approval. There is record of absence in infotype 2001. It is imported using function P2001.
3	Employee is at work or is working off-site. There is record of attendance in infotype 2002 or there is clock-in/clock-out entry with time events pertaining to off-site work. It is imported using function P2011 or P2002.

28.6 TIME TYPES

Functional Consultant	User	Business Process Owner	Senior Management	My Rating	Understanding Level
A	B	B	C		

28.6.1 Purpose

What is it?

In SAP, there are two main outputs of time management—time wage types and time balances. Time balances are maintained against time types. Time types serve as buckets for presenting a summarized picture. You may want to know how many hours a person worked, how many hours within work schedule, how many hours overtime, etc. Each of these would be a time type, and the balances, whether daywise, or monthwise, would answer your questions.

Therefore, it is very important to plan your time types in advance and write down their descriptions so that people pick up the correct time type to get answers to their questions.

SAP has predefined some time types, which are used in the PCRs in standard schemas. You could use them. In addition, you could define your own time types. You have to take care that they are correctly formed in the schema.

How is it determined?

Time types are determined primarily by function TIMTP using table T555Z, where employees record time, and by function TYPES using table T555Y where they don't. Where the time types are determined by function TYPES, the naming convention for time types is 1yzz, where y is the pair type and zz is the processing type/time type class.

In table TIP, time type of a pair can be overwritten by operation COLOP, while transferring the pair to table TOP. This operation is used in PCRs TD40, TP10, TB10, TB11, TO20, TO21, TO10, TO16, TO11 and TO15 in schema TM00, but time type is overwritten only in PCRs TD40 and TO11.

Day balances are formed by operation ADDDB, which creates records in table TES. This operation is used in PCRs TE20, TF10, TP20, TB11, TO21, TO11, TC40, TC41, TC42, TR10 and TR30 in schema TM00.

Function CUMBT transfers time balances from table TES to table ZES, and cumulates them in table SALDO. Operation ADDMB adds time balance to a time type directly to table SALDO. Function DEFTP also creates two time types—0000 and 0001.

When you do time transfer using infotype 2012, the system adds or subtracts time balances to time types based on the entries in table T555J.

You can limit the value of a time type using function LIMIT. While doing so, you can transfer the difference to another time type. You can also store original value in another time type. These are specified in table V_T559P.

When overtime is worked, it is checked for approval specified in attendance quota in PA2007. Attendance quota specifies attendance quota type. If overtime is approved, it is accumulated in the time type specified 'TmType' field in view V_556P_B. If overtime is not approved, it is accumulated in the time type specified in the 'alt.TT' field in the same view.

Where is it stored?

A time type can have both day balance and period balance. Time balances are stored in tables ZES (day balance) and SALDO (period balance) in cluster B2. During time evaluation, they are also temporarily stored in internal table TES.

How is it used?

The most important use of time types is to provide data for payroll. This is done through time wage types. Another important use of time balances is for quota generation. Automatic absence quota generation can use time types in various ways. For more details, see chapter 7.4. You can also generate absence quotas from time types so that employees can use excess time worked to take time off.

Attendance/absence data is required for various purposes in the organization, e.g. determination of productivity, discipline, identification of high absenteeism employees, etc. All these purposes can be served through time types.

You can transfer time balances to other time types, wage types and absence quotas, based on employee request through infotype 2012. Time balances in specified time types can provide default values for infotype 2012.

Time types can be cumulated into other time types in PCRs, e.g. in PCR TR10, TR11. Time balances can be reported in time statement and other reports. They can be seen in time manager's workplace and shift planning. They can be downloaded to attendance recording systems. Time balances can be read in PCRs using operation HRS. Their cumulative values can be read using operation SUM.

28.6.2 IMG Node

SM30 ➢ V_T555A

28.6.3 Screen

28.6.4 Primary Key

PS Grouping for Time Recording + Time Type + End Date

28.6.5 Important Fields

PS grouping for time recording

The set of time types you use and their definition can depend on the PS grouping for time recording.

Time type

Time types serve as buckets for presenting a summarized picture. You may want to know how many hours a person worked, how many hours were within work schedule, how many hours were overtime, etc. Each of these would be a time type, and the balances, whether daywise, or monthwise, would answer your questions. One may like to think of time types as primary time types, which are assigned to a time pair, and secondary time types, which are cumulated from the primary time types.

Start and end date

Validity period of the record.

Save as day balance

In this field you can define whether day balance is formed or not. This indicator is interpreted by function CUMBT in the time evaluation schema to decide whether table ZES should be populated or not.

Blank or 0	No balance formation	These time types are not stored in table ZES. For example, utility time types which are used internally during time evaluation and should not be saved.
1	Balance formation	These time types are stored in table ZES.
2	Balance formation without preceding cancellation (Caution!)	The day balance is not deleted if there is a recalculation.

Cumulate in period balance

In this field you can define whether period balance is formed or not. This indicator is interpreted by function CUMBT in the time evaluation schema to decide whether table SALDO should be populated or not.

Blank or 0	No balance formation	These time types are not stored in table SALDO. For example, utility time types which are used internally during time evaluation and should not be saved.
1	Balance formation	These time types are stored in table SALDO.
2	Balance formation without preceding cancellation (Caution!)	The period balance is not deleted if there is a recalculation.

Transfer from previous period

At the start of a new period, you can decide whether or not to transfer the period balance from the previous period for cumulations.

Blank or 0	No transfer	The period balance is not transferred from the previous period.
1	Transfer	The period balance is transferred from the previous period and used as a basis for the cumulation for the new period.
		In the first period in January, the indicator transfer from previous year is used to transfer December's period balance.

Transfer from previous year

At the start of a new year, you can decide whether or not to transfer the period balance from the previous year for cumulations. This overrides the transfer from previous period indicator.

Blank or 0	No transfer	The period balance is not transferred from the previous year.
1	Transfer	The period balance is transferred from the previous year and used as a basis for the cumulation for the new year.

Period balance of previous period

The period balance of previous period may be transferred to a different time type. Here you specify the time type to which the balance should be transferred.

Period balance of previous year

The period balance of previous year may be transferred to a different time type. Here you specify the time type to which the balance should be transferred.

Store for time accounts and download to time recording systems

Here you specify which time types are to be stored in table ST in cluster B1, so that they can be downloaded to the time recording systems. Then, in view V_T555I, PDC Master

Record Information, you can specify from this list for the actual download, which may be different for different groups of employees.

| Blank or 0 | No storage | Not stored in table ST and therefore cannot be downloaded to time recording systems. |
| 1 | Storage | Stored in table ST and therefore can be downloaded to time recording system. |

28.6.6 Flow of Time Types when Recording Clock Times

Function TIMTP determines time types using table T555Z. SAP provides following pre-configured values.

Time ID	Time ID description	At work	Recorded absence	Off-site/recorded attendance
02	Fill time	0110	0120	0130
03	Core time	0210	0220	0230
01	Overtime	0310	0320	0330
04	Core time break			
05	Fill time break	0510	0520	0530
07	Unpaid overtime break			
09	Overtime break			
06	Paid break		0540	
08	Paid overtime break			

In the case of overtime approvals, the time type in table TIP is updated to 0040 from 0310 and 0330. PCR TR10 cumulates these time types into larger time types.

Time type	Description	Sum of time types
0003	Skeleton time	0110, 0210, 0120, 0220, 0130, 0230, 0411 and 0540
0010	Attendance	0110 and 0210
0020	Absence	0120 and 0220
0030	Off-site work	0130 and 0230
0100	Fill time	0110, 0120 and 0130
0200	Core time	0210, 0220 and 0230
0301	Overtime	0310, 0320 and 0330.
		Before cumulation by function TR10 takes place, time type of approved overtimes has been changed to 0040.
		Thus, time types 0310, 0320, 0330 and 0301 in tables TES, ZES and SALDO are unapproved overtimes. Approved overtimes are in 0040, 0041, 0042, 0043 and 0410.
0500	Break	0510, 0520, 0530 and 0540

Time type balances may also change by function P2012, or LIMIT. This happens before updation of balances in cluster B2 by function CUMBT.

28.6.7 Flow of Overtime Time Types when Recording Clock Times

Overtime coming from infotype 2005 is assigned time type 0040 by PCR TD40. This remains unchanged when function TIMTP generates time types for pairs in table TIP.

Function TIMTP generates time types 0310, 0320 and 0330 for overtimes. You may also see PCR TE10, which updates time id to 01 in certain cases, so that overtime time types are generated by function TIMTP.

PCRs TO10, TO15, TO16 and TO11 check for overtime approval, and update the time type of approved pairs in TIP to 0040. In this process, for some pairs, time types get updated from 0310 or 0330 to 0040.

Function GWT processes table TIP (time pairs with processing type M) and creates records in table ZML.

PCR TC40 processes wage types in table ZML, and depending on processing class 17 of wage types and overtime compensation type of records, generates time types 0041, 0042, 0043 and 0410 in table TES.

Time type balances may also change by function P2012 or LIMIT. Function P2012 processes time transfers in infotype 2012, and makes time transfer between time types, wage types and quotas. Function LIMIT applies predefined capping rules to time types. It may transfer excess balance in time types to other time types. This happens before updation of balances in cluster B2 by function CUMBT.

28.7 PROCESSING TYPE

Functional Consultant	User	Business Process Owner	Senior Management	My Rating	Understanding Level
A	B	B	C		

28.7.1 Purpose and Overview

One of the most important uses of time management is to generate time wage types which can be paid in payroll. For salaried employees, these payments are usually for overtime. There may also be other payments, e.g. night shift allowance and holiday allowance. For hourly paid employees, their entire wages may be determined from time wage types.

SAP provides you a flexible method of generating time wage types, which depends on the concept of processing type. Let us say, you want to pay the salaried employees differently for attendance (P), absence (A), overtime (M) and breaks (K). You would define these processing types. Then you would define a table as under, and put it in configuration table T555Z of SAP.

Time ID	Time ID description	Pair type 0 no info	Pair type 1 recorded time	Pair type 2 absence	Pair type 3 off-site work
	Within work schedule				
02	Fill time	K	P	A	P
03	Core time	K	P	A	P
04	Core time break	K	K	Blank	K
05	Fill time break	K	K	Blank	K
06	Paid break	K	P	A	P
	Outside work schedule				
01	Overtime	Blank	M	Blank	M
07	Unpaid overtime break	K	K	Blank	K
08	Paid overtime break	Blank	M	M	M
09	Overtime break	K	K	Blank	K

A similar template for hourly paid employees could be as under, where processing type S is planned time.

Time ID	Time ID description	Pair type 0 no info	Pair type 1 recorded time	Pair type 2 absence	Pair type 3 off-site work
	Within work schedule				
02	Fill time	Blank	S	S	S
03	Core time	Blank	S	S	S
04	Core time break	Blank	K	Blank	K
05	Fill time break	Blank	K	Blank	K
06	Paid break	Blank	S	S	S
	Outside work schedule				
01	Overtime	Blank	M	Blank	M
07	Unpaid overtime break	Blank	K	Blank	K
08	Paid overtime break	Blank	M	M	M
09	Overtime break	Blank	K	Blank	K

When you are doing time evaluation, you have time pairs in internal table TIP. For these time pairs, time id and pair type are determined by the system. Function TIMTP then determines processing type from the configuration table T555Z, and update for each pair in internal table TIP.

Where you keep the processing type blank, you are either planning to fill it later in a PCR, or you have decided that no time wage type is to be generated for those time pairs.

As time evaluation proceeds further, you may stamp processing type of certain time pairs based on the logic written in the PCRs. The operation used to stamp processing type is FILLP. This is commonly done for overtime where you would check approval for overtime, so that only approved overtimes are paid (see PCRs TO10, TO15, TO16 and TO11, for example).

Finally, operation GWT would create time wage types, depending on processing type in accordance with rules defined in table T510S.

If you are not working with recorded times, the processing type gets determined by function TYPES using table T555Y.

Unlike time types, where pre-defined time types have reasonably fixed meaning, processing types are heavily dependent on your company's requirements. The templates given above are only to explain the concept.

28.7.2   IMG Node

SM30 ➤ V_T510V

28.7.3   Screen

Processing Type	Processing type text
A	Absence
C	On-call shift
G	Guaranteed hours
H	Assumed overtime
J	Break for "as if" time
K	Break
M	Overtime
N	Overtime (paid + comp)
O	Overtime (comp only)
P	Attendance
R	On-call duty
S	Planned work
X	Public holiday

28.7.4   Primary Key

Language Key + Processing Type

28.8 TIME WAGE TYPE SELECTION RULE

Functional Consultant	User	Business Process Owner	Senior Management	My Rating	Understanding Level
A	B	C	X		

28.8.1 Purpose

One of the most important uses of time management is to generate time wage types which can be paid in payroll. For salaried employees, these payments are usually for overtime. There may also be other payments, e.g. night shift allowance and holiday allowance. For hourly paid employees, their entire wages may be determined from time wage types. This table is used to define the rules for generating time wage types.

A wage type selection rule in table T510S consists of several subrules. Only those subrules, which meet the specified conditions, are selected.

Operation GWT would create time wage types, depending on processing type in accordance with rules defined in table T510S. Time wage types for overtime (processing type M) are inserted in table ZML, whereas time wage types for other processing type are inserted in table DZL.

If overtime is to be compensated, time wage types from ZML are also moved into table DZL. Finally entries of table DZL are stored in table ZL in cluster B2, from where they are picked up for payroll.

28.8.2 IMG Node

SM30 ≻ V_T510S

28.8.3 Screen

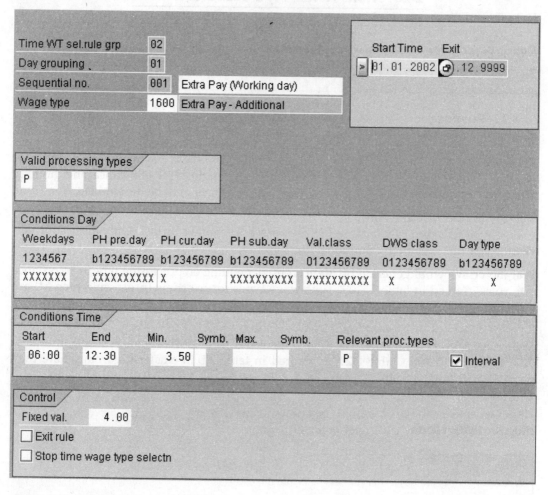

28.8.4 Primary Key

Country Grouping + Time Wage Type Selection Rule Group + Day Grouping for the Time Wage Type Selection + End Date + Number of Infotype Record with Same Key

28.8.5 Important Fields

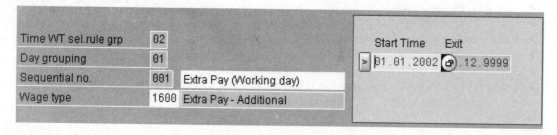

Time wage type selection rule group

In time evaluation, this field is set by function MOD, PCR MODT, value W.

Day grouping for the time wage type selection

The function DAYMO or the operation MODIF D=xx can be used to define which entry should be used for the rule group in the DAYMO field. This entry is usually defined on the basis of the features of the day to be evaluated.

Sequential number

This identifies the subrule.

Start and end dates

Validity period of the record.

Wage type

Wage type which is generated if the conditions are fulfilled.

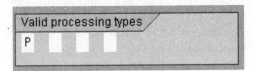

Valid processing types

Here you specify the processing types to which the rule applies. You can enter up to four processing types, but you must enter at least one.

Conditions Day						
Weekdays	PH pre.day	PH cur.day	PH sub.day	Val.class	DWS class	Day type
1234567	b123456789	b123456789	b123456789	0123456789	0123456789	b123456789
XXXXXXX	XXXXXXXXXX X		XXXXXXXXXX	XXXXXXXXXX	X	X

Here you specify the days for which the wage type is generated. The applicability can be affected by:

➢ The day of the week
➢ Public holiday class for previous day
➢ Public holiday class of current day
➢ Public holiday class for next day
➢ Valuation class (matched with valuation class of the employee's period work schedule)
➢ Daily work schedule class (matched with daily work schedule class of the employee's daily work schedule)
➢ Day type

Conditions Time							
Start	End	Min.	Symb.	Max.	Symb.	Relevant proc.types	
06:00	12:30	3.50				P	☑ Interval

Here you can specify the time conditions for which wage type should be generated.

➤ If you want that the wage type should be generated only if the time pair is within a specified time period of the day, you can specify that here.

➤ You can also specify that the employee must put in a certain minimum number of hours of the specified processing type, before the wage type is generated.

➤ Instead of specifying fixed number of hours as minimum, you can specify that the employee must complete planned hours, average working time per day etc.

➤ Similarly, you can specify the maximum number of hours of relevant processing type for which the wage type is generated. If the number of hours is exceeded, the wage type is generated only for specified maximum hours.

➤ Instead of a fixed value, the maximum value can be specified in terms of planned hours, average working time per day, etc.

➤ You specify processing types which should be considered for applying minimum and maximum limits. If you do not specify any processing types here, the system uses the processing type specified in parameter 2 when function GWT is called up.

➤ In the interval check box you specify whether minimum/maximum are to be counted within specified time period only. For more details, see field help.

Control	
Fixed val.	4.00
☐ Exit rule	
☐ Stop time wage type selectn	

Fixed value

If you want to generate the wage type with a fixed value you specify that here. In that case, it is only necessary that employee's time pair overlaps with the time period in time condition. This is useful, for example, if you want to pay your employees a night shift allowance. The fact that they were present during the night is enough. How long were they present is unimportant.

Exit rule

If you tick this field, as soon as conditions for a subrule are satisfied and wage type generated, further subrules of that rule are not processed. The system goes to the next rule.

Stop time wage type selection

If you tick this field, as soon as conditions for a rule are satisfied and wage type generated, further rules are not processed. The system exits wage type selection for that time pair.

28.9 LIMITS FOR TIME BALANCES

Functional Consultant	User	Business Process Owner	Senior Management	My Rating	Understanding Level
A	B	C	X		

28.9.1 Purpose

This view defines limits on time balances. Multiple rules may be defined for PS grouping for time recording and time balance rule group combination. All these rules are applied to an employee belonging to this combination.

28.9.2 IMG Node

SM30 ➤ V_T559P

28.9.3 Primary Key

Country Grouping + PS Grouping for Time Recording + Time Balance Rule Group + Rule for Balance Formation + End Date

28.9.4 Important Fields

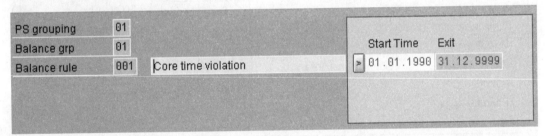

PS grouping for time recording

Limits for time balance can be different for different locations.

Balance group

In time evaluation, this field is set by function MOD, PCR MODT value L.

Balance rule

You can define multiple rules, which apply to an employee belonging to a PS grouping for time recording and time balance rule group. All rules apply to the employee. This field gives a number to each rule.

Start and end date

Validity period of the record.

Value limit for time balance			Type of value limit
Constant value		⬚	⦿ Maximum
From operation HRS	Origin	⬚	○ Lower limit
	Parameters	⬚	

Value limit for time balance

If the limit is a constant value in hours, you specify it in constant value field. You can also determine the value limit from your employees' planned working time, time balances etc. This option gives a lot more flexibility.

Type of value limit

You can specify whether this rule is enforcing an upper limit, or a lower limit. You can have one rule enforcing an upper limit, and another enforcing a lower limit.

Time balance

Time type   0235   Core time violation

Day balance processed over		Period balance	
⦿ Current day		○ Current period Incl. PPs ⬚	
○ Time evaluation period	Incl. PPs ⬚		
○ Payroll period	Incl. PPs ⬚		
○ Working week	Incl. PPs ⬚		
○ Period ⬚	Incl. PPs ⬚		
○ Period	⬚		

Processing in period

⦿ Cumulate   ○ Find maximum   ○ Find minimum

Time type

You specify the time type which is to be limited.

Day balance processed over

When limiting day balance, you can include a number of previous days defined in terms of various periods.

Period balance

When limiting period balance, you can include multiple previous periods.

Processing in period

The limit is not necessarily applied to the sum of day or period balance, but may be applied to the maximum or minimum as well.

```
Processing if value limit is exceeded

Messages          44       Core time violation
  ● Note               ○ Information        ○ Error            ○ Termination
  ☐ Capping
  ┌─ Store surplus in time balance ─┐      ┌─ Store surplus in wage type ─┐
  │                                 │      │                              │
  │ ☐ Replace value                 │      │ Infotype                     │
  │ ☐ Reverse +/- sign              │      │ ☐ Reverse +/- sign           │
  └─────────────────────────────────┘      └──────────────────────────────┘
```

Messages

If the value limit is exceeded, you can give a message, which may be note, information, error (causes recalculation), or termination (terminates time evaluation).

Capping

You would tick capping, if you want the balance to be changed to the value limit. If you don't tick this, the value does not change, you only get message.

Store surplus in time balance

If you change the time balances by capping, you can transfer the difference to another time type. When transferring this value, you can ignore or retain the existing value in the time type, and add or subtract the difference you want to transfer.

Store surplus in wage type

You can also transfer the difference to a wage type. Here, you give additional information called 'Information type'. You can also specify whether the sign is to be reversed.

```
Processing if value limit is reached

Message
Tolerance                          ☐ Percentage
```

Processing if value limit is reached

You can also give a message when the value limit is reached, or is about to be reached. If the message is to be given before the limit is reached, you specify the tolerance in hours or percentage.

```
Store time balance in time type

                                    ☐ Replace value
```

Store time balance in time type

The LIMIT function may, or may not, change the time balance. If you want to store the original value, you can specify a time type here. In the new time type, the balance may be added, or replaced.

```
Check point

  During day processing                    During final processing

  ◉ Daily                                    ○ End of time eval. period
  ○ End of time evaluation period            ○ End of period
  ○ End of payroll period
  ○ End of working week
  ○ End of period
```

Check point

The check point specifies when the limits are to be checked.

```
Age limit

  From          ──────
```

Age limit

Your limit rules can depend on the age of the employee, which you enter here.

28.10 TIME EVALUATION MESSAGES

Functional Consultant	User	Business Process Owner	Senior Management	My Rating	Understanding Level
A	B	C	X		

28.10.1 Purpose

In this view you define your own message types and specify how you want the system to handle the message types. You set the number of the message type xx in a personnel calculation rule using operation COLER xx. Here you define the meaning of message type xx.

28.10.2 IMG Node

SM30 ➢ V_T555E

28.10.3 Screen

	PSG	Ty.	MessTy	Message long text	Mail	List ID	Balance	Generate ...
	01	1	00	Employee at work although OFF	0	0		☐
	01	1	01	Employee not at work	1	1		☐
	01	1	02	At work despite full-day absence	1	1		☐
	01	1	03	Clock-in cannot be delimited	1	1		☐
	01	1	04	Clock-out cannot be delimited	1	1		☐

28.10.4 Primary Key

PS Grouping for Time Recording + Category of Message Type + Number of Message Type

28.10.5 Important Fields

PS grouping for time recording

Messages may vary depending on an employee's location.

Category of message type

Category	Origin
1	Error set via operation COLER in time evaluation
2	(do not use anymore) Customer-specific message for pair formation
3	Technical error in pair formation
4	Technical error in time evaluation
5	Warnings and notes generated by time evaluation

Number of message type

Number of the message that is generated and stored in table FEHLER if a particular situation arises in pair formation and/or time evaluation.

Mail indicator

SAP provides for messages to be communicated to employees through time recording terminals. If this field is ticked, and this message is generated, the transaction Transfer HR master record to PDC subsystems, which supplies the time recording system with the mini-master records, sets a mail indicator in the mini-master record according to the entry in this field.

List indicator

The indicator enables message types to be categorized. In the standard system, you can query the list indicator in report RPTERR00 (Time Management: Error Handling). You can use the indicator for the time management pool (transaction PT40) to control which employees process which messages.

Balance indicator

In the case of some errors, displaying balances at the time recording terminals does not make sense. If you do not want balances to be displayed at the time recording terminal in the case of particular errors, set an X in this field.

Generate time evaluation messages once

If time evaluation is repeated before corrective action is taken, the same messages are repeated. This can become a nuisance for those responsible for processing the messages. If you tick this field, the messages are not repeated in the case of a recalculation.

28.11   TIME PARAMETERS

Functional Consultant	User	Business Process Owner	Senior Management	My Rating	Understanding Level
A	B	C	X		

28.11.1   Purpose and Overview

It goes without saying that you should study each and every PCR in the time management schema you implement. Some of them use global constants. SAP lets you maintain global constants in table T511K, which can change with time. You must make sure that they contain correct values. You may read value of a parameter, using operation HRS (5th character C) in a PCR and make decisions or use in calculations. Some of the constants used in configuration are given below. You may read the exact use in help given with each constant.

Constant	Explanation
GLMAX	Flextime maximum for a month
GLMIN	Flextime minimum (negative)
LVACR	Leave accrual per payroll period
OVERT	Limit value–overtime (week)
OVTWH	Maximum overtime (week)
OVTWL	Minimum overtime (week)
OVTWY	Annual overtime limit (week)
TGMAX	Daily maximum working time
ZEDEG	Delimit off-site work automatically
ZETOL	Time tolerance for work end
ZMRND	Rounding factor for overtime

28.11.2 IMG Node

SM30 ➤ V_T511K

28.11.3 Screen

Constant	Info	Payroll constant	Start Date	End Date	Value
ADDSS	H	Employee Address	01.01.1999	31.12.9999	1.00
ARTDS	H	Arrear Payment - TDS %	01.01.1999	31.12.9999	30.00
BNNPR	H	Bonus-Minimum %	01.04.1998	31.03.9999	8.33
BNTDS	H	Bonus Payment - TDS %	01.01.1999	31.12.9999	30.00
BNXPR	H	Bonus-Maximum %	01.04.1998	31.03.9999	20.00
CADTR	H	COA/CLA Delta Treatment	01.04.1998	31.03.9999	1.00

28.12 ENHANCEMENT OF BUSINESS LOGIC FOR TIME DATA

Functional Consultant	User	Business Process Owner	Senior Management	My Rating	Understanding Level
B	X	X	X		

You can implement BAdI PT_BLP_USER to enhance business logic for time data.

Cluster B1

29.1 GENERAL

Functional Consultant	User	Business Process Owner	Senior Management	My Rating	Understanding Level
A	B	C	X		

The data in cluster B1 is stored for individual personnel numbers. You can see the data in cluster B1 by running transaction PT_CLSTB1. When you run this transaction at the highest level, you get one record per person. Personnel number is the cluster key. Transparent table PCL1 contains one record for each cluster key. All information in the cluster is at cluster key level. You can drill down these records. When you drill down a record for a person, you see all the tables and the number of records in them. As you drill down further, you see the list of records displaying data.

29.2 NT1–UNPROCESSED TIME EVENTS

Functional Consultant	User	Business Process Owner	Senior Management	My Rating	Understanding Level
A	B	C	X		

29.2.1 Purpose and Overview

Table NT1 contains pointers to all unprocessed time events. It is used in pair formation and to recognize the necessity for a recalculation. All time events are stored in table TEVEN. NT1 contains only the unprocessed ones.

When time events data is entered into infotype 2011 (table TEVEN), it is simultaneously entered in table NT1 also. It is used in pair formation during time evaluation. If the time event is successfully used, it is deleted from NT1, otherwise it is transferred to NT2. After time evaluation is run, table NT1 becomes empty, as all time events, which could not be processed (due to error in pair formation), are shifted to NT2.

The earliest date in this table is considered for determining the date from which time evaluation should start. The structure of table NT1 is PDCMT.

29.2.2 Screen

Date	Time	EntDate	EntTime	OIn	I/D/U	Time event type	current no.
15.04.2005	08:23:00	15.04.2005	12:49:59	M	I	P10 Clock-in	000050674059
15.04.2005	17:00:00	15.04.2005	12:49:59	M	I	P20 Clock-out	000050674058
16.04.2005	08:23:00	16.04.2005	16:10:08	M	I	P10 Clock-in	000050740227
16.04.2005	17:00:00	16.04.2005	16:10:08	M	I	P20 Clock-out	000050740226

29.2.3 Important Fields

Date and time of time event

This is automatically assigned by the time recording system when the time event is recorded.

Date and time of data entry in SAP

This is automatically assigned by SAP when the data record of time event is created in SAP.

Origin indicator of PDC message

The origin indicator shows whether the time event was entered manually in the SAP system. An M in the field denotes a manual entry. The field is blank if the data was uploaded into the system.

Insert/delete/update

This indicates whether the record is inserted, deleted or updated.

Time event type

Time event types, e.g. clock-in, clock-out, start of break, end of break are predefined by SAP.

Sequential number for PDC messages

When time events are loaded in SAP, each time event gets a unique number which is stored here. Using this number, you can see all the data in TEVEN table.

29.3 NT2–TIME EVENTS TO BE REPROCESSED

Functional Consultant	User	Business Process Owner	Senior Management	My Rating	Understanding Level
A	B	C	X		

29.3.1 Purpose and Overview

Table NT2 contains pointers to time events that lead to a processing error. It contains time events, which had problem in pair formation. These are transferred from NT1 to NT2. When time pair formation takes place next time, these time events are also considered. If they are successfully used, they get deleted from this table.

The earliest date in this table is considered for determining the date from which time evaluation should start. If an employee has time management status 9, he is not supposed to record attendance. However, if he does so on some occasions, these time events end up in NT2. Since no pair formation takes place for these employees, they remain there, and therefore influence the date from which time evaluation starts. It is therefore necessary to delete time events of these employees from table NT2. You can use program RPUP1D00 to delete time events from table NT2. However, you may read the caution in program's document.

The structure of table NT2 is PDCMT (same as NT1). Hence the fields are not described here.

29.3.2 Screen

Date	Time	EntDate	EntTime	OIn	I/D/U	Time event type	current no.
13.04.2005	08:22:00	13.04.2005	12:08:37	M	I	P10 Clock-in	000050593431
13.04.2005	17:00:00	13.04.2005	12:08:37	M	I	P20 Clock-out	000050593430

29.4 ERT–MESSAGES

Functional Consultant	User	Business Process Owner	Senior Management	My Rating	Understanding Level
A	B	C	X		

29.4.1 Purpose and Overview

Table ERT contains the messages from the last time evaluation run. There are different types of messages. Type 3 errors are technical error from pair formation according to the Time Evaluation Errors table (T555E).

Internal table ERT contains errors not only of type 3, but also of others. Type 3 errors get cleared and are freshly evaluated, when time evaluation runs again. The messages in table ERT are processed by function PERT which only reads type 3 errors. If such an error is found, PCR TD20 stops time evaluation of that person.

The structure of table ERT is PC2B8.

29.4.2 Screen

Field name	Field content
Date	13.06.2004
Cat. of Message Type	1
Message type number	14 Absence < 1 day exceeded
Message type	
Message supplement	
SeqNo. time event	000000000000
Time	00:00:00
Historical record	
Processing status	
Agent	YVD114891
Processing date	23.06.2004
Origin	00000000

29.4.3 Important Fields

Date

Time evaluation takes place for a person and date. This field contains the date that was being processed when the message was generated.

Category of message type

Category	Origin
1	Error set by operation COLER in time evaluation
2	(No longer use) User-specific message from pair formation
3	Technical error from pair formation
4	Technical error from time evaluation
5	Warnings and notes, generated by time evaluation

Message type number

This specifies the message generated.

Message type

This field specifies whether the message is an Error (E), a Cancellation (A) or a Note (blank).

Message supplement

Sequence number of time event

If this message refers to a time event, its sequential number is specified here. This number uniquely identifies a time event record.

Time

Time of the time event.

Historical record flag

If you mark a record historical, it is permanently stored in the database and is available for reporting. However, it cannot be changed.

Processing status

Blank	New
1	In process
2	Completed
3	Confirmed

Agent

User id of the last user who acted on this message.

Processing date

The date when this message was processed last.

Origin

This field is relevant only if you use time evaluation for concurrent employment.

29.4.4 Data Flow

Input	Processing	Output	Details
		ERT	Created during pair formation
ERT	PERT TD20	FEHLER, ERT	Terminates processing for an employee if there is a technical error from pair formation in table ERT.

29.5   NCT–DAYS TO BE RECALCULATED

Functional Consultant	User	Business Process Owner	Senior Management	My Rating	Understanding Level
B	C	X	X		

29.5.1   Purpose and Overview

Table NCT contains date specifications for days for which the entire pair formation process must be carried out again. If an error occurs for a day in pair formation, then the error is written to table NCT. When the pair formation happens correctly for this day, the error is cleared. This is one of the dates which is considered for determining the date from which time evaluation should start. The structure of table NCT is PDC07.

29.5.2   Screen

Logical date

01.09.2004

29.6   IFT1–INTERFACE TO LOGISTICS

Functional Consultant	User	Business Process Owner	Senior Management	My Rating	Understanding Level
B	C	X	X		

29.6.1   Purpose and Overview

Table IFT1 is only used internally by SAP. The structure of table IFT1 is PDCIFT.

29.7   IFT2–INTERFACE TO INCENTIVE WAGES

Functional Consultant	User	Business Process Owner	Senior Management	My Rating	Understanding Level
B	C	X	X		

29.7.1   Purpose and Overview

Table IFT2 is the interface table for incentive wages. It describes the changes in table WST (time tickets, other documents) from cluster B2 to the time tickets that have already been updated in incentive wages. The structure of table IFT2 is PDCIFT.

29.8   ST–SELECTED PERIOD BALANCES

Functional Consultant	User	Business Process Owner	Senior Management	My Rating	Understanding Level
B	C	X	X		

29.8.1   Purpose and Overview

Table ST contains selected balances which are transferred to the time recording systems for employees' information the next time a download is performed. In 'Store for time accounts' field of table T555A, you specify which time types are to be stored in table ST, so that they can be downloaded to the time recording systems. Then, in view V_T555I, PDC Master Record Information, you can specify from this list for the actual download, which may be different for different groups of employees. The structure of table ST is PC2B5.

29.8.2   Screen

Time type	Number
0003 Skeleton time	88.00
0110 Fill time Attendance	88.00

29.9 QT–VARIOUS FIELDS

Functional Consultant	User	Business Process Owner	Senior Management	My Rating	Understanding Level
A	B	C	X		

29.9.1 Purpose and Overview

Unlike other tables, which have daywise records, table QT contains a single record, giving status of various items for a personnel number. Starting date for time evaluation in table QT of cluster B1 is one of the dates, which determines the starting point of time evaluation. The structure of field string QT is PDC06.

29.9.2 Screen

Field name	Field content
Starting date for time evaluation	13.04.2005
Att./absence status	5
Index for table PT	000
Last day processed (*)	12.04.2005
Start of plnd work from (*)	08:30
End of plnd work from (*)	17:00
Holiday class from (*)	0
Daily WS class from (*)	1
Day type from (*)	0
Recalculation triggered by PB for ZA	00.00.0000
Last error processing	00.00.0000

29.9.3 Important Fields

Starting date for time evaluation

This table contains one of the dates which determines when time evaluation for an employee starts.

Attendance or absence status in pair formation

Status	Description
Blank	Start (absent before clock-in)
0	On break
1	At work
3	Off-site
4	Absent before clock-in (do not use for new pair formation)
5	Absent after clock-out
6	Absent before clock-in with interim postings
7	Absent after clock-out with interim postings
E	Error
R	Restart after error

This field is also present in table PT Time pairs.

Index for table PT

Index of pair formation table.

Last day processed

Last day for which pair formation was started.

Start of planned work from

Start time of planned work for last day processed.

End of planned work from

End time of planned work for last day processed.

Holiday class from

Public holiday class for last day processed.

Daily work schedule class from

Daily work schedule class for last day processed.

Day type from

Day type for last day processed.

Recalculation triggered by PB for ZA

If pair formation triggers retro time evaluation, the date from which time evaluation must be run is stored here.

Last error processing

Last error processing date.

29.10   VERSION–B1 VERSION

Functional Consultant	User	Business Process Owner	Senior Management	My Rating	Understanding Level
B	C	X	X		

29.10.1   Purpose and Overview

This table contains details of SAP version, which can be useful information when analyzing errors. This also contains a single record.

29.10.2   Screen

```
Imported B1 version

SAP Release                        470
Version no.                        04
Created by
Created on                         00.00.0000    00:00
Created using
```

30

Cluster B2
(Time Evaluation Results)

30.1 GENERAL

Functional Consultant	User	Business Process Owner	Senior Management	My Rating	Understanding Level
A	A	A	C		

The data in cluster B2 is stored for individual personnel numbers and periods. You can see the data in cluster B2 by running transaction PT_CLSTB2. When you run this transaction at the highest level, you get one record per person per period.

Personnel number, year, month and cluster type together form the cluster key (Structure PC2B0). Transparent table PCL2 contains one record for each cluster key. All information in the cluster is at cluster key level. You can drill down these records. When you drill down a record for a person for a period, you see all the tables and the number of records in them. As you drill down, you see the list of records displaying important data. On drilling down further, you see all the data of a record.

30.2 WPBP–BASIC DATA

Functional Consultant	User	Business Process Owner	Senior Management	My Rating	Understanding Level
A	A	A	C		

30.2.1 Purpose and Overview

When an employee's master data in infotype 0000, 0001, 0007, 0008, or 0027 changes, the period is split. There is one record for each split period in this table, which contains information from these infotypes. This information applies to the whole split period. All the split periods together cover the entire payroll period, plus one day before and one day after.

Note that cost center changes in infotype 0027 are not routed through table C1, but through table WPBP. This table contains many fields of the above infotypes. You can see them in the structure PC205. To understand the fields, refer to the infotypes listed above.

30.2.2 Screen

Field name	Field cont.
Assignment number (APZNR)	01
Validity period	31.03.2003 - 31.03.2003
Action Type	Z1 Hiring
Reason for Action	
Company Code	010
Personnel area	PAP
Personnel subarea	PSAP
Cost Center	
Employee group	2
Employee subgroup	Z1
Cust.-specific stat.	
Employment status	3
Spec.payment status	1
Active	J
ES grouping for PCR	
Position	99999999
Business Area	
Organizational unit	00000000
Job key	00000000
Organizational key	PAP
Work contract	
Time Mgmt status	0 0 - No time evaluation
Work schedule rule	
Employment percent	0.00
Dyn.daily work schedule	
Daily working hours	0.00
Weekly workdays	0.00
Work hours/period	0.00
Capacity util. level	0.00
Pay scale type	
Pay scale Area	
Pay Scale Group	
Pay scale level	

30.2.3 Data Flow

Input	Processing	Output	Details
		WPBP	Created before the time management schema executes
WPBP	MOD MODT GEN		Determines groupings for each record in WPBP table
WPBP, PSP, AB, ZES, SALDO, ABWKONTI	QUOTA	ABWKONTI, QTACC, QTBASE, QTTRANS	Generates absence quotas

30.3 PSP–PERSONAL WORK SCHEDULE

Functional Consultant	User	Business Process Owner	Senior Management	My Rating	Understanding Level
A	A	A	C		

30.3.1 Purpose and Overview

This table contains the work schedule of the employee that was considered during time evaluation. It contains one record for each day of the period, including Sundays and holidays. There is also a record for one day each before and after the period.

Dynamic work schedule updation is shown. Personal work schedule is not affected by attendances and absences, but is affected by substitution. See the fields of this table in the structure PC2BA. To understand the fields, see work schedule.

30.3.2 Screen

Date	Grpg	DWS	Variant	Class	DyTyp	HolCl	PWS	No. hrs	Break	Actve
31.03.2003	40	PG		1	0	0	PG	8.00	PBG	X
01.04.2003	40	PG		1	0	0	PG	8.00	PBG	X
02.04.2003	40	PG		1	1	1	PG	8.00	PBG	X
03.04.2003	40	POFF		0	0	0	PG	0.00		X

30.3.3 Data Flow

Input	Processing	Output	Details
		PSP	Created before the time management schema executes. The basic data comes from table T552A (Monthly work schedule). Work schedule substitution has already taken place.
PSP, time pairs	P2011	TIP, TZP	Inserts time pairs in TIP. Converts the information in table PSP into time pair format and store it in table TZP.
AB	ACTIO TD60 AB	TZP, PSP	In the case of reduced work hours (infotype 0049) and full day absence, daily work schedule is replaced in both TZP and PSP.
PSP	P2000	TIP, TZP	Converts the information in table PSP into time pair format and store it in table TZP.
TIP, TZP	ACTIO TD30	TZP, PSP	Changes work schedule in PSP and TZP, depending on first clock-in time from TIP.
TIP, TZP, PSP	DYNWS	TIP, TZP, PSP	Changes work schedule in TZP and PSP, depending on the overlap between permitted work schedules and employee's presence.
PSP, TZP	DYNBR TF10	PSP, TZP	Changes in break schedules change TZP table, but not PSP table.
			Most important use of work schedule is made by function TIMTP, which uses table TZP to compare the work schedule TZP and actual time in TIP, and creates multiple records based on their overlap.
WPBP, PSP, AB, ZES, SALDO, ABWKONTI	QUOTA	ABWKONTI, QTACC, QTBASE, QTTRANS	Function QUOTA reads table PSP.

30.4   ZES–TIME BALANCES FOR EACH DAY

Functional Consultant	User	Business Process Owner	Senior Management	My Rating	Understanding Level
A	A	A	C		

30.4.1   Purpose and Overview

All time types that are formed or processed in schema processing are stored in the internal table TES (daily balances) during time evaluation. This table contains balances only for the current day.

At the end of day processing, the balances in TES are transferred to table ZES, which contains time balances for each day of the period. Table ZES is stored in B2 cluster. The fields of table ZES can be seen in structure PC2B6.

At the end of day processing, the balances in TES are also cumulated in table SALDO, which contains cumulative time balances for the current period. Table SALDO is also stored in B2 cluster.

30.4.2   Screen

Relative day		Time type	Number
01	01.04.2003	0110 Fill time Attendance	8.00
01	01.04.2003	0100 Fill time	8.00
01	01.04.2003	0010 Attendance	8.00
01	01.04.2003	0003 Skeleton time	8.00
01	01.04.2003	0500 Break	0.50

30.4.3   Data Flow

Input	Processing	Output	Details
	LIMIT	TES, SALDO, DZL, FEHLER	Table TES may be updated by function LIMIT which affects ZES.
TES, DZL, DVS	CUMBT	ZES, SALDO, ZL, VS, CVS	CUMBT inserts TES records in ZES and cumulates them in SALDO. (TES ≻ ZES, SALDO)
			It also transfers DZL to ZL. (DZL ≻ ZL)
			It transfers DVS to VS and cumulates DVS in CVS. (DVS ≻ VS, CVS)
WPBP, PSP, AB, ZES, SALDO, ABWKONTI	QUOTA	ABWKONTI, QTACC, QTBASE, QTTRANS	Generates absence quotas. Reads ZES.

30.5 SALDO–CUMULATED TIME BALANCES

Functional Consultant	User	Business Process Owner	Senior Management	My Rating	Understanding Level
A	A	A	C		

30.5.1 Purpose and Overview

All time types that are formed or processed in schema processing are stored in the internal table TES (daily balances) during time evaluation. This table contains balances only for the current day.

At the end of day processing, the balances in TES are transferred to table ZES, which contains time balances for each day of the period. Table ZES is stored in B2 cluster.

At the end of day processing, the balances in TES are also cumulated in table SALDO, which contains cumulative time balances for the current period. Table SALDO is also stored in B2 cluster. The fields of table SALDO can be seen in structure PC2B5. Whether the information is for the month or the year depends on time type.

30.5.2 Screen

Time type	Number
0003 Skeleton time	208.00
0020 Absence	16.00
0110 Fill time Attendance	168.00
0120 Fill time Absence	16.00
0130 Fill time Off-site	24.00
0500 Break	13.00

30.5.3 Data Flow

Input	Processing	Output	Details
TES, DZL, DVS	CUMBT	ZES, SALDO, ZL, VS, CVS	CUMBT inserts TES records in ZES and cumulates them in SALDO. (TES ≻ ZES, SALDO)
			It also transfers DZL to ZL. (DZL ≻ ZL)
			It transfers DVS to VS and cumulates DVS in CVS. (DVS ≻ VS, CVS)
WPBP, PSP, AB, ZES, SALDO, ABWKONTI	QUOTA	ABWKONTI, QTACC, QTBASE, QTTRANS	Generates absence quotas. Reads SALDO.
	LIMIT	TES, SALDO, DZL, FEHLER	Table SALDO may be updated by function LIMIT.

30.6 ZKO–TIME QUOTAS

Functional Consultant	User	Business Process Owner	Senior Management	My Rating	Understanding Level
B	C	X	X		

30.6.1 Purpose and Overview

This table contains time quotas. It is populated by operation GENOT, which is called by function GOT (Generation of Overtime Time Pairs). The structure of table ZKO is PC2B7.

30.6.2 Screen

Relative day	QTyp	Infty	Subt	OID	SeqNo	Validity period	Number
01 01.04.2003	P	2007	01		000	01.04.2003 - 01.04.2003	4.00000
06 06.04.2003	P	2007	01		000	06.04.2003 - 06.04.2003	2.00000
28 28.04.2003	P	2007	01		000	28.04.2003 - 28.04.2003	2.00000
29 29.04.2003	P	2007	01		000	29.04.2003 - 29.04.2003	2.00000

30.6.3 Data Flow

Input	Processing	Output	Details
ANWKONTI, TIP	GOT TO20 01	TIP, ANWKONTI, ZKO	Table ZKO is populated by operation GENOT, which is called by function GOT.
ANWKONTI, TIP	GOT TO20 02	TIP, ANWKONTI, ZKO	Table ZKO is populated by operation GENOT, which is called by function GOT.

30.7 ZL–TIME WAGE TYPES

Functional Consultant	User	Business Process Owner	Senior Management	My Rating	Understanding Level
A	A	A	C		

30.7.1 Purpose and Overview

Table ZL represents the interface between time management and payroll. In time evaluation, there are three tables for time wage types: ZML, DZL and ZL. Tables ZML and DZL are internal tables, which exist only during time evaluation. Their information is transferred to table ZL, which is stored in B2 cluster.

Function GWT creates table ZML for overtime (GWT M ZML). Function POVT appends records in table ZML to table DZL. Function GWT also appends records to table DZL directly. Function CUMBT appends DZL records to ZL, which is stored in cluster B2 and used in payroll.

Table ZL is used in payroll by function ZLIT. The entries in table ZL contain pointers to the following tables:

➢ ALP—alternative payment
➢ C1—cost distribution
➢ AB—absences (column heading 'Fr')

ITy specifies the type of employee time data used to generate the time wage type. It describes the origin of the wage type. Payroll can then use this identifier (information category) to perform different types of processing. Its possible values are:

➢ S—planned work
➢ M—overtime
➢ A—absence

The structure of table ZL is PC2BF. There is also a function PZL for processing ZL table, but it is not used in schemas TM00–TM04.

30.7.2 Screen

Date	Time	A1	C1	Fr	WType	ITy	Number
01.04.2003	15:00 - 19:00	00	0000	00	1505 Ex-gratia	M	4.00
06.04.2003	15:00 - 17:00	00	0000	00	1505 Ex-gratia	M	2.00
28.04.2003	15:00 - 17:00	00	0000	00	1505 Ex-gratia	M	2.00
29.04.2003	15:00 - 17:00	00	0000	00	1505 Ex-gratia	M	2.00

30.7.3 Data Flow

Input	Processing	Output	Details
TES, DZL, DVS	CUMBT	ZES, SALDO, ZL, VS, CVS	CUMBT inserts TES records in ZES and cumulates them in SALDO. (TES ≻ ZES, SALDO)
			It also transfers DZL to ZL. (DZL ≻ ZL)
			It transfers DVS to VS and cumulates DVS in CVS. (DVS ≻ VS, CVS)

30.8 ALP–DIFFERENT PAYMENT

Functional Consultant	User	Business Process Owner	Senior Management	My Rating	Understanding Level
B	C	X	X		

30.8.1 Purpose and Overview

If you create different payment data in time management infotype 2001, 2002, 2003, 2004, 2005, 2010 or 2011, it is stored in table ALP of cluster B2. A pointer to this table is kept in tables TIP, ZML, DZL and finally ZL. This data can be accessed in payroll via table ZL.

Table ALP contains the specifications on a different rate of payment. To understand the fields in this table, you may see chapter 24, 'Different Payment'. The structure of table ALP is PC20E.

30.8.2 Screen

Field name	Field cont.
ALP assignment	01
Validity period	01.06.2005 - 12.06.2005
Time	-
Number/unit	0.00
Unit of time/meas.	
Valuation basis	0.00
Currency	
Amount	0.00
Extra pay ID	
Object type	
Position	00000000
Premium number	
Premium ID	0000
Pay Scale Group	E-1
Pay scale level	
Overtime comp. type	
Tax Area	

30.8.3 Data Flow

Input	Processing	Output	Details
P2003	A2003	TIP, ALP, C1	Inserts position substitution in these tables.
P2002	P2002	TIP, ALP, C1	Imports attendances from infotype 2002.
P2005	P2005	TIP, ALP, C1	Creates entry in TIP for records in infotype 2005. Delimits existing records depending on parameters.

30.9 C1–COST DISTRIBUTION

Functional Consultant	User	Business Process Owner	Senior Management	My Rating	Understanding Level
A	B	C	X		

30.9.1 Purpose and Overview

If you do cost assignment or activity allocation in time management infotype 2001, 2002, 2003, 2004, 2005, 2010 or 2011, it is stored in table C1 of cluster B2. A pointer to this table is kept in tables TIP, ZML, DZL and finally ZL. This data can be accessed in payroll via table ZL. Note that cost center changes in infotype 0027 are not routed through table C1, but through table WPBP.

Information about sender cost objects is filled in activity allocation. To understand the fields in this table, you may see chapter 22 on 'Cost Assignment' and chapter 21 on 'Activity Allocation'. The structure of table C1 is PC25X.

30.9.2 Screen

C1ZNR	CCode	BArea	CArea	CCtr	Order no.	SCCde	SBsAr	SCoCe	ActType
0001	0100	P010	0100	1112035					

30.9.3 Data Flow

Input	Processing	Output	Details
P2003	A2003	TIP, ALP, C1	Inserts position substitution in these tables.
AB	P2001	TIP, C1	Imports absences of infotype 2001
P2002	P2002	TIP, ALP, C1	Imports attendances from infotype 2002.
P2005	P2005	TIP, ALP, C1	Creates entry in TIP for records in infotype 2005. Delimits existing records depending on parameters.

30.10 VS–VARIABLE BALANCES

Functional Consultant	User	Business Process Owner	Senior Management	My Rating	Understanding Level
B	C	X	X		

30.10.1 Purpose and Overview

Table VS contains variable balances which can be defined by the user. These balances can be entered in the table during time evaluation using operation ADDVS, where they are available for customer-specific evaluations. Function CUMBT appends DVS to VS and cumulates DVS in CVS. The structure of table VS is PC2BH.

30.10.2 Screen

Date	ID	Variable key	Number
08.04.2005	PAIR		1.00
09.04.2005	PAIR		1.00

30.10.3 Data Flow

Input	Processing	Output	Details
TES, DZL, DVS	CUMBT	ZES, SALDO, ZL, VS, CVS	CUMBT inserts TES records in ZES and cumulates them in SALDO. (TES ≻ ZES, SALDO)
			It also transfers DZL to ZL. (DZL ≻ ZL)
			It transfers DVS to VS and cumulates DVS in CVS. (DVS ≻ VS, CVS)

30.11 CVS–ACCRUED VARIABLE BALANCES

Functional Consultant	User	Business Process Owner	Senior Management	My Rating	Understanding Level
B	C	X	X		

30.11.1 Purpose and Overview

Table VS contains variable balances which can be defined by the user. These balances can be entered in the table during time evaluation using operation ADDVS where they are available for customer-specific evaluations.

Function CUMBT appends DVS to VS and cumulates DVS in CVS. Table CVS is not initialized when period changes. The structure of table CVS is PC2BI.

30.11.2 Screen

ID	Variable key	Number
PAIR		205.00

30.11.3 Data Flow

Input	Processing	Output	Details
TES, DZL, DVS	CUMBT	ZES, SALDO, ZL, VS, CVS	CUMBT inserts TES records in ZES and cumulates them in SALDO. (TES ≻ ZES, SALDO) It also transfers DZL to ZL. (DZL ≻ ZL) It transfers DVS to VS and cumulates DVS in CVS. (DVS ≻ VS, CVS)

30.12 FEHLER–MESSAGES

Functional Consultant	User	Business Process Owner	Senior Management	My Rating	Understanding Level
B	B	C	X		

30.12.1 Purpose and Overview

All messages generated during time evaluation are stored in table FEHLER. Operation COLER transfers errors to table FEHLER. It includes errors, information and notes. The structure of table FEHLER is PC2B8.

30.12.2 Screen

Field name	Field cont.
Date	02.04.2003
Cat. of Message Type	1
Message type number	08 At work despite day type "1"
Message type	
Message supplement	
SeqNo. time event	000000000000
Time	00:00:00
Historical record	
Processing status	
Agent	YVD114891
Processing date	17.01.2004
Origin	00000000

30.12.3 Important Fields

Date

Time evaluation takes place for a person and date. This field contains the date that was being processed when the message was generated.

Category of message type

Category	Origin
1	Error set by operation COLER in time evaluation
2	(No longer use) User-specific message from pair formation
3	Technical error from pair formation
4	Technical error from time evaluation
5	Warnings and notes generated by time evaluation

Message type number

This specifies the message generated.

Message type

This field specifies whether the message is an Error (E), a Cancellation (A) or a Note (blank).

Message supplement

Sequential number of time event

If this message refers to a time event, its sequential number is specified here. This number uniquely identifies a time event record.

Time

Time of the time event.

Historical record flag

If you mark a record historical, it is permanently stored in the database and is available for reporting. However, it cannot be changed.

Processing status

Blank	New
1	In process
2	Completed
3	Confirmed

Agent

User id of the last user who acted on this message.

Processing date

This is the date when this message was processed last.

Origin

This field is relevant only if you use time evaluation for concurrent employment.

30.12.4   Data Flow

Input	Processing	Output	Details
ERT	PERT TD20	FEHLER, ERT	Terminates processing for an employee if there is a technical error from pair formation in table ERT. Table FEHLER gets populated by operation COLER, which can be used in any PCR.
TIP	PTIP TE30 GEN	TIP, FEHLER	TE30 checks the status1 of the time pairs and completes them if possible. Otherwise, it gives error message.
	LIMIT	TES, SALDO, DZL, FEHLER	Messages are generated by function LIMIT.
	LIMIT	TES, SALDO, DZL, FEHLER	Messages are generated by function LIMIT.

30.13 KNTAG–WORK BRIDGING TWO CALENDAR DAYS

Functional Consultant	User	Business Process Owner	Senior Management	My Rating	Understanding Level
C	X	X	X		

30.13.1 Purpose and Overview

The string KNTAG shows whether or not the employee performs core night work (Germany only). The structure of field KNTAG is PC2BY.

30.13.2 Screen

Relative day	....x....1....x....2....x....3.
Indicator	0000000000000000000000000000000000000

30.14 QTACC–ABSENCE QUOTA GENERATION

Functional Consultant	User	Business Process Owner	Senior Management	My Rating	Understanding Level
B	C	X	X		

30.14.1 Purpose and Overview

Table QTACC contains the accrual entitlements that were generated by time evaluation on the relevant date of the accrual. You can view detailed information on the generation by double-clicking the appropriate line.

The structure of table QTACC is PC2BJ. This table is also updated by function P2013. However, this function is required only for employees having concurrent employment. For others, function QUOTA takes care of quota corrections entered in infotype 2013.

30.14.2 Data Flow

Input	Processing	Output	Details
WPBP, PSP, AB, ZES, SALDO, ABWKONTI	QUOTA	ABWKONTI, QTACC, QTBASE, QTTRANS	Generates absence quotas.

30.15 QTBASE–BASE ENTITLEMENT

Functional Consultant	User	Business Process Owner	Senior Management	My Rating	Understanding Level
B	C	X	X		

30.15.1 Purpose and Overview

Table QTBASE contains the information on the base entitlement that was used as a basis for calculating the accrual entitlements. Any changes to the base entitlement within an accrual period are flagged accordingly. The structure of table QTBASE is PC2BK.

30.15.2 Data Flow

Input	Processing	Output	Details
WPBP, PSP, AB, ZES, SALDO, ABWKONTI	QUOTA	ABWKONTI, QTACC, QTBASE, QTTRANS	Generates absence quotas.

30.16 QTTRANS–TRANSFER POOL

Functional Consultant	User	Business Process Owner	Senior Management	My Rating	Understanding Level
B	C	X	X		

30.16.1 Purpose and Overview

Table QTTRANS indicates the status of the transfer pool for each day. The cumulated entitlements are indicated until they have been transferred to the absence quotas infotype (2006) or until the entitlement has expired. You can view detailed information on the transfer pool and on the transfer by double clicking the appropriate line.

The structure of table QTTRANS is PC2BL. This table is also updated by function P2013. However, this function is required only for employees having concurrent employment. For others, function QUOTA takes care of quota corrections entered in infotype 2013.

30.16.2 Data Flow

Input	Processing	Output	Details
WPBP, PSP, AB, ZES, SALDO, ABWKONTI	QUOTA	ABWKONTI, QTACC, QTBASE, QTTRANS	Generates absence quotas.

30.17   URLAN–LEAVE ACCRUAL

Functional Consultant	User	Business Process Owner	Senior Management	My Rating	Understanding Level
C	X	X	X		

30.17.1   Purpose and Overview

Table URLAN contains information on the updating of the leave entitlement infotype (0005). The structure of table URLAN is PC2BG.

30.18   PT–TIME PAIRS

Functional Consultant	User	Business Process Owner	Senior Management	My Rating	Understanding Level
A	A	A	B		

30.18.1   Purpose and Overview

Table PT contains the time pairs generated in pair formation. This table is required only if you use time recording systems. This table contains records only for those days when attendance was recorded. The structure of table PT is PDCPT.

30.18.2   Screen

Field name	Field cont.
Date	01.04.2003
Time	08:22:00 - 17:00:01
Time event pair start	P10
Beg.att./abs.reason	
Terminal ID begin entry	6354
MP field for begin	
SeqNo. clock-in entry	000001000256
Time event pair end	P20
End att./abs.reason	
End terminal ID	6354
MP field for end	
SeqNo. clock-out entry	000001000255
Att./absence status	1
Pair form. status	
Time evaluation st.	
Change status	3

30.18.3 Important Fields

Attendance/absence status

Status	Description
Blank	Start (absent before clock-in)
0	On break
1	At work
3	Off-site
4	Absent before clock-in (do not use for new pair formation)
5	Absent after clock-out
6	Absent before clock-in with interim postings
7	Absent after clock-out with interim postings
E	Error
R	Restart after error

This field is also present in table QT, Various fields.

Pair formation status

Status	Description
0 or Blank	Pair is error-free and complete.
1	No start and end times. These are only interim entries.
2	No clock-in (first time event of the day is missing).
3	No clock-out (last time event of the day is missing).
4	No end time for break. Employee is absent for a brief period. The system expects a second time event.
5	No start time for break.
7	No start time for off-site work.
8	No end time for off-site work.
E	Order confirmation missing.
A	Pair delimited in time evaluation.

This status field is also there in table TIP.

Time evaluation status

This field contains attendance status of pair in time evaluation. This field is also present in table TIP and is usually called pair type. It indicates whether the employee is at work is absent, and how his or her data has been recorded. If a record comes from infotype, the status is assigned when the infotypes are imported. It can have the following values:

Status	Description
0	Non-recorded absence or employee is on break. The employee is not at work, and it has not been recorded. If there are gaps in time pairs, function TIMTP creates the required pairs, and assigns them pair type 0.
1	Employee is at work. If the employee is recording time, there is clock-in/clock-out entry. If he is recording deviations from daily work schedule, this comes from planned time. It is imported to time evaluation using function P2011 or P2000.
2	Employee is absent with approval. There is record of absence in infotype 2001. It is imported using function P2001.
3	Employee is at work or is working off-site. There is record of attendance in infotype 2002, or there is clock-in/clock-out entry with time events pertaining to off-site work. It is imported using function P2011 or P2002.

Change status

The change status of a pair indicates whether the first, last or both time postings of the pair were entered manually. The change status can be queried in time evaluation. Possible values are:

Status	Description
Blank	Both time postings were entered in the time recording system.
1	The start (first) time posting was entered manually.
2	The end (last) time posting was entered manually.
3	Both time postings were entered manually.

30.19 WST–TIME TICKETS, OTHER DOCUMENTS

Functional Consultant	User	Business Process Owner	Senior Management	My Rating	Understanding Level
C	X	X	X		

30.19.1 Purpose and Overview

Table WST contains the generated time tickets. The structure of table WST is PDCWST.

30.20   CWST–CUMULATED TIME TICKETS

Functional Consultant	User	Business Process Owner	Senior Management	My Rating	Understanding Level
C	X	X	X		

30.20.1   Purpose and Overview

Table CWST contains the cumulated time tickets. The structure of table CWST is PDCWST.

30.21   AT–LINK PAIRS/TIME TICKETS

Functional Consultant	User	Business Process Owner	Senior Management	My Rating	Understanding Level
C	X	X	X		

30.21.1   Purpose and Overview

Table AT is an assignment table which links time pairs and time tickets. The structure of table AT is PDC04.

30.22   AB–ABSENCES

Functional Consultant	User	Business Process Owner	Senior Management	My Rating	Understanding Level
A	A	A	B		

30.22.1   Purpose and Overview

Table AB contains absences which have been entered using the absences infotype (2001). Infotype 2001 is copied in both table AB and P2001 before time evaluation schema processing.

In schema processing, table AB is directly updated, and later saved in cluster B2. You therefore see table AB in time evaluation log, and not table P2001. The structure of table AB is PC20I.

30.22.2 Screen

Field name	Field cont.
Split number (ABZNR)	01
Att./Absence type	M0 SL (Sick Leave Certifd)
Validity period	27.04.2003 - 27.04.2003
Time	-
Prev. day indicator	
Full-day	X
Set hours	
Absence days	1.00
Absence hours	8.00
ESG for PCR	
Subtype	M0
Object ID	
Infotype record no.	000
Lock indicator	
Payroll days	1.00
Payroll hours	8.00
Calendar days	1.00
Subs.sickness ind.	0
Ind. for repeated illness	0
Valuation rule	02
% work incapacity	0.00
Reference fields exist (cost assign.)	
Conf. fields exist	
Offcycle Indicator	
Previous valid period	27.04.2003 - 27.04.2003
Assign. for alt. payment	00
Document number	00000000008109372001

30.22.3 Data Flow

Input	Processing	Output	Details
AB	ACTIO TD60 AB	TZP, PSP	In the case of reduced work hours (infotype 0049) and full day absence, daily work schedule is replaced in both TZP and PSP.
AB	P2001	TIP, C1	Import absences of infotype 2001
	ACTIO TD90	AB, P2002	If a full-day absence and attendance record is generated automatically by PCR TD80 during the previous day's time evaluation run, that time pair is inserted in the internal table TIP.
WPBP, PSP, AB, ZES, SALDO, ABWKONTI	QUOTA	ABWKONTI, QTACC, QTBASE, QTTRANS	Generates absence quotas.
			This table is also updated by function ADJAB, but it is not in any schema. It is also read by function TYPES.

30.23 ANWES–ATTENDANCES

Functional Consultant	User	Business Process Owner	Senior Management	My Rating	Understanding Level
A	A	A	B		

30.23.1 Purpose and Overview

Table ANWES contains attendances which have been entered using the attendances infotype (2002). Attendances are copied from infotype table PA2002 to temporary table P2002. After schema processing is over, the records in table P2002 are appended to table ANWES, which is stored in cluster B2.

As a result, you do not see table ANWES in time evaluation log. For data flow, see temporary table P2002. Fields are primarily those of infotype 2002. The structure of table ANWES is PC2BD.

30.23.2 Screen

Field name	Field cont.
Att./Absence type	WØ CERTIFIED ATTD. (MISC.)
Validity period	08.04.2003 - 08.04.2003
Time	-
Prev. day indicator	
Full-day X	
Set hours	
Attendance days	1.00
Attendance hours	8.00
Payroll days	1.00
Payroll hours	8.00
Calendar days	1.00
Eval.type atts/abs	
Overtime comp. type	Depends on wage type
Reference fields exist (cost assign.)	
Conf. fields exist	
Wage type	
Subtype	WØ
Object ID	
Infotype record no.	000

30.24   VERT–SUBSTITUTIONS

Functional Consultant	User	Business Process Owner	Senior Management	My Rating	Understanding Level
B	B	B	C		

30.24.1   Purpose and Overview

Table VERT contains substitutions entered in the substitutions infotype (2003). Substitutions are copied from infotype table PA2003 to temporary table P2003. After schema processing is over, the records in table P2003 are appended to table VERT, which is stored in cluster B2.

As a result, you do not see table VERT in time evaluation log. For data flow, see temporary table P2003. Fields are primarily those of infotype 2003. The structure of table VERT is PC2B4.

30.24.2 Screen

Field name	Field cont.
Substitution type	02 Shift substitution
Validity period	22.04.2005 - 22.04.2005
Time	-
Object ID	
Infotype record no.	000
Prev. day indicator	
Daily work schedule	PB
Daily WS variant	
Daily WS class	
DWS grouping	40
Day type	
ES grouping	
Holiday calendar ID	
PS grouping	00
Work schedule rule	
Company Code	
Personnel area	
Position	00000000

Breaks			
Break	Time	Paid break period	Unpaid break period
1	-		
2	-		

30.25 RUFB–ON-CALL DUTY

Functional Consultant	User	Business Process Owner	Senior Management	My Rating	Understanding Level
C	X	X	X		

30.25.1 Purpose and Overview

Table RUFB contains availability records for on-call duty entered in the availability infotype (2004). Availabilities are copied from infotype table PA2004 to temporary table P2004. After schema processing is over, the records in table P2004 are appended to table RUFB, which is stored in cluster B2.

As a result, you do not see table RUFB in time evaluation log. For data flow, see temporary table P2004. Fields are primarily those of infotype 2004. The structure of table RUFB is PC2BE.

30.26   MEHR–OVERTIME

Functional Consultant	User	Business Process Owner	Senior Management	My Rating	Understanding Level
B	C	X	X		

30.26.1   Purpose and Overview

Table MEHR contains all overtime data entered in the overtime infotype (2005). Overtimes are copied from infotype table PA2005 to temporary table P2005. After schema processing is over, the records in table P2005 are appended to table MEHR, which is stored in cluster B2.

As a result, you do not see table MEHR in time evaluation log. For data flow, see temporary table P2005. Fields are primarily those of infotype 2005. The structure of table MEHR is PC2BC.

30.27   ABWKONTI–ABSENCE QUOTAS

Functional Consultant	User	Business Process Owner	Senior Management	My Rating	Understanding Level
B	C	X	X		

30.27.1   Purpose and Overview

Table ABWKONTI contains relevant absence quotas from the absence quotas infotype (2006). Infotype 2006 is copied in both table ABWKONTI and P2006 before time evaluation schema processing. In schema processing, table ABWKONTI is directly updated, and later saved in cluster B2.

You therefore see table ABWKONTI in time evaluation log, and not table P2006. The structure of table ABWKONTI is PC2B9.

30.27.2 Screen

Field name	Field cont.
Absence quota type	30 Casual leave
Validity period	01.04.2003 - 31.12.2003
Time	-
Quota number	8.00000
Unit of time/meas.	010
Quota deduction	8.00000
Infotype	2006
Subtype	30
Object ID	
Infotype record no.	000
Prev. day indicator	
Update indicator	
Deduction period	01.04.2003 - 31.12.2003

30.27.3 Data Flow

Input	Processing	Output	Details
P2012	P2012	TES, DZL, ABWKONTI	Function P2012 may create time quota while processing time transfer specifications infotype (2012).
WPBP, PSP, AB, ZES, SALDO, ABWKONTI	QUOTA	ABWKONTI, QTACC, QTBASE, QTTRANS	Generates absence quotas. Also processes quota correction.
ANWKONTI	P2007 TS20 GEN	ANWKONTI, ABWKONI	

Absence quota may be created:

➢ Manually in infotype 2006.
➢ Automatically using RPTQTA00.
➢ By function QUOTA (Automatic quota generation, quota correction).
➢ By function P2013 (Quota correction for concurrent employment).
➢ By function P2012 (Time transfer).
➢ By operation UPDTQ.

Function QUOTA creates absence quota. It also processes quota correction for normal cases.

This table is also updated by function P2013. However, this function is required only for employees having concurrent employment. For others, function QUOTA takes care of quota corrections entered in infotype 2013.

Function P2012 may create time quota while processing time transfer specifications infotype (2012).

Absence quota can be generated by operation UPDTQ and updated in table ABWKONTI.

➢ Operation UPDTQ may be used in a PCR called by function P2006, which processes table ABWQONTI. However, this function is not called in schemas TM00–TM04.
➢ Operation UPDTQ may also be used in a PCR called by functions other than P2006.
  ▶ It is called by function P2007 TS20 GEN in schema TM00.
  ▶ It is also called in PCR TC20 called by function POVT. However, this PCR is not called in schemas TM00–TM04.

30.28 ANWKONTI–ATTENDANCE QUOTAS

Functional Consultant	User	Business Process Owner	Senior Management	My Rating	Understanding Level
B	C	X	X		

30.28.1 Purpose and Overview

Table ANWKONTI contains relevant attendance approvals from the attendance quotas infotype (2007). Infotype 2007 is copied in both table ANWKONTI and P2007 before time evaluation schema processing. In schema processing, table ANWKONTI is directly updated, and later saved in cluster B2.

You therefore see table ANWKONTI in time evaluation log, and not table P2007. The structure of table ANWKONTI is PC2BB.

30.28.2 Screen

Field name	Field cont.
Attendance quota type	01 App. XGR/ Addn. Stipend
Validity period	01.04.2003 - 01.04.2003
Time	-
Quota number	4.00000
Unit of time/meas.	001
Quota deduction	4.00000
Infotype	2007
Subtype	01
Object ID	
Infotype record no.	000
Overtime comp. type	
Update indicator	1
Approval before	
Approval after	
Approval full-day	

30.28.3 Data Flow

Input	Processing	Output	Details
ANWKONTI, TIP	GOT TO20 01	TIP, ANWKONTI, ZKO	
ANWKONTI, TIP	GOT TO20 02	TIP, ANWKONTI, ZKO	
ANWKONTI	P2007 TS20 GEN	ANWKONTI, ABWKONI	

Note that attendance quotas are not created during time evaluation. You may also note that operation UPDTQ creates only absence quota, and not attendance quota.

Operation GENOT updates the quota used field on infotype 2007 & ANWKONTI. This operation is called in PCR TO20 processed by function GOT. Function GOU also works like function GOT, but it does not update the quota used field.

Function P2007 processes table ANWKOTI as per specified PCR. Operation COLTQ increases the amount of an attendance quota used by the current number of hours field.

30.29 SKO–TIME TRANSFER SPECIFICATIONS

Functional Consultant	User	Business Process Owner	Senior Management	My Rating	Understanding Level
B	C	X	X		

30.29.1 Purpose and Overview

Table SKO contains time transfer specifications recorded in the time transfer specifications infotype (2012). Time transfer specifications are copied from infotype table PA2012 to temporary table P2012. After schema processing is over, the records in table P2012 are appended to table SKO, which is stored in cluster B2.

As a result, you do not see table SKO in time evaluation log. For data flow, see temporary table P2012. Fields are primarily those of infotype 2012. The structure of table SKO is PC2B3.

30.29.2 Screen

Validity period	Time transfer specification	OID	SeqNo	Number
01.01.2005 - 01.01.2005	ZEPL Earned PL for Prev. Year		000	30.00

30.30 BEZUG–RECALCULATION DATA

Functional Consultant	User	Business Process Owner	Senior Management	My Rating	Understanding Level
B	B	C	X		

30.30.1 Purpose and Overview

This table shows the recalculation dates for time evaluation, the time statement and a third-party payroll system. The structure of field string BEZUG is PC2B2.

30.30.2 Screen

Recalculation data	
Last day evaluated (RPTIME00) Recalculation period for time statement Recalculation period for third-party payroll	30.04.2003

30.31 VERSION–B2 VERSION

Functional Consultant	User	Business Process Owner	Senior Management	My Rating	Understanding Level
B	C	X	X		

30.31.1 Purpose and Overview

This table contains the information about the SAP version and the program used for creating the B2 cluster entry. This is useful if you are doing some investigation.

30.31.2 Screen

```
Imported B2 version

SAP Release          46C
Version no.          04
Created by           YVD114891
Created on           06.05.2004    16:37
Created using        RPTIME00
```

Internal Tables

When time evaluation is run, certain tables are created, which are not preserved. These tables are described here. Tables, which are stored in clusters, also participate in time evaluation. Those are not discussed here.

31.1 GENERAL STATUS FIELDS

Functional Consultant	User	Business Process Owner	Senior Management	My Rating	Understanding Level
A	A	A	C		

When time evaluation is being run, the system has a lot of information, which you can use for defining your logic in a PCR. The fields below can be queried through operation VARST.

Field	Description
DAYTY	Day type
HOLCL	Holiday class
NDYHC	Holiday class (next day)
FREE	Daily work schedule off?
DAYPG	Daily work schedule
VARIA	Daily work schedule variant
DPRCL	Daily work schedule class
BREAK	Work break schedule
TIMMD	Period work schedule
TIMCL	Valuation class of period work schedule

(Contd.)

Field	Description
SUBST	Substitution type
PRSNT	Employee at work?
PRSWD	Employee at work for full day? (infotype 2002)
ABSCE	Employee absent?
ABSWD	Employee absent for full day?
NDYPO	Time Management status (infotype 0007) '1' or '2' on next day?
NDYNE	Time Management status '9' on next day?
NDYAC	Employee active on next day?
FIRST	First pair in TIP?
LAST	Last pair in TIP?
NOTIM	Entries without clock times in TIP?
P2000	Planned pair generated from DWS?
P2001	Record imported from Absences infotype (2001)?
P2002	Record imported from Attendances infotype (2002)?
P2004	Record imported from Availability infotype (2004)?
P2005	Record imported from Overtime infotype (2005)?
P2011	Time pair imported from time postings?
TPLN	Was time evaluation called from the target plan from Shift Planning?
WEDAY	Relative weekday
WDY x	Relative weekday = x?
LDWDY	Relative weekday where week frame specified by feature LDAYW
LWDYx	Relative weekday = x? (in relation to feature LDAYW)
CURMO	Current time evaluation period
CURYR	Current year
REDAY	Relative day of time evaluation period
LDAYP	Last day of time evaluation period?
RDYPP	Relative day of payroll period
FDYPP	First day of payroll period?
LDYPP	Last day of payroll period?
RDYxx	Relative day of payroll period with period modifier xx?
FDYxx	First day of payroll period with period modifier xx?
LDYxx	Last day of payroll period with period modifier xx?
RDYWW	Relative day of working week
FDYWW	First day of working week?
LDYWW	Last day of working week?
LRDxy	Leave type xy deducted? xy = SPACE means that the query is made for all leave types

(Contd.)

Field	Description
OVPOS	Overtime automatically from Daily Work Schedules Table (T550A). Value is X if T550A-OVPOS is X, otherwise it is *.
MOD W	Time wage type selection rule group from Time Wage Type Selection Rule Table (T510S), see operation MODIF
MOD T	Time type determination group for Time Type Determination Table (T555Z), see operation MODIF
MOD A	Employee grouping for absence valuation for Absence Valuation Table (T554C), see operation MODIF
MOD D	Day grouping for wage type generation for Time Wage Type Selection Rule Table (T510S) See function DAYMO operation MODIF
MOD S	Type for daily work schedule assignment for Dynamic Assignment of DWS—Planned/Actual Overlap Table (T552W) See operation MODIF
MOD Q	Quota type selection rule group for Absence Quota Type Selection Table (T559L) See function QUOTA operation MODIF
MOD L	Time balance rule group for Value Limits for Time Balances Table (T559P) See operation MODIF
SIM	Simulation?

31.2 TIP–ONE DAY'S TIME DATA FOR TIME EVALUATION

Functional Consultant	User	Business Process Owner	Senior Management	My Rating	Understanding Level
A	A	A	C		

31.2.1 Purpose and Overview

The internal table TIP (daily input) is the work table for time evaluation. It is the most important table in time evaluation. The time pairs determined on the basis of the time postings are inserted in TIP. Most infotypes are also imported in table TIP. In the course of time evaluation, the time pairs in TIP are processed, changed and made available for further processing.

Table TIP takes the output of a previous step and provides it as input to the current step. The time pairs are then transferred individually to a personnel calculation rule for processing. After processing, the new results are inserted in the internal table TOP (daily output).

There are no more time pairs in TIP at this stage. TOP is renamed as TIP for the next function, so that further processing can be performed from a different perspective.

Operation OUTTP can be used to read a variable in TIP and perform necessary action. Operation FILLP can be used to update a variable in table TIP. Operation COLOP is used to transfer an entry from TIP to TOP. The structure of table TIP is PZI01 (include RPTDAT20).

31.2.2 Screen

From	To	1	P	ID	CT	P	TTyp	BR	ER	C	0	I	BPin	EPin	PT	ALP	C1	AB	Number
08.3500	17.0000		1		00			P10	P20		E				0001				8,6500

31.2.3 Important Fields

Start time (From)

Decimalized start time of time pair

End time (To)

Decimalized end time of time pair

Status from pair formation (1)

Table TIP contains time pairs; this field contains the status of a time pair. Each pair is assigned a status during pair formation and indicates whether it was possible to form an error-free time pair, or if the start or end time could not be delimited. The status can be queried in time evaluation's rule processing. The status can have the following values:

Status	Description
0 or Blank	Pair is error-free and complete.
1	No start and end times. These are only interim entries.
2	No clock-in (first time event of the day is missing).
3	No clock-out (last time event of the day is missing).
4	No end time for break. Employee is absent for a brief period. The system expects a second time event.
5	No start time for break.
7	No start time for off-site work.
8	No end time for off-site work.
E	Order confirmation missing.
A	Pair delimited in time evaluation.

Pair type—Attendance status of pair in time evaluation (P)

The pair type of a TIP entry indicates whether the employee is at work or absent, and how his or her data has been recorded. If a record comes from infotype, the status is assigned when the infotypes are imported. The pair type can have the following values:

Pair type	Description
0	Non-recorded absence or employee is on break. The employee is not at work and it has not been recorded. If there are gaps in time pairs, function TIMTP creates the required pairs, and assigns them pair type 0.
1	Employee is at work. If the employee is recording time, there is clock-in/clock-out entry. If he is recording deviations from daily work schedule, this comes from planned time. It is imported to time evaluation using function P2011 or P2000.
2	Employee is absent with approval. There is record of absence in infotype 2001. It is imported using function P2001.
3	Employee is at work or is working off-site. There is record of attendance in infotype 2002, or there is clock-in/clock-out entry with time events pertaining to off-site work. It is imported using function P2011 or P2002.

Time identifier for daily work schedule (ID)

The identifier denotes the relation of the time interval to the daily work schedule as a whole. Pair type and time identifier combination is used to determine time type and processing type from T555Z. It can have the following values:

Time identifier	Description
Blank	It is initially blank when entry comes from 2001.
01	Overtime (time outside of daily work schedule)
02	Fill time (during planned working time, without core times) All 24 hours on an off day.
03	Core time
04	Core time break
05	Fill time break
06	Paid break
07	Unpaid overtime break (infotype 2005)
08	Paid overtime break (infotype 2005)
09	Overtime break

Processing type/time type class (CT)

In table TIP, this field comes from table T554S (Attendance and Absence Types). For other time pairs it is 00. It is used for determining processing type and time type by function TYPES using table T555Y.

You can use the processing type/time type class to group absence and attendance types, which are to be processed identically in time evaluation. A time type and a processing type are assigned to the absence and attendance times in time evaluation according to the processing type/time type class.

Time balances can be formed by means of the time type. The formation of time wage types is controlled by the processing type. This is not required when you work with clock times and use table T555Z to determine time type and processing type.

Processing type for time evaluation (P)

One of the most important uses of time management is to generate time wage types which can be paid in payroll. SAP provides you a flexible method of generating time wage types, which depends on the concept of processing type.

When you are doing time evaluation, you have time pairs in internal table TIP. For these time pairs, time id and pair type are determined by the system. Function TIMTP then determines processing type from the configuration table T555Z, and updates for each pair in internal table TIP.

As time evaluation proceeds further, you may stamp processing type of certain time pairs based on the logic written in the PCRs. The operation used to stamp processing type is FILLP. This is commonly done for overtime, where you would check approval for overtime, so that only approved overtimes are paid (for example, see PCRs TO10, TO15, TO16 and TO11).

Finally, operation GWT would create time wage types, depending on processing type in accordance with rules defined in table T510S. If you are not working with recorded times, the processing type gets determined by function TYPES using table T555Y. Important processing types are:

Processing type	Description
S	Planned work
M	Overtime
A	Absence
P	Attendance
K	Break

Time type (TTYP)

This field contains the time type of the time pair. Time type is determined by function TIMTP using table T555Z, or by function TYPES using table T555Y.

The time types are defined in view V_T555A, Time Types. They are used to form day balances in TES (RTIP TR10). These are stored for all days of the period in ZES and cumulated in SALDO by function CUMBT.

You may see chapter 28.6 (view V_T555A) for understanding the concept of time types, list of important time types, and how they are processed in schema TM00.

Time event pair start (BR)

A time pair starts with one time event and ends with another time event. This field contains the time event, which started the time pair.

Time event pair end (ER)

A time pair starts with one time event and ends with another time event. This field contains the time event which ended the time pair.

Overtime compensation type (C)

If the employees have a choice of deciding whether they want to receive payment or time off or a combination of the two, that choice is shown here. For more details, see chapter 11.4 (T555R).

OT comp. type	Description
Blank	Depends on wage type
1	Remuneration
2	Time off plus overtime rate
3	Compensation (time off)

Origin indicator for time pairs (O)

The origin indicator of a TIP entry shows where the time data has come from.

Origin indicator	Description
E	Time event
O	Overtime from Overtime infotype (2005)
A	Absence from Absences infotype (2001)
P	Attendance from Attendances infotype (2002)
R	Availability from Availability infotype (2004)
D	Generated planned pair (e.g. on a paid public holiday)
C	Attendance/absence reasons

Internal key for availability duty (I)

This key is used in the payroll program for civil service, Germany. When a record from infotype 2004 is imported, it has an availability type. For that availability type, the internal key for availability duty is specified in view V_T557, Availability Type.

Attendance/absence reason for begin entry (BPin)

If an attendance/absence reason has been entered when the first time event of the time pair was recorded, it is stored here.

Attendance/absence reason for end entry (EPin)

If an attendance/absence reason has been entered when the last time event of the time pair was recorded, it is stored here.

Pointer to time pairs from time events (PT)

Additional data on the time pairs is stored in table PT in order to keep the amount of information in table TIP to a minimum. If you click on this pointer, you can see more details of the time pair.

Assignment for alternative payment (ALP)

This field contains pointer to table ALP.

Pointer to cost accounting (C1)

This field contains pointer to table C1.

Pointer to absences (AB)

This field contains pointer to table AB.

Number of hours (Number)

This field shows the number of hours of a time pair. The number is displayed as a decimal figure.

31.2.4 Data Flow

Since table TIP participates in most of the steps of schema TM00, you may see the overview of schema TM00.

31.3 TOP

Functional Consultant	User	Business Process Owner	Senior Management	My Rating	Understanding Level
A	A	A	C		

31.3.1 Purpose and Overview

Table TIP takes the output of a previous step, and provides it as input to the current step. The time pairs are then transferred individually to a personnel calculation rule for processing.

After processing, the new results are inserted in the internal table TOP (daily output). There are no more time pairs in TIP at this stage. TOP is renamed as TIP for the next function, so that further processing can be performed from a different perspective.

31.4 TZP–TIMES OF DAY

Functional Consultant	User	Business Process Owner	Senior Management	My Rating	Understanding Level
A	A	A		C	

31.4.1 Purpose and Overview

The system requires two pieces of information in order to calculate employees' time balances:

➢ The planned specifications: These stipulate how the employee has to work (according to his/her work schedule).
➢ The actual specifications: These indicate when the employee actually worked.

At the start of time evaluation, the system gets an employee's daily work schedule in table PSP. This contains the name of the daily work schedule (substitutions are also taken into consideration). The system needs the details. It gets these from the customizing tables and fills in table TZP.

Table TZP contains details of the full day. It divides it into periods, identifies what type it is, e.g. working time, break time, non-working time, etc. A record is inserted in table TZP by function P2011. The fields of table TZP are in structure PZI09.

31.4.2 Screen

Table TZP

Time	Time ID	Paid break period	Unpaid break perio
000000	01	0.0000	0.0000
085000	02	0.0000	0.0000
125000	05	0.0000	0.5000
130000	02	0.0000	0.0000
170000	01	0.0000	0.0000

31.4.3 Important Fields

Point in time

The daily work schedule specifies start times for breaks, core time and so on as decimalized values. Times outside of the daily work schedule are also taken into account. Although the record has only the starting time point, actually the record is for a time period. The starting time point of the next record is the end time point of the previous record. The day is broken up based on the work schedule.

Time identifier for daily work schedule

Time identifier field here is same as that in TIP. Here it is for the time pair of daily work schedule. A time identifier is assigned to each time period to describe its place in the daily work schedule. The breaks are taken from the work break schedule that is assigned to the daily work schedule.

Time ID	Description
Blank	It is initially blank when entry comes from 2001.
01	Overtime (time outside of daily work schedule)
02	Fill time (during planned working time, without core times)
	All 24 hours on a Sunday.
03	Core time
04	Core time break
05	Fill time break
06	Paid break
07	Unpaid overtime break (infotype 2005)
08	Paid overtime break (infotype 2005)
09	Overtime break

Paid break period

The duration of the paid break period is specified. The time wage types formed from this information are evaluated in payroll.

Unpaid break period

The duration of the unpaid break period is specified.

Break type 1, Break type 2

Each line of table TZP is a time pair. These time pairs are based on the work schedule which includes break schedule. Thus, some of these lines correspond to breaks, and the system has the details of that break in table T550P. That table contains two fields, 'Break type 1' and 'Break type 2'. These are brought in table TZP. Although you do not see these fields on the screen, they are available. If the break is an overtime break, Break type 1 contains O, otherwise it is blank. Break type 2 is a free field where you can specify a 1 character Break type, and use in PCR using function PBRKS.

31.4.4 Data Flow

Input	Processing	Output	Details
PSP, time pairs	P2011	TIP, TZP	Inserts time pairs in TIP. Converts the information in table PSP into time pair format and store it in table TZP.
PSP	P2000	TIP, TZP	Converts the information in table PSP into time pair format and store it in table TZP.
AB	ACTIO TD60 AB	TZP	In the case of reduced work hours (infotype 0049) and full day absence, daily work schedule is replaced in both TZP and PSP.
TIP, TZP	ACTIO TD30	TZP, PSP	Changes work schedule in PSP and TZP, depending on first clock-in time from TIP.
TIP, TZP, PSP	DYNWS	TIP, TZP, PSP	Changes work schedule in TZP and PSP, depending on overlap between permitted work schedules and employee's presence.
PSP, TZP	DYNBR TF10	PSP, TZP	Changes in break schedules change TZP table, but not PSP table.
TZP, TIP, P2002	TIMTP	TZP, TIP	Compares the work schedule TZP and actual time in TIP, and creates multiple records based on their overlap in TOP.

31.5 TES–TIME BALANCES FOR DAY TO BE EVALUATED

Functional Consultant	User	Business Process Owner	Senior Management	My Rating	Understanding Level
A	A	A	C		

31.5.1 Purpose and Overview

All time types that are formed or processed in schema processing are stored in the internal table TES (daily balances) during time evaluation. This table contains balances only for the current day. The fields of this table can be seen in structure PZI02. At the end of day processing, the balances in TES are appended to table ZES, which contains time balances for each day of the period. Table ZES is stored in B2 cluster. At the end of day processing, the balances in TES are also cumulated in table SALDO, which contains cumulative time balances for the current period. Table SALDO is also stored in B2 cluster.

31.5.2 Screen

Time type	Number
0110 Fill time Attendance	8,0000
0100 Fill time	8,0000
0010 Attendance	8,0000
0003 Skeleton time	8,0000
0500 Break	0,5000

31.5.3 Data Flow

Input	Processing	Output	Details
	DEFTP	TIP, TES	Function DEFTP fills time types 0000 and 0001 for planned time pairs from table TIP.
ZML	POVT TC40 GEN	TES, DZL, ZML	If a wage type in table ZML needs to be paid, it goes into table DZL. If it is to be compensated by time off, it goes in TES.
TIP	RTIP TR10	TES	PCR TR10 updates time types 0100, 0010, 0003, 0020, 0030, 0200, 0301 and 0500 based on time type of TIP entries.
P2012	P2012	TES, DZL, ABWKONTI	Function P2012 adds to (or subtracts from) time types based on configuration in table T555J.
	ACTIO TR30	TES	PCR TR30 updates time types 0002, 0005, 0040, 0050, 0051.
	LIMIT	TES, SALDO, DZL, FEHLER	Function LIMIT applies limit as per table T559P, limits for time balances. Modifies tables TES and SALDO.
TES, DZL, DVS	CUMBT	ZES, SALDO, ZL, VS, CVS	CUMBT inserts TES records in ZES and cumulates them in SALDO. (TES ≻ ZES, SALDO) It also transfers DZL to ZL. (DZL ≻ ZL) It transfers DVS to VS and cumulates DVS in CVS. (DVS ≻ VS, CVS)

(Contd.)

Input	Processing	Output	Details
	LIMIT	TES, SALDO, DZL, FEHLER	Here, Function LIMIT applies monthly limit as per table T559P, limits for time balances. It modifies SALDO. It can't modify TES and ZES.
			Table TES can be processed using function PDB. However, it is not in schema TM00.
			This table is read by operation HRS (option D). It is updated by operations ADDDB. The data is usually prepared by function HRS. It can be sorted using function SORT. It can be printed in time evaluation log using function PRINT.

31.6 ZML–OVERTIME WAGE TYPES FOR ONE DAY

Functional Consultant	User	Business Process Owner	Senior Management	My Rating	Understanding Level
B	B	B	X		

31.6.1 Purpose and Overview

Internal table ZML serves as an interim table in time evaluation. Only overtime wage types are stored in ZML during time evaluation. This makes it possible to process overtime wage types separately. The structure of this table is PZI08.

Function GWT generates time wage types from time pairs in table TIP, according to the rules in table T510S, Time Wage Type Selection Rule. Only time pairs with processing type M are used to generate wage types and populate table ZML.

The wage types in table ZML may be paid, compensated by time off or a combination of both. For some wage types, company rules may permit an employee to choose from these options. These specifications come from processing class 17 of wage type. If employee has an option, that information, overtime compensation type, comes from the infotypes. Function POVT processes table ZML and PCR TC40 creates appropriate time type balances in table TES. It also creates entries in table DZL where the employee needs to be paid.

This two-step processing gives you the flexibility to decide when you want to pay for overtime, and when you want to compensate in other ways. Further, function CUMBT transfers DZL to ZL, which is used in payroll.

31.6.2   Screen

From	To	Wage type	Comp.	IT	ALP	C1	AB	Number
23:30	27:30	1505 Ex-gratia		M				4.0000
28:00	30:30	1505 Ex-gratia		M				2.5000

31.6.3   Important Fields

From and To

Start and end time for which the wage type is to be paid.

Wage type

Wage type under which overtime is to be paid.

Overtime compensation type

If the employees have a choice of deciding whether they want to receive payment or time off, or a combination of the two, that choice is captured here. For more details, see chapter 11.4 (T555R).

If the overtime is to be remunerated, a wage type is generated and inserted in table DZL. If the employee is granted time off for overtime, the system forms a time balance which can then be converted in an absence quota. Possible values of overtime compensation type are:

OT comp. type	Description
Blank	Depends on wage type
1	Remuneration
2	Time off plus overtime rate
3	Compensation (time off)

IT

Wage types are flagged using an information type. The standard identifiers are:

IT	Description
S	Planned work
M	Overtime
A	Absence

ALP

If there is alternative payment, this field contains a pointer to that.

C1

If there is cost assignment, this field contains a pointer to that.

AB

This field contains a pointer to absences.

Number

Number of hours for the wage type.

31.6.4   Data Flow

Input	Processing			Output	Details
TIP	GWT	M	ZML	ZML	This step generates time wage types from overtime pairs in table TIP, according to the rules in table T510S.
ZML	POVT	TC40 GEN		TES, DZL, ZML	If a wage type in table ZML needs to be paid, it goes into table DZL. If it is to be compensated by time off, it goes in TES.

31.7   DZL–TIME WAGE TYPES IN DAY PROCESSING

Functional Consultant	User	Business Process Owner	Senior Management	My Rating	Understanding Level
A	A	A	C		

31.7.1   Purpose and Overview

All wage types that are generated during time evaluation are stored in the internal table DZL for the employee for the day. The structure of the table is PTM_DZL.

Function GWT generates time wage types from time pairs in table TIP, according to the rules in table T510S, Time Wage Type Selection Rule. Time pairs with processing type S are directly inserted in table DZL.

The wage types in table ZML may be paid, compensated by time off, or a combination of both. For some wage types, company rules may permit an employee to choose from these options. These specifications come from processing class 17 of wage type. If employee has an option, that information, overtime compensation type, comes from the infotypes. Function POVT processes table ZML and PCR TC40 creates appropriate time type balances in table TES. It also creates entries in table DZL where the employee needs to be paid.

Function P2012 processes infotype 2012, where you can transfer balances in time types, wage types and absence quotas, from one to another. It thus updates table DZL.

If you apply a limit to time type, you can also transfer the difference to a wage type. The specification for this comes from table T559P and is processed by function LIMIT. Function CUMBT transfers the entries of table DZL to ZL, which is stored in cluster B2 and used in payroll. Table DZL is also processed by function PZL, but it is not in schemas TM00-TM04.

31.7.2 Screen

Date	From	To	Wage type	IT	ALP	C1	AB	Number
05.04.2003	23:30	27:30	1505 Ex-gratia	M				4.0000
05.04.2003	28:00	30:30	1505 Ex-gratia	M				2.5000

31.7.3 Important Fields

From and to

Start and end time for which the wage type is to be paid.

Wage type

Wage type which is to be paid.

Overtime compensation type

If the employees have a choice of deciding whether they want to receive payment or time off or a combination of the two, that choice is captured here. For more details, see chapter 11.4 (T555R).

If the overtime is to be remunerated, a wage type is generated and inserted in table DZL. If the employee is granted time off for overtime, the system forms a time balance, which can then be converted in an absence quota.

Possible values of overtime compensation type are:

OT comp. type	Description
Blank	Depends on wage type
1	Remuneration
2	Time off plus overtime rate
3	Compensation (time off)

IT

Wage types are flagged using an information type. The standard identifiers are:

IT	Description
S	Planned work
M	Overtime
A	Absence

ALP

If there is alternative payment, this field contains a pointer to that.

C1

If there is cost assignment, this field contains a pointer to that.

AB

This field contains a pointer to absences.

Number

Number of hours for the wage type.

31.7.4 Data Flow

Input	Processing			Output	Details
TIP	GWT	S	DZL	DZL	Generates time wage types from time pairs in table TIP, according to the rules in table T510S, Time Wage Type Selection Rule.
ZML	POVT	TC40	GEN	TES, DZL, ZML	If a wage type in table ZML needs to be paid, it goes into table DZL. If it is to be compensated by time off, it goes in TES.
P2012	P2012			TES, DZL, ABWKONTI	Function P2012 may create time quota while processing time transfer specifications infotype (2012).
	LIMIT			TES, SALDO, DZL, FEHLER	Function LIMIT applies limit as per table T559P, limits for time balances, modifies tables TES and SALDO. It can also store surplus time balance in a wage type.

(Contd.)

Input	Processing	Output	Details
TES, DZL, DVS	CUMBT	ZES, SALDO, ZL, VS, CVS	CUMBT inserts TES records in ZES and cumulates them in SALDO. (TES ≻ ZES, SALDO) It also transfers DZL to ZL. (DZL ≻ ZL) It transfers DVS to VS and cumulates DVS in CVS. (DVS ≻ VS, CVS).

31.8 TEMPORARY TABLES FOR TIME INFOTYPES

Functional Consultant	User	Business Process Owner	Senior Management	My Rating	Understanding Level
A	A	A	C		

SAP needs to process data from time infotypes in time evaluation. During time evaluation it brings this data in temporary tables P2001, P2002, P2003, P2004, P2005, P2006, P2007, P2011 and P2012. After time evaluation, it stores this data in B2 cluster. It is necessary to store the data as it existed during time evaluation, because the data in master infotype tables may change. While storing data in B2 cluster, SAP does not use the same table names as temporary tables, but different ones. These are given below.

Further, in some cases, the tables to be stored in B2 cluster, get copied before schema processing starts. You see these tables in time evaluation log. In other cases, the tables to be stored in B2 cluster are appended after schema processing is over. In these cases, you see temporary tables in the log. Table P2011 is not stored. Closest data stored in B2 cluster is table PT.

Infotype	Temporary tables in schema processing	Copied before schema processing and updated directly in schema	Updated after schema processing
2001	P2001	AB	
2002	P2002		ANWES
2003	P2003		VERT
2004	P2004		RUFB
2005	P2005		MEHR
2006	P2006	ABWKONTI	
2007	P2007	ANWKONTI	
2011	P2011		
2012	P2012		SKO

31.9 P2001–ABSENCES

Functional Consultant	User	Business Process Owner	Senior Management	My Rating	Understanding Level
A	A	A	C		

31.9.1 Purpose and Overview

This internal table is used only by function COLLI which is used only if you use time evaluation for concurrent employment. In other cases internal table AB is used instead.

31.10 P2002–ATTENDANCES

Functional Consultant	User	Business Process Owner	Senior Management	My Rating	Understanding Level
A	A	A	C		

31.10.1 Purpose and Overview

This table contains infotype 2002 data during time evaluation. It is also an input to function COLLI, which is used only if you use time evaluation for concurrent employment. It is also used as an input to function TYPES. After time evaluation, the data is stored in table ANWES in cluster B2.

31.10.2 Data Flow

Input	Processing	Output	Details
P2002	P2002	TIP, ALP, C1	Import attendances from infotype 2002.
	ACTIO TD90	AB, P2002	If a full-day absence and attendance record is generated automatically by PCR TD80 during the previous day's time evaluation run, that time pair is inserted in the internal table TIP.
TZP, TIP, P2002	TIMTP	TZP, TIP	Compares the work schedule TZP and actual time in TIP, and creates multiple records based on their overlap in TOP.

31.11 P2003–SUBSTITUTIONS

Functional Consultant	User	Business Process Owner	Senior Management	My Rating	Understanding Level
A	A	A	C		

31.11.1 Purpose and Overview

This table contains infotype 2003 data during time evaluation. It is also an input to function COLLI which is used only if you use time evaluation for concurrent employment. After time evaluation, the data is stored in table VERT in cluster B2.

31.11.2 Data Flow

Input	Processing	Output	Details
P2003	A2003	TIP, ALP, C1	Inserts position substitution in these tables.

31.12 P2004–AVAILABILITY

Functional Consultant	User	Business Process Owner	Senior Management	My Rating	Understanding Level
B	B	B	X		

31.12.1 Purpose and Overview

This table contains infotype 2004 data during time evaluation. It is an input to function P2004 which puts it in TIP, ALP and C1. It is not used in schemas TM00-TM04, but can be included if required. After time evaluation, the data is stored in table RUFB in cluster B2.

31.13 P2005–OVERTIME

Functional Consultant	User	Business Process Owner	Senior Management	My Rating	Understanding Level
A	A	A	C		

31.13.1 Purpose and Overview

This table contains infotype 2005 data during time evaluation. After time evaluation, the data is stored in table MEHR in cluster B2.

31.13.2 Data Flow

Input	Processing	Output	Details
P2005	P2005	TIP, ALP, C1	Creates entry in TIP for records in infotype 2005. Delimits existing records depending on parameters.

31.14 P2006–ABSENCE QUOTAS

Functional Consultant	User	Business Process Owner	Senior Management	My Rating	Understanding Level
A	A	A	C		

13.14.1 Purpose and Overview

This internal table is used only by function COLLI which is used only if you use time evaluation for concurrent employment. In other cases internal table ABWKONTI is used instead.

31.15 P2007–ATTENDANCE QUOTAS

Functional Consultant	User	Business Process Owner	Senior Management	My Rating	Understanding Level
A	A	A	C		

31.15.1 Purpose and Overview

This internal table is used only by function COLLI which is used only if you use time evaluation for concurrent employment. In other cases internal table ANWKONTI is used instead.

31.16 P2011–TIME EVENTS

Functional Consultant	User	Business Process Owner	Senior Management	My Rating	Understanding Level
A	A	A	C		

31.16.1 Purpose and Overview

This internal table is used only by function COLLI which is used only if you use time evaluation for concurrent employment. Table P2011 is not stored. Closest data stored in B2 cluster is table PT.

31.17 P2012–TIME TRANSFER SPECIFICATIONS

Functional Consultant	User	Business Process Owner	Senior Management	My Rating	Understanding Level
B	B	B	X		

31.17.1 Purpose and Overview

This table contains infotype 2012 data during time evaluation. After time evaluation, the data is stored in table SKO in cluster B2.

31.17.2 Data Flow

Input	Processing	Output	Details
P2012	P2012	TES, DZL, ABWKONTI	Function P2012 may create time quota while processing time transfer specifications infotype (2012).

31.18 P2013–QUOTA CORRECTIONS

Functional Consultant	User	Business Process Owner	Senior Management	My Rating	Understanding Level
B	B	B	X		

31.18.1 Purpose and Overview

This table contains infotype 2013 data during time evaluation. It is an input to function P2013. However, this table and function are required only for employees having concurrent employment. For others, function QUOTA takes care of quota corrections entered in infotype 2013.

31.19 DVS–VARIABLE BALANCES

Functional Consultant	User	Business Process·Owner	Senior Management	My Rating	Understanding Level
B	C	X	X		

31.19.1 Purpose and Overview

During time evaluation, you can define your own variables and use them. These are stored in internal table DVS. Operation ADDVS populates table DVS. Function CUMBT transfers DVS to VS and cumulates DVS in CVS. Operation HRS can read table VS.

31.19.2 Data Flow

Input	Processing	Output	Details
TES, DZL, DVS	CUMBT	ZES, SALDO, ZL, VS, CVS	CUMBT inserts TES records in ZES and cumulates them in SALDO. (TES ≻ ZES, SALDO)
			It also transfers DZL to ZL. (DZL ≻ ZL)
			It transfers DVS to VS and cumulates DVS in CVS. (DVS ≻ VS, CVS)

Time Evaluation with Clock Times (Schema TM00)

32.1 TIME EVALUATION FROM USER'S PERSPECTIVE

Functional Consultant	User	Business Process Owner	Senior Management	My Rating	Understanding Level
A	A	A	A		

Time evaluation is one of the most important activities in time management. Many rules of the company are implemented through time evaluation. It is during time evaluation that the system generates time balances, time wage types and time quotas. It also detects anomalies in time management data and generates messages. You run time evaluation using transaction PT60 which gives the following selection screen.

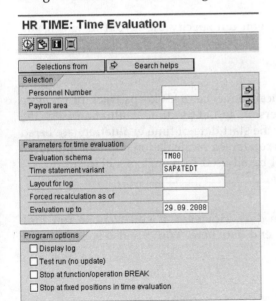

Personnel number

You can run time evaluation for specified personnel numbers. You can also exclude personnel numbers.

Payroll area

You can run time evaluation for specified payroll areas. If this field is not visible, click on 'Further selections' to get this field. Note that you cannot run it for a personnel area, or employee group etc.

Evaluation schema

Time evaluation is controlled by time evaluation schema. As a time administrator, you would be answerable to employees that the company rules are correctly applied. Thus, whereas you may never look at the configuration of the system, you must understand each step of your time evaluation schema. Day in and day out, you will be looking at its logs to understand why you got a certain result.

You must use the correct time evaluation schema. Ideally, there should be only one active time evaluation schema. However, if different schemas are to be used for different employees, you must have clear guideline and you must stick to it meticulously. Remember that if you use wrong schema, you are inviting trouble.

Time statement variant

If you want to see time statement after executing time evaluation, you specify a time statement variant here. To see the time statement, choose Goto ➤ Display form from the menu.

Layout for log

You can create and save layouts for log. Here you can specify the layout in which you want to see the log.

Forced recalculation as of

Time evaluation is always done in chronological sequence. SAP keeps track of the date till which time evaluation is done for each person, and starts time evaluation from the day after that date. Other factors, which affect the start date of time evaluation, are listed later in this chapter. However, you may need to run forced recalculation if the configuration or schema is changed. In such cases, you will be advised by your consultant to do so.

Evaluation up to

Normally time evaluation runs till the system date. However, if you want to run time evaluation for future also, you can specify the end date here. You can also specify a past date.

Display log

You should be careful not to run your regular time evaluation with 'Display log'. It takes more time and space. This option should be used for troubleshooting.

Test run (no update)

Test run is a very useful option, which lets you simulate the scenarios without updating the database. This is particularly useful for troubleshooting. If you can't understand why you got a certain result, you can run that period again in test mode with display log. You may need to use forced recalculation to ensure that the time evaluation is not skipped.

Stop at function/operation BREAK

The BREAK function allows you to interrupt processing at any point in the schema and branch into the break mode. Similarly, the BREAK operation interrupts the processing of rules and branches into the debugging mode. This option is for troubleshooting and is normally used by the consultants.

Stop at fixed positions in time evaluation

This option is for troubleshooting and is normally used by the consultants.

32.2   OVERVIEW

Functional Consultant	User	Business Process Owner	Senior Management	My Rating	Understanding Level
A	A	A	A		

32.2.1 Time Evaluation Program

You do time evaluation by running transaction PT60. It runs program RPTIME00. Program RPTIME00 triggers function pool SAPFP51T to valuate the time data. The function pool calls application components which process the time data.

In the selection screen you specify the time management schema, whether you want to run forced retro and the date till which you want to do time evaluation. In program options you can specify that you want to do a test run.

32.2.2 Employee Selection

Time evaluation takes place only for active employees (employment status 3 in infotype 0001). One of the important considerations for selecting employees is their time management status. This is specified through function CHECK. See documentation of function CHECK for more details. The processing takes place one employee at a time in personnel number sequence.

32.2.3   Period Selection

Time evaluation starts from the earliest of the following dates, unless forced retro date is specified:

➢ PDC date in infotype 0003
➢ Date in NCT table of cluster B1
➢ Earliest date in NT1 table of cluster B1
➢ Earliest date in NT2 table of cluster B1
➢ Forced retro date of time evaluation run
➢ One day after last day processed in table QT of cluster B1

However, it cannot start before the earliest personal recalculation date in infotype 0003. It also cannot start before the earliest recalculation date for time evaluation defined in table T569R.

32.2.4   Pair Formation

If your employees record time at time recording system, that forms one of the most important inputs to time evaluation. When time events data is loaded, it goes both in table TEVEN, as well as in table NT1. There may also be data lying in table NT2 (time events to be reprocessed). Time pairs are formed from these time events to determine periods when employees were at work. View V_T705B controls the pair formation process.

32.2.5   Schema Processing

Most of the logic of time evaluation is built in time management schema. There are different schemas for different scenarios. Schema TM00 serves as a model for employees who record time at time recording systems.

Schema TM00, time evaluation with clock times, is used to compare the employees' recorded time with their work schedule to determine whether they have adhered to the work schedule. The employees may work more or less than their schedule. You define how to handle these cases. The standard schema TM00 is explained here so that you can get an insight into the working of SAP time evaluation.

Schema calls functions. Functions may take a PCR as a parameter. PCRs call operations, or other PCRs. Schema can also call subschemas.

32.2.6   Database Updation in Schema Processing

The results of time evaluation are stored mainly in clusters B1 and B2. However, there are also some infotypes, which are updated by time evaluation. These are infotype 0003 (PDC recalculation date and PDC error indicator), 2011 (day assignment), 2006 (by function QUOTA), 2007 (quota deduction), locked records in 2001 and 2002 (attendance/absence reasons).

32.2.7 Time Evaluation Log

When you perform time evaluation, you have the option to select 'Display log'. This option permits you to see how the processing took place at each stage, and is very helpful in diagnosing the problem.

Time evaluation log is a structured document. In schema, you specify this structure by 'BLOCK BEG' and 'BLOCK END' functions. For each step, the log shows the input and output tables, and the processing that took place.

The tables, which are shown in input and output, are specified in table T52BW. If you wish to add or delete tables from log display, you can maintain it through SM30. If you wish to temporarily see the contents of some tables during schema processing, you can use function PRINT with table name to print an internal table.

32.3 SCHEMA TM00–INITIALIZATION

Functional Consultant	User	Business Process Owner	Senior Management	My Rating	Understanding Level
A	A	B	X		

32.3.1 Initialization

BINI

Function BINI

Function BINI marks the start of the processing block that precedes day processing. The block is used for setting employee-dependent modifiers, for example. Function EINI ends the processing block. In this block you set the groupings, which are used to access time management tables. The PCR MOD used for this purpose usually depends on organizational assignment. Therefore, processing in this block is done once for each record in table WPBP. Depending on the day being processed, appropriate data is made available.

32.3.2 Define Groupings

MOD MODT GEN

Function MOD

Function MOD calls a personnel calculation rule in which groupings for table access can be set using operation MODIF. Function MOD must only be used in the initialization block (between functions BINI and EINI). Since function MOD takes table WPBP into account, function MOD can be used to set the groupings on the basis of WPBP splits. If there is more than one record in WPBP, the PCR is called multiple times and sets groupings for each period. You can read table WPBP using operation OUTWP.

PCR MODT

PCR MODT sets groupings for employees, which are needed to access various tables, as below:

W	Time wage type selection rule group for the Time Wage Type Selection Rule Table (T510S)
T	Time type determination group for the Time Type Determination Table (T555Z). Also T555Y.
A	Employee grouping for absence valuation for the Absence Valuation Table (T554C)
D	Day grouping for wage type generation for the Time Wage Type Selection Rule Table (T510S)
S	Type for daily work schedule assignment for the Dynamic Work Schedule Assignment: Planned/Actual Overlap Table (T552W)
Q	Quota type selection rule group for the Absence Quota Type Selection Table (T559L)
L	Time balance rule group for the Value Limits for Time Balances Table (T559P)

Input

WPBP

Output

Modifiers set.

32.3.3 End of Processing Block

EINI

32.4 SCHEMA TM00–DAY PROCESSING

Functional Consultant	User	Business Process Owner	Senior Management	My Rating	Understanding Level
A	A	B	X		

32.4.1 Day Processing

BDAY

Function BDAY

Function BDAY indicates the start of day processing. This block is processed once for each employee and each day evaluated. Function EDAY marks the end of the day processing block.

32.4.2 Set Retro. Acc. for Payroll, if Required

CHECK RPR

Function CHECK

Function CHECK can be used for multiple purposes. It can be used for selecting employees, which infotypes are read, and to control time evaluation. Here it is specified that the retroactive accounting indicator is set if results change for periods that have already been processed in a payroll run.

32.4.3 Allow Evaluations for Future Periods

CHECK FUT

Evaluations of future days: You specify the last day of the evaluation when you start report RPTIME00. The system does not check whether it is a future date.

32.4.4 Process Reduced Hours

DKG

Function DKG

Function DKG references the data in the reduced hours infotype (0049) when the personal work schedule is created.

Applicability

If using infotype 0049

32.4.5 Mail to Administrator if Errors Occur

*OPTT MAIL 1   ***

Function OPTT

Function OPTT is used to set program parameters for the e-mail function.

32.4.6 Provide Time Data (Begin)

BLOCK BEG

Function BLOCK

Function BLOCK is used to structure the time evaluation log. It marks the start and end of a semantic sequence of time evaluation functions. The functions then appear under the same node in the log.

32.4.7   No Simulation for Future Periods

IF NOT SIMF

The else part of this statement is applicable if you are running time evaluation for a future period in simulation mode. Hence, this section is normally applicable.

32.4.8   Evaluate Errors from Pair Formation

PERT TD20

Function PERT

Function PERT calls a personnel calculation rule in which the errors of type 3 (technical error from pair formation) of the input table ERT are processed according to the specified rules. All pair formation errors are transferred to time evaluation error table FEHLER. Type 3 errors (technical error from pair formation) get cleared when the time evaluation starts. So, only the fresh errors impact.

PCR TD20

PCR TD20 terminates processing if there is an error in ERT table. If infotype 0050 is not maintained, you get an error here.

Input

ERT

Output

FEHLER, ERT

32.4.9   Provide Time Pairs and Daily WS

P2011

Function P2011

Function P2011 puts time pairs in the internal table TIP. It takes personal work schedule from table PSP. Work schedule substitution has already taken place while creating input table PSP. It takes information from PSP to create table TZP. Table TZP has multiple records which account for the entire day. The day is split into several periods and each period has a time identifier.

Input

PSP, time pairs formed earlier

Output

TIP, TZP

32.4.10   End if Daily Work Schedule still Active

ACTIO TD10

Function ACTIO

Function ACTIO calls and processes a personnel calculation rule. Depending on the parameter, it does the following:

➢ Process the PCR exactly once regardless of whether or not there are time pairs
➢ Call the PCR for each Absence
➢ Call the PCR for each attendance

Here it processes PCR TD10 exactly once.

PCR TD10

Personnel calculation rule TD10 checks if the daily work schedule for the day to be evaluated is still active, and if it is, terminates processing of that day. This ensures that processing is done only after all the events for the day have come in.

32.4.11   Process Work Center Substitution

A2003

Function A2003

Function A2003 processes the positions that involve a different rate of payment. If an employee has a position substitution on the day being evaluated, an ALP split indicator is set for all pairs in table TIP, that come within the period of substitution. Function A2003 processes only position substitutions. Other substitutions are already taken in table PSP, and are not processed here.

Input

P2003

Output

TIP, ALP, C1

32.4.12   Convert Daily WS if RWH and Leave

ACTIO TD60 AB

ACTIO calls TD60 once for every absence, as par2 is AB.

PCR TD60

TD60 (Processing leave during reduced working hours period): The personnel calculation rule checks whether the current day is within a RWH period. If it is, and there is no substitution or substitution 03, it calls PCR TD61.

PCR TD61

TD61 replaces the daily work schedule by a fixed daily work schedule 0007, in the case of full day absences where the absence category is 0100.

Applicability

If using infotype 0049

Input

AB

Output

TZP

32.4.13 Provide Absence Data of the Day

P2001

Function P2001

Function P2001 imports the absences for the day being evaluated from table AB (source PA2001) into table TIP. Partial day absences are entered in TIP with the recorded time interval. For full day absences, the system generates a pair based on the normal working time in the Daily Work Schedules table T550A.

If parameter 1 is blank, absences are only imported on workdays (daily work schedule class other than 0 and day type 0 or 1). If parameter 1 is EVER, absences are imported regardless of whether or not it is a workday.

When time pairs are imported, they may overlap with existing time pairs in table TIP. If parameter 2 is blank, existing time pairs are not delimited. You can delimit existing time pairs of only certain pair types by specifying those pair types as parameter 2.

Input

AB

Output

TIP, C1

32.4.14 Provide Attendance Data of the Day

P2002

Function P2002

Function P2002 imports the attendances from P2002 and enters them in table TIP. Partial day attendances are entered in TIP with the recorded time interval. For full day attendances, the system generates a pair based on the normal working time in the Daily Work Schedules table T550A. Different payment in infotype 2002 creates an entry in ALP. If cost assignment is done, entry comes in C1. Existing time pairs may be delimited based on parameter 2.

Input

P2002

Output

TIP, ALP, C1

32.4.15 Process Absence/Attendance Reasons

PTIP TD80 GEN

Function PTIP

Function PTIP calls a personnel calculation rule in which the contents of the input table TIP are processed according to the specified rules.

PCR TD80

Personnel calculation rule TD80 evaluates the attendance and absence reasons (PIN codes) that have been entered with time events. The Attendance/Absence Reasons Subsystem table V_T705A specifies how the attendance or absence reason should be processed.

The PCR generates a locked record of partial absence for current day, or full day absence for subsequent or previous day, and puts it in TIP.

Decide whether your employees should be permitted to enter attendance and absence reasons at the terminal. If not, deactivate function PTIP TD80 GEN. If needed, customize the PCR TD80 as per your needs.

Applicability

Attendance and absence reasons

Input

TIP

Output

TIP

32.4.16 Process Generated Locked Records

ACTIO TD90

PCR TD90

This PCR is required only if PCR TD80 is used. A time pair is inserted in the internal table TIP and is included provisionally in time evaluation. The time pair is based on full day absence and attendance records generated automatically by operation PPINC during the previous day's time evaluation run.

If there is only one automatically generated absence/attendance on the day to be processed, the day is accounted provisionally. A recalculation indicator is set however, and the record has to be unlocked to allow a final evaluation of the day. If there are several such records, the personnel calculation rule generates an error message. If the current day is a day off (daily work schedule class '0' or day type > '0'), the automatically generated record is extended by one day.

Applicability

Attendance and absence reasons

Output

AB, P2002

32.4.17 Provide Overtime Data of the Day

*P2005 ***

Function P2005

Function P2005 imports the overtime data for the day being evaluated to table TIP. Depending on the parameter, it may delimit existing TIP pairs. The overtime pairs generated in TIP by function P2005 are assigned

➢ Pair type '1'
➢ Origin indicator 'O'
➢ Overtime compensation type from the record
➢ Time ids
  ▸ Overtime pair: '01'
  ▸ Unpaid overtime break: '07'
  ▸ Paid overtime break: '08'.

Applicability

If using overtime infotype 2005

Input

P2005

Output

TIP, ALP, C1

32.4.18 Set PTYPE/TTYPE for Overtime

*PTIP TD40 GEN   ***

PCR TD40

This PCR sets the processing type of the overtime pairs imported from infotype 2005 (time identifier '01', origin indicator 'O') to 'M' and adds hours in time type 0040. Since function GOT does not select time pairs with processing type M, these time pairs are not considered for the approval process set up by function GOT.

Input

TIP

Output

TIP

Applicability

If using overtime infotype 2005

32.4.19 Dynamic DWS Assignment: Clock-in Entry

ACTIO TD30

PCR TD30

If there is no substitution, TD30 changes work schedule in TZP, depending on first clock-in time and T552V configuration, and gives message.

RC	DYNDP condition	DWS change	TD30 Msg
0	Dynamic DWS found and matches employee's DWS.	No	
2	Dynamic DWS found and does not match employee's DWS.	Yes	24
3	No TIP entry with pair type 1.	No	
4	Clock-in entry does not match with any Dynamic DWS.	No	23
5	Variant to be assigned does not exist	No	
8	No entry in T552V	No	

Input

TIP, TZP

Output

TZP, PSP

32.4.20 Dynamic DWS Assignment: Overlap

DYNWS *

Function DYNWS assigns an employee a new daily work schedule dynamically in time evaluation. The daily work schedule is determined from a set of work schedules as the one where the planned specifications show the 'best' overlap with the employee's actual times.

The set of daily work schedules is defined on the basis of the period work schedule using the 'Dynamic Daily Work Schedule Assignment: Planned/Actual Overlap' view (V_T552W). Unlike in PCR TD30, the daily work schedule is not assigned on the basis of the first clock-in entry, but according to the overlap between the planned specifications and the actual times. The calculation of the overlap is based only on pairs that specify clock times.

Input

TIP, TZP, PSP

Output

TIP, TZP, PSP

32.4.21 Simulation for Future Period

ELSE

32.4.22 Provide Time Data for Simulation

COPY TDT0 *

This subschema is expanded below.

32.4.23 Planned Pair and Daily Work Schedule

P2000

Function P2000

During the evaluation of future periods, no information is available about the employee's actual working time. Therefore, the time evaluation generates the daily information using function P2000. It places the daily work schedule in table TZP and a planned pair in the TIP.

Input

PSP

Output

TIP, TZP

32.4.24 Process Work Center Substitution

A2003

32.4.25 Provide Absences

P2001 1

32.4.26 Provide Attendances

P2002 1

32.4.27 Set Attendance Flag

RTIPA TD70 GEN

This function is called only in future simulation.

Function RTIPA

Function RTIPA is identical to RTIP, but it is only processed if there is an absence on the current day.

PCR TD70

The system checks if there is an attendance record on the current day. If there is, the attendance flag is set to '1'. If there are only absence pairs on the day, the attendance flag is set to '0'.

Input

TIP

Output

Attendance flag

32.4.28 Endif (Simulation)

ENDIF

32.4.29 Provide Time Data (End)

BLOCK END

At this point, you have all the data in tables TIP and TZP.

32.4.30 Tolerances and Error Checks (Begin)

BLOCK BEG

While doing online entry in infotypes, the system ensures that there is no conflicting information. However, such conflicting information has to be handled during time evaluation. Some conflicts can be resolved by changing information based on rules, while in other cases manual intervention is required.

32.4.31 Adjust Absences

PTIPA TE10 GEN

Function PTIPA

The only difference between this function and function PTIP is that it is only processed if there is an absence on the current day.

PCR TE10

TE10 adjusts any inserted absences of less than one day relative to the attendance pairs. It adjusts absence records in TIP, if needed. There are 2 parts of this rule:

➤ Full day absence: For full-day absences, any attendances are assigned the time identifier 01 (unapproved overtime) so that they can be handled as overtime.
➤ Non full day absence: If there is overlap of absence and attendance, absence record is adjusted. If there is gap, error message is issued.

Note that adjustment of absences is a functionality of time evaluation, which does not result in a pay change. The absences infotype (2001) is not updated. Also see Help of the Configuration Node of PCR TE10.

Input

TIP

Output

TIP

32.4.32   Check for Day with Error

ACTIO TE20

PCR TE20

This PCR compares information (or lack of it) about an employee's presence and absence with his work schedule and takes various actions. This is one of the most complex and important PCR and should reflect business policy. At present, depending on the combination of conditions, it does one of the following:

➤ An error is generated.
➤ A planned pair is generated.
➤ The day is processed as if it were a day off.

Parameters for operation VARST	
FREE	Daily work schedule off? Y for planned hours=0 from T550A for DWS
PRSNT	Employee at work? Pair type 1 or 3, data coming in TIP from TEVEN or infotype 2002
ABSCE	Employee absent? Pair type 2, data coming in TIP from infotype 2001
ABSWD	Employee absent for whole day from infotype 2001, field ALLDF = X
DAYTY	Day Type Rule Table (T553A)

32.4.33   Error Checks for Each Pair

PTIP TE30 GEN

TE30 checks the status1 of the time pairs and completes them if possible. Otherwise, it gives error message. You can also use PCR TE31, which does not delimit incomplete time pairs automatically, but cancels time evaluation with an appropriate message.

Status	*Description*
Blank	Correct pair Pass on.
2	No clock-in entry Error message
3	No clock-out entry Query: Is the employee still at work? Yes: The end of planned working time is used as the clock-out entry for the time event. Retroactive accounting is performed during the next payroll run. No: Error message—No clock-out entry

(Contd.)

Status	Description
4	No end time for break Error message
5	No start time for break Error message
7	No clock-in entry for off-site work The start time specified in daily work schedule is used to delimit the record. Retroactive accounting is not performed.
8	No clock-out entry for off-site work Query: Is the employee expected to return? Yes: The end time specified in the daily work schedule is used to delimit the record. A recalculation is performed. No: The end time specified in the daily work schedule is used to delimit the record. No recalculation is performed.
E	Error message

Input

TIP

Output

TIP, FEHLER

32.4.34 Process Daily Work Schedule Tolerances

DPTOL

Function DPTOL processes time pairs according to the tolerances specified in the daily work schedule and changes the begin or end time of the time pair.

Input

TIP

Output

TIP

32.4.35 Tolerances and Error Checks (End)

BLOCK END

32.4.36 Determine Planned Working Times (Begin)

BLOCK BEG

32.4.37 Round First/Last Pair

*PTIP TL10 GEN   ***

PCR TL10

The personnel calculation rule TL10 rounds the start and end times of postings recorded by employees. If the start and end times of the pair are within the working time frame, the first and last pair of the day (from table TIP) are rounded.

For example, an employee's planned working time starts at 8 a.m. He arrives 5 minutes late, however, which means that he clocks in at 8.05 a.m. You wish to deduct 15 minutes for late arrival, i.e. the system should process the first time pair as if the employee had clocked in at 8.15 a.m.

Input

TIP

Output

TIP

32.4.38 Set Dynamic Breaks

*DYNBR TF10   ***

Function DYNBR

Deactivate function DYNBR, if you have only fixed breaks. It is required only for dynamic breaks.

Function DYNBR is used to determine how dynamic breaks are distributed within the daily work schedule. Dynamic breaks are breaks for which there is no start/end time in the Work Break Schedules table (T550P). Instead, a number of hours is specified in the 'After hrs' field; the break is calculated as of this number of hours. It updates TZP table, but not PSP table.

The time as of which the number of hours is calculated (referred to as the starting point) is the start of planned working time stipulated in the daily work schedule. You can change the default starting point using function DYNBR.

PCR TF10

TF10 (Starting point for dynamic breaks): On days of day type 1, personnel calculation rule TF10 sets the starting point for calculating the distribution of dynamic breaks to the start of planned working time in the daily work schedule.

On a day of day type 1, the distribution of dynamic breaks in the daily work schedule is not determined according to the employee's first time posting, but according to the start of planned working time. This means that the breaks for the daily work schedule (as for non-dynamic break schedules) only apply to the planned pair generated on a public holiday (personnel calculation rule TE20) and not to any overtime the employee has worked.

You can use schema TOB0 if you want daily work schedule breaks to be counted for overlapping overtime pairs.

Input

PSP, TZP

Output

PSP, TZP

32.4.39 Assign Time Type to Time Pair

TIMTP

This function compares the work schedule TZP and actual time in TIP, and creates multiple records in TIP based on their overlap. These records are evaluated for time identifier and pair type. Based on these, processing type and time type is determined from T555Z. All these four fields are updated in TIP.

Input

TZP, TIP, P2002

Output

TZP, TIP

32.4.40 Evaluate Breaks

PBRKS 1 ALL

Function PBRKS evaluates all breaks in the daily work schedule (table T550A) or work break schedule (T550P). You use function PBRKS for variable breaks which specify that employees must take a break within a specified break frame, for example, a half-hour break between 12 noon and 1 p.m.

Input

TIP

Output

TIP

Applicability

Variable breaks

32.4.41 Determine Planned Pairs

DEFTP

Function DEFTP determines the planned working time pairs in table TIP. They are assigned processing type 'S'. The function checks that only pairs within the maximum daily working time are flagged as planned working time pairs. Processing type P is changed to S. Time type 0000 and 0001 (total of working time) created in TES (Daily Balances).

Output

TIP, TES

32.4.42 Reduce Absences

PTIPA TP10 GEN

PCR TP10

In SAP, for each absence type, you define whether it is compensated by the employer, or not in the field 'Time evaluation class of table T554S. If an employee has a partial day absence, and the employer pays for the absence, and if the employee works extra time, he does not accrue flextime credit. Instead, his absence is shortened. However, if the employer is not paying for the absence, then the employee accrues flextime balance.

Input

TIP

Output

TIP

Applicability

Flextime

32.4.43　Absences with Time Compensation

RTIPA TP20 GEN

Function RTIPA

Function RTIPA is identical to RTIP, but it is only processed if there is an absence on the current day.

PCR TP20

You can use this rule as a model to allow employees to get their absences deducted from accumulated flextime hours or the overtime account. The employee uses an absence type, which determines the account (time type) from which the deduction should take place.

Input

TIP

Applicability

Flextime

32.4.44　Shorten Automatically Delimited Off-site Records

PTIP TB10 GEN　　*

PCR TB10

If your employee has worked off-site but not recorded end time, you may like to delimit the record. But if this results in too much flextime, you may like to limit it using this PCR.

Certain off-site work records, which are still open, are delimited automatically in personnel calculation rule TB10. If the record is delimited too generously, resulting in excess flextime, personnel calculation rule TB10 shortens the record.

If an automatically delimited off-site work record exists, and the flextime balance is greater than the value of constant TEDEG in the Constants table (T511K), the off-site work record is shortened to make the working time equal to the planned hours plus the constant TEDEG.

If the day's flextime balance is greater than the planned hours plus the constant TEDEG without the off-site work record, the off-site record is deleted.

You can see whether an off-site work record has been delimited automatically in field STAT1 = A of table TIP.

Input

TIP

Output

TIP

Applicability

Flextime

32.4.45 Shorten Autom. Delimited OS (with OT)

COPY TB00 *

32.4.46 Determine Planned Working Times (End)

BLOCK END

32.4.47 Determine Overtime (Begin)

BLOCK BEG

Overtime is time id 01 (outside DWS), and processing type P.

32.4.48 Calculate Overtime with Quota 2007 01

GOT TO20 01

You call function GOT for each quota type you want to process.

Function GOT

Function GOT compares the time pairs in table TIP with the overtime approvals for the current day (infotype 2007). The 'approved' times are made available for processing in the specified personnel calculation rule, where they can be flagged as overtime pairs.

PCR TO20 (Form overtime pairs)

Personnel calculation rule TO20 determines overtime from employees' attendances and absences. The following prerequisites must be met before overtime can be determined:

➤ Time type 0000 (attendance and absence time) must exceed the planned hours in the daily work schedule.
➤ Time type 0001 (attendance time) must be less than the constant TGMAX from table T511K to ensure that the maximum daily working time is not exceeded.
➤ There is an overtime approval in infotype 2007.

The unapproved time pairs are passed on to personnel calculation rule TO20 and the following conditions are checked:

➢ Overtime is only allowed after the employee has completed the number of planned hours (covered by the basic wage) in the daily work schedule.
➢ Overtime is only credited up to the maximum daily working time.
➢ The time pairs are sorted in descending order to calculate overtime in the standard system.

Input

ANWKONTI, TIP

Output

TIP, ANWKONTI, ZKO

32.4.49 Overtime on the Basis of Quota 2007 02

GOT TO20 02

Here function GOT processes quota type 02. For all details, see above.

Input

ANWKONTI, TIP

Output

TIP, ANWKONTI, ZKO

32.4.50 Evaluate Overtime Approval in I0050

*PTIP TO10 GEN *

SAP offers three methods of automatic overtime approval.

➢ For specified employees (PCR TO10).
➢ For employees in specified daily work schedules (PCR TO15).
➢ For all employees (PCR TO16).

The main processing is in PCR TO16. PCRs TO10 and TO15 call PCR TO16 appropriately. Hence, see the detailed logic in PCR TO16 in the following subsection.

PCR TO10 (Standard overtime approval – P0050)

If an employee has standard overtime approval in infotype 0050, this step converts an unapproved overtime pair into an approved one. It also ensures that the employee has worked the planned hours before getting overtime, and that his total work including overtime does not exceed TGMAX value in table T511K.

Input

TIP

Output

TIP

32.4.51 Evaluate Overtime Approval in Daily WS

PTIP TO15 GEN *

PCR TO15 (Evaluate overtime approval from daily work schedule – T550A)

If an employee has a daily work schedule for which 'automatic overtime' is allowed in the Daily Work Schedule View V_T550A, this step converts his unapproved overtime pair into an approved one (processing type M). It also ensures that the employee has worked the planned hours before getting overtime, and that his total work including overtime does not exceed TGMAX value in table T511K.

Input

TIP

Output

TIP

32.4.52 Determine Overtime without Approval

PTIP TO16 GEN *

PCR TO16 (Calculating overtime for time pairs outside of planned)

If time id is 01, and pair type is 1 or 3, call PCR TO11.

PCR TO11 (Determining overtime pairs)

If time type 0000 > planned working time, then time type 0001 is compared to TGMAX from T511K. If it is greater than or equal to, TIP record is written to TOP. If it is less, then it is added to time type 0001, processing type is set to M, time type is set to 0040, and the record is added to TOP. However, if by adding the hours of the current record, TGMAX is exceeded, the number of hours is so reduced that TGMAX is not exceeded.

If time type 0000 < planned working time, and does not exceed the planned time, even if the current pair is taken into account, a planned pair is generated with time identifier 02 and processing type S (Planned time). However, if time type 0000 + current pair exceed planned working time, a time pair is generated which contains difference between planned time and time type 0001. It has time id 02, processing type M and time type 0040. TGMAX restriction is applied before creating this time pair.

It ensures that you have worked the planned hours before getting overtime, and that your total work including overtime does not exceed TGMAX.

Input

TIP

Output

TIP

32.4.53   Calc. Overtime using Rounding and Quota

*COPY TO00   ***

32.4.54   Weekly Overtime Analysis

*COPY TPOW   ***

32.4.55   Determine Indicator for Core Night Work

KNTAG   K

Function KNTAG refers to the time pairs to determine whether the employee is performing core night work. In this case, core night work means that the employee starts night work before midnight (24.00). Deactivate the function KNTAG if core night work does not feature in your company (relevant for Germany).

32.4.56   Determine Overtime (End)

BLOCK END

32.4.57   Select Time Wage Types (Begin)

BLOCK BEG

32.4.58   Set Day Grouping for T510S

DAYMO 01 02 02 02

Function DAYMO

You can use function DAYMO to set the day grouping for time wage type selection from the Time Wage Type Selection table T510S to a particular value. The value is set as follows:

	Monday to Saturday	*Sunday*
Not a public holiday	Parameter 1	Parameter 2
Public holiday	Parameter 3	Parameter 4

DAYMO must always be set before function GWT in day processing. If this assignment is not detailed enough for your requirements, you can also set the day grouping for time wage type selection in personnel calculation rules using operation MODIF.

32.4.59 Adjust Pay for Lost Time/OT on Holidays

*COPY TOH0   **

32.4.60 Process Guaranteed Hours

*COPY TG00   **

32.4.61 Wage Type Selection for Planned Work

*GWT   S DZL   **

Function GWT generates time wage types from time pairs in table TIP, according to the rules in table T510S, Time Wage Type Selection Rule. The function is part of the interface between payroll and time management. If you use it for payroll, it should be in the day processing schema.

S: Only time pairs with processing type S are used to generate wage types.

DZL: The generated wage types are entered in the internal table DZL.

Input

TIP

Output

DZL

32.4.62 Wage Type Selection for Overtime

*GWT   M ZML **

Function GWT generates time wage types from time pairs in table TIP, according to the rules in table T510S, Time Wage Type Selection Rule. The function is part of the interface between payroll and time management. If you use it for payroll, it should be in the day processing schema.

M: Only time pairs with processing type M are used to generate wage types.

ZML: The generated wage types are entered in the internal table ZML.

Input

TIP

Output

ZML

32.4.63   Select Time Wage Types (End)

BLOCK END

32.4.64   Compensate Overtime Wage Types (Begin)

BLOCK BEG

32.4.65   Overtime: Higher WT after 10 Hrs/Week

*COPY TW00   ***

32.4.66   Overtime Compensation

POVT TC40 GEN

Function POVT

POVT: Process table ZML (Overtime wage types)

PCR TC40 (Compensate overtime)

The wage types in table ZML may be paid, compensated by time off, or a combination of both. For some wage types, company rules may permit an employee to choose from these options. These specifications come from processing class 17 of wage type. If employee has an option, that information, overtime compensation type comes from the infotypes. Function POVT processes table ZML and PCR TC40 creates appropriate time type balances in table TES. It also creates entries in table DZL where the employee needs to be paid.

Input

ZML

Output

TES, DZL, ZML

32.4.67   Compensate Overtime Wage Types (End)

BLOCK END

32.4.68   Manage Time Accounts (Begin)

BLOCK BEG

32.4.69   Form Day Balances

RTIP TR10

Personnel calculation rule TR10 cumulates the number of hours of the respective time type in various other time types to form daily totals.

Input

TIP

Output

TES

32.4.70   Process Time Transfer Specifications

P2012

Function P2012 imports the time transfer specifications for the day being evaluated. You can enter time transfer specifications in the time transfer specifications infotype (2012). The function can be called either with or without a personnel calculation rule.

Input

P2012

Output

TES, DZL, ABWKONTI

32.4.71   Flextime Balance/Overtime/Productive Hrs

ACTIO TR30

ACTIO calls TR30 only once.

PCR TR30 (Calculating flextime balances)

The personnel calculation rule TR30 forms the flextime balance for the current day by subtracting the planned time (time type 0002) from the skeleton time (time type 0003). The number of overtime hours worked and the productive hours are also calculated.

Output

TES

32.4.72   Limits for Time Balances

LIMIT

Function LIMIT applies the rules defined in T559P to limit an employee's time balance. It checks time balances to see if they reach or exceed specified value limits. Typical examples of the function are the capping of flextime at the end of a period, checking the maximum working time allowed by working time regulations, maximum values for time-off credit, minimum length of work breaks, and so on. You can also total day balances over various periods; if required, you can define the periods yourself.

Output

TES, SALDO, DZL, FEHLER

Applicability

Flextime

32.4.73   Update Balances, Wage Types...

CUMBT

CUMBT inserts TES records in ZES and cumulates them in SALDO. (TES ≻ ZES, SALDO)

It also transfers DZL to ZL. (DZL ≻ ZL)

It transfers DVS to VS and cumulates DVS in CVS. (DVS ≻ VS, CVS)

Input

TES, DZL, DVS

Output

ZES, SALDO, ZL, VS, CVS

32.4.74   Generate Absence Quotas

QUOTA

Function QUOTA generates quota automatically during time evaluation. Alternatively, quota can be generated by running Generate Absence Quotas report (RPTQTA00), or through manual entry. Function QUOTA generates absence quotas according to the rules in the 'Quota Type Selection' view cluster VC_T559L. The results of the generation process are stored in tables QTACC and QTTRANS in the evaluation cluster. They can be checked in the Quota Overview screen using transaction PT50, and corrected or supplemented if necessary. For more information see chapter 7.4.

Input

WPBP, PSP, AB, ZES, SALDO, ABWKONTI

Output

ABWKONTI, QTACC, QTBASE, QTTRANS

32.4.75   Manage Time Accounts (End)

BLOCK END

32.4.76   End of Day Processing

EDAY

32.5   SCHEMA TM00–PERIOD END PROCESSING

Functional Consultant	User	Business Process Owner	Senior Management	My Rating	Understanding Level
A	A	B	X		

32.5.1   Final Processing

BEND

This block is processed only once for each employee and evaluation. Function EEND marks the end of the period processing block.

32.5.2   If Last Day of Period

IF EOM

32.5.3   Transfer Excess Flextime to Overtime

*P2007 TS20 GEN   ***

Function P2007

Function P2007 calls a personnel calculation rule in which the contents of the input table ANWKONTI are processed according to the specified rules.

TS20 (Transfer excess flextime to overtime)

TS20 compares the current flextime balance with the value of constant GLMAX in the Constants table T511K. If the balance is greater, the excess is transferred from the flextime to the overtime account.

Input

ANWKONTI

Output

ANWKONTI, ABWKONTI

32.5.4   Adjust Flextime Balance

LIMIT

Function LIMIT

Here function LIMIT applies monthly limit as per table T559P, Limits for Time Balances. It modifies SALDO. It cannot modify TES and ZES.

Output

TES, SALDO, DZL, FEHLER

32.5.5   Endif (Last Day of Period)

ENDIF

32.5.6   Export Evaluation Results

EXPRT

Function EXPRT instructs time evaluation to store the results. The function can come at any point in the schema. If you only want to perform a simulation, you should deactivate function EXPRT.

32.5.7   End of Processing Block

EEND

Schemas, Functions PCRs, Operations, Features

33.1 TIME MANAGEMENT SCHEMAS

Functional Consultant	User	Business Process Owner	Senior Management	My Rating	Understanding Level
A	B	C	C		

You manage time management schemas through transaction PE01. Designing the schema is the most important activity in implementing time management. It is through the schema that you achieve the results you want. SAP supplies model schemas which you study to understand what is possible. You then copy and modify them in customer name space.

SAP stores the schemas in tables. SAP supplied schemas are stored in T52C0 (text in T52C2). Customer schemas are stored in table T52C1 (text in T52C3). There are also tables T52CC (schema directory for customer) and T52CD (schema directory for SAP).

You may have different schemas for different category of employees, e.g. internal and external employees. You can avoid the risk of running the wrong schema, by calling both the schemas in a common schema and use If statement. After If, use function CHECK, followed by COPY subschema number. Do the same after Else statement.

For the schemas, which are not to be run, e.g. subschema or old version, remove the tick from 'Schema can be executed' check box in attributes. This reduces the chances of running a wrong schema. You eliminate this risk if there is only one executable schema.

33.2 TIME MANAGEMENT FUNCTIONS

Functional Consultant	User	Business Process Owner	Senior Management	My Rating	Understanding Level
A	B	C	C		

You manage functions through transaction PE04. SAP supplies you the functions. You need to understand their behaviour by going through the documentation. You also study how they are called in SAP supplied schemas. The functions have to be called at the right places in the schema, so that the internal tables have the right data at that point. You are usually guided by the model schema.

The documentation of the function also indicates what parameters the function takes. Depending on your requirement you select the parameters. In many cases, a PCR is a parameter of the function.

You don't normally modify a SAP function, certainly not unless you are absolutely competent. However, SAP permits you (i) create your own function, and (ii) to modify SAP's function. In PE04 transaction, if you specify a function, and click on change, you get the following screen:

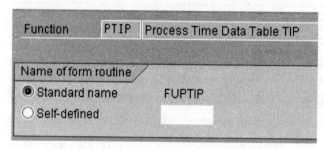

You can choose the radio button self-defined, write the form routine name and click on source text (Ctrl+F7). It takes you to an include, where you can write your own code, that is executed instead of standard code.

Using SAP's standard function name and modifying the text has following advantages/ disadvantages, compared to writing a Z function.

➤ You can use standard SAP schema/subschema. If you created a Z function, you have to write Z schemas to call it.
➤ You consistently use the same code. If you created a Z function, there is a possibility that at some places, you use SAP function, while at other places you use Z function. If you consciously want this to happen, it is an advantage, otherwise a disadvantage.
➤ While looking at the schema, you may not realize that the function is your creation, and not SAP's. By creating Z function, you make it self-evident.
➤ If you modify a function, you must remember to modify its documentation. If you don't, one might expect certain behaviour from a function by reading its documentation, whereas the function's actual behaviour might be different.

You can see the parameters that a function can take and valid values for each of these parameters. You can also see the tables that will be displayed in the log before and after the function is called (these can depend on function parameters). These are stored in tables T52B6, T52B7, T52B8, T52BB and T52BW. If you see the delivery class of these tables, it shows that there can be customer entries in them. However, be very careful before you make any changes. T52BW is safe to change, particularly if you will like the log to display some additional relevant tables.

You can see the parameters that a function can take and valid values for each of these parameters in tables T52B6, T52B7, T52B8 and T52BB. The delivery classes of these tables show that there can be customer entries in them. However, be very careful before you make any changes.

You can also see the tables that are displayed in the log before and after the function is called in table T52BW. This table can be safely changed, if you want the log to display some additional relevant tables.

There are different types of functions:

> Functions that set a switch: They can come in any position within a schema. They are not called again while the current schema is being executed. They can not be processed in IF-ELSE-ENDIF loop. Example: OPPT, CHECK, EXPRT.
> Functions that import data: e.g. P2001.
> Functions that call a PCR
  ‣ Functions for processing status information, e.g. ACTIO.
  ‣ Functions that process an internal table line by line, e.g. PTIP.
  ‣ Functions with fixed processing, e.g. PBRKS.

33.3 TIME MANAGEMENT PCRs

Functional Consultant	User	Business Process Owner	Senior Management	My Rating	Understanding Level
A	B	C	C		

You manage PCRs through transaction PE02. Understanding and writing PCRs is one of the most complex and important jobs in implementing SAP time management. It is through PCRs that you achieve most of your objectives.

A PCR lets you test conditions and take actions. You can nest condition testing up to a certain extent. It builds a variable key, which has a limited length. The actions can modify data in internal tables and sometimes even in database.

Bulk of the work in PCRs is done by operations. Operations are used both for testing conditions, as well as for taking actions. There are two predefined parameters, which are available in all time management PCRs. These are ES grouping for PCR and time type.

SAP stores the PCRs in tables. All PCRs are stored in T52C5. Directory of PCRs is in table T52CE.

33.4 TIME MANAGEMENT OPERATIONS

Functional Consultant	User	Business Process Owner	Senior Management	My Rating	Understanding Level
A	B	C	X		

33.4.1 Overview

You manage operations through transaction PE04. The real skill in SAP time management lies in your ability to write PCRs, for which a good knowledge of what you can achieve with which operation is a must. In particular you need to know with which operation, you can read/update which table, be it a transparent table, cluster table or internal table.

Understanding the operations is critical to achieving your goal in time evaluation. The main source of information is the documentation of operation provided by SAP. Seeing how they are used in PCRs given by SAP is also useful. To find the PCRs, where an operation is used, you can use the 'where used' icon.

Until you achieve a mastery over operations, the description of operations given below will help you narrow down the search of operations for a given purpose.

Like function, you can modify the code of an operation. However, use this facility with extreme caution.

33.4.2 Important Operations

While you should study all operations, there are some that are very frequently used. You may like to study them first. These are OUTWP, TABLE, VARAB, VARPR, VARST, ADDDB, ADDMB, COLER, COLOP, FILLP, HRS, TFLAG, GCY and PCY.

33.4.3 Operations that Provide Information for Decision Making in PCRs

These operations can be used to read a variety of information in the variable key of the PCR, and building required logic on its basis.

Operation	Description
ALLDT	Check 24-hour coverage from start of period For Germany
LDPAY	Query end of continued pay
OUTAL	Provide data for different payment Operation OUTAL enters data from the internal table ALP (alternate payment) in the variable key. OUTAL is a decision operation.
OUTAQ	Retrieve information from absence quotas Operation OUTAQ enters data from table ABWKONTI (absence quotas) in the variable key. It is a decision operation.

(Contd.)

Operation	Description
OUTER	Error information Operation OUTER enters data on the error being processed in the variable key. The operation can only be used in a personnel calculation rule called by function PERT.
OUTOT	Provide data on overtime wage types Depending on the parameters set, operation OUTOT enters the overtime compensation type or the wage type of an overtime wage type in the variable table key.
OUTPQ	Retrieve information from attendance quotas Operation OUTPQ enters information from table ANWKONTI (attendance quotas) in the variable table key. OUTPQ is a decision operation.
OUTTI	Retrieve fields from the 'Time Recording' infotype Operation OUTTI enters the values of the specified parameter from the time recording Information infotype (0050) in the variable table key.
OUTTP	Provide time pair data Operation OUTTP enters data from the current time pair in the variable table key.
OUTWP	Provide work center data Operation OUTWP transfers the values of the parameters listed below from the work center to the variable key. Company code, PA, PSA, cost center, EG, ESG, payroll area, position, job, org unit, work schedule rule, time management status, pay scale type/area/group/level, ES grouping for CAP, action, employment status, sex, etc.
OUTZL	Provide information from time wage types Operation OUTZL enters information from table ZL (time wage types) or DZL (daily time wage types) in the variable key. Operation OUTZL is a decision operation.
R555D	Read abs./attendance reasons for subsystem Operation R555D reads the Attendance/Absence Reasons for Subsystem table (V_T705A) for the attendance or absence reason that is specified in the start or end pin code of the time pair being processed. This is a decision operation.
TABLE	Prepare access to table fields You can use this operation to read data from the following tables:

001P	Personnel areas/subareas
503	Employee groups/subgroups
508A	Work schedule rule
510I	Standard working time
559A	Working week

(Contd.)

Operation	Description
TIMAP	Have the infotypes imported by Time Evaluation been checked? Operation TIMAP checks the infotypes processed by time evaluation for their release date in the test procedures infotype (0130).
TIPOS	Determine relative position of a time pair Operation TIPOS checks where the current time pair comes in relation to the previous and subsequent pairs (see function PTIP).
TKUZR	Query Reduced Working Hours (RWH) period Operation TKUZR checks whether the day being processed comes within a reduced working hours (RWH) period.
VALEN	Length of variable key Operation VALEN limits the enhancement of the variable key to length 'n'; this makes sense if not all positions are to be queried by a decision operation for a field, which is 'n' characters long.
VAOFF	Offsetting Variable Key This operation allows you to check a field as of the nth position, using a decision operation.
VARAB	Provide information on absences Operation VARAB enters data on the current absence in the variable key, according to the parameters given below.

	TYP	Absence category
	CAT	Class for time evaluation from view V_554S_E
	VCL	Absence valuation rule from view V_554S_G
	DAY	Query: Full day absence? Y = Full day absence N = Partial day absence * = No absence
	TIM	Processing type/time type class from T554S
	OCABS	Indicator for absence valuation in off-cycle payroll
	ABSTP	Absence category from calendar entry
	PSS	Public sector only

Operation	Description
VARPR	Provide Data on current attendance Operation VARPR enters data on the current attendance in the variable key, according to the parameters given below.

	TYP	Attendance type
	CAT	Class for time evaluation from view V_554S_F
	VCL	Absence valuation rule from view V_554S_H
	DAY	Query: Full day attendance? Y = Full day attendance N = Partial day attendance * = No attendance
	TIM	Processing type/time type class from T554S

Operation	Description
VARST	Provide general fields Queries many fields including work schedule related fields. Depending on the parameters set, operation VARST can be used to query general status fields, or fill the variable key of the current personnel calculation rule with status information.
VWTCL	Provide processing class of wage type Operation VWTCL enters the value of the processing classes of wage types from the wage type valuation table (T512W) in the variable key.

33.4.4 Operations that Change Contents of Internal Tables

Operation	Description
ADDDB	Cumulate in day balance table TES Add to the same or another time type. Control indicator can be used to overwrite. It can also be used to add planned hours.
ADDMB	Cumulate in monthly balance table SALDO Add to the same or another time type. Control indicator can be used to overwrite. It can also be used to add planned hours.
ADDOT	Transfer to table ZMO Operation ADDOT enters the wage types in table ZML.
ADDVS	Cumulate in variable balances table Operation ADDVS adds the value of the number of hours field for each day to the internal table of variable balances.
ADDZL	Cumulate in time wage types table Operation ADDZL adds the current number field to the internal table ZL.
COLER	Transfer to error table Operation COLER transfers errors to the internal table FEHLER.
COLOP	Transfer data to internal table TOP Operation COLOP transfers data from the internal table TIP to the internal table TOP. The time type can be changed.
COLPA	Transfer to pair table You can use operation COLPA to change a generated time pair in Pairs table (PT) in cluster B2. The operation is intended for delimiting open time pairs (PCR TE30).
COLTQ	Increase amount of quota taken Operation COLTQ increases the amount of an attendance quota used by the current number of hours field. You can only call operation COLTQ using function P2007.

(Contd.)

Operation	Description
COMOT	Overtime pairs analysis Operation COMOT compares TIP pairs according to their processing type. The operation is used to fill periods that contain several (overlapping) time pairs in TIP with only one (new) time pair.
DAYPG	Replace daily work schedule Operation DAYPG can be used to override an employee's current daily work schedule or day type. A return code is set.
DELIM	Delimit time pair Operation DELIM delimits time pairs with times from the daily work schedule.
DYNDP	Dynamic daily work schedule assignment Operation DYNDP assigns a new daily work schedule dynamically to an employee based on first clock-in time using V_T552V.
FILLP	Change time pair information (in TIP) Operation FILLP enters the status and time data for a time pair. The data entered in the fields is either read from the current number field or directly specified in the parameter.
FILLW	Fill wage type data Entries in the internal wage type tables are assigned additional information during time evaluation. You can use operation FILLW to make manual changes to the fields for the subsequent operations ADDZL and ADDOT.
GENOT	Generate time pairs for overtime As long as the overtime quota being processed has not been used up, operation GENOT flags the time pair (or parts of the time pair) as an overtime time pair.
GENOW	Generate wage type in ZML Operation GENOW splits the wage type being processed and enters one part in the table of overtime wage types, ZML. The number of hours field (filled using operation HRS) specifies how much of the wage type should be separated off. The rest of the wage type can then be processed.
GENTG	Generate a TIP entry Operation GENTG enters a new entry in the internal table TIP. The operation can be used in personnel calculation rules that are called using function ACTIO.
GENTP	Split TIP entry Operation GENTP separates a part of the current TIP entry and enters it in the daily output table TOP. The number of hours field (filled by operation HRS) specifies the size of the partial pair. Processing can then be resumed with the (reduced) current time pair.

(Contd.)

Operation	Description
GENTW	Generate wage types Operation GENTW separates a part of the wage type being processed and enters it in the time wage types table ZL. This is required for wage types that specify start and end times. The number of hours field (filled by operation HRS) specifies how much of the wage type should be split. Processing can then be resumed with the (reduced) current wage type.
HRS	Edit number of hours field Operation HRS can be used to change the number of hours field or to compare it with other values. HRS may or may not be a decision operation, depending on the parameters set.
INSLR	Insert locked records in table TIP Operation INSLR inserts automatically generated absences and attendances that have not yet been locked in table TIP.
INSTP	Correctly setup pair Operation INSTP adjusts time pairs in the daily input table TIP according to the end time of the previous pair and the start time of the subsequent pair.
RNDOT	Round time pairs Operation RNDOT rounds time pairs so that their total number of hours for a specific processing type observes a predefined value.
ROUND	Round clock times or number of hours field Operation ROUND rounds the start and/or end time of the current time pair, the duration of the current time pair, or the number of hours field.
SORTP	Sort daily input table TIP Operation SORTP sorts the time pairs in the daily input table TIP.
SUM	Cumulation of a time type over a particular period
TMBRE	Generate break time You can use operation TMBRE to convert time pairs within the break frame to paid or unpaid break or working time.
TSORT	Sort internal tables Operation TSORT sorts internal tables within time evaluation.
VSTRG	Provide strings in variable key Operation VSTRG is used to enter strings in the variable key of the current personnel calculation rule.

33.4.5 Operations that Change Overall Status

Operation	Description
MODIF	Set groupings Operation MODIF is used to set groupings for table access.
PAYTP	Setting ES grouping for Personnel Calculation Rule You can use operation PAYTP to re-determine the ES grouping for PCR.
TFLAG	Change status data of a day Operation TFLAG can be used to (re)set various status indicators (absence flag, attendance flag, core night work indicator, break processing flag) that control the way in which the day is processed.

33.4.6 Operations that Change Contents of Database Tables

Operation	Description
BITQU	Generate batch input session for attendance quotas Operation BITQU creates an attendance quota in the attendance quotas infotype (2007).
PPINC	Process attendance/absence reasons (PIN codes) Operation PPINC processes the attendance or absence reason that has been entered for the current time pair and positioned using operation R555D.
UPDLE	Absence quota accrual Operation UPDLE can be used to automatically accrue an employee's entitlement to specific leave types (leave entitlement infotype 0005).
UPDTQ	Accrue absence quota Operation UPDTQ can be used to update the employee's entitlement to specific absence quotas automatically (infotype 2006).

33.4.7 General

Operation	Description
BREAK	Set a break point Using operation BREAK, rule processing can be interrupted at any point to branch to the break mode.
GCY	Branch to other Personnel Calculation Rule Operation GCY terminates processing of the current personnel calculation rule and branches to a new one.
GOTC	Request internal recalculation run for time evaluation This operation starts a recalculation for a given period.

(Contd.)

Operation	Description
LEAVE	Exit processing of Personnel Calculation Rule Operation LEAVE exits the current personnel calculation rule. Processing continues with the next line in the schema.
MESSG	Message output Operation MESSG outputs a message containing the personnel number.
NEXTR	Process a continuation lineOperation NEXTR can also be replaced by '*'. In this case, sequence numbers 1 through 9 are permitted.
PCY	Branch to a Personnel Calculation Subrule Operation PCY is used to call a personnel calculation subrule. The system then continues to process the original personnel calculation rule.
PLOOP	Nth execution of command sequence Operation PLOOP can be used to specify the nth execution of operations.
RETCD	Query return code Operation RETCD enters the return code in the variable key. The return code can be set during processing.
RJCT	RJCT: Rejection of employee If operation RJCT is processed, the system cancels processing for the current employee. The operation is always processed if non-existing operations are used in a personnel calculation rule.
SCOND	Set Validity of Condition (IF ... EIF) Operation SCOND is used to set the condition to true or false for function IF.
SUBST	Substitutions Operation SUBST checks if there is a substitution for an employee.
TEXIT	Exit Schema Processing

33.5 TIME MANAGEMENT FEATURES

Functional Consultant	User	Business Process Owner	Senior Management	My Rating	Understanding Level
A	B	C	C		

You manage features through transaction PE03. Features are powerful decision-making tools in SAP HR. In a feature, you can specify a field for decision making operation, and for various values of that field, define return values.

When the feature is invoked, the specified field is read, and depending on its value, the return value is sent back to the calling program, which uses it for the required purpose. You can create several layers of decision making fields before specifying the return value. You can also call another feature or a program inside a feature. A feature must be activated before it can be used.

The decision-making fields available in a feature are from a structure, which is associated with the feature. You can see the fields available (Goto ➤ Structure). If you want a field which is there in the structure, but not available in the list of decision-making fields, ask your ABAP consultant, if it can be made available.

Common uses of features include supplying default values for online data entry, determining the value of a column (typically employee grouping) for reading a configuration table and so on.

SAP supplies you pre-configured features. You can modify them. SAP maintains both versions, the one supplied by SAP, and the one maintained by you (in different tables). It uses the customer version, if there is one, otherwise it uses SAP version. If you were to delete a feature, the customer version gets deleted, and SAP version comes in use again. Features are stored in tables T549B, T549BT, T549C, T549CT and T549D.

Time Manager's Workplace

34.1 TIME DATA MAINTENANCE

Functional Consultant	User	Business Process Owner	Senior Management	My Rating	Understanding Level
A	A	A	B		

34.1.1 Screen

In time manager's workplace (transaction PTMW), you can do time data maintenance, or message processing. You can switch from one to the other in Goto menu. The screen for time data maintenance is given on next page.

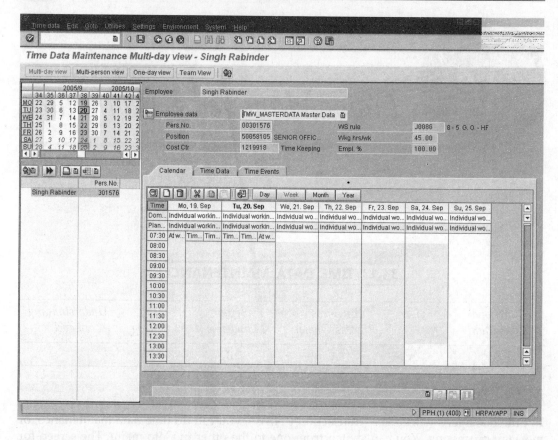

Time manager's workplace has been so designed that time administrators can do most of their work from this single interface. An inexperienced user may find it complex. The more you use it and experiment with it, the more you like it. Time manager's workplace screen is divided into the following sub-screens.

34.1.2 Sub-screens

Menu		
Calendar	Employee Information	
Employee List	Time Data	
	Details	
	System Messages	

34.1.3 Menu

In time manager's workplace you can do two things. You can switch from one to the other in Goto menu.

➢ Maintain time data
➢ Process messages

In Environment, you can do the following:

➢ Maintain HR master data
➢ Display HR master data

In Utilities, you can do the following:

➢ Start time evaluation
➢ Display time statement form
➢ Call employee
➢ Temporarily insert employees

In Maintain time data, there are four icons. You can change the view in the time data sub-screen using these.

➢ Multi-day view
➢ Multi-person view
➢ Team View
➢ One-day view

In Process messages, there are two icons. You can change the view in the messages sub-screen using these.

➢ Employee view
➢ Message view

You may find that some of these features are disabled. SAP lets you define which user should be able to do what. These are defined for a profile, which is assigned to a user. Therefore, if you find that some of these features are disabled for you, then you may contact your system administrator.

34.1.4 Calendar

You can use the calendar in the time manager's workplace to select the time period for which you want to process or display time data. Using the calendar, you can also enter data for the entire period at the same time. In the calendar, a period is selected by default. This is based on the settings in your profile. To show or hide the calendar, choose Settings ➢ Show/Hide calendar.

34.1.5 Employee List

As a time administrator, you are usually responsible for a group of employees. You may divide them into employee lists, based on some characteristics, e.g. PA/PSA, EG/ESG, organizational units etc. This helps you organize and control your work. For example, you may do message processing for all employee lists, taking one employee list at a time.

The employee lists used by you as time administrator may be pre-selected, or you may select it yourself by going to Settings ➢ Choose IDs, provided your profile gives you that authorization. You may also insert an employee temporarily in the list.

If you change the period selection in the calendar, you get a message, 'Employee list not current'. If you wish, you can refresh the employee list.

You can select an employee to work on. You can also select several employees together if you are using Multi-Person view. Do not forget to transfer the employees you have selected using ▶▶ icon.

The layout of your employee lists is set by your consultants according to your requirement. They would set up the data to be shown for each employee, and whether it is a plain list, or a hierarchy of one or two levels. The list is also sorted as per your requirement. The layout of employee list for maintaining time data can be different from the layout of employee list for message processing.

34.1.6 Employee Information

When you select an employee in the employee list, the system shows you his information, e.g. his name, leave balance etc. This information is organized in logical layouts, which are shown in the drop down list. When you choose a layout from the list, corresponding information is shown. Both the number of layouts, as well as information in a layout, can be customized as per your requirement.

34.1.7 Time Data

In this part of the screen you see the time data for the selected employees. SAP lets you choose from multiple views for your convenience.

View	Persons	Days
Multi-day view	One	Multiple
Time data		
Time events		
Annual Calendar		
Monthly Calendar		
Weekly Calendar		
One-Day Calendar		
Multi-person view	Multiple	One
One-day view	One	One
Team View	Multiple	Multiple

34.1.8 Details

When you select an entry in time data, you can see, or change, its details in this sub-screen. On the left hand side, you see the key information, and on the right hand side you see data in one or more tabs. If you find this area very cluttered, with tabs and fields you don't need, ask your consultants to simplify it for you.

31.1.9 System Messages

This sub-screen shows system messages. Usually it is at the bottom as shown in the screen shot above. But, it can be shifted to top, if you prefer it that way.

34.1.10 Profile

In time manager's workplace, you can configure each screen area as per your requirement. But what would you do, if two users require the same screen area to look different? Fortunately, SAP allows this flexibility. For each screen area, you can have multiple layouts or field selections. You can assign the appropriate layouts to a profile and a profile to a user. Having the layouts assigned to a profile has an advantage. If a new user is added, in all probability an existing profile would meet his requirement. In that case, you just need to assign the profile to the user, and not individual screen area layouts to the user. Profiles can be assigned to user using the user parameter PT_TMW_PROFILE, or by creating a parameter transaction using transaction SE93 and assigning it to a user via a role. If neither is used, the system prompts you to enter the profile.

34.1.11 Multi-day View: Time Data

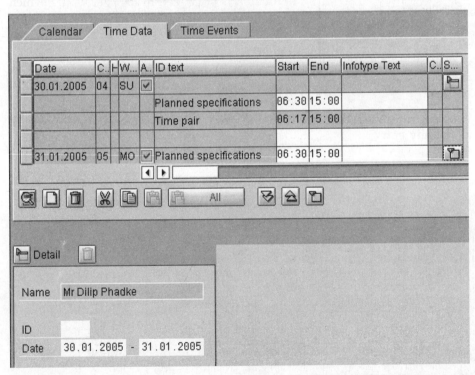

The time data sub-screen is very important and you should have a feel of its look in different views. In multi-day view, there are three tabs, as shown in the screenshot. In time data tab, you see data for each date in a row. You can expand 🗂 to show all entries for a day. You can create, or delete entries, or see details of any entry.

34.1.12 Multi-day View: Time Events

	Calendar	Time Data	Time Events				

	Date	Date	Ti...	Time	C	Att./...	Ter...
	30.01.2005	30.01.2005	P10	06:17:00	+		6414
		30.01.2005	P20	15:00:00	+		6414
	31.01.2005	31.01.2005	P10	06:20:00	+		6414
		31.01.2005	P20	15:00:00	+		6414

Detail			Time Event	Different Payment

Name	Mr Dilip Phadke		Time	06:17:00
			Time event type	P10 Clock-in
ID	?11 Time event		Day assignment	+
Date	30.01.2005		Att./absence reason	
			Terminal ID	6414

In time events tab, you see all time event data in rows. You can create, or delete entries, or see details of any entry.

34.1.13 Multi-day View: Annual Calendar

	Calendar	Time Data	Time Events

IDs for T...						Day	Week	Month	Year								
	MN	13	14	15	16	17	18	19	20	21	22	23	24	25	26	27	28
AB	Jan	WS	WS	WS	WS	WS	WS	WS	WS	WS	WS	WS	WS	WS	WS	WS	WS
AT			IN	IN	IN	IN	IN	IN		IN	IN	IN	IN	IN		IN	IN
IN			IO	IO	IO	IO	IO	IO		IO	IO	IO	IO	IO		IO	IO
OU			OU	OU	OU	OU	OU	OU		OU	OU	OU	OU	OU		OU	OU
WS	Feb	WS	WS	WS	WS	WS	WS	WS	WS	WS	WS	WS	WS	WS	AT	WS	AB
		IN	IN	IN	IN		IN	IN	IN	IN	IN	IN		IN		IN	
		IO	IO	IO	IO		IO	IO	IO	IO	IO	IO		IO		IO	
		OU	OU	OU	OU		OU	OU	OU	OU	OU	OU		AB		OU	
														OU			

The look of the calendar tab depends on the calendar you choose. In annual calendar, you can see an overview of all time data. Each cell contains a time data id. A time data id may represent an attendance, an absence, a work schedule etc. You can create, or delete entries, or see details of any entry. Entries may be color coded. This helps in quickly locating absences, for example.

34.1.14 Multi-day View: Monthly Calendar

Calendar	Time Data	Time Events						
IDs for T...		Day	Week	Month	Year			
AB	WN	Friday	Saturday	Sunday	Monday	Tuesday	Wednes...	Thursday
AT	1	31	1	2	3	4	5	6
IN			Individua...	Individua...	Individua...	Individua...	Individua...	Individua...
OU			Clock out	Clock out	Clock out	Clock out	Clock out	
WS			Time pair	Time pair	Time pair	Time pair	Time pair	
			Clock out	Clock out	Clock out	Clock out	Clock out	
	2	7	8	9	10	11	12	13
		Individua...	Individua...	Individua...	Individua...	Individua...	Individua...	Individua...
		Clock out	Clock out	Clock out	Clock out	Clock out	Clock out	
		Time pair	Time pair	Time pair	Time pair	Time pair	Time pair	
		Clock out	Clock out	Clock out	Clock out	Clock out	Clock out	

Monthly calendar is similar to annual calendar, but has more column width. You can create, or delete entries, or see details of any entry.

34.1.15 Multi-day View: Weekly Calendar

Calendar	Time Data	Time Events			
IDs for T...		Day	Week	Month	Year
AB	Time	Friday, 04.February2005	Saturday, 05.February2...	Sunday, 06.February20...	Monday, 07.February20...
AT		Individual working time	Individual working time	Individual working time	Individual working time
IN		06:30-15:00	06:30-15:00	06:30-15:00	15:00-23:30
OU					
WS	06:00	Time pair Clock out	Time pair Clock out	Time pair Clock out	
	06:30	06:13-15:00	06:14-15:00	06:13-15:00	
	07:00				
	07:30				
	08:00				
	08:30				
	09:00				

In weekly calendar, you see details of the day. You can create, or delete entries, or see details of any entry.

34.1.16 Multi-day View: One-day Calendar

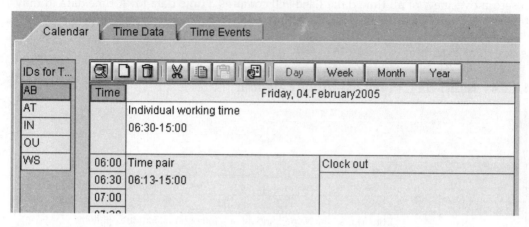

One-day calendar is similar to weekly calendar, but has more column width. You can create, or delete entries, or see details of any entry.

34.1.17 Multi-person View

Pers.No.	Valid From	End Date	M.	A.	H	Pla...	ID	ID text	Start	End	P.	Infotype Text	S...
113303	04.02.2005	04.02.2005	✓	✓		WS	WS	Individual working time	06:30	15:00	☐		🗂
113914			✓	✓		WS	WS	Individual working time	06:30	15:00	☐		🗂
114649			✓	✓		WS							🖿
							WS	Individual working time	06:30	15:00	☐		
							IO	Time pair	06:17	15:00	☐		
											☐		
116408			✓	✓		WS							🖿
							WS	Individual working time	08:30	17:00	☐		
							IO	Time pair	08:22	17:00	☐		
											☐		

Multi-person view of time data enables you to maintain time data for more than one employee for one day. You can see an overview of all time data for the day selected in the calendar for all the employees assigned to you. You process time data in a list-oriented view.

34.1.18 One-day View

	ID	ID text		Start	End	P..	Pay Scal...	H..	WS rule	Daily WS	Day type
						☐					

Time Data

Dominant WS Individual working time

One-day view of time data enables you to process time data for one employee for one day. You can see an overview of all time data for the day selected in the calendar for one employee. You process time data in a list-oriented view.

34.1.19 Team View

Time Data: Team View

IDs for Ti...
AB
AT
WS

Name	Fr, 30	Sa, 1	Su, 2	Mo, 3	Tu, 4	We, 5	Th, 6
Mr Deepak Kondha...	AB	WS	AB	WS	AB	AB	WS
Mr Dilip Phadke	AB	WS	WS	WS	WS	WS	WS
Mr Vishnudeo Raw...	WS	WS	WS	WS	WS	WS	WS
Mr Sanjay Chandane	WS	WS	WS	WS	WS	WS	WS
Mr Dnyaneshwar K...	WS	WS	WS	WS	WS	WS	WS
Mr Shirish Upadhye	WS	WS	WS	WS	WS	WS	WS

Team view is very useful in seeing data of multiple employees for multiple days at a glance. It shows full day absence/ attendance/ work schedule. Suppose you want to see how many people would be available each day, you can use this view to see it at a glance.

You may want the system to show you the count of people who would be present/ absent. SAP provides a facility of adding rows below, or above, your team to show such data. You have to specify the requirement, and your consultants would set it up. You can have multiple summary rows. One can show the number of people present, while others may show their shift wise break up.

Just as you can have rows, which summarize a day, you can also have columns, which summarize a person's data. For example, you may want to see how many days a person is absent. Just as you can have a number of summary rows, you can have a number of summary columns. You can have some columns on the left side of your data, and some on the right side.

34.2 MESSAGE PROCESSING

Functional Consultant	User	Business Process Owner	Senior Management	My Rating	Understanding Level
A	A	A	B		

34.2.1 Messages

During time evaluation, SAP generates some messages. Messages represent conditions, which need attention. They may be errors, warnings, or information. Someone needs to attend to all these messages, take the necessary action or confirm that no action is required.

You can select the employees, for whom you want to process the messages. The period selection in the calendar does not restrict the messages. However, you can see messages only after a certain date by setting 🔲.

When you select a message, the time data of the concerned employee is shown for reference. Depending on the view selected, the data is shown for the corresponding day, week, month, or year.

34.2.2 Message View

When you start processing time evaluation messages, you soon realize that there are some messages, which can be dealt with quickly. They require similar processing. You are much more comfortable dealing with them together, regardless of the employees for whom they are.

To facilitate processing of such messages, time manager's workplace provides a message view. The system creates a message list, grouping the messages by message types, and further grouping them in message functional areas. Message processing is driven by the message list, instead of the employee list. Also, for a message type or message functional area, you see messages, instead of employee information.

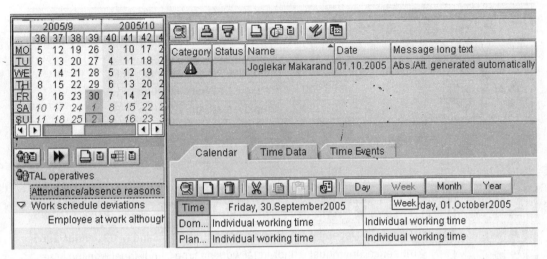

Message list structure

A message list is structured as under:

➢ Message functional area	Having a processing method which applies to all message types under it
➢ Message functional area	Not having a processing method
▸ Message types	Belonging to the message functional area above
➢ Message types	Not belonging to any message functional area

34.2.3 Employee View

After having dealt with simple and routine messages in the message view, you process more complex messages. For processing these messages, the employee view may be more appropriate, as you can see messages for the employee on previous or subsequent day. Sometimes these help in understanding why a particular message was generated. In employee view, you select employees from the employee list; there is no message list.

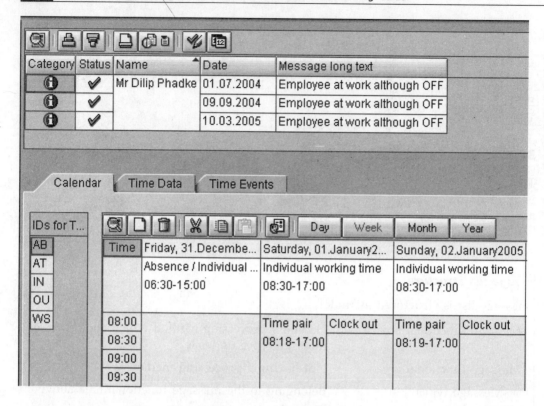

34.2.4 Contextual Information on Messages

When you are analyzing a message, you need information, which helps you understand the message. For example, if there is a message that the employee came in wrong shift, you want to know, in which shift the employee came, and in which shift he was supposed to come.

However, if the message was that the employee came late, the information you need is, at what time he was supposed to come, and at what time he came. Thus, the information you need may differ from message to message. Your system is configured in such a way that you can see appropriate contextual information along with the messages.

34.2.5 Message Processing

After you process a message, you want to mark it as completed, so that they don't get mixed up with unprocessed messages. You do so by clicking on the status field of the message. You can also complete all the messages together by clicking on [icon].

At this stage, if you exit time manager's workplace, and come back, you still see the messages. To make them permanently disappear from the screen, you click on [icon]. The messages disappear only if they are information messages. Error messages do not disappear unless corrective action is taken and time evaluation is run.

34.3 FLEXIBLE SCREEN DESIGN

Functional Consultant	User	Business Process Owner	Senior Management	My Rating	Understanding Level
A	C	C	C		

34.3.1 Sub-screens

The time manager's workplace shows a comprehensive view of all time data. Its screen is divided into a number of sub-screens. Consequently, each sub-screen occupies a small area on the screen. Some sub-screens also have a number of views. In each sub-screen, SAP has huge amount of data, and it is a challenge to fit so much data in it.

	Menu
Calendar	Employee Information

Employee List
Layout
Employee Selection
	Time Data
	  Multi-day view
	  Calendar
	    Annual
	    Monthly
	    Weekly
	    One-Day
	  Time Data
	  Time Events
	  Multi-person view
	  One-day view
	  Team View

	Details
	System Messages

34.3.2 Screen Areas

SAP has solved this problem through a concept called, 'Screen area'. Each screen area is about a particular aspect of a sub-screen, e.g. layout of fields, or tabs in a sub-screen, or menu items that are enabled or disabled.

For each screen area, you can define one or more field selections, or options, in view clusters. Since there are some differences in the definitions of field selections, SAP has five view clusters (see chapters 34.4 to 34.8) in which field selections of different screen areas are defined.

Finally, you assign the field selections to a profile for each screen area. In most cases, you assign one field selection to a profile. In some cases, you assign two field selections to a profile; one to maintaining time data, and another to processing message. Thus, you can have one layout of employee list while maintaining time data, and another in the employee view of message processing. In some cases, the assignment of field selections to a profile depends on the context. For example, information displayed about absences can be different for different absence types.

However, even if you don't do any customization, SAP provides excellent defaults. By customizing, you make the screen of time manager's workplace, less cluttered and more powerful. Rest of this chapter explains how you can customize each sub-screen.

34.3.3 Menu

Screen area	Description	Use
TSK	Task Selection	In time manager's workplace, there are two tasks. ➢ Maintain time data ➢ Process messages You can use this screen area to enable a user to perform one or both of these tasks.
VTD	Views for Time Data Maintenance Task	In Maintain time data, there are four views. ➢ Multi-day view ➢ Multi-person view ➢ Team View ➢ One-day view You can use this screen area to enable a subset of these views for a user. By default, all views are enabled.
VWL	Views for Message Processing Task	In messages processing, there are two views. ➢ Employee view ➢ Message view You can use this screen area to enable one or both of these views for a user. By default, both views are enabled.

MEN	Menu Functions	The menu contains the following items.
		➢ Environment
		  ▸ Maintain HR master data
		  ▸ Display HR master data
		➢ Utilities
		  ▸ Start time evaluation
		  ▸ Display time statement form
		  ▸ Call employee
		  ▸ Temporarily insert employees
		You can use this screen area to enable a subset of these menu items for a user. By default, all menu items (except Call employee) are enabled.

(Contd.)

Screen area	Description	Use
		You may not want to use the same time statement form (RPTEDT00) for all employees. SAP lets you create different variants of time statement form and runs the appropriate variant for an employee. Similarly, time evaluation (RPTIME00) can also have multiple variants, and the appropriate variant is run for the employee. You define these in feature LLREP.

34.3.4 Calendar

You can use the calendar in the time manager's workplace to select the time period for which you want to process or display time data. Using the calendar, you can also enter data for the entire period at the same time. In the calendar, a period is selected by default. This is based on the settings in your profile. To show or hide the calendar, choose Settings ➤ Show/Hide calendar.

SAP also gives an option to choose an enhanced calendar, instead of a simple one. This is defined in configuration view VV_PT_TMW_GCCAL.

Usage indicator	PTMW
Short description	

Set Up Calendar for the Time Manager's Workplace	
Object ID	Class

If you select the calendar CL_PT_GUI_TMW_CALENDAR2, you can implement BAdI PT_GUI_TMW_CALENDAR to fill default values in the calendar.

34.3.5 Employee List

Layout of employee list

Screen area	Description	Use
EMP	Layout of employee list	You can use screen area EMP to determine the layout of employee list, which can be a hierarchy of up to two levels. The layout for maintaining time data can be different from the layout for processing messages. This is done while assigning the layout to Profile. By default, the layout has only full name and personnel number of employees without any hierarchy.

Employee selection

➢ SAP lets you define employee lists in a number of ways.
  ▸ You can define employee lists based on structural reporting, e.g. all persons in an organization unit.
  ▸ You can also define employee lists whose attributes match selection criteria defined in terms of infotype field values.
  ▸ If neither of these meets your requirements, you can define function modules, which return a list of employees.
  ▸ You can also define employee lists, which are a combination of these.
➢ Each list is identified by a selection id.
➢ You can group the selection ids in groups, which can then be assigned to a profile.
➢ Thus, you can create multiple employee lists, and assign one or more employee lists to a time administrators.
➢ Time administrators can also create/ change/ delete their own employee lists, if permitted (see interactive selection in profile).
➢ They may also insert an employee temporarily in the list.
➢ When your period selection in the calendar changes, you get a message, 'Employee list not current'. If you wish, you can refresh the employee list.
➢ You can select an employee to work on. You can also select several employees together, if you are using Multi-Person view.
➢ Employee lists must be created. SAP does not provide any employee list by default.
➢ For more details, see chapter 34.9, Employee Selection.

34.3.6 Employee Information

Screen area	Description	Use
INF	Employee information	When you select an employee in the employee list, the system shows you his details, e.g. his name, leave balance etc. in a set of logical layouts.
		You can create a number of layouts, create their sets, and assign a set to screen area INF in a profile.
		By default, SAP shows employee information under master data.

34.3.7 Time Data

Views

In Time data sub-screen, there are four views.

➢ Multi-Day View
➢ Multi-Person View
➢ One-Day View
➢ Team View

Depending on the view you choose, the layout changes. SAP gives you flexibility to define the layout of each of these. Details of each of these are discussed in this chapter.

Tabs

In each of the above views, SAP has pre-defined tabs. SAP also lets you create your own tabs and assign them to any of these views. The tabs are created in the views given below.

View	Screen area	View for creating tabs
Multi-Day View	VN1	VV_PT_TMW_GCLTN1
Multi-Person View	V1M	VV_PT_TMW_GCLT1M
One-Day View	V11	VV_PT_TMW_GCLT11
Team View	VNM	V_PT_TMW_GCLTNM

The layout of all the views is the same.

Define Tabs	
Layout ID	Short Text

Fields

Usually SAP fills the time data fields with data. However, SAP lets you populate them yourself using customer enhancement PTIMTMW. After activating the enhancement, you must insert the new fields in the field selections for time data in the individual views. Be aware that the fields cannot be used in the time events table.

Degree of detail for time data maintenance screen area

Screen area	Description	Use
TEC	Degree of detail for time data maintenance screen area	When you open the screen, you may want to see the data in summary form, or in details form. This initial setting is controlled by this screen area. Thereafter, you can expand to see details, or collapse to see summary.
		The row with the dominant of the day cannot be hidden because this row contains the most important information on the day. You can hide any of the other rows displayed besides the day dominant row.

(Contd.)

Screen area	Description	Use
		You can use the degree of detail for the multi-day view and the multi-person view. There are three fields, of which only one can be selected. ➢ Collapse All in Initial Screen ➢ Expand All in Initial Screen ➢ Expand All Partial-Day Time Data in Initial Screen

34.3.8 Time Data: Multi-day View

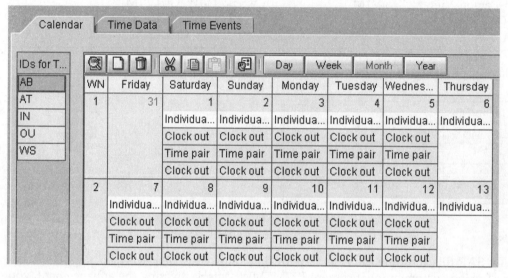

Tabs

Screen area	Description	Use
VN1	Tabs for Multi-Day View	In Multi-Day view, you see three tabs by default: Calendar, Time data, and Time events. If you want to add/ delete any tabs, you can do it through this screen area. You can define your own tabs in view VV_PT_TMW_GCLTN1.

Calendar tab

Screen area	Description	Use
CAI	Calendar Views: Time Data to be Selected	You can determine from which of the following data sources you want to display information in the calendars. ➢ Time Management infotypes except infotype 2011. ➢ Time pairs formed from the time events in table PT (cluster B2) or table TEVEN if time evaluation has not yet formed pairs for periods. ➢ Time events from table TEVEN. By default all are available.
CAL	Calendar Views: Selection of Views	The information displayed in the calendars is split into information blocks such as dominants, planned time, time data without clock times (for example, full-day data records, employee remuneration information), and so on. You can decide the information blocks that are displayed and the sequence in which they are sorted. By default, you get dominant, planned working time, full-day, time data with clock times.
CAD	Calendar Views: Dominant Fields	When one looks at the calendar of an employee, one would prefer to see the important information in the top line. You can determine the information you want to see in the top line, called dominant line. You can create several dominant layouts. When you assign them to a profile, you can specify different dominants for daily, weekly, and monthly calendar. This is important because the width of the column for a day in these calendars vary. It is recommended not to have a dominant for annual calendar, as the width of the columns is too small. However, technically it is possible to define one. SAP provides you a set of dominants by default.
CAA	Calendar Views: Appointments with Clock Times	If partial-day information is output in the weekly or daily calendar, there are often several lines for displaying important information for time data extending over several hours. You can use these lines to display additional information on the time data. You can output a large quantity of additional information depending on how many additional lines are available. In this screen area, you determine the type of information you want to display and the sequence in which you want to display it.

Time data layout

Screen area	Description	Use
TN1	Time data in multi-day view	In Multiple-Day View, the Time Data tab has a layout. You can create multiple layouts and assign one to a profile. SAP provides a default layout.

Time events layout

Screen area	Description	Use
EN1	Time events in multi-day view	In Multiple-Day View, the Time Events tab has a layout. You can create multiple layouts and assign one to a profile. SAP provides a default layout.

34.3.9   Time Data: Multi-person View

	Pers.No.	Valid From	End Date	M.	A.	H	Pla...	ID	ID text	Start	End	P.	Infotype Text	S...
	113303	04.02.2005	04.02.2005	✓	✓		WS	WS	Individual working time	06:30	15:00	☐		🗍
	113914			✓	✓		WS	WS	Individual working time	06:30	15:00	☐		🗍
	114649				✓	✓	WS							🗀
								WS	Individual working time	06:30	15:00	☐		
								IO	Time pair	06:17	15:00	☐		
												☐		
	116408			✓	✓		WS							🗀
								WS	Individual working time	08:30	17:00	☐		
								IO	Time pair	08:22	17:00	☐		
												☐		

Tabs

Screen area	Description	Use
V1M	Tabs for Multi-person View	In Multi-Person View, there is only one tab by default: Time data. If you want to add any tabs, you can do it through this screen area. You can define your own tabs in view VV_PT_TMW_GCLT1M.

Layout

Screen area	Description	Use
T1M	Time Data in Multi-Person View	In Multiple-Person View, in the Time Data tab, you get a layout. That layout can be customized to your requirements. SAP provides a default layout.

34.3.10 Time Data: One-day View

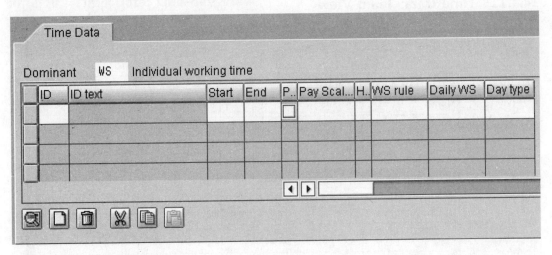

Tabs

Screen area	Description	Use
V11	Tabs for One-day View	In One-Day View, there is only one tab by default; Time data. If you want to add any tabs, you can do it through this screen area. You can define your own tabs in view VV_PT_TMW_GCLT11.

Layout

Screen area	Description	Use
T11	Time Data in One-day View	In One-Day View, in the Time Data tab, you get a layout. That layout can be customized to your requirements. SAP provides a default layout.

Dominants/processing instructions

Screen area	Description	Use
TDO	Dominants/Processing Instructions for Time Data Maintenance	The TDO screen area corresponds to the area above the time data table in the time manager's workplace. Here you can display the dominant as well as checkboxes for processing instructions. By default, no data is displayed.

34.3.11 Time Data: Team View

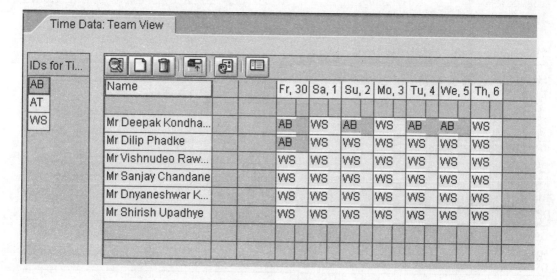

Tabs

Screen area	Description	Use
VNM	Team View: Tab Strips	In Team view, there is only one tab by default; Time Data: Team View. If you want to add any tabs, you can do it through this screen area. You can define your own tabs in view V_PT_TMW_GCLTNM.

Layout

Screen area	Description	Use
TNM	Team View: Additional Fields from Dominant	In the Time Data: Team View tab, you get a layout. That layout can be customized to your requirements.

Lines on the left, right, top and bottom

Screen area	Description	Use
CFL, CFR, CFT, CFB	Customer columns on left, right, top, bottom	You can create customer fields for display in lines which are above, below, or on left or right of time data. You can also specify the size of the fields for CFL and CFR. You can use the BAdI PT_TMW_NM_BADI_EXMPL (Fill Customer Fields) to populate these fields. By default, there are no customer fields.

34.3.12 Processing Instructions

Screen area	Description	Use
CHK	Processing instructions	Processing instructions are used to create check boxes in time data, which time administrators can tick to create time transfers which get processed in time evaluation.

You can use processing instructions to reduce data entry effort of time administrators. Processing instructions are displayed as checkboxes, which time administrators tick. When data is saved, the system creates appropriate infotype records (usually time transfer of specified time transfer type). In time evaluation, PCR TOF0 processes these records.

You can have several processing instructions which can be grouped in processing instruction groups. Master list of processing instruction groups is defined in view cluster VC_PT_FIELD_SELECTION (CHK).

Screen area	CHK	Processing Instructions

Field Selection Attributes	
Field sel.	Field selection text
TML	Tata Motors Ltd.

Each processing instruction group can have up to seven processing instructions. Processing instructions belonging to a processing instruction group are also defined in view cluster VC_PT_FIELD_SELECTION (CHK).

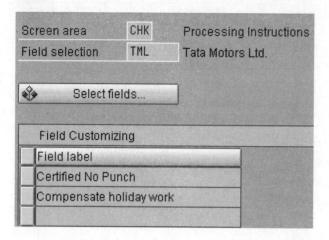

A processing instruction group is assigned to a profile in screen area CHK. Thereafter, the checkboxes appear in time data of time manager's workplace. In multi-day and multi-person view, checkboxes are in the table for time data. In one-day view, checkboxes are in a row above the table for time data.

34.3.13 Details

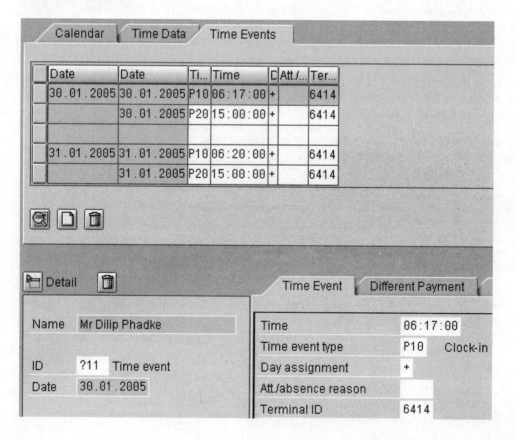

Screen area	Description	Use
C01 - C12, D01 - D12, CWS, DWS		In time manager's workplace, you have a details sub-screen, which shows you details of time data. Most of the time you see infotype data there. You can also enter data in this sub-screen.

In this sub-screen, you may see data for personal work schedule, substitution, availability, absences, attendances, time events, employee remuneration information, absence quotas and time transfer specification.

In each of these infotype, SAP has a lot of fields. SAP has grouped them in tabs, so that they can be viewed in a limited space. However, even then the layout remains complex. In absences, there are 13 tabs and 86 fields.

By default, you get all the tabs, and all the fields. But, most of the time you may not require all the tabs, and all the fields in a tab. SAP lets you simplify your screen by selecting only the required tabs, and required fields.

Further, SAP realizes that the data you need to view depends on the context. If you are viewing an absence, which can be only in full days, you don't need the time fields, but if you are viewing a partial day absence, you need the time fields as well. Hence, SAP gives you the flexibility of using different layouts in different contexts.

To do so, SAP gives you two screen areas for each infotype. For infotype 2001, these are C01 & D01.

In C01, you define the tabs you want. You can select from all the tabs, which are available for infotype 2001. You can create multiple tab sets.

In D01, you define the fields you want. Thus, even from selected tabs, you can remove unwanted fields. You can create multiple field selections.

You assign tab sets with corresponding field selections to a profile. You can do that at subtype + PSG level. Thus, for one absence type, you may select one layout, while for another absence type you may select a different layout. |

(Contd.)

Screen area	Description	Use
		To reduce configuration, you can assign a tab set and a field selection to all remaining absences. If you do not use 'All remaining absences' provision, the default layout contains all tabs and all fields.
		Finally, you assign a profile to a user.
		The tabs that you see for detail screens have SAP defined names. If you want, you can change tab names in view V_PT_TMW_GCSLYT.

Alternative texts for details tabs

You can use view V_PT_TMW_GCSLYT to give your own description to the tabs in details area.

Alternative Texts for Details Tabs		
Layout ID	Short Text	Standard Short Text

34.3.14 System Messages

If you so prefer, you can move the system messages area from bottom to top. This is set in the profile.

34.4 SCREEN AREAS (INFORMATION)

Functional Consultant	User	Business Process Owner	Senior Management	My Rating	Understanding Level
A	C	X	X		

34.4.1 Purpose and Overview

This view cluster is used to create sets of tabs, drop down lists and menu items. For each screen area, you can define multiple field selections which are sets of fields provided by SAP. Field selections are assigned to profiles, which in turn are assigned to users. Thus, the layout created here become applicable to users.

34.4.2 Screen Areas

Screen area	Description
	Menu
TSK	Task Selection
VTD	Views for Time Data Maintenance Task
VWL	Views for Message Processing Task
MEN	Menu Functions
	Employee Information
INF	Employee Data Selection
	Time Data Tabs
VN1	Tabs for Multi-Day View
V1M	Tabs for Multi-Person View
V11	Tabs for One-Day View
	Details Tabs
C01	Details: Tabs for Absence Infotype (2001)
C02	Details: Tabs for Attendances Infotype (2002)
C03	Details: Tabs for Substitutions Infotype (2003)
C04	Details: Tabs for Availability Infotype (2004)
C07	Details: Tabs for Attendance Quota Infotype (2007)
C10	Details: Tabs for EE Remuneration Info Infotype (2010)
C11	Details: Tabs for Time Events Infotype (2011)
C12	Details: Tabs for Time Transfer Specs Infotype (2012)
CWS	Details: Tabs for Personal Work Schedule
	Calendar Views
CAI	Calendar Views: Time Data to Be Selected
CAL	Calendar Views: Selection of Views
CAD	Calendar Views: Dominant Fields
CAA	Calendar Views: Appointments with Clock Times
	Team Views
TNM	Team View: Additional Fields from Dominant
CFT	Team View: Customer Rows in Upper Screen Area
CFB	Team View: Customer Rows in Lower Screen Area
	Others
CHK	Processing Instructions
TDT	Display Type of Time Data ID List
TEC	Degree of Detail for Time Data Maintenance Screen Area
WLI	Groups of Display Objects for Message Processing

34.4.3 IMG Node

SM34 ➢ VC_PT_FIELD_SELECTION_INF

34.4.4   Screen

Screen area   MEN   Menu Functions

Field Selection Attributes	
Field sel.	Field selection text
ALLFUNC	All functions

Screen area   MEN   Menu Functions

Field selection   ALLFUNC All functions

Field Customizing
Field label
Maintain HR master data
Display HR master data
Start time evaluation
Display time statement form
Temporarily insert employees

34.5   SCREEN AREAS (DETAILS)

Functional Consultant	User	Business Process Owner	Senior Management	My Rating	Understanding Level
A	C	X	X		

34.5.1   Purpose and Overview

This view cluster is used to create sets of fields for details area. For each screen area, you can define multiple field selections which are sets of fields. Note that the fields which are seen in each tab are pre-determined. Therefore, if you select a field, you must also select corresponding tab (C01 for D01). In this view, you can also specify.

➢ Display width. If you do not specify display width, the system uses the values specified in the data dictionary as default.

➢ Whether the field is display only, or enterable by user. This characteristic is only for user enterable fields. The fields, which are system determined, are permanently disabled.

Usually SAP fills the time data fields with data. However, SAP lets you populate them yourself using customer enhancement PTIMTMW. Field selections are assigned to profiles, which in turn are assigned to users. Thus, the layout created here become applicable to users.

34.5.2   Screen Areas

Screen area	Description
	Details Fields
D01	Details: Fields for Absences Infotype (2001)
D02	Details: Fields for Attendances Infotype (2002)
D03	Details: Fields for Substitutions Infotype (2003)
D04	Details: Fields for Availability Infotype (2004)
D07	Details: Fields for Attendance Quota Infotype (2007)
D10	Details: Fields for EE Remuneration Info Infotype (2010)
D11	Details: Fields for Time Events Infotype (2011)
D12	Details: Fields for Time Transfer Specs Infotype (2012)
DWS	Details: Fields for Personal Work Schedule

34.5.3   IMG Node

SM34 ➢ VC_PT_FIELD_SELECTION_DTL

34.5.4   Screen

Screen area	DWS	Details: Fields for Personal Work Schedule

Field Selection Attributes

Field sel.	Field selection text
TML	TML PWS

Screen area	DWS	Details: Fields for Personal Work Schedule
Field selection	TML	TML PWS

Field Customizing

Field label	Disp.length	Ready for input
Substitution hours	9	☐
Substitution Type	2	✔
Daily Work Schedule	4	✔
Day Type	1	✔
Planned working hours	8	☐

34.6 SCREEN AREAS (DOMINANTS)

Functional Consultant	User	Business Process Owner	Senior Management	My Rating	Understanding Level
A	C	X	X		

34.6.1 Purpose and Overview

This view cluster is same as VC_PT_FIELD_SELECTION_DTL, except that you cannot define the display length here. But, you can determine whether the field is enterable or not. Field selections are assigned to profiles, which in turn are assigned to users. Thus, the layout created here become applicable to users.

34.6.2 Screen Areas

Screen area	Description
TDO	Dominants/Processing Instructions for Time Data Maintenance
VNM	Team View: Tab Strips

34.6.3 IMG Node

SM34 ➤ VC_PT_FIELD_SELECTION_TDO

34.6.4 Screen

Screen area	TDO	Dominants/Processing Instructions for Time Data Maintenance

Field Selection Attributes	
Field sel.	Field selection text
TML	One day dominant view

Screen area	TDO	Dominants/Processing Instructions for Time Data Maintenance
Field selection	TML	One day dominant view

❖ Select fields...

Field Customizing

Field label	Ready for input
Dominant	☑

34.7 SCREEN AREAS (LISTS)

Functional Consultant	User	Business Process Owner	Senior Management	My Rating	Understanding Level
A	C	X	X		

34.7.1 Purpose and Overview

This view cluster is same as VC_PT_FIELD_SELECTION_DTL. In addition, here you can also specify the number of columns, which remain fixed, when you move the scroll bar. Field selections are assigned to profiles, which in turn are assigned to users. Thus, the layout created here become applicable to users.

34.7.2 Screen Areas

Screen area	Description
CFL	Team View: Customer Columns in Screen Area on Left
CFR	Team View: Customer Columns in Screen Area on Right
EN1	Time Events in Multi-Day View
T11	Time Data in One-Day View
T1M	Time Data in Multi-Person View
TN1	Time Data in Multi-Day View

34.7.3 IMG Node

SM34 ➢ VC_PT_FIELD_SELECTION_LST

34.7.4 Screen

Screen area   T11   Time Data in One-Day View

Field Selection Attributes

	Field sel.	Field selection text	No. of fixed columns
	TML	One Day View for TML	4

Screen area   T11   Time Data in One-Day View

Field selection   TML   One Day View for TML

Field Customizing

	Field label	Disp.length	Ready for input
	Time Data ID Type	4	☑
	Time Data ID Text	20	☐
	Start Time	5	☑
	End Time	5	☑
	Previous Day Indicator	2	☑
	Pay Scale Group	8	☑
	Public Holiday Calendar	2	☑
	Work Schedule Rule	8	☑
	Daily Work Schedule	4	☑
	Day Type	1	☑

34.8 SCREEN AREA (EMPLOYEE LIST LAYOUT)

Functional Consultant	User	Business Process Owner	Senior Management	My Rating	Understanding Level
A	C	X	X		

34.8.1 Purpose and Overview

You can display the employee list using a hierarchy of up to two levels. The employee list is then displayed in a hierarchy tree. You can choose the following display forms:

> Employees are sorted using the criteria in the first field of the field selection. There is no tree display.
> The tree display has one level. Employees are displayed under the first field of the field selection in the hierarchy tree. Under this node, employees are sorted according to the second field of the field selection.
> The tree display has two levels. Employees are displayed under the first two fields of the field selection in the hierarchy tree. Under these nodes, employees are sorted according to the third field of the field selection.

The display can differ for Maintain time data and for Process messages. This is done while assigning to the layout to profile.

34.8.2 Screen Areas

Screen area	Description
EMP	Employee List

34.8.3 IMG Node

SM34 ➢ VC_PT_FIELD_SELECTION_EMP

34.8.4 Screens

Screen area	EMP	Employee List	

Field Selection Attributes

Field sel.	Field selection text	Number of hierarchy levels
EL1S001	1 Level Emp List, CC Hier, Per No, Name	One-level hierarchy displa…

Screen area	EMP	Employee List
Field selection	EL1S001	1 Level Emp List, CC Hier, Per No, Name

Select fields...

Field Customizing

Field label	Display type	Update	Sort field	Sort descend.	Add	Hide column
Cost Center	Display value	☐		☐	☐	☐
Personnel Number	Display value	☐		☐	☐	☐
Employee Name (…	Display text …	☐		☐	☐	☐

34.8.5 Important Fields

Field label

Fields are entered in the sequence in which they are required in the employee list layout.

Display type

You can display either value, or text, or icon.

Update

If you select this option, the field value is updated after every change. This can affect system performance.

Sort field

If you do not wish to display a field, but sort by it, you can specify a different sort field here.

Sort descending

By default, the system sorts the list in ascending order of the sort field. If you want the sort to be in descending order sequence, you tick this field.

Add

If this option is selected, then the total of the values in the columns of this hierarchy level in the employee selection are displayed. This option can only be used for columns containing numerical values.

Hide column

If you select this field, the column is not displayed in employee list by default. However, a user can go to 'change layout' and display it. He can also save the layout. You may use this facility to provide a number of columns, which the users can choose from, while maintaining a simple default layout.

34.9 EMPLOYEE SELECTION

Functional Consultant	User	Business Process Owner	Senior Management	My Rating	Understanding Level
A	X	X	X		

34.9.1 Overview

SAP lets you define employee lists in a number of ways.

> You can define employee lists based on structural reporting, e.g. all persons in an organization unit.
> You can also define employee lists whose attributes match selection criteria defined in terms of infotype field values.
> If neither of these meets your requirements, you can define function modules, which return a list of employees.
> You can also define employee lists, which are a combination of these.

Each list is identified by a selection id. You can group the selection ids in groups, which can then be assigned to a profile. Thus, you can create multiple employee lists, and assign one or more employee lists to a time administrators. Employee lists must be created. SAP does not provide any employee list by default.

Time administrators can also create/ change/ delete their own employee lists, if permitted (see interactive selection in profile). They may also insert an employee temporarily in the list.

When your period selection in the calendar changes, you get a message, 'Employee list not current'. If you wish, you can refresh the employee list. You can select an employee to work on. You can also select several employees together if you are using Multi-Person view.

34.9.2 Selections

Dialog Structure		Selection ID	Selection text
▽ 🗀 Selections		BUDGET	Budget allocation
⠀⠀🗀 Combination		CMP_COMP_ADMIN	Compensation manager
▽ 🗀 Structure		CMP_FOREIGN_ORGUNIT	Processor of external org. unit
⠀⠀🗀 Root Objects		CMP_LINE_MANAGER	Line manager
▽ 🗀 Table		ESS_WHOS_WHO	ESS Who's Who selection
⠀⠀🗀 Ranges		MGE_HRINT_ADMIN	Administrator international HR
▽ 🗀 Function		ORGA	Persons along organizational structure
⠀⠀🗀 Data for Function		ORGEH	Organizational units along org.structure

You define the master list of selection ids in view HRSEL_IDS of view cluster HR_SELECTIONS.

34.9.3 Combination

Selection ID	No.	No.	Sel.type	Op.		No.	Sel.type	Ob
TMW_TIME_ADMIN	1	1	A	+		2	A	P

You can create selections, which are combinations. The components of a combination are defined in Structure, Table, Function as well as Combination nodes. In each of these nodes, you can create components, which are identified by their selection id + sequence number. Here, you take two such components, and create either their union set (operation −), or their intersection set (operation +). Combinations are stored in view HRSEL_COMBINE.

34.9.4 Structure

Structure									
Sel.ID	S..	P..	O..	ID..	Eval.path	Stat...	Tech....	Period	FM	O..
PPOME_STRUC_P	1		0		SBESX	12		A11 📋	HR_GET_OR_KEEP_ROOTS	P
								📋		
								📋		

Here you can define employee selection from a structure, e.g. organization structure. You can define starting object type and object id, evaluation path, and how many levels the structure should be traversed. You can also specify a function module to determine the root object of the structural authorization. Structures are stored in view HRSEL_STRUCTURE.

34.9.5 Root Objects

Root Objects				
Sel.ID	S...	S...	O..	Ext.obj ID

This view contains the objects (object type and object id), which you can use in the structure for employee selection. Root Objects are stored in view HRSEL_ROOTOBJ.

34.9.6 Table

Table									
Sel.ID	S..	S..	Obj.class	Inf...	Field name	Field type	O..	Rel.spec.	R...	R..
ZENGINE-PCBU	1	1	Persons 🗐	0001	WERKS	Infotype field 🗐	P		🗐	
ZENGINE-PCBU	1	2	Persons 🗐	0001	BTRTL	Infotype field 🗐	P		🗐	
			🗐				🗐		🗐	

Here you can define employee selection from a table, e.g. infotypes. Tables are stored in view HRSEL_TABFIELD.

34.9.7 Ranges

Selection ID	No.	No.	No.	INCL/EXCL	Option	Selection ...	Selection ...	Function module
TMW_TIME_ADMIN	1	1	1					HR_GET_GPA_FO...

In this view, you can maintain ranges for use in the table option of employee selection. A range definition can be in multiple lines (identified by first enterable sequence number). You can include, or exclude a range. For ease of understanding, you should first define all inclusions, then exclusions. The system is anyhow going to take it that way. If you follow this practice, it is easier to understand for you. You can give a single value, or a range. You can even use pattern matching. If your requirement is not met even by using all these features, you can specify a function module, which returns the values desired by you. Ranges are stored in view HRSEL_RANGES.

34.9.8 Function

Function		
Sel.ID	Seq. no.	FM
CMP_COMP_ADMIN	1	HRCM_COMP_ORGUNIT_EMPL_GET

Here you can define employee selection based on a function module. Functions are stored in view HRSEL_FUNCTIONS.

34.9.9 Data for Function Module

	Sel.ID	Seq. no.	Seq. no.	Data FM
Data for Function Module				

Here you can specify data for the function module. Data for function module is stored in view HRSEL_FUNC_DATA.

34.9.10 Groups

Dialog Structure	Groups			
▽ 🗁 Groups	Group	O	Q	InfoSet
⬜ Grouping	TMW_INTERACTIVE	P	G	/SAPQUERY/HR_XX_PT_TMW

Groups and Groupings are maintained through view cluster HRSEL_GROUPINGS. Here you can create groups of employees either based on infosets, or selection ids (specified in Grouping), or both. You can create your own infosets using transaction SQ02. Groups are stored in view HRSEL_GROUPIDS. Groups can be assigned to a profile, thereby making the employee selection available to a user.

34.9.11 Grouping

Dialog Structure	Grouping			
▽ ⬜ Groups	Group	User	Seq. no.	Sel.ID
🗁 Grouping	TMW_INTERACTIVE		001	TMW_TIME_ADMIN

A Group, defined above, may consist of a set of selection ids. One selection id can go in multiple groups. If you specify user in the screen below, the employee list is available only to that user. From a user, you get a profile; from profile, group; and from group selection ids. Selection ids determine the employee lists available to the user. Groupings are stored in view HRSEL_GROUPING.

34.9.12   Assignment of Groups to Profile

Employee selection	
Standard selection using selection criteria	
User-specific selections according to group	
Multiple-user selections according to group	ZTML

Interactive selection	
Selection criteria according to group	TMW_INTERACTIVE

Finally, you assign the groups to profile in view V_PT_TMW_PROFILE (see chapter 34.13).

34.10   EMPLOYEE INFORMATION

Functional Consultant	User	Business Process Owner	Senior Management	My Rating	Understanding Level
A	X	X	X		

34.10.1   Overview

When you select an employee in the employee list, the system shows you his details, e.g. his name, leave balance etc. These details are organized in logical layouts, e.g. master data, time accounts etc., which are shown in the drop down list. The layouts contain display objects. If you want, you can create your own display objects. After you define the layouts, they become available to you for including in a field selection through view cluster VC_PT_FIELD_SELECTION_INF (Screen area INF). The field selection is then assigned to a profile, and the profile to a user. This is how you get a set of layouts. By default, SAP shows employee information under master data.

34.10.2   Layouts for Employee Data

Definition: Layout for Employee Information	
Layout	Short Text
TMW_TIME_ACCOUNTS	Time Accounts
Y_TMW_MASTERDATA	Master Data

You create a layout for employee data in view V_HEAD_INFOGRP. You then assign display objects to it in view V_HEAD_INFOGSTR.

34.10.3 Display Objects in Layouts

Layout ID	ZTIMEACCOUNTS
Short description	Time Accounts

◈ Select object

Display Objects for Employee Information

	Column/row	Display object	Short text
1	1	EMPLOYEENAME	Employee Name
1	2	EMPLOYEE_SUBGROUP	Employee Subgroup
1	3	TIME_STATUS	Time Management Status
2	1	WORKSCHEDULE_RULE	Work Schedule Rule
2	2	PLANNED_TIME	Planned hours

A layout contains display objects assigned to it in view V_HEAD_INFOGSTR. You can select the objects by clicking on the select object icon.

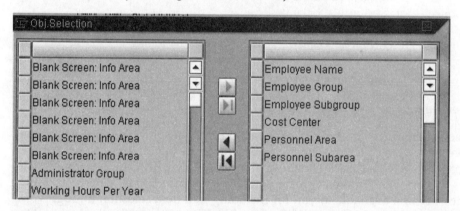

Here you can choose from the objects available to display in layout. SAP provides you standard objects, from which you can choose. However, in case your requirement is not fulfilled by these standard objects, SAP also provides you the ability to create your own objects of type HR Master Data, Reporting Quota Types and Reporting Time Types.

34.10.4 Display Objects for HR Master Data

① Standard objects

Display Object: Master Data Infotype Fields

	DisplayObj	Short Text	Inftyp.	IT text	Type	Field	TMW Field Label
	WSR	Shift Pattern	0007	Planned Working Time		SCHKZ	

In view V_MDAT_OBJ_CTS you can define your own object, based on infotype, subtype and field.

34.10.5   Reporting Quota Types

Dialog Structure	RptgQ	Quota types text	
▽ 🗁 Define Reporting Quota Types	00000001	Leave Entitlement	▲
🗀 Assign Absence Quotas	00000002	Time Off from Overtime	▼
🗀 Assign Attendance Quotas	00000003	Sick Leave Entitlement	
🗀 Assign Monthly Balances (SALDO)	00000006	Approved Overtime	
	00000007	Education/Training Quota	
	10000005	Flextime Balance	
	10000006	Flextime Excess/Deficit	
	LEAVE	Leave	

You can create reporting quota type through view cluster VC_T557LTMW. Note the difference with VC_T557L. A reporting quota type can be assigned to multiple absence quotas, attendance quotas, monthly balances, or a combination of these. While defining a reporting quota type, you can base it on a rule group, which is determined for an employee using feature GRDWK.

34.10.6   Grouping of Reporting Quotas

This feature is used to determine an employee's rule group, which is used in the definition of reporting quota types.

```
GRDWK Feature for grouping of reporting quotas
   └──── 01
```

34.10.7   Display Objects for Reporting Quota Types

Display Object: Employee Time Quotas				
DisplayObj	Short Text	RptgQTy...	Quota	TMW Field ...
ABSENCE_QUOTA_FROM_OVER...	Time off from overtime	00000002	Time Off from Ov...	
FLEXTIME_BALANCE	Flextime balance	10000005	Flextime Balance	
FLEXTIME_BALANCE_CUT_OFF	Flextime excess/deficit	10000006	Flextime Excess/...	
FURTHER_EDUCATION_ENTIT...	Education/training quota	00000007	Education/Traini...	
LEAVE_ENTITLEMENT	Leave entitlement	00000001	Leave Entitlement	Paid Lvs
OVERTIME_APPROVED	Approved overtime	00000006	Approved Overti...	

In view V_ABQT_OBJ_CTS, you assign the reporting quota type to a display object, after which it becomes available for layouts.

34.10.8 Reporting Time Types

Dialog Structure
▽ 🗁 Define Reporting Time Types
📁 Attendances/Absences Assignment
📁 Time Types Assignment
📁 Wage Types Assignment

Define Reporting Time Types

RptgTm...	Time type	Hrs.	Days
00000001	Leave	○	◉
00000002	Illness	○	◉
00000003	Plnd time (DWS time eval)	◉	○
00000004	Overtime	◉	○
00000005	Productive time	◉	○
00000009	Planned time accdg to PWS	◉	○

You can create reporting time type through view cluster VC_T557TMW. Note the difference with VC_T557I. A reporting time type can be assigned to multiple absences, attendances, time types, wage types, or a combination of these. While defining a reporting time type, you can base it on a rule group, which is determined for an employee using feature GRDWT.

34.10.9 Grouping of Reporting Time Types

This feature is used to determine an employee's rule group, which is used in the definition of reporting time types.

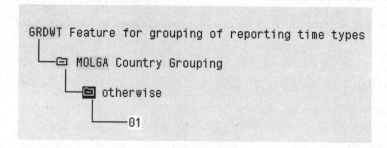

```
GRDWT Feature for grouping of reporting time types

    └─🗐 MOLGA Country Grouping

        └─🗐 otherwise

            └─── 01
```

34.10.10 Display Objects for Reporting Time Types

Display Object: Employee Time and Labor Data				
DisplayObj	Short Text	RptgTm...	Time Type	TMW field
CORE_VIOLATION	Core time violation	10000235	Core time violation	Core viol.
LEAVE	Unpaid Absence	00000001	Leave	Unpaid Abs
OVERTIME	Overtime	10000040	Overtime hours	More
PLANNED_TIME	Planned hours	10000002	Planned working ho...	Planned

In view V_TBAL_OBJ_CTS, you assign the reporting time type to a display object, after which it becomes available for layouts.

34.11 TIME DATA ID

Functional Consultant	User	Business Process Owner	Senior Management	My Rating	Understanding Level
A	X	X	X		

34.11.1 Overview

Time data ids are synonyms for various time data. For example, you may have time data ids CL, PL and SL, corresponding to casual leave, privilege leave, and sick leave, which are subtypes of infotype 2001. Similarly, you may have time data ids, TRN for training and TOUR for official tour, which are subtypes of infotype 2002.

You can create time data ids for infotypes 2001, 2002, 2003, 2004, 2007, 2010, 2011 and 2012. You can also create time data ids for time pairs. There is also provision to create time data ids for 'work schedule data', which is inactive now.

One time data id cannot span across infotypes, but one infotype can have multiple time data ids, by specifying subtypes. However, it is not necessary that you must create one time data id for each subtype. You can create one time data id, which represents one set of subtypes, and another, which represents a different set of subtypes.

You create a time data id record for each subtype. SAP internally assigns an entry number to distinguish between them, which you don't see on the screen.

Time data ids are displayed on the left hand side in the calendar view, and they can be dragged and dropped on a day in the calendar view. Details are filled in the details sub-screen.

When time data for a day, or part of a day, already exists in the time data sub-screen, clicking on it shows its details in details sub-screen. This sub-screen shows the time data id, and its details. You can also drag and drop an id on a day, and enter its details in details sub-screen.

It is important to keep the list of time data ids short and meaningful. If the list became too big, it would lose its main benefit of ease-of-use. You can create ids, which specify both infotype and subtype, or you may create ids, which specify only infotype. In the former case you save on data entry effort; in the latter, you have a short list of ids. You may be guided by the frequency of use to determine when to take the former approach, and when to take the latter.

Note that time data ids are meant to simplify display and updation of time data. Time manager's workplace offers only an alternative method. Time data could also be created through transaction PA61, or PA30.

Non-availability of time data id does not compromise the time administrator's ability to view or update data in time manager's workplace. If a suitable time data id does not exist, but the data exists, the system displays a time data id, starting with a '?'.

You can assign different colors to a time data id. You can also specify if the color should be intense, or inverse.

Time data ids are defined in a definition set. Each user is assigned a definition set, which determines the ids available to him. Why would one want to create multiple definition sets in an enterprise? One may think of the following reasons:

➤ Time data ids must be intuitive. If different users speak different languages, what is intuitive to one may not be intuitive to the other.
➤ If the users deal with employees in different locations, or different grades, their needs of time data ids may be different.

Apart from a definition set for ids, SAP also provides a definition subset for ids. Each user is also assigned a definition subset for ids. At definition subset level you can define the properties of a time data id. Is it inactive, display only or usable for data entry? In case an id represents multiple subtypes of an infotype, which is the default subtype. Thus, by assigning different definition subsets to different users, you can control their actions.

There are two ways of assigning definition set and definition subset to a user. You can enter them in user parameter PT_TMW_TDLANGU as <definition set>/<definition subset>, or you may create a parameter transaction in which profile, definition set and definition subset are specified. You then assign the transaction to role, and role to user.

The time data ids you see in time manager's workplace depend on the definition set and definition subset assigned to you. Out of this list also, only those ids, which are not inactive in view V_TMW_TDSUBLA are seen.

You can give freedom to your users to choose definition subset, within definition sets assigned to them. To do so, you enable it in the profile by ticking the field, 'Subset IDs can be changed'. If you do that, in time manager's workplace, the user can change his definition subset through menu (Settings ➤ Choose IDs).

SAP lets you decide whether you want to see the id in the calendar, or its text. Experienced users, who remember the ids, may want to hide it altogether, so that they save on screen space. You can make your choice (in screen area TDT, view VC_PT_FIELD_SELECTION_INF) and assign it to the profile, which is attached to users.

34.11.2 Definition Sets

You define definition sets in view V_TMW_TDLAN.

Definition Set for IDs		
Definition set	ID	
0S1	Abbreviation Language 1	

34.11.3 Definition Subsets

A definitions set may have multiple definition subsets. You define them in view V_TMW_TDSLAN.

Subset IDs		
Definition set	Subset	Subset
OS1	001	Secondary Language 1

34.11.4 Time Data Id

You define time data ids for each definition set in view V_TMW_TDTYPE.

Def...	ID	ID text	Category	Data...	P..	A/A...	P..	S..	A.	D.	Dai...	V	Sta...	En...	S..	E	P..	A..	C.	WT	A	Ti...	P..	Tra...	C
OS1	A	Absence	IT	2001		00		00							☐		00	00					00		
OS1	AN	At work from time ...	TIMPAIR	PT	00		00		00						☐		00	00			1		00		
OS1	B	Availability	IT	2004	00										☐		00	00					00		
OS1	D6	Off-site work from ...	TIMPAIR	PT	00		00		00						☐		00	00			3		00		
OS1	E	Remuneration info	IT	2010	00		00		00						☐		00	00					00		
OS1	G	Attendance approv.	IT	2007	00		00		00						☐								00		
OS1	I	Individual working ..	IT	2003	00										☐		00	00					00		
OS1	K	III	IT	2001	01	0230	00		00						☐		00	00					00		
OS1	K	III	IT	2001	01	0200	00		00						☐		00	00					00		
OS1	K	III	IT	2001	01	0210	00		00						☐		00	00					00		

When you create a new record, you select from multiple tabs presented to you. That tab determines the category and data type. Based on this choice, only appropriate fields are open for input. In case of infotypes, these are infotype fields. In case of time pairs, there is only one field, 'Attendance or absence status in pair formation', which has a set of values. The data entered in the fields here is matched with the record being displayed to determine the id.

34.11.5 Time Data IDs in a Definition Subset

Each user is assigned a definition subset for ids. At definition subset level you can define the properties of a time data id. Is it inactive, display only or usable for data entry? In case an id represents multiple subtypes of an infotype, which is the default subtype. These are defined in view V_TMW_TDSUBLA.

| Definition set | OS1 | OS1 |
| Subset | 001 | Secondary Language 1 |

Use of IDs in a Subset						
	ID	ID text	Default ID	Input ID	Displ.only	Inactive
	A	Absence	⦿	○	○	○
	AN	At work from time posting	○	○	⦿	○
	B	Availability	⦿	○	○	○
	DG	Off-site work from time p...	○	○	⦿	○
	E	Remuneration info	⦿	○	○	○

34.11.6 Color Attributes for Time Data Ids

You can assign different colors to a time data id in view V_TMW_TD_ATTRIB. You can also specify if the color should be intense (darker shade), or inverse (lighter shade). Note that these properties cannot vary at definition subset level. They are also the same for all entries of an id (do not vary at entry number level).

| Definition set | OS1 | OS1 |

Set Colors of Time Data IDs for Calendar View					
	ID	Short text	Color	Intense	Inverse
	A	Absence	Red (negative threshold valu...🖹	☐	☐
			🖹		
			🖹		
			🖹		

34.11.7 Display Type of Time Data Id List

SAP lets you decide whether you want to see the id in the calendar, or its text. Experienced users, who remember the ids, may want to hide it altogether, so that they save on screen space. You can make your choice in screen area TDT of view cluster VC_PT_FIELD_SELECTION_INF.

Dialog Structure
▽ 🗁 Field Selection Attributes
🗀 Field Customizing

Screen area   **TDT**   Display Type of Time Data ID List

Field Selection Attributes	
Field sel.	Field selection text

34.11.8 Display Type of Time Data Id List to Profiles Assignment

Assignment of all screen areas to profile is covered in VC_PT_TMW_PROFILE_STR. screen area TDT is the only exception, which does not get covered through that node but the concept is identical. You need to do this assignment in view cluster VC_PT_TMW_PRF_TDT.

Dialog Structure	Define Profile	
▽ 🗂 Define Profile	Profile	Text
☐ Assign Field Selection		

34.12 MESSAGE LIST AND CONTEXTUAL INFORMATION

Functional Consultant	User	Business Process Owner	Senior Management	My Rating	Understanding Level
A	X	X	X		

34.12.1 Overview

Message type

All messages are classified into message types.

Contextual information

For different messages, you need to see relevant contextual information. If there is a message that the time events had errors, you want to see the time events. If the message is that core time was violated, you want to know what was the core time, and when did the employee come and go.

Processing method

You can have a number of processing methods, which determine the contextual information for a message based on its message type. Sometimes a processing method may be assigned to a message functional area and apply to all message types belonging to it.

Message functional area

Message types are grouped in message functional areas. Using this relationship, the message list is shown as a two-tier hierarchy. In some cases, processing method may be assigned directly to a message functional area, and apply to all message types belonging to that message functional area.

Grouping message types in message functional areas

There is no guideline on grouping message types in message functional areas. However, you may like to consider the following criteria:

➢ Messages that relate to the same subject, such as violations of working time regulations.
➢ Messages that require a similar or identical method of processing, such as incorrect or missing time events.
➢ Messages that are of the same category, for example, notes, info messages, or errors.

Message functional area having a processing method

If a message functional area is assigned a processing method, then

➢ All messages in the message functional area are processed in a similar manner.
➢ You need same contextual information for them.
➢ All messages under that message functional area are grouped together in the message list. They are not displayed message type wise. They are also displayed together in the message area.
➢ All message types under a message functional area inherit the processing method of the message functional area. These message types cannot be assigned their own processing methods.

Message functional area not having a processing method

If a message functional area is not assigned a processing method, messages under that message functional area are grouped and displayed message type wise.

Message types not belonging to a message functional area

If some message types do not belong to any message functional area, they are displayed at the same level as message functional areas.

Message list structure

A message list is structured as under.

➢ Message functional area	Having a processing method which applies to all message types under it
➢ Message functional area	Not having a processing method
▸ Message types	Belonging to the message functional area above
➢ Message types	Not belonging to any message functional area

34.12.2 Processing Methods

Processing method determines the contextual information and layout of a message. Master list of processing methods is defined in view TPT_WLIST_PROC.

	ProcMethod	Processig method text	Start Date	End Date
	TCOTIVI	Info Field: Core Time Violation	01.01.1990	31.12.9999
	TDPWS	Info Field: Personal Daily Work Schedule	01.01.1990	31.12.9999
	TEVENTS	Time Events with Errors	01.01.1990	31.12.9999
	TFLEX	Info Field: Flextime Status	01.01.1990	31.12.9999
	TOVER	Info Fields: Overtime and Planned Hours	01.01.1990	31.12.9999
	TPINC	Attendance/Absence Reasons: Processing	01.01.1990	31.12.9999
	TSKELTI	Info Field: Skeleton Time	01.01.1990	31.12.9999

Message Processing: Methods

34.12.3 Message Functional Areas

Message functional areas are defined in view VV_TPT_WLI_AREA.

Message Processing: Create Message Functional Areas

	Func. area	Func. area
	CUST	Customizing errors
	PINCODES	Attendance/absence reasons
	PWS	Work schedule deviations
	TECH	Technical errors
	TESTPROC	Test procedures
	TIMEACC	Time account checks
	TIMEEVENT	Time events with errors
	WAGESLIP	Time tickets with errors
	WORKSCHED	Daily work schedule changes
	WOTIREG	Working time order violation

34.12.4 Contextual Information

For a message, you need contextual information. Contextual information provides additional data for time administrators to help them process messages. The contextual information you need for messages of one type may be different from the contextual information you need for messages of another type. You define the master list of contextual information in view cluster VC_PT_FIELD_SELECTION_WLI (WLI).

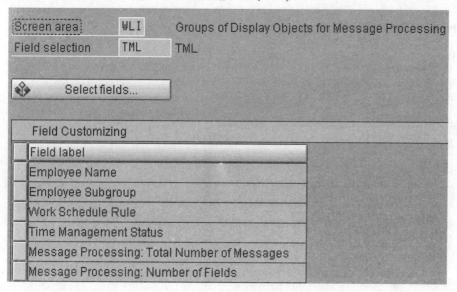

You also define the display objects that constitute the contextual information in view cluster VC_PT_FIELD_SELECTION_WLI (WLI).

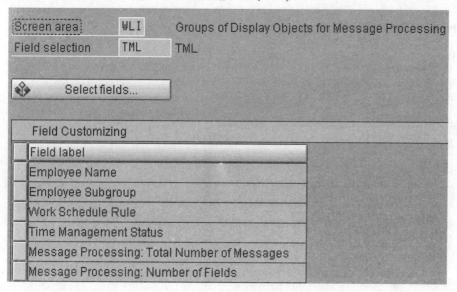

34.12.5 Contextual Information for Processing Methods

You then assign contextual information to processing methods in view VV_PT_TMW_PRF_FL. If a processing method is not assigned contextual information, no contextual information is displayed for the message functional area or message type, which use that processing method.

Screen area	WLI	Groups of Display Objects for Message Processing

Assign Field Selection to Processing Step		Field sel.	Field text
Info Field: Core Time Violation	🗏	TML	TML
Info Field: Personal Daily Work Schedule	🗏	TML	TML
Time Events with Errors	🗏	TML	TML
Info Field: Flextime Status	🗏	TML	TML
Info Fields: Overtime and Planned Hours	🗏	TML	TML
Attendance/Absence Reasons: Processing	🗏	TML	TML
Info Field: Skeleton Time	🗏	TML	TML
	🗏		

WLI is the only screen area, which is not profile dependent. Hence, it is not assigned to any profile. It is same for all users.

34.12.6   Processing Methods and Message Functional Areas for Message Types

Message types are assigned a processing method, so that appropriate contextual information can be displayed for messages belonging to that message type.

Message types are assigned a message functional area, so that all message types belonging to a message functional area can be grouped and displayed under that message functional area.

Both these attributes of a message type are defined in view V_T555E_WLIST. You do not need view VV_T555E_WLIST, which shows only message functional area for a message type.

Message Processing: Message Types							
PSG	T..	M...	Text	Func. area	Functional area	ProcMethod	Processig method text
01	1	00	Employee at work although OFF	PWS	Work schedule deviations	TOVER	Info Fields: Overtime an..
01	1	01	Employee not at work	WOTIREG	Working time order violation		
01	1	02	At work despite full-day absence				
01	1	03	Clock-in cannot be delimited	TIMEEVENT	Time events with errors	TEVENTS	Time Events with Errors
01	1	04	Clock-out cannot be delimited	TIMEEVENT	Time events with errors	TEVENTS	Time Events with Errors
01	1	05	Off-site start cannot be delimited	TIMEEVENT	Time events with errors	TEVENTS	Time Events with Errors
01	1	06	Off-site end cannot be delimited	TIMEEVENT	Time events with errors	TEVENTS	Time Events with Errors
01	1	07	Off-site< 1 day cannot be delim...	TIMEEVENT	Time events with errors	TEVENTS	Time Events with Errors
01	1	08	At work despite day type "1"	PWS	Work schedule deviations	TOVER	Info Fields: Overtime an..
01	1	09	Clock ID: PDC terminal				

Sometimes, all method types belonging to a message functional area have the same processing method. In such cases, a processing method is assigned directly to the message functional area. This is done in view V_TPT_WLIST_AREA.

Message Processing: Functional Area			
Func. area	Func. area	ProcMethod	Processig method text
CUST	Customizing errors		
PINCODES	Attendance/absence reasons	TPINC	Attendance/Absence Reasons: Processi...
PWS	Work schedule deviations		
TECH	Technical errors		
TESTPROC	Test procedures		
TIMEACC	Time account checks		
TIMEEVENT	Time events with errors	TEVENTS	Time Events with Errors
WAGESLIP	Time tickets with errors		
WORKSCHED	Daily work schedule changes	TDPWS	Info Field: Personal Daily Work Schedule
WOTIREG	Working time order violation		

This assignment also has an effect on the message list; under the message functional area, message types are not shown. When you select such a message functional area in the message list, all message types are displayed together in employee sequence. Same contextual information is made available.

If a message type is not assigned a processing method, but is assigned a message functional area which has a processing method, the messages of that message type get contextual information through that link.

If a message type is neither assigned a processing method, nor a message functional area, the messages of that message type cannot display contextual information.

If a message type is not assigned a processing method, and the message functional area it is assigned does not have a processing method, the messages of that message type cannot display contextual information.

If some message types are not assigned a message functional area they are displayed in the message list after all message functional areas. They are displayed at the same level as message functional areas.

34.13   PROFILE

Functional Consultant	User	Business Process Owner	Senior Management	My Rating	Understanding Level
A	C	C	X		

34.13.1   Purpose and Overview

Profile

All time managers may not work in the same way. They may be allowed to perform only a subset of all activities. The employees for whom they work may differ. Also, the layouts they need may differ. The time manager's workplace allows this flexibility to time managers through a concept called profile. You can define multiple profiles and assign one to each time manager.

A profile specifies details, e.g. default period, employee selection etc. under tab Settings. For each screen area, you also specify field selections, which control the layout and behaviour of time manager's workplace for the user.

Default values in profile

When you create a profile, what is it that you must specify, and what happens to those aspects where you specify nothing? You can create an almost blank profile; the only thing you are required to specify is at least one method for employee selection. SAP supplies excellent default values in most cases. Thus, while SAP would let you customize the time manager's workplace screen to your requirement, it is not a pre-requisite. You can start with default values, and make your choices when both users and management understand the significance of these choices.

Assignment of profile to user

Each user of time manager's workplace needs to be assigned a profile. This can be done in two ways:

➤ By creating a parameter transaction using transaction SE93 and assigning it to a role. For more details, see help of IMG node Time Management ➤ Time Manager's Workplace ➤ Profiles ➤ Create Parameter Transactions.
➤ By using the user parameter PT_TMW_PROFILE.

If a user is assigned a profile by both a role and a user parameter, the role specification overrides the user parameter. If no profile is specified in either of the two methods, SAP prompts you to specify a profile when you execute transaction PTMW (Time manager's workplace).

34.13.2 IMG Node

SM34 ➤ VC_PT_TMW_PROFILE_STR (V_PT_TMW_PROFILE)

34.13.3 Primary Key

Time Manager's Workplace: Profile

34.13.4 Screen

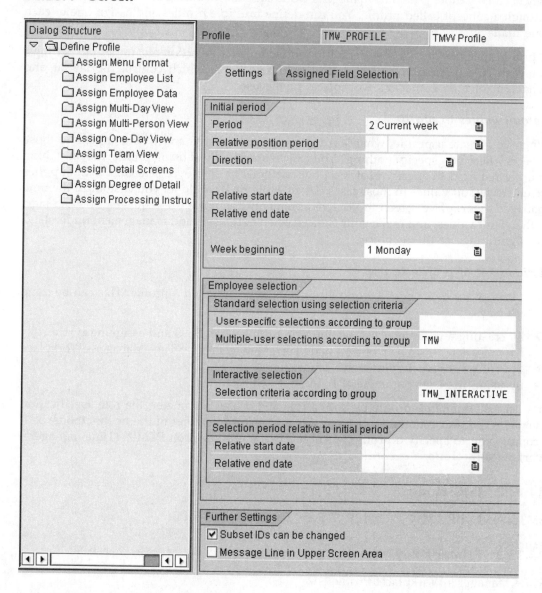

34.13.5 Initial Period Settings

Profile

Here you name the profile and give a suitable description.

Initial period

When you enter time manager's workplace, the calendar on the left top corner has a period pre-selected. The fields in this block determine that.

Period

The period is specified in terms of Current day/ Current week/ Current month. If no offset is specified, this is the initial period. If this field is left blank, the current day is selected by default.

Relative position period with unit and direction

The initial period can be shifted into the future or the past by specified number of days/ weeks/months. Forward direction shifts the initial period into the future, backwards in the past.

Relative start and end date with units

You can expand the initial period by extending the start date backwards, and end date forward.

Week beginning

The calendar shows all days of a week in one column, and the week can be selected by selecting the column. You would like the calendar to show your working week, which may be different from other companies. You can set that here.

34.13.6 Employee Selection Settings

User-specific selections according to group

You enter a group in this field. Definition of that group may have several employee lists; some with user field blank, and some with user field specified. Only those employee lists are taken where the content of the user field matches the current user.

Multiple-user selections according to group

You enter a group in this field. Definition of that group may have several employee lists; some with user field blank, and some with user field specified. Only those employee lists are taken where the user field is blank.

Interactive selection

You enter a group in this field. Definition of that group may have several employee lists. The time administrator can add these own employee lists to his own in a session, interactively.

Employee selection period relative to initial period

The employee selection depends on the period selected in the calendar. However, you can expand the employee selection period on both sides. You may do this in the calendar manually. This changes the employee selection temporarily. However, if you expand the period here, the expansion applies all the time.

34.13.7 Further Settings

Subset ids can be changed

If this check box is ticked, the user can choose between different subsets ids via Settings ➤ Choose Ids for time data entry.

Message line in upper screen area

If this checkbox is ticked, the message line is displayed in the upper screen area. By default the message line appears at the lower screen area.

34.13.8 Field Selection Assignments

Field selection assignments

Time manager's workplace contains 46 screen areas. Each screen area controls the layout or behaviour of some aspect of time manager's workplace. For each screen area, you assign one or more field selections to a profile. If you do not assign any field selections to a profile in a screen area, SAP uses default values. Through this view cluster, you can assign field selections for 44 screen areas to a profile. The assignments you make are displayed in the tab 'Assigned Field Selection'. In the view cluster, these screen areas are grouped by sub-screens.

Types of assignment

When you assign field selections to profiles, depending on the screen area, you see three types of layouts.

➢ Independent of task and context
➢ Dependent on task
➢ Dependent on context

Field selection assignment independent of task and context

For screen areas, which are independent of task and context, you can assign one field selection to a profile. You can see these assignments in tab 'For Multiple tasks' under tab 'Assigned Field Selection'.

Profile	TMW_PROFILE	TMW Profile
Screen area	TSK	Task Selection

Assign Field Selection	
Field s...	Field text
ALL	All Tasks

Field selection assignment dependent on task

For screen areas which are dependent on task, in a profile, you can assign one field selection to 'Maintain time data' and one to 'Process messages'. You may assign different field selections to these tasks, or the same field selection to both the tasks. There are only three such screen areas: EMP, MEN and TEC. You can see these assignments in tabs 'Maintain time data' and 'Process messages' under tab 'Assigned Field Selection'.

Profile	TMW_PROFILE	
Screen area	EMP	Employee List

Assign Field Selection

TMW Task	Field sel.	Field text
Maintain time data ▤	EL1S001	1 Level Emp List, CC Hier, Per No, Name
Process messages ▤	EL1S001	1 Level Emp List, CC Hier, Per No, Name
▤		

Field selection assignment dependent on context

For some screen areas, assignment of field selection to profile is context dependent. Context is a flexible concept. In most cases, the context is self-explanatory. For absences, the context is absence type, including 'All remaining absences'. For these screen areas, you can assign one field selection to each context in a profile. You can see these assignments in tab, 'For Multiple tasks' under tab, 'Assigned Field Selection'.

Profile	TMW_PROFILE	TMW Profile
Screen area	D01	Details: Fields for Absences Infotype (2001)

Assign Field Selection

	Field s...	Field text
All remaining absences ▤	CL	Casual Leave
40,P0/PL (Privilege Leave) ▤	PL	Privilege Leave
▤		
▤		

35 Time Management Pool

35.1 SCREEN

Functional Consultant	User	Business Process Owner	Senior Management	My Rating	Understanding Level
A	A	A	C		

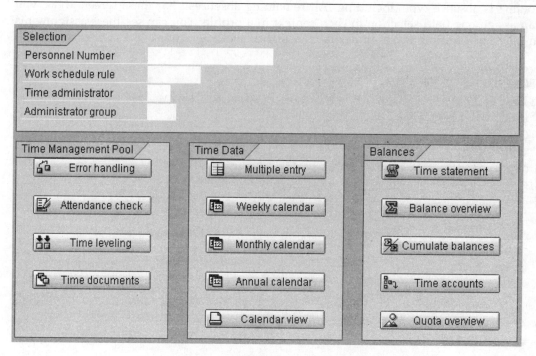

35.2 OVERVIEW

Functional Consultant	User	Business Process Owner	Senior Management	My Rating	Understanding Level
A	A	A	C		

SAP provides two major interfaces for time administrator: time management pool and time manager's workplace. Time management pool (transaction PT40) provides you a menu from which you can perform most activities, you need to perform. Time manager's workplace is even more comprehensive. For details refer to chapter 34. The screen of time management pool shows the following options. Some of these call programs, which can be directly called through their own transactions. This mapping is given below.

Item	Transaction	Remarks
Error handling		Functionality similar to that of transaction PT_ERL00
Attendance check	PT62	
Time leveling	PW61	You may see chapter 37.26, Incentive Wages.
Time documents		You may see chapter 35.5
Multiple entry	PT69	
Weekly calendar	PA61, infotype 2052	You may see chapter 5.18
Monthly calendar	PA61, infotype 2051	You may see chapter 5.17
Annual calendar	PA61, infotype 2050	You may see chapter 5.16
Calendar view	PT90, PT90_ATT	
Time statement	PT61	
Balance overview	PT_EDT_TELU	
Cumulate balances	PT_BAL00	
Time accounts		Result same as transaction PT_DOW00
Quota overview	PT50	

35.3 ERROR HANDLING

Functional Consultant	User	Business Process Owner	Senior Management	My Rating	Understanding Level
A	A	A	C		

This screen is for message processing. If you select a message and click on [icon], you see the document view, which shows you all relevant data for that day, a day before, and a day after. This data helps you understand the context of the message.

You can maintain time events, absences, attendances, absence quotas and attendance quotas from here. This functionality is similar to that of transaction PT_ERL00–Time Evaluation Messages. You can also do error handling in time manager's workplace.

35.4 ATTENDANCE CHECK

Functional Consultant	User	Business Process Owner	Senior Management	My Rating	Understanding Level
A	A	A	C		

When you run attendance check program using transaction PT62, you get a selection screen, which gives you more flexibility than when you run it from time management pool. Hence, this program is explained with respect to that transaction.

The purpose of this program is to show you the status of employees who are expected to be present at a given date and time. The expected presence takes into account the employee's daily work schedule, substitution and dynamic substitution.

Pers.No.	Employee/app.name	Stat.	Status text	TET	Meaning	TimeUnit	A/AType	Att./abs. type text	Time
110858	Sahasrabudhe Shashikant	1	At work	P10	Clock-in	08:26:00			
111048	Gracias Noel	7	Full-day At work				W0	CERTIFIED ATTD. (MISC.)	
111417	Kamat Shashikant	5	Full-day Absent				M0	SL (Sick Leave Certifd)	
111426	Sawant Shrikant	1	At work	P10	Clock-in	06:28:00			
111431	Sapre Satich	1	At work	P10	Clock-in	08:27:00			

This program is very useful for knowing which employees are present or absent at any given time. However, the following may dampen the enthusiasm somewhat.

> ➤ This program cannot be run unless time evaluation has been run. Therefore, if you are in a hurry to find which people have or have not reported for work at the start of the shift, you have to wait until time evaluation is done first.
> ➤ You can't see the daily work schedule of the employees in this list.
> ➤ If you tick the checkbox 'Evaluate work schedule', the records selected change. It is not clear why that happens.
> ➤ Take care to select employment status 3 in the selection screen if you want the system to show only active employees.

35.5 TIME DOCUMENTS

Functional Consultant	User	Business Process Owner	Senior Management	My Rating	Understanding Level
A	A	A	C		

The document view shows all time information for an employee for specified period. The information shown is absences, attendances, substitutions, absence quotas, and time transfer specifications. It calls program RPLTIM00.

35.6 MULTIPLE ENTRY

Functional Consultant	User	Business Process Owner	Senior Management	My Rating	Understanding Level
A	A	A	C		

Through this user interface, you can enter data for multiple infotypes at the same time. However, if you select too many infotypes, the layout becomes very cluttered. You can also run this program through transaction PT69.

35.7 CALENDAR VIEW

Functional Consultant	User	Business Process Owner	Senior Management	My Rating	Understanding Level
A	A	A	C		

Calendar view is very similar to annual calendar. Additional facilities include statistics, legend, seeing only selected attendances and absences if you so desire and highlighting of holidays. However, you cannot create attendances/absences directly from here, which is possible in annual calendar. You can also run this program through transactions PT90, PT90_ATT.

35.8 TIME STATEMENT

Functional Consultant	User	Business Process Owner	Senior Management	My Rating	Understanding Level
A	A	A	C		

You can use time statement to present the results determined by time evaluation. It can be generated only after time evaluation. The time statement is an overview of an employee's time accounts and time wage types. It is used by time administrators to check the time evaluation results. It can also be sent to employees for information.

Your consultants define the format of time statement in consultation with you. This is the format you see when you create time statement. Time balances and time wage types formed by time evaluation, are output for individual days. If you create a time statement for an entire period that has already been accounted, the time statement displays a totals overview of the balances calculated for the evaluated period.

You can output a time statement for periods for which time evaluation triggers a recalculation. You can also output a time statement for employees who have errors in time evaluation.

You can go from the list screen to the time data records to receive detailed information. You can display collapsed views of the results, such as weekly totals and summarized time wage types.

You can add a letterhead to the form so that you can send time statements to your employees. Alternatively, you can allow your employees access to the self-service application for the time statement so that they can view the time statement in the internet or intranet.

You can specify an output language for the time statement. For example, if you choose employee's language, the time statement is displayed in the employee's language.

When you generate time statement, you specify a form name in the selection screen. SAP provides different forms, which display different views of the information. You can also run this program through transactions given as follows:

Form	Use	Transactions
TF00	Lists the most important time balances by day	PT61, PZ34
TF01	Lists the most important time balances by day, letterhead with address, additional information	
TF02	Lists the most important time balances by day, letterhead with address, additional information in a clearer layout.	PT_EDT_TEDT
TFL1	Overview list of the cumulated time balances	PT_EDT_TELU

(Contd.)

Form	Use	Transactions
TFL2	Overview list of the cumulated time balances. Form is only printed under particular conditions (which you can set in Customizing). For example, the flextime surplus or deficit is only printed if it is < 0.	

35.9 BALANCE OVERVIEW

Functional Consultant	User	Business Process Owner	Senior Management	My Rating	Understanding Level
A	A	A	C		

This is also time statement, called with form TFL1 and shows overview list of the cumulated time balances. You can also run this program through transaction PT_EDT_TELU.

35.10 CUMULATE BALANCES

Functional Consultant	User	Business Process Owner	Senior Management	My Rating	Understanding Level
A	A	A	C		

You can use this transaction to see day balances of time types, cumulated balances of time types, or time wage types generated during time evaluation. SAP allows you to highlight employees whose day balances, cumulated balances or time wage types are more than specified values. You set specified values for day balances, cumulated balances and time wage types in features LIMIE, LIMIS and LIMIZ respectively. You can also run this program through transaction PT_BAL00.

35.11 TIME ACCOUNTS

Functional Consultant	User	Business Process Owner	Senior Management	My Rating	Understanding Level
A	A	A	C		

When you define time types, you specify which time types are downloaded to the time recording systems. These are stored in table ST in cluster B1. Time accounts shows balances for these time types. This is an alternative to time statement. Whereas time statement shows balances for all time types, this one shows only the important ones. This report can also be generated by executing transaction PT_DOW00.

35.12 QUOTA OVERVIEW

Functional Consultant	User	Business Process Owner	Senior Management	My Rating	Understanding Level
A	A	A	C		

You can use quota overview to display how much absence quota and attendance quota an employee has, and how much absence quota has accrued to him. The first tab shows the summary, while the other three show details. Before you use this transaction, you should be familiar with the concepts associated with absence quota infotype 2006, and attendance quota infotype 2007. The data displayed is for the periods you select. You can also run this program through transaction PT50. You can also display absence quota information using transaction PT_QTA10.

35.13 MENU ITEMS

Functional Consultant	User	Business Process Owner	Senior Management	My Rating	Understanding Level
A	A	C	X		

Most items in time management pool menu are already covered above. For the remaining, reference is given below.

Menu path	Program	Chapter
Time Management pool ➤ Employee expenditures errors ➤ Records with errors	RPIEWT00	26.8
Time Management pool ➤ Employee expenditures errors ➤ Errors in sessions	RPIEWT03	26.11
Time Management pool ➤ Time events errors	RPAFRV00	25.14
Time Management pool ➤ Logistics errors ➤ Confirmations with errors	RPWI1100	27.4
Time Management pool ➤ Logistics errors ➤ Errors in sessions	RPWI3000	27.4

35.14 TABLES SHOWN IN TIME MANAGEMENT POOL

Functional Consultant	User	Business Process Owner	Senior Management	My Rating	Understanding Level
B	C	X	X		

35.14.1 Purpose

You can use feature REPTA to decide the infotypes and tables that are shown in time management pool.

35.14.2 IMG Node

PE03 ➤ REPTA

35.14.3 Screen

```
REPTA Preselection of infotypes and tables
  └─□ ZTERF Employee Time Management Status
       ├─□ 0 No time evaluation
       │      └─REPT1 Subfeature of REPTA, preselection of infotypes
       ├─□ 9 Time evaluation of planned times
       └─□ otherwise
```

```
REPT1 Subfeature of REPTA, preselection of infotypes and tables
  ├─REPTA = 2001
  ├─REPTA = 2002
  ├─REPTA = 2003
  ├─REPTA = 2004
  ├─REPTA = 2005
  ├─REPTA = 2006
  ├─REPTA = 2007
  ├─REPTA = 2010
  ├─REPTA = 2012
  ├─REPTA = PSP
  ├─REPTA = ERT
  ├─REPTA = LE
  └─REPTA = IFT
```

35.14.4 Fields for Decision Making

Personnel Area
Personnel Subarea
Employee Group
Employee Subgroup
Employee Time Management Status

35.14.5 Return Value

Tables that are shown in time management pool.

35.15 REACTION TO ERROR TRANSACTION

Functional Consultant	User	Business Process Owner	Senior Management	My Rating	Understanding Level
B	X	X	X		

35.15.1 Purpose

If you want to display different information for different errors, you can specify that here. If you do not make any settings, all available information is displayed for all the errors.

35.15.2 IMG Node

SM30 ➤ V_T705E

35.15.3 Screen

PS grouping	01	
Cat. of Message Type	1	Error set by operation COLER in time evaluation
Message type number	01	Employee not at work

Reaction to Error Transaction

Function part

PSP/2001/2002/2011

35.15.4 Primary Key

PS Grouping for Time Recording + Category of Message Type + Number of Message Type + ABAB Dictionary: Two-Digit Numeric Field

35.15.5 Important Fields

PS grouping, category of message type, message type number

A message is uniquely defined for combination of these fields.

Function part

Infotypes and tables, which are to be displayed if an error occurs.

35.16 HOURLY LIMITS FOR DAY BALANCES

Functional Consultant	User	Business Process Owner	Senior Management	My Rating	Understanding Level
B	C	X	X		

35.16.1 Purpose

In time management pool when you run 'Cumulate Balances' program, you can highlight employees whose day balances, cumulated balances or time wage types are more than specified values.

Limiting values for day balances are specified in feature LIMIE. It can be a number with a maximum of 2 decimal places.

35.16.2 IMG Node

PE03 ➢ LIMIE

35.16.3 Screen

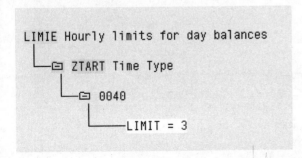

35.16.4 Fields for Decision Making

Personnel Area
Personnel Subarea
Employee Group
Employee Subgroup
Cost Center
Pay Scale Type
Pay Scale Area
Pay Scale Group
Pay Scale Level
Time Type
Gender Key

35.16.5 Return Value

Limiting values for day balances.

35.17 HOURLY LIMITS FOR CUMULATED BALANCES

Functional Consultant	User	Business Process Owner	Senior Management	My Rating	Understanding Level
B	C	X	X		

35.17.1 Purpose

In time management pool when you run 'Cumulate Balances' program, you can highlight employees whose day balances, cumulated balances or time wage types are more than specified values.

Limiting values for cumulated balances are specified in feature LIMIS. It can be a number with a maximum of 2 decimal places.

35.17.2 IMG Node

PE03 ≻ LIMIS

35.17.3 Screen

```
LIMIS Hourly limits for cumulated balances
   └─▭ ZTART Time Type
         └─▭ 0005
               └────LIMIT = 15
```

35.17.4 Fields for Decision Making

Personnel Area
Personnel Subarea
Employee Group
Employee Subgroup
Cost Center
Pay Scale Type
Pay Scale Area
Pay Scale Group
Pay Scale Level
Time Type
Gender Key

35.17.5 Return Value

Limiting values for cumulated balances.

35.18 HOURLY LIMITS FOR TIME WAGE TYPES

Functional Consultant	User	Business Process Owner	Senior Management	My Rating	Understanding Level
B	C	X	X		

35.18.1 Purpose

In time management pool when you run 'Cumulate Balances' program, you can highlight employees whose day balances, cumulated balances or time wage types are more than specified values.

Limiting values for time wage types are specified in feature LIMIZ. It can be a number with a maximum of 2 decimal places.

35.18.2 IMG Node

PE03 ➢ LIMIZ

35.18.3   Screen

```
LIMIZ Hourly limits for time wage types
    │
    └─🗀 LGART Wage type
          │
          ├─🗀 MM10
          │     │
          │     └──LIMIT = 2
          │
          └─🗀 MM20
                │
                └──LIMIT = 1
```

35.18.4   Fields for Decision Making

Personnel Area
Personnel Subarea
Employee Group
Employee Subgroup
Cost Center
Pay Scale Type
Pay Scale Area
Pay Scale Group
Pay Scale Level
Wage Type
Gender Key

35.18.5   Return Value

Limiting values for time wage types.

Cross-Application Time Sheet

36.1 TIME SHEET

Functional Consultant	User	Business Process Owner	Senior Management	My Rating	Understanding Level
A	A	B	C		

36.1.1 A Simple Scenario

The Cross-Application Time Sheet (CATS) is a tool for your employees to record how they spent their time. They can specify the work they did; the cost center or project to which it is to be charged, etc. They can also specify if they were on leave, attending training, etc. When an employee runs transaction CAT2 (Record Working Times), he gets the following screen.

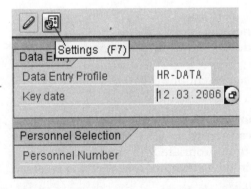

He enters the data entry profile, which the consultant has set up for him, the personnel number (usually one's own) for which he wants to record the time, and the key date which determines the period for which he records time. When he selects the change icon, he gets the following screen.

509

| | | Personnel Number | | 125866 | | | | | | Cost Ctr | | 1119054 |
| | | Data Entry Period | | 13.03.2006 - 19.03.2006 | | | | | | Week | | 11.2006 |

Data Entry Area

LT	A/A...	Wa...	MO ...	TU ...	WE ...	TH ...	FR ...	SA ...	SU ...
🕒			8.00	8.00	8.00	0.00	8.00	8.00	8.00
Σ			8.00	4.00	0.00	0.00	0.00	0.00	0.00
	M0		8.00	4.00					
		1560		3.00					

Here he enters the attendance or absence type, and day wise hours. The hours he enters on several lines for the same day are totaled in the line marked Σ. The hours he is expected to work are displayed in the line marked 🕒. After this he can save his entries and his time recording is done.

If your requirement is this simple, so is the solution. But rest assured that CATS has the ability to address requirements of much greater complexity, and the rest of this chapter explains what else can you do with CATS.

36.1.2   Objectives of Time Recording

Does one record working and non-working time merely to account for it? Usually a company wants to make much better use of time data. Some of the important objectives of time recording may be:

> Costing of the companies' product and services and determining profitability of various lines of businesses.
> Billing based on resources consumed/activity performed.
> Determining what work the employee did and how much time he took, in order to compare with what work he was expected to do, and how much time he was expected to take.
> Determining the time for which employee was present or absent, so as to determine the salary payable to him.

All these objectives require that the employee not only records his time; but also time attributes. There are various time attributes he can record in CATS. Depending on the time attributes recorded, the data is transferred to appropriate SAP module where it is processed further. One of the important concepts in time attributes is sender and receiver.

> Sender objects get credit for the time spent/work done.
> Receiver objects are debited for the time spent/work done.
> There are various methods of determining the value of time spent/work done. It may be based on actual cost or activity allocation.

36.1.3 Settings (Data Entry Profile)

Most of the flexibility of CATS is controlled by the data entry profile, which you enter in the initial screen. When you are in the initial screen, you see an icon 🖼 (Settings). You also see this icon in the data entry screen. If you click on this icon (or select in the menu: Goto ➤ Settings), you see the following screen, which shows, under various tabs, the settings applicable to you. These settings have been done in configuration.

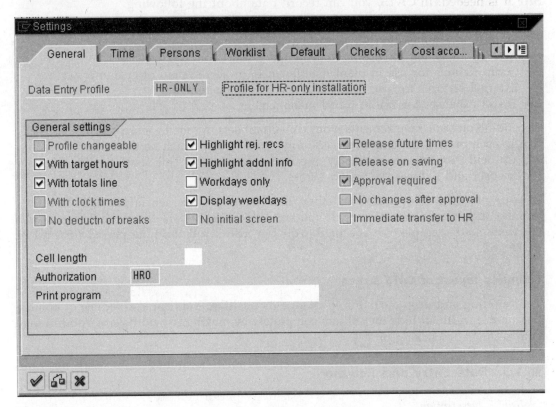

You can always change some of these settings, e.g. 'With totals line'. These are harmless changes, which you are always allowed to do. There are some settings, e.g. 'Approval required', which you can never change as a user. If they are to be changed, they must be changed in the profile. There are also certain settings, which you can change, if 'profile changeable' is ticked.

By experimenting with the settings, you can make the user interface better suited to your needs and likings. If you want to understand the data entry profile in greater detail, you may like to study chapter 36.2.

36.1.4 Screen Layout and Personalization

Layout of CATS screen

One of the most important things you define in a profile is the set of fields which are available for entry. The power of CATS lies in its ability to capture every possible piece of information you can associate with an employee's time, no matter in which module of SAP it is needed. In CATS, you can record data about the following:

> Employee attendances and absences, for use in time management.
> Employee remuneration for use in payroll.
> Activity allocation for use in controlling.
> Confirmations for use in plant maintenance, project system or customer service.
> External services for use in external services management.
> Travel expenses for use in travel management.

Depending on your requirements, your consultant sets up one or more profiles, ensuring that in each profile, the employee sees only those fields, which he needs to fill. He also sets up field properties, e.g. display, input and mandatory. This simplifies the interface for the user and reduces data entry errors.

In your profile it is specified whether your data entry screen is for daily/weekly/semimonthly/monthly data entry. If you are doing weekly data entry, the day on which the week starts can also be specified. You can also scroll the time period forward or backward.

Changing layout of CATS screen

You can drag and drop a column to change its position. You can also reduce or enlarge the column width, or hide the column completely by making its width zero. You can save your settings by clicking on ▥.

36.1.5 Data Entry and Release

Icon	Description
▣▣	You can use these icons to change the period. Your data entry profile determines how many periods you can go forward and backward.
Σ	In data entry area, you may want to see total hours for each day. This line can be displayed or hidden by clicking on this icon.
�🕐	One would like to see completeness of time recording by comparing total recorded hours with hours the employee is expected to work. The hours an employee is expected to work is called target hours. You can display or hide the target hours line by clicking on this icon. For more details of target hours, you may see chapter 36.2, 'Data Entry Profile'.

(Contd.)

Icon	Description
	You have a choice of seeing the days either as dates or as weekdays (Monday, Tuesday, etc.). Using this icon, you can switch from one mode to the other.
	If you click on this icon, you see details of the full line.
	If you want to store some information about the time recorded, you can do so by clicking on this icon.
	You can click on this icon to enter travel information, provided it has been set up for you.
	The data you enter needs to be consistent with other data you have entered, as well as with the data that has been entered earlier in the system. When you save the data, these checks are carried out. You can use this icon to perform these checks anytime.
	When you perform data entry check, it creates a log. You can access this log by clicking on this icon.

	Not a workday according to calendar
12.34	Hours - without additional information
12.34	Hours - with additional information
12.34	Hours - rejected

Icon	Description
	This icon shows you the meaning of different colors on your screen.
	Your data entry screen is customized to your requirements in your data entry profile. By clicking on this icon, you can see these settings. You can even change some of them. If you want to understand what each setting means, you may see chapter 36.2, 'Data Entry Profile'.
	If you choose a line with account assignment, and click on this icon, remaining target hours are copied in that line.
	If you select a cell and click on this icon (split row), a new row is created with same account assignment, but without any time data (in the case of copy row, even time data is copied).
	You can use this icon to save the current information as personal template.
	You can use this icon to delete your personal template.

Cell information

If you are in a time data entry cell, and press F2 (Edit ≻ Choose), you see the following screen. This lets you see information which cannot be shown in a cell due to space constraint.

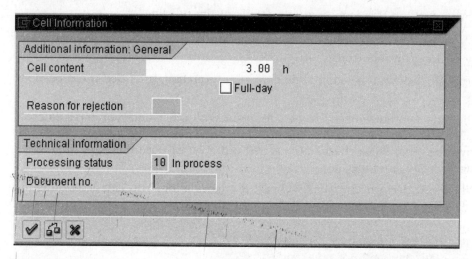

Copy target hours

If you choose a line with account assignments, and click on Edit ≻ Propose times ≻ Target hours, remaining target hours are copied in that line.

Distribute hours

If you click on Edit ≻ Propose times ≻ Distribute hours, you get the following screen:

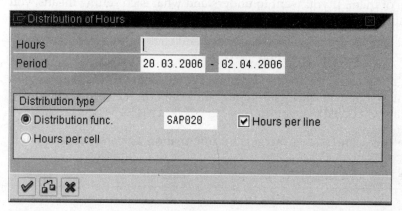

Here you can copy a given number of hours in all the cells of a given period, or distribute specified number of hours in a given period. Note that the hours are distributed only among those days where target hours are non-zero. Also, the distribution is limited to a maximum of planned hours in the case of absences. If you plan to use different distribution functions, you must understand from your consultant how each one behaves.

Hiding off days

You may not want to see the off days of your company in time sheet. This requires that plant is maintained in infotype 0315 record, and a factory calendar is associated with the plant. If these prerequisites are met, you can hide the off days in time sheet by clicking on Edit ➢ Days Off On/Off.

Views

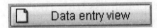

The data entry view is the view you use to enter data in time sheet.

Your data entry process may sometimes be interrupted, and you may like to save your entries. At the same time, you don't want them to be processed further. SAP provides you a two-step process; in step 1 you save the data, and in step 2 you release it.

However, for some users, the interruption may not be frequent, and they would prefer that as soon as they save the data, it be released. In doing so, they accept that if their data entry is interrupted, they will not save, and thereby lose, the data. The checkbox 'Release on saving' in your data entry profile, lets you choose between the two alternatives.

If you are using the two-step process, you use release view to release data that you have entered, but not yet released. You select the cell, or lines, you want to release, and then click on the release icon 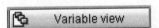. Before releasing, check the data for consistency, and after release, save the data.

If your data needs to go through an approval process, it is triggered when you release the data. Depending on your data entry profile, the approver may be automatically determined by the system, or you may be asked to specify the approver.

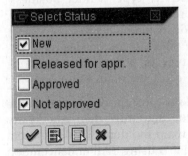

When you click on the variable view icon, you see the dialog box given below. You can use this view to filter the data you want to see.

Predecessor

If you correct the time sheet after the data has been approved or transferred to the interface tables, a new record is created. The new original record and its predecessor are linked and stored in the database table for the time sheet. The predecessor is transferred as a cancellation document.

Travel expenses

You can use the time sheet to enter working times you spent on a business trip. You can branch directly from the screen where you process working times to the component where you maintain trip data.

Material withdrawal

You may have used material during an activity for which you are entering working times. By branching directly to the materials management (MM) component, you can post a material withdrawal.

36.1.6   Data Entry Aids

Skipping initial screen

If you are entering your own data, you may like to skip the initial screen. Ask your consultant to tick 'No initial screen' in your profile. You need to maintain default data entry profile in user parameter CVR, and default personnel number in user parameter PER (alternatively, you maintain subtype 0001 of infotype 0105, linking personnel number to user id).

Additional data in initial screen

You can use the SAP enhancement CATS0007 to allow users to enter data on the initial screen that applies to all time sheet records.

Default values

Since CATS is primarily for data entry, it is important to make this process efficient. Default values help reduce data entry time. SAP provide infotype 0315, which can be used to maintain default values of sender cost center, activity type, sender business process, vendor, sending purchase order, sending purchase order item and service number. Apart from maintaining infotype 0315, your profile also needs to enable them. Controlling area and cost center can also be picked up from infotype 0001, if you so desire. Your profile also contains either a default attendance/absence type or a default wage type. Maintaining one of them in profile is mandatory and you can't maintain both.

You can also get default values for personnel number and data entry profile, as described in 'Skipping initial screen'. Normally, default values are proposed only when you create a new record and not when you are changing data. If you want the default values to be proposed during change also, your consultant can implement it using SAP enhancement CATS0002.

If default values are available from multiple sources, the highest priority is to infotype 0315, then to infotype 0001, followed by work center or activity and finally from CATS0002.

You can also get default values based on task type, task component and task level. These are defined in the configuration. BAdI CATS_DERIVATIVES can change the values coming from configuration.

Worklist

Another method of reducing effort in entering time data is by providing a worklist, which contains the data an employee is most likely to enter. Your profile must enable worklist and define its content. A worklist can be used only if you are entering data for a single personnel number, and not for multiple personnel numbers.

Often people work on the same project for many days. The data you entered a few days back is an excellent source to copy from. In each profile you can define how many days data is shown in the worklist, so as to avoid unnecessary cluttering of the worklist.

If an employee has been assigned some work in logistics modules of SAP that can be shown in the worklist. If an employee is assigned to a work center, the operations performed in that work center are displayed in his worklist. The worklist can also display data from the pool of confirmations, if the employee specifies the name of the confirmations pool in settings in the initial screen or in data entry screen.

Your consultants can also write your organization specific logic to determine what is shown in the worklist. This can be done using the SAP enhancement CATS0001 (Set Up Worklist) or using the Business Add-In (BAdI) CATS_WORKLIST_ADDIN.

Using the copy function, users can transfer data from the worklist to the data entry section. When you copy from worklist, usually you would copy the data without hours. However, if you were copying data from planning, it would make sense to copy the data with hours. You can make the choice of copying with or without hours in settings.

Just as the layout of your data entry screen is customized to your requirements, so also is the layout of your worklist.

Personal templates

If you do the same kind of work repeatedly, every time you are entering the same information except for time worked, which may be different. In such a situation, you can save account assignment rows entered in the data entry area as a personal template (Extras ➤ Save as Template). If a personal template already exists, the system overwrites it with the new one.

Whenever you go to a new period, the personal template is displayed. You can have a personal template for each profile. So, if you are using a different profile, you can have a different personal template.

You can use program RCATSTMP to define any user's existing personal template as the standard template for a particular data entry profile. If a user has not created a personal template, the system uses the standard template when the user accesses time recording using this data entry profile.

You can delete your personal template (Extras ➤ Delete Template). If you delete your personal template, the standard template gets reactivated.

36.1.7 Data Validation

Collision

It makes no sense to enter data which is contradictory, e.g. full day attendance and full day absence for the same day. If you were to enter such a data, your profile determines whether to give error, warning, or no message? The collision can be checked both with CATS records as well as with HR records.

Working for more than 24 hours in a day

Should the system accept if an employee records more than 24 hours for a day? Should the system give error, warning, or no message? If you want the data to be transferred to HR, you cannot enter more than 24 hours (regardless of whether or not it is allowed in CATS). The number of hours entered is reduced to the maximum working time permitted per day.

Target hours

When you are recording time in CATS, should it not be cross-checked against the time you recorded on the company's attendance recording system? However, there may be complexities. For example, you may have worked part of the day outside the company's premises, for which the time may not have been recorded on the attendance recording system.

SAP provides a flexible solution. You define the logic for determining target hours in time evaluation and fill a time type. CATS shows the target hours from that time type. If you don't specify any time type, the system picks up target hours from the planned hours.

If your employees apply for leave directly in SAP HR (time management), then they should not be entering the same data in CATS. In that case, your profile specifies that HR hours should be subtracted while determining target hours.

Should overtime entered in infotype 2005 be added to the target hours? You may take care of it while filling the time type for target hours in time evaluation, or you may choose to add it directly. This is specified in the profile.

What should happen if the hours, recorded by an employee in CATS, differ from target hours? Should you accept it, reject it, or accept it if it is within certain tolerance? In your profile both the tolerance and reaction is specified. They are specified independently for over-recording (recorded hours are more than target hours) and under-recording (recorded hours are less than target hours).

Absences cannot exceed target hours. If you enter an absence, which is more than the target hours, it is reduced to target hours. If you are recording clock times, an absence must be within the employee's planned working time.

Insufficient quota

When you enter an absence or attendance, it may result in deduction from quota. If you do not have sufficient quota, the system does not let you create the absence or attendance record. This check can take place at the time of data entry in CATS itself.

Locked period

When CATS data is posted to controlling, time data must be recorded before the period is closed. Although it is possible to change the posting date, some organizations discourage such a practice and require their employees to record their time promptly. If your organization has such a policy, you may get an error message, if you try to record time for a date, whose period is closed.

Special checks

SAP also lets you define your own checks in CATS0003 (validate recorded data) and CATS0006 (validate entire time sheet).

Data entry for future

Your profile determines whether data for future can be released. This is useful when you apply for leave in advance, which need approval before you actually take leave.

36.1.8 Data Entry for Several Personnel Numbers

CATS is often used by employees for recording their own time data. However, CATS can also be used for central data recording, where a secretary, supervisor or administrator record data for other employees. These are appropriately controlled through authorizations.

In such a scenario, the user may want to enter data of multiple employees at the same time. This can be set in your profile. There are four ways in which employees can be displayed in your initial screen, from which you may select the employees whose data you want to enter. For each of these, you need to maintain the user parameters, as given below:

Time administrator	SGR (Administrator group)
	SAZ (Time administrator)
Organizational unit	PON (Object ID–PD)
Cost center	CAC (Controlling area)
	KOS (Cost center)
Selection report	VSR (Personnel number selection report variant)

From the initial screen, you can either choose a single personnel number or choose multiple personnel numbers. If you choose a single personnel number, the screen is same as that for your own data.

In case you select multiple personnel numbers, the screen shows existing data for all personnel numbers. If there is no existing data, only target and totals line is shown. You enter data at the bottom. The system automatically transfers the line below the summary of appropriate personnel number.

Data Entry Period	13.03.2006 - 19.03.2006	☑ ☑	Week	11.2006

Data Entry Area

	LT	Pers.No.	A/A...	Wa...	MO ...	TU ...	WE ...	TH ...	FR ...	SA ...	SU ...
	🕐	125962			8.00	8.00	8.00	0.00	8.00	8.00	8.00
	Σ	125962			4.00	0.00	0.00	0.00	0.00	0.00	0.00
		125962	10		4.00						
	🕐	125866			8.00	8.00	8.00	0.00	8.00	8.00	8.00
	Σ	125866			8.00	4.00	0.00	0.00	0.00	0.00	0.00
		125866	M0		8.00	4.00					
		125866		1560		3.00					

36.1.9   Approval, Rejection, Cancellation

In normal course, you would enter data and release it. It will then get approved. After that the data is ready for transfer to other modules of SAP. In certain cases, release may take place on saving, and in some cases approval may not be required.

At the same time, you may have contingency processes. You may want to change or delete data, which may be unreleased, released or approved. Your request for approval may be rejected. SAP handles these by keeping a status for every record.

Whenever you save time sheet data, it creates a record in table CATSDB. For each cell of time data, which is for a personnel number a date and working time characteristics, a record is created, which contains the time data and its attributes. Each record also has a processing status. How the processing status of a record changes is explained below.

Processing status	Action	Release on saving	Approval required	Processing status
In process	Change			In process
In process	Save	No		In process
In process	Save	Yes	Yes	Released for approval
In process	Save	Yes	No	Approved
In process	Release		Yes	Released for approval
In process	Release		No	Approved

(Contd.)

Processing status	Action	Release on saving	Approval required	Processing status
Released for approval	Approve			Approved
Released for approval	Reject			Rejected
Released for approval	Change			In process
Approved	Change			In process + Changed after approval
Approval rejected	Change			In process
Changed after approval	Approve			Cancelled

When an approved document is changed, it marks the original record as 'changed after approval' and creates a new record with 'in process' status. When the new record is approved, the approver acknowledges that the earlier approved record, which is currently 'changed after approval', is no longer valid, and hence its status is changed to 'cancelled'. A cancelled document cannot change further.

Dummy infotype 0328 represents the authorization for reporting and approval. You can use transactions CATS_APPR_LITE–Approve Working Times and ACTEXP_APPR_LITE– Approve Working Times and Travel Expenses, to approve time sheet entries.

36.1.10 Data Transfer

When a time sheet record is approved or cancelled, apart from creating/updating an entry in CATSDB, it also creates entries in the following interface tables. The system determines which interface tables are relevant based on the record's working time attributes.

> ➤ Human Resources (PTEX2000, PTEX2010 and others)
> ➤ Controlling (CATSCO)
> ➤ Plant Maintenance/Customer Service (CATSPM)
> ➤ Project System (CATSPS)
> ➤ Materials Management (CATSMM)

This gives you flexibility to transfer data to respective module when you desire. If the data was transferred immediately, it could cause performance problems. Also, if the data could not be transferred because a record is locked, for example, the employee will not be able to do time recording at all.

A two-step process gives you more flexibility and control. However, it also creates a potential that the status of the target system might change causing problem in data transfer. For example, if an absence record is created in HR time management after the data for the same date is entered in the time sheet, it will result in collision when you attempt to transfer time sheet data.

For HR, if you wish to do immediate data transfer, you can tick 'Immediate transfer to HR' in the data entry profile. For transferring data to HR, you can use transaction CAT6. You get the following selection screen.

Transfer Time Data to HR Time Management

⊕	🅷

Processing Control

Mode   ⦿ Backgr   ○ Fore   ○ Error   ○ Direct

✔	Initial Transfer	Repeat Transfer	Transfer/Delete
	Delete Only	Lock/Unlock	

Data Selection for Initial Transfer

Personnel number		to		⇨
Date		to		⇨
Customer field		to		⇨

Infotypes

☑ Attendances/absences
☑ EE remuneration info
☑ Substitutions

Other Data

☑ Output log
☐ Send mail
☑ Test run

Using 'Initial Transfer', you can transfer data to appropriate infotypes. You can execute a test run to see the data that would be transferred. When you execute actual transfer, appropriate infotype records are created in HR. The system also updates transfer details in tables PTEX2000 and PTEX2010.

You can perform a repeat transfer if there was problem in transfer of some data records. The system does not select the records which were transferred successfully. However, if you explicitly specify that even those records, which were successfully transferred, should also be transferred (by ticking 'Last retrieval successful'), the system attempts to transfer even those records. However, if the corresponding records already exist in HR time management, it results in collision, and the transfer is unsuccessful. Hence, this option should be used only if the data in HR has got deleted for some reason.

Since the data in interface tables is only for the purpose of data transfer to the respective module, after successful data transfer the data should be deleted. You can do that here too. The system takes care not to delete records, which are not successfully transferred.

SAP also provides a report RCATSRIF (Reorganize Time Sheet Interface Tables), which deletes time sheet data that has already been transferred to the target components from the interface tables. If your time sheet data is transferred to multiple target components, you may want to use this report. If your data needs to be transferred only to HR, this report is optional. It is executed via transaction CATR.

36.1.11 Checking Time Sheet

You would like to ensure that your employees are

➢ Recording time, if they are expected to.
➢ Not recording more time than they worked.
➢ Not recording less time than they worked.

You can perform these checks using transaction CATC—Time Leveling. If there are employees whose time sheets are inconsistent, you can notify them automatically by mail. You can schedule the report as a background job that sends mails automatically. Since all employees may not be required to do time recording, you can maintain which employees are required to do time recording in infotype 0315. When you run transaction CATC, you can restrict the checking to only these employees. There are several options in the selection screen, which can be used to correctly identify the population and to restrict your search to key offenders. You may see program documentation for more information.

36.1.12 Different User Interfaces of CATS

There are two basic variants of CATS

➢ CATS classic
➢ CATS for service providers

They offer different layouts, even though the basic data entered remains the same. Apart from these, there are some variants of CATS classic, depending on the device used. These are:

➢ CATS regular (for employee self service)
➢ CATS notebook (for employees recording time on PC notebook in offline mode)
➢ CATS instant (for recording from portal)
➢ CATS phone (for recording from phone)

CATS instant and CATS phone have limited functionality. Through them, you can make basic entry, but cannot do everything that is possible through CATS classic, regular or CATS for service providers.

There is also CATS calendar. It displays for which days you still need to enter time data. By clicking on a week in the calendar, you are taken to CATS regular for data entry. The information displayed in the CATS calendar depends on the settings you make in the ALERT variant of the RCATSCMP program.

36.1.13 CATS for Service Providers

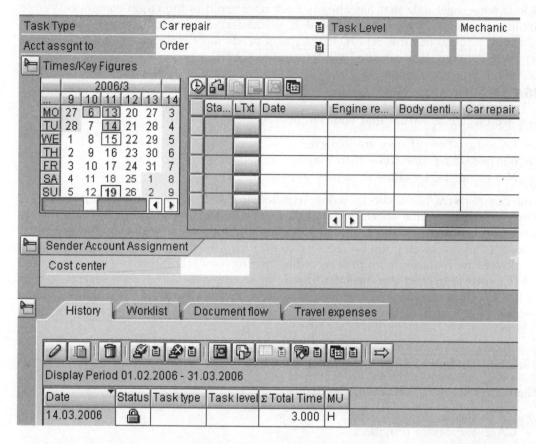

CATS for service providers offers a user interface which is completely different from CATS classic. Here the focus is on entering the quantum of service provided. The service may be in terms of hours spent or may be in completely different units, e.g. distance traveled, weight carried, etc.

The key concepts here are task type, task level and task component. You basically record different types of task performed and the level at which they were performed. Once these are specified, the system shows you various components of the task you could perform, and you enter date wise quantities. These quantities would be in different units, which are determined by combination of task type, task level and task component.

You also specify the account assignment, which applies to all the entries. You also have sender account assignment. You can copy data from history or worklist, and see document flow and travel expenses.

When you open CATS for service provider, you find that it looks same as when you closed it. This is because the system automatically saves your settings, e.g. which subscreens were open, etc., and uses it when you open the screen again. The settings determine how your system behaves. You can click on the settings icon and change some of the settings. If you save the settings, they are always used until you change them again.

Unlike CATS classic, in CATS for service provider, data entry profile is determined based on task type and employee characteristics.

When you enter data for a day, that date in the calendar is shown in light green highlight. When the data is saved, it is shown in dark green. Red color indicates non-working day.

You can use transaction CATSXT to record own working times and CATSXT_ADMIN to record own and other employees' working times.

36.1.14 Reports

Display working times (CATS_DA)

You can use this report to display working time data. This report is suitable for data entered through CATS classic and similar user interfaces. You can pick up employees based on organizational structure or other groups (using search help). There are also many other selection parameters to filter records displayed. You can also select the fields you want displayed.

Display working times and tasks (CATSXT_DA)

You can use this report to display working time data. This report is suitable for data entered through CATS for service provider.

Working times and tasks: Display details (CATSXT_DTL)

This report displays detailed data for working times. This report is suitable for data entered through CATS for service provider.

Display single documents (CAT8)

You can use this report to access data records saved in the database table for the time sheet (CATSDB).

36.2 DATA ENTRY PROFILE

Functional Consultant	User	Business Process Owner	Senior Management	My Rating	Understanding Level
A	C	X	X		

36.2.1 Purpose

Data Entry Profile is among the most critical settings for CATS. The interface that a user gets depends on it. For a data entry profile, you define what fields are available to users, and what are their properties. Some of the settings shown here do not apply to CATS for service providers. If you go to appropriate nodes in configuration, you see the applicable view. However, the concepts remain the same.

36.2.2 IMG Node

SM30 ➤ TCATS/V_TCATSXC

36.2.3 Primary Key

Data Entry Profile

36.2.4 Important Fields

Data Entry Profile	HR-DATA	Data Entry Profile for HR

General settings

- ☐ Profile changeable
- ☐ With target hours
- ☐ With totals line
- ☐ With clock times
- ☐ No Deductn of Breaks
- ☐ Highlight rej. recs
- ☐ Highlight addnl info
- ☐ Workdays only
- ☐ Display weekdays
- ☐ No initial screen
- ☐ Release future times
- ☐ Release on saving
- ☐ No changes after approval

Cell length

Trip schema

Authorization

Print program

Profile changeable

If you tick this checkbox, the user can change the profile through settings icon. However, he cannot change sensitive settings, e.g. approval required.

With target hours

If you tick this checkbox, the target hours are displayed in a separate line marked with a symbol 🕐 in the data entry section.

With totals line

If you tick this checkbox, the system shows day wise total hours in a line marked with a symbol Σ. While computing total hours, hours recorded against wage type are not considered.

With clock times

If you wish to record start time and end time instead of hours, you tick this checkbox. The system automatically computes hours after taking into account unpaid breaks from the daily work schedule.

No deduction of breaks

If you do not wish to subtract unpaid breaks while computing hours from clock times, tick this checkbox.

Highlight rejected records

If you tick this checkbox, rejected records are highlighted. By double-clicking on the field, you can correct the number of hours in the rejected record.

Highlight additional information

If you tick this checkbox, the system highlights the records for which there is additional information.

Workdays only

If you tick this checkbox, you can enter data only for workdays as per factory calendar, which is determined from the plant specified for the employee in infotype 0315.

Display weekdays

If you tick this checkbox, the system displays the day of the week (e.g. Monday), in addition to the date.

No initial screen

Usually the system displays an initial screen, where you enter the profile, personnel number and key date. If you are entering your own data, you may like to skip this screen. You can do that by ticking this checkbox and by providing defaults for these fields as under:

Data entry profile	You maintain default data entry profile in user parameter CVR.
Personnel number	You maintain default personnel number in user parameter PER. Alternatively, you maintain subtype 0001 of infotype 0105, linking personnel number to user id.
Key date	By default this is usually the system date. However, the default can be set to a different value using the profile field 'Start date relative'.

Release future times

This determines whether data for future can be released. This is useful when you apply for leave in advance which needs approval before you actually take leave.

Release on saving

When you release data, you indicate that the data is complete and correct. It can be used for further processing. If you want to enter data, save incomplete data, check it and release after you are satisfied, you don't tick this checkbox. This gives you greater flexibility, but requires you to explicitly release the data. If you tick this checkbox, the data is released on saving. In such a scenario, if your data entry is incomplete, you should not save the data, thereby losing the data you entered.

No changes after approval

If you tick this checkbox, the approved records cannot be changed.

Cell length

Default length of the cells in the time sheet is 4. Here you can change that to any value from 4 to 20.

Trip schema

If you enter travel data from time sheet, this trip schema is used.

Authorization

You can group several data entry profiles in a profile authorization group. A user is assigned a role which contains his profile authorization group in infotype 0316. The user can use any profile from that group.

Print program

You may want to print the time sheet. SAP provides a standard program (RCATSP01) for this purpose. However, if you want to use your own program, you can specify that here.

Time settings				
Period type	2	Weekly data entry	Periods	2
First day of week		Monday		
Start date relative		Lower limit relative	Upper limit relative	

Period type

It determines how often users should enter data in the time sheet. The following options are available:

➢ Daily data entry
➢ Weekly data entry
➢ Semimonthly data entry
➢ Monthly data entry

First day of week

When you are doing weekly data entry, you can specify the day on which the week starts. If you leave it blank, the week starts on Monday.

Periods

For daily and weekly period types only, the number of times the 'period type' is repeated on the data entry screen.

Start date relative

The period, for which the data entry screen is shown, depends on the key date. The period contains the key date. By default, the key date is system date. However, you can change this default to give a past or future date.

Period type	Value	Key date
Daily and weekly period	Blank	System date
Daily and weekly period	1+	System date + 1
Daily and weekly period	1–	System date – 1
Semimonthly and monthly period	Blank	First day of the current period
Semimonthly and monthly period	1+	First day of the next period
Semimonthly and monthly period	1–	First day of the last period

Lower limit relative, upper limit relative

Next to the data entry period, you see [icons]. Lower limit relative indicates how many times you can scroll to the left and upper limit relative indicates how many times you can scroll to the right.

```
Person selection
  ☐ Enter for several personnel nos
  ☐ Select via pers. list
  ◉ Time administrator      ○ Organizational unit      ○ Cost center
  ○ Selection report       [                                    ]
```

If you want to enter data in CATS for only one person, you leave this sub-screen blank. If you want to enter data in CATS for several persons, you specify that here.

Enter for several personnel numbers

If you tick this checkbox, you can enter data in CATS for several persons at the same time. Note that if you select this option, you cannot use worklist.

Select via personnel list

If you are allowed to enter data in CATS for several persons, you tick this check box. Note that it is possible to have this checkbox ticked and the previous checkbox un-ticked. In that case, you get a list of personnel numbers, but you can select only one at a time to enter time data.

Source of personnel list

SAP provides you four options to determine the list of personnel numbers from which you select one. If you select selection report, you specify the report name here. If you leave this field blank, the system uses the standard report RPLFST01. Depending on your choice, you need to maintain the following user parameters.

Time administrator	SGR (Administrator group)
	SAZ (Time administrator)
Organizational unit	PON (Object ID–PD)
Cost center	CAC (Controlling area)
	KOS (Cost center)
Selection report	VSR (Personnel number selection report variant)

Approval procedure

Here you specify whether data entered using this data entry profile requires approval, does not require approval, or requires approval only in exceptional cases. If data requires approval only in exceptional cases, the logic to identify the data requiring approval is built in feature CATEX for 'Rules for special approval', and a group of such rules is specified in the data entry profile.

Immediate transfer to HR

Time data entered in CATS is usually transferred to SAP HR time management. By ticking this checkbox, you automate this transfer process. However, immediate transfer to HR takes place only for the data that does not require approval.

With SAP business workflow

If you tick this checkbox, the approval procedure is triggered using workflow specified in the field 'Task'.

With automatic determination of recipient

If you tick this checkbox, the system selects the recipient of the approval workflow automatically.

Task

If the workflow requires an approval, the approver is determined based on the task specified here. SAP provides three single step tasks to choose from.

TS31000004	CATS ApprovalYou may use this workflow if you want the employee to select the approver manually, or if it is determined using SAP enhancement CATS0008. If you are using this workflow, you should not select the checkbox 'With Auto. Determination of Recipient'.
TS31000006	CATS Approval by Time AdministratorYou may use this workflow if you want the CATS data to be approved by the time administrator of the employee. If you are using this workflow, you should select the checkbox 'With Auto. Determination of Recipient'. You also need to maintain user parameters SGR (Administrator Group (HR)) and SAZ (Time Data Administrator).
TS31000007	CATS Approval by SupervisorYou may use this workflow if you want the CATS data to be approved by the line manager of the employee. The line manager is determined from the organizational structure. If you are using this workflow, you should select the checkbox 'With Auto. Determination of Recipient'.

If you use BADI_CATS_APPROVAL along with a workflow, the data for which BADI_CATS_APPROVAL is able to determine recipients are sent to those recipients. If BAdI is not able to determine a recipient, the recipient determined by the workflow is used. This design can be used to determine approver for certain data based on the attributes of the data, and for the remaining data based on the employee entering the data.

```
Cost accounting variant
⦿ Assignmnt of personnel costs to master cost center
◯ Assignment of personnel costs to receiver object
◯ Assignment of personnel costs to sender
◯ Activity allocation master/sender
☐ Acct assgmt to acty type
```

Cost accounting variant

Here you specify where the personnel costs are assigned. If the 'Assignment of personnel costs to the receiver object' indicator is set, you cannot use default values for the sender cost center and activity type.

If you select activity allocation, the checkbox 'Account assignment to activity type' can also be set. If you want to use default activity type, do not tick this checkbox. If you want to enter activity type while entering time data in CATS, you select this checkbox.

Default values		
☐ Controlling area	☐ Master cost center	☐ Cost center
☐ Activity type	☐ Sender bus. process	
☐ Purchase order	☐ Service master	☐ Wage type
☐ Att./absence type		

Since CATS is primarily for data entry, it is important to make this process efficient. Default values help reduce data entry time. In this section of data entry profile, you set the default values, which are proposed by the system, when one is entering data in CATS.

Controlling area

If you tick this checkbox, default controlling area for the personnel number is determined from infotype 0001.

Master cost center

If you tick this checkbox, default sender cost center for the personnel number is determined from infotype 0001. You can overwrite the value if required.

Cost center

If you tick this checkbox, default sender cost center for the personnel number is determined from infotype 0315. You can overwrite the value if required.

Activity type

If you tick this checkbox, default activity type for the personnel number is determined from infotype 0315. You can overwrite the value if required.

Sender business process

If you tick this checkbox, default sender business process for the personnel number is determined from infotype 0315. You can overwrite the value if required.

Purchase order

If you tick this checkbox, default purchase order for the personnel number is determined from infotype 0315. You can overwrite the value if required.

Service master

If you tick this checkbox, default service number for the personnel number is determined from infotype 0315. You can overwrite the value if required.

Wage type

If you tick this checkbox, and specify wage type, the same is proposed in CATS. You can overwrite the value if required.

Attendance/absence type

If you tick this checkbox and specify attendance/absence type, the same is proposed in CATS. You can overwrite the value if required. You have to specify either default attendance/absence type or default wage type, and you cannot specify both.

Worklist		
☐ With worklist	☐ In Process	In proc. since ⬜ Days
☐ From resource plng	☐ By work center	☐ Workdays only
☐ From pool of confs	☐ Customer enhancement	☐ From Project Assignment
☐ Copy without hours		

Another method of reducing effort in entering time data is by providing a worklist, which contains the data an employee is most likely to enter.

With worklist

This is the basic switch which activates the worklist. A worklist can be used only if you are entering data for a single personnel number and not for multiple personnel numbers.

In process and since

Through these fields, you can specify that the user is shown data which he has already entered in the system, and which he can copy from. If you do not specify anything in 'since' field, only current day's data is shown. Specifying a positive number results in worklist containing past data of that many days. A negative number shows future data.

From resource planning

If you have assigned some work to an employee in logistics modules of SAP, that is shown in the worklist.

By work center

If an employee is assigned to a work center, the operations performed in that work center are displayed in his worklist.

Workdays only

This field determines whether the hours displayed in the worklist should be distributed for workdays only, or whether non-workdays should also be included.

From pool of confirmations

This field determines whether the time sheet worklist displays data from the pool of confirmations. Users must specify the name of the confirmations pool they want to display in settings, either on the initial screen or inside the time sheet.

Customer enhancement

If you select this option, the worklist is set up using the SAP enhancement CATS0001.

From project assignment

You select this option to specify that the data from projects is to be displayed in the worklist of the time sheet.

Copy without hours

If you tick this checkbox, hours are not copied.

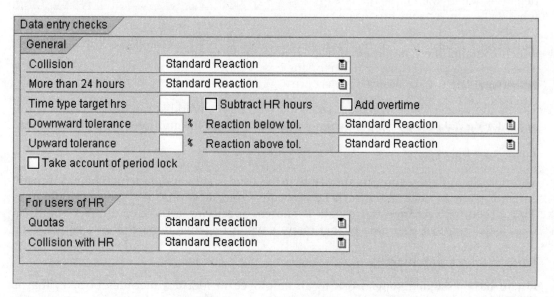

Collision

If there is collision between time data, e.g. full day attendance and full day absence for the same day, should the system give error, warning, or no message? Note that this is collision check within CATS records only, and not with HR records.

More than 24 hours

Should the system accept if an employee records more than 24 hours for a day? Should the system give error, warning or no message? If you want the data to be transferred to HR, you cannot enter more than 24 hours (regardless of whether or not you select this field). The number of hours entered is reduced to the maximum working time permitted per day.

Time type target hours

Here you specify the time type (usually 0050) from which target hours are to be picked. If you don't specify any time type, the system uses the planned hours.

Subtract HR hours

Should the employees apply for leave also through CATS, or is that data entered in SAP HR (time management) directly? In the former case, you should not subtract HR hours. In the latter, you should, because the employee is not required to enter this data in CATS.

Add overtime

If you tick this field, overtime from infotype 2005 is added to the target hours. You must decide whether the employee is expected to account for overtime or not. If yes, decide whether it comes from time type or directly from infotype 2005 through this tick.

Downward tolerance (%), reaction below downward tolerance

These two fields determine what happens if an employee does not account for the target hours fully. In the downward tolerance (%), you specify acceptable tolerance, and in reaction, you specify whether the system gives error, warning, or no message.

Upward tolerance (%), reaction above upward tolerance

These two fields determine what happens if an employee records more than the target hours. In the upward tolerance (%), you specify acceptable tolerance and in reaction, you specify whether the system gives error, warning or no message.

Take account of period lock

The data you enter in CATS may be used for costing. In costing, each document has a posting date. The posting date of the document created from CATS is the same as the date for which you entered data. Further, in costing, each period is closed for posting after a certain date. If an employee entered data for a very old date, the posting document would have the same date. When you post this document, the period would be closed and you would not be able to post the document.

There are two ways of handling this. One is to discipline your employees. If you tick this checkbox, they would not be able to enter data for a period which is already closed in costing. Once it happens a few times, the employees would learn to do it in time. The second approach is to change the posting date in the transfer program RCATSTCO (Transfer to Controlling) manually.

Insufficient quota

When you enter an absence, or attendance, it may result in deduction from quota. In the case of insufficient quota, the system does not let you create the absence, or attendance, record. If you tick this field, this check is carried out when you enter data in CATS as well. It is recommended that you specify error here, because otherwise you can not transfer CATS data to SAP HR time management.

Collision with HR records

If there is collision between CATS data and HR data, should the system give error, warning or no message? It is recommended that you specify error here, because otherwise you cannot transfer CATS data to SAP HR time management.

36.3 SCREEN LAYOUT

Functional Consultant	User	Business Process Owner	Senior Management	My Rating	Understanding Level
B	X	X	X		

36.3.1 Purpose and Overview

When you want to enter data in time sheet, you get a layout. This layout depends on the profile you are using and is defined in this node. You specify the layout at two levels. At global level, you specify which fields you are going to use and what are their properties. These settings are applicable to all profiles. At profile level, you can further restrict these settings. For example, a field, which is displayed at global level, can be hidden at profile level. However, you cannot give more authorization at profile level. You cannot display a field, which is hidden at global level.

Apart from the layout for the data entry, you can also specify the layout of a worklist here in screen group 'Worklist'.

General behaviour of your screen is defined in profile. One of the parameters in your profile says whether you can change it. If you are allowed to change the settings you may do so either in the initial screen or in the time sheet (Goto ➢ Settings). Even if you are allowed to change the settings, there are certain settings you cannot change, e.g. approval required. If you want to further restrict change in setting by the employee, you can do so in screen group 'settings' in this node.

You can add your own fields in addition to the fields provided by SAP.

36.3.2 IMG Node

Cross-Application Components ➢ Time Sheet ➢ Settings for All User Interfaces ➢ Time Recording ➢ Choose Fields

Transaction CAC2   Time Sheet: Field Selection

36.3.3 Screen

Screen Grp
Settings
Worklist
Data entry section

Screen group   Data entry section

Modifiable fields

Modifiable field	Field name	Input	Req.	Disp.	Hide	HiLi
Controlling Area	CATSD-KOKRS	○	○	◉	○	☐
Cost Center	CATSFIELDS-HDRKOSTL	◉	○	○	○	☐
Currency	CATSD-WAERS	○	○	○	◉	☐
Description	CATSFIELDS-KOSTLLT...	○	◉	○	○	☐
Det. status auto.	CATSFIELDS-AUSTAT	○	○	○	◉	☐

Screen group	Data entry section
Influencing field	Data Entry Profile
Contents	HR-ONLY

Modified fields

Modifiable field	Field name	Input	Req.	Disp.	Hide	HiLi
Att./Absence type	CATSD-AWART	◉	○	○	○	☐
Capacity Category	CATSD-KAPAR	○	○	○	◉	☐
Controlling Area	CATSD-KOKRS	◉	○	○	○	☐
Cost Center	CATSFIELDS-HDRKOSTL	○	○	○	◉	☐
Currency	CATSD-WAERS	◉	○	○	○	☐
Description	CATSFIELDS-KOSTLLT...	◉	○	○	○	☐

36.3.4 Customer Fields

No	Field	Name

You can add to the fields in the database table for the Time Sheet (CATSDB) by defining your own fields in Customer Field Enhancements (CATS0005). Insert the fields you want to add to the Time Sheet database table into the structure CI_CATSDB. Only the data dictionary types NUMC and CHAR are permitted.

Assign the fields created above to the view TCAFI. You can include up to 10 additional fields in the data entry section. Assign a number from 1 - 10 and specify the name of the field. The number you assign to the additional field corresponds to the number of the customer field in the field selection.

Add customer fields to field selection as described in chapter 36.3.3 and maintain the attributes of these fields (display field, input field, and so on).

You can fill customer field enhancements automatically using the SAP enhancement Supplement Recorded Data (CATS0002), and specify whether they are display-only or ready for input.

36.4 APPROVAL PROCEDURE

Functional Consultant	User	Business Process Owner	Senior Management	My Rating	Understanding Level
B	X	X	X		

36.4.1 Overview

SAP provides you various components so that you can build the approval process as per your requirement. The manner in which SAP addresses the key questions in the approval process are discussed below.

What data needs approval?

In the data entry profile, you specify whether approval is needed for all data, no data, or exceptional data. If approval is needed for exceptional data, the logic to identify the data requiring approval is built in feature CATEX or BADI_CATS_APPROVAL.

Who approves the data?

The approver of data can be determined either based on the employee, or based on the attributes of the data. If the approver is to be determined based on the employee, you specify the workflow task in the data entry profile assigned to the employee. . If the approver is to be determined based on the attributes of the data, you implement BADI_CATS_APPROVAL. If you specify the workflow task and also implement BADI_CATS_APPROVAL, the data for which BADI_CATS_APPROVAL is able to determine approver is sent to those approvers. If BAdI is not able to determine an approver, the approver determined by the workflow is used. This design can be used to determine approver for certain data based on the attributes of the data, and for the remaining data based on the employee entering the data.

Which application is used for the approval process?

You can approve CATS data using program RCATS_APPROVE_ACTIVITIES in the SAP system. BAdI CATS_REPORTING can be used to enhance this program. Alternatively, you may use the 'Approve working times' web application in MSS.

36.4.2 Special Approval

Sometimes you want the critical data entered by the employees to be approved. At the same time, you do not want non-critical data to go through the approval process and create unnecessary load on the approvers. In such a scenario, you can use the special approval functionality provided in CATS. When you use special approval, the system segregates the data into 'approval required' and 'no approval required' categories based on the attributes of the data. The logic for this segregation is built in feature CATEX. If you don't want to define the same set of rules for all employees, you can do that too. You divide your entire logic into a set of rules. In feature CATEX, you build the logic for each rule. You then create rule groups, which are subset of rules, and assign a rule group in each employee's data entry profile. You can also implement BADI_CATS_APPROVAL and write your data segregation logic in it. In this BAdI, apart from segregating the data, you can also decide the approver of the data based on the attributes of the data.

36.4.3 Rules for Special Approval

You can define rules for special approval in view V_CATS_EXC_RULE. This view contains just the list of rules. The logic for segregating the data into 'approval required' and 'no approval required' categories based on the attributes of the data is written in feature CATEX for each rule.

Rule	Description

36.4.4 Logic for Special Approval

Feature CATEX contains the logic for segregating the data into 'approval required' and 'no approval required' categories based on the attributes of the data for each rule.

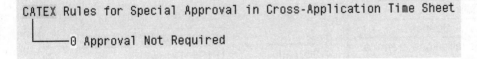

```
CATEX Rules for Special Approval in Cross-Application Time Sheet
  |
  |————0 Approval Not Required
```

36.4.5   Rule Groups for Special Approval

The rule groups for special approval are defined in view cluster VC_CATS_EXC. Each rule group consists of a set of rules. A rule group is specified in the data entry profile of each employee for whom special approval is applicable. This rule group determines the rules which are applicable to the employee.

Dialog Structure	Define Rule Groups	
▽ 🗁 Define Rule Groups	Group	Description
🗀 Link to Rule		

36.4.6   Rejection Reasons

In the approval process, if a record is rejected, you can specify the reason for rejection. Master list of rejection reasons is maintained in view TCATSD. If the long text field is ticked, the approver can further explain why the recorded time is rejected. This is included in the mail sent to the employee (provided 'Send Notification of Rejection' option is active), but not saved.

CATS: Rejection Reasons		
Reason	Text	LT
REJ1	Needed for urgent work	☐
REJ2	Fictitious time booking	☑
REJ3	Too much time taken for the job	☑

36.4.7   Method for Executing UWL Item

If you are not using the web application 'Approve working times' and want to start the HTML version of an approval program; you should delete the entries for the standard tasks TS31000004, TS31000006, TS31000007, TS20000459, TS40007901, and TS20000460 from view cluster SWFVT.

Dialog Structure	Task Visualization	
▽ 🗁 Task Visualization	Task	Visualization Type
🗀 Visualization Parameter	TS00700042	IVIEW iView 🗎
▽ 🗀 Object Visualization	TS00700049	WD_JAVA Java WebDynpro 🗎
🗀 Visualization Parameter	TS00700057	PCOMP Portal Component 🗎
	TS00700059	PCOMP Portal Component 🗎

36.5 NUMBER RANGE INTERVALS FOR CATS

Functional Consultant	User	Business Process Owner	Senior Management	My Rating	Understanding Level
B	X	X	X		

36.5.1 Purpose and Overview

This IMG node covers the following number ranges:

➤ Number range for the document number for the time sheet.
➤ Number range for the internal key for the time sheet.
➤ Number range for the internal key for the task.

36.5.2 IMG Node

Cross-Application components ➤ Time Sheet ➤ Specific Settings for CATS for Service Providers ➤ Define Number Range Intervals

Transaction CAC7   Number Range Maintenance: CATS
Transaction CAC8   Number Range Maintenance: CATS_INTRN
Transaction CAC_XT1   Number Range Maintenance: CATS_XTEND

36.5.3 Screen

Number Range Obj.	Task Counter

Ranges

No	From number	To number	Current number	Ext
1	0000000001	0000999999	0	☐

36.6 DISTRIBUTION FUNCTION, STRATEGY, TYPE

Functional Consultant	User	Business Process Owner	Senior Management	My Rating	Understanding Level
B	X	X	X		

36.6.1 Purpose and Overview

One of the tools provided by SAP, to reduce data entry effort, is 'Distribute Hours'. When you use this facility, you can specify the total hours and the system distributes it in the cells in a line. You can build different logic to do distribution.

You can use distribution function to specify whether you want to distribute equally, or you want to put more hours towards the end, or more hours towards the beginning.

Distribution strategies define whether you want to distribute between earliest or latest dates, whether you want continuous or discrete distribution, and whether you want to use factory calendar, Gregorian calendar or operating time.

A combination of distribution function and distribution strategy is called distribution type, which you specify while distributing time.

36.6.2 Distribution Function

SM34 ➤ VC0C12

Here you specify, during what % duration what % requirement is to be completed.

36.6.3   Distribution Strategy

SM30 ➤ V_TC29S

	Strat	Description	E/L	Type	Basis
	S01	Earliest dates, continuous, Greg. calend	01	01	01
	S02	Earliest dates, continuous, fact. calend	01	01	02
	S03	Earliest dates, continuous, oper. time	01	01	03
	S04	Earliest dates, discrete, Greg. calend.	01	02	01
	S05	Earliest dates, discrete, factory calend	01	02	02
	S06	Earl. dates, discrete, operating time	01	02	03
	S07	Latest dates, continuous, Greg. calendar	02	01	01
	S08	Latest dates, continuous, factory calend	02	01	02
	S09	Lat. dates, continuous, operating time	02	01	03
	S10	Latest dates, discrete, Greg. calendar	02	02	01
	S11	Latest dates, discrete, factory calendar	02	02	02
	S12	Lat. dates, discrete, operating time	02	02	03

Earliest/latest dates

Here you specify whether the time distribution is between earliest dates or between latest dates.

Type of distribution (continuous or discrete)

Here you specify whether the time distribution is continuously through time or according to discrete points.

Basis for distribution (factory calendar/Gregorian calendar)

Here you specify whether the time distribution is according to Gregorian calendar, factory calendar or operating time.

36.6.4   Distribution Type

SM30 ➤ V_TC29

	Distrib.	Description	Strat	Function
	SAP000	Overall load for latest start date	S11	S10
	SAP010	Overall load for earliest start date	S05	S10
	SAP020	Equal distrib. earliest dates, fact.cal.	S02	S20
	SAP030	Equal distrib. latest dates, fact. cal.	S08	S20
	SAP040	Equal distrib. latest dates, discrete	S11	S30
	SAP050	Equal distrib. earliest dates, oper.time	S03	S30
	SAP060	Equal distr. latest dates, operat. time	S09	S20
	SAP070	Overall load at latest finish date	S11	S50

36.7   SUMMARIZATION IN CO DOCUMENTS

Functional Consultant	User	Business Process Owner	Senior Management	My Rating	Understanding Level
B	X	X	X		

36.7.1   Purpose and Overview

Here you define whether CO documents are created at summary level or detailed level.

36.7.2   IMG Node

SM30 ➤ CCATSCOSUM

36.7.3   Screen

- ◉ One CO document per record
- ◯ All data records in one CO document
- ◯ All data records of a personnel number in a CO document
- ◯ All data records are summarized in one CO document
- ◯ All data records of a personnel no. summarized in a CO doc.

36.8 PROFILE AUTHORIZATION GROUPS

Functional Consultant	User	Business Process Owner	Senior Management	My Rating	Understanding Level
B	X	X	X		

36.8.1 Purpose and Overview

Profile authorization groups are used to group data entry profiles. Users are assigned profile authorization groups in subtype of infotype 0316. Through this linkage, a user is authorized to use certain data entry profiles.

36.8.2 IMG Node

SM30 ➤ TCATSA

36.8.3 Screen

Auth	Text
HR1	Authorization group for Finance users
HR0	Authorization group for HR-only installation

36.9 ADDITIONAL INFORMATION FOR ESS PROFILE

Functional Consultant	User	Business Process Owner	Senior Management	My Rating	Understanding Level
B	X	X	X		

36.9.1 Purpose and Overview

When you are using CATS regular through ESS, you can further control your profile. The features are self explanatory. For more details, see field help.

36.9.2 IMG Node

SM30 ➤ TCATS_ITS

36.9.3 Screen

Entry Profile	HR-ONLY	

Web settings

☑ Initial lines

☐ "Goto" function active
☐ "Copy prev. period" function active   ☐ Copy including hours
☐ "Insert line" function active   Insert lines at same time
☐ "Delete line" function active
☐ "Show/Hide all details" active   ☐ Show all details now

☐ Display data entry profile   ☐ Choose data entry profile

36.10 POSSIBLE ENTRIES HELP IN INTERNET

Functional Consultant	User	Business Process Owner	Senior Management	My Rating	Understanding Level
B	X	X	X		

36.10.1 Purpose

For some fields in CATS regular, SAP provides a choice of search helps. You can use it if needed. For more details, see the documentation of the configuration node.

36.10.2 IMG Node

SM30 ➢ TCATS_SHLP_ITS

36.10.3   Screen

Field Name	BEMOT

Time Sheet: Possible Entries Help in Internet	
Search help name	H_TBMOT
Help type	Search help
Selection field 1	BEMOT
Selection field 2	BEMOT_TXT
Selection field 3	
Selection field 4	
Display field 1	BEMOT
Display field 2	BEMOT_TXT
Display field 3	
Display field 4	
Display field 5	
Display field 6	

36.11   DEACTIVATION OF ATTENDANCE/ABSENCE TYPES IN ESS

Functional Consultant	User	Business Process Owner	Senior Management	My Rating	Understanding Level
B	X	X	X		

36.11.1   Purpose

In SAP, you create all the attendance/absence types you require. However, you may not want all of them to be available to employees for entry in CATS through ESS. For example, you may want training data to be entered by the training administrator, and not by the employee. You can use this view to restrict the attendance/absence types, which are available to employees for entry in CATS through ESS. Note that this restriction does not apply to CATS classic.

36.11.2   IMG Node

SM30 ➤ V_T554S_ESSEX

36.11.3 Screen

PSG	A/AType	A/A type text	End Date	Deact
2	0155	Unpaid leave	31.12.9999	☐
2	0160	Unpaid absence/no SI d...	31.12.9999	☐
2	0200	Illness more than 3 days	31.12.9999	☐
2	0210	Illness less than 3 days	31.12.9999	☐
2	0220	Doctor and treatment	31.12.9999	☐
2	0300	Paid absences	31.12.9999	☐

36.12 ALLOWED PRINT REPORTS FOR CATS

Functional Consultant	User	Business Process Owner	Senior Management	My Rating	Understanding Level
B	X	X	X		

36.12.1 Purpose and Overview

SAP provides a program, RCATSP01, to print time sheet data. If you want to copy and modify this program, you may do so. You maintain list of such programs here. In data entry profile, you can specify one of these print programs.

36.12.2 IMG Node

SM30 ➤ TCATP

36.12.3 Screen

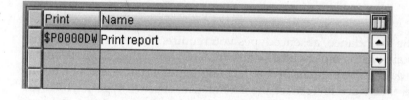

Print	Name
$P0000DW	Print report

36.13 TASK TYPE, TASK LEVEL, TASK COMPONENT

Functional Consultant	User	Business Process Owner	Senior Management	My Rating	Understanding Level
B	X	X	X		

36.13.1 Purpose and Overview

Task type, task level and task component are key concepts in CATS for service providers. However, they can be used in other user interfaces of CATS also. You basically record different types of task performed and the level at which they were performed. Once these are specified, the system shows you various components of the task you could perform, and you enter datewise time/other quantities. These quantities would be in different units, which are determined by combination of task type, task level and task component.

36.13.2 IMG Node

SM34 ➤ VC_CATSXC_ZUORD

36.13.3 Task Type

Ta...	Task Type Description	Default Acct Assgnmt	Program	Screen
TTY1	Car repair	Order		
TTY2	Goods transport	Order		
TTY3	Passenger transport - bus	Order		
TTY4	Passenger transport - car	Order		
TTY5	Car rental	Order		
TTY6	Driver on hire	Order		

You may perform different types of tasks for which you want to record time. For each task type, you can have a default account assignment, which is shown when you enter CATS for service provider screen. You can choose other account assignments if you want to.

A part of CATS for service provider screen can depend on task type. You can specify that here. Remaining subscreens are defined in 'Customizing Interface for CATS for service provider'. Task types are stored in view TCATX_TASKTYPES.

36.13.4 Task Level

Task levels	
TaskLevel	Text
TASKLE1	Mechanic
TASKLE10	Heavy goods vehicle
TASKLE11	Chauffer
TASKLE12	Driver
TASKLE2	Supervisor
TASKLE3	Unskilled worker
TASKLE4	Painter
TASKLE5	Luxury seat (bus)
TASKLE6	Economy seat (bus)
TASKLE7	Luxury car
TASKLE8	Economy car
TASKLE9	Medium goods vehicle

You may be able to perform a task at different levels (e.g. competency levels). This is a master list of task levels for all task types. Task levels are stored in view TCATX_LEVELS.

36.13.5 Task Component

Task components		Co...	Unit	Max....	Incr...	Default ...	Hist.pos.	Help...
TaskCo...	Text							
TASKC01	Engine repair	☐	H					🗐
TASKC02	Body denting and painting	☐	H					🗐
TASKC03	Car repair (other items)	☐	H					🗐
TASKC04	Car servicing	☐	AU					🗐
TASKC05	Mumbai Pune	☐	AU					🗐
TASKC06	Mumbai Delhi	☐	AU					🗐
TASKC07	Car rental	☐	H					🗐
TASKC08	Driver	☐	H					🗐

Within a task type, you may have different components. For example, within car repair, you may have engine repair, body repair, etc.

'Component is Activity Type' indicator determines the fields you can specify for a combination of task type, task component and task level. Both these screens are discussed later.

A task component has a unit, a maximum value, an increment, a default value, and a position in history display. All these fields are self-explanatory and are needed only if you are using CATS for service providers. Task components are stored in view TCATX_COMPONENTS.

36.13.6 Task Type + Task Level

Task type	TTY1	Car repair

Assign task level				
	Task Level		Valid From	End Date
	Mechanic	🗎	01.01.0001	31.12.9999
	Supervisor	🗎	01.01.0001	31.12.9999
	Unskilled wor…	🗎	01.01.0001	31.12.9999
	Painter	🗎	01.01.0001	31.12.9999
		🗎		

Here you specify valid combinations of task type and task level. Task Type + Task Level combinations are stored in view V_TCATX_LEVE2TYP.

36.13.7 Task Type + Task Component

Task type	TTY1	Car repair

Assign components				
	Task component		ValidFrom	Valid to
	Engine repair	🗎	01.01.0001	31.12.9999
	Body denting and pa…	🗎	01.01.0001	31.12.9999
	Car repair (other i…	🗎	01.01.0001	31.12.9999
	Car servicing	🗎	01.01.0001	31.12.9999
		🗎		

Here you specify valid combinations of task type and task component. Task Type + Task Component combinations are stored in view V_TCATX_ COMP2TYP.

36.13.8 Task Type + Task Component + Task Level

Here you specify valid combinations of task type, task component and task level. If 'Component is Activity Type' indicator is set in task component, you get the following screen:

	Task Type	TTY1	Car repair					
	Task component	TASKCO1	Engine repair					

Derivations

	Task Level	Valid From	End Date	A/A Ty...	Wage...	Acty Ty...	Send.Bus...	Service Number
	Mechanic ☰	01.01.0001	31.12.9999					
	Supervisor ☰	01.01.0001	31.12.9999					
	Unskilled... ☰	01.01.0001	31.12.9999					
	Painter ☰	01.01.0001	01.01.0001					
	☰							

If 'Component is Activity Type' indicator is not set in task component, you get the following screen:

	Task Type	TTY1	Car repair			
	Task component	TASKCO1	Engine repair			

Derivations

	Task Level	Valid From	End Date	Wage type	StatKeyFig	Service Number
	Mechanic ☰	01.01.0001	31.12.9999			
	Supervisor ☰	01.01.0001	31.12.9999			
	Unskilled worker ☰	01.01.0001	31.12.9999			
	Painter ☰	01.01.0001	01.01.0001			
	☰					

From task type, task component and task level you can determine attendance/absence type, wage type, activity type, statistical key figure, sender business process and service number. Depending on whether the 'Component is Activity Type' indicator is set or not you can specify a subset of these fields.

You can create a statistical key figure in Accounting ➢ Controlling ➢ Cost Center Accounting ➢ Master Data ➢ Statistical Key Figures ➢ Individual Processing ➢ KK01– Create. You only see those Statistical Key Figures, where category is 2 (Total value).

You can create a service in Materials Management ➢ Service Master ➢ Service ➢ AC03–Service Master.

Task Type + Task Component + Task Level combinations are stored in view V_TCATX_DEDUC.

36.14 DATA ENTRY PROFILE FOR A TASK TYPE

Functional Consultant	User	Business Process Owner	Senior Management	My Rating	Understanding Level
B	X	X	X		

36.14.1 Purpose and Overview

CATS for service providers lets you specify the data entry profile for a task type and the organizational assignment of the employee. If this feature is not maintained, you will not see task types in list of values in CATS for service provider.

36.14.2 IMG Node

PE03 ≻ CATSX

36.14.3 Screen

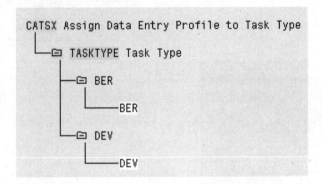

36.14.4 Fields for Decision Making

Activity Type
Company Code
Personnel Area
Cost Center
Controlling Area
Employee Group
Employee Subgroup
Business Area
Personnel Subarea
Organizational Unit

36.14.5 Return Value

Data Entry Profile

36.15   DATA ENTRY TABLE FOR CATS FOR SERVICE PROVIDER

Functional Consultant	User	Business Process Owner	Senior Management	My Rating	Understanding Level
B	X	X	X		

36.15.1   Purpose and Overview

In this view you define which task components are displayed for a data entry profile and in which order. You also specify whether a field is mandatory or not. Only those task components, which are valid for task type and task level specified in CATS for service provider entry screen, are displayed.

36.15.2   IMG Node

SM30 ➤ TCATX_GRID

Cross-Application Components ➤ Time Sheet ➤ Specific Settings for CATS for Service Providers ➤ Set Up Data Entry Table

36.15.3   Screen

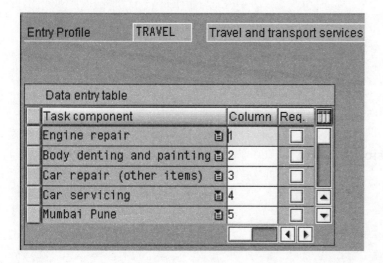

36.16 CUSTOMIZING INTERFACE FOR CATS FOR SERVICE PROVIDER

Functional Consultant	User	Business Process Owner	Senior Management	My Rating	Understanding Level
B	X	X	X		

36.16.1 Purpose

Usually the screen of CATS for service provider would meet your requirements. However, if you want, you can define multiple user interfaces and select one based on the employee's organizational assignment.

36.16.2 Access Key for Transaction Control

The screen consists of subscreens and tabs which are determined from an access key. The access key for SAP's standard screens is CATSXT. If you want to create your own customized interface, you define your own access keys in view TCATX_AK.

CATX: Access Key for Transaction Control	
Access	Text

36.16.3 Determination of Access Key for Transaction Control

SAP lets you have different interfaces for CATS for service provider, from which one would get selected. Depending on the organizational assignment of the employee, you can get an access key which is used for determining the layout. You define the logic for determining access key in feature CATSS.

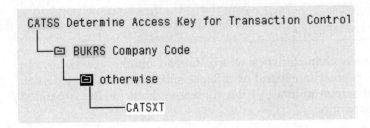

36.16.4 Tab Control

In CATS for service provider screen, you see the following tabs:

These can be customized depending on the settings below (Cross-Application Components ➤ Time Sheet ➤ Specific Settings for CATS for service providers ➤ Customize Interface ➤ Define Tab Control). View TCATX_TCR.

CATX: Tabstrip Control

	Access	Tabstrip		Text	Program	Screen	Inactive
	CATSXT	Tabstrip 01 🖹		History	SAPLCATSXT	0940	☐
	CATSXT	Tabstrip 02 🖹		Worklist	SAPLCATSXT	0930	☐
	CATSXT	Tabstrip 03 🖹		Document flow	SAPLCATSXT	0950	☐
	CATSXT	Tabstrip 04 🖹		Travel expenses	SAPLCATSXT	0960	☐
			🖹				

36.16.5 Subscreen Control

CATS for service provider screen consists of several subscreens. These are defined in view TCATX_SCR.

Text	Prog.	Scr...	Prog ...	Scr...	F C...	Open	Resvd	Inactive
Header Data	SAPLCA...	0204				☑	☐	☐
Receiver Account Assgnt	SAPLCA...	1200				☑	☐	☐
Reserved For Task Type						☐	☑	☐
Long Text	SAPLCA...	0220	SAPLC...	0210	CX_...	☐	☐	☐
Times/Key Figures	SAPLCA...	0820	SAPLC...	0810	CX_...	☑	☐	☐
Sender Account Assign...	SAPLCA...	0720	SAPLC...	0710	CX_...	☐	☐	☐
History/Worklist	SAPLCA...	0920	SAPLC...	0910	CX_...	☑	☐	☐
Logistics Data	SAPLCA...	0420	SAPLC...	0410	CX_...	☐	☐	☐

You can define further subscreen characteristics which depend on the access key. In CATS for service provider screen you can expand or collapse subscreen. In this node you specify the program name and screen number of the subscreen, both for the expanded mode as well as for the collapsed mode.

When you open CATS for service provider screen, the subscreen may be open or closed. You specify this in the checkbox titled 'Open'.

You can specify one subscreen per access key, which can depend on task type (by using checkbox Reserved). The program and screen number for this subscreen is defined in properties of task type.

You can deactivate a subscreen.

36.16.6 Central Functions

CATX: Central Functions						
Access	Unit	LTxtC	LtxtD	CB ...	StatW	Auto.Deletion
CATSXT		☑	☑	☐		

You get the above screen through IMG path: Cross-Application Components ≻ Time Sheet ≻ Specific Settings for CATS for service providers ≻ Customize Interface ≻ Set Up Central Functions. View TCATX_CC.

You can define a unit of measure for sum column. By default it is hours.

If you set the long text per day indicator, you can enter long text for each day. Otherwise, you can enter a single long text for all the days of a task.

Long text is usually for internal use. However, if you want to use long text for external purpose, e.g. printing on an invoice for the customer, you can set long text division field.

Normally the clipboard is displayed as part of the history. However, if you set clipboard as dialog box indicator, the clipboard is displayed in a separate dialog box.

SAP lets you save the data without releasing. However, as soon as you complete data entry for a period, you are expected to release it. If you don't, the system can give you warning. You can specify here the number of days after which warning should be given.

You can also set a time limit after which in process records are automatically deleted.

36.16.7 Customer-specific Fields and Data Checks for CATSXT

You can use BAdI CATSXT_EVENT to implement customer-specific fields and data checks for CATSXT.

36.17 SPECIFIC SETTINGS FOR CATS NOTEBOOK

Functional Consultant	User	Business Process Owner	Senior Management	My Rating	Understanding Level
B	X	X	X		

You can implement CATS notebook for those employees who would record time data on a notebook/laptop. The laptop may not be always connected to SAP. CATS notebook users can record their working time data on the notebook and then transfer it to SAP when they are able to set up a connection. After they set up a connection, they click on 'Synchronize'. During the synchronization process, they also download the master data to their laptops. For procedure to install CATS notebook, see SAP Library help: Cross-Application Time Sheet ≻ User Interfaces ≻ CATS notebook ≻ Installation.

36.17.1   Fields for Data Entry Section

In view cluster VC_PT_FIELD_SELECTION, you specify which fields are to be used in the data entry section when recording working times using CATS notebook, and define their properties.

Dialog Structure	Screen area	OCA	CATS notebook		
▽ 🗁 Field Selection Attributes					
🗋 Field Customizing	**Field Selection Attributes**				
		Field sel.	Field selection text	No. of fixed columns	Number of hier.
					🗒
					🗒
					🗒

36.17.2   Fields for Detail Area

In view cluster VC_PT_FIELD_SELECTION, you specify which fields are to be used in the detail area when recording working times using CATS notebook. By default, the detail view is the same as the data entry view, but it may be useful to see additional data in the detail view.

Dialog Structure	Screen area	OCB	CATS Notebook, Detail Screen		
▽ 🗁 Field Selection Attributes					
🗋 Field Customizing	**Field Selection Attributes**				
		Field sel.	Field selection text	No. of fixed columns	Number of hier.
					🗒
					🗒
					🗒

36.17.3   Data Entry Profiles to Field Selections Link

In view CATS_MY_FIELDSEL, you can assign more than one field selection to a data entry profile. You can also specify the one which is to be used as the default field selection.

Profile	Field Sel.	Default
		☐
		☐
		☐

36.17.4 Synchronization of Static Objects

When you synchronize CATS notebook, you download customizing and master data from SAP to notebook. Some of these objects rarely change. Therefore, there is no point in downloading them during each synchronization. However, you would want to download them, when they change. You specify what to download when in view CATS_MY_PUSH. Objects in this view are automatically transferred during first synchronization.

Object	Date	Time	Not Used	Not Used

36.17.5 Periods for Target Hours and Data Storage

Different users may have different synchronization frequency. If you synchronize more often, you need to download target hours data for smaller period. If you synchronize less often, you need to download target hours data for longer period. In view CATS_MY_DATES you define the period (with respect to synchronization date) for which you download target hours data. Also, to free the memory, you specify, the period for which data is retained. Older data is deleted in synchronization process.

Profile	Target Hours (Past)	Target Hours (Future)	Data Storage (Past)	N	N	N

36.17.6 Creation and Distribution of HTML Documentation

SAP provides a document, MYCATS_USERDOCU under document class general text. If you want, you can copy and modify the same using transaction SE61. Include the document you have created in this view CATS_MY_DOCU. When synchronization takes place, this document is converted in HTML, and transferred to the notebook.

Profile	ID	Text Name	Text Name	Ind.	File

36.17.7 User Interface Texts

You can use view CATS_MY_TEXTS_C to provide more user friendly field descriptions.

Field Name	Lang.	Short Description	Heading	Short	Medium	Long

36.18 ENHANCEMENTS

Functional Consultant	User	Business Process Owner	Senior Management	My Rating	Understanding Level
B	X	X	X		

SAP provides you a number of enhancements and BadIs to implement your own logic. Depending on your requirement, you need to explore these.

Enhancement	Description	CATS classic	CATS regular	CATS for service providers	CATS notebook	Refer to
CATS0001	CATS: Set up worklist	Yes	Yes	Yes	Yes	36.1.6
CATS0002	CATS: Supplement recorded data	Yes	Yes	Yes	Yes	36.1.6
CATS0003	CATS: Validate recorded data	Yes	Yes	Yes	Yes	36.1.7
CATS0004	CATS: Deactivate functions in the user interface	Yes	No	No	No	
CATS0005	CATS: Customer field enhancements	Yes	No	No	No	36.3.4
CATS0006	CATS: Validate entire time sheet	Yes	Yes	Yes	Yes	36.1.7
CATS0007	CATS: Subscreen on initial screen	Yes	No	No	No	36.1.6
CATS0008	CATS: Determine workflow recipients for approval	Yes	Yes	Yes	Yes	36.2.4
CATS0009	CATS: Customer-Specific Text Fields in Data Entry Section	Yes	Yes	No	No	
CATS0010	CATS: Customer-Specific Text Fields in Worklist	Yes	Yes	Yes	No	

(Contd.)

Enhancement	Description	CATS classic	CATS regular	CATS for service providers	CATS notebook	Refer to
CATS0011	CATS: Customer functions	Yes	No	No	No	
CATS0012	CATS: Subscreen on data entry screen	Yes	No	No	No	
CATP0001	Determine target hours	Yes	Yes	Yes	Yes	
MYCATS01	Enhancement of Picklists for CATS notebook	No	No	No	Yes	
MYCATS02	Sending Customer-Specific Tables or Standard Texts to CATS notebook	No	No	No	Yes	
MYCATS03	Change or Supplement Working Time Data During Transfer to SAP	No	No	No	Yes	
CATSBW01	Customer Exit for Time Sheet Data Transfer -> BW	Yes	Yes	Yes	Yes	
CAWAO_TS	Format Text in Worklist	Yes	Yes	Yes	Yes	

Incentive Wages

37.1 TYPES OF INCENTIVE WAGES

Functional Consultant	User	Business Process Owner	Senior Management	My Rating	Understanding Level
A	A	A	A		

37.1.1 Performance Based Payments

You can pay your employees based on performance. For some jobs, the employee payment may be based on individual performance, whereas for some jobs the performance can be determined only for a group of employees. To determine employee performance, you need to know

➢ Work done
➢ Time taken
➢ Time expected to be taken

These are captured in time tickets. There are different types of time tickets. Performance based payments can be either for an individual employee or for groups of employees.

37.1.2 Time Based Payments

You can also pay your employees based on target or actual time. When you pay based on output produced or target time, you are paying by piecework rate. In this case you use wage type ML01. When you pay based on actual time spent, you can pay by average rate. In this case you use wage type ML02. Data for time based payments is also captured in time tickets.

37.2 TIME TICKETS

Functional Consultant	User	Business Process Owner	Senior Management	My Rating	Understanding Level
A	B	C	X		

37.2.1 What is a Time Ticket

A time ticket is a record of work done and time spent in doing so. They are used in incentive wages to determine incentive (premium) or time based payments.

37.2.2 Types of Time Ticket

You need to capture different data depending on whether you are using individual or group incentives, and whether you are making performance based or time based payments. For this reason, SAP provides you the following types of time ticket.

➢ Premium time ticket
➢ Quantity time ticket
➢ Person time ticket
➢ Time-related time ticket
➢ Foreman time ticket

The use of these types of time ticket are summarized below:

Type of incentive	Group/ Individual	Time ticket type for capturing quantity information	Time ticket type for capturing time information
Performance	Group	Quantity time tickets	Person time tickets
	Individual	Premium time tickets	Premium time tickets
Time-based	Individual		Premium time tickets, or Time-related time tickets

Foreman time tickets are different from other type of time tickets. Here the employee is paid based on individual efficiency, but his efficiency is also included in determining the result of the group to which he belongs. They are similar to premium time tickets, except that you also capture group number, in which his efficiency is to be included.

37.2.3 Premium Time Ticket

You can record time tickets using transaction PW03. When you run this transaction, you get the following screen.

Group number	
Personnel Number	

Time ticket type	

Selection of time tickets

Time ticket number		Order number	
		Sequence	
Confirmation number		Operation	
Confirmation counter		Suboperation	

Period

Entry period	04 2006
Valid From	01.04.2006 - 30.04.2006

This is merely a selection screen. You need to specify time ticket type here (because the subsequent screen depends on that), and the period. Other fields are optional. After entering these, you go to full screen (F5 or Screens ➤ Full screen, or [⊞]), given below:

Personnel No.	
Time ticket no.	

Confirmation

Confirmation	

Order		Seqnce	Operation	Suboperation	

Time Ticket

Posting date	01.04.2006	Company code	
Wage type		Cost center	
Premium formula	· Target/Actual		
Result	0.000 % Labor Utilization	Yield	
Pay Scale Group		Scrap quantity	
PS level		Scrap reason	
Amount		Base quantity	

	From	To	Conf. value	Standard value	Target value
Labor time					
Setup time					
Teardown time					
Machine time					
Variable acti					

New time ticket type

Time tkt type	01	Personnel Number		Group

Types of time

In the above screen, you enter labor time, setup time, teardown time, machine time and variable activity time.

Confirmation value

You can enter the actual time spent directly as hours in confirmation value column, or you may enter the start and end time, from which the system computes the confirmation value.

Target value

You also enter target value for each of these. Target values represent time you were expected to take.

Standard value

If your output (yield + scrap) is different from input (base quantity), you may compute target value as (yield + scrap) * standard value/ base quantity.

Quantities

On this screen, you see three quantity fields. Yield represents quantity produced, scrap quantity is the quantity scrapped and base quantity is the quantity consumed. You can also enter the reason for scrap.

Result

Based on the data you have entered, the system immediately shows you the labor utilization of this time ticket in result field. SAP lets you define how you want to compute labor utilization. This is done in the premium formula which your consultant sets up for you. While defining the formula, he can use the fields in which you fill data. He also has other flexibilities, so that he can define the formula to meet your company's requirement.

It is not necessary that the result must be labor utilization. It can also be a premium. What the result is depends on the premium formula. Note that it is possible to define multiple premium formula, and you may choose the appropriate one while recording the time ticket.

37.2.4 List Screen

If you find that you are entering too little data in the full screen, you may find it more convenient to enter data in a list screen. Your consultant can provide you a list screen, containing only those fields, which you most often enter. From the list screen, you can always go to full screen, if you want to enter additional data for some peculiar case, and come back. Thus, using list screen does not compromise your ability to enter all the data you wish to enter. You can use list screen to enter data for a single employee, or you may enter data for several persons. These are displayed as tab pages in the screen.

	List	List for several persons	

Personnel Number	125866	Joglekar Makarand	Period

TimeTickets

	Posting date	TT no.	Actual labor	Yield	Standard value	Wage type	Result	Lock
	04.04.2006		6.000	1.000	6.000	ML01	100.000	☐
								☐

37.2.5 Cumulations

You saw that for each time ticket, labor utilization was computed. However, result at time ticket level is possible only for premium time tickets and foreman time tickets, as these time tickets contain both input and output data. For other types of time tickets, the result cannot be computed at time ticket level. It can only be computed for a period.

Even for premium and foreman time tickets, the more important information is daily or monthly performance, rather than time ticket level performance. SAP computes period performance, based on time tickets entered. This can be seen by executing transaction PW01 and clicking on ![icon]. You see the screen below, which shows day and period summaries under tab cumulations. Apart from result, it shows cumulation of six time fields which SAP provides as standard.

Personnel no.	125866	Joglekar Makarand		Entry period	04 2006
Group number					
Premium formula		Target/Actual			
Result		92.353	% Labor Utilization Rate (LU)		

	Cumulations	Result types	Parameters	

Cumulations from period

Result	Actual labor	Target labor	Actual setup	Target setup	ActTeardown	TgtTeardown
92.353	17.000	15.700	0.750	1.000	0.000	0.000

◀ ▶

Cumulations from day

Date	Result	Actual labor	Target labor	Actual setup	Target setup	ActTeardown	TgtTeardown
01.04.2006	111.667	6.000	6.700	0.750	1.000	0.000	0.000
02.04.2006	83.333	6.000	5.000	0.000	0.000	0.000	0.000

However, SAP provides more flexibility than standard cumulations. It lets you define one or more premium formulas. The premium formula determines how cumulation would take place. You can disable cumulation for some of the fields which are cumulated in normal course.

When you save a premium or foreman time ticket, the premium formula specified for it, if any, also gets saved. However, not all types of time ticket have a premium formula.

To determine period result, you need to specify premium formula. You do that here by specifying the premium formula for an individual or group and save. The premium formula uses the cumulated values in predefined manner and produces result.

37.2.6 Result Types

Cumulations	Result types	Parameters

Result types from period

Order	TT no.	Res.	Result type long text	Value

◀ ▶

Result types from day

Date	Order	TT no.	Res.	Result type long text	Value

In most cases, standard cumulations are sufficient to determine performance or result. However, sometimes you want the result to be more intricately computed. SAP lets you do additional summarizations using result types.

Result type permits you to cumulate machine time and variable activity type as well, which you cannot do with standard cumulations. It also lets you do cumulation for splits. Using this feature, you can cumulate at order level, cost center level, or even time ticket level.

For each result type, a value is computed for each day and period which can be used in premium formulas. All these are predefined by your consultant while configuring your system. When you go to result type tab, you see which result types are computed, and their values.

37.2.7 Parameters

Parameters provide still more flexibility in determining performance or result. In some premium formula, you may use parameters. They may have predefined values or default values that can be overwritten. When you click on parameters tab, these values are shown. If they are permitted to be overwritten, you can change them.

37.2.8 Premium Formula

Based on your company's requirement, your consultant defines the premium formula, which determines result. The user needs to select the right premium formula and save.

37.2.9 Result

One of the basic purposes of creating time tickets is to determine performance or result. Result is computed by premium formula, which uses cumulations, result types and parameters to compute result. The method of doing cumulations and computing result types is defined for each premium formula. Similarly, the parameters which can be used and their values are also defined at premium formula level.

37.2.10 Foreman Time Ticket

Foreman time tickets are identical to premium time ticket. Only group number field is extra and mandatory. Also, group result is shown. It contributes to both time ticket result and group result.

37.2.11 Time-related Time Tickets

Personnel No.	125866	Joglekar Makarand		
Time ticket no.				

Time Ticket

Posting date	01.04.2006		Company code	
Wage type			Cost center	
Amount				

	From	To	Conf. value
Labor time			
Setup time			
Teardown time			
Machine time			
Variable acti			

New time ticket type

Time tkt type	04	Personnel Number	125866	Group	

You use time-related time tickets, when you want to record only time spent, and not work done, e.g. when employee is to be paid based on time spent. These time tickets do not have a time ticket result. There is no target value or order confirmation. For time-related time tickets, you use wage type ML02 so that payment is at average rate.

37.2.12 Quantity Time Tickets

Group number	1				
Time ticket no.					

Confirmation

Confirmation					
Order		Seqnce	Operation	Suboperation	

Time Ticket

Posting date	01.04.2006			Yield	
				Scrap quantity	
				Scrap reason	
				Base quantity	

	From	To	Conf. value	Standard value	Tgt value
Labor time					
Setup time					
Teardown time					
Machine time					
Variable acti					

You use quantity time tickets to record output for group incentive schemes. In quantity time tickets, you do not record the actual time taken; that is recorded in person time tickets. Here you record quantities produced and the target value of labor, set-up and teardown time. Target value may be derived from standard value, as explained earlier. For machine time and variable activity, you can record all the information.

37.2.13 Person Time Tickets

You use person time tickets to record time spent by employees for group incentive schemes. In person time tickets, you do not record the output, as the output is the result of group activity and not individual activity.

Personnel No.						Group	1	
Time ticket no.								

Confirmation

Confirmation								
Order			Seqnce		Operation		Suboperation	

Time Ticket

Posting date	01.04.2006			Company code	
Wage type				Cost center	
Pay Scale Group					
PS level					
Amount					

	From	To	Conf. value	
Labor time				
Setup time				
Teardown time				
Machine time				
Variable acti				

37.2.14 Viewing Incentive Wages Data

The data on incentive wages is kept in clusters. You may use the following transactions to view this data.

PT_CLSTL1 – Display Individual Incentive Wages (Cluster L1)
PT_CLSTG1 – Display Group Incentive Wages (Cluster G1)

37.3 TIME TICKET TYPES

Functional Consultant	User	Business Process Owner	Senior Management	My Rating	Understanding Level
A	A	B	B		

37.3.1 Purpose and Overview

SAP provides five time ticket types. Their properties are described below.

Premium time ticket

Premium time ticket is for a person and not for a group. It has a result at time ticket level. In premium time ticket, logistics data can be used. Premium time ticket is used in individual incentive wages. It can be used both in piecework or premium wages. If your payment is based on piecework, you normally use wage type ML01 and standard cumulations. If your payment is based on time spent, you normally use wage type ML02 and average result type.

Quantity time ticket

Quantity time tickets are for a group (group incentive wages), and not for a person. They have group result. They can use logistics data. They contain both quantities completed as well as corresponding target times for groups. The actual time spent by each group member is recorded in person time tickets.

Person time ticket

Person time tickets are used to record actual times worked by the individual members of the group. In person time ticket, you specify both personnel number and group number. It has a group result and is used in group incentive wages. Logistics data can be used in it. Target times of the group are recorded using quantity time tickets.

Time-related time ticket

You specify only personnel number and not the group number. It has neither individual nor group result. It leads to individual incentive wages based on average rate. Time-related time tickets use wage type ML02 (average from paid times).

Foreman time ticket

In foreman time ticket, you specify both personnel number and group number. It has both individual and group result. Logistics data can be used. It leads to individual incentive wages. Foreman's labor utilization contributes to group's labor utilization, but he is not part of group incentive scheme.

Properties of time ticket types

The properties of time ticket types described above are not hard coded by SAP. These are also defined in configuration views described below.

View	Purpose
V_T703L	In this view, properties of time ticket type are defined. These include whether person number is required, group number is required, time ticket has individual result, employee has result and group has result.
V_T703K	This view defines which wage types are permitted for each time ticket type.
V_T703JP, V_T703JG	These views define how time ticket types are cumulated.
V_T703D	This view defines the screen properties of time ticket types.
VC_T703U	This view cluster defines, for each time ticket type which screen types are valid, and what is their layout.

37.3.2 IMG Node

SM30 ➤ V_T703L

37.3.3 Screen

Time tkt type	02	Quantity time tickets
Payroll indic.		Not valuated during accounting

Time ticket attributes

☐ Personnel number required

☑ Group number required

☐ Time ticket has individual result

☑ Integration with Logistics

37.3.4 Primary Key

Time Ticket Type

37.3.5 Important Fields

Time ticket type

Time ticket type being defined.

Payroll indicator

This field determines whether time tickets of this type lead to individual incentive (1), group incentive (2), or no incentive (Blank).

Personnel number required

In all types of time tickets except quantity time tickets, personnel number must be specified.

Group number required

Group number is required in quantity time tickets, person time tickets and foreman time tickets.

Time ticket has individual result

Only for premium and foreman time tickets, you can get labor utilization at time ticket level. The result is calculated on the basis of the premium formula of the time ticket.

Integration with logistics

You can get logistics data for all types of time tickets, except time-related time tickets.

37.4 RESULT TYPES

Functional Consultant	User	Business Process Owner	Senior Management	My Rating	Understanding Level
A	B	C	X		

37.4.1 Purpose

Usually you would compute result based on standard cumulations. However, sometimes you want the result to be more intricately computed. SAP lets you do additional summarizations using result types. Result type permits you to cumulate machine time and variable activity type as well, which you cannot do with standard cumulations. It also lets you do cumulation for splits. Using this feature, you can cumulate at order level, at cost center level, or even at time ticket level. For each result type, a value is computed for each day and period, which can be used in premium formulas.

37.4.2 IMG Node

SM30 ➤ V_T703W

37.4.3 Screen

	Result type	Result type long text	Result type short te
	DSCHN	Average	Average
	LEIST	Activity time	Activ.time

37.5 CUMULATION RULES

Functional Consultant	User	Business Process Owner	Senior Management	My Rating	Understanding Level
A	C	X	X		

37.5.1 Purpose and Overview

In a time ticket you can enter labor time, setup time, teardown time, machine time and variable activity type. Each of these can have actual value and target value. In this view you define how they should be cumulated. In standard cumulation, you can cumulate actual value and target value of labor time, setup time, and teardown time. You cannot cumulate machine time and variable activity type. If you want to cumulate in result type, you can cumulate actual value and target value of all five types of time. You can also specify whether cumulation is split by order, cost center or time ticket type. This view contains cumulation rules for both employees and groups. You access them using different views.

37.5.2 IMG Node

SM30 ➤ V_T703JP
SM30 ➤ V_T703JG

37.5.3 Screen

		Start Time	Exit
Time tkt type			
Wage type		➤	
Premium formula			

Cumulation for employees

☐ Actual labor   ☐ Target labor

☐ Actual setup   ☐ Target setup

☐ Act.teardown   ☐ Tgt teardown

Cumulation in result types for employees

Cumulation of actual values

	Result type	Split
Labor time		
Setup time		
Teardown time		
Machine time		
Var. acty type		

Cumulation of target values

	Result type	Split
Labor time		
Setup time		
Teardown time		
Machine time		
Var. acty type		

37.5.4 Primary Key

Country Grouping + Time Ticket Type + Wage Type + Premium Formula + End Date

37.6 PREMIUM FORMULA

Functional Consultant	User	Business Process Owner	Senior Management	My Rating	Understanding Level
B	X	X	X		

37.6.1 Purpose and Overview

One of the basic purposes of time tickets is to determine result. This is done by premium formula. This can be at any of the following levels.

➤ Time ticket level
➤ Employee level
➤ Group level

Time ticket level results are possible only for premium time tickets and foreman time tickets. While entering these time tickets, you can specify premium formula.

When you go to cumulations in transaction PW01 by clicking on ![icon], you can enter premium formula for an employee or group. Note that if you do not specify premium formula, the system assumes premium formula 000 by default.

The premium formula determines the method of standard cumulations and the result types that are computed (T703J). It also determines if parameters can be entered (T703H).

Depending on standard cumulations, result types and parameters, the result is computed. The formula for computing result is defined in V_T703F.

Master list of premium formulas and whether it can be used in time ticket or in period result is defined in V_T703Q. It also specifies what the result, arising from the premium formula, is called.

Groups can be assigned a default premium formula in V_T703G.

37.6.2 IMG Node

SM30 ➤ V_T703Q

37.6.3 Screen

37.6.4 Primary Key

Country Grouping + Premium Formula + End Date

37.6.5 Important Fields

Premium formula

The premium formula being defined.

Validity period

Premium formula properties can change with time. There can be multiple records for a premium formula, each having a different validity period.

Use

Here you can specify whether this premium formula can be used in time tickets, period results (cumulations, result types, parameters), or both.

Premium result

For each premium formula, you can specify what the result, produced by premium formula, is called. This is displayed by the side of result in the time tickets and cumulations.

Value limits

Here you maintain value limits in % for the premium result. The system issues warnings or error messages if these are not observed. The value limits are only validated when time tickets are entered or maintained. They are used in the time leveling report to determine which data is highlighted.

Error message if target time exceeds

Here you can specify the limit of target time. If the target value calculated for the labor, setup, teardown or machine time is greater than the value specified here, you get an error message. If this field is blank, you do not get error messages on this account.

37.7 PREMIUM CALCULATION FORMULA

Functional Consultant	User	Business Process Owner	Senior Management	My Rating	Understanding Level
B	X	X	X		

37.7.1 Purpose

In incentive wages, result is computed using premium calculation formula which is defined here. If a formula continues in multiple lines, the lines should be numbered. The formula is written in postfix notation. For more details, see configuration node help.

The premium formula can be used to calculate the result of the individual time ticket or for the day and month. In the formula to calculate the result of the individual time ticket, you can use numeric fields of time ticket. In the formula to calculate the result for the day and month, you can use cumulated values, result types and parameters. In both you can use fixed constants, routines and step functions. Before you use them in a premium formula, you must first create the corresponding parameters, result types, premium functions and routines.

37.7.2 IMG Node

SM30 ➤ V_T703F

37.7.3 Screen

	Formula	No.	Calculation rule
	0		SOW01 RUW01 /
	100		SOW01 SOW02 + RUW01 RUW02 + /
	101		(PRAEMIE100)
	300		SOW01 ZSOLZ + RUW01 ZISTZ + / $100
	400		SOW01 ZSOLZ + RUW01 ZISTZ + / &100.000 *
	400	1	ZGMAX < ZGMIN > &100.000 /

37.8 FUNCTIONS FOR ROUNDING OF RESULT

Functional Consultant	User	Business Process Owner	Senior Management	My Rating	Understanding Level
B	X	X	X		

37.8.1 Purpose

You can use this feature to round the result computed by premium formula. You can define a range and a target value. If the result is in specified range, the target value is used instead. If you do not specify a target value, the result remains unchanged.

37.8.2 IMG Node

SM30 ➤ T703P

37.8.3 Screen

	Premium func.	Start Date	End Date	Key	Value
	100	01.01.1990	31.12.9999	000080000	000080000
	100	01.01.1990	31.12.9999	000150000	
	100	01.01.1990	31.12.9999	999999999	000150000

37.8.4 Primary Key

Premium Function + End Date + Key for Premium Function

37.8.5 Important Fields

Premium function

Premium function (also called step function) being defined.

Start and end date

Validity period of the record.

Key and value

In both key and value, last 3 digits are after decimal place. The value range is from the key of the previous record to the key of the current record. Thus, the entries in the screen shot have following meaning:

From	To	Target
> 0.000	80.000	80.000
> 80.000	150.000	No change
> 150.000	999999.999	150.000

37.9 PARAMETERS FOR INCENTIVE WAGES

Functional Consultant	User	Business Process Owner	Senior Management	My Rating	Understanding Level
B	X	X	X		

37.9.1 Purpose

Here you maintain a master list of parameters. Which premium formulas can use which parameters is specified in V_T703H.

37.9.2 IMG Node

SM30 ➤ V_T703C

37.9.3 Screen

Parameters	Parameter long text	Parameter short text
ZGMAX	Max. Labor Utilization Rate	MaxLURate
ZGMIN	Min. Labor Utilization rate	MinLURate
ZISTZ	Additional actual time	Add'l act.
ZSOLZ	Additional target time	Add'l tgt.

37.10 PREMIUM FORMULA PARAMETERS

Functional Consultant	User	Business Process Owner	Senior Management	My Rating	Understanding Level
B	X	X	X		

37.10.1 Purpose

Here you specify the parameters of a premium formula, default value of a parameter and whether the parameter value can be changed by the user.

37.10.2 IMG Node

SM30 ➤ V_T703H

37.10.3 Screen

37.10.4 Primary Key

Country Grouping + Premium Formula + Parameters for Premium Formula

37.10.5 Important Fields

Premium formula, parameters

Here you specify the parameters a premium formula can take.

Constant

Here you can specify a constant from table T511K. The value of parameter is taken from there.

Value

Here you can enter a specific value directly which is taken as parameter value. If there is an entry in constant field, that gets priority.

Can overwrite

If this check box is ticked, the parameter value is modifiable when displaying period results.

37.11 ES GROUPING FOR INCENTIVE WAGES PARTICIPATION

Functional Consultant	User	Business Process Owner	Senior Management	My Rating	Understanding Level
B	X	X	X		

37.11.1 Purpose

You can use this view to bar certain employee group, employee subgroup combinations from participating in incentive wages. This can be queried in a PCR using operation OUTWP (INWID) and used for decision making (see PCR XW3).

37.11.2 IMG Node

SM30 ➤ V_503_I

37.11.3 Screen

EE group	Name of Employee ...	Employee subgroup	Nam...	Partic. IW
1	Permanent	1A	1A	☐
1	Permanent	1B	1B	☐
1	Permanent	2A	2A	☐
1	Permanent	2B	2B	☐

37.12 GROUPING FOR EARLIEST RECALCULATION DATE

Functional Consultant	User	Business Process Owner	Senior Management	My Rating	Understanding Level
B	X	X	X		

37.12.1 Purpose

Earliest recalculation date for incentive wages can be different for different sets of employees. Here you create these sets of employees. This is used in VV_T569R_V1.

37.12.2 IMG Node

PE03 ≻ TIMMO

37.12.3 Screen

```
TIMMO Defining the modifier for table T569R
  └─────01
```

37.12.4 Fields for Decision Making

Company Code
Personnel Area
Personnel Subarea
Employee Group
Employee Subgroup
Country Grouping

37.12.5 Return Value

Modifier for determining earliest recalculation date.

37.13 EARLIEST RECALCULATION DATES FOR INCENTIVE WAGES

Functional Consultant	User	Business Process Owner	Senior Management	My Rating	Understanding Level
B	X	X	X		

37.13.1 Purpose

Earliest recalculation date for incentive wages can be different for different sets of employees. Here you define the dates for each set of employees. The sets of employees are determined using feature TIMMO.

37.13.2 IMG Node

SM30 ≻ VV_T569R_V1

37.13.3 Screen

Recalculation cat.   01 Incentive wages

EarliestRecalcDates		
Mod.	Earliest recalc.date	
01	01.01.2002	

37.14 PARAMETERS FOR INCENTIVE WAGES

Functional Consultant	User	Business Process Owner	Senior Management	My Rating	Understanding Level
B	X	X	X		

37.14.1 Purpose

Here you specify whether break time is to be subtracted from the time spent by the employee, and whether daily cumulation is required or not.

37.14.2 IMG Node

Transaction PW91   Incentive Wages: Control Parameters

37.14.3 Screen

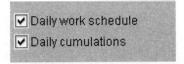

37.14.4 Important Fields

Daily work schedule

When you specify start time and end time in a time ticket, the system computes the time spent. This duration may include a break taken by the employee as per his daily work schedule. If you want to deduct the duration of break while computing hours, you tick this checkbox.

Daily cumulations

Apart from period cumulations, which you need for making payment to employee, SAP also lets you do daily cumulations. These can be useful in analyzing performance, and working out action plans for improvement. If you don't plan to do that, you should leave this checkbox blank, and avoid unnecessary cluttering of screen and system load.

If you activate this facility at a later date, you can do recalculation for earlier periods. To do this, choose Human resources ➤ Time management ➤ Incentive wages ➤ Tools ➤ Recalculation (PW70, PW71, PW72).

37.15 LOGISTICS INTEGRATION PARAMETERS

Functional Consultant	User	Business Process Owner	Senior Management	My Rating	Understanding Level
B	X	X	X		

37.15.1 Purpose

Here you specify what data can be brought in time tickets from logistics. You can further enhance integration with logistics using transaction CMOD (HRPINW01).

37.15.2 IMG Node

Transaction PW94   Inc. Wages: Logistics Parameters

37.15.3 Screen

☑ Read order data
☑ Retrieve confirmations online
☐ Maintain PDC time tickets

37.15.4 Important Fields

Read order data

If you want to read order data from logistics, you set this switch and specify either the confirmation number of the operation or the order number, sequence and operation when recording the time ticket. The system transfers the specifications for the activity types to the time ticket.

Read confirmations online

If this switch is set, the retrieve confirmations function is active on the entry screen for time tickets. You can specify the requested confirmations on a subsequent screen. The selection criteria are as follows: confirmation number, confirmation counter, personnel number, order number, sequence and operation. Time tickets entered in this way can be changed independently of the original confirmations.

Maintain PDC time tickets

Select this field if you want to be able to change time tickets that were generated from time events. A changed time ticket is not overwritten in incentive wages after the applicable confirmation is corrected in logistics. Both time tickets must be manually compared using the error handling function in time management.

37.15.5 Enhanced Integration with Logistics

The integration between Logistics and Human Resources enables you to retrieve confirmations from Logistics and store them as time tickets in a batch input session. You can add your own data to time tickets before storing them in the session by implementing user exit EXIT_SAPLHRIW_001 in enhancement HRPINW01.

37.16 TRANSACTION PARAMETERS FOR INCENTIVE WAGES

Functional Consultant	User	Business Process Owner	Senior Management	My Rating	Understanding Level
B	X	X	X		

37.16.1 Purpose

In this view you specify the properties of transactions used for maintaining incentive wages (PW01, PW02 and PW03).

37.16.2 IMG Node

SM30 ➢ V_T7032

37.16.3 Screen

```
┌─────────────────────────────────────────────────────────────────────────────┐
│  Incentive wages transaction          PW01    Maintain Incentive Wages Data   │
│                                                                                │
│  ┌─ Transaction Parameters ──────────────────────────────────────────────┐   │
│  │  Transaction status        1     Display, maintain and create time tickets │
│  │                                                                          │   │
│  │  ┌─ Selection screen ──────────────────────────────────────────────┐   │   │
│  │  │  Default date            0     Period corresponding to current date │   │
│  │  │  Payroll area                                                     │   │   │
│  │  └──────────────────────────────────────────────────────────────────┘   │   │
│  └──────────────────────────────────────────────────────────────────────────┘   │
│                                                                                │
│  ┌─ Messages ────────────────────────────────────────────────────────────┐   │
│  │  ☑ Check entry                                                          │   │
│  │  ☑ Check entry in lists                                                 │   │
│  │  ☑ Confirm deletion                                                     │   │
│  │  ☑ Display warnings                                                     │   │
│  │  ☑ Display notes                                                        │   │
│  └──────────────────────────────────────────────────────────────────────────┘   │
└─────────────────────────────────────────────────────────────────────────────┘
```

37.16.4 Primary Key

Incentive Wages Transaction

37.16.5 Important Fields

Transaction status

Here you can specify whether you can create, maintain or display time tickets using this transaction.

Default date

Default date proposed on selection screen.

Payroll area

If default date is linked to payroll area, you specify that here.

Check entry

If this switch is set, the system requests that you check your entries in full screen for results and cumulations. On confirmation, corrections are made immediately.

Check entry in lists

If this switch is set, the system requests that you check your entries in list screen for results and cumulations. On confirmation, corrections are made immediately.

Confirm deletion

If this switch is set, you have to confirm a delete request by pressing the delete key for a second time. It is not permitted to leave the selected line in list screens.

Display warnings

If you set this switch, the system displays all general warnings which have to be confirmed by pressing 'Enter'.

Display notes

The system displays notes if you set this switch; it is not necessary to confirm by pressing 'Enter'.

37.17   USER PARAMETERS FOR INCENTIVE WAGES

Functional Consultant	User	Business Process Owner	Senior Management	My Rating	Understanding Level
B	X	X	X		

37.17.1   Purpose

In transaction parameters, you defined messages at transaction level. Here you can specify them at user level within a transaction. All the concepts remain the same. By using this feature you can save matured users from the irritation of unnecessary messages, while helping inexperienced users with appropriate messages.

37.17.2   IMG Node

SM30 ➢ V_T7033

37.17.3   Screen

37.18   USER EXITS FOR INCENTIVE WAGES

Functional Consultant	User	Business Process Owner	Senior Management	My Rating	Understanding Level
B	X	X	X		

37.18.1   Purpose

SAP allows you to write your own logic to replace standard SAP logic. Here you specify the areas in which you want to write your own logic. Where to write this logic is specified in configuration node help.

37.18.2   IMG Node

Transaction PW92   Incentive Wages: User Exits

37.18.3   Screen

Calculations
- [ ] Determine time ticket type
- [ ] Read daily work schedule
- [ ] Determine target labor time
- [ ] Determine target setup time
- [ ] Determine target teardown time
- [ ] Determine target machine time
- [ ] Tgt time: var. activity type
- [ ] Premium formula for employee
- [ ] Premium formula for group
- [ ] Time ticket premium formula
- [ ] Calculate LU rate
- [ ] Cumulate time ticket data
- [ ] User-specific fields

Validations
- [ ] Validate group number
- [ ] Validate wage type
- [ ] Validate pay scale group
- [ ] Validate cost center

Logistics integration
- [ ] Read own order data
- [ ] Retrieve own confirmations

37.19 VALIDATION OF GROUP NUMBERS

Functional Consultant	User	Business Process Owner	Senior Management	My Rating	Understanding Level
B	X	X	X		

37.19.1 Purpose

Here you specify whether creation of group membership is automatic or manual. You also specify whether group numbers are restricted to certain ranges.

37.19.2 IMG Node

Transaction PW93   Incentive Wages: Group Parameters

37.19.3 Screen

37.19.4 Important Fields

Validate group membership

If this switch is set, you can enter group time tickets only for employees who already belong to the group. The system ignores time tickets of employees who do not belong to this group. If the switch is not set and you enter group time tickets for employees who do not belong to the group, the system assigns them to the group.

Validate group

If you want to restrict group numbers to valid ranges, you specify number of digits here. Then you make the required entries in V_T703G. When a group is created, its first n digits (n specified in this field) is picked up and matched with first n digits of all entries in V_T703G (Incentive Wages: Groups). If a match is found, the entry is allowed, otherwise not.

37.20   VALID RANGES OF GROUP NUMBERS

Functional Consultant	User	Business Process Owner	Senior Management	My Rating	Understanding Level
B	X	X	X		

37.20.1   Purpose and Overview

In this view you define range of valid group numbers. If you have group incentive scheme, you are going to create groups whose members are employees. Here you can define sets of groups, their validity period and country grouping. You can also specify a default premium formula, which is proposed in time ticket recording.

37.20.2   IMG Node

SM30 ➢ V_T703G

37.20.3   Screen

Group	Start Date	End Date	CGrpg	PFo	Premium formula
00000000	01.01.1990	31.12.9999	99		Target/Actual
00100000	01.01.1990	31.12.9999	01		Target/Actual
00200000	01.01.1990	31.12.9999	02		
00300000	01.01.1990	31.12.9999	03		

37.20.4   Primary Key

Group Number + End Date

37.21   FULL SCREENS FOR TIME TICKET TYPES

Functional Consultant	User	Business Process Owner	Senior Management	My Rating	Understanding Level
B	X	X	X		

37.21.1   Purpose and Overview

You can use this node to define different full screens for different time ticket types. You should make entries only for screen type 0 (full screen). The other screen types are for internal use only. Personnel number checkbox specifies whether personnel number can be entered. Similarly, group number checkbox specifies whether group number can be entered. Usually, you do not need to change this view.

37.21.2 IMG Node

SM30 ➢ V_T703D

37.21.3 Screen

	Screen	ScreenType	Screen type	PersNo	GrpNo	Time tkt type	Time ticket type text
	0100		Initial screen	☐	☐		
	0101	0	Full screen	☑	☐	01	Premium time tickets
	0160	9	Internal usage	☑	☑		
	0201	0	Full screen	☐	☑	02	Quantity time tickets
	0301	0	Full screen	☑	☑	03	Person time ticket
	0305	5	Employees in group	☑	☑		

37.21.4 Primary Key

Data Entry Screen

37.22 LIST SCREENS FOR TIME TICKET TYPES

Functional Consultant	User	Business Process Owner	Senior Management	My Rating	Understanding Level
B	X	X	X		

37.22.1 Purpose and Overview

SAP has defined all list screens for use in incentive wages. Here you can specify display length of the fields, and whether data can be entered in them.

37.22.2 IMG Node

SM34 ➢ VC_T703U

37.22.3 Screen

	TT	Time ticket type text	ScreenType	Screen type
	*	All time ticket types	4	List for several persons and groups
	01	Premium time tickets	1	List
	01	Premium time tickets	2	List for several persons
	02	Quantity time tickets	1	List
	02	Quantity time tickets	3	List for several groups

Time tkt type	01	Premium time tickets
ListScreenType	1	List

TimeTicketFields			
Field Name	Field Label	Disp.lngth	Input
BUDAT	Posting date	10	☑
RUCKR	Time ticket number	8	☑
RUW01	Confirmation Value	13	☑
LMNGR	Yield	13	☑

37.23 WAGE TYPES PERMITTED FOR TIME TICKET TYPES

Functional Consultant	User	Business Process Owner	Senior Management	My Rating	Understanding Level
B	X	X	X		

37.23.1 Purpose

Here you define wage types that are permitted for each time ticket type. When you pay based on output produced or target time, you are paying by piecework rate. In this case you use wage type ML01. When you pay based on actual time spent, you pay by average rate. In this case you use wage type ML02.

For some time ticket types, e.g. quantity time tickets, wage types are not relevant. In time related time tickets, information on target time is not captured. Hence, wage type ML01 is not permitted. For each time ticket type, you can assign a default wage type.

37.23.2 IMG Node

SM30 ➤ V_T703K

37.23.3 Screen

TT type	TT type text	Start Date	End Date	Wage type	Text	Default
01	Premium time tickets	01.01.2000	31.12.9999	ML01	PieceWrk	☑
01	Premium time tickets	01.01.2000	31.12.9999	ML02	Avg PWkT	☐
03	Person time ticket	01.01.2000	31.12.9999	ML01	PieceWrk	☑
03	Person time ticket	01.01.2000	31.12.9999	ML02	Avg PWkT	☐
04	Time-related time tickets	01.01.2000	31.12.9999	ML02	Avg PWkT	☑
05	Foreman time tickets	01.01.2000	31.12.9999	ML01	PieceWrk	☑
05	Foreman time tickets	01.01.2000	31.12.9999	ML02	Avg PWkT	☐

37.23.4 Primary Key

Country Grouping + Time Ticket Type + Wage Type + End Date

37.24 WAGE TYPES TO WAGE TYPE GROUPS ASSIGNMENT

Functional Consultant	User	Business Process Owner	Senior Management	My Rating	Understanding Level
B	X	X	X		

37.24.1 Purpose

Here you assign wage types you want to use in time tickets to wage type group 0LL1.

37.24.2 IMG Node

SM30 ➤ VV_52D7_B_0LL1_AL0

37.24.3 Screen

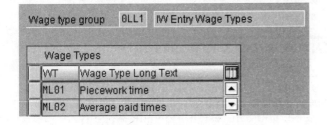

37.25 WAGE TYPE PROPERTIES FOR INCENTIVE WAGES

Functional Consultant	User	Business Process Owner	Senior Management	My Rating	Understanding Level
B	X	X	X		

37.25.1 Purpose

The wage type entered on a time ticket in incentive wages determines whether the time ticket is paid using a piecework rate or an average rate. These characteristics are defined in processing class 46 of the wage type, which is queried in PCRs and logic written as per your requirement. SAP provides PCR XW10 which can be used as a model for logic based on processing class 46. Unless a wage type is in wage type group 0LL1, it does not appear in this view.

37.25.2 IMG Node

SM30 ➤ V_512W_D

37.25.3 Screen

37.26 INCENTIVE WAGES REPORTS

Functional Consultant	User	Business Process Owner	Senior Management	My Rating	Understanding Level
A	A	B	C		

Time leveling (PW61)

You can use this report to compare the employees' working time with the time documented by their time data or incentive wages data. Working time comes from a time type, which is filled based on attendance recording or where the employee is not recording attendance, from planned working time. Documented time comes from incentive wage time tickets, infotype 2002 (attendances), and infotype 2010 (Employee remuneration specifications). You can see data in period view, day view, or detailed document view. From this report, you can access and correct master data.

Working times of time- and incentive wage earners (PW62)

This report gives a list of employees whose working time in incentive wages during the payroll period either falls short of or exceeds certain percentage rates.

Reassignment proposals for wage groups (PW63)

This report checks to what extent employees working for incentive wages scheme should be assigned to a different master wage group for the following payroll period.

Before gross pay (PW_CEDTX0_BEFORE)

This transaction shows the remuneration statement without subsequent time tickets.

After gross pay (PW_CEDTX0_AFTER)

This transaction shows the remuneration statement with subsequent time tickets.

Shift Planning

38.1 SHIFT PLANNING

Functional Consultant	User	Business Process Owner	Senior Management	My Rating	Understanding Level
A	B	C	X		

38.1.1 Overview

You can create a shift plan for an organizational unit by running transaction PP61 (PP60 for display). You can also do so for a work center. You can switch between them by going to Settings ➤ Choose profile. You can also use transaction PP66 (Choose profile).

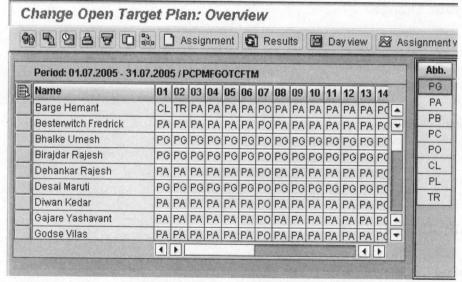

In the overview you see all the employees in the organizational unit. It also shows you the shifts in which they are scheduled to come. If you wish, you can restrict the employees to be selected in shift plan. In the entry screen, go to Edit ➢ Employee selection.

The shifts are picked up from the work schedule rule assigned to them in infotype 0007. This view also shows if there is any attendance or absence information in infotype 2001 or 2002 (e.g. CL & TR in the first line of the screen above). If the shift is changed in infotype 2003, the changed shift is shown.

If you find a * instead of a shift, it means that the shift group of the organizational unit does not have the shift that the employee has. Shift groups are discussed later in this chapter.

38.1.2 Employee Selection

The employees you see for shift planning depends on profile definition. In general, you see employees belonging to an organizational unit. These are selected through the evaluation path O-P.

During shift planning, an employee can be deployed to another organizational unit. It is stored in Relationships table HRP1001 as relationship 067 (Exclusive temp. assignment). It is used to show the employee in his new organizational unit, and hide him from his old organizational unit for appropriate period.

You can also create relationship 071 (Parallel temp. assignment), in Relationships table HRP1001. These employees are seen in both organizational units.

If you do not want to do shift planning for an employee, you can create relationship 068 (No shift planning), between the organizational unit and person. These employees are not shown in shift planning.

38.1.3 Layout Change

If you, or your user got upset that you can't see the personnel numbers of the employees, don't worry. SAP gives you a choice of several fields from which you can choose to customize the display to your liking. Go to Views ➢ Edit information columns, and select the fields you want to display. You can save the settings, so that you don't have to do it every time.

Your consultant can also set these columns, if there is general agreement on what needs to be displayed. The settings are done in table T77EJ. These are only defaults, and can be changed by the users. You can even add your own fields by defining them in table T77EI.

SAP also provides you options to display data in different colors. For example, you could show absences in different colors. These are customized by your consultant.

38.1.4 Shift Abbreviations

The shift plan shows the shift in which each employee is going to come on each day. In case an employee is going to be absent on a particular day, then one would like to know that, rather than the shift in which he was expected to come. Similarly, if an employee is going to attend a training program, or be away on official tour, that information is more important.

The shift plan takes this into account and shows either the employee's shift, or his absence/ attendance information, as appropriate. There can also be abbreviations for availability. The shifts, and absence/attendance types are also shown in an abbreviation bar on the right hand side of a shift plan.

38.1.5   Shift Plan Change through Work Schedule Rule

If an employee has a regular working time pattern (for example morning and night shifts in alternate weeks), you can specify it in the period work schedule, which is assigned to an employee in infotype 0007 through a work schedule rule.

If you largely work that way, but need to change the working pattern of an employee for some reason, the best way is to change his work schedule rule, through which you can either shift the work pattern in time scale, or change the work pattern itself. After the change, the work pattern continues week after week.

38.1.6   Shift Plan Change through Substitution

Another way of changing a person's shift plan is through substitution. You can do that through transaction PA30/PA61 (infotype 2003). SAP also lets you do this through the shift plan overview. You can go to any cell, and change the shift (either by typing, or selecting from the list, or clicking on the shift bar). When you save the data, SAP automatically creates the substitution records. The substitution type used for creating these records is determined by your configuration.

You can also select multiple cells, which may involve multiple employees, and change the shift of all by clicking on the appropriate shift abbreviation. If you want to change the shifts for a period, instead of doing it one by one, you can go to Edit ➢ Shifts during period, and change the shifts for the whole period together. You can specify a single shift, or you may specify a pattern (the patterns must be predefined).

Sometimes employers wish to know when shift change was done at employee's request. SAP supports this requirement. To implement this, you create a substitution type, which indicates that the shift is changed at employee's request, and specify it in table T77S0 (PEINS+VARWI). When you want to change shift because of employee preference, in the menu you select Goto ➢ Employee preferences. Whatever shift changes you do in this view, are recorded in infotype 2003 with the substitution type, you created for this purpose.

38.1.7   Attendance/Absence Entry

If you have information that an employee is going to be absent, the system shows absence instead of the work schedule. However, if it has not been entered in the system, you can do that here itself. Instead of replacing one shift by another, you replace it by the code of the absence. You can similarly replace a work schedule by an attendance. The codes in the shift bar include attendances and absences as well.

38.1.8 Availability Entry/Display

If you click on Views ➤ Show/hide availability view, you see an additional line for each employee, which shows availability information if any. You can also create/change availability information here.

38.1.9 Manpower Deployment

If your organizational unit has surplus manpower, and there is a need elsewhere, you can deploy your manpower. Select the employee to be deployed and go to Edit ➤ Employee ➤ Temporarily assign. Here you specify the organizational unit to which the person is to be deployed, and the period for which he is deployed. You can also specify the shift while deploying. If, as a result of deployment, the employee is to be paid differently, you can enter even that in 'Temp. paid by' field.

After you have deployed a person in your overview, those cells are displayed blank, as can be seen in the picture below. If the deployment covers the entire period of the overview, the person does not appear at all.

Name	01	02	03	04	05	06	07
Barge Hemant		CL	TR	PA		PA	PO

SAP also lets you deploy a person, such that he is available to both organizational units for assignment. Such deployment is done through relationship 071. This is included in profile SAP_000004. If you are using this profile, when you do temporary assignment, you see a check box, where you can specify that the employee has shared availability. If so specified, the employee is not excluded from the shift plan of the deploying organizational unit. The manpower deployment is only for a specific period. After that he is available to you.

The manpower deployment data is kept in table HRP1001 (Relationship) as relation A/B067 (Exclusive temp. assignment) or as A/B071 (Parallel temp. assignment). If a person has been deployed to your organizational unit, you can deploy him to another organizational unit or return to the organizational unit, which sent him to you. This can be done only for the period he has been deployed with you.

Remember that you can only give people; you can't take any. If you need employees from other organizational units, their owners must deploy them out to you.

38.1.10 Target and Actual Plan

When you are carrying out the planning process, you know who is coming in which shift, who is going to be absent, who is attending training, who is going for a tour, etc. If you know of absences/attendances, which are not updated in the system, you may update them. You may change shifts of employees, so as to meet the requirement of each shift. Finally, you freeze the plan and print it for information to employees and supervisors.

However meticulously you may plan, changes may still take place. An employee may fall ill; another employee's shift may have to be changed, either because the management wants it, or because the employee wants it. You would like to see the plan, which was originally made, and changes that took place after that separately.

SAP lets you do that by having a target plan and an actual plan. You start your planning process in target plan. After you have completed your planning, you freeze the plan by clicking on Target plan ➤ Complete. Once you do that, the target plan is frozen, and cannot be modified. You can only display it.

Freezing the target plan does not mean that the changes cannot take place. However, if you see the target plan, you do not see them (the frozen data is stored in table PSOLL). You can see the changes in the actual plan which shows the frozen target plan, and subsequent changes in two separate lines. Changes can be made in actual plan screen also.

Period: 01.11.2005 - 30.11.2005 / PCPMFGOTCFTM					
Name	**TU 01**	**WE 02**	**TH 03**	**FR 04**	**SA 05**
Barge Hemant	PA	PA	PO	PA	PG
		CL			
Besterwitch Fredrick	PA	PA	PO	PA	PA

If you have a situation where you want to unfreeze the target plan, you can do so by using transaction PP6C—Undo completed target plan.

38.1.11   Locking/Unlocking Employees

If you are doing shift planning in change mode, SAP locks the employees so that other users cannot change their data. If you do not wish to change the data of an employee, you can select that employee and unlock him. This allows other users to change his data.

If you unlock an employee, his name is shown in italics as shown below. If you make any changes in the shift plan of an unlocked employee, they do not get saved when you save the shift plan. Hence, be careful while using this feature.

Name	**MO 02**	**TU 03**
Barge Hemant	PA	PA
Besterwitch Fredrick	PA	PA
Bhalke Umesh	PG	PG

38.1.12   Requirements

The methods discussed so far are manual methods. They help you implement your decisions. They don't help you in making those decisions.

When you are doing shift planning, the basic question that would arise is, what is the requirement of employees in each shift and how much of it is fulfilled? The requirements may vary from day to day, shift to shift. Also, the requirement is not just number of men. They should have the requisite skills and knowledge.

The method of defining the requirements is discussed in detail in chapter 38.2. In this chapter, how to fulfill these requirements is discussed.

38.1.13 Assignment of Employees to Requirements

Having created requirements, you can display both the available manpower as well as the requirements one below the other in the same screen. To do so, Goto ➢ Assignment view.

Period: January 2006 / PCPMFGOTCFTM

Name	07	Assi...	from	to	08	Assi...	from	to
Barge Hemant	PA				PA			
Besterwitch Fredrick	PA				PA			
Bhalke Umesh	PG				PG			
Bhosale Sanjay	PG				PG			
Birajdar Rajesh	PG				PG			
Dehankar Rajesh	PA				PA			

Ab	From	To	Ext.	Tgt	Min.	Max.	ID	SU 01	MO 02	TU 03	WE ...
PG	08:30	17:00	☐	10	8	12	☐		■	■	■
PA	06:30	15:00	☐	8	7	9	☐		■	■	■
PB	15:00	23:30	☐	4	4	5	☐		■	■	■
PC	23:30	06:30	☐	2	2	2	☐		■	■	■
PG	08:30	17:00	☐	1	1	1	☐	■			

At this point, the manpower is not yet assigned to the requirements. Hence, the assignment fields are blank. The red squares in the picture indicate that the requirement is unfulfilled.

The last line of requirement is for weekends. Hence, for Sunday, unfulfilled requirement is shown in the last line, and not in the lines above that.

You may create the assignments manually if you want. When you do so, the organizational unit to which the employee is assigned is shown in the assignment field. The time for which he is assigned is shown in the from and to fields. Unless you specifically change the time of assignment, the from and to fields show start and end of the shift, in which the employee is expected to work for this organizational unit.

The assignment may not be for full day. You can specify the time for which an employee is assigned to a requirement. Thus, you can assign an employee to different requirements for different parts of a day.

If you click on any icon, you can see the people who are assigned to a particular requirement.

38.1.14 Assignment Proposal

Assigning employees to requirements manually can be a time consuming task. SAP can help you in this by making assignment proposals for you. If you go to Edit ➢ Determine assignment proposal, SAP automatically creates the assignment of employees to requirements. While doing so, it takes into account the job, skills (qualifications) and employee preferences into account. It displays the extent of requirement fulfillment for each requirement for each day.

Period: January 2006 / PCPMFGOTCFTM					
Name	01	Assignment	From	to	
Barge Hemant	PB				
Besterwitch Fredrick	PA				
Bhalke Umesh	PG	PCPMFGOT…	08:30	17:00	
Bhosale Sanjay	PG				
Birajdar Rajesh	PG				
Dehankar Rajesh	PA				

Ab	From	To	Ext.	Tgt	Min.	Max.	ID	SU 01	MO 02
PG	08:30	17:00	☐	10	8	12	☐		△14
PA	06:30	15:00	☐	8	7	9	☐		△ 8
PB	15:00	23:30	☐	4	4	5	☐		■ 4
PC	23:30	06:30	☐	2	2	2	☐		■
PG	08:30	17:00	☐	1	1	1	☐	● 1	

For each requirement for each day, you see one of the three types of icons, along with a number. These icons and related formatting can be customized in view V_T77RQ_ICON.

➢ Green circular icon indicates that the target requirement is fulfilled.
➢ Yellow triangular icon indicates that the target requirement is either short or exceeded, but minimum requirement is fulfilled.
➢ Red square icon indicates that the minimum requirement is not yet fulfilled.

The numbers in these icons indicate the number of employees involved. Since it is possible that some of these employees may not be assigned full time, do not compare these numbers with requirement numbers.

If you click on an icon, you can see the persons who are assigned to a requirement. You can add or delete a person to a requirement.

While determining assignment proposal, look at the options. These affect the proposal generated by the system.

If there is an employee, who perfectly matches the requirement both in terms of time and competence, the system has no difficulty in assigning him. However, sometimes the match may be less than perfect. Some people may have the requisite competence, but the time may not match, whereas in other cases the time may match but there may be a gap qualitatively. You can specify what to do in such cases by going to Settings ➢ Prioritize proposal determination. You may also see, Settings ➢ Assignment options and Settings ➢ Select strategy.

The data on assignment proposal is kept as relationship A/B065 (Planned assignment) in table HRP10001.

38.1.15 Time Evaluation

If you wish to see the impact of your shift plan, you can do time evaluation and look at time balances. You can even print time statements. These are useful, for example, if you have working time quotas.

When time evaluation is run for future dates, it is assumed that the employees are going to be present as per their assignment in the shift plan. These are treated as attendances. You need to define the attendance type, which is used for these assignments during simulation in T77S0. You also need to define the program variant for calling time evaluation in T77S0.

38.1.16 Shift Planner Authorization

You need to ensure that the shift planners can do shift planning only for the organizational units for which they are authorized. You may also have situations where one shift planner does shift planning for multiple organizational units. It is, therefore, necessary to specify the shift planner position for an organizational unit. This is done using relationship B072.

Thereafter, you build structural authorization. From user code you determine person (using infotype 0105, subtype 0001), from person to position (using organization structure), and from position to organizational unit (using relationship B072). These are coded in a function module (similar to RH_GET_MANAGER_ASSIGNMENT).

You specify the function module and evaluation path in transaction OOSP (Authorization Profiles). Your evaluation path needs to include employees who are deployed in your organizational unit, so that you are able to change their master data, e.g. substitution, absence, attendance, etc.

38.1.17 OM in Shift Planning

In time management, shift planning is the only area where you work with organizational management concepts. You do shift planning for an organizational unit or work center. You pick up or exclude employees in an organizational unit using evaluation paths. The employees are picked up primarily through Organizational unit ≻ Position ≻ Person link. You maintain the following relationships between an organizational unit and a person.

> ➤ 067—Exclusive temporary assignment
> ➤ 068—No shift planning
> ➤ 071—Parallel temporary assignment

You maintain the following infotypes for an organizational unit:

> ➤ Shift groups are assigned to organizational units in infotype 1039.
> ➤ Factory calendar is assigned to an organizational unit in infotype 1027.

You can maintain all these using transaction PP01 in SAP Menu. There are also some transactions in shift planning menu, e.g. PP65, PPOME, PPPD, PPPM and PEPM, which should be used by OM user. Shift planning user may at best use them for display.

SAP provides a generic facility of using multiple plan versions (transaction PP64). You usually use current plan. If you change the plan version, you do not see the data, you expect to see.

Requirement definitions are stored as object type SR (Planned staff requirement) in the database. The infotypes used are 1000 and 1049. It also has the following relationship with other objects (infotype 1001):

> ➤ A Requirement (SR) may require (A031) Qualification (skill) (Q).
> ➤ A Requirement (SR) may have a requirement description (A062), which is a Job (C).
> ➤ A Requirement (SR) may be the requirements definition (B064) of an Organizational unit (O) or Work center (A).
> ➤ A Person (P) may be assigned (A065) to a Requirement (SR).

38.1.18 Shift Planning Reports

Apart from printing the shift plan, you can print:

> ➤ 'Personal shift plan', which shows employee wise shifts (transaction PP6A).
> ➤ 'Attendance list', which shows date wise employees' assignment to organizational units (transaction PP6B).
> ➤ 'Temporary assignment list' (transaction PP6I)
> ➤ 'Time statement list'

38.2   REQUIREMENTS

Functional Consultant	User	Business Process Owner	Senior Management	My Rating	Understanding Level
A	B	C	C		

38.2.1   Purpose and Overview

An organizational unit has requirements. Instead of defining requirements for each specific day, you can define them in a generic way, e.g. requirements on a working day, requirements on weekends, requirements on public holidays etc. These generic definitions are called requirements type. You may see chapter 38.4 for a better understanding of requirements types.

An organizational unit can work in several shifts on each day. Therefore, you specify the shift for which you are defining manpower requirement. For a shift, you specify target, minimum and maximum manpower required.

You don't just specify the head count, you can also specify the kind of people you want. You may specify that you want six electricians (people whose job is that of an electrician). Or you may specify that you want people who have certain skills (stored in infotype 0024 in SAP). For example, you may say that you want two persons who can translate from English to German with proficiency level two. In this way, your total requirement of manpower may be specified in several lines on the requirement screen.

You can also specify different manpower requirements during different times of the shift by clicking on 🖾.

If the ID field of a requirement is 'Yes', that requirement can be met by people who are already assigned to a shift plan (Exclusive manpower is not required).

If you don't have any requirement in some shift on some day, you can create blank requirements (Edit ➤ Insert ➤ Blank requirements).

Requirement overview translates the requirements and shows the exact requirement daywise. You use transaction PP67 to create, PP63 to change and PP62 to display requirements. Requirements can be copied. If you want to copy a requirement into another requirements, you can use Edit ➤ Copy to clipboard, followed by Edit ➤ Insert from clipboard.

Requirement definitions are stored as object type SR (Planned staff requirement) in the database. The infotypes used are 1000 and 1049. It also has following relationship with other objects (infotype 1001):

➤ A Requirement (SR) may require (A031) Qualification (skill) (Q).
➤ A Requirement (SR) may have a requirement description (A062), which is a Job (C).
➤ A Requirement (SR) may be the requirements definition (B064) of an Organizational unit (O) or Work center (A).
➤ A Person (P) may be assigned (A065) to a Requirement (SR).

38.2.2 Screen

Organizational unit	CAR PLANT - MFG - TRIM & ASSEMBLY
Selection period	From 01.06.2005 To 30.06.2005
Reqmnts type	Working day

	Ab	Shift	From	To	Tar...	Min...	Ma...	Job	Qualif.	ID	Comments	Start date	End date
	PG	G Shift	08:30	17:00	10	8	12		⇨	No		23.06.2005	31.12.9999
			00:00	00:00					⇨	No		27.06.2005	31.12.9999
			00:00	00:00					⇨	No		27.06.2005	31.12.9999

38.2.3 Important Fields

Organizational unit

Organizational unit for which the requirement is being defined.

Selection period

The period for which you are viewing the requirements. If some requirement has start and end date which is totally outside the selection period, that requirement is not seen. Actual validity of requirement is shown in start date and end date fields.

Requirements type

The type of day for which requirement is being defined. Note that only those requirements types are shown here, which are valid for the shift group to which the organizational unit belongs. You may see chapter 38.5 on Shift Group for more details.

Abbreviation and shift

A day can have multiple shifts. Hence, the requirements are defined for each shift. Only in the case of blank requirements, these fields are blank.

From and to time

These fields display the shift time. However, you can change this time interval. The manpower requirement is for this time interval.

Target, minimum and maximum manpower

For each requirement you can define how many persons you want with a tolerance on either side. If the manpower assigned is equal to target, the requirement in assignment view of shift planning shows a green circle. If the assigned manpower is less than minimum manpower, the requirement is shown as a red square. In all other cases, it is shown as a yellow triangle. Thus, you can visually see where you have a problem in meeting manpower requirement.

Job

In case you need people who have a specific job (In SAP, jobs are linked to positions, which in turn are linked to persons), you can specify that here. If you need one supervisor, six welders and four fitters in general shift, you would create three requirement records specifying job in each case. This ensures that you get right kind of people. SAP uses this information for making assignment proposal.

Qualification (Skill)

In the case of qualifications, you can specify multiple qualifications. You can also specify if some qualifications are essential qualifications. SAP uses this information also for making assignment proposal.

ID

If the ID field of a requirement is 'Yes', that requirement can be met by people who are already assigned to a shift plan (Exclusive manpower is not required).

Comments

If you have multiple requirements in a shift, you need to give it a description, which you do in this field.

Start and end date

These dates specify the validity period of the requirement. Note that a requirement may not be valid for the entire selection period. When you see requirements in shift planning, these dates specify periods of requirements.

38.2.4 Requirement Overview

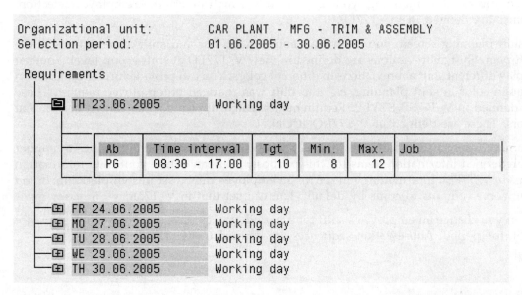

Requirement overview translates the requirements and shows the exact requirement day wise. If there are no requirements on a day, that day is not shown.

38.3 SHIFT PLANNING CONFIGURATION OVERVIEW

Functional Consultant	User	Business Process Owner	Senior Management	My Rating	Understanding Level
A	B	C	X		

This chapter explains what configuration you can do in shift planning, except those under 'Additional Settings for Public Sector Germany'.

You do shift planning for an organizational unit.

You need to assign a factory calendar to the organizational units or maintain it in global settings. Factory calendar is needed to show weekly offs.

For an organizational unit you may define requirement of manpower. Requirements are defined in terms of requirements types. SAP provides predefined requirements types. You may create your own requirements types in T77RD, if needed.

Organizational units are grouped in shift groups. These are defined in VC_T77DB. Shift groups are assigned to organizational units in infotype 1039. Thus, for an organizational unit, shift group is known.

When you define requirements for an organizational unit, you use requirements types. In doing so, you see only those requirements, which are valid for a shift group. Valid requirements for a shift group are defined in V_T77RB.

When you do shift planning, you use a profile which determines employee selection. Profiles are defined in VC_T77EP.

In shift planning screen, you see a shift abbreviation bar and shift abbreviations in the shift plan. Shift abbreviations are defined in view V_T77ED at shift group level. You can display different shift abbreviations in different colors. You can provide further information through color in shift planning, e.g. the shift was changed on employee request. These are defined in V_T77SP_STYLE. Requirements match up can also be shown in different colors. These are defined in V_T77RQ_ICON.

You may want to see additional information about employees. SAP provides a number of predefined information items for this purpose. You can define your own information items in V_T77EI. Information you see for an employee can be set in shift planning. If you want some columns to come by default, you can set that in V_T77EJ.

When you change an employee's shift for a period, you can use an abbreviation sequence to fill the period. Abbreviation sequences are defined in VC_T77SP_CE.

When you change an employee's shift, the system creates a substitution. The substitution type can be taken from global settings. If you want the user to manually specify it, you specify valid substitution types in V_T77ER.

During shift planning, you may want the system to do automatic assignment of employees to requirements. While doing so, how the system should behave is defined as strategies in V_T77EVOPT. In defining strategy, you use suitability criteria. You can create your own suitability criteria in V_T77EH. A shift group can have a default assignment strategy, which can be configured in V_T77EVOPT_DEF.

During shift planning, a user can change assignment options. Which options he can change, and which he cannot are specified in V_T77EOPT.

During shift planning, you can display the day details in multiple Tabs. You can configure these tabs in VC_77EDAYCUST.

Normally you use RPTIME00 for time evaluation during shift planning. If you want to use some other program, you can specify that in table T596F.

There are several global settings for shift planning. These are specified in table T77S0 (Group PEINS).

38.4 REQUIREMENTS TYPE

Functional Consultant	User	Business Process Owner	Senior Management	My Rating	Understanding Level
A	C	X	X		

38.4.1 Purpose and Overview

In shift planning, you need to specify shiftwise manpower requirement of an organizational unit or work center for each day. Instead of asking you to specify the requirement for each day, SAP lets you specify the requirement in a generic way, e.g. requirements on a working day, requirements on a weekly off day, requirements on a public holiday, etc.

In order to determine whether a day is a working day, a weekly off day or a public holiday, you need to specify the logic. This logic is written in the function module associated with the requirements type. SAP supplies you function modules for common requirements, e.g. Sunday, Public holiday, New Year's Day. If you define your own requirements types, you have to see if a suitable function module exists. If not you have to write one.

Some days may qualify the criteria of more than one requirements type. A public holiday may fall on a working day, or it may fall on an off day. When that happens, you get two requirements for the same day. You need to define which one gets priority. This is defined at requirements type level.

You may notice a requirements type SPECIFIC, which has priority number 1, i.e. highest priority. This requirements type is valid for all days. Hence, if you want 10 persons on 15th November 2005, regardless of any other criteria, you include a requirement with requirements type SPECIFIC, for 15th November 2005.

Requirements types are assigned to shift groups, and are available only in those shift groups, and hence in the associated organization units.

38.4.2   IMG Node

SM30 ≻ T77RD

38.4.3   Screen

ReqmtsType	Name	Pr	Function module
BEFHOLIDAY	Before public holiday	3	RH_REQUEST_ON_BEFOREHOLIDAYS
BRIDGEDAY	Bridge day	3	RH_REQUEST_ON_BRIDGEDAYS
CHRISTEVE	Christmas Eve	2	RH_REQUEST_ON_CHRISTMASEVE
DAYOFF	Workfree day	3	RH_REQUEST_ON_DAYOFF
EASTERMON	Easter Monday	2	RH_REQUEST_ON_EASTERMONDAY
EASTERSUN	Easter Sunday	2	RH_REQUEST_ON_EASTERSUNDAY

38.4.4   Primary Key

Requirements Type for Shift Planning

38.4.5   Important Fields

Requirements type for shift planning

An organizational unit or work center may have different types of requirements, e.g. requirements on weekdays, requirements on weekly offs, etc. These are identified by requirements types.

Priority of requirements type

If multiple requirements types are valid for a given date, the requirement with highest priority (lowest priority number) is taken.

Function module

These function modules read the necessary data, including factory calendar, for a given date and determine whether the date meets the criteria coded in the function module. If the criteria are not met, that requirement does not apply to that date.

38.5 SHIFT GROUP

Functional Consultant	User	Business Process Owner	Senior Management	My Rating	Understanding Level
A	X	X	X		

38.5.1 Purpose and Overview

What is it?

In your organization, you may have many shifts. All of these may not be applicable to all organizational units. SAP lets you group your organizational units in shift groups. The basic criterion is that they should have the same set of shift abbreviations (shifts, attendances, absences). A shift group should not cut across DWS groupings. For reasons, see DWS grouping field in V_T77ED.

How is it determined?

Shift group is determined from the organizational units for which shift planning is being done. You can link organization units to a shift group through infotype 1039. All organizational units below that organizational unit will inherit the shift group, unless a shift group is specifically assigned to them. If no shift group is assigned to an organizational unit, default value for shift group is taken from table T77S0 (PEINS+GROUP).

How is it used?

A shift group is associated with shift abbreviations. These shift abbreviations are available to all organizational units in the shift group. Similarly, a shift group is associated with certain requirements types. These requirements types are available to all organizational units associated with the shift group.

A shift group also has color and character formatting, which are assigned to a predefined list. For a cell, the characteristic is determined and it is displayed in the color and character format associated with it.

Abbreviation sequences are defined at shift group level, and thereby become available to an organizational unit.

Substitution types which can be used in target plan, and substitution types which can be used in actual plan, are defined at shift group level.

A shift group can have a default assignment strategy.

38.5.2 IMG Node

SM34 ➤ VC_T77DB (V_T77DB)

38.5.3 Screen

Dialog Structure
▽ 🗁 Shift groups
📁 Shift abbreviation
📁 Requirements types
📁 General color and ch

Shift groups	
Shift group	Name
STANDARD	Standard Shift Group

38.5.4 Primary Key

Shift Group for Organizational Units

38.6 SHIFT ABBREVIATION

Functional Consultant	User	Business Process Owner	Senior Management	My Rating	Understanding Level
A	X	X	X		

38.6.1 Purpose and Overview

Shift abbreviations present a consolidated picture in shift planning. Through them, you can specify daily work schedule/attendance/absence/availability.

An organizational unit is linked to a shift group, which has shift abbreviations. When you are doing shift planning for an organizational unit, these shift abbreviations are shown in the shift abbreviation bar. They are also shown in the list of values. Moreover, an employee's shift is shown using shift abbreviations. You can change a day's plan directly in shift planning. SAP automatically creates appropriate infotype record.

If an employee's shift/attendance/absence/availability does not match with any shift abbreviation, it is shown as * by the system. In this way, you can immediately recognize a shift abbreviation that is not permitted while you are still in the planning process.

You can define shift abbreviation sequences (you may see chapter 38.9), so that instead of assigning one shift abbreviation at a time, you can assign a whole sequence.

38.6.2 IMG Node

SM34 ➤ VC_T77DB (V_T77ED)

38.6.3 Screen

Shift group   STANDARD

Shift abbreviation

Shift	Shift	D.	Dai...	V...	From	To	Break	Abs.	Att.	Auth	Sort.	Color	N...	Hi...	In...	B...	It...	U...
//	Off	01	FREI		00:00	00:00	00:00	☐	☐	☐		Backg... ▤	◉	○	○	☐	☐	☐
B	On-call duty	01	RUFB		08:00	20:00	00:00	☐	☐	☑		Backg... ▤	◉	○	○	☐	☐	☐
FR	Early shift	01	F-11		05:30	14:15	01:00	☐	☐	☐		Backg... ▤	◉	○	○	☐	☐	☐
GL	Flextime	01	GLZ		08:00	17:00	01:00	☐	☐	☐		Backg... ▤	◉	○	○	☐	☐	☐
K	III	01			00:00	00:00	00:00	☑	☐	☐		Backg... ▤	◉	○	○	☐	☐	☐
NA	Night shift	01	N-11		22:30	05:45	01:00	☐	☐	☐		Backg... ▤	◉	○	○	☐	☐	☐
SP	Late shift	01	S-11		14:00	22:45	01:00	☐	☐	☐		Backg... ▤	◉	○	○	☐	☐	☐
T	Seminar/Course	01			00:00	00:00	00:00	☐	☑	☐		Backg... ▤	◉	○	○	☐	☐	☐
U	Leave	01			00:00	00:00	00:00	☑	☐	☐		Backg... ▤	◉	○	○	☐	☐	☐

38.6.4 Primary Key

Shift Group for Organizational Units + Shift Abbreviation for Shift Planning

38.6.5 Important Fields

Shift group

Shift abbreviations are defined for a shift group.

Shift abbreviation and description

Shift abbreviations present a consolidated picture in shift planning. Through them, you can specify daily work schedule/attendance/absence/availability. You can change a day's plan directly in shift planning. SAP automatically creates appropriate infotype record.

DWS grouping

Since a daily work schedule is defined at DWS grouping (PS grouping for daily work schedules) level, you specify the DWS grouping along with daily work schedule. Therefore, your shift group should not cut across a DWS grouping. If you have too many DWS groupings, this could create a problem. You must ensure that every organizational unit is within a DWS grouping and that appropriate shift group is attached to it.

Daily work schedule and daily work schedule variant

If a shift abbreviation represents a daily work schedule (including variant), you specify that here. When an employee's shift is replaced by this shift abbreviation, SAP creates a substitution in infotype 2003 specifying this daily work schedule as the new work schedule.

From and to

If you specify a daily work schedule, the system automatically picks up the shift time. If you are not specifying a daily work schedule, you can enter the shift start and end time directly.

Break

Break hours are picked up directly from the daily work schedule.

Attendance/absence/availability indicator

If the shift abbreviation represents an attendance/absence/availability, you click on Attendance | Absence | Availability . They open a window where you enter relevant details. Attendance/absence/daily work schedule are mutually exclusive. When defining availability, you define it along with a daily work schedule.

Sort

Your users may like to see the shifts in a certain order in the shift abbreviation bar. This can be achieved by specifying the sort order in this field.

Color, normal/highlight/inverted, bold, italics, underlined

You can display different shifts in different ways using these characteristics. For example, you may want to show absence in a different color.

38.7 REQUIREMENTS TYPES FOR A SHIFT GROUP

Functional Consultant	User	Business Process Owner	Senior Management	My Rating	Understanding Level
A	X	X	X		

38.7.1 Purpose

This view contains the requirements types permitted for a shift group, and thereby for an organizational unit. Requirements types, which are defined in T77RD, can be made available to a shift group.

38.7.2 IMG Node

SM34 ➤ VC_T77DB (V_T77RB)

38.7.3 Screen

	ReqmtsType	Reqmts type text
	DAYOFF	Workfree day
	FRIDAYS	Friday
	HOLIDAYS	Public holiday
	MONDAYS	Monday
	SATURDAYS	Saturday
	SPECIFIC	Special daily requirements
	STANDARD	General requirements
	SUNDAYS	Sunday

Shift group: STANDARD

Requirements types

38.7.4 Primary Key

Shift Group for Organizational Units + Requirements Type for Shift Planning

38.8 GENERAL COLOR AND CHARACTER FORMATTING

Functional Consultant	User	Business Process Owner	Senior Management	My Rating	Understanding Level
A	X	X	X		

38.8.1 Purpose and Overview

You can use this view to format the output of your shift plan. Depending on the logical determination of the status of a field, the formatting is applied. If a field satisfies multiple status conditions, e.g. the shift is changed on employee's request, at the same time the employee is already assigned to a requirement; you need to decide which formatting is to be applied. This decision is based on the priority field.

38.8.2 IMG Node

SM34 ➤ VC_T77DB (V_T77SP_STYLE)

38.8.3   Screen

Shift group	STANDARD

General color and character formattings

	Status	Color	Normal	Highlight	Inverted	Priority	Bold	Italics	Und...
	Req... 🗐	Background col... 🗐	⦿	◯	◯		☐	☐	☐
	Cha... 🗐	Background col... 🗐	⦿	◯	◯		☐	☐	☐
	🗐	Background col... 🗐	⦿	◯	◯		☐	☐	☐
	🗐	Background col... 🗐	⦿	◯	◯		☐	☐	☐
	🗐	Background col... 🗐	⦿	◯	◯		☐	☐	☐

38.8.4   Primary Key

Shift Group for Organizational Units + Planning Status of Color and Character Formatting

38.8.5   Important Fields

Shift group

Color and character formatting can differ from shift group to shift group.

Status

SAP has identified a number of conditions for which you may want the day's plan to be highlighted. For example, you may want to know if the shift is changed on employee's request, or whether a person is already assigned to a requirement. You may also want to identify shift changes you have done.

Color

Depending on the status of a field, you can specify the color in which the information should be displayed.

Normal/highlight/inverted

Apart from the color, you can specify whether the information should be highlighted or inverted.

Priority

If a field satisfies multiple status conditions, e.g. the shift is changed on employee's request, at the same time the employee is already assigned to a requirement; you need to decide which formatting is to be applied. This decision is based on the priority field.

Bold, italics, underlined

These checkboxes can be used to highlight the information further.

38.9 ABBREVIATION SEQUENCE

Functional Consultant	User	Business Process Owner	Senior Management	My Rating	Understanding Level
A	X	X	X		

38.9.1 Purpose

When you are changing shifts of an employee in shift planning, you would like to save effort by changing shifts for an entire period, rather than one day at a time. Sometimes you would assign a single shift to the entire period for an employee. However, there may be occasions when you want to assign shifts, which follow a pattern. For example, you may want the employee to alternate between morning shift and afternoon shift. SAP lets you create abbreviation sequences. When the employee has to follow shifts in a sequence, you can specify the abbreviation sequence for the period. The employee's shifts are replaced as per the abbreviation sequence. Abbreviation sequences can differ from shift group to shift group.

38.9.2 IMG Node

SM34 ➤ VC_T77SP_CE. Views V_T77SP_CD and V_T77SP_CE

38.9.3 Screen

	Shift group	Seq. name	Description
	STANDARD	5XGL+2X//	Standard: Flextime model for one week
	STANDARD	FR+SP+NA	Standard: Rolling shift system with availability
	STANDARD	SAP_F_S_N	Sequence: 1 week early shift/ 1 week late/ 1 w
	STANDARD	SAP_GLZ	Sequence: 5 days flextime/ 2 days off work
	STANDARD	SAP_GLZ_B	Sequence: 1 week flextime & on-call duty

Dialog Structure
▽ Define sequence
  Assign shift abbrevia

Shift group   STANDARD
Sequence name   FR+SP+NA

	Day no.	Item no.	Ab	Start Time	End Time	Shift description
	1	1	FR	05:30:00	14:15:00	Früh
	2	1	FR	05:30:00	14:15:00	Früh
	3	1	FR	05:30:00	14:15:00	Früh
	4	1	FR	05:30:00	14:15:00	Früh
	5	1	FR	05:30:00	14:15:00	Früh

38.9.4 Primary Key

Shift Group for Organizational Units + Name for Abbreviation Sequence + Day Number + Item Number

38.9.5 Important Fields

Shift group

Abbreviation sequences are defined for a shift group.

Sequence name

Name of the abbreviation sequence.

Day number

When you are assigning an abbreviation sequence to an employee's planning period, the abbreviations get applied in day number sequence.

Item number

You can use this field if you want to assign both shift and availability for the same day.

Shift abbreviation and description

Shift abbreviation which is to be assigned to an employee depending on day number.

Start and end time

Start and end time is automatically picked up for the shift. You cannot change it.

38.10 SUBSTITUTION TYPES IN SHIFT PLANS

Functional Consultant	User	Business Process Owner	Senior Management	My Rating	Understanding Level
A	X	X	X		

38.10.1 Determination of Substitution Type in Shift Planning

When you change a shift in shift plan, a substitution record is created in infotype 2003. Each substitution record must have a substitution type. SAP offers various methods of determining this substitution type.

You can specify three different substitution types, one for changes in target plan, one for changes in actual plan, and one for shift changes on employee request. Appropriate substitution type is automatically selected when a substitution record is created. These are specified in table T77S0 (PEINS + VARTI/VARTS/VARWI).

SAP also lets you specify the substitution type manually, if you so desire. To activate this, you set system switch PEINS+VTART in table T77S0.

It further lets you control which substitution types are available for target plan, and which for actual plan. These are set in this table T77ER.

When you want to manually determine substitution type, you open Edit shift window, either by double clicking on a cell in shift plan, or by navigating through Edit ≻ Shift details. You specify substitution type in the indicator field in this window.

Note that if table T77ER is not maintained, or does not return any row, the indicator field is not shown in this window. Indicator field is also not shown if system switch PEINS+VTART in table T77S0 is not active.

38.10.2 IMG Node

SM30 ≻ V_T77ER

38.10.3 Screen

	Shift grp	PSG	Type	Text	TargetPlan	ActualPlan
	STANDARD	01	01	Foreman substitution	☑	☐
	STANDARD	01	02	Shift substitution	☑	☐
	STANDARD	01	05	Actual plan substitution	☐	☑
	STANDARD	01	06	Requested working time	☑	☑

38.10.4 Primary Key

Shift Group for Organizational Units + PS Grouping for Substitution/Availability Types + Substitution Type

38.10.5 Important Fields

Shift group

Substitution types, which are available for target plan and actual plan depend on shift group.

PS grouping

Substitution types, which are available for target plan and actual plan, also depend on PS grouping for substitution/availability types.

Substitution type

Substitution types, which are available for manual selection in the target plan or actual plan.

Target plan

This checkbox determines whether the substitution type is available for manual selection in the target plan.

Actual plan

This checkbox determines whether the substitution type is available for manual selection in the actual plan.

38.11 SHIFT GROUP ASSIGNMENT TO ORGANIZATIONAL UNIT

Functional Consultant	User	Business Process Owner	Senior Management	My Rating	Understanding Level
A	X	X	X		

38.11.1 Purpose

Shift groups are assigned to an organization unit in infotype 1039. Shift group can also be assigned to a work center. For an organizational unit, the following are determined through shift group:

> Shift abbreviations
> Requirements types
> Color and character formatting
> Abbreviation sequences
> Substitution types for manual selection in target and actual plan
> Default assignment strategy

If the shift group is assigned to an organizational unit, it is available to all organizational units under it through the principle of inheritance. If no shift group is assigned to an organizational unit, default value for shift group is taken from table T77S0 (PEINS+GROUP).

38.11.2 IMG Node

Transaction	PO10	Maintain Organizational Unit
Transaction	S_AHR_61004980	Maintain shift group infotype for organizational unit

38.11.3 Screen

Shift Group	01 O 100000001 1
Shift group	

38.12   FACTORY CALENDAR

Functional Consultant	User	Business Process Owner	Senior Management	My Rating	Understanding Level
A	C	X	X		

38.12.1   Purpose and Overview

In shift planning you need to identify weekly offs, because on those days you may require less manpower. In factory calendar you define which days of a week are working days and which days are non-working days.

You can also specify whether public holidays are working days or non-working days. For identifying public holidays, you also associate a public holiday calendar with a factory calendar.

Finally, you can specify any specific day as working or non-working, in special rules. Each working day of a factory can be given a unique factory date. Since the factory calendar of a factory may change, you need to specify from what number the factory date should begin.

38.12.2   IMG Node

Transaction OY05   Factory calendar

38.12.3   Screen

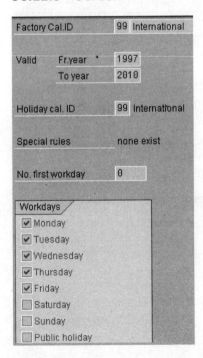

38.13 FACTORY CALENDAR ASSIGNMENT TO ORGANIZATIONAL UNIT

Functional Consultant	User	Business Process Owner	Senior Management	My Rating	Understanding Level
A	C	X	X		

38.13.1 Purpose and Overview

In shift planning, you need to identify weekly offs, because on those days you may require less manpower. The weekly offs are identified in factory calendar.

If you have only one factory calendar, you can specify it in table T77S0 (PEINS+CALID). However, if different organizational units follow different factory calendar, you specify it in infotype 1027 'Site-Dependent Info' for the organizational unit. If, for an organizational unit, no factory calendar is specified, it is taken from table T77S0 (PEINS+CALID).

Factory calendar is used in function modules, which define requirements type. You can use transaction PP01 to maintain 'Factory calendar assignment to organizational unit'.

38.14 STRATEGIES FOR AUTOMATIC ASSIGNMENT PROPOSAL

Functional Consultant	User	Business Process Owner	Senior Management	My Rating	Understanding Level
B	X	X	X		

38.14.1 Purpose

Here you define the strategies which determine how the automatic assignment proposal works. Strategies are assigned to shift plans at three levels. These are given below in the decreasing order of priority

➢ Specifically selected strategy during shift planning (Settings ➢ Select strategy)
➢ Strategy for a shift group (T77EVOPT_DEF)
➢ Strategy for a client (PEINS + RULE in T77S0)

Apart from selecting the strategy, you can change the assignment options during shift planning (Settings ➢ Assignment options).

38.14.2 IMG Node

SM30 ➢ V_T77EVOPT

38.14.3   Screen

Strategy   SAP_1   No 1

Working time
- ☐ Adjust working time to reqs   ☐ Use current settings
  - ◉ By altering working time
  - ○ By increasing working time
    - with

- ☑ Do not split requirements interval   ☐ Use current settings
- ☑ Do not split working time   ☐ Use current settings
- ☑ Membership relevant   ☐ Use current settings
- ☑ Job relevant   ☐ Use current settings
- ☐ Reqmts with ID

Priority
- Priority 1   ☑ Use current settings
- Priority 2
- Priority 3
- Priority 4

Target   1

38.14.4   Primary Key

Strategy for Automatic Proposal Determination + Serial Number for Proposal Determination Strategy

38.14.5   Important Fields

Strategy

You can have various strategies for automatic proposal determination. This field contains the name of the strategy being defined.

Number

After you have done assignment of employees to requirements using a strategy, the entire requirement may not get fulfilled. You may then like the system to relax the strategy rules, so that it can do more assignment. You can do this by creating multiple parts of a strategy using this field. It also specifies the sequence in which the strategy is applied.

Adjusting working time, alter working time, increase working time, attendance type

Your strategy may be to adjust employees' working time to meet the requirement. This can be done by altering working time or increasing working time. In case you are altering working time, a substitution is created. In case you are increasing working time, an attendance record is created with specified attendance type.

Do not split requirements interval

If you do not have an employee, who completely covers your requirement, the system has two choices, it can split the requirement interval, covering different interval by different employees, or leave the requirement unassigned. You make that choice here.

Do not split working time

Here you specify that an employee should be assigned to a requirement only if he is fully utilized. If not, he should not be assigned.

Membership relevant

If you select this checkbox, the employees of an organizational unit are assigned only to the requirement of that organizational unit.

Job relevant

If you select this checkbox, an employee is assigned to a requirement only if his job is same as that specified in the requirement.

Requirements with ID

Normally, once an employee is assigned to a requirement, he is occupied and cannot be used for other requirements. However, there are some requirements, which may not require the employee to devote much time, but take responsibility. For example, among many shift supervisors, you may want to specify one, who is shift in-charge.

You can do so, by creating a requirement of shift in-charge, but turn on the ID, so that the system knows that the person fulfilling this requirement can be assigned to other requirements as well. Here you specify whether you want the system to fill these requirements also, during automatic assignment proposal.

Priority 1 to priority 4

When the system is creating an automatic assignment proposal, there may be several employees available to meet a requirement. The system needs to decide who should be assigned first. The system gives you the following options, on which the system can base its decision:

➤ Employment percentage
➤ Qualitative essential requirements fulfilled
➤ Qualitative suitability
➤ Length of service

You can decide the order in which you want to apply these criteria. Applying each criterion narrows the choice. Finally, when the choice cannot be narrowed any further, the system assigns an employee randomly. It then repeats the process to assign the next employee.

Target

When you define a requirement, you define minimum, target and maximum manpower required. When the system is assigning manpower to requirement, should it try to assign the minimum, target, maximum, or more than the maximum manpower? You specify that here.

Use current settings

If you tick this checkbox, the shift planner can change these settings in the shift plan (Settings ➤ Assignment options). You see this checkbox against various items on the screen. These can be set independently. By doing so, you can determine what settings the user can change during shift planning.

38.15 DEFINITION OF PROPOSAL LISTS

Functional Consultant	User	Business Process Owner	Senior Management	My Rating	Understanding Level
B	X	X .	X		

38.15.1 Purpose and Overview

When you define strategies for automatic assignment proposal in V_T77EVOPT, you can control which employees are proposed by the system first. This is done by defining suitability criteria and assigning them priorities. SAP has provided four suitability criteria. If you need more suitability criteria, you need to define them here.

38.15.2 IMG Node

SM30 ➤ V_T77EH

38.15.3 Screen

Name	EMPCT
Name	Employment percentage
☐ Inactive	

Function module	HRSP_HITLIST_EMPLOYMENT_PCT

Sort
- ○ Ascending
- ◉ Descending
- ○ Undefined

38.15.4 Primary Key

Hitlist of Suitability Criteria for Proposal Determination

38.15.5 Important Fields

Name of suitability criteria and description

For each suitability criterion, you give a name and description.

Inactive

If you select this checkbox, the suitability criterion becomes inactive, and is not available for priority assignment in table V_T77EVOPT.

Function module

Here you specify the function module which determines an employee's suitability.

Sort ascending/descending/undefined

The function module sequences the employees as per criteria. For some criteria, e.g. length of service, in some strategy you may want to select the senior most person, while in some other strategy, you may want to select the junior most person. This can be achieved by using the sort field, instead of creating another function module. If you want to use the default sort of the function module, you choose undefined.

38.16 ASSIGNMENT STRATEGY DEFAULTS

Functional Consultant	User	Business Process Owner	Senior Management	My Rating	Understanding Level
B	X	X	X		

38.16.1 Purpose

Here you can assign default strategies to shift groups. Strategies are assigned to shift plans at three levels. These are given below in the decreasing order of priority.

➢ Specifically selected strategy (Settings ➢ Select strategy during shift planning)
➢ Strategy for a shift group (T77EVOPT_DEF)
➢ Strategy for a client (PEINS + RULE in T77S0)

38.16.2 IMG Node

SM30 ➢ V_T77EVOPT_DEF

38.16.3 Screen

Default Value for Assignment Strategy		
Shift group	Strategy	Text

38.16.4 Primary Key

Shift Group for Organizational Units

38.16.5 Important Fields

Shift group

Shift group for which strategy is being defined.

Strategy

Default strategy for the shift group.

38.17 ASSIGNMENT OPTIONS

Functional Consultant	User	Business Process Owner	Senior Management	My Rating	Understanding Level
B	X	X	X		

38.17.1 Purpose

When you want the system to do automatic assignment, it uses the strategy defined in view V_T77EVOPT. However, you may want to give the users flexibility in changing the strategy when doing their shift planning. In shift planning, if you go to Settings ➤ Assignment options, you see the following dialog box:

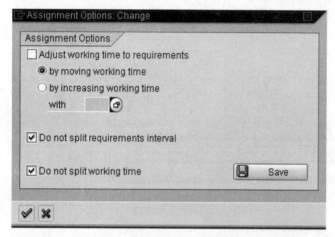

The options which are enabled for the user is specified in view V_T77EOPT. Through this, you can provide the users restricted flexibility. Note that these restrictions apply to all users.

38.17.2 IMG Node

SM30 ➤ V_T77EOPT

38.17.3 Screen

Option	Name	Value	Changble	Saveable
ADOPT	Adjust working time to reqs		✔	✔
ADOPTATT	Extend working time by attendance		✔	✔
ADOPTAWART	Attendance type for extension		✔	✔
ADOPTSUB	Adjust by substitution	X	✔	✔
SPLIT1	Do not split requirements interval	X	✔	✔
SPLIT2	Do not split working time	X	✔	✔

38.17.4 Primary Key

Assignment Option

38.17.5 Important Fields

Option and name

This field specifies what flexibility is to be allowed. These are predefined by SAP.

Value

Through this field you activate the option.

Changeable

If you select this checkbox, the user can change the option in the dialog box.

Saveable

If you select this checkbox, the user can save the dialog box option. When he opens the dialog box again, he finds the value he had saved.

38.18 INFORMATION COLUMNS DEFINITION

Functional Consultant	User	Business Process Owner	Senior Management	My Rating	Understanding Level
B	C	X	X		

38.18.1 Purpose and Overview

When you are doing shift planning, you may like to see certain information about the employee. For example, you may want to see how much overtime he has done, or how much flex balance he has. You can modify the shift planning layout to see up to four columns of information about employees at a time (Views ➤ Edit information columns). But you can choose these four columns from a list created by SAP, or those defined by you.

This node is for defining your own information content, which can be seen in shift planning. You can create it either by associating a function module, time type or wage type. You can also display time evaluation errors in a column. If you do not wish anyone to use some information, instead of deleting it, you can make it inactive.

38.18.2 IMG Node

SM30 ➤ V_T77EI

38.18.3 Screen

Name	ORGEH
Name	Organizational unit
☐ Inactive	

Function module	
Function module	HR_INFOCOLUMN_ORG_ASSIGNMENT

or time type	
PS grouping	
Time type	

or wage type	
Ctry Grouping	
Wage type	

or error	
☐ Time eval. errors	

38.18.4 Primary Key

Contents and Description of Info Column in Shift Plan

38.19 INFORMATION COLUMNS DEFAULTS

Functional Consultant	User	Business Process Owner	Senior Management	My Rating	Understanding Level
B	C	X	X		

38.19.1 Purpose and Overview

In this view you can specify the information, which is available in shift plan by default. You choose from the fields defined in V_T77EI. Note that in a shift plan, your choice is not restricted only to these information columns. You have all the information columns available, except those, which are marked inactive.

If you want the information to be visible by default in the shift plan, you tick the field visible. If you want the user to be able to change the settings in the shift plan, you tick the field changeable. If you want to permit the users to be able to save the non-standard settings in the shift plan, you tick the field saveable.

38.19.2 IMG Node

SM30 ➢ V_T77EJ

38.19.3 Screen

Column	Name	Name	Visible	Changble	Saveable
INFO_01	PERNR	Personnel number	☐	☑	☑
INFO_02	JOBS	Job	☐	☑	☑
INFO_03	ORGEH	Organizational unit	☐	☑	☑
INFO_04	GENERAL	General info	☐	☑	☑

38.19.4 Primary Key

Physical Info Column in the Shift Plan

38.20 REQUIREMENTS MATCHUP ICONS

Functional Consultant	User	Business Process Owner	Senior Management	My Rating	Understanding Level
B	C	X	X		

38.20.1 Purpose

Here you define the icons, colors and fonts for different types of requirement coverage.

Requirement coverage exceeds the maximum number of employees
Requirement coverage matches the maximum number of employees
Requirement coverage does not meet the minimum number of employees
Requirement coverage matchup matches the minimum number of employees
Requirement coverage exceeds the target number of employees
Requirement coverage does not meet the target number of employees
Requirement coverage matches the target number of employees

38.20.2 IMG Node

SM30 ➢ V_T77RQ_ICON

38.20.3 Screen

Status   SAP_MAX_+

Set Requirements Matchup Icons

Status   Requirement coverage exceeds the maximum number of employees

Icon   △   ICON_LED_YELLOW

Formatting for color

Color   Background color (background dependent on GUI)

● Normal
○ Intensive
○ Inverse

Formatting for fonts

☐ Bold
☐ Italics
☐ Underlined

38.20.4 Primary Key

Current status of requirements coverage in requirements matchup.

38.21 PERMITTED TAB PAGES

Functional Consultant	User	Business Process Owner	Senior Management	My Rating	Understanding Level
B	C	X	X		

38.21.1 Purpose

During shift planning, if you go to Edit ➢ Shift details, the system displays the day details in multiple tabs. In permitted tab pages, you specify all the tab pages. You can add your own for which you need to create the screens first. In displayed tab pages, you specify which tab pages are displayed. You also need to activate the switch (PEINS + DCUST) in table T77S0. If this field is blank, the system shows default tab pages. For more details, see IMG node help.

38.21.2 IMG Node

SM34 ➤ VC_77EDAYCUST (T77EDAYCUST_E and V_T77EDAYCUST)

38.21.3 Permitted Tab Pages

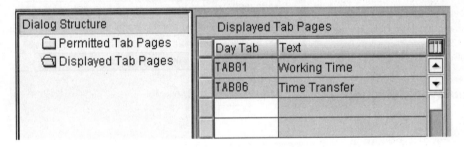

38.21.4 Displayed Tab Pages

38.22 SHIFT PLANNING PROFILE

Functional Consultant	User	Business Process Owner	Senior Management	My Rating	Understanding Level
A	X	X	X		

38.22.1 Purpose

When you start shift planning, you start with a profile. The profile determines which employees are selected for shift planning. Most commonly used and default profile is SAP_000001. It includes all the employees belonging to an organizational unit, except those who are deployed out (exclusive temporary assignment), plus those who are deployed in. The employees who are exclusively deployed out are not shown in an organizational unit's shift plan.

SAP also lets you deploy a person, such that he is available to both organizational units for assignment. Such deployment is done through relationship 071. This is included in profile SAP_000004. If you are using this profile, when you do temporary assignment, you see a checkbox, where you can specify that the employee has shared availability. If so specified, the employee is not excluded from the shift plan of the deploying organizational unit.

In the profile you specify the evaluation paths of employees to be included and excluded. These configurations are stored in tables T77EP and T77EC. You can set the profile before you start shift planning using transaction PP66.

38.22.2 IMG Node

SM34 ➢ VC_T77EP

38.22.3 Screen

Dialog Structure
▽ ☐ Define profiles
☐ Employee selection
☐ Remove employee from selection
☐ Employee assigned elsewhere
☐ Requirements source for entry objects

Profile	Description	E...
SAP_000001	Employees in organizational units	0
SAP_000002	Work center view	0
SAP_000003	Work center view accdg. to OrgStructure	0
SAP_000004	EE in org. units (parallel temp.assgmt)	0
SAP_000005	Employees along organizational structure	0
SAP_PT50	Quota overview / Worklist	0

38.22.4 Employee Selection

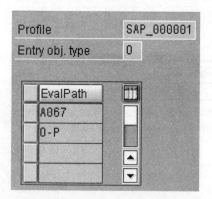

Profile	SAP_000001
Entry obj. type	0

EvalPath	
A067	
O-P	

Here you can specify the evaluation paths, which are used to include employees in shift planning for a given organizational unit (entry object). The entry object comes from the selection screen of shift planning. Evaluation path O-P shows the employees in the organizational unit and evaluation path A067 shows the employees deployed to that organizational unit. Employee selection is stored in view V_T77EC_I.

38.22.5 Remove Employee from Selection

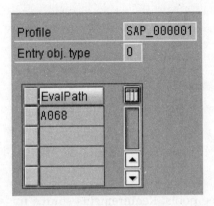

Here you can specify the evaluation paths, which are used to exclude employees in shift planning for a given organizational unit (entry object). The entry object comes from the selection screen of shift planning. Evaluation path A067 excludes the employees for whom shift planning is not to be done. Remove employee from selection is stored in view V_T77EC_E.

38.22.6 Employee Assigned Elsewhere

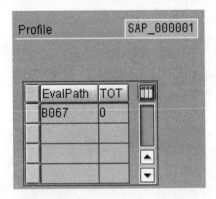

'Employee assigned elsewhere' is also used to exclude employees in shift planning. Evaluation path B067 excludes the employees who are deployed to other organizational units. Employee assigned elsewhere is stored in view V_T77EC_T.

38.22.7   Requirements Source for Entry Objects

You can use this node to get employees from employee pools. Requirements source for entry objects is stored in view V_T77EC_R.

38.23   HR SUBROUTINES

Functional Consultant	User	Business Process Owner	Senior Management	My Rating	Understanding Level
B	X	X	X		

38.23.1   Purpose

You only need to carry out this step if you have copied the standard time evaluation report (RPTIME00), and you want to call the copied version in shift planning. In that case, maintain the entry 'RPTIME00' in the field 'Symb.Name'. In the field 'Module pool', enter the name of the program to be called.

38.23.2   IMG Node

SM30 ≻ T596F

38.23.3   Screen

Symb.name	Start Date	End Date	Mod. pool	Module	Ty.
RPTIME00	01.01.1800	31.12.9999	RPTIME00	EXTCALL	R

38.24 GLOBAL SETTINGS FOR SHIFT PLANNING

Functional Consultant	User	Business Process Owner	Senior Management	My Rating	Understanding Level
A	C	X	X		

38.24.1 Purpose

This view stores global settings. Group for shift planning is PEINS. Note that all these settings are current. They cannot change with time.

38.24.2 IMG Node

SM30 ➢ T77S0

38.24.3 Settings for Shift Planning

Sem. abbr.	Description	Remarks
	Define Substitution Types	
VARTI	Substitution type for shifts in the actual plan	When you change a shift in actual plan, a substitution is created. Here you specify the substitution type of that record.
VARTS	Substitution type for shifts in the target plan	When you change a shift in target plan, a substitution is created. Here you specify the substitution type of that record.
VARWI	Substitution type for working time preferences	When you change a shift due to employee preference, a substitution is created. Here you specify the substitution type of that record.
	Define Report Variant for Time Evaluation	
SCEME	Report variant for time evaluation	Specify here the report variant you want to use when you call time evaluation from within shift planning.
	Set Up Assignments as Simulated Attendances	
AWART	Attendance type of assignments for simulation	When you do simulated time evaluation for shift planning, it is assumed that the employee is present as per the shift plan. Here you specify the attendance type used for that purpose.
VARIA	Report variant for calling time evaluation	In this field, you specify the report variant used for the simulated evaluation of an employee's assignment to a requirement or shift.

(Contd.)

Sem. abbr.	Description	Remarks
	Set Employee Status for Simulation	
PZTEF	Org. employee status from time management	Here you specify whether the time evaluation simulation is carried out with time management status according to the target working time infotype (0007) or status 9 (time evaluation–target).
	Define Shift Abbreviations for Special Functions	
TIM_V	Shift abbreviation for time substitution in plan	Which shift abbreviation or symbol is displayed in the shift plan if an employee was assigned a working time that deviates from his or her actual shift (time substitution) and for which there is no shift abbreviation.
	Define Standard Shift Group	
GROUP	Default value for shift group of Shift Planning	An organizational unit is linked to a shift group in infotype 1039 either directly or through inheritance from higher organizational unit. If a shift group is not defined for an organizational unit in either of these ways, the shift group given here is taken.
	Define Groupings	
MOABW	Personnel subarea grouping for absence/attendance	Here you define default values for PS grouping for attendance/absence types, which are used when you create a new shift group.
MOTPR	Personnel subarea grouping for daily work schedule	Here you define default values for PS grouping for daily work schedules, which are used when you create a new shift group.
MOVER	Personnel subarea grouping for substitution/availability	Here you define default values for PS grouping for substitution/availability types, which are used when you create a new shift group.
	Specify Factory Calendar	
CALID	Calendar ID of the Shift Planning factory calendar	This entry contains the id of the factory calendar relevant to shift planning if a specific factory calendar has not been entered in infotype 1027 'Site-Dependent Info' for the organizational unit.
	Set Up Automatic Proposal Determination	
RULE	Strategy for automatic assignment proposal	Here you can define the base strategy, which should be followed in automatic assignment proposal. This applies to all entry objects by default. However, while doing shift planning, you can go to Settings ➤ Select strategy, and change the strategy.
SMUDR	Period for assignment proposal	If you activate this switch, the shift planner can set the period in the shift plan overview that is to be used for automatic proposal determination.

(Contd.)

Sem. abbr.	Description	Remarks
SMUCD	Assignment proposal only on days with changes	If you activate this switch, the shift planner can restrict the automatic proposal determination in the shift plan overview to the days on which changes were made. This function is active only if the PEINS SMUDR switch is also activated.
RULE2	Strategy for automatic assignment if plan changes	Here you specify the strategy that the system uses to assign an employee to a requirement when his/ her shift/working times have been changed. You can also do that in the shift plan.

View for Employee Selection

DBSEL	Selection view to restrict employee selection	

Indicator for Shifts in Shift Plan

VTART	Change of substitution type in shift plan active	Here you specify whether substitution types can be specified when you change shift in a shift plan. You may see table T77ER for more details.

Reaction to Different Assignment

MJOB	Error message for different job	If you assign an employee to a job other than his own, should the system give error, warning, subsequent screen, or information message?
MORG	Error message for different organizational object	If you assign an employee to an organizational unit other than his own, should the system give error, warning, subsequent screen, or information message?

Settings for Assignment View

ARBPL	Save work center substitute schedule	If an employee is temporarily assigned to an alternative work center, and he is to be paid for that, you need to create a work center substitution, so that time evaluation can trigger the appropriate payment. Here you specify whether that substitution is needed or not.

Day Details: Set Up Dialog Box

DCUST	Detail Dialog Box:	During shift planning, if you go to Edit ➤ Shift details,
	Allow Subscreen Selection	the system displays the day details in multiple tabs. If this switch is not active, the system shows default tab pages. If it is active, it shows tab pages as per view V_T77EDAYCUST.

(Contd.)

Sem. abbr.	Description	Remarks
	Deactivate Different Payment (Position)	
PLSTE	Different payment (position) active	Here you specify whether a different payment of an employee according to the payment method of another position is possible. You can also specify that although a different payment is not possible, information can still be displayed.
	Lock Setting	
LOCK	Activate lock for employee in shift plan	When you are doing shift planning, the system locks that employee by default. If you do not want to lock the employee during shift planning, you can blank out this field. In that case, you have to first lock an employee before making a change in his shift plan.
	Activate Assignment of Shift Abbreviation	
PSESK	Get Shift Abbreviation	This activity controls whether the system determines the most suitable abbreviation when clock time is changed or retains the original abbreviation and instead displays the changes by using a special display format for the abbreviation.
	Activate Update of Time Data/Temporary Assignments on Saving	
RFRSH	Refresh Time Data/ Temp. Assignments on Saving	If you activate this field, the shift plan can be refreshed (to show any changes done by others), when you click on save icon.
	Activate Temporary Assignment Despite Attendance/Absence	
TASSA	Temporary assignment despite attendance/ absence	Normally you would not create temporary assignments if the employee has a fullday attendance or absence. However, if you want this to be allowed, you can activate this switch. This enables you to assign an employee for a particular period even if the employee has a fullday attendance or absence in the period. If you carry out a temporary assignment where the employee has a fullday attendance or absence, a dialog box notifies you of this fact. You can create the temporary assignment despite the message.
	Specify Control Parameters for Printout	
EXBDA	Name of MS Excel Print Macro for Reqmts Matchup	Here you enter the name of the print macro that enables the requirements match up using Microsoft Excel.

(Contd.)

Sem. abbr.	Description	Remarks
EXCDR	Automatic printout of the shift plan via MS Excel	When you print shift plan, normally (value 0) you are taken to formatted excel sheet. You have to give print command from the excel file. If you enter 1 here, the print gets fired automatically.
EXCFV	Name of the MS Excel style for the shift plan	Here you enter the name of the Microsoft Excel worksheet you want to use to format data in Microsoft Excel.
EXCMA	Name of the MS Excel print macro the shift plan	Here you enter the name of the Microsoft Excel print macro for the shift plan.
EXCME	Environment for path of Excel macro	This field contains the variable for determining the path in which the Microsoft Excel macro is stored.
Define Time Types for Connecting to Microsoft Excel		
TTYP1, TTYP2, TTYP3, TTYP4	Time type for output of shift plan via MS Excel	In the output of shift plan, SAP has provided four columns, one before daywise shift schedule, and three after. In these you can print balances of time types which are printed in first, second, third and fourth free columns of the shift plan using Microsoft Excel.

Utilities

39.1 FUNCTIONALITY

Functional Consultant	User	Business Process Owner	Senior Management	My Rating	Understanding Level
A	A	B	B		

39.1.1 Users

Logging on

If you are going to work in SAP, your system administrator will create a SAP logon pad on your desktop/ laptop. The logon pad can be accessed either through a shortcut on your desktop, or through the Windows Start icon. When you open the SAP logon pad, you will find one or more entries in it.

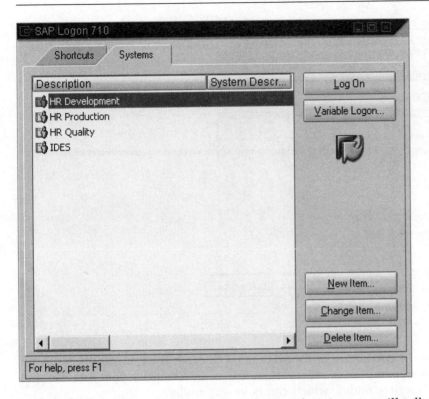

Each entry represents a server. Your system administrator will tell you the purpose for which each server is to be used. You select the server you want to work on, and click the 'Lon On' icon. The system gives you the logon screen.

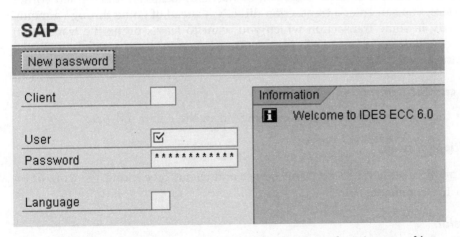

You enter the details given to you by your system administrator. You can change your password or press Enter to logon. The system gives you the SAP menu.

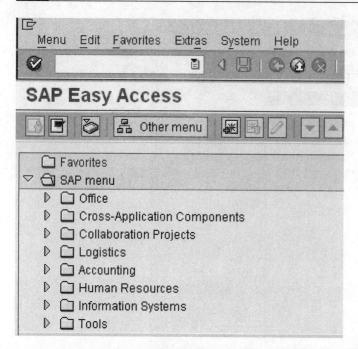

You can open the tree like structure of the SAP menu to reach the transaction you want to carry out. You can switch to user menu, if one has been set up for you. You can add transactions to the Favorites folder, which can have sub-folders.

Executing a transaction in the command field

An important part of all SAP screens is the command field, located in the top left corner of the screen. Here, you can enter a transaction directly, instead of going through a menu. If you are already in some transaction which you want to leave, prefix the transaction with /n, e.g. /nPA30. If you want to run the new transaction in a new session, prefix the transaction with /o, e.g. /oPA30.

Aborting the current transaction

You can abort the current transaction by entering /n in the command field.

Opening multiple sessions

You can open another session of SAP (same server and client) by clicking ▦ icon, or by entering /o in the command field.

Closing a session

You can close a session by entering /i in the command line or by closing the window. If the session you are closing is the only session on a client, you are logged off. The system asks you to confirm that you want to log off.

Logging off

You can log off by entering /nend or /nex in the command line. In the former case, the system asks you to confirm that you want to log off. All the sessions on the client are closed.

Displaying transactions

You work in SAP either through menu, or through transactions. Experienced users often prefer the latter method. Therefore, they need to know the transactions of various menu items. You can display the transactions in the menu by ticking the checkbox ☑ Display technical names in Extras ➢ Settings. The menu display changes as shown below.

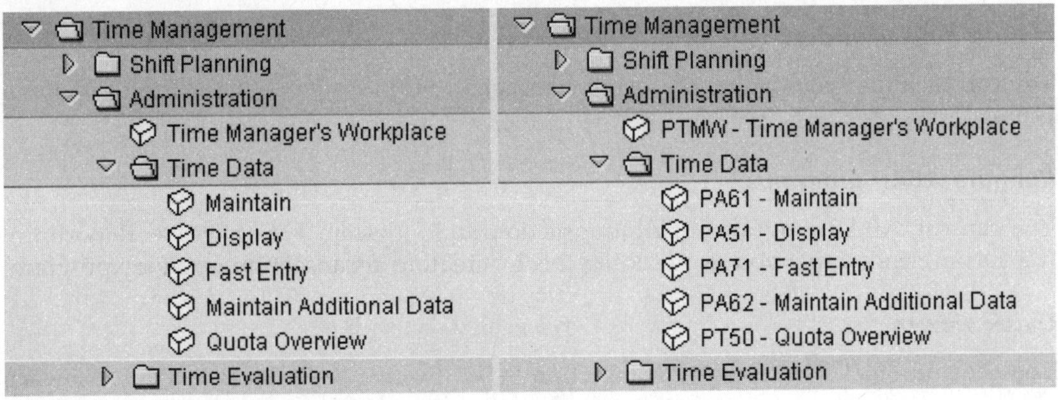

▽ 🗁 Time Management	▽ 🗁 Time Management
▷ 🗀 Shift Planning	▷ 🗀 Shift Planning
▽ 🗁 Administration	▽ 🗁 Administration
�} Time Manager's Workplace	🔸 PTMW - Time Manager's Workplace
▽ 🗁 Time Data	▽ 🗁 Time Data
🔸 Maintain	🔸 PA61 - Maintain
🔸 Display	🔸 PA51 - Display
🔸 Fast Entry	🔸 PA71 - Fast Entry
🔸 Maintain Additional Data	🔸 PA62 - Maintain Additional Data
🔸 Quota Overview	🔸 PT50 - Quota Overview
▷ 🗀 Time Evaluation	▷ 🗀 Time Evaluation

Displaying keys in drop down lists

In many fields, SAP provides a drop down list from which you can choose a value. These list of values usually have a key and a description. Users who like to see the key in addition to description can tick ☑ Show Keys in All Dropdown Lists . They can even sort the dropdown list by the key by ticking ☑ Sort Items by Key . You access these checkboxes by clicking 🖼 ➢ Options ➢ Expert.

Quick copy and paste

SAP provides a method of quick copy and quick paste. You enable this by ticking ✔ Quick Cut and Paste in 🖼. After that, if you press the left button of the mouse, move the mouse on some text, and leave it, the text gets copied to the clipboard. The text is not selected, as would be the case, if this feature is not enabled. Also, if you press the right button of the mouse in any field of SAP, the text is pasted from the clipboard. The text may have been copied on the clipboard from any application, e.g. Microsoft Word.

Business workplace

SAP provides a wide range of office functionality, e.g. mail, workflow, etc., in business workplace. You can access it using transaction SBWP, or by clicking the icon as shown.

You can create document and send by selecting 'New message' from business workplace, or by running transaction SO00, or through menu (System ➤ Short Message).

Maintaining own data

You can maintain your own data using transaction SU3 (System ➤ User Profile ➤ Own Data).

Running ABAP programs

You can run ABAP programs using transaction SA38 (System ➤ Services ➤ Reporting). It is recommended that you avoid doing this by creating a transaction for every program.

Quick viewer

You can run quick viewer using transaction SQVI (System ➤ Services ➤ QuickViewer).

Output control

You can run transaction SP01 (System ➤ Services ➤ Output Control) to list the spool requests and output requests for a user id in a specific period. You can display their contents, print them and delete them. You can run transaction SP02 (System ➤ Own Spool Requests) to list your own spool requests.

Batch input

You can run transaction SM35 (System ➤ Services ➤ Batch Input ➤ Sessions) to monitor, process and analyze the batch input sessions. You can see the logs using transaction SM35P (System ➤ Services ➤ Batch Input ➤ Logs). You can do recording for batch input using transaction SHDB (System ➤ Services ➤ Batch Input ➤ Recorder).

Computer aided test tool

You can use transaction SECATT (System ➤ Services ➤ ECATT ➤ Record) to perform computer aided testing.

Background jobs

You can use transaction SM36 to define and schedule a background job (System ≻ Services ≻ Jobs ≻ Define Job). You can use transaction SM37 (System ≻ Services ≻ Jobs ≻ Job Overview) to monitor and manage jobs. You can release a job, stop an active job, delete a job, display spool list, display job log and display step list. You can also check status, change status from released to scheduled, copy job, change job, repeat scheduling and move the job to a different server. You can also run transaction SMX to see your own jobs (System ≻ Own Jobs).

Queue

You can use transaction SM38 (System ≻ Services ≻ Queue) to display queue.

Reporting authorization problems

You can use transaction SU53 (System ≻ Utilities ≻ Display Authorization Check) to see details of authorization problems and to report to the Basis team for resolution. Immediately after you encounter the authorization problem, enter /nSU53. The system will show a comparison between authorization available and authorization required.

Archiving documents

You can use transaction OAAD to store and assign a new document in the content server. The transaction also provides a facility to search the archived documents.

Downloading file

You can use transaction CG3Y to download a file from the application server to your desktop.

Uploading file

You can use transaction CG3Z to upload a file from your desktop to the application server.

SAP query

You can start SAP queries using transaction SQ00.

39.1.2 Functional Consultants

Customizing

Transaction SPRO is used for accessing the customizing environment. You can customize the SAP system using the SAP Reference IMG or you can define projects for customization, e.g. adapting the SAP Reference IMG to the needs of your company and/or subdivide the customization task into different subprojects.

View maintenance

Transactions SM30 (System ➢ Services ➢ Table Maintenance ➢ Extended Table Maintenance) and SM31 are used for maintaining data in one or more tables through a maintenance view. This transaction also provides a facility to navigate to the underlying IMG node for a particular maintenance view. Transaction SM34 (System ➢ Services ➢ Table Maintenance ➢ View Cluster Maintenance) is used for maintaining view clusters.

Customizing comparison

You can compare customizing of two systems or two clients in the same system by using transaction SCMP. You can also create comparison runs involving multiple objects using transaction SCU0 or OY19.

Transport management

You can use transactions SE09 and SE10 for creating and releasing a customizing or workbench transport request.

Data migration, computer aided testing, BDC

You can use transaction LSMW to migrate legacy data to SAP. You can use transaction SCAT or SECATT for creating a test case by recording a transaction and creating and loading test data. You can record or modify a BDC and run it using transaction SHDB.

Viewing data in tables

You can view data in a table using transaction SE11, SE16, SE16N or SE17.

Logging on to OSS

You can use transaction OSS1 (System ➢ Services ➢ SAP Service) to log on to OSS. It is generally used to import and apply SAP notes.

Searching string in programs

You can use program RPR_ABAP_SOURCE_SCAN to search strings in programs.

Searching in SAP menu

You can use transaction SEARCH_SAP_MENU to search in SAP menu.

Searching in user menu

You can use transaction SEARCH_USER_MENU to search in user menu.

SAP query

You can use transaction SQ01 to maintain SAP queries, transaction SQ02 to maintain infoset and SQ03 to maintain user groups. You can start SAP queries using transaction SQ00.

Workflow builder

You can use transaction SWDD for creating and editing workflows.

System status

You can see SAP version, operating system and the database by clicking System ➤ Status. You can also see the transaction, program and screen number.

Translation

You can use transaction SE63 to translate texts for various ABAP and non-ABAP objects.

39.1.3 ABAP

ABAP programs

You can create, modify, delete, and display source code of ABAP programs using transaction SE38. You can also execute ABAP programs using transaction SA38 or SE38. You can compare ABAP programs using transaction SE39.

Function modules

You can create, modify, delete, display and test function modules using transaction SE37. You can also maintain a function group.

Dialog modules

You can create, modify, delete, display and test dialog modules using transaction SE35. You can create menus using transaction SE41. Screens can be painted using transaction SE51 and its underlying flow logic defined.

Classes

You can create, modify, delete, display and test classes using transaction SE24.

Logical databases

You can create, modify, delete, display and test logical databases using transaction SE36. SAP provides several logical databases for HR, e.g. PAP, PCH, PNP, PNPCE. If you use logical databases in your ABAP programs, authorization checks are automatically taken care of; otherwise you must explicitly build authorization checks in your programs.

Enhancements

You can create enhancements through transaction CMOD. Enhancements are created in projects, which are logical groups of enhancements. You can test the enhancements using transaction SMOD.

BAdIs

You can use transaction SE19, to implement a Business Add-In. SAP provides predefined BAdIs for use by the customers. If you want to define your own BAdI, you can use transaction SE18.

Area menus

You can create area menus using transaction SE43. Area menus can be used in creating role menus in transaction PFCG.

Tables and views

You can create, modify, delete and display tables and table fields using transaction SE11. You can view data in a table using transaction SE11, SE16, SE16N or SE17. You can display/change technical settings of a table in transaction SE13.

Documentation

You can create documentation using transaction SE61.

SAP scripts

You can create SAP scripts using transaction SE71. Other transactions related to SAP script are SE72, SE73, SE74, SE75, SE75TTDTGC, SE75TTDTGD, SE76, SE77 and SO10.

Messages

You can maintain messages using transaction SE91. You can then call them in your own programs. You can also use SAP defined messages in your own programs.

Transactions

You can maintain transactions using transaction SE93. It is recommended that you have a transaction for every program so that the users are not required to run programs using transaction SA38 or SE38. This provides better control on authorizations. It is also recommended that you keep the transaction the same as the program name.

Repository information

SAP has created a lot of software objects. You can use transaction SE15/ SE85/ SE84 to find them.

HR form editor

You can create/ change/ delete HR forms, e.g. remuneration statements, payroll account, wage type statement or payroll journal using transaction PE51. Alternatively, you may use HR Forms Workplace, transaction HRFORMS. You can also use transaction SMARTFORMS to create and maintain forms in the SAP system.

BAPIs

You can see the BAPIs provided by SAP using transaction BAPI.

Object navigator

You use transaction SE80 to organize your programming in an integrated development environment. Development objects are arranged together in object lists. Each object list contains all of the objects in a certain category, such as package, program and global class. From the object list, you can select an object by double clicking it. When you open an object, the workbench calls up the development tool with which the object was created.

ABAP dump analysis

You can use transaction ST22 to see details of any runtime error or short dump. This helps in analyzing the root cause of the dump and finding its solution.

39.1.4 Basis

System administration

You can use transaction S002 to get the menu for system administration.

Users

You can maintain users using transaction SU01. You can get a variety of information about users, roles and authorizations using transaction SUIM. You can view users' logon dates and password changes using transaction RSUSR200. You can use transaction SM04 to check the status of the users; for example, how many users have logged on and how many sessions a user is working on.

Roles

You can maintain roles using transaction PFCG. The system automatically inserts authorization objects based on transactions selected by you (These can be maintained using transaction SU22 or SU24). You update them with appropriate values. You can see change documents for roles using transaction RSSCD100_PFCG. The same program is called by transaction RSSCD100_PFCG_USER. Transaction S_BCE_68001403 gives the list of critical authorizations.

Transport management

You can manage transports using transactions SE01, SE03, SE09 and SE10.

SAP connect

You can use transaction SCOT for monitoring the status of the inbound and outbound traffic through SAPconnect.

ALE

Customizing of ALE can be done using transaction SALE. You can monitor ALE messages using transaction BD87.

Displaying and deleting locks

Transaction SM12 is used for checking and releasing lock entries.

Locking/unlocking transactions

You can use transaction SM01 to lock/unlock transactions.

39.2   TABLES AND VIEWS

Functional Consultant	User	Business Process Owner	Senior Management	My Rating	Understanding Level
A	A	B	B		

39.2.1   Schemas, Functions, PCRs, Operations, Features

Schemas

SAP stores the schemas in tables. SAP supplied schemas are stored in table T52C0 (text in table T52C2). Customer schemas are stored in table T52C1 (text in table T52C3). There are also tables T52CC (schema directory for customer) and T52CD (schema directory for SAP).

Functions

You can see the parameters that a function can take and valid values for each of these parameters in tables T52B6, T52B7, T52B8 and T52BB. You can also see the tables that are displayed in the log before and after the function is called in table T52BW.

PCRs

SAP stores the PCRs in tables. All PCRs are stored in table T52C5. Directory of PCRs is in table T52CE.

Operations

Operation models, their assignment to operations and operation parameters are stored in tables T52BM, T52BN, T52BO and T52BP.

Features

Features are stored in tables T549B, T549BT, T549C, T549CT and T549D.

39.2.2 Data Dictionary

Domains

View DD01V contains the list of domains. View DD07V contains values for domains.

Data elements

View DD04V contains data elements and their descriptions.

Tables

View DD02V contains the list of tables.

Table fields

Table DD03L contains table fields and DD03T their descriptions. Table DD03M contains table fields with data elements, text, and domains. View DDVAL contains fixed values for table fields.

Foreign key fields

View DD08V contains foreign key relationship definitions.

Pool/cluster structures

View DD06V contains pool/cluster structures.

Technical settings of tables

Table DD09L contains technical settings of tables.

Matchcode objects

View DD20V contains matchcode objects. Table DD24S contains fields of a matchcode id.

Views

Table TVDIR contains directory of views. Table DD25T contains views, matchcode objects and lock objects. Table DD27S contains fields in a view, matchcode object or lock object.

39.2.3 Software Repository

Packages

All objects are developed under Packages (earlier called Development Classes), which are logical grouping of objects. Table TDEVC contains list of Packages. Packages of SAP HR can be identified by selecting entries from table TDEVC where software component is SAP_HR. Some of the important Packages are:

PINC	Incentive Wages: Customizing
PINW	Incentive Wages
PP08	Shift Planning
PP8C	Shift Planning-Customizing
PPTM	PT Application Components
PTCA	HR Time Management Cross-Application Components
PTIC	HR Time Data: Customizing
PTIM	HR Time Management Application Development
PT_IW	Incentive Wages: Core Development

Repository objects

Table TADIR contains the directory of repository objects, along with their development class. Tables and structures are identified by object type TABL.

Objects

Objects are stored in OBJ series of tables.

ABAP programs

Table TRDIR contains list of ABAP programs. Table D010TAB contains the tables used by ABAP programs.

Transactions

View TSTCV contains list of transactions and programs associated with them.

39.2.4 Users, Roles and Authorization

User data

User data is stored in USR series of tables. Table USR01 stores the master list of users. Table USR04 contains the profiles attached to a user. A user's parameter IDs and their values are stored in table USR05.

Role maintenance

You can create, delete, or modify roles using transaction PFCG. Role related data is stored in tables starting with AGR.

Authorization objects

Authorization objects and their field names are in table TOBJ.

Authorization objects for roles

Table AGR_1250 contains authorization objects for a role which you see in transaction PFCG.

Master list of roles

Table AGR_DEFINE contains master list of roles.

Transactions for a role

Table AGR_TCODES contains transactions for roles.

Users having a role

Table AGR_USERS contains users for roles. Also see table AGR_USERT.

39.2.5 IMG Menu

Table CUS_IMGACH contains master list of IMG activities including documentation object and transaction.

39.2.6 Forms and SAP scripts

Forms

Master list of forms is in table T514D. Details of forms are stored in T514 series of tables.

SAP scripts

SAP scripts are stored in STX series of tables.

39.2.7 Others

Documentation

Documentation header is stored in table DOKHL and text in table DOKTL.

Reserved names

Reserved Names for Customizing Tables/Objects are stored in table TRESC.

39.2.8 Delivery Classes of Tables

SAP stores data in tables. Each table is assigned a delivery class which determines whether the data in the table is controlled by SAP or by the customer. Delivery class of a table can be seen in the 'Delivery and Maintenance' tab in transaction SE11.

Code	Delivery class	Explanation
A	Application table (master and transaction data)	A Support Pack of SAP is not expected to update these tables in any client.
L	Table for storing temporary data, delivered empty	A Support Pack of SAP is not expected to update these tables in any client.
G	Customizing table, protected against SAP Upd., only INS all.	A Support Pack of SAP is not expected to update these tables in any client.
C	Customizing table, maintenance only by cust., not SAP import	A Support Pack of SAP updates these tables in client 000 only. In other clients, these tables have to be adjusted from client 000 to get these entries.
E	Control table, SAP and customer have separate key areas	A Support Pack of SAP updates these tables in all clients.
S	System table, maint. only by SAP, change = modification	A Support Pack of SAP updates these tables in all clients.
W	System table, contents transportable via separate TR objects	A Support Pack of SAP updates these tables in all clients.

39.2.9 Search Help

When SAP designs tables, for each column it tries to provide search help. If search help is provided, you can choose a value from it. By assigning search help to table columns, the help becomes standardized. There are different types of search help. In transaction SE11, if you go to tab 'Entry help/check', you can see which columns have got entry help and of which type in the column 'Origin of the Input Help'. Different types of search help are listed below.

Code	Search help	Explanation
T	Input help based on data type	For example Date (Calendar), Time.
D	Explicit search help attachment to data element	Attachment of a search help to the data element assigned to the field.
X	Explicit search help attachment to field	Data integrity is checked against search help. There is no check table.
P	Input help implemented with check table	Data integrity is checked using a check table.
F	Input help with fixed values	The field can take values only from a fixed list, which is defined in the Domain.
Blank	No input help	There is no input help.

39.3 IMPLEMENTATION GUIDE

Functional Consultant	User	Business Process Owner	Senior Management	My Rating	Understanding Level
A	B	B	B		

When a consultant implements SAP HR Time Management for a client, how does the consultant determine the client requirement and do configuration, and how does the client know that the right configuration is done for him? The answers to these twin questions lie in the methodology you follow.

The consultant can use the structure of this book to guide the implementation. He can ask specific questions to the users, record their answers and use the answers to do the configuration. Having done the configuration, he can explain it to the users and get it approved. If the users do not have enough SAP knowledge to confirm the configuration, the consultant should record the user input and get it signed off. An auditor should then confirm that the configuration reflects the user input. The source of all configuration should be user input.

Whereas many factual inputs can come from a knowledgeable power user, policy inputs should come from senior management. In large companies, senior management is often surprised at the diversity of practices followed in different parts of the company. Implementation of SAP provides an opportunity to senior management to either commonize the practice, or approve diversity. Even when there is no diversity, decisions on policy should be approved by management.

Both user inputs and the corresponding configuration should be recorded in a configuration manual. The configuration manual should explain what has been configured and, if necessary, why. If you use the following table as the Table of Content of your configuration manual, your configuration manual will be easy to understand. Apart from what you configure, you should also indicate what is not implemented (NR) and what is SAP standard (SS). You should also add all Z developments done by you in respective chapters. Feel free to add chapters in the table of contents, but don't delete any line which has configuration in it. The support team needs to know if something is not implemented. If some configuration is not implemented, you can keep the chapter number blank, instead of creating empty chapters in the configuration manual. The Reference column contains the chapter number in the book.

In the 'Approved by' column, you should record the name of the person who has approved that particular configuration. The entries in the table below show the suggested approving level: SM – Senior Management/ Steering Committee, PO – Business Process Owner, US – Power User, FC – Functional Consultant. If users are not knowledgeable enough to sign off the configuration, the users should sign off their input, and the auditor should sign off the configuration.

Chapter	Description	Configuration	NR/SS/ Done	Reference	Approved by
1	**Infotypes**			1	
1.1	Time Management Infotypes			1.8	PO
2	**Employee Groupings**			2	
2.1	Personnel Area	T500P		2.2	SM
2.2	Assignment of Personnel Area to Company Code	V_T500P		2.3	SM
2.3	Personnel Subarea	V_001P_ALL		2.4	PO
2.4	PS Grouping for Daily Work Schedules	T508Z		2.4.7	PO
2.5	Employee Group	T501		2.5	SM
2.6	Employee Subgroup	T503K		2.6	SM
2.7	Country Assignment for Employee Group/Subgroup	V_T503Z		2.7	PO
2.8	Employee Group/Subgroup	V_503_ALL		2.8	PO
2.9	ES Grouping for Work Schedules	V_T508T		2.9	PO
3	**Work Schedule**			3	
3.1	Employee Time Management Status	T555U		3.3	PO
3.2	Default Time Management Status	Feature TMSTA		3.4	PO
3.3	Working Hour Fields Control	Feature WRKHR		3.5	PO
3.4	Daily Work Schedule	V_T550A		3.6	PO
3.5	Work Break Schedule	V_T550P		3.7	PO
3.6	Daily Work Schedule Selection Rule	V_T550X		3.8	FC
3.7	Daily Work Schedule Selection Rule	V_550X_B		3.8	DC
3.8	Period Work Schedule	V_T551A		3.9	PO
3.9	Period Work Schedule Valuation	V_T551C		3.10	FC
3.10	Period Work Schedule Valuation	V_551C_B		3.10	FC
3.11	Work Schedule Rule	V_T508A		3.11	FC
3.12	Default Work Schedule Rule	Feature SCHKZ		3.12	PO
3.13	Day Type	V_T553T		3.13	FC
3.14	Day Type Rule	T553A		3.14	FC
3.15	Day Types for Special Days	T553S		3.15	FC
3.16	Public Holiday	Transaction OY05		3.16	PO
3.17	Public Holiday Calendar	Transaction OY05		3.17	PO
3.18	Monthly Work Schedule	Transaction PT01		3.18	FC
3.19	Dynamic Shift Change Based on Clock-in Time	V_T552V		3.19	PO
3.20	Dynamic Shift Change Based on Planned/Actual Overlap	V_T552W		3.20	PO
3.21	Working Week	T559A		3.21	FC
3.22	Default Working Week	Feature WWEEK		3.22	FC

(Contd.)

Chapter	Description	Configuration	NR/SS/ Done	Reference	Approved by
4	**Substitution**			4	
4.1	Substitution Type	V_T556		4.2	PO
4.2	Default Substitution Type	Feature VTART		4.3	PO
5	**Absence**			5	
5.1	Multiply Payroll Hours and Payroll Days	BAdI TIM00ATTABS COUNTING		5.1.6	FC
5.2	Free Determination of Payroll Hours and Payroll Days	BAdI PT_ABS_ATT_ COUNTRY		5.1.6	FC
5.3	Attendance and Absence Types	T554S		5.2	PO
5.4	Time Constraint Reaction for Time Management Infotypes	V_554Y_B		5.3	FC
5.5	Counting Rule for Attendances and Absences (for Quota Deduction)	T556C		5.4	FC
5.6	Deduction Rules for Absence Quotas	V_556R_B		5.5	FC
5.7	Rounding Rule	V_T559R		5.6	FC
5.8	Absence Valuation	V_T554C		5.7	FC
5.9	Absence Valuation Rules	V_T554L		5.8	FC
5.10	Counting Classes for Absence Valuation	V_T554E		5.9	FC
5.11	Day Rules for Absence Valuation	V_T554R		5.10	FC
5.12	Breakdown of Absences after Quota Deduction	V_T554A		5.11	FC
5.13	Symbol for Attendance and Absence	V_T554P		5.12	FC
5.14	Processing Type/Time Type according to Att./Absence Class	T555Y		5.13	FC
5.15	Clock Time Generation in Attendance and Absence	Feature HRSIF		5.14	FC
5.16	Illness Texts	T572B		5.15	FC
5.17	Default attendance/absence type in weekly screen	Enhancement PTIM2005		5.18.2	FC
5.18	Completeness check in weekly screen	Enhancement PTIM2006		5.18.2	FC
5.19	Daily Standard Time Determination	Feature TIMTA		5.19	FC
5.20	Last Day of a Week	Feature LDAYW		5.20	FC

(Contd.)

Chapter	Description	Configuration	NR/SS/ Done	Reference	Approved by
6	**Attendance**		6		
6.1	Deduction Rules for Attendance Quotas	V_T556R		5.5	FC
6.2	Evaluation Type for Attendances	V_T554H		6.2	FC
7	**Absence Quota**		7		
7.1	Number Range for Attendances and Absences	Transaction PT10		7.2	FC
7.2	Number Range for Time Quotas	Transaction PT11		7.2	FC
7.3	Absence Quota Type	V_T556A		7.3	PO
7.4	Absence Quota Generation	VC_T559L		7.4	FC
7.4.1	Selection Rules	V_T559L		7.5	FC
7.4.2	Quota Types (Automatic Generation)	V_556A_B		7.6	FC
7.4.3	Base Entitlement	V_T559E		7.7	FC
7.4.4	Validity/Deduction Interval	V_T559D		7.8	FC
7.4.5	Validity Period for Default Values	T559V		7.9	FC
7.4.6	Reduction Rules	T559M		7.10	FC
7.4.7	Reduction Indicators for Absences	V_554S_M		7.11	FC
7.4.8	Rounding Rule	V_T559R		7.12	FC
7.5	Quota Type Selection Rule Group Determination	Feature QUOMO		7.13	FC
7.6	Applicability of the selection rule	EXIT_SAPLHR V_001		7.14	FC
7.7	Defaults for processing accrual entitlements	EXIT_SAPLHR V_002		7.14	FC
7.8	Rules for reducing quota entitlements	EXIT_SAPLHR V_003		7.14	FC
7.9	Defaults for determining base entitlements	EXIT_SAPLHR V_004		7.14	FC
7.10	Default for transfer: Change results of quota generation	EXIT_SAPLHR V_005		7.14	FC
7.11	Determining the employee's entry and leaving dates	EXIT_SAPLHR V_006		7.14	FC
8	**Quota Correction**		8		
9	**Attendance Quota**		9		
9.1	Attendance Quota Type	V_T556P		9.2	PO
9.2	Attendance Quota Type	V_556P_B		9.2	FC
10	**Quota Compensation**		10		
10.1	Quota Compensation Types	V_T556U		10.2	FC
10.2	Wage Type Assignment to Quota Compensation Method	V_T556W		10.3	FC

(Contd.)

Chapter	Description	Configuration	NR/SS/ Done	Reference	Approved by
11	**Overtime**			11	
11.1	Overtime Compensation Types	T555R		11.4	FC
12	**Availability**			12	
12.1	Availability Type	V_T557		12.2	PO
12.2	Daily Work Schedules: Permissibility for Availability	V_550A_B		12.3	PO
12.3	Work Schedule Rule: Availability	V_508A_B		12.4	PO
13	**Time Recording**			13	
13.1	Work Time Event Type Groups	T705F		13.2	FC
13.2	Time Event Types in Work Time Event Type Groups	T705P		13.3	FC
13.3	Grouping of Attendance/Absence Reasons	V_T705I		13.4	FC
13.4	Attendance/Absence Reasons for Subsystem	V_T705A		13.5	PO
13.5	Groupings for Connection to Subsystem	V_T705T		13.6	FC
13.6	Time Profiles	V_T555O		13.7	PO
13.7	PDC Master Record Information	V_T555I		13.8	PO
13.8	Employee Grouping for the Time Evaluation Rule	T555N		13.9	FC
14	**Time Events**			14	
14.1	Number Range for Time Events and Acct Assignment Data	Transaction PA06		14.2	FC
14.2	Communication Parameters	Transaction PT41		14.3	FC
15	**Time Transfer**			15	
15.1	Employee Time Transfer Type	V_T555P		15.2	PO
15.2	Time Transfer to Time Types	V_T555J		15.3	PO
15.3	Time Transfer to Wage Types	V_T555K		15.4	PO
15.4	Time Transfer to Absence Quotas	V_T555L		15.5	PO
16	**Employee Remuneration**			16	
17	**Maternity Leave**			17	
17.1	Parental Leave Eligibility	Feature MASEX		17.2	PO
17.2	Absence: Input Checks	V_T554S		17.3	PO
17.3	Types of Birth	V_T554G		17.4	PO
17.4	Maternity Leave Rules	V_T554M		17.5	FC
17.5	Defaults for Absence Types	V_T554V		17.6	FC
18	**Military Service**			18	
18.1	Military Service Eligibility	Feature DFSEX		18.2	PO
18.2	Absence: Input Checks	V_T554S		18.3	PO

(Contd.)

Chapter	Description	Configuration	NR/SS/ Done	Reference	Approved by
18.3	Defaults for Absence Types	V_T554V		18.4	FC
18.4	Subtype Characteristics	VV_T591A_008 1___AL0		18.5	PO
18.5	Periods of Military Service	V_T554W		18.6	PO
18.6	Military Service Ranks	V_T554D		18.7	PO
19	**Additional Absence Data**			19	
19.1	Subtype Characteristics	VV_T591A_008 2___AL0		19.2	PO
19.2	Control Table for Additional Absence Data	V_T572E		19.3	FC
19.3	Permitted Values for Events	V_T572G		19.4	FC
19.4	Supplementary Absence Data	V_554S_P		19.5	FC
20	**Flextime**			20	
21	**Activity Allocation**			21	
21.1	Default Values for Activity Allocation	Enhancement PTIM2001		21.1	FC
21.2	Check Activity Allocation Data	Enhancement PTIM2004		21.1	FC
21.3	Control Table for PA Time Management	T582Z		21.2	FC
21.4	Screen Modification for Assignment Data	T588O		21.3	FC
21.5	Screen Modification for Account Assignment Block	V_T588N		21.3	FC
21.6	Subscreens for Controlling Objects	Transaction OXK1		21.3	FC
21.7	Number Range for Additional Time Data	Transaction PA05		21.4	FC
21.8	Number Range for Posting Documents	Transaction PT12		21.5	FC
21.9	Data Transfer to Activity Allocation	Transaction PT68		21.6	US
22	**Cost Assignment**			22	
22.1	Default Values for Cost Assignment	Enhancement PTIM2002		22.1	FC
23	**External Services**			23	
23.1	Default Values for External Services	Enhancement PTIM2003		23.1	FC
23.2	Wage Types Permitted for Transfer to MM-SRV	V_T510X		23.2	FC
24	**Different Payment**			24	

(Contd.)

Chapter	Description	Configuration	NR/SS/ Done	Reference	Approved by
25	**Time Data Collection**			25	
25.1	Enhancement for Link to Time Recording Systems (HR-PDC)	Enhancement HRPTIM05		25.1	FC
26	**Employee Expenditure Collection**			26	
26.1	Grouping for Employee Expenses	V_T705J		26.3	PO
26.2	Employee Expenditures from Subsystem	V_T705K		26.4	FC
27	**Logistics Integration**			27	
28	**Time Evaluation Configuration**			28	
28.1	Pair Formation: Status Table	TPT_PAIRSTAT2		28.1	FC
28.2	PDC Processing Statuses	V_T705B		28.2	FC
28.3	Earliest Recalculation Dates for Time Management	V_T569R		28.3	PO
28.4	Grouping for Earliest Recalculation Date	Feature TIMMO		28.4	FC
28.5	Time Type Determination	V_T555Z		28.5	FC
28.6	Time Types	V_T555A		28.6	FC
28.7	Processing Type	V_T510V		28.7	FC
28.8	Time Wage Type Selection Rule	V_T510S		28.8	FC
28.9	Limits for Time Balances	V_T559P		28.9	PO
28.10	Time Evaluation Messages	V_T555E		28.10	FC
28.11	Time Parameters	V_T511K		28.11	FC
28.12	Enhancement of Business Logic for Time Data	BAdI PT_BLP_ USER		28.12	FC
29	**Time Evaluation with Clock Times (Schema TM00)**			32	
30	**Schemas, Functions, PCRs, Operations, Features**			33	
31	**Time Manager's Workplace**			34	
31.1	Variants of Time Management Reports	Feature LLREP		34.3.3	FC
31.2	Enhanced Calendar	VV_PT_TMW_ GCCAL		34.3.4	FC
31.3	Default Values in TMW Calendar	BAdI PT_GUI_ TMW_CALENDAR		34.3.4	FC
31.4	Tabs for Multi-Day View	VV_PT_TMW_ GCLTN1		34.3.7	PO
31.5	Tabs for Multi-Person View	VV_PT_TMW_ GCLT1M		34.3.7	PO
31.6	Tabs for One-Day View	VV_PT_TMW_ GCLT11		34.3.7	PO

(Contd.)

Chapter	Description	Configuration	NR/SS/ Done	Reference	Approved by
31.7	Tabs for Team View	V_PT_TMW_ GCLTNM		34.3.7	PO
31.8	Customer Enhancement to Fill Fields	Enhancement PTIMTMW		34.3.7	FC
31.9	Fill Customer Fields	BAdI PT_TMW_ NM_BADI_EXMPL		34.3.11	FC
31.10	Processing Instructions	VC_PT_FIELD_ SELECTION (CHK)		34.3.12	FC
31.11	Alternative Texts for Details Tabs	V_PT_TMW_ GCSLYT		34.3.13	PO
31.12	Screen Areas (Information)	VC_PT_FIELD_ SELECTION_INF		34.4	FC
31.13	Screen Areas (Details)	VC_PT_FIELD_ SELECTION_DTL		34.5	FC
31.14	Screen Areas (Dominants)	VC_PT_FIELD_ SELECTION_TDO		34.6	FC
31.15	Screen Areas (Lists)	VC_PT_FIELD_ SELECTION_LST		34.7	FC
31.16	Screen Area (Employee List Layout)	VC_PT_FIELD_ SELECTION_EMP		34.8	FC
31.17	Employee Selection	HR_SELECTIONS		34.9	FC
31.18	Groups	HRSEL_GROU PINGS		34.9.10	FC
31.19	Employee Information	VC_PT_FIELD_ SELECTION_INF		34.10	FC
31.20	Layouts for Employee Data	V_HEAD_INF OGRP		34.10.2	FC
31.21	Display Objects in Layouts	V_HEAD_INF OGSTR		34.10.3	FC
31.22	Display Objects for HR Master Data	V_MDAT_OBJ_CTS		34.10.4	FC
31.23	Reporting Quota Types	VC_T557LTMW		34.10.5	FC
31.24	Reporting Quota Types	VC_T557L		34.10.5	FC
31.25	Grouping of Reporting Quotas	Feature GRDWK		34.10.6	FC
31.26	Display Objects for Reporting Quota Types	V_ABQT_OBJ_CTS		34.10.7	FC
31.27	Reporting Time Types	VC_T557TMW		34.10.8	FC
31.28	Reporting Time Types	VC_T557I		34.10.8	FC
31.29	Grouping of Reporting Time Types	Feature GRDWT		34.10.9	FC
31.30	Display Objects for Reporting Time Types	V_TBAL_OBJ_CTS		34.10.10	FC
31.31	Time Data Id			34.11	FC
31.32	Definition Sets	V_TMW_TDLAN		34.11.2	FC

(Contd.)

Chapter	Description	Configuration	NR/SS/ Done	Reference	Approved by
31.33	Definition Subsets	V_TMW_TDSLAN		34.11.3	FC
31.34	Time Data Id	V_TMW_TDTYPE		34.11.4	FC
31.35	Time Data IDs in a Definition Subset	V_TMW_TDS UBLA		34.11.5	FC
31.36	Color Attributes for Time Data Ids	V_TMW_TD_ ATTRIB		34.11.6	FC
31.37	Display Type of Time Data Id List	VC_PT_FIELD_ SELECTION_ INF (TDT)		34.11.7	FC
31.38	Display Type of Time Data Id List to Profiles Assignment	VC_PT_TMW_ PRF_TDT		34.11.8	FC
31.39	Message List and Contextual Information			34.12	FC
31.40	Processing Methods	TPT_WLIST_PROC		34.12.2	FC
31.41	Message Functional Areas	VV_TPT_WLI_ AREA		34.12.3	FC
31.42	Contextual Information	VC_PT_FIELD_ SELECTION_ WLI (WLI)		34.12.4	FC
31.43	Contextual information for processing methods	VV_PT_TMW_ PRF_FL		34.12.5	FC
31.44	Processing Methods and Message Functional Areas for Message Types	V_T555E_WLIST		34.12.6	FC
31.45	Processing Methods for Message Functional Areas	V_TPT_WLIST _AREA		34.12.6	FC
31.46	Profile	VC_PT_TMW_ PROFILE_STR		34.13	FC
31.47	Parameter Transaction	Transaction SE93		34.13.1	FC
32	**Time Management Pool**			35	
32.1	Tables Shown in Time Management Pool	Feature REPTA		35.14	FC
32.2	Reaction to Error Transaction	V_T705E		35.15	FC
32.3	Hourly Limits for Day Balances	Feature LIMIE		35.16	FC
32.4	Hourly Limits for Cumulated Balances	Feature LIMIS		35.17	FC
32.5	Hourly Limits for Time Wage Types	Feature LIMIZ		35.18	FC
33	**Cross-Application Time Sheet**			36	
33.1	BAdI: Change Derived Values	BAdI CATS_DERI VATIVES		36.1.6	FC

(Contd.)

Chapter	Description	Configuration	NR/SS/ Done	Reference	Approved by
33.2	BAdI: Influence Setup of Worklist	BAdI CATS_WORK LIST_ADDIN		36.1.6	FC
33.3	Data Entry Profile	TCATS		36.2	FC
33.4	Data Entry Profile	V_TCATSXC		36.2	FC
33.5	Screen Layout	Transaction CAC2		36.3	FC
33.6	Customer Fields	TCAFI		36.3.4	FC
33.7	BAdI: CATS Approval	BAdI BADI_CATS_ APPROVAL		36.4.1	FC
33.8	BAdI: Display and Approval of Working Times	BAdI CATS_REPORTING		36.4.1	FC
33.9	Rules for Special Approval	V_CATS_EXC _RULE		36.4.3	FC
33.10	Logic for Special Approval	Feature CATEX		36.4.4	FC
33.11	Rule Groups for Special Approval	VC_CATS_EXC		36.4.5	FC
33.12	Rejection Reasons	TCATSD		36.4.6	FC
33.13	Method for Executing UWL Item	SWFVT		36.4.7	FC
33.14	Number Range Interval for Document Number	Transaction CAC7		36.5	FC
33.15	Number Range Interval for Internal Key	Transaction CAC8		36.5	FC
33.16	Number Range Interval for Task	Transaction CAC_XT1		36.5	FC
33.17	Distribution Function	VC0C12		36.6.2	FC
33.18	Distribution Strategy	V_TC29S		36.6.3	FC
33.19	Distribution Type	V_TC29		36.6.4	FC
33.20	Summarization in CO Documents	CCATSCOSUM		36.7	PO
33.21	Profile Authorization Groups	TCATSA		36.8	FC
33.22	Additional Information for ESS Profile	TCATS_ITS		36.9	FC
33.23	Possible Entries Help in Internet	TCATS_SHLP_ITS		36.10	FC
33.24	Deactivation of Attendance/ Absence Types in ESS	V_T554S_ESSEX		36.11	PO
33.25	Allowed Print Reports for CATS	TCATP		36.12	FC
33.26	Task Type, Task Level, Task Component	VC_CATSXC_ ZUORD		36.13	FC
33.27	Data Entry Profile for a Task Type	Feature CATSX		36.14	FC
33.28	Data Entry Table for CATS for Service Provider	TCATX_GRID		36.15	FC
33.29	Access Key for Transaction Control	TCATX_AK		36.16.2	FC
33.30	Access Key for Transaction Control Determination	Feature CATSS		36.16.3	FC
33.31	Tab Control	TCATX_TCR		36.16.4	FC

(Contd.)

(Contd.)

Chapter	Description	Configuration	NR/SS/ Done	Reference	Approved by
34.19	Validation of Group Numbers	Transaction PW93		37.19	FC
34.20	Valid Ranges of Group Numbers	V_T703G		37.20	FC
34.21	Full Screens for Time Ticket Types	V_T703D		37.21	FC
34.22	List Screens for Time Ticket Types	VC_T703U		37.22	FC
34.23	Wage Types Permitted for Time Ticket Types	V_T703K		37.23	FC
34.24	Wage Types to Wage Type Groups Assignment	VV_52D7_B_0 LL1_AL0		37.24	FC
34.25	Wage Type Properties for Incentive Wages	V_512W_D		37.25	FC
35	**Shift Planning**			38	
35.1	Requirements Type	T77RD		38.4	FC
35.2	Shift Group	V_T77DB		38.5	FC
35.3	Shift Abbreviation	V_T77ED		38.6	PO
35.4	Requirements Types for a Shift Group	V_T77RB		38.7	PO
35.5	General Color and Character Formatting	V_T77SP_STYLE		38.8	PO
35.6	Abbreviation Sequence	VC_T77SP_CE		38.9	FC
35.7	Substitution Types in Shift Plans	V_T77ER		38.10	FC
35.8	Shift Group Assignment to Organizational Unit	Transaction PO10		38.11	FC
35.9	Factory Calendar	Transaction OY05		38.12	PO
35.10	Factory Calendar Assignment to Organizational Unit	T77S0		38.13	PO
35.11	Strategies for Automatic Assignment Proposal	V_T77EVOPT		38.14	FC
35.12	Definition of Proposal Lists	V_T77EH		38.15	FC
35.13	Assignment Strategy Defaults	V_T77EVOPT_DEF		38.16	FC
35.14	Assignment Options	V_T77EOPT		38.17	FC
35.15	Information Columns Definition	V_T77EI		38.18	FC
35.16	Information Columns Defaults	V_T77EJ		38.19	FC
35.17	Requirements Matchup Icons	V_T77RQ_ICON		38.20	FC
35.18	Permitted Tab Pages	VC_77EDAYCUST		38.21	PO
35.19	Shift Planning Profile	VC_T77EP		38.22	FC
35.20	HR Subroutines	T596F		38.23	FC
35.21	Global Settings for Shift Planning	T77S0		38.24	FC

39.4 TRANSACTIONS

Functional Consultant	User	Business Process Owner	Senior Management	My Rating	Understanding Level
A	X	X	X		

Transactions given in this chapter can be used for authorization design.

39.4.1 Time Management

Category	Transaction	Description
User	ACTEXP_APPR_LITE	Approve Working Times
Customizing	CAC_XT1	Number Range Maintenance: CATS_XTEND
Customizing	CAC2	Time Sheet: Field Selection
Customizing	CAC7	Number Range Maintenance: CATS
Customizing	CAC8	Number Range Maintenance: CATS_INTRN
User	CAT2	Record Working Times
User	CAT3	Display Working Times
User	CAT6	Human Resources
User	CAT8	Display Single Documents
User	CATC	Time Leveling
User	CATR	Reorganize Interface Tables
User	CATS_APPR_LITE	Approve Working Times
User	CATS_DA	Display Working Times
User	CATSXT	Record Own Working Times
User	CATSXT_ADMIN	Record Working Times
User	CATSXT_DA	Display Working Times and Tasks
User	CATSXT_DTL	Working Times and Tasks: Display Details
Customizing	OXK1	Coding Block: Maintain Subscreens
Customizing	OY05	Factory calendar
Customizing	PA05	Number Range Maintenance: RP_COIFT
Customizing	PA06	Number Range Maintenance: PD_SEQ_NR
User	PA20	Display HR master data
User	PA51	Display time data
User	PA61	Maintain time data
User	PA62	Maintain Additional Data
User	PA71	Fast Entry
User	PC00_M99_TLEA30	Create Leave Entitlement
User	PE01	Maintain Schemas
User	PE02	Maintain Personnel Calculation Rules

(Contd.)

Category	Transaction	Description
User	PE03	Maintain Features
User	PE04	Functions/Operations
User	PEPM	Profile matchup
Customizing	PO10	Maintain Organizational Unit
User	PP01	Detail maintenance
User	PP60	Display shift plan
User	PP61	Change shift plan
User	PP62	Display requirements
User	PP63	Change requirements
User	PP64	Choose plan version
User	PP65	Simple maintenance
User	PP66	Choose profile
User	PP67	Create requirements
User	PP6A	Display personal shift plan
User	PP6B	Display attendance list
User	PP6C	Undo completed target plan
User	PP6I	Display temporary assignment list
User	PPOME	Change organization and staffing
User	PPPD	Display profile
User	PPPM	Change profile
User	PT_55400	Find Attendance/Absence
User	PT_BAL00	Cumulated Time Balances/Wage Types
User	PT_BPC00	Generate Personal Calendar
User	PT_BPC10	Revaluate Leave Quota
User	PT_CLSTB1	Display Temporary TE Results (Cluster B1)
User	PT_CLSTB2	Display Time Evaluation Results (Cluster B2)
User	PT_CLSTG1	Display Group Incentive Wages (Cluster G1)
User	PT_CLSTL1	Display Individual Incentive Wages (Cluster L1)
User	PT_CLSTPC	Display Personal Calendar (Cluster PC)
User	PT_DOW00	Time Accounts
User	PT_DSH20	Daily Work Schedule
User	PT_EDT_TEDT	Time Statement
User	PT_EDT_TELU	Time Balances Overview
User	PT_ERL00	Time Evaluation Messages
User	PT_ILVA00	Leave Accrual
User	PT_LEACONV	Transfer Remaining Leave
User	PT_QTA00	Generate Absence Quotas
User	PT_QTA10	Display Absence Quota Information
User	PT_REOPC	Personal Calendar Reorganization

(Contd.)

Category	Transaction	Description
User	PT_SHF00	Create Period Work Schedule
User	PT_UPD00	Recalculate Attendance/Absence Records
User	PT_UTPR00	Revaluate Daily Work Schedules
User	PT_UWSH00	Revaluate Planned Working Time
User	PT01	Create Work Schedule
User	PT02	Change Work Schedule
User	PT03	Display Work Schedule
Customizing	PT10	Number Range Maintenance: PTM_DOCNR
Customizing	PT11	Number Range Maintenance: PTM_QUONR
Customizing	PT12	Number Range Maintenance: HRAA_PDOC
User	PT40	Time Management Pool
Customizing	PT41	Customizing CC1 Communication Param.
User	PT50	Quota Overview
User	PT60	Time Evaluation
User	PT61	Time Statement
User	PT62	Attendance Check
User	PT63	Personal Work Schedule
User	PT64	Attendance/Absence Data Overview
User	PT65	Attendance/Absence Overview Graphic
User	PT68	Activity Allocation
User	PT80	Subsystem Connection
User	PT90	Absence Data: Calendar View
User	PT90_ATT	Attendance Data: Calendar View
User	PT91	Absence Data: Multiple Employee View
User	PT91_ATT	Attendance Data: Multiple Employee View
User	PTMW	Time Manager's Workplace
User	PU03	Change Payroll Status
User	PW_CEDTX0_AFTER	After Gross Pay
User	PW_CEDTX0_BEFORE	Before Gross Pay
User	PW01	Maintain
User	PW02	Display
User	PW03	Record
User	PW61	Time Leveling
User	PW62	Working of Time and Incentive Wage Earners
User	PW63	Reassignment Proposals for Wage Groups
User	PW70	Individual Incentive Wages
User	PW71	Group Incentive Wages
User	PW72	Withdrawal from Group
Customizing	PW91	Incentive Wages: Control Parameters
Customizing	PW92	Incentive Wages: User Exits

(Contd.)

Category	Transaction	Description
Customizing	PW93	Incentive Wages: Group Parameters
Customizing	PW94	Inc. Wages: Logistics Parameters
User	S_AHR_61004980	Maintain shift group infotype for OU
User	S_AHR_61004989	Specify shift groups
User	S_AHR_61005002	Define time types for Excel
User	S_AHR_61008856	E R for Pair Formation/Time Evaluation
User	S_AHR_61010096	Earliest recal. for incentive wages
User	S_AHR_61010745	Earliest Recal. for the Time Statement
User	SCAL	Holiday Calendar

39.4.2 Utility

Category	Transaction	Description
ABAP	BAPI	Bapi explorer
Basis	BD87	Status monitor for ALE messages
User	CG3Y	Download file
User	CG3Z	Upload file
ABAP	CMOD	Enhancements
ABAP	HRFORMS	HR forms workplace
Consultant	LSMW	Legacy system migration workbench
User	OAAD	Archivelink administration documents
Consultant	OSS1	Logon to SAPNet
Consultant	OY19	Customizing cross-system viewer
ABAP	PE51	HR form editor
Basis	PFCG	Role maintenance
Basis	RSSCD100_PFCG	Change documents for role admin.
Basis	RSSCD100_PFCG_USER	For role assignment
Basis	RSUSR200	List of users per login date
Basis	S_BCE_68001403	With critical authorizations
Basis	S002	Menu administration
User	SA38	ABAP reporting
Basis	SALE	Display ALE customizing
User	SBWP	SAP business workplace
Consultant	SCAT	Computer aided test tool
Consultant	SCMP	View/table comparison
Basis	SCOT	SAPconnect–administration
Consultant	SCU0	Customizing cross-system viewer
Basis	SE01	Transport organizer (extended)
Basis	SE03	Transport organizer tools

Category	Transaction	Description
Consultant, Basis	SE09	Transport organizer
Consultant, Basis	SE10	Transport organizer
Consultant, ABAP	SE11	ABAP dictionary maintenance
ABAP	SE13	Maintain technical settings (tables)
ABAP	SE15	ABAP/4 repository information system
Consultant, ABAP	SE16	Data browser
Consultant, ABAP	SE16N	General table display
Consultant, ABAP	SE17	General table display
ABAP	SE18	Business add-ins: definitions
ABAP	SE19	Business add-ins: implementations
ABAP	SE24	Class builder
ABAP	SE35	ABAP/4 dialog modules
ABAP	SE36	Logical database builder
ABAP	SE37	ABAP function modules
ABAP	SE38	ABAP editor
ABAP	SE39	Splitscreen editor: (new)
ABAP	SE41	Menu painter
ABAP	SE43	Maintain area menu
ABAP	SE51	Screen painter
ABAP	SE61	SAP documentation
Consultant	SE63	Translation: initial screen
ABAP	SE71	SAPscript form
ABAP	SE72	SAPscript styles
ABAP	SE73	SAPscript font maintenance
ABAP	SE74	SAPscript format conversion
ABAP	SE75	SAPscript settings
ABAP	SE75TTDTGC	SAPscript: change standard symbols
ABAP	SE75TTDTGD	SAPscript: display standard symbols
ABAP	SE76	SAPscript: form translation
ABAP	SE77	SAPscript styles translation
ABAP	SE80	Object navigator
ABAP	SE84	Repository information system
ABAP	SE85	ABAP/4 repository information system
ABAP	SE91	Message maintenance
ABAP	SE93	Maintain transactions
Consultant	SEARCH_SAP_MENU	Find in SAP menu
Consultant	SEARCH_USER_MENU	Find in user menu
User, Consultant	SECATT	Extended computer aided test tool
User, Consultant	SHDB	Batch input transaction recorder

(Contd.)

Category	Transaction	Description
Consultant	SLG1	Application log: display logs
Basis	SM01	Lock transactions
Basis	SM04	User list
Basis	SM12	Display and delete locks
Consultant	SM30	Call view maintenance
Consultant	SM31	Call view maintenance like SM30
Consultant	SM34	Viewcluster maintenance call
User	SM35	Batch input monitoring
User	SM35P	Batch input: log monitoring
User	SM36	Schedule background job
User	SM37	Job overview
User	SM38	Queue maintenance transaction
ABAP	SMARTFORMS	SAP smart forms
ABAP	SMOD	SAP enhancement management
User	SMX	Display own jobs
User	SO00	SAPoffice: short message
ABAP	SO10	SAPscript: standard texts
User	SP01	Output controller
User	SP02	Display spool requests
Consultant	SP11	TemSe directory
Consultant	SPRO	Customizing-edit project
User, Consultant	SQ00	SAP query: start queries
Consultant	SQ01	SAP query: maintain queries
Consultant	SQ02	SAP query: maintain infoset
Consultant	SQ03	SAP query: maintain user groups
User	SQVI	Quickviewer
ABAP	ST22	ABAP dump analysis
Basis	SU01	User maintenance
Basis	SU21	Maintain the Authorization Objects
Basis	SU22	Auth. object usage in transactions
Basis	SU24	Auth. object check under transactions
User	SU3	Maintain users own data
User	SU53	Display authorization check
Basis	SUIM	User information system
Consultant	SWDD	Workflow builder

Index

World Government
For a World Free from War, Terrorism and Poverty

Facts

- The world spends trillions of dollars every year on military and war equipment, while its people go hungry.
- Today the world is incapable of resolving any dispute through military actions.
- Terrorism thrives because of covert support of country governments.
- Enormous expenditure on militaries all over the world is not only a waste, but also extremely dangerous as it increases the destructive power of country governments.

We want

- A world free from war, terrorism and poverty.

How can it be done?

- Establish a world parliament, a world government and a world court.
- Disband militaries of all countries simultaneously.
- Use the savings to alleviate poverty.

Will all countries agree?

- Yes! When people of the countries want it.
- We have to awaken the people of the whole world.

How will it work?

- The world parliament will be formed through direct election of members of parliament all over the world. These members of parliament will form the world government.
- The world government will have limited but sufficient power to provide security to all countries, manage global environment and combat terrorism all over the world.
- The world government will secure the borders of all countries to ensure that there is no unauthorized entry or exit.
- The country governments will continue to manage their affairs.
- Disputes between countries will be resolved with the help of the world parliament and the world court.
- No country will disband its military first. All countries will disband their militaries simultaneously in a phased manner,

under the supervision of the world government, which will verify that the militaries are actually disbanded.

- Countries will retain their police to maintain law and order.
- Countries may have special forces to deal with terrorism and to provide relief in the event of natural disasters.

Is it possible?

- Many people say that this is an impossible task because other people will not agree.
- This task is possible if we talk only about ourselves, and not about others. This task is big but not impossible.
- We have only one world, we can't give up on it.
- We can succeed only if we try.

What should I do?

- Level 1: Register with WIII and become a world citizen. Even children can join.
- Level 2: Spread the message to your family, friends and neighbours. Convince five persons to join.

- Level 3: Convince five persons that each one of them would enroll five more persons.
- Level 4: Become an active volunteer.

Act now

- Act now. Don't give up because of enormity of the task.

You have nothing to lose

- There is no membership fee.
- You are not required to work unless you want to. But if you want, there is a lot of work to do.
- You are not required to follow any person or any belief.

Contact

World Integration and Improvement Initiative (WIII)
L/A-4/303, Ajmera Housing Complex, Pune 411018 India.
E-mail: agrawal.prem@gmail.com
Phone: 91(20)27462635

World Language

Need for a World Language

Perhaps the most important gift of nature to mankind is the ability to communicate using a language. However, this gift is not unmitigated, because we have got too much of it. We do not have a single language, but a large number of them, which sometimes is as bad as not having any language.

Lack of a common world language can greatly handicap a person, as more and more people travelling around the world discover to their dismay. With the world becoming smaller and smaller, as a result of advances in transportation and communication, the need for a common world language is felt more and more acutely. One option to overcome this hadicap is for a person to learn multiple languages, which is not only wasteful, but can be done only to a limited extent. Another way to overcome this handicap is through translation and interpretation, for which we pay a heavy price in terms of cost, time, and timeliness, and achieve at best partial communication. Scientific and technical literature available in one language cannot be used by people who do not know that language.

There is probably no one, who does not agree with the need for a world language. Only, people do not want to discuss it, fearing that accepting any language, other than their own, as world language will put them at a disadvantage. Also, people are strongly attached to their mother tongue, often considering it as revered as their mother, and feel a sense of guilt in accepting another language.

While there are some, who do not want to discuss this issue fearing that they may have to accept another language, there are others who do the same hoping that their language may become world language by default. This may well happen, but is it desirable even for them?

Importance of a good world language

A language is a tool for communication, and we must evaluate it as we would evaluate any other tool. How effective is it in meeting its objective; and how much resources does it consume in doing so? People who hope that their language may become world language, should think again. Do we just want a common language, or do we want a really good world language—a language which provides effective, unambiguous communication with minimum effort.

This article shows that existing languages score quite badly in a rational evaluation. Let us remember that many of us use almost

693

our entire non-sleeping time in reading, writing, and thinking—activities which depend on the efficiency of language. If we can design a language, which is more efficient than our existing language, we will gain that much extra time, which can be used for productive or recreational purposes. It has also been well accepted that languages influence our thinking, making the role of language even more important.

We must, therefore, consider ourselves lucky that we do not have a single language in the world. This gives us a choice. It is possible for us to have a well designed world language. If we had only one language, we would not have this choice, as we have no choice today in numbering system, computer keyboard, etc. We must not squander this choice away, by letting an existing language become the world language. It will be like losing a fortune, just because we refused to decide. It is also important that we decide to develop a world language as early as possible. The more time we lose, the more will be the backlog of translation, which must necessarily be done.

Should an existing natural language be world language?

Some of the existing natural languages, particularly English, aspire to become world language. Their claim is based primarily on their widespread use in dominant segments of society all over the world, e.g. science, law, business, industry, government, etc. However, if we objectively examine their effectiveness and efficiency, they do not perform too well. Let us take a look at 'English'.

Let us start from the alphabet. English does not have a phonetic alphabet. The same letter is associated with different sounds in different words. This puts tremendous load on people learning the language. They have to learn both the pronunciation as well as the spelling. Many languages of the world have this problem, while many are free from it.

The length of the words in a language determines the effort in communication to a large extent. If the words are long, the communication time and effort is more. Natural languages being product of evolution, have not paid much attention to length of words. Consequently, the words tend to be long. The best proof of this defect in a language is the existence of short forms for long words. 'Info' for information, and 'ad' for advertisement, amply demonstrate that words can be shorter.

All languages use prefixes and suffixes to add additional meaning to the meaning of a word. By doing so, they avoid the need to define and learn a word. This practice is very good, but often there are exceptions, which are not desirable. Also, usually this concept is not utilized fully. We do not need separate words for boy and girl. We need only one word with a prefix or a suffix for gender.

The meanings of words is another area of concern. Many times the words have contextual meanings. This increases the learning effort, as all the meanings of the words have to be learnt. Also, the words often suffer from overprecision, and underprecision. There are many words which mean exactly, or nearly, the same. On the other hand there are some words, whose meaning is not precise enough.

Grammars of natural languages are usually quite complex. Agreement of number and gender between noun and verb is a case in point. Really speaking, there is no need to alter the verb for number and gender; they should be attributes of noun alone. If that was done, the language will become simpler. By unnecessarily modifying the verb for number and gender, we make the language complex, and introduce the possibility of making mistakes. Needless complexity of grammar is best understood by learners of a foreign language, who constantly compare the grammar of the new language with that of their mother tongues.

Ambiguity or lack of clarity in the meaning of a sentence also exists.

It might be argued that the defects of English may be removed to prepare it for the role of world language. However, the changes may be so many, that we may not recognise it as English at all. Also, however much we improve it, it can never be as good as a language designed from scratch. We are going to build the world language only once, and it must be the best. Evaluation of other natural languages is likely to bring us to the same conclusion.

Also, we must remember that adopting an existing language as world language will be more repugnant to the rest of the world, than adopting a newly designed language.

Should Esperanto be world language?

If natural languages do not qualify to be the world language, what about Esperanto? After all it was created precisely for this purpose. There is no doubt that Esperanto is better suited to be the world language, than any other natural language. However, the question remains: is it possible to design a language better than Esperanto? The answer would be in affirmative, primarily because even Esperanto is based on some natural languages, and has not exercised freedom of choice in design to the fullest. However, Esperanto has definitely proved a major point—that it is possible to design a language.

How to develop a world language?

Designing a language is not a very difficult job, but designing a good language is. Designing a language involves making a large number of decisions. How much effort is put in arriving at these decisions will determine the quality of language. Also, the process should involve wide ranging cosultations with experts in various fields. After an initial decision is made based on expert opinion, it should be widely publicized, and feedback and comments of all the people should be considered, before finalizing the decision. Even then, if there is a good reason to alter a decision previously made, it should be done. In no case should we compromise on the quality of the world language. Some ideas are discussed here to illustrate the kind of improvements possible. Obviously, they are at best the tip of the iceberg.

Objectives of the world language

Some of the objectives of the world language would be as under. These need to be debated and enlarged. They also need to be interpreted for each sub-activity.

1. Achieve effective and unambiguous communication
   1.1 Between humans
   1.2 Between humans and machines
2. Minimize effort in communication
   2.1 Minimize effort in speaking and hearing
   2.2 Minimize effort in writing and reading
3. Minimize effort in learning the language
   3.1 Minimize the length and number of words
   3.2 Maximize the use of rules to form words and sentences. Have no exceptions.

Designing alphabet and script

One of the most fundamental components of a language is its alphabet. The alphabet is in two forms—written and spoken. While designing the alphabet, the spoken alphabet should be designed first. The sounds produced by human beings are not discrete. From a continous spectrum, we have to select a set of sounds. If we select too few sounds, the alphabet will be small and words will be longer. On the other hand, too many sounds may cause problems in distinguishing between them. Fortunately, this science, called phonetics, is well developed, and can be used for selecting a set of sounds. The sounds should be selected in such a way that we get the maximum distinction between sounds, and the effort required in production of sound is minimum. In addition, pleasant-ness of sound in hearing may also be considered. The ability of machines to produce these sounds, and distinguish between them on hearing may also be considered.

In order to minimize learning effort, each sound should be assigned a character. Frequently occurring sound combinations may also be assigned an additional character, as in shorthand. The language should be phonetic. We already have natural languages which are phonetic, and they demonstrate the advantages offered by a phonetic language.

The script for the world language should be designed keeping in mind the ability of human hand for writing, and human eye for reading. In writing, the script should provide continuity. There should be no dotting the 'i', or cutting the 't'. This will minimize the movement of hand, and save effort. Each character should be independent, and combined sequentially. In some scripts, a part of the character is outside the main writing area, e.g. a part of 'g' is below the main line of writing. This should be avoided to conserve space. Characters should be as uniform in size as possible. Each character should be written in only one way. There should be no concept of upper and lower case, wherein the same character is written in two ways.

The effort in writing can be greatly reduced, if natural movements of body are used in the design of characters. Research should be conducted to determine which movements are easy for human hands, and which are not. For example, it is common experience that people find it easier to write 'u' than to write 'n'. So much so, that often 'n' looks like 'u'. This is not accidental, because its opposit never happens. This is an interesting example, because the two characters are mirror images of one another. It can perhaps be said that human hand can turn in quickly, but cannot turn out as quickly. Perhaps it has a natural tendency to move towards the chest as observed in case of an electric shock. Similarly, research should be conducted to determine if the human eye has any preferences in pattern recognition. We should also consider, whether the writing will be from left to right, right to left, top to bottom, or bottom to top. The suitability of the script for machine production and recognition should also be considered.

Designing words

Words, even in natural languages, consist of parts which have independent meaning. For example, both 'un' and 'well' in unwell have independent meanings, which determine the meaning of unwell. These parts are called morphemes by linguists; we may call them roots. All languages use the concepts of roots, prefixes, suffixes, etc. But they do not use it to the fullest. For example, the word 'bad' is not needed; 'ungood' could be used in its place.

We should design word roots in such a way that their meanings are, as far as possible, independent of each other. For the same meaning there should not be more than one word root. If word roots are well defined, the learning effort will greatly reduce. Let me illustrate.

We need word roots to indicate the number and the gender. We may decide that there will be three genders—masculine, feminine, and unknown or unspecified. Similarly, we may decide that there will be three numbers—singular, plural, and unknown or unspecified. We may combine both these attributes, and assign a vowel to each of the nine combinations. We then use these vowels to suffix nouns and pronouns. Let us see the power of this simple design. We now need only one word for father, mother, and parent. Similarly, only one word will be needed for brother, sister, and sibling. Not only that the number of words will be reduced, some new words will become available, e.g. a word for either son or daughter. Speakers of Hindi, will find new words like parent and sibling, which they never had before. Also, we do not often know the sex of a bird, and use masculine, feminine, or neuter gender, depending on convention. In the new scheme, we can use the unspecified gender most of the time, and can specify it if we know the gender. Also, legal documents often use words like person(s). This is because there is no concept of unknown, or unspecified, number. We can, thus, see the power of a simple well-defined word root.

The above example is not an isolated one. By defining just three morphemes, for parent, child, and spouse, hundreds of existing and non-existing words for family relations can be eliminated. A large number of words describing young members of a species can be eliminated by using a single prefix with the word for species. Also, we can have a prefix each for first half, second half, first quarter, second quarter etc. of age, and so on. Thus, the communicator can choose the precision with which he wants to convey the age.

Word roots will be formed by assigning a sequence of characters to each concept. This should be done, using principles of classification and codification. In many branches of science, e.g. zoology and botany, such classification already exists. These should be used, so that there is no need to have a separate scientific name. Also, the frequency of their use should be considered. Highly used roots should be identified by few characters, so that the words are short.

Rules should be defined to combine roots into words. Where classification and codification gives a large word, but the frequency of use requires a small word, a synonym may be defined. Thus, synonyms will exist only for the purpose of making the language more efficient.

Designing grammar

Grammar defines how to combine words into sentences. These rules should be as simple as possible, and there should be no exceptions. The sequence of words in a sentence should not affect its meaning. Also, preferably the sequence of words should not change, as it happens in English, where changing a sentence from affirmative to inquisitive requires a change in the sequence of words.

In many existing languages, attributes which should affect only words, are defined at the level of sentence. Number and gender are attributes of noun, and they have nothing to do with verb. Similarly, tense is an attribute of verb, and should not affect the noun. We think that a sentence is affirmative, or inquisitive (asks a question). Let us consider a simple sentence, "Are you going?". This may be interpreted as, "Are you going? (or not going)", or as "Are you? (or someone else) going". Here we can see that the question is an attribute of word, and not of sentence. Research will be needed to determine whether enquiry is always at word level, or sometimes at word level, and sometimes at sentence level.

What do we do next?

There is no doubt that it is possible to develop a language, which is far superior to existing languages. The development of such a language will be an iterative process. It will go through several cycles of improvement, before it becomes reasonably good. If we can assign even 1% of resources being spent in linguistic research, we can easily build such a language. Then it can be improved, and compared with existing languages. Only after its superiority is clearly demonstrated, do we have to think of adopting it. This project is definitely worthy of research, and I call upon the world community to take it up.

Good Governance

Many countries of the world face a number of problems. Are there any solutions? I believe that there are. Here are some ideas that could be helpful in solving some of our problems. There could be a structured public debate on these, and those which meet public approval could be implemented.

Minimize government functions

- Often governments try to do too many things.
- It is not government's job to provide goods and services. It should facilitate their production and distribution and ensure competitiveness, efficiency and non-exploitation of customers.
- Government should not be looked upon to provide direct employment. It should ensure a vibrant economy in which people are gainfully engaged.

Minimize government expenditure

- Whatever functions the government must perform, must be performed in the most efficient way, thereby reducing the cost of governance to a minimum.
- Methods of governance should be regularly reviewed, debated in public, and benchmarked with other countries and states to ensure that they are most effective and efficient.

Taxation

- There should be a single authority in each country which can levy taxes. No one else should be allowed to collect tax from any one. However, governments should be allowed to sell specific goods and services, which the citizens should be free to buy, or not to buy.
- The taxes collected by the taxation authority should be distributed among country, state and local governments as per a pre-defined agreed formula.
- The distribution of revenue from taxes should consider both the needs of governments and their contribution to revenue.
- The needs should be determined by estimating the cost of functions the governments are expected to provide.
- It will be citizens' right to get the services for which money is provided by the tax authority.
- The tax structure should be simplified. There should be only two forms of taxes. Excise for all goods and services produced in the country, and Custom for all goods and services brought in a country from outside.
- Sales tax, octroi, income tax, etc. should be abolished.
- Collection of excise and custom should be made effective by allocating more

resources which would become available because of abolition of other taxes. In addition, the penalty for tax evasion should be very heavy, and corruption should be severely dealt with.

- It may be argued that income tax is applicable to only affluent sections of population. But, the same effect can be achieved by levying more excise on items which are consumed by these sections.

Norm-based governance

- People have started thinking that what the government does for them is charity. As a result, while some people get too much, others don't get even the basic minimum.
- This tendency is clearly visible. Constituencies of VIPs, e.g. prime minister, railway minister, etc. get generous allocation, which suddenly dries up if the concerned minister no longer holds office.
- This tendency is often justified by saying that at least somewhere something is getting done. This argument shows how little we have come to expect from our governments.
- In order to ensure that justice is done to all, we must define the functions of government, the levels in each function, and the entitlement criteria.
- For example we may say that all villages with population between 100 and 1000 will be linked with brick road, while those with a population of more than 1000, will be linked with tar road.
- Such norms will ensure fairness to all.
- Along with norms, the mechanism to redress grievances arising from not following the norms should be specified. In case of deliberate victimization, those responsible should be punished.

Government as service provider

- Where the government provides service, e.g. water, health care, education, roads, etc. it should be paid by the government treasury to the concerned government department for quantity and quality of service provided. This mechanism should replace the current mechanism of budgetary allocation.
- Government departments should be run as business. Their units should earn revenue, pay bills, and make profit or loss. The employees of each individual unit should be rewarded based on the financial performance of the unit.
- Citizens should be treated as customers and given bills for the service provided, showing the amount payable by them and the subsidies.
- Where possible, the quantity and quality of service should be certified by the individual customers. Where it is not possible, it should be certified by customer bodies.
- If private parties offer to provide service at a cheaper rate, the job should be given to them.

Accountability

- Government functionaries seem to have all power but no accountability.
- For example, the encroachment department of a municipal corporation has powers to demolish an illegal building. But such powers are often exercised selectively to demolish some and leave others. The municipal corporation is not accountable to people as to why rules are being applied selectively.
- Lack of accountability breeds corruption.
- Whenever someone is given power, he should also be made accountable, preferably to the public.

- For example, if an illegal construction is found in the jurisdiction of an anti-encroachment department, its officers should be punished.

Citizens role in governance

- Governance can be much better and easier if citizens are involved in it.
- Schemes to involve citizens in governance should clearly specify how the citizens are going to contribute.
- Citizens can contribute by providing information, monitoring situations and taking action.
- The schemes involving citizens' role should be planned keeping their convenience in mind and should utilize their contribution in a most effective way.
- For example, 'Each one teach one' is not a viable and effective method; but asking a citizen to teach for two hours in a week is both convenient to the citizen and also effective in spreading education.
- Citizens should be able to see the effect of their contribution.
- One way of involving citizens would be to have a well publicised telephone number, which citizens can use to report situations such as street lights being kept on in daytime, engine of a parked bus running, leakage in a water pipe, etc. The person manning such a telephone should contact the concerned officer, who in turn should remedy the situation. Only when citizens see their involvement resulting in action, they would participate more and more.
- Another way to involve citizens would be to assign them a small neighbourhood, which they will look after to ensure its cleanliness and orderliness. If someone digs up a road in their area, they will ensure that it is mended. They will also ensure that conservancy staff keeps their area clean. There can be many ways in which citizens can help.

Innovation

- Innovation can greatly help in good governance. Chronic problems faced by government can be solved by innovative methods.
- For example, a municipal corporation should never award a contract merely for building roads. It should always be a contract to build and maintain roads. Then the contractor will do a good job in building the road, as he will have to spend less on its maintenance. This will benefit everyone.

Political system

- In many countries, political system is corrupt because politics is not an economically viable profession.
- Every profession, except politics, offers a regular income.
- It is futile to argue that MLAs and MPs are paid a salary. These are the highest levels to which people reach in politics. The corruptionalisation is completed much before such levels are reached.
- We cannot expect to have politicians for free. If we do, we pay through our nose.
- Unless politics can attract young men and women and provide them a descent secure career, it is futile to expect politicians to be honest.
- Many countries have administrative or civil services. They should also create a political service in which young men and women should be recruited in an open competition. This service should conduct competitive examinations on the lines of the administrative or civil services.
- Those qualifying in the competitive examination should be trained and given

pay and perks at par with the administrative or civil services.

- Those selected for political service, should be barred from taking up any other job, or doing any business.
- They should not be given any regular work. They should do political or social work of their choice.
- Their work should be monitored by Judiciary to ensure that they do adequate amount of work. If the quantum of their work is found inadequate, they must be withdrawn from political service and assigned administrative work. If they are found to be corrupt, their services should be terminated.
- They will contest election like any other person, and if they get elected, they will be entitled to only one salary, either of the service or of the elected office.
- Only if we can attract young students, and allow them to make an honest career in politics, can we hope to end corruption some day.

Education

- The objective of the education system is not clearly defined.
- People claim that education system has failed without even defining what education is expected to achieve.
- The objective of primary and secondary education should be to impart skills in languages and mathematics, and to create general awareness and scientific temperament.
- The objective of higher level education should be to impart skills and knowledge which a person will need in his career.
- The availability of different courses should be based on the manpower needs of a country. Consequently, in a country like India a large number of students should be educated in agriculture, horticulture, fishery, cattle rearing, etc.

- Education should not be fashionable; it should be need based and add value. It should also be easy to obtain, preferably without sacrificing the earning capacity of students.

Judiciary

- The effectiveness of judiciary determines how civilized a society is.
- The objective of judiciary is not merely to hear cases and pronounce judgement, but also to create confidence in people that if they are wronged, judiciary will help remedy the problem. It should also create the impression that no one can do wrong and get away with it.
- From the above point of view, judiciary in many countries has failed miserably.
- Failure of judiciary is the primary reason of corruption in society.
- Judiciary must work out and implement a strategy to achieve the above objectives. Judicial management should be a part of judiciary.
- Judiciary must get its workload studied to see what part of it can be eliminated by improving the rules governing those situations. For example, Judiciary handles a large number of cases related to motor vehicle accident compensation. If rules are framed to determine this compensation based on relevant factors like age, earning capacity, number of dependants, etc. insurance companies will be able to settle most of the cases, and the number of such cases going to court will drastically reduce.
- Judiciary should work on cases in a time bound manner. It should fix time norms for different types of cases and endeavour to finish a case in the allotted time.
- Judiciary can work in a time bound manner only if it has a reasonable number of cases in hearing. Therefore, new cases should go in a queue from which they should be taken for hearing.

The cases may not be taken for hearing on a first-come first-served basis, but based on some guidelines which take into account the importance and urgency of a case.

- Judiciary must augment its capacity to meet the workload. The major resource that the judiciary requires is manpower. It is ironic that even in countries with excess manpower, this function is poorly performed due to lack of resources.
- Judiciary may take help of retired citizens to augment its capacity.
- Judiciary should review its policies to ensure that they are concomitant with speedy and effective justice.

E-Governance

- Information Technology (IT) is having a major impact on governance. Many country and state governments are changing their business processes to take advantage of the benefits that IT offers. However, if we have to get the most efficient e-governance at minimum cost, we need to do two things: commonize business processes and develop soft IT infrastructure.

Commonize business processes

- At present, the same business process gets computerized by different agencies in different ways. This creates islands of information which cannot talk to each other.
- A case in point is the computerization of RTO (Regional Transport Office) operations in India. Initially, different RTOs created their systems independently, and now it is proposed to scrap all those systems and replace them with a common central system. Needless to say the expenditure in independent systems could have been avoided.

Develop soft IT infrastructure

- We are aware of the importance of IT infrastructure in the development of IT. However, we usually think only of hardware infrastructure. It is high time we start thinking of soft IT infrastructure as well, and understand its importance in the development of IT. Let me explain.
- Any computerization project requires creation of master data, e.g. citizens, business entities, real estate properties, etc. At present each system creates its own master data. In India, a citizen has one id for income tax department, another for his driving licence, and yet another for his bank. He also has an id in each of the hospitals he visits, and so on. Obviously, these systems cannot talk to each other. If each person in the world were to be given a unique person id, that id would get used by all these systems, instead of trying to create their own. This not only would save development effort but also would enable diverse systems to talk to each other.
- It is not only the persons we need to identify uniquely but also every legal entity such as businesses, each piece of land and real estate, etc. The list is endless and so are the benefits of creating such unique identities.
- Wherever possible, we should look for natural attributes in giving id to an entity. For example, we can give a number to land and real estate based on its longitude, latitude and altitude. Similarly, we can codify the primary relation between two persons as Father (F), Mother (M), Brother (B), Sister (C), Husband (H), Wife (W), Son (S) and Daughter (D). All other relations can be derived by combining these primary relations.

- It is important that standards for master data creation and codification are discussed and agreed in international bodies such as International Standards Organization. If this is not done, the world will have to incur additional cost later either in changing the systems, or in building interfaces.
- The benefits of unique identification are enormous. If each person is given a unique numeric id, we can store a telephone number and an e-mail id against him. For calling a person, you would make the call on his person id with a prefix, say 1. The prefix will indicate to the telephone system that the following number is a person id which has to be converted into telephone number. If the person's telephone number changes, only the link needs to be changed. The callers will still call the same number. Similarly, a person can be contacted on the same e-mail id, even if he changes his service provider.
- E-governance should not be creating islands of computer systems. We must have a clear vision, strategy and master plan. We must understand what to do and what not to do, if we are not to waste our precious time and resources.

Pledge your time (samay daan)

- We citizens only criticize. We do nothing concrete.
- Things are not going to change if we expect others to change them. They will change if we act to change them.
- Those who want to change the world for better should pledge 1% of their time for society. This works out to less than 15 minutes a day and less than two hours a week.
- They can spend this time to pursue the cause of their choice. They can join an NGO, or form local groups to discuss and debate what can be done.
- Even if they just meet once a week to discuss what can be done, ideas will emerge and things will begin to happen.
- Their own efforts will shape their actions and organizations.
- The key thing is commitment and doing; not idle criticism.
- Register your time pledge (samay daan) with World Integration and Improvement Initiative (agrawal.prem@gmail.com)

City without Traffic Lights

Are you fed up with traffic lights? Traffic lights at every junction. Stop, start. Stop, start. Stop, start. Do you sometimes wish that the roads of your city were like expressway. Where your car would compete with the wind and you would reach your destination in minutes.

Fortunately, this is possible. In order to use this plan, the main roads of the city need to be like a grid, as shown in Figure 1.

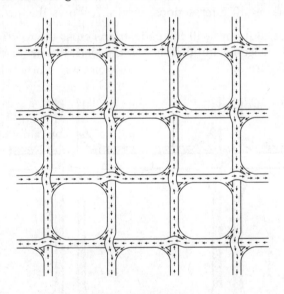

Figure 1

All roads will be one-way. When one road meets another at an intersection, there are two possibilities; you may either continue on your road, or you may turn on the other road in the direction of the traffic on that road. This is shown in Figure 2.

If you turn on the other road, there is no problem. But if you continue on your road, you will run into the traffic going straight on the other road. This is solved by a flyover or grade separator. Traffic on one road will go above the flyover, and the traffic on the other

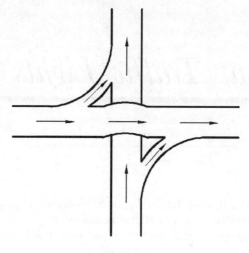

Figure 2

road will go under the flyover. This will ensure smooth flow of traffic without traffic light. This will be done on all intersections. Figure 1 shows this arrangement.

Sounds like a good idea. But how will the pedestrians cross the road? If the traffic moves at a fast speed, it will become impossible for the pedestrians to cross the road. The solution to this is in Figure 3.

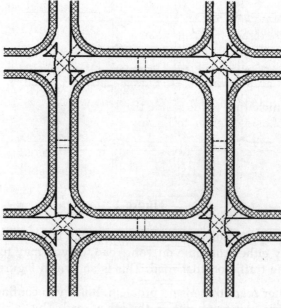

Figure 3

There will be a ring road for pedestrians and cyclists in each sector (the area bounded by main roads on all four sides). This pedestrian ring road will be connected to the pedestrian ring roads of adjoining sectors through subways. Thus, no pedestrian or cyclist will ever come on the main roads, allowing the vehicles to move freely on the main roads. Pedestrian roads will not be one-way. Pedestrians and cyclists will move on the pedestrian roads in both directions.

But how will a person take public transport, e.g. bus or taxi? This is explained in Figure 4.

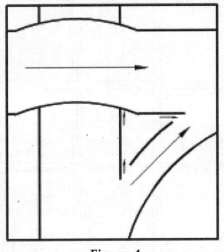

Figure 4

At each intersection, there are two triangular areas. Buses and taxis will go inside these triangular areas. There they will drop and pickup the passengers and come out of the triangle on the road they wish to take. These triangular areas will be connected to the pedestrian roads through subways.

Figure 5 shows the vehicle ring roads inside the sectors. This ring road will be connected to all the four main roads as well as to the internal roads of the sector. These roads will be two-way.

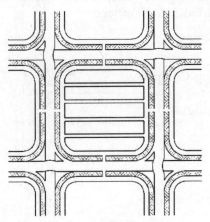

Figure 5

Figure 6 shows how the vehicles will move from one sector to another sector. Draw a horizontal and a vertical line from the source sector to the destination sector. You can do this in two ways. You can take either of these two ways to travel to your destination. You come out of the source sector taking the exit according to your travel path, move to the destination sector and enter it.

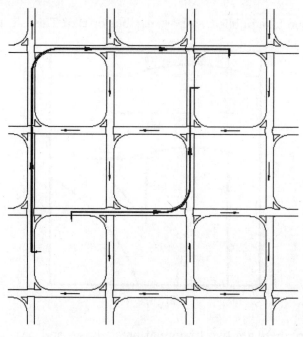

Figure 6

The main roads will be fenced on both sides so that no one can enter or exit them except through designated entry and exit roads. No pedestrian or cyclist will enter these roads. The vehicles will enter these roads, move to their destination and exit. Vehicles will neither stop on the main roads, nor be parked on it. Public transport will not stop on the main roads. There will be no shops or vendors on the main roads. Main roads will be like expressways. Enter, Move, Exit. No stoppage.

For further information, contact

P K Agrawal
L/A-4/303, Ajmera Housing Complex,
Pimpri, Pune 411018
E-mail: agrawal.prem@gmail.com
Phone: +91(20)27462635
Mobile: +919822847682

INDEX
(675–690)